Six-Guns and Saddle Leather

A Bibliography of
Books and Pamphlets
on Western Outlaws and Gunmen

Six-Guns and Saddle Leather

Compiled by RAMON F. ADAMS

New Edition, Revised
and Greatly Enlarged

Books by RAMON F. ADAMS

Cowboy Lingo (Boston, 1936)
Western Words: A Dictionary of the Range, Cow Camp, and Trail (Norman, 1944)
Charles M. Russell, the Cowboy Artist (with Homer E. Britzman) (Pasadena, 1948)
Come an' Get It: The Story of the Old Cowboy Cook (Norman, 1952)
The Best of the American Cowboy (compiler and editor) (Norman, 1957)
The Rampaging Herd: A Bibliography of Books and Pamphlets on Men and Events in the Cattle Industry (Norman, 1959)
A Fitting Death for Billy the Kid (Norman, 1960)
The Old-Time Cowhand (New York, 1961)
Burs Under the Saddle: A Second Look at Books and Histories of the West (Norman, 1964)
From the Pecos to the Powder: A Cowboy's Autobiography (with Bob Kennon) (Norman, 1965)
The Legendary West (Dallas, 1965)
The Cowman and His Philosophy (Austin, 1967)
The Cowboy and His Humor (Austin, 1968)
Western Words: A Dictionary of the American West (Norman, 1968)
The Cowman and His Code of Ethics (Austin, 1969)
Six-Guns and Saddle Leather: A Bibliography of Books and Pamphlets on Western Outlaws and Gunmen (Norman, 1954; revised and enlarged edition, 1969)

STANDARD BOOK NUMBER: 8061–0849–5

LIBRARY OF CONGRESS CATALOG CARD NUMBER: 69–16729

 Composed and printed at Norman, Oklahoma, by the University of Oklahoma Press. New edition.

Dedicated

*with sincere personal regards to William A. Blakley,
whose encouragement and warm friendship has helped
in compiling the revision of this work.*

Acknowledgments for the Revised Edition

First I wish to repeat my thanks to all those who gave such willing assistance while I was compiling the first edition. That edition was the result of my travels over the western states. This revised edition is the result of travels and research throughout the eastern part of the United States after the original edition was published. In my home town of Dallas, Texas, my undying gratitude is extended to my benevolent friend, Mr. William A. Blakley, for financial aid for research on the eastern journey.

In Topeka, Kansas, my thanks to Mr. Nyle H. Miller, secretary of the Kansas State Historical Society, whose wonderful library was one of the high spots of my eastern trip. I am also grateful to Mr. Miller for driving me to Kansas City, Missouri, for a meeting of the Westerners Posse of that city, where I, together with the late Homer Croy, were honored guests. My thanks also to Miss Alberta Pantle, acting librarian, and to Miss Portia Anderson, cataloguer, of the same institution. My thanks, too, to Mr. Harry Lose, of the Hotel Jayhawk, Topeka, for inviting me to examine his private library.

Miss Laura Neiswanger, librarian, Kansas Collection, Kansas State University, Lawrence, Kansas, and Miss Sandra Updike, assistant librarian, of the same department, were indeed kind and co-operative.

In Kansas City, Missouri, my friend the late Martin E. Ismert, an outstanding collector, allowed me the privilege and freedom of his home more than once to examine his most unusual collection. I am grateful to Mr. Brice J. Mansfield, also of that city, for his hospitality, for allowing me to examine his library and for transporting me over a goodly portion of Missouri to show me the Jesse James country.

Mrs. Viola A. Perotti, curator of the Snyder Memorial Library, University of Kansas City, gave her time and knowledge to assist my research in that institution, where I found a few books not seen anywhere else. Mr. Alan W. Farley, of Kansas City, Kansas, was also kind enough to let me spend some time in his private collection, for which I thank him.

My thanks to the entire staff of the Library of Congress, Washington, D.C., where I spent many days, both in the general library and in the rare-book room. My good friend, the well-known book collector and writer, Mr. Jeff C. Dykes, of College Park, Maryland, took me to his home as a guest and not only drove me to points of interest in Washington and its environs but also dug out many, many books packed away in cartons in an attic—quite a labor in the heat of summer, but done with his characteristic enthusiasm—and his courtesies, and those of his good wife, will never be forgotten. In Washington, also, I had the pleasure of examining the private library of Mr. Frederic G. Renner, an opportunity I deeply appreciate.

Continuing north, I spent a week examining the Philip A. Rollins Collection in the Rare Book and Special Collection Department, Princeton University. For a most pleasant and profitable week there I wish to thank Mr. Howard C. Rice, Jr., chief of staff, and his staff assistant, Mr. Lucien Bergeron, Jr., for their many favors in making this one of the most memorable stops of my trip.

In New York, it was a pleasure to receive the willing assistance of Mr. Leon Weidman, first assistant of the American History Room, New York Public Library, and of Miss Shirley L. Spranger, reference assistant in the same department, as well as Mrs. Maude D. Cole, of the Rare Book Department of this excellent library. Also in New York, my thanks to Mr. R. W. G. Vail, director of the New York Historical Society, and to Miss Geraldine Beard, a member of his staff, for the trouble she went to in helping assure success in my work there.

Also while in New York, I visited such old friends and rare-book dealers as the Eberstadts, Mr. Peter Decker and Mr. William F. Kelleher, of Cliffside Park, New Jersey, in whose home I had the pleasure of being a guest. All these dealers have helped me for years in finding rare and valuable additions to my library.

One of the most enjoyable occasions of this trip was a luncheon at which I was the guest of the late Mr. Thomas W. Streeter, of Morristown, New Jersey, to whose home I was driven by Mr. Nick Eggenhofer, my artist friend and the illustrator of several of my books. We spent some time examining Mr. Streeter's unusual collection, for he was one of the really great book collectors of the United States.

At New Haven, Connecticut, I spent many profitable days working in the Coe Collection at Yale University, and for this privilege I wish to thank Mrs. Ruth Smith, assistant librarian of the collection.

Mr. Robert H. Haynes, assistant librarian and curator of the Theodore Roosevelt Collection, Harvard University, Cambridge, was most kind in helping me locate books in that collection. In Boston, I must thank Mr. Mike J. Walsh, of the Goodspeed Book Shop, for his valuable suggestions as we chatted in his office. In that city, too, I wish to thank Mr. Walter Muir Whitehill, director of the Boston Athenaeum Library and his assistants, and also the staff of the Boston Public Library.

Mr. Clarence S. Brigham, well-known authority on rare books and director of the American Antiquarian Society Library, of Worcester, Massachusetts, and his assistant, Miss Mary E. Brown, were most gracious and co-operative. I appreciate indeed the interest Mr. Brigham expressed in my work.

During my attendance of the Oklahoma City meeting of the Western History Association in 1964, I was fortunate in meeting Mr. Jim L. Edwards, a collector and book dealer of that city, and he was kind enough to take me to visit his collection, and doubly kind in letting me take back to my hotel some rare items for a closer and more thorough examination.

During a special trip to Tucson, Arizona, for further research in the University of Arizona Library, my friend Mr. John D. Gilchriese, field historian of the university, met me at the plane and did everything in his power to make my stay pleasant and profitable. He not only gave me free access to their special collection stacks but dined me and drove me to such historical places as Tombstone and Bisbee. I wish to thank Dr. Robert K. Johnson, librarian of the same institution, and Mr. Joseph F. Park, curator of Western Americana. Both were most helpful.

I wish to thank Mr. T. N. Luther, a book dealer of Kansas City, Missouri, for the loan of some rare books from his catalogues. I am no less appreciative of the help given by my friends Mr. Everett L. DeGolyer, Jr., and Miss Sue Hertzog, both of the DeGolyer Foundation of Dallas. I also wish to thank Mrs. Virginia Hoke and Mrs. Emma Hamilton, both of the Southwest Reference Department of the El Paso, Texas, Public Library. They were most gracious and co-operative.

Some of my greatest assistance has come from a personal friend and fellow bibliophile, Mr. Robert G. McCubbin, of El Paso, who during his travels has constantly been on the lookout for those little-known books and pamphlets privately printed or printed in limited editions in small towns by small print shops. He has told me about such publications, bought them for me, or loaned me copies from his own library. Without his help many items in this revised edition would not have been included.

Others who have been helpful and who bring back pleasant memories as close personal friends include the late Walter S. Campbell (Stanley Vestal), of the University of Oklahoma, and the late Floyd B. Streeter, librarian of the Fort Hays Kansas State College. No less appreciated is the help rendered by such good friends as the late Edward N. Wentworth, of Chesterton, Indiana, and Mr. Don Russell, of Chicago, all collectors of books on various subjects.

On my journeys from coast to coast I found that librarians and book collectors everywhere were happy and eager to extend every help. This has made the many hours spent in research a pleasant memory; and to express my appreciation in mere words hardly seems adequate. Yet I trust these words will suffice to make all these good people realize that my appreciation is sincere and deeply felt. The many new friends made and the old friendships renewed certainly made this work pleasant and seem worthwhile, even though it has been a most difficult and exacting task. So, once more, thanks to all, and may your reward be richly abundant.

Ramon F. Adams

Dallas, Texas
March 15, 1969

Acknowledgments for the First Edition

Although a large percentage of the books listed herein are in my own private library, I needed to search far and wide to see and examine certain rare items which I do not possess. To do this, I needed help, and I am happy to say that this world is still filled with co-operative souls if one but looks for them. I wish to thank the Texas State Historical Association for a Rockefeller Foundation grant which made it possible for me to visit libraries of various states and institutions, as well as several important private libraries. In these travels I met many old friends and, I hope, made a few new ones. I found librarians and book collectors everywhere most co-operative and willing helpers, and if by chance I overlook any who took the trouble and time to search their shelves for me, it is not intentional.

I would like to express my appreciation to the Henry E. Huntington Library, of San Marino, California, and its Grant-in-Aid Committee for extending me a second grant for extended research in that institution. My thanks to Dr. Robert Glass Cleland and Dr. Godfrey Davies of the Committee; Dr. John E. Pomfret, director of the Library; Mr. Leslie E. Bliss, librarian; Mr. Carey Bliss, assistant curator of rare books; Miss Mary Isabel Fry, reference librarian and registrar; Mrs. Margaret L. Packer, supervisor of the rare reading room; and Dr. French Fogle for the many favors extended me.

Aside from the members of the staff of the Huntington Library, my greatest benefactor in California was my friend and an outstanding collector of books on western outlaws, Loring Campbell. He not only went to a great deal of trouble to dig out books for my examination, but cheerfully transported me over wide areas of Los Angeles County to inspect other private libraries. Among these was that of my good friend Mr. Robert J. Woods, of Hollywood, in which I spent one whole day and where I found some unusual and rare books in what is perhaps the greatest private collection it has been my pleasure to examine.

My friend Mr. Paul W. Galleher, of the Arthur H. Clark Company, Glendale, was most kind in helping me locate certain books and in allowing me to take his valuable time discussing points of reference in first editions, and I shall ever be in his debt for acting as my cordial host at two dinners given by the Westerners of Los Angeles.

I wish to thank my old friend Mr. Glen Dawson, of the Dawson Book Shop, Los Angeles, for the many favors extended me and for transportation to places not easily accessible.

Mrs. Ella L. Robinson, librarian of the Southwest Museum Library, Los Angeles, was most kind to let me spend a day searching the shelves of this institution. Her welcome and help made this day a very pleasant memory.

My gratitude is extended to Dr. E. E. Dale, curator of the Phillips Collection, University of Oklahoma; to Miss Ina T. Aulls, Western History Room, Denver Public Library; to Mrs. Agnes Wright Spring, a friend of long standing, of the same department, but now of the Colorado Historical Society, for digging out many books for me; to Miss Frances Shea, librarian, Colorado State Historical Society, for her help and interest; to Mrs. Eulalia Chapman, of the Bibliographical Center for Research, Denver Public Library, for her valuable aid in locating certain rare titles; to Miss Mae Cody, of the Wyoming State Library, Cheyenne; to Miss Mary E. Marks, librarian, University of Wyoming, Laramie; and to Miss Lola Homsher, archivist of the Western Room, University of Wyoming, and her able assistant, Miss Henryetta Berry. Not only did the last two accord me every courtesy among the bookshelves, but they also took the time to show me some of the beautiful scenery of that section of the country.

My thanks also to Mr. Frederick Cromwell, librarian of the University of Arizona, Tucson, and his assistants for allowing me to search through the bookshelves of that institution; to Mr. Mulford Winsor, director of the State Library and Archives of Arizona, Phoenix, and Mrs. Alice Good, librarian, for giving me free access to their shelves; to Miss Harriett Smither, archivist, Texas State Library, for research and photostats; to Mr. E. W. Winkler, University of Texas Library, Austin; and to Miss Llerna Friend, University of Texas, Texas Collection, for her untiring effort to locate new acquisitions not yet catalogued by that institution. My thanks are also extended to Mrs. Margaret D. Ulridge, University of California Library, Berkeley; Mrs. Eleanor A. Bancroft, assistant to the director of the Bancroft Library of the same institution, and Mr. Walter Muir Whitehill, director and librarian of the Boston Athenaeum Library.

Many personal friends are due my thanks for assistance in varied directions: Mr. J. C. Dykes, of College Park, Maryland, for calling my attention to certain books and giving me pointers on them; Mr. and Mrs. John J. Lipsey, of Colorado Springs, in whose home and library I spent several days; and Mr. Don Bloch, of Denver, for his constant words of encouragement.

I wish especially to acknowledge my indebtedness to my good friends Mr. J. Frank Dobie, Mr. Frank Caldwell, and Captain R. W. Aldrich, all of Austin, Texas, for allowing me the freedom of their private libraries. They possess a number of unusual books and a great willingness to help others. My gratitude to that experienced bookman and good friend Mr. Fred A. Rosenstock, of Denver, for inviting me to his home to search through his private library and examine his most precious collection. My thanks also to Mr. Thomas M. Bogie, Interlibrary Loan Department of the Dallas Public Library, for his most friendly co-operation.

I wish to thank the Reverend Robert W. Shields, of Alcester, South Dakota, for his help with some books and stories on the Reno brothers, on whom he has perhaps done more genuine research than any other man. My thanks also to Mrs. Elsie D. Hand, librarian of the Oklahoma Historical Society, Oklahoma City, for her aid in securing a photostat of one of the very rare books in that collection. Mr. Don Russell, associate editor, *American Peoples' Encyclopedia*, Chicago, has given me helpful information and suggestions.

My friend and fellow collector of Dallas, Texas, Mr. Dan Ferguson, was most kind to bring me books from his office to read and examine, and to allow me to visit his home library with every freedom to examine its contents. My friend Mr. Wayne Gard, of the *Dallas Morning News*, has extended me every help and encouragement. My thanks to Mr. Walter S. Campbell, University of Oklahoma; to Mr. F. B. Streeter, librarian, Fort Hays Kansas State College; and to Miss Joyce McLeod, assistant reference librarian, University of Kansas, Lawrence, for their cordial co-operation.

Among the book dealers who have helped me in locating rare volumes for my own library, and to whom I am grateful, are Mr. Charles Eberstadt and Mr. Peter Decker, both of New York; Mr. H. M. Sender, Kansas City, Missouri; and Mr. H. C. Revercomb, Kansas City, Kansas; Mr. M. J. Walsh, of Goodspeed's, Boston; and Glen Dawson, Paul Gallaher, Fred Rosenstock, John J. Lipsey, and that good bookman Mr. William F. Kelleher, of Cliffside Park, New Jersey.

I would indeed be ungrateful if I did not express appreciation to my good wife for her encouragement, the giving of her time that I might work on this project which has taken unlimited hours, and her willingness for me to buy expensive books with money which could well have been used for her own comfort.

A compilation of this kind demands much time, labor, travel, and expense, with the expectation of only a limited financial return, but when the compiler takes into consideration the many friends made during his excursions, he feels that his reward is richly abundant.

RAMON F. ADAMS

Dallas, Texas
January 19, 1954

Introduction to the First Edition

One of the phenomena of our times is the vitality of the western tradition and the strength and continuity of its claim upon the interest of Americans. The late Eduard Lindeman, writing in the *Saturday Review* shortly before his death, called attention to the fact that "the frontier is a cherished element in our experience as a people. Every American is a potential pioneer. In every American there lies dormant the feeling that he too might play the part of a hero. Every American is a latent out-of-doors person. . . . In short, the West is 'in our blood.' "

Of all the figures of the American frontier, the bad man with a single-action Colt's revolver in his hand has surest claim upon the attention of American readers. A latecomer to the western scene, and a social product of settlement rather than of self-sufficient isolation, he treads in the footsteps of four great predecessors: the mountain man, the explorer, the military man, and the Indian. Arrayed against the virtuous settler or small townsman, he is the stuff of which action is made. Without him, the more or less orderly processes of settlement could have been as dull as neighborhood gossip in a country store. With him, the West was in ferment from the moment of its social emergence.

The outlaw antedates the Civil War, but he becomes the most notable mark upon the western landscape after 1865. He was a natural product of his time. Men from more settled sections of the country flocked west when they got into trouble at home, often dropping their real names when they reached the frontier, for this was a new land where every man was a law unto himself and where there was a "longer distance between sheriffs." Many of the early Texas outlaws got a start because of their quick-tempered resistance to carpetbagger rule after the Civil War and their rebellion against the Negro police. At a time when six-guns were necessary accouterment, thorough familiarity with them bred contempt for bloodshed, and hasty use led to a career of "ridin' the high line."

When a working cowhand found his boss mavericking calves under the guise of legitimate branding, he saw no crime in trying to build a herd of his own with rope and running iron. But the big cattleman viewed things in a different light, and the ambitious cowboy soon found himself considered a cow thief and outlaw—unless he was clever enough to "steal himself rich" and become another influential cattleman, free of the threat of a long rope. The horse thief, on the other hand, was not tolerated by any westerner except one of his own kind. If captured, he seldom was accorded a trial by law, but was taken to the nearest tree, where his body was left to sway in the breeze as an example to others.

No matter what form of outlawry he might follow—stage or train robbing, cattle rustling, horse stealing, or killing—the bad man led an exciting and colorful life. Often his name became celebrated in both deed and legend around campfires, and his exploits epitomized the daring and excitement of chase and battle. His survival depended upon quick thinking, good judgment, and abundant practice of the fast draw. Generally speaking, he trusted no man. When he sat, he did so with his back to the wall, facing the door, cat-eyed to every movement around him. If his reputation had become widespread, he knew that there were other gunmen of lesser caliber seeking to down him for the fame it would bring them. It is natural for men to become fascinated by such adventurous characters and easily mistake cold nerve for bravery, for killers are rarely brave. The brave man never shoots until he has to. As Struthers Burt once wrote, "The real heroes of the West saved their cartridges."

It is true that some of the western outlaws followed a code which might be considered honorable, such as never shooting an unarmed man, or shooting a man in the back, or molesting a decent woman. But this code resulted from fear of an enraged citizenry rather than any conception of honor. Most outlaws were bloodthirsty killers thinking of self-preservation first and last. Biographers of bad men often seek to justify their subjects' outlawry on the grounds of persecution of themselves or their families, but such was rarely the case. Usually they got their first start from their own foolhardiness, hot tempers, or desire for a reputation of being feared by other men. Once they took the fatal step, there was no turning back. As one of them once said, "You couldn't stop no more'n a loser in a poker game."

Although most outlaws departed from physical life with their boots on, some of the more famous ones—such as Billy the Kid, Joaquín Murieta, Jesse James, Sam Bass, and John Wesley Hardin—live on forever in both song and legend. Many books have been written about them and their kind. Numbers of books on the cattle industry and cowboy life have included outlaws because many men outside the law were associated with the range. It was easy for the reckless cowboy to drift into outlawry. Not a few reminiscences of westerners include accounts of outlaws because it seemed inevitable that most men in the West would sooner or later run into some of them.

Because of the widespread interest in, and extensive writing about, outlaws, I have compiled this bibliography of books which have come under my personal observation, many of them diligently sought by the great number of collectors of outlaw material. Please bear in mind that this compilation has been made as a book collector, not a professional bibliographer. No doubt the latter would have followed certain rules which have been grossly neglected in this work. I have merely tried, in a manner dictated by common sense and, I hope, unconfusing simplicity, to slant this whole collection toward the antiquarian bookman, the book collector, and the librarian, with the added hope that the future historian may take notice, particularly of the margin I have tried to establish between fact and fancy, between contemporary truth and subsequent legend.

The perfect bibliography has not yet been compiled, and perhaps never will be, even by the professional bibliographer. This one, like others preceding it, will be criticized, I am sure. Many critics will accuse me of leaving out this or that, or of including items of no importance. No one man can know every elusive book or pamphlet, even in a narrowly delimited field or for a brief historical period. Too many are memoirs of old-timers, printed without copyright by country presses in small editions and not distributed beyond the bounds of their place of origin. By the time the outside world has discovered them, they have been lost or thrown away, or the pulp paper upon which they were printed has disintegrated.

I freely confess that I have omitted a number of possible items in this bibliography, some on purpose and some through my ignorance of their existence. While the ink is still fresh on its pages, I will undoubtedly discover other outlaw books and wish they had been included. I think this happens to every compiler.

Perhaps it would be in order here to discuss some of the volumes excluded purposely from this compilation. The first large category consists of county and state histories. To include all such books which deal with or touch upon the western outlaw, I would have to list practically every state and county history for all the states west of the Mississippi. This would pose a problem of space, and therefore of practicality. Hence, if you find some favorite work of this nature omitted, the reason may not be my ignorance, but rather the necessity of using the space for books of larger importance, or for those needing severe criticism. I have attempted, however, to list enough of these volumes to give them representation.

There are many books of poetry and of cowboy songs which refer to western outlaws, but these, too, have been excluded because they do not serve the purpose of this work.

Almost every state and territory of the early West had vigilance committees, and the California committees were perhaps the most publicized. Books concerned with these California committees I have also purposely excluded, because they do not deal with the true western outlaw. The work of California vigilance committees was mostly against petty thieves, arsonists, "Sydney Ducks," and political enemies. The vigilantes of territories such as Montana, Idaho, New Mexico, and the like dealt with road agents such as the Plummer gang and killers such as Vicente Silva and Joel Fowler of New Mexico—genuine western outlaws and gunmen—and are therefore included.

It would be impractical to attempt to include all the "butcher boy" books, "penny dreadfuls," and dime novels written about the western outlaws in a work of the proportions I have chosen. All are wild fiction of no historical value, written to enrich the publishers and to thrill and stir young imaginations. I have tried, however, to include enough of those which appeal to collectors to provide more than a sampling of the class. Some of the old *New York Police Gazette* publications, especially, are expensive collectors' items, and some, like *Bella Starr*, unfortunately have provided the foundation for "histories" by careless writers who have sought the sensational rather than the true. It has seemed necessary to list a number of the latter in order to point out the pitfalls they contain for the researcher. To include all would be but a waste of space, of no value to the historian, and of little value to the collector.

There were a few female outlaws in the West, notably Belle Starr and Pearl Hart, and I have tried to list books containing information about them. In addition, although Calamity Jane, Poker Alice, and Madame Moustache cannot be classed as outlaws, it seems to me that these unique characters deserve a place here as part of the gunman's West.

In including many less worthy books than some I have omitted, I have had a definite purpose. Very little that is trustworthy has been printed about the old outlaws, aside from the court records and the accounts in the honest but scattered newspapers of their day. In all truth, one would not have to use an adding machine to count the really reliable books on the subject; they are greatly outnumbered by the unreliable ones.

For many years I have collected books pertaining to our western outlaws, but only when I approached the task of compiling this bibliography did I attempt to relate, analyze, and refine the information they contain. Now, after reading hundreds, I am like many another researcher before me: never would I have believed, before my investigations began, that so much false, inaccurate, and garbled history could have found its way into print.

Unfortunately, no matter how historically worthless many books are, they remain collectors' items. The book collector often fails to make, or disregards, the distinction between trustworthy and inaccurate accounts. It is not entirely his own fault, because the search for books is an end in itself, whereas the evaluation of them is a science which has history for its name. There are few among us, however, who would pass up a book like John Rollin Ridge's *Life and Adventures of Joaquín Murieta,* even though it does not contain the materials of historical accuracy. To know when to honor a legend is a fine act of judgment which will always be in dispute. Collecting the book that contains it is quite a different thing from arriving at the past event which is sought by other, historical, means.

But the historian or biographer should be concerned with the veracity of what he reads, and I think it extremely important to point out inaccurate sources so that the student of history can better appreciate factually reliable accounts. Many historians and would-be historians and biographers in the past have perpetuated false statements because they did not take the trouble to question what they had read or make investigations of their own.

A characteristic of the western American, as I have pointed out, has ever been to create legends about outlaws. Billy the Kid's living out his natural life in Mexico, Tom Horn's being seen walking the streets of Denver after his hanging in Cheyenne, a dummy's having been hanged in Giddings, Texas, instead of Bill Longley, and the half-dozen men during the last generation claiming to be Jesse James at various times—all of these tales and improvisations are by-products of western hero worship. Cumulatively, they offer a distortion of character and career which makes the search for the real man an almost impossible task. And I might add that not even the most heedless collector can escape, in time, the attraction of recognizable facts. Nor is it necessary to embellish a fourteen-carat hero in order to make him worthy of worship.

I know of no more striking example of handing down false history from author to author, and from generation to generation, than the account of Wild Bill Hickok's fight with the McCanles faction. This spurious report was started by Colonel George Ward Nichols in an article published in *Harper's Magazine,* in February, 1867. Purported to be an interview with Wild Bill himself, it has now been proved highly imaginary and exaggerated sensationalism, pure fabrication throughout. Nevertheless, most of the subsequent books on Wild Bill rehashed this legend, and Wild Bill himself made the story credible by not denying it.

In order to contrast the fabrications of these early unreliable historians with what actually happened, it may be desirable to give a brief account of the truth of this fight as it took place.

David McCanles had sold the Rock Creek Station property to the Overland Stage Company, which had fallen behind in its payments to him. He went to the station to talk with Wellman, its keeper, about the delinquency, taking with him his twelve-year-old son, Monroe, and two friends, Gordon and Woods. The four comprised the notorious "McCanles gang" of "cutthroats" which, through the efforts of certain yellow journalists, became so identified in the minds of the public.

If McCanles had expected trouble, he certainly would not have taken his young son along. In addition, he was a powerful man physically and did most of his fighting with his fists. There is no evidence that any of his party were armed.

Wellman refused to come out and talk with McCanles, but Wild Bill stepped to the door. Surprised at seeing Hickok, McCanles asked for a drink of water to gain time to collect his thoughts. After handing the dipper back to Hickok, he walked to another door to try again to talk with Wellman. It was then that Wild Bill shot him through the heart from a concealed position behind a curtain, using a rifle which McCanles had left at the station.

Woods and Gordon, meantime, had gone to the barn. Hearing the shots, they came running to see what was going on. Wild Bill stepped to the door and shot Woods, severely wounding him; then he shot Gordon as he was running away from the trouble. The brave Wellman now came out and finished the wounded Woods by beating his brains out with a heavy hoe, and would have done the same to the McCanles boy had the youngster not fled.

Simply told, these are the facts of the so-called "fight" with the "McCanles gang."

J. W. Buel, in nearly all his books, repeated the false Nichols story; then Emerson Hough seized it and enlarged upon it, and with his popularity and reputation convinced the public of its truth even more. Today it is still being repeated by writers who, for lack of better evidence, assume it to be reliable.

Many books and pamphlets have been written about Billy the Kid, concerning whose career most writers are in agreement on one point: he killed a man for every year of his life. However, writers disagree as to his age when he was killed by Pat Garrett, despite the commonly accepted statement that he died at the age of twenty-one years after having killed twenty-one men. His age and the number of men killed vary up to twenty-seven. From my own investigations, I think it is doubtful that he killed a total of ten men.

Even to the initiated, it is astonishing to discover how many accounts of his life have been written. Many have appeared in autobiographies of men who claimed acquaintance with the young outlaw. Others deal only with Billy. Most of them contain preposterous statements which will be discussed in the comments I make on individual works in this volume.

Joaquín Murieta of California is hardly second to Billy the Kid in demonstrating the power of legend to overcome fact. And it may be worthy to note at this point that the development of this kind of legend is of the order of conscious artifice, not of accident in an oral or unwritten tradition. If the study of human institutions and conventions teaches us anything, it is that an oral tradition has a singular purity, even among the most primitive. Nor do I think that Joaquín is necessarily the product of a bookless frontier, admitting, however, that it is upon the frontier that the tall tale and its characters—Paul Bunyan and Pecos Bill, for example—are developed. The tall tale is of another order: it exhibits a knowing wink and a conscious sense of tongue in cheek.

Today's historians have proved that Joaquín Murieta was nothing more than a low, brutal, and vicious cutthroat, but in the early 1850's he was seized upon by Californians as a subject to fill men's folk-memories. In 1854, John Rollin Ridge wrote a story of Murieta which was issued in an unpretentious little paper-bound book. Ridge was anything but a historian and biographer, but he could write with a certain rhetorical flourish. His account, though pure fiction, was greedily received by the waiting public, and it was believed. Ridge's creation was pirated, copied, made into plays and poems, and translated into foreign languages until it was, and is, accepted as truth.

An unsuccessful newspaperman with a vivid imagination, Ridge was merely trying to make enough money to pay some debts. But in common with many of his contemporaries, he possessed in abundance those techniques of the dime novelist which were to make the last half of the nineteenth century notable in the history of mass-reading phenomena. Indeed, he acknowledged that he wrote his book for the profit he expected to make from it. He could not guess how strongly it would appeal to an adventure-hungry people, or how little money he would realize from it because of difficulties with his own publishers and widespread pirating by others.

His story was seized and, with a few changes, published by the *California Police Gazette,* running serially for ten issues. It was illustrated by Charles Christian Nahl, a well-known artist of his day, and issued in book form in 1859, five years after the publication of Ridge's original story. By this time the legend was well on its way. Soon afterward it began to appear, with slight changes and under different authors' names, in Mexico, Spain, France, and Chile. Later this same legend was used by Walter Noble Burns and such careful historians as Bancroft and Hittell until now it is hard to convince the reader that it is fiction. Thus the history of Ridge's fabrication demonstrates the peculiar credibility and vitality of a fabrication, once it gets under way.

It may also demonstrate an even larger principle, namely the search for a series of writing conventions which would make a vast and little-inhabited land beyond the Missouri understandable to American society in the nineteenth century. It is only unfortunate that the search was not always conducted by well-informed writers, with a regard for the line of distinction between legitimate factual narrative and gross distortion of events. But to inveigh against the fabrications in this field is to miss the essential point that, in a developing urban and industrial society east of the Mississippi, the "penny dreadful" was the order of the day, and the pattern it set could hardly miss application to an exciting land and adventurous personalities needing no embellishment.

After studying hundreds of books on our western outlaws, I have classed the writers into four groups. The earliest writers were those of the penny dreadfuls and dime novels. They were hired by the publishers to turn out sensational stories in modern production-line style. By no stretch of the imagination could they be classed as lovers of the truth. They merely wrote what was expected of them—and here the word "expect" is of the essence, for it represents not so much a concession to popular taste as it does a hard-pressed hack's view of what the public should have. It must never be forgotten that this was still the age of marvels.

My chief complaint against such writers is not their fictitious histories, but their attempt at deception by leaning so heavily upon the disarming words "true" and "authentic" in their titles and subtitles. This was their stock in trade. But for the careful reader these misleading words serve as a warning, and rarely do they fail to prove the book so identified to be historically questionable.

The second type of author in the western outlaw field who has posed problems for us is the old-timer who attempts a book of memoirs. To begin with, he has rarely had previous writing experience, a handicap which often causes him to choose a worse instead of a better writing model, usually something dimly appreciated from his younger years. Memory, even in youth, is never entirely reliable, but in old age it offers pitfalls of an alarming kind. By a special variety of osmosis, the story heard around a campfire becomes an established fact of personal experience. Dates become transposed haphazardly, family connections take bizarre turns, and action which was fast enough at the time acquires extra tempo.

If the old-timer places his work in the hands of an editor, the latter is often enough quite ignorant of the West, its language and history, and like the average reader is too ready to accept the author's statements as gospel truth, mainly because none can dispute remembered events not of his own knowing. Old-timers' books are usually entertaining when they have not been spoiled by academic editing, but the serious student of western life and history is urged to accept them only with several grains of salt.

The third group of writers I call "rocking chair historians." They do not have the energy nor the acumen to dig out for themselves the records requisite to authentic narrative, or the critical powers needed to analyze the secondary sources upon which they mainly rely. Rewriting earlier spurious accounts in their own words—oftentimes not even taking the trouble to change the original phrasing—they sometimes succeed in passing along unreliable information from generation to generation. The complicating factor here is that highly respected writers occasionally accept, quite unwittingly, the substance of transmitted error, thus hardening into accepted doctrine the false and untrustworthy. From this point on, the public is unwilling to discount the word of a favored and competent author, even if subsequent research casts doubt upon his findings. As Mr. E. DeGolyer, the well-known collector of Western Americana, has said, any attempt to make Billy the Kid a character less admirable than Robin Hood is practically foredoomed to failure, in spite of the facts.

My fourth class of writers on the western outlaw consists of those thoroughly able and scrupulous men who, by their tireless efforts, their imagination, and their grasp of the methods of history, can in fact be called true historians. These are the men who go back to the newspaper files and court records, who check and compare, and who reconstruct personalities and events with a careful regard for manner and action and conflicting claims. The work of many of these will appear in this bibliography.

It is my earnest hope that the facts, as I have found them, will be valuable to librarians, to book collectors, and to followers of the western tradition in history, letters, and the arts. To say that my informal bibliographical effort has been a labor of love is tempting but untrue. In the words of a cowhand grown old, having just roped a Brahma bull, "it sweated the hell out of me."

Contents

Six-Guns and Saddle Leather

Table of Abbreviations

adv.	advertisement, advertisements
cm.	centimeters
co.	company
col.	colored
dec.	decorated
diagr., diagrs.	diagram, diagrams
dif.	different, differs
ed.	edition, editor, edited
facsm., facsms.	facsimile, facsimiles
fold.	folding, folded
front.	frontispiece
geneal.	genealogy, genealogical
illus.	illustrated, illustration, illustrations
imt.	imitation
incl.	including
l.	leaf, leaves
ltd.	limited
n.d.	no date
No., Nos.	number, numbers
n.p.	no place
OP.	out of print
p.	page, pages
pict.	pictorial
p.l.	preliminary leaf, leaves
port., ports.	portrait, portraits
prelim.	preliminary
pseud.	pseudonym
pub.	publisher, published, publishers
pub. device	publisher's device
t.p.	title page
Vol., Vols.	volume, volumes

A Bibliography of Books and Pamphlets on Western Outlaws and Gunmen

A

1. Abbott, E. C. (Teddy Blue)

We pointed them north; recollections of a cowpuncher, by E. C. Abbott ("Teddy Blue") and Helena Huntington Smith. Illustrated with drawings by Ross Santee, and photographs. New York, Toronto, Farrar & Rinehart, inc. [1939]. Pict. cloth.

xv p., 1 l., 3–281 p. front. (map), illus., ports., facsm. map, music. 22 cm.
Index: p. 271–281.
Half title; vignette; t.p. magenta; first edition "F R" in device on copyright p.
Reprinted in 1955, with illustrations by Nick Eggenhofer, by University of Oklahoma press.

This is one of the best books in recent years depicting cowboy life, and although it was recorded by a woman, she was wise enough to leave in all the flavor and saltiness of the cowboy lingo. Too often an erudite editor spoils a work of this kind by making it conform to academic standards. The book contains many references to the outlaws of the period covered, but the author's knowledge of outlaws, like that of most old-timers, was from hearsay and thus unreliable. He is mistaken in saying Sam Bass was his father's wagon boss before he went to Texas. Bass had very little cattle experience before helping drive a herd to Kansas with Joel Collins. He makes other mistakes such as having Calamity Jane die later than 1907. She died in 1903.

2. Abbott, Newton Carl

Montana in the making, by Newton Carl Abbott. . . . Billings, Mont., Gazette printing co., 1931. Cloth. Scarce.

5 p.l., 3–520 p. front. (relief map), illus., plates, ports., maps, facsm. 20 cm.
Appendix: p. 504–514; index: p. 515–520.
Map on end papers (dif.).

Although this book went through several editions, the eighth being a complete revision issued on March 15, 1943, it is difficult to find a copy, perhaps because it was used as a textbook. It contains chapters on Henry Plummer, his gang of outlaws, and the vigilantes of Montana. As a textbook, there are "Questions for Thought and Study" after each chapter.

3. **Abernathy, John R. (Jack)**

"Catch-'Em-Alive Jack"; the life and adventures of an American pioneer, by John R. Abernathy. New York, Association press, 1936. Cloth. OP.

4 p.l., 9–224 p. front. (port.), plates, ports. 20.8 cm.

This is a reissue, with extensive variations in the text, of the author's *In Camp with Roosevelt.* It contains a chapter on the author's activities as a United States marshal in Oklahoma, and the arrest of Jim Miller and other outlaws, and tells of the hanging of Miller at Ada, Oklahoma.

4. ———

In camp with Roosevelt; or, the life of John R. (Jack) Abernathy. John R. (Jack) Abernathy, author. Oklahoma City, Okla., published by the Times-Journal publishing co. [1933]. Pict. cloth. OP.

2 p.l., [9]–279 p. front. (ports.), plates (1 fold.), ports. 20 cm.

The author tells of some of his experiences as a deputy sheriff in Oklahoma and his captures of some of its outlaws. He tells of his efforts in helping capture Jim Miller, the noted killer, after which Miller was mobbed and lynched. He writes of knowing Frank James and repeats a lot of tall tales Frank told him, though he took them to be the truth. For instance, he says Frank told him that Civil War soldiers shot off his mother's arm and killed his little brother and that when he and Jesse came home and discovered it they left and "captured at least half of the soldiers who took part in it."

5. **Abney, H. A.**

Life and adventures of L. D. Lafferty; being a true biography of one of the most remarkable men of the great southwest, from an adventurous boyhood in Arkansas, through a protected life of almost unparalleled sufferings and hair-breadth escapes upon the frontier of Texas. . . . By H. A. Abney, of Rockport, Texas. New York, H. S. Goodspeed & co. [1875]. Dec. cloth. Scarce.

4 p.l., [15]–219 p. front. (port.), plates, ports. (all with tissues). 19 cm.

Contains some material on outlaws.

6. Adams, James Truslow (ed.)

Album of American history. Vol. II, 1853–1893. James Truslow Adams, editor in chief. R. V. Coleman, managing editor, Atkinson Dymock, art director. New York, Charles Scribner's sons [1946]. Dec. cloth. OP.

xi, 435 p. illus., plates. 28.5 cm.

Has some unreliable information on Wild Bill Hickok and Calamity Jane.

7. Adams, Ramon Frederick

Burs under the saddle. A second look at books and histories of the west, by Ramon F. Adams. Norman, University of Oklahoma press [1964]. Cloth.

x p., 2 l., [3]–610 p. 24.2 cm.
Index: p. [585]–610.
Half title; double column; "First edition" on copyright p.

A critical analysis of 424 books and pamphlets dealing with western outlaws and an attempt to correct some of the false history which has been written about them for many years.

8. ———

Cowboy lingo, [by] Ramon F. Adams. With illustrations. Boston, Houghton Mifflin co., 1936. Cloth. Scarce.

6 p.l., [3]–257 p. front., illus., cattle brands. 19.7 cm.
Index: p. [241]–257.
Half title; pub. device; first edition: 1936 under imprint.

Has a chapter on cattle rustlers and outlaws.

9. ———

A fitting death for Billy the Kid, by Ramon F. Adams. Norman, University of Oklahoma press, [1960]. Cloth.

ix p., 1 l., 3–310 p. plates, ports. 22 cm.
Index: p. 299–310.
Half title; "First edition" on copyright p.

An attempt to correct some of the false accounts that have been written about Billy the Kid for the past eighty years.

10. ———

From the Pecos to the Powder. A cowboy's autobiography as told to Ramon F. Adams by Bob Kennon. With drawings by Joe Beeler. Norman, University of Oklahoma press, [1965]. Pict. cloth.

xi [1] p., 1 l., 3–251 p. front., illus. (1 double p.), plates, map, plan. 23.5 cm.
Index: p. 242–251.
Half title; "First edition" on copyright p.

Has a chapter on Kid Curry and his killing of Pike Landusky, tells of the hanging of Black Jack Ketchum, and gives some new information on Henry Plummer.

11. ———

The legendary west. An exhibit by the Friends of the Dallas Public Library. Mayor Erik Jonsson, honorary exhibit chairman. . . . [By] Ramon F. Adams. Dallas, Texas, 1965. Stiff col. wrappers.

[64] p (no pagination). front., illus., plates, ports., map, facsms. 23 cm.

A catalogue with descriptions of the rare books shown in a library exhibit, among them books dealing with Wild Bill Hickok, Jesse James, Belle Starr, Calamity Jane, Sam Bass, and others.

12. ———

The old-time cowhand, [by] Ramon F. Adams. Illustrated by Nick Eggenhofer. New York, the Macmillan co., 1961. Cloth.

x p., 1 l., 3–354 p. illus. 24 cm.
Double illus. t.p.

Also published in a de luxe edition numbered and signed by both the author and the artist and in a slip case.

Has a chapter on cattle rustlers and one on outlaws.

13. ——— **(ed.)**

The best of the American cowboy. Compiled and edited by Ramon F. Adams, with drawings by Nick Eggenhofer. Norman, University of Oklahoma press, [1957]. Cloth.

xiv p., 1 l., 3–289 p. illus. 23.6 cm.
Half title; illus. double t.p.; "First edition" on copyright p.

Has a chapter on Elfego Baca and some material on Jim Averill and Cattle Kate.

14. ———**, and Homer Britzman**

Charles M. Russell, the cowboy artist. A biography by Ramon F. Adams and Homer Britzman, with bibliographical check list by Karl Yost. Pasadena, Calif., published by Trail's End publishing co., inc., [1948]. Cloth. OP.

xii p., 3 l., 350 p. front. (col.), 111 plates (12 col.), 37 chapter headings from pen-and-ink drawings by Charles M. Russell, facsm. 23.6 cm.

Index: p. 327–335; bibliographical check list: p. 339–350; col. illus. end papers from Russell's oil painting "Where Great Herds Came to Drink"; "First edition" on copyright p.

Also published in a deluxe edition limited to six hundred sets in two volumes.

Vol. I, same as trade edition except bound in three-quarter leather.

Vol. II, Charles M. Russell, the cowboy artist. A bibliography by Karl Yost, with a note by Homer Britzman and Frederic G. Renner, Pasadena, Calif., the Trail's End publishing co., inc., [1948]. Three-quarter leather.

8 p.l., 19–218 p. front. (facsm.), 20 illus. 23.6 cm.
Vol. II also published separately.

Both volumes boxed and issued with envelope of separate sets of colored illustrations.

Also issued in twenty-five sets bound in saddle leather and initialed in metal for recipient and signed by authors.

Vol. I has some material on Kid Curry and his killing of Pike Landusky.

15. Adler, Alfred

"Billy the Kid; a case study in epic origins." Berkeley, Calif., University of California press, 1951. Pamphlet. Scarce.

[10] p. (no pagination). stapled. 25.4 cm.

A reprint from *Western Folklore*, Vol. X, No. 2 (April, 1951), published for the California Folklore Society by the University of California Press. The author traces the steps by which Billy the Kid became a folk hero.

16. Agee, George W.

Rube Burrow, king of outlaws, and his band of train robbers. An accurate and faithful history of their exploits and adventures, by G. W. Agee. . . . Chicago, the Henneberry co., publishers [1890]. Cloth. Rare.

x, 194 p. front., ports. 19 cm.
Published same year by the C. J. Krehbiel co., Cincinnati.

The author was superintendent of the Western Division of the Southern Express Company and gives a fairly accurate account of Burrow's life and activities.

17. Ahern, L. Dale

Down one hundred years, by L. Dale Ahern. With illustrations by Clair B. Watson. Des Moines, Iowa, Wallace-Homestead co., 1938. Pict. cloth. OP.

6 p.l., 13–266 [1] p. front., illus. 19.8 cm.
Historical appendix: p. 195–266; chronological table: p. [267].
Half title.

In a chapter entitled "Hot Lead and Bad Blood," the author tells of the Mercer brothers of Decatur, Iowa.

18. Aiken, Albert W.

Rocky Mountain Rob, the California outlaw; or, the vigilantes of Humbug Bar, by Albert W. Aiken. New York, Beadle & Adams, 1871. Pict. wrappers. Rare.

206 p. 17 cm.

A wildly imaginary account of western outlawry, like many of Beadle & Adams' novels of the period. Robert Ernest Cowan, in *A Bibliography of the History of California and the Pacific West, 1510–1906* (San Francisco, Book Club of California, 1914), gives the 1871 date for the publication of this book; but Albert Johannsen, in *The House of Beadle and Adams and Its Dime and Nickel Novels* (Norman, University of Oklahoma press, 1950), does not show publication until 1873 as a serial in the *Saturday Journal*, with subsequent reprints in book form in 1875, 1878, and 1897.

19. Aikman, Duncan

Calamity Jane, and the lady wildcats, by Duncan Aikman. New York, Henry Holt and co., [1927]. Cloth. OP.

xii p., 1 l., 3–347 p. front., illus., plates, ports. 21 cm.
Illus. end papers (col.); vignette; untrimmed.
Republished, New York, Blue Ribbon, inc., 1937.
vii p., 2 l., 347 p. front., ports. 19.5 cm.

This book deals with Calamity Jane, Belle Starr, Cattle Kate, Pearl Hart, Poker Alice, and some other female characters of the early West. It is better written than some of its predecessors, but still fails to separate some of the legend from fact. In the Belle Starr chapter the author admits drawing liberally from Harman's *Hell on the Border* and also follows some of the legends created by the *Police Gazette's Bella Starr.*

Most of his information on Calamity Jane and Belle Starr is unreliable, and most of his errors have been pointed out in an earlier work. He deals rather sarcastically with Jane, and in spite of his seemingly thorough research states that she died on August 2, on "the 27th anniversary of Mr. McCall's stupendous play for fame in the annals of homicide." Actually she died on August 1.

20. ——— (ed.)

The taming of the frontier.... By ten authors. Edited by Duncan Aikman. New York, Minton, Balch & co., 1925. Cloth. Op.

xv p., 1 l., 3–319 p. front., plates. 21.5 cm.
Half title; pub. device.

One chapter tells the story of El Paso, Texas, in its six-gun days, and another, on Cheyenne, Wyoming, tells something of the Johnson County War.

21. Allan, A. A. (Scotty)

Gold, men and dogs. By A. A. "Scotty" Allan. Illustrated. New York and London, G. P. Putnam's sons. . . , 1931. Cloth. OP.

vii p., 1 l., 3–337 p. front. (port.), plates. 21 cm.
Half title; illus., end papers; vignette.

In a chapter entitled "Soapy Smith" the author tells a new story about this noted con man.

22. Alldredge, Eugene Perry

Cowboys and coyotes, by Eugene Perry Alldredge. [Nashville, Marshall & Bruce co., 1945.] Cloth. OP.

v, 7–184 p. illus., plates. 23.5 cm.
Illus. chapter headings.

The author makes some mention of Billy the Kid and Pat Garrett, but makes the erroneous statement that Pete Maxwell's daughter lured Billy the Kid upon the front porch where he was shot from ambush. In a footnote he refers to Mrs. Sophie Poe's book, *Buckboard Days,* pages 111–116, but she tells no such tale as that of the Kid's being lured to his death.

23. Allen, Allyn

The real book about the Texas Rangers, by Allyn Allen. Illustrated by C. L. Hartman. Edited by Helen Hoke. Garden City, New York, Garden City Books, by arrangement with Franklin Watts, inc. [1952]. Dec. boards. OP.

4 p.l., 9–192 p. front., illus., plates. 20.2 cm.
Index: p. 189–192.
Half title; illus., end papers; pub. device.

Contains a chapter on the capture of John Wesley Hardin and another on Sam Bass.

24. Allen, Ruth A.

The great southwest strike. [By] Ruth A. Allen. . . . Bureau of Research in the Social Sciences. Austin, Texas, University of Texas publications, 1942. Wrappers. OP.

4 p.l., [9]–174 p. illus., plates, facsms. 22 cm.
Appendix: p. [159]–163; bibliography: p. [164]–168; index: p. [169]–174.
At head of title: "The University of Texas Publications, No. 4214, April 8, 1942."

Has some information on Jim Courtwright when he was marshal at Fort Worth, Texas, and the trouble there during the railroad strike.

25. **Allen, Stookie**

Men of daring, by Stookie Allen. . . . New York City, Cupples & Leon co. [1933]. Pict. boards. OP.

[86] p. (no pagination). illus. 22.3 cm.

The author has a section on Tom Horn and must have taken his material from Coolidge's *Fighting Men of the West* because he makes the same mistakes. He states that Horn killed the Yapless boy, but the boy was Willie Nickells. He also states that Horn identified his killings by leaving a .30-30 shell on the victim's breast, but his identifying mark was a rock placed under the victim's head.

26. **Allen, Dr. William A.**

Adventures with Indians and game; or, twenty years in the Rocky mountains, by Dr. William A. Allen. Illustrated. Chicago, A. W. Bowen & co., 1903. Leather and boards. Scarce.

8 p.l., [19]–302 p. front. (port.), plates. 23 cm.

In relating a story about Calamity Jane and the killing of Wild Bill Hickok, the author quotes Buffalo Bill, who tells a most preposterous tale. He says that Jack McCall (which he spells McCaul), the murderer of Wild Bill, "was a cold-blooded one, and it was the general opinion that lynching was only too mild for him. Calamity Jane [was] in the lead of the lynching party and it was she who captured the desperado. She had left her rifle at home, but with a butcher's cleaver she held him up, and a very few minutes later McCaul's body was swinging from a cottonwood tree and his soul had passed over the Great Divide." History tells us that Calamity Jane was nowhere near when McCall was captured, and we know that he was not lynched.

27. **Aloutte (pseud.)**

Quantrell [*sic*], the terror of the West, Aloutte. . . . New York, M. J. Ivers & co., 1881. Pict. wrappers. Rare.

[15]–59 p. 18 cm.

An example of the wild fiction of the period.

28. **Altrocchi, Julia Cooley**

Traces of folklore and furrow. The old California trail, by Julia Cooley Altrocchi. Illustrated from photographs by the author. Caldwell, Idaho, the Caxton printers, ltd., 1945. Cloth.

12 p.l., [25]–327 p. front., plates, ports. 23.6 cm.
Bibliography: p. [317]–320; index: p. [321]–327.
At head of title: "The Old California Trail"; map on end papers; pub. device.

Has some information on the killing of Jesse James by Bob Ford and on some other western outlaws, but the author misnames Clell Miller as Clem.

29. Alvarez, N.

The James boys of Missouri. A western drama in four acts, by N. Alvarez. To which is added a description of the costumes—cast of characters—entrances and exits—relative positions of the performers on the stage, and the whole of the stage business. . . . [N.p.], Ames' publishing co., 1906. Wrappers. (Cover title.) Scarce.

[3]–31 p. 19.3 cm.

This little four-act play is wildly imaginary and has no historical value, but is a scarce collector's item.

30. American Guide Series

Arizona, a state guide. Compiled by workers of the Writers' Program of the Work Projects Administration in the state of Arizona. . . . Illustrated. . . . New York, Hastings House, publishers, MCMXL. Cloth.

xxv p., 1 l., 3–530 p. illus., plates, ports., maps. 21 cm.
American guide series.
Appendix: p. 499–[520]; index: p. 521–530.
Half title; map on end papers.

Contains some information on many of the outlaws and gunmen of Arizona, including the robbery of the Southern Pacific by Alvord and Stiles, the O K Corral fight in Tombstone, and the Tonto Basin War.

31. ———

California. A guide to the golden state. Compiled and written by the Federal Writers' Project of the Works Progress Administration for the state of California. . . . New York, Hastings House, publishers, MCMXXXIX. Cloth.

xxxl p., 1 l., 3–713 p. plates, ports., maps. 20.2 cm.
American guide series.
Chronology: p. 687–693; selected reading list: p. 694–698; index: p. 699–713.
Half title.

Sheds some light on California outlaws and stage robbers, such as Murieta, Vasquez, Black Bart, Tom Bell, and Jack Powers.

32. ———

Colorado. A guide to the highest state. Compiled by workers of the Writers' Program of the Works Projects Administration in the state of Colorado. . . . Illustrated. . . . New York, Hastings House, publishers, MCMXLI. Cloth.

xxxiii p., 1 l., 3–511 p. illus., plates, ports., maps. 21 cm.
American guide series.
Appendix: p. 467–[496]; index: p. 497–511.
Half title; map on end papers.

Contains reliable information on such outlaws as Butch Cassidy, the Espinosas, Joseph Slade, and Soapy Smith, and gives an account of Alferd Packer, the "man eater" (Packer himself signed his name Alferd). The book tells of the killing of Bob Ford, but misnames his killer Ed O'Kelly instead of Ed O. Kelly. This has been a common error, probably because Kelly's full name sounded as such.

33. ———

Idaho, a guide in word and picture. Prepared by the Federal Writers' Project of the Works Progress Administration. . . . Illustrated. Sponsored by the secretary of the state of Idaho. New York, Oxford University press, 1937. Cloth.

xiv p., 1 l., 3–300 p. plates, ports. 20.8 cm.
American guide series.
Appendices, origin of names: p. 279–286; bibliography: p. 287–289; index: p. 291–300.
Half title; map on end papers.

Contains some information on the Plummer gang, Bob Zachary, Cy Skinner, and the rest.

34. ———

Kansas. A guide to the sunflower state. Compiled and written by the Federal Writers' Project of the Works Projects Administration for the state of Kansas. . . . Illustrated. New York, the Viking press, MCMXXXIX. Cloth.

xviii [2] p., 538 p. front., plates, ports., map. 20.8 cm.
American guide series.
Chronology: p. 511–522; bibliography: p. 523–529; index: p. 531–538.
Half title.

Contains material on Wild Bill Hickok and other Kansas cowtown gunmen.

35. ———

Mississippi, a guide to the magnolia state. Compiled and written by the Federal Writers' Project of the Work Projects Administration. . . . Illustrated.

Sponsored by the Mississippi Agricultural and Industrial Board. New York, Hastings House, publishers, MCMXXXVIII. Cloth.

xxiv p., 1 l., [3]–545 p. plates, ports., maps. 21 cm.
American guide series.
Appendices: p. [509]–521; bibliography: p. [523]–530; index: p. [533]–545.
Half title; map on end papers; device.

Has some material on Rube Burrow, his train robberies, and his capture.

36. ———

Missouri. A guide to the "show me" state. Compiled by workers of the Writers' Program of the Work Projects Administration in the state of Missouri. . . . Illustrated. New York, Duell, Sloan and Pearce [1941]. Cloth.

15 p.l., 3–652 p. plates, ports., maps. 20 cm.
American guide series.
Chronology: p. 577–595; selected bibliography: p. 596–611; map section: p. 614–[627]; index: p. 629–652.
Half title.

Gives some information on Sam Hildebrand, the James and Younger boys, and the killing of Jesse James by Bob Ford.

37. ———

Montana. A state guide book. Compiled and written by the Federal Writers' Project of the Work Projects Administration for the state of Montana. . . . Illustrated. . . . New York, the Viking press, MCMXXXIX. Cloth.

xxiii [3] p., 3–430 [12] p. illus., plates, ports., fold. map in pocket at end. 21 cm.
American guide series.
Appendices: p. 413–423; bibliography; p. 425–429; index: p. 430–[442].
Half title; map on end papers; device.

Has some reliable information on Calamity Jane, Kid Curry, the vigilantes of Montana, and many of the state's outlaws. The writers misname James Butler Hickok as Charles Butler Hickok.

38. ———

Nebraska. A guide to the cornhusker state. Compiled and written by the Federal Writers' Project of the Works Progress Administration for the state of Nebraska. . . . Illustrated. . . . New York, the Viking press, MCMXXXIX. Cloth.

xxiii [3] p., 3–424 p. front., plates, ports., maps, plans, fold. map in pocket at end. 21 cm.
American guide series.

Chronology: p. 401–406; bibliography: p. 407–412; index: p. 413–424.
Half title; map on end papers.

Gives an account of the so-called Hickok-McCanles fight. It is claimed that the shooting of McCanles and his two companions by Hickok was "magnified into the 'McCanles massacre' in order to glorify the name of 'Wild Bill.'" Hickok and Wellman were tried at Beatrice in July, 1861, in the first criminal trial in the county.

39. ———

New Mexico. A guide to the colorful state. Compiled by workers of the Writers' Program of the Works Projects Administration in the state of New Mexico. . . . Illustrated. . . . New York, Hastings House, publishers, MCMXL. Cloth.

xxxvii p., 1 l., 3–458 p. illus., plates, ports., maps. 21 cm.
American guide series.
Appendices: p. 423–439; index: p. 441–458.
Half title; map on end papers; vignette.
Republished by University of New Mexico press, 1945, with a road map in pocket at end.

Has material on the Lincoln County War, Billy the Kid, Elfego Baca, Clay Allison, Black Jack Ketchum, and other outlaws. In the account about Billy the Kid, Jesse Evans is called Joe, and the writers make the statement that the Kid was twenty-two years old when he was killed.

40. ———

Oklahoma. A guide to the sooner state. Compiled by workers of the Writers' Program of the Work Projects Administration in the state of Oklahoma. . . . Illustrated. . . . Norman, University of Oklahoma press, MCMXLI. Cloth.

xxvi p., 1 l., 3–442 p. plates, ports., maps (6 on 1 fold. map in pocket at end). 20 cm.
American guide series.
Chronology: p. 415–421; selected reading list: p. 422–426; index: p. 427–442.

Contains material on the outlaws and law officers of Oklahoma. Also gives information on some of the lesser-known outlaws, such as Ray Terrell, Mat Kimes, and Wilbur Underhill.

41. ———

The Oregon Trail, U.S. 30, the Missouri river to the Pacific ocean. Compiled and written by the Federal Writers' Project of the Works Progress Administration. Sponsored by Oregon Trail Memorial Association, inc., New York, Hastings House, publishers [1939]. Pict. cloth.

xii, 244 p. front., plates, fold. map at end. 21 cm.
American guide series.
Appendices: p. 215–227; bibliography: p. 228–230; index: p. 233–244.
Half title.

Contains some material on Butch Cassidy, Tom Horn, and Joseph Slade.

42. ———

Provo, pioneer Mormon city. Compiled by the workers of the Writers' Program of the Work Projects Administration for the state of Utah. . . . Illustrated. . . . Portland, Oreg., Binfords & Mort, publishers [1942]. Cloth.

8 p.l., [17]–223 p. plates. 20.3 cm.
American guide series.
Notes: p. [190]–201; bibliography: p. [202]–208; index: p. [209]–223.
Half title; map on front end papers; plan on rear end papers; pub. device.

Contains some material on Butch Cassidy and his gang.

43. ———

Santa Barbara. A guide to the channel city and its environs. Compiled and written by the Southern California Writers' Project of the Work Projects Administration. . . . Illustrated. Sponsored by Santa Barbara State College. New York, Hastings House, publishers, MCMXLI. Cloth.

xviii p., 1 l., 3–206 p. illus., plates, map. 21 cm.
American guide series.
Chronology: p. 187–193; bibliography: p. 194–197; index: p. 199–206.
Half title; maps on end papers (dif.).

Has some slight material on Jack Powers.

44. ———

A South Dakota guide. Compiled by the Federal Writers' Project of the Works Progress Administration for the state of South Dakota. Sponsored by the state of South Dakota. [Pierre, State publishing co.], 1938. Cloth.

xxii p., 1 l., illus., plates, ports., maps, facsms. 21 cm.
[American guide series.]
Bibliography: p. 429–435; index: p. [436]–441.

Tells of the killing of Wild Bill Hickok by Jack McCall. The authors give Calamity Jane's birthplace as LaSalle, Illinois, and the date of her birth as May 1, 1852.

45. ———

Tennessee. A guide to the state. Compiled and written by the Federal Writers' Project of the Work Projects Administration for the state of Tennessee. Illustrated. Sponsored by Department of Conservation, Division of Information. New York, Hastings House, publishers, MCMXXXIX. Cloth.

xxiv p., 1 l., 3–558 p. plates, ports., maps, plans. 21 cm.
American guide series.
Chronology: p. 521–528; selected bibliography: p. 529–535; index: p. 537–558.
Half title; map on front end papers; device.

Contains some information on John Murrell.

46. ———

Texas. A guide to the lone star state. Compiled by the workers of the Federal Writers' Program of the Work Projects Administration in the state of Texas. . . . Illustrated. New York, Hastings House, publishers, 1940. Cloth.

xxxiii [3] p., 3–718 p. plates, ports., maps. 20.2 cm.
American guide series.
Glossary: p. 669–670; chronology: p. 671–676; selected reading list: p. 677–682; index: p. 701–718.
Half title; illus. end papers.

Goes to some extent into the activities of such outlaws as Sam Bass, King Fisher, Ben Thompson, and John Wesley Hardin.

47. ———

Tulsa. A guide to the oil capital. Compiled by the workers of the Federal Writers' Project of the Works Progress Administration in the state of Oklahoma. Sponsored by the Tulsa Federation of Women's Clubs. Tulsa, Okla., published by the Mid-West printing co., 1938. Stiff pict. wrappers. OP.

3 p.l., 9–79 p. front., plates, map, plans. 21.3 cm.
American guide series.
Bibliography: p. 75; index: p. 76–79.

This little book has a section on the Oklahoma outlaws who hung out near Tulsa, such as the Glass gang, the Dalton boys, the Buck gang, Bill Doolin's gang, Cherokee Bill, and Henry Starr. None of these outlaws ever bothered the people of Tulsa; for the most part they rode to town to drink and gamble.

48. ———

Utah. A guide to the state. Compiled by workers of the Writers' Program of the Works Projects Administration for the state of Utah. . . . Illustrated. . . . New York, Hastings House, publishers, MCMXLI. Cloth.

xxvi p., 1 l., 3–595 p. illus., plates, ports., maps. 21 cm.
American guide series.
Appendices: p. 531–566; index: p. 567–595.
Half title; map on end papers.

Has some information on Butch Cassidy, Joseph Slade and other bad men.

49. ———

Wyoming. A guide to its history, highways, and people. Compiled by workers of the Writers' Program of the Works Projects Administration in the state of Wyoming. . . . Illustrated. . . . New York, Oxford University press [1941]. Cloth.

xxvii p., 1 l., 3–490 p. illus., plates, ports., maps, fold. map in pocket at end. 21 cm.
American guide series.
Appendices: p. 441–468; index: p. 469–490.
Half title; map on end papers.

Has some information on Butch Cassidy, the Johnson County War, Calamity Jane, Bill Carlisle, Cattle Kate, Nate Champion, and others.

50. American Heritage

American Heritage, August, 1960, Vol. XI, No. 5, Pict. boards.

3–112 p. front. (col.), illus., plates, (part col., some double p.), ports., facsms. 28.5 cm.

Debunks such western characters as Wild Bill Hickok, Jesse James, Wyatt Earp, Bat Masterson, Billy the Kid, Belle Starr, and Calamity Jane.

51. Anderson, A. M.

Wild Bill Hickok, by A. M. Anderson. Emmett A. Betts, editor. . . . Illustrations by Jack Merryweather. Chicago, Wheeler publishing co. [1947]. Pict. cloth. OP.

2 p.l., 252 p. illus. 19 cm.
Illus. end papers (col.).
One of a series entitled "The American Adventure Series."

A highly fictionized account for young readers, all the more unfortunate because it teaches American youth what purports to be history.

52. Anderson, Abraham C.

The pioneer life of George W. Goodhart, and his association with the Hudson's bay and American fur company's traders and trappers. Trails of early Idaho, as told to Abraham C. Anderson. Illustrations: photos by Abraham C. Anderson, drawings by Jo G. Martin. Caldwell, Idaho, the Caxton printers, ltd., 1940. Cloth.

9 p.l., [15]–368 p. front. (col.), plates, ports. 23.5 cm.
Half title; map on end papers; pub. device.

Contains some first-hand material on some of Plummer's road agents.

53. Anderson, E. T.

A quarter-inch of rain, [by] E. T. Anderson. Emporia, Kans., 1962. Pict. cloth.

7 p.l., 15–220 p. illus., plates. 22.3 cm.

Contains a chapter on Henry Starr and also some information on the Dalton gang.

54. Anderson, Frank W.

Bill Miner, train robber, by Frank W. Anderson. [Calgary, Alberta, published by Frontiers unlimited, n.d.] Pict. wrappers.

2 p.l., 5–56 p. plates (4 full p.), ports. (full p.), 4 maps. 21 cm.
References: p. 56.

Gives a complete life of Bill Miner and his train robberies in both Canada and the United States.

55. Anderson, George B. (ed.)

History of New Mexico, its resources and people. Illustrated. Los Angeles, Chicago, New York, Pacific States publishing co., 1907. Pub. in two volumes. Three-quarter leather. Scarce.

Vol. I, xxvii, 522 p. front. (port.), plates, ports. (part with tissues). 26 cm.
Vol. II, biographical.
Both volumes paged continuously.

Volume I contains a long chapter entitled "Local Wars and Crimes," and deals with the Lincoln County War and Billy the Kid; the Horrell War; the train robbery of Taggart, Joy, and Lee; and the capture and trial of Black Jack Ketchum and other criminals. As in many accounts of this period, quite a few proper names are misspelled. Much material is quoted from the unreliable writings of Emerson Hough.

56. Andreas, A. T.

History of the state of Nebraska, containing a full account of its growth from the uninhabited territory to a wealthy and important state; of its early settlement; its rapid increase in population and the marvelous development of its great natural resources. . . . Illustrated. Chicago, the Western Historical co. . . . , 1882. Cloth. Scarce.

4 p.l., [32]–1506 p. illus., plates, ports., large fold. map (col.) in front. 30.2 cm.

Perhaps the first publication to give the true account of the "fight" at Rock Creek Station between Hickok and McCanles. Being a large, 1,506-page book, it received very little circulation. The author criticizes a preceding biography of Wild Bill, probably that by Buel, saying: "Perhaps most of this is true, but if the biographer knew that the first noted incident, namely the fight at Rock Creek, was basely exaggerated, he would have been less enthusiastic in his preface. From the fact that this incident is so far from correct, the citizens of Jefferson are inclined to look upon all the facts given as exaggerations, and many as entire fiction. This biographer states that Wild Bill killed eight men at Rock Creek, but after a most thorough examination we find that he only killed three, and in a manner that did not display bravery or courage but simply skill in the use of firearms."

Yet this author, after a good start toward the truth, suddently also gets his facts wrong and misspells names, for example, McCaulas for McCanles. He does, however, make Wild Bill a cowardly bushwhacker of the worst kind. He also tells of the trouble between I. P. Olive and Mitchell and Ketchum, and the burning of the latter two.

57. **Andrews, C. L.**

The story of Alaska, by C. L. Andrews. Illustrated. Caldwell, Idaho, the Caxton printers, ltd., 1938. Pict. cloth.

10 p.l., [21]–332 p. front. (port. with signature in facsm.), plates, ports., maps (1 large fold. map in pocket at end). 23.6 cm.

Appendix: p. [259]–261; notes: p. [265]–317; bibliography: p. [321]–326; index: p. [327]–332.

Half title; pict. map on end papers; vignette.

Has a short chapter devoted to Soapy Smith and his activities in Skagway.

58. **Angel, Myron (ed.)**

History of Nevada, with illustrations and biographical sketches of its prominent men and pioneers. Oakland, Calif., Thompson & West, 1881. Leather. Scarce.

xiv p., 2 l., [17]–680 p. illus., plates (1 double p.), ports. (part with tissues), facsm., tables. 20.5 cm.

Double column.

Republished in 1958 at Berkeley, Calif., with an introduction by David Myrick.

One chapter, which includes a short sketch of Sam Brown and Langford Peal, gives a long list of the killings by years.

59. ———

History of Placer county, California, with illustrations and biographical sketches of its prominent men and pioneers. Oakland, Calif., Thompson & West, 1882. Three-quarter leather. Scarce.

viii, [9]–416 p. front. (with tissue), plates (1 fold.), ports. 31 cm.

In a long chapter on crime, the author deals at length with Richard Barter, alias Rattlesnake Dick, one of the notorious outlaws of California.

60. ———

History of San Luis Obispo County, California, with illustrations and biographical sketches of its prominent men and pioneers. Oakland, Calif., Thompson & West, 1883. Three-quarter leather. Scarce.

viii, [9]–391 p. plates, ports. 30.8 cm.

This scarce book has three long chapters on crime and criminals, giving accounts of such California outlaws as Jack Powers, Joaquín Murieta, and Joaquín Valenzuela.

61. Angle, Paul M.

Bloody Williamson. A chapter in American lawlessness, by Paul M. Angle. New York, Alfred A. Knopf, 1952. Cloth. OP.

xiv p., 2 l., 3–299 [1] p., i–xiv p. maps. 22 cm.

[Summary of] principal events: p. 277–291; sources: p. 292–299 [1]; index: p. i–xiv.

Half title; pub. device; untrimmed.

Though not strictly about western outlaws, it does contain much on lawlessness and the murder of S. Young Glenn.

62. Ankeny, Nesmith

The West as I knew it. By Nesmith Ankeny. [Lewiston, Idaho, printed by the R. G. Bailey printing co., 1953]. Stiff pict. wrappers.

viii, 148 [1] p. plates, 1 port., map. 23 cm.

Chapter V deals with Henry Plummer's gang and other outlaws of the Northwest.

63. Anthony, Irvin

Paddle wheels and pistols, by Irvin Anthony. . . . Illustrated and decorated by Manning De V. Lee and Lyle Justis. Philadelphia, Macrae Smith co., publishers [1929]. Pict. cloth. OP.

5 p.l., 13–329 p. front. (col.), illus., plates (4 col. incl. front.). 23.7 cm.

Illus. half title; illus. end papers; illus. t.p.; "First edition" on copyright p.

64. Antwerp, Albert van

La Fiesta, a one act play with music. (Type of music suggested.) Based upon an incident in the life of the Southwest's romantic boy bandit, Billy the Kid.

By Albert van Antwerp. Sioux City, Iowa, Wetmore Declamation Bureau, publishers [1935]. Wrappers. OP.

15 p. 19 cm.

Another example of the prolific output concerning a greatly exaggerated folk hero.

65. Appell, George C.

Belle's castle. [By] George C. Appell. New York, the Macmillan co., 1959. Cloth.

3 p.l., 134 p. 20.8 cm.
Half title; "First printing" on copyright p.

A highly fictionized story about Belle Starr. The author says her home was known as the "Castle," but it was known as "Younger's Bend."

66. Applegate, Frank G.

Native tales of New Mexico. Introduction by Mary Austin with illustrations in color by the author. Philadelphia and London, J. B. Lippincott co. [1932]. Cloth. Scarce.

7 p.l., 15–263 p. front. (col.), plates (all col.). 21 cm.
Half title; t.p. in brown and black; untrimmed.
Frank G. Applegate at head of title.

Contains a chapter on the Apache Kid.

67. Appleman, Roy E.

Charlie Siringo, cowboy detective, by Roy E. Appleman. Washington, D.C., Potomac Corral, the Westerners, 1968. Stiff pict. wrappers.

2 p.l., 19 [1] p. front., plates, port. 22.5 cm.
Bibliography: p. 18.
No. 3 of the Great Western Series.

A short biography of Siringo, mostly about his detective years.

68. Appler, Augustus C.

The guerrillas of the West; or, the life, character and daring exploits of the Younger brothers. With a sketch of the life of Henry W. Younger, father of the Younger brothers, who was assassinated and robbed by a band of Jayhawkers. . . . Also a sketch of the life of the James boys whose names are familiar to every household in the country, and whose reputed deeds of blood, robbery & crime of almost every kind, equal the most desperate brigand of the nineteenth century, etc., etc., by Augustus C. Appler. . . . St. Louis, John T. Appler, publisher and proprietor, 1875. Cloth. Rare.

iv, 208 p. front., plates, ports. 19 cm.
Cover title: "Younger Brothers."
Reprinted in 1876, St. Louis, Eureka publishing co.
iv, 5–224 p. front., plates, ports. 21.2 cm.

Reprinted with same imprint in 1878 with 215 pages, 8 pages of the Northfield Bank robbery being omitted at the end. Another edition was printed in Chicago by Bedford, Clark and Company, with 287 pages. The original illustrations are used, but have a different placement. Although the text is the same, there are more pages because larger type was used. "The Guerrillas of the West" is omitted at head of title page. On page 32 the word "Ohio" is substituted for "Iowa" on page 23 of the original. This edition has no date of publication.

Another edition, entitled "The True Life . . . of the Younger Brothers," with 287 pages, was published in Chicago in 1880. Still another edition was published in Chicago in 1882, two parts in one and reprinted with the same imprint in 1884. Reprinted again in a cloth edition in the Pinkerton Detective Series, No. 48, by Chicago, Laird and Lee in 1893.

viii, [9]–287 p. front., plates, ports. 19 cm.

The author painted the Youngers with a kindly brush and did much to prove that these outlaws did not commit all the crimes of which they were accused. However, such accusations were a part of the lives of all outlaws. As long as they were free and active, they received credit for many crimes committed by others. Editor of the Osceola, Missouri, *Democrat*, the author had the honesty of the old-time newspaperman, and most of his statements concerning the war years are fairly accurate, though he does tell several yarns which are untrue. His information of the Youngers' outlaw years is unreliable.

One of the untrue stories Appler told did Cole Younger some damage later, when he was trying to secure a pardon. That was the tale in which Cole was supposed to have shot fifteen prisoners with a powerful new Enfield rifle captured the day before. Someone remarked that he had heard the rifle would shoot a mile, and Cole replied that if such was the case a bullet should go through ten men. The fifteen prisoners were lined up, one behind the other, and Cole continued to shoot until they were all dead. The story came up before the Board of Pardons when the Youngers were seeking a pardon from the Minnesota prison. Appler took this story, along with several others, from some of the *Police Gazette* publications. Another such story is the one about Cole making his escape in the night by walking in his sock feet for several miles on top of a plank fence. Appler also errs in saying that Cole killed his cousin, Captain Charles Younger of the Union Army; the whole account, together with Cole's escape, is a fabrication. Appler's book, being one of the earliest ones, served as a fountainhead for many later and even less accurate volumes.

69. ———

The Younger brothers, their life and character, by A. C. Appler. With a foreword by Burton Rascoe. New York, Frederick Fell, inc., publishers [1955]. Cloth.

14 p.l., 25–245 p. front., plates, ports. 21 cm.

In his foreword Burton Rascoe makes many unreliable statements, for example, that the Jameses and the Youngers were related and that the author of *John Wesley Hardin, as Written by Himself*, "was very likely a reporter on the staff of an Austin, Texas, newspaper and a correspondent for the *National Police Gazette*."

70. Archambeau, Ernest R. (ed.)

Old Tascosa, 1885–1888. . . . Canyon, Texas, published by the Panhandle-Plains Historical society, 1966. Imt. leather.

viii p., 2 l., 195 p. 1 plate, 1 map. 22.5 cm.
Index: p. 185–195.
Copyright notice on t.p.; partly double column.

This book consists of excerpts from the old *Tascosa Pioneer* for the years 1886 to 1888 and preserves some of the forgotten history of that famous cow town. It repeats that old fable about Clay Allison pulling his dentist's teeth in revenge for pulling the wrong one; in this telling the incident takes place in Cheyenne, Wyoming. There is a short account of the killing of Jim Courtright by Luke Short, and a longer account about the Catfish Kid. It is disappointing that the famous Tascosa gun battle is omitted.

71. Argall, Phyllis

The truth about Jesse James, by Phyllis Argall. . . . A post mortem presentation of little-known facts about the famous American character. Sullivan, Mo., published by Lester B. Dill and Rudy Turilli, 1953. Wrappers. Scarce.

3–28 p. plates, ports., facsms. 20.5 cm.

This little book upholds the claim that J. Frank Dalton was the real Jesse James, but the author advances no conclusive proof.

72. [Arizona]

Historical anecdotes of old prison days. . . . [Yuma, Ariz., n.d.] Pict. wrappers.

[20] p., (no pagination). plates. 23 cm.

Has some material on various Arizona outlaws who were imprisoned at Yuma.

73. ———

History of Arizona territory, showing its resources and advantages; with illustrations descriptive of its scenery, residences, farms, mines, mills . . ., from original drawings. San Francisco, Calif., Wallace W. Elliott & co., publishers, 1884. Three-quarter leather. Scarce.

5 p.l., [25]–332 [2] p. front. (with tissue), plates (2 double p.), ports., charts (1 col.), cattle brands, tables. 34.8 cm.

Double column; last p. adv.

Tells of the hanging of John Heath and his gang.

74. ———

Outlawry and justice in old Arizona. By various members of the History Club of Sunnyside High School. Tucson, Ariz., L. A. Printers, 1965. Stiff pict. wrappers.

6 p.l., 119 [1] p. illus. 23.5 cm.

Bibliography after each chapter; printed on one side of paper only.

Has chapters on Luke Short, the Apache Kid, Pearl Hart, Curly Bill Brocius, Johnny Ringo, the Earps, Bat Masterson, the O K Corral, Arizona Rangers, Billy Breakenridge, John Slaughter, Pat Garrett, and Billy the Kid. The author of the chapter on the Earps is mistaken when she says that Wyatt spent most of his life as a U.S. marshal and that after the O K Corral fight he "disappeared into the desert." The author of the chapter on Garrett is mistaken in saying that Olinger was killed by the Kid from a balcony. I fail to see why Garrett and Billy the Kid are included in a book about Arizona, except that most authors writing about western outlaws feel that they must bring these characters into their stories.

75. ———

Souvenir of Tombstone, Arizona. [N.p., n.d.] Wrappers.

[20] p. (no pagination). plates, ports., map. 22.5 cm.

Double column; 8 p. adv. (incl. verso and recto of covers).

Has a chapter on the O K Corral fight and material on the Earps, Doc Holliday, Johnny Behan, and Russian Bill.

76. Armor, Samuel (ed.)

History of Orange county, California, with biographical sketches of the leading men and women of the county, who have been identified with the growth and development from the early days to the present. History by Samuel

Armor. Illustrated. . . . Los Angeles, Calif., Historic Record co., 1911. Leather. Scarce.

x, [5]–705 p. plates, ports. (part with tissues), fold. map. 28.2 cm.

Chapter XXI deals with the killing of Sheriff Barton and the capture and lynching of Juan Flores and his gang.

Rewritten ten years later (1921) and published by the same company.

11 p.l., [33]–1669 p. plates, ports. 27.6 cm.

Chapter XXIV again tells of Barton's murder and gives the story of the capture and lynching of Juan Flores, written by an eyewitness to the hanging.

77. Armstrong, J. B.

The raw edge, by J. B. Armstrong. Missoula, Montana State University press [1964]. Stiff pict. wrappers.

xi, 90 [1] p. illus., plates, ports. 21 cm.

This little book gives a good picture of the early-day Texas Panhandle and life in Oklahoma Territory. It tells the story of the "big fight" at Tascosa, Texas.

78. Arnold, Oren

Thunder in the southwest. Echoes from the wild frontier, by Oren Arnold, with drawings by Nick Eggenhofer. Norman, University of Oklahoma press [1952]. Cloth. OP.

ix p., 1 l., 3–237 p. illus. 21.9 cm.

Half title; "First edition" on copyright p.

The author here tells of lawlessness in the Southwest, some of which is legendary. In one chapter he repeats the Murieta legend and uses the Carmen version of the *California Police Gazette*. Like several other authors, he misspells Murieta's name. He has Carmen raped and killed before the very eyes of the wounded Murieta. He repeats the old legend about the reward notice and Murieta's writing beneath the poster doubling the reward. This incident never happened. The author says that three movies have been made about Murieta's life, "none of them historically accurate"; yet his chapter on Murieta is inaccurate in every detail. In his chapter on the Earp-Clanton feud, he is favorable to the Earps.

There is one typographical error which may later identify the first printing of this work. On page 39, line 11, the word "beheld" is spelled "behld."

79. ———, and John P. Hale

Hot irons. Heraldry of the range, by Oren Arnold and John P. Hale. New York, the Macmillan co., 1940. Pict. Cloth. OP.

viii p., 2 l., 242 p. illus., cattle brands. 21.7 cm.

Half title; cattle brands on end papers.

This excellent book has a long chapter on cattle rustlers.

80. Arrington, Alfred W. (pseud. of Charles Summerfield)

The desperadoes of the southwest; containing an account of the Cane-Hill murders. Together with the lives of several of the most notorious regulators and moderators of that region, by Charles Summerfield [pseud.]. New York, William H. Graham, 1847. Pict. wrappers. Rare.

iv, [5]–48 p. front., illus. 24.5 cm.
Illus. t.p.

There were three issues of this book, one with only forty-two lines on the last page and with the printer's name on the verso of the title page, and two with forty-four lines on the last page, one with and one without the printer's name on the title page. These now rare books, published to sell for fifteen cents, bring very high prices today.

81. ———

Duelists and dueling in the south-west. With sketches of southern life. Being the second and concluding part of "The Desperadoes of the South-West," by Charles Summerfield [pseud.] of Texas. New York, William H. Graham; H. Long and brother; Philadelphia, Zeiber and co.; St. Louis, E. K. Woodward, 1847. Pict. wrappers. Rare.

iv, [5]–54 p. front. 22.4 cm.
2 p. adv. at end.

A sequel to Item 80 and reissued in later editions.

82. ———

Illustrated lives and adventures of the desperadoes of the new world; containing an account of the different modes of lynching; the Cane-Hill murders . . . , together with the lives of the notorious regulators and moderators in the known world, by Charles Summerfield [pseud.]. . . . Philadelphia, T. B. Peterson [1849]. Wrappers. Rare.

2 p.l., 11–117 p. wood-block engravings. 24 cm.

83. ———

The lives and adventures of the desperadoes of the south-west; containing an account of the duelists and dueling; together with the lives of several of the most notorious regulators and moderators of that region, by Charles Summerfield [pseud.]. New York, W. H. Graham, 1849. Wrappers. Rare.

iv, [5]–98 p. wood-block engravings. 24 cm.

84. ———

The rangers and regulators of the Tenaha; or, life among the lawless. A tale of the republic of Texas, by Charles Summerfield [pseud.]. . . . New York, Robert M. DeWitt, publisher . . . [1856]. Cloth. Very scarce.

xi, [13]–397 p. front., plates (all with tissues). 19.2 cm.
5 l. adv. at end.

Reprinted in New York in 1874 with Mayne Reid's name as the author on the spine. Later published under the title *A Faithful Lover* by G. W. Carleton and co., 1884.

1 p.l., [13]–396 p. front. 19.5 cm.

All Judge Arrington's books are fictionized accounts of life in Texas during the Shelby County War between the Regulators and the Moderators and were written in the flowery style of the period. Most of his writings were repetitions of the same theme.

85. Arthur, George Clinton

Bushwhacker, by George Clinton Arthur. A true history of Bill Wilson, Missouri's greatest desperado; a story of blood. Rolla, Mo., Rolla Printing co., 1938. Thin pict. cloth. OP.

x, [11]–108 [1] p. front., illus., ports. 17.8 cm.
Half title.

The only book I know devoted to this famous Missouri outlaw. It tells of Wilson's hardships and daring exploits.

86. Artrip, Louise, and Fullen Artrip

Memoirs of Daniel Fore (Jim) Chisholm and the Chisholm trail, by Louise and Fullen Artrip. [Boonville, Ark, published by Artrip publications, 1949.] Stiff wrappers. OP.

4 p.l., 11–89 [1] p. front., plates, ports. 19.6 cm.

The authors erroneously claim that Daniel Chisholm bossed the first herd of cattle to leave Texas and that the Chisholm Trail was named for him. They also state that the trail led through Vernon, Texas, and crossed Red River at Doan's Crossing. This was not the original Chisholm Trail, but the Western Trail, which was established several years later when the railroads had moved farther west and the settlers had begun to fence their claims. The authors' account of the Sutton-Taylor feud and John Wesley Hardin's participation in it is more reliable.

87. ———, and ———

Memoirs of (the late) Daniel Fore (Jim) Chisholm and the Chisholm Trail, by Louise and Fullen Artrip. [N.p. [Yermo, Calif.,], published by Artrip publications, 1949]. Stiff wrappers. OP.

4 p.l., 9–185 p. illus., plates, ports. 18.5 cm.

This edition is much the same as the first edition through Chapter V, except for a change in tenses and in chapter arrangements. After Chapter V there is much new material which the authors could not publish until after Chisholm's death. The authors, however, still insist that Jim Chisholm's father drove the first herds of cattle out of Texas to the northern markets and that the trail led through Mineral Wells, Graham, Vernon, and Doan's Crossing, though history differs with them. They say that the trail went through Norman, Oklahoma City, Sapulpa, and Tulsa, though they do not explain why it should lead as far west as Oklahoma City to reach Tulsa, which is to the northeast.

They tell a great deal about Chisholm's life as an outlaw in Arizona, but the book is filled with errors. It is also characterized by irritating and unnecessary capitalization of words and by many miniature stock illustrations which do not fit the text. Many of the authors' errors have been discussed in my *Burs under the Saddle* (Item 7).

88. Asbury, Herbert

Sucker's progress. An informal history of gambling in America from the Colonies to Canfield. By Herbert Asbury. Illustrated. New York, Dodd, Mead & co., 1938. Cloth and pict. boards. OP.

x p., 1 l., 3–493 p. illus., plates, ports., facsm. 22.6 cm.
Bibliography: p. 470–478; index: p. 479–493.
Half title; untrimmed.

Makes mention of many gunmen, such as John Wesley Hardin, Bat Masterson, King Fisher, the killing of Hickok, Soapy Smith, and the Clantons. The author tells of the killing of Bob Ford but makes the common mistake of spelling Ed O. Kelly as Ed O'Kelly. His account of the killing of Phil Coe by Hickok is not true, and he is mistaken in giving the year of Doc Holliday's death as 1897. He died in 1887.

89. [Ash, George]

Captain George Ash. His adventures and life story as cowboy, ranger, soldier. . . . Eastleigh, [England], Eastleigh printing works. . . . [N.p., n.d. [ca. 1933]]. Pict. boards. Scarce.

6 p.l., 17–180 p. plates, ports. 18.8 cm.

This scarce little book tells about cattle rustling and outlawry in the Mexican border country.

90. Ashton-Wolfe, H.

Outlaws of modern days, by H. Ashton-Wolfe . . ., with eight plates. London, Toronto, Melbourne & Sydney, Cassell & co., ltd. [1927]. Cloth. OP.

xiii, 277 [1] p. front., plates, ports., facsm. 22.2 cm.
Half title; device.

Republished in the United States with the same contents except for one added chapter, a different title, and a different order of arrangement. American title: Crimes of violence and revenge, by H. Ashton-Wolfe . . . with illustrations. Boston and New York, Houghton Mifflin co. . . ., 1929. Cloth. OP.

vii p., 3 l., 3–359 [1] p. front., plates, ports., facsms. 19.7 cm.
Half title; device; untrimmed; first American edition: 1929 under imprint.

Both books contain a chapter on Red López, but it is unreliable.

91. Aten, Ira

Six and one-half years in the ranger service. The memoirs of Ira Aten, sergeant, Company D, Texas rangers. Bandera, Texas, published by Frontier Times, 1945. Pict. wrappers. (Cover title.) OP.

64 p. front. (port.), plates. 26.7 cm.
Double column.

A separate reprint of a series which ran in the *Frontier Times.* Aten tells of his efforts to suppress wire cutting and other lawlessness in Texas.

92. Atherton, Lewis

The cattle kings, by Lewis Atherton. Bloomington, Indiana University press [1961]. Pict. cloth.

xii, 308 p. front., plates, ports. 24 cm.
Notes: p. [279]–298; index: p. [299]–308.
Half title; map on end papers.

Has some information on the Johnson County War and a mention of such gunmen as Wild Bill Hickok and Billy the Kid.

93. Atkinson, S. W.

Adventures of Oklahoma Bill. [By S. W. Atkinson, n.p., n.d.] Pict. wrappers. Very rare.

16 p. 21.5 cm.
Adv. on verso and recto of wrappers.

Tells about the deaths of Jesse James and of Wild Bill Hickok.

94. Ault, Phillip H. (ed.)

The home book of western humor. Edited with an introduction by Phillip H. Ault. New York, Dodd, Mead & co. [1967]. Cloth.

xx p., 1 l., 3–364 p. 23.5 cm.
Half title.

An anthology with a section about Black Bart from Ghost Town by G. Ezra Dane.

95. Austin, Charles H. (publisher)

"Old Mother Osborne, the female road agent." Dies destitute in a lonely cabin in the Yellowstone country, after a stirring life of outlawry in the Black hills. Copied and reprinted from the *Police Gazette* of the early '80s, by Chas. H. Austin. Philadelphia, Pa., 1939. Pamphlet. Pict. wrappers. (Cover title). Scarce.

[5] p. (no pagination). 14.5 cm.

A separate reprint of one of the numerous imaginary tales about outlaws published by the *New York Police Gazette.*

96. Axford, Joseph Mack

Around western campfires, by Joseph "Mack" Axford. New York, Pageant press, inc. [1964]. Cloth.

5 p.l., 262 p. plates. 21 cm.
Half title.

The personal experiences of an early settler of Arizona whom I met in Tombstone, where he had formerly been a deputy and the jailer. He writes about many of the early outlaws of Arizona and New Mexico, such as Curly Bill Brocius, Billy Claiborne, Buckskin Frank Leslie, the McLaurys, the Clantons, Billy Stiles, Burt Alvord, John Ringo, Doc Holliday, the Ketchums, Billy the Kid, Will Carver, Will McGinnis, Butch Cassidy, and the Earps. He also gives an account of the O K Corral fight. He is mistaken, however, in saying that Russian Bill was hanged in Galeyville. He was hanged at Shakespeare, New Mexico, with Sandy King.

97. Axtell, Gov. Samuel B.

Message of Gov. Samuel B. Axtell to the legislative assembly of New Mexico, twenty-third session. Santa Fé, N.M., Manderfield & Tucker, public printers [1878]. Wrappers. (Cover title.) Rare.

16 p. 20.2 cm.

In the speech the governor laments the escape from jail of Billy the Kid, discourses on the "bad white man," and urges the repeal of the statute against carrying arms.

98. Ayers, I. Winslow

Life in the wilds of America, and wonders of the West in and beyond the bounds of civilization. Illustrated. . . . By I. Winslow Ayers. . . . Grand Rapids, Mich., published by the Central publishing co., 1880. Cloth. Scarce.

5 p.l., [11]–528 p. front., illus., plates. 22 cm.

Contains some minor material on road agents and the vigilantes of Montana.

99. Ayers, Col. James J.

Gold and sunshine; reminiscences of early California, [by] Colonel James J. Ayers. Illustrated from the collection of Charles B. Turrill. Boston, Richard G. Badger. . . . [1922]. Cloth. OP.

xiv p., 1 l., 11–359 p. front. (port.), plates, ports. 21 cm.
Index: p. 347–359.
Illus. end papers; pub. device; untrimmed.

Has a chapter devoted to the capture of Tiburcio Vásquez.

100. Ayers, Nathaniel M.

Building a new empire, by Nathaniel M. Ayers. A historical story of the settlement of the wild west. Taking up the wild scenes incident to the settlement of a country inhabited by buffalo and hostile Indians. . . . New York, Broadway publishing co. . . . [1910]. Cloth. Scarce.

3 p.l., 7–221 p. front. (port. with tissue), illus., plates. 20 cm.
Pub. device; untrimmed.

Has several chapters on horse thieves and outlaws.

B

101. Baber, Daisy F.

Injun summer. An old cowhand rides the ghost trails, by Daisy F. Baber as told by Bill Walker. Illustrated with photographs. Caldwell, Idaho, the Caxton printers, ltd., 1952. Cloth. OP.

9 p.l., [19]–223 p. front., plates, ports. 23.5 cm.
Half title; headpieces; vignette; pub. device.

The teller of this tale, Bill Walker, claims to have talked with Billy the Kid in Colorado, but much of his information, like that of most old-timers, is incorrect. He repeats the old legend about the Kid's killing a man who insulted his mother and claims that the Kid later became a bank and stage robber. Walker adds that when the law was closing in on him in Colorado, "and he knew his gun was going empty, Billy the Kid took a high dive into the Missouri River, but he saved one last shot for Black Bess" (his horse, which the posse wanted). Walker mixes up his history and geography.

He claims that the Kid was a great favorite in Lincoln County and had many good points and many friends. He severely condemns Pat Garrett for hiding in the dark *"and behind a curtain"* to shoot the Kid. He says that Garrett "was small-time and small-town before he shot Billy the Kid." He further states that grass, flowers, and trees will not grow above the Kid's grave; yet on the next page is a photograph of the Kid's grave covered with grass and a bush in bloom.

102. ———

The longest rope; the truth about the Johnson county cattle war, by D. F. Baber as told by Bill Walker. Illustrated by R. H. Hall. Caldwell, Idaho, the Caxton printers, ltd., 1940. Pict. cloth. OP.

9 p.l., [19]–320 p. front., illus., plates. 23.5 cm.

Appendix: p. [297]–320 (George Dunning's confession).

Half title; map on end papers; headpieces; double illus. t.p. in red.

Reprinted with same imprint in 1947.

This is a much better book than Item 101 and gives some inside information never before told about the Johnson County War and the battle between the invaders and Nate Champion.

The author writes, however, that Calamity Jane learned her shooting from Wild Bill Hickok, to whom she was married at the age of fifteen, a ridiculous claim.

"Bill had got his rep as a gunman," Bill Walker says, "when he shot and killed several of the McCanles boys—a bunch of unarmed farmers who had gone to his place to settle a small argument. Wild Bill had got by a long time by shooting men in the back, and that is how he died. A big percentage of these so-called western heroes didn't deserve the name, and Bill Hickok was as big a counterfeit spy as any. Nobody mourned him much when he died, except Calamity Jane, and I sure don't know why she did. He made a good profit off of her for several years, then dropped her to shift for herself. She always had a weakness for him, and she rode at the head of the posse that run down and killed Jack McCaul [*sic*], the gambler that shot Hickok in the back." All this, as we know, is incorrect, and reads as though Mr. Walker was a little prejudiced.

103. Baca, Carlos Cabeza de

Vicente Silva, New Mexico's vice king of the nineties. [N.p., n.d.] Wrappers. Rare.

2 p.l., [5]–39 p. 15.3 cm.

The author admits he used Manuel Cabeza de Baca's book (Item 106) as the basis for his own, and the two books are very similar, but he does add a little new material.

104. [Baca, Elfego]

Political record of Elfego Baca and a brief history of his life. [By Elfego Baca] candidate for district attorney of the second judicial district, composed of Bernalillo, Sandoval, and Valencia counties. Albuquerque, Albuquerque printing house, [n.d.]. Pict. wrappers. Rare.

[6] p. (no pagination). port. 20.3 cm.

Tells about Baca's battle with the cowboys at Frisco, New Mexico.

105. Baca, Fabiola Cabeza de

We fed them cactus, by Fabiola Cabeza de Baca. With drawings by Dorothy L. Peters. [Albuquerque], University of New Mexico press [1954]. Pict. cloth. OP.

x p., 1 l., 186 p. illus. 21.6 cm.
Glossary: p. 179–180; index: p. 181–186.
Half title.

Contains several chapters on Vicente Silva and gives some new stories about Billy the Kid and Black Jack Ketchum. The man who wrote the first book about Silva—Manuel Cabeza de Baca (see Item 106)—was an uncle of the author of this book.

106. Baca, Manuel Cabeza de

Historia de Vicente Silva sus cuarenta bandidos sus crímenes y retribuciones. Escrita por Manuel C. de Baca. Corregida y aumentada por Francisco L. Lopez. Las Vegas, N.M., Spanish-American publishing co. [n.d.]. Wrappers. Exceedingly rare.

4 p.l., 97 p. 21.3 cm.

An exceedingly rare and crudely printed little volume dealing with the reign of Vicente Silva and his band of criminals. I have in my private library another edition [112 pages, plates, and ports., 17.7 cm.], the most crudely printed and bound book it has ever been my privilege to examine. The author was a police reporter for a Spanish-language newspaper in Las Vegas, New Mexico, and wrote the first account of that gang of killers.

107. ———

Historia de Vicente Silva sus cuarenta bandidos sus crímenes y retribuciones. Escrita por Manuel C. de Baca. Las Vegas, N.M., Imprenta la voz del Pueblo, 1896. Wrappers. Rare.

5 p.l., 128 p. front., plates, ports. 18.4 cm.

108. ———

Vicente Silva & his 40 bandits, [by] Manuel C. de Baca. Translation by Lane Kauffmann. Illustrations [by] Fanita Lanier. Washington, Edward McLean, Libros escogidos, 1947. Boards and cloth. OP.

vi p., 3 l., 7–77 [1] p. illus. 32.5 cm.

Illus. chapter headings; lettering in red and black.

Colophon: "500 copies of this book have been printed by E. L. Hildreth and company of Brattleboro, Vermont, for *Libros Escogidos* under the supervision of Edward McLean. The text is set in Intertype Garamond Bold; the paper is Strathmore's all rag Old Stratford. Miss Lanier's drawings are adapted from the illustrations of the edition in Spanish.

"25 numbered copies hand bound in full Niger Goatskin signed by the translator, the illustrator, and the binders, Hazel Dries and Edward McLean.

"300 copies case bound and signed by the translator and illustrator.

"175 copies in French wrappers."

A translation of the original.

109. Badger, Joseph E., Jr.

Joaquín, the saddle king. A romance of Murieta's first fight, by Joseph E. Badger, Jr. New York, Beadle & Adams, 1881. Pict. wrappers. Rare.

29 p. 31.5 cm.

Beadle's Dime Library, Vol. XIII, No. 154.

Triple column.

110. ———

Joaquín, the terrible. The true history of the three bitter blows that changed an honest man into a merciless demon, by Joseph E. Badger, Jr. New York, Beadle & Adams, 1881. Pict. wrappers. Rare.

29 p. 31.5 cm.

Beadle's Dime Library, Vol. XIII, No. 165.

Triple column.

111. ———

Pacific Pete. The prince of the revolver, by Joseph E. Badger, Jr. New York, Beadle & Adams, 1875. Pict. wrappers. Rare.

172 p. 17 cm.

Ernest Cowan's *A Bibliography of the History of California and the Pacific West, 1510–1906,* gives the above information. But according to Albert Johannsen, in his *The House of Beadle and Adams and Its Dime and Nickel Novels, Pacific Pete* appeared serially in the *Saturday Journal* in 1875–76 and was published as a twenty-cent novel in 1876.

112. ———

The pirate of the placers; or, Joaquín's death-hunt, by Joseph E. Badger, Jr. New York, Beadle & Adams, 1882. Pict. wrappers. Rare.

29 [3] p. 31.5 cm.
Beadle's Dime Library, Vol. XVI, No. 201.
Triple column.

All the Badger novels are exceedingly rare and are placed in this work as examples of the early writings on outlaws. None of them are of any value historically, being mostly wild fiction, but they have become valuable as collector's items.

113. Bailey, Harry H.

When New Mexico was young, by Harry H. Bailey. His autobiography. Edited by Homer E. Gruver. [Las Cruces, N.M., published by the Las Cruces Citizen, 1948.] (Copyright 1946.) Pict. wrappers. Scarce.

202 [1] p. illus., ports. 22.8 cm.
Double column; port. of author on cover; foreword on verso of t.p.; copyright notice on verso of flyleaf preceding t.p.

This book tells of life in early New Mexico and contains some material on Jim Miller and the Oliver-Lee feud, but the author makes a statement I have not seen before when he says that Billy the Kid was married to Pete Maxwell's daughter and that they had two children. The book is a separate reprint from a series which ran in the *Las Cruces Citizen* from 1946 to 1948, which accounts for the fact that the copyright antedates the book by two years. The author pictures Billy the Kid as one who shot his victims in the back.

114. Bailey, Robert G.

River of no return. (The great Salmon river of Idaho.) A century of central Idaho and eastern Washington history and development, together with the wars, customs, myths, and legends of the Nez Percé Indians, by Robert G. Bailey. . . . Lewiston, Idaho, Bailey-Blake printing co., 1935. Pict. cloth. Scarce.

xxiv p., 2 l., 5–515 p. front., illus., plates, ports., maps. 23.4 cm.
Half title; pub. device.
Colophon: "There are not to exceed 1400 copies printed of the 'River of No Return.' Each is autographed by the author and the copies numbered from 1 to 1400 inclusive. Signed ——. No. ——."
Revised in 1947 in an edition of two thousand copies with 754 pages, including an index. The colophon calls for signed and numbered copies, but the author died

in his sleep before signing them. This edition has a tipped-in notice of his death by his son and a newsprint notice of his death.

There are chapters on Idaho's first vigilance committee, Henry Plummer, Cherokee Bob, Hank Vaughn, the courts of early days, and other information on the outlaws of that section. The author explains for the first time why the real leader of the vigilantes of Montana was not named in Dimsdale's book. His name was James Williams, and he had given strict orders that his name must not be given.

115. Bair, Everett

This will be an empire, by Everett Bair. New York, Pageant press, inc. [1959]. Cloth.

8 p.l., 11–292 p. plates, ports. 20.7 cm.
Half title; "First edition" on copyright p.

Has material on the Espinosa gang and other outlaws in Colorado.

116. Baird, Josie

Tom Bond, bronc-buster, and trail driver, by Josie Baird. Illustrated by Delila Baird. Sweetwater, Texas, printed by Watson-Focht co. [1960]. Cloth.

x, 135 p. illus., 2 ports. 21.8 cm.
Index: p. 131–135.
Half title; illus. t.p.

Has some mention of Sam Bass.

117. Bakarich, Sarah Grace

Empty saddles. A new version of the Earp-Clanton fight, by Sarah Grace Bakarich. [N.p., 1946.] Pict. wrappers. (Cover title.) Scarce.

8 p. 19.2 x 8.1 cm.

The author, partial to the Clantons, is mistaken when she says that the Earps came to Tombstone in 1877. They arrived in late 1879.

118. ———

Gun-smoke, by Sarah Grace Bakarich. . . . [N.p.], 1947. Pict. wrappers.

3–152 [1] p. 15.3 cm.
Device.

This little book deals with the gunmen and outlaws of Tombstone, Arizona. There are many errors of fact, and the book is full of typographical errors and is crudely printed. The author misspells the names of many of her characters, for example, Chisholm for Chisum, and Seringo for Siringo. When I see a supposedly factual book filled with conversation, I believe that it has been more or less fictionized.

119. ———, and Kathelen M. Bennett

There's treasure in our hills, by Sarah Grace Bakarich [and] Kathelen M. Bennett. [N.p., 1947.] Pict. wrappers. (Cover title.)

15 p. 19.6 x 8.6 cm.

Contains some information about Curly Bill Brocius, Zwing Hunt, Burt Alvord, Billy Stiles, and other outlaws.

120. Baker, Joseph E. (ed.)

Past and present of Alameda county, California. Joseph E. Baker, editor. Illustrated. Chicago, the S. J. Clarke co., 1914. Pub. in two volumes. Three-quarter leather. Scarce.

Vol. I, 4 p.l., 7–463 p. front. (port.), plates, ports., map. 26.8 cm.
Vol. II, biographical.

Chapter X deals with the outlaws of this county, such as Juan Soto, José Pizzarro, and Tomaso Rondedo, alias Procopio.

121. Baker, Pearl

The Wild Bunch at Robbers Roost, by Pearl Baker. Los Angeles, Westernlore press, 1965. Fabrikoid.

7 p.l., [15]–255 p. plates, ports., maps. 21 cm.
Index: p. [249]–255.
Half title.

The author has the killing of Pike Landusky all wrong according to all other accounts, and she tells the well-worn story of the widow and the mortgage, this time with a member of the Wild Bunch. She is also wrong in claiming that Black Jack Ketchum was with a gang when his arm was "shot off." He was alone in that robbery attempt. There are other errors.

122. Ball, Eve

Ma'am Jones of the Pecos, by Eve Ball. Tucson, Ariz., University of Arizona press, [1968]. Cloth.

xiii p., 1 l., 3–238 p. plates, ports., maps. 23 cm.
Sources: p. 228–233; index: p. 234–238.
Half title.

Has information about Billy the Kid and the Lincoln County War.

123. ———

Ruidoso. The last frontier, by Eve Ball. San Antonio, Texas, the Naylor co. . . . [1963]. Stiff pict. wrappers.

vii p., 27 p. 21 cm.
Sources: p. 25–27.

Has information about the Lincoln County War, Billy the Kid, the Olingers, the Jones boys, and others.

124. Ballenger, T. H.

Around Tahlequah council fires. By T. H. Ballenger. Muskogee, Okla., Motter bookbinding co., 1935. Pict. cloth. OP.

7 p.l., 17–172 p. plates, ports. 21 cm.
Republished in a revised edition in 1945 by the Cherokee publishing co., Oklahoma City.

Has a chapter on the James boys when they visited Tahlequah, and one on Ned Christie, the Oklahoma outlaw.

125. Ballou, Robert

Early Klickitat valley days, by Robert Ballou. . . . [Goldendale, Wash., printed at the Goldendale Sentinel, 1938.] Cloth. Scarce.

3 p.l., 7–496 p. front., illus., ports. 23.5 cm.
Double column; errata on last p.

This little-known book contains material on bank and stagecoach robbers, the vigilantes of Idaho, and, most surprisingly, a correct version of the Hickok-McCanles "fight" as reported by a pony-express rider who arrived at Rock Creek Station immediately after the shooting.

126. Bancroft, Hubert Howe

Works of Hubert Howe Bancroft. Vol. XVII. History of Arizona and New Mexico, 1530–1888. San Francisco, the Historical co., publishers, 1889. Calf. Scarce.

xxxvii, 829 p. maps (1 fold.). 23.6 cm.
Index: p. 802–829.

Contains some material on Billy the Kid and Pat Garrett.

127. ———

Works of Hubert Howe Bancroft. Vol. XXV. History of Nevada, Colorado, and Wyoming, 1540–1888. San Francisco, the Historical co., publishers, 1890. Calf. Scarce.

xxxii, 828 p. illus., maps. 23.6 cm.
Index: p. 802–828.
Half title.

128. ———

Works of Hubert Howe Bancroft. Vol. XXXI. History of Washington, Idaho, and Montana. San Francisco, the Historical co., publishers, 1890. Calf. Scarce.

xxvi, 836 p. maps. 23.6 cm.
Index: p. 809–836.

Contains some material on George Ives, Henry Plummer, and the Montana vigilantes.

129. ———

Works of Hubert Howe Bancroft. Vol. XXXIV. California pastoral, 1769–1848. San Francisco, the Historical co., publishers, 1888. Calf. Scarce.

vi, 808 p. 23.6 cm.
Glossary: p. 793–800; index: p. 801–808.

Information on train and stagecoach robberies, Murieta, Juan Soto and Vásquez.

130. ———

Works of Hubert Howe Bancroft. Vol. XXXVI. Popular tribunals. San Francisco, the Historical co., publishers, 1887. Calf. Scarce.

Vol. I, xiii, 749 p. fold. map. 23.6 cm.
Half title.
Vol. II, viii, 772 p. 23.6 cm.
Index: p. 749–772.
Half title.

All these works of Bancroft's give some history of the outlaws of the various states treated in the volumes.

131. Banditti of the Rocky Mountains

and vigilance committee in Idaho. . . . Chicago, Post-office box 3179, 1865. Pict. wrappers. Exceedingly rare.

vi, [25]–143 [6] p. illus. 22.7 cm.
Last 6 p. adv.
Another edition published by Wilson and Co., New York, 1865.

There are only three known copies of this rare book, one at the University of Washington, one in the Coe Collection, Yale University, and one in the Library of Congress. The first two were published in Chicago, and the Library of Congress copy was published in New York. The book contains 83 pages of actual text, but owing to faulty pagination it reached 144. This pagination is thought to have been caused by the hope of securing advertisements for pages throughout to help with the expenses of publication. Both imprints were of the same year, 1865, the publisher of the Chicago issue simply listed as Post-office box 3179, and the New York issue published by Wilson and Company.

It is a history of the Plummer gang of outlaws published a year earlier than the well-known one by Dimsdale. Though some claim that this is a plagiarized version of Dimsdale's work, the latter was not published in book form until 1866, though it was serialized in 1865. An article in the *Montana Post,* dated Saturday, August 26, 1865, announced the first publication of the first installment of Dimsdale's book in that paper and condemned this book, but Dimsdale admitted that he owned a copy of this book when he wrote the criticism of it in his paper.

No one seems to know the author of this book, but many think it was written by John Lyle Campbell, a reporter for the *Chicago Tribune* who had earlier written a guidebook to the gold fields and had it published both in Chicago and New York, just as this book was published.

The author repeatedly misspells Slade's name as Slaid, and misnames Mrs. Vedder as Mrs. Venard. Plummer murdered her husband when the latter came home unexpectedly one night and caught Plummer in bed with her. The author says Plummer was tried and released, but actually he received a change of venue and was sentenced to ten years in prison. The author says that Plummer and Cleveland fell in love with a Miss "D" ("whose real name we omit"), but her name was Electra Bryan. He refers to Cyrus Skinner as Charles Skinner.

This book was reprinted in 1964 by Ross and Haines, with a preface and introduction by its editor, Jerome Peltier. Cloth.

14 p.l., [31]–190 p. illus. 22.2 cm.
Footnotes: p. [153]–175; bibliography: p. 177–184; index: p. [185]–190.
Half title.

The Peltier edition has valuable footnotes. On page 15 there is a typographical error: 1965 for 1865.

132. [Bank of Douglas]

Bank of Douglas, Arizona, 1887–1950. [Phoenix, Ariz., 1949, published by the Bank of Douglas, 1949.] Wrappers. OP.

2 p.l., 7–30 p. plates, ports. 30.6 cm.
Illus. t.p.; double column.

This booklet of pictures and short sketches contains material on many of the outlaws and gunmen of Arizona and on the hanging of the Heath gang.

133. Bankson, Russell A.

The Klondike nugget, by Russell A. Bankson. Caldwell, Idaho, the Caxton printers, ltd., 1935. Cloth. OP.

5 p.l., [11]–349 p. front. (port.), plates. 19.5 cm.
Half title; pub. device.

Contains a chapter on Soapy Smith and also mentions Calamity Jane.

134. Banning, Capt. William, and George Hugh Banning

Six horses, by Captain William Banning and George Hugh Banning, with a foreword by Major Frederick Russell Burnham. . . . New York, London, the Century co. [1930]. Pict. cloth. Scarce.

xx p., 1 l., 3–410 p. front. (port.), illus., plates, ports., map, facsms. 21 cm.
Bibliography: p. 377–387; appendix: p. 391–398; glossary: p. 399–402; index: p. 403–410; acknowledgments signed: G.H.B.
Half title; map on end papers; vignette.

A well-written history of the western stage lines containing some information about the early stage robbers, with much on Tom Bell.

135. [Bannorris, Amanda]

The female land pirate; or, awful, mysterious, and horrible disclosures of Amanda Bannorris, wife and accomplice of Richard Bannorris, a leader of that terrible band of robbers and murderers, known far and wide as the Murrell men. . . . Cincinnati, printed for and published by E. E. Barclay, 1848. Pict. wrappers. Exceedingly rare.

3 p.l., [7]–32 p. front. (2 full p. plates), illus. 22 cm.

A very rare and curious work. "The following manuscripts were found in the cell of Amanda Bannorris, who, as all will recollect who have noticed the lists of crime in the New Orleans papers, within the past year, was found dead in her cell, from having taken poison. As she has narrated the case, it is senseless to say more; save that these manuscripts procured from the jailer, who claimed them as his property, at a heavy expense, and are now, for the first time, put before the world."—Publisher's note on verso of title page.

136. Bard, Floyd C.

Horse wrangler. Sixty years in the saddle in Wyoming and Montana, by Floyd C. Bard as told to Agnes Wright Spring. Norman, University of Oklahoma press [1960]. Cloth.

xi [1] p., 1 l., 3–296 p. front., plates, port., map. 22 cm.
Index: p. 285–296.
Half title; "First edition" on copyright p.

Contains material on the Johnson County War, Nate Champion, Nick Ray, Jim Averill, and Cattle Kate Watson.

137. Barker, John T.

Missouri lawyer, by John T. Barker, of the Missouri bar. Philadelphia, Dorrance & co. [1949]. Cloth. OP.

vii, 9–391 p. front. (port.). 21 cm.

Has a long chapter on Frank and Jesse James, the Youngers, and Bob Ford. The author calls attention to the fact that neither Governor Crittenden, who offered the reward for the James boys, nor William H. Wallace, who prosecuted Frank, was ever re-elected to office. The author is mistaken, however, in saying that Bob Ford was killed in Cripple Creek, Colorado. He was killed at Creede. The author is mistaken, too, in saying that Frank and Jesse were buried on the old home place near Kearney. Jesse was originally buried there, but later his body was removed to a cemetery in Kearney. Frank was never buried there, but in a little private cemetery on the outskirts of the present day Kansas City, Missouri. He also repeats the old fable about the widow whom Jesse helped with her mortgage.

138. ———

The trial of Frank James. An address given by General John T. Barker before a meeting of the Boone County Bar Association held at Columbia, Missouri, August 7th, 1952. [N.p., n.d., ca. 1952.] Pamphlet. (Cover title.)

3–12 p. 23 cm.

The author gives a list of witnesses for the state and a list for the defense. He spells Quantrill's name wrong as so many others do.

139. Barkley, Mary Starr

History of Travis county and Austin, 1839–1899, by Mary Starr Barkley. [Waco, Texas, printed by Texian press, 1963.] Cloth.

vii, 388 p. plates, maps, plats. 23.8 cm.
Appendix: p. 337–348; references: p. 349–364; index: p. 365–388.
Pub. device.

Scattered throughout the book is information on Ben Thompson, his army life, and his killings; the killing of Phil Coe by Wild Bill Hickok at Abilene; and Thompson's death in San Antonio, shot down with King Fisher in the Variety Theater.

140. Barler, Miles

Early days in Llano, by Miles Barler. Personal reminiscences. [Llano, Texas, ca. 1898.] Stiff wrappers. (Cover title.) Rare.

68 p. 14.6 cm.

Later reprinted (ca. 1905) in a small edition with seventy-six pages. It is also rare.

141. Barnard, Evan G.

A rider of the Cherokee Strip, [by] Evan G. Barnard. With illustrations. Boston, New York, Houghton Mifflin co., 1936. Cloth. OP.

xviii p., 1 l., 233 p. front., plates, ports. 21.3 cm.

Appendix: p. [225]–227; index: p. [229]–233.

Half title; map on end papers; pub. device; untrimmed; first edition: 1936 under imprint.

Contains information on some Oklahoma outlaws, such as Tulsa Jack, Dick Yeager, and the Daltons. It also has an account of the battle between Charlie Bryant and Ed Short.

142. Barnes, William Croft

Apaches & longhorns; the reminiscences of Will C. Barnes, edited and with an introduction by Frank C. Lockwood . . . ., with a decoration by Cas Duchow. Los Angeles, the Ward Ritchie press, MCMXLI. Pict. cloth. OP.

xxiii p., 1 l., 3–210 p. front., plates, ports., plan. 21.5 cm.

Half title; vignette.

An interesting book containing accounts of the Tonto Basin War and the killing of Andy Cooper by Commodore Perry Owens.

143. [Barnum, G. H., Pub.]

Rube Burrow, the famous outlaw, murderer, and train robber. With a complete history of his eventful life, from his birth to his startling capture and sensational death on October 8th, 1890. . . . Chicago. G. H. Barnum, publisher, 1890. Wrappers. Scarce.

3–64 p. front. (port.), illus., plates. 18.6 cm.

144. Barrows, John R.

Ubet, by John R. Barrows. Caldwell, Idaho, the Caxton printers, ltd., 1934. Pict. cloth. OP.

3 p.l., 7–278 p. illus., plates. 19.5 cm.

Half title; illus. end papers; illus. t.p., headpieces.

Two chapters on the Robbers' Roost dealing with rustlers, Rattlesnake Jake Fallon, and Longhaired Owens.

145. Barrows, William

The United States of yesterday and of tomorrow, by William Barrows, D.D. . . . Boston, Roberts Brothers, 1887. Cloth. Scarce.

viii, [9]–432 p. 18.5 cm.

Index: p. [421]–432.
Half title; 16 numbered p. adv. at end.

In a long chapter entitled "Lynch Law" the author gives a full account of the Montana vigilantes and the activities of the Plummer gang, ending with their hangings.

146. Barsness, Larry

Gold camp. Alder Gulch and Virginia City, Montana, by Larry Barsness. New York, Hastings House, publishers [1962]. Pict. cloth.

x, 312 p. 21 cm.
Notes: p. [285]–298; bibliography: p. [299]–304; index: p. [305]–312.
Half title.

Has chapters on the Montana vigilantes and the outlaws of the Plummer gang.

147. Bartholomew, Ed

The biographical album of western gunfighters, by Ed Bartholomew. Containing more than a 1,000 biographical entries together with over six hundred rare photographs of the most famous sheriffs, outlaws, marshalls [*sic*] and celebrated personalities in the history of the western frontier. Houston, Texas, the Frontier press of Texas, 1958. Pict. cloth.

[76] p. (no pagination). illus., plates, ports., fascms. 34.5 x 51.8 cm. (Oblong.)
Biographical entries: p. [74–75]; bibliography: p. [76].

Contains short biographical sketches of many western gunmen and outlaws. Owing to its shape it is awkward to read.

148. ———

Black Jack Ketchum, last of the hold-up kings. An authentic biography of the old west, by Ed Bartholomew. Houston, the Frontier press of Texas, 1955. Cloth.

1 p.l., 5–116 p. plates, ports. 21.6 cm.
Illus. t.p.; last 8 p. plates and ports. from the Rose collection; edition limited to 1,000 copies.

149. ———

Cullen Baker, premier Texas gunfighter, by Ed Bartholomew. Illustrated from the Rose collection. Houston, Texas, the Frontier press of Texas, 1954. Cloth.

1 p.l., [9]–139 p. plates, ports. 22.2 cm.
Last 7 p., plates and ports.
Colophon: "A limited edition of 1000 copies, printed at Houston, Texas, March, 1954."

The rare book on Baker edited by Thomas Orr is reprinted on pages 85 to 132.

150. ———

The hanging of Three-Fingered Jack and his Nevada gang, by Ed Bartholomew. [N.p., 1955.] Wrappers. Scarce.

23 p. 18 cm.

Only 25 copies printed.

A story of Nevada outlawry and of Three-Fingered Jack McDowell.

151. ———

Jesse Evans, a Texas hide-burner, by Ed Bartholomew. Houston, Texas, the Frontier press of Texas, 1955. Cloth. Also pub. in wrappers.

1 p.l., 3–75 p. plates, ports. 22 cm.

500 copies printed, 18 bound in wrappers by the author, and 482 bound in cloth by a bindery.

The first book devoted exclusively to this well-known outlaw. It contains material on Billy the Kid, Tom O'Folliard, Charlie Bowdre, George Coe, and Henry Brown.

152. ———

Kill or be killed, by Ed Bartholomew. A record of violence in the early southwest. . . . Houston, Texas, the Frontier press of Texas, 1953. Cloth.

2 p.l., 148 [16] p. plates, ports. 22.3 cm.

Last 16 p., plates and ports. from the Rose collection.

This book deals with many of the gunmen of the Southwest, such as John Wesley Hardin, John Selman, John Scarborough, and Tom Ketchum.

153. ———

Some western gunfighters, compiled by Ed Bartholomew. . . . Toyahvale, Texas, Frontier Book co., publisher [n.d.]. Cloth.

2 p.l., [5]–56 p., [2] l. plates, ports. 21 cm.

A collection of the compiler's reprints of earlier reprints. It contains chapters on Clay Allison, Cherokee Bill Goldsby, Belle Starr, and Robert McKemie.

154. ———

Western hard-cases; or, gunfighters named Smith, by Ed Bartholomew. Ruidoso, N.M., Frontier Book co., 1960. Cloth.

2 p.l., 5–191 p. 20 cm.

Half title.

A treatise on gunmen named Smith, some well known, others not so well known. There are many errors.

155. ———

Wild Bill Longley, a Texas hard-case, by Ed Bartholomew. . . . Illustrated from the famous Rose collection. Houston, Texas, the Frontier press of Texas, 1953. Cloth.

1 p.l., 5–117 [3] p. front. (port.), plates. 22.3 cm.
3 p. plates at end.

Published in both cloth and wrappers. This book gives some previously undisclosed facts about Bill Longley, but there are many misspelled words. Crudely printed, but a genuine contribution to western Americana.

The first plate shows Longley standing between his two captors, both of whom wear long, heavy beards. It is said that he requested this photograph be made to prove to the world that he was not captured by two "boys."

156. ———

Wyatt Earp, 1848 to 1880. The untold story, by Ed Bartholomew. Toyahvale, Texas, Frontier Book co., 1963. Cloth.

2 p.l., [5]–328 p. 22.3 cm.
Bibliography: p. 318–328.
Half title follows t.p.

An account of Wyatt Earp's Kansas and Dodge City years. The author has unearthed some surprising material from the records. He claims that Bat Masterson's middle name was Bartholomew and calls him Bart throughout, giving his reason in the last chapter. I have never seen this contention elsewhere. The book is an important addition to the Earp controversy. Unfortunately it is repetitive and written in a rather dull manner. There are some errors, but readers of western Americana should be grateful to Mr. Bartholomew for the material he has unearthed. See also Item 157.

157. ———

Wyatt Earp, 1879–1882. The man & the myth. A sequel to "The Untold Story," by Ed Bartholomew. Toyahvale, Texas, Frontier Book co., 1964. Cloth.

1 p.l., [3]–335 p. 4 ports. 22.3 cm.
Chronological bibliography: p. 328–333.
Last 2 p. ports.

The second volume of the author's study of Wyatt Earp (Item 156), dealing with his Arizona years. Many of the outlaws of that period are also discussed, among them Dave Rudabaugh, Jesse Evans, Russian Bill, Frank Stillwell, Pete Spence, Johnny Ringo, Frank Leslie, Kit Joy, the Clantons, and the McLaurys. Indexes would have made both volumes much more useful to readers.

158. ——— (ed.)

Henry Plummer, Montana outlaw boss. From old newspaper files by unknown newspapers. Limited edition. Ruidoso, N.M., Frontier Book co., 1960. Wrappers.

4–47 p. 19.6 cm.

500 copies printed.

Excerpts from an unnamed Montana newspaper and from a scrapbook of newspaper clippings.

159. Bartlett, I. S. (ed.)

History of Wyoming. I. S. Bartlett, editor. Chicago, the S. J. Clarke Publishing co., 1918. Pict. cloth. Pub. in 3 vols.

Vol. I, 8 p.l., 17–667 p. front. (col. flag), plates, ports. (part with tissues). 27.2 cm.

Vol. II, [5]–652 p. front. (port. with tissue), ports. (part with tissues). 27.2 cm.

Vol. III, [5]–659 p. front. (port. with tissue), ports. (part with tissues). 27.2 cm.

Volume I has a chapter on the Johnson County War and information on Tom Horn and Doc Middleton. Volumes II and III are biographical.

160. Barton, O. S.

Three years with Quantrell [*sic*]. A true story told by his scout John McCorkle, written by O. S. Barton. Armstrong, Mo., Armstrong Herald print. [n.d.]. Wrappers. OP.

2 p.l., 1 p., [6]–157 p. front., ports. 23 cm.

An account of Quantrill and his activities, repeating disproved legends about the notorious guerrilla. The author also tells about some of the escapades of Cole Younger and Frank James while they were guerrillas.

161. Baskin, R. N.

Reminiscences of early Utah, by R. N. Baskin. . . . [N.p., n.d., Salt Lake City, ca. 1914.] Cloth. OP.

3 p.l., 5–252 p. front. (port.), ports. 23.5 cm.

Contains much material on John D. Lee and the Mountain Meadow Massacre.

162. [Bass, Sam]

Life and adventures of Sam Bass, the notorious Union Pacific and Texas train robber, together with a graphic account of his capture and death—sketch of the members of his band, with thrilling pen pictures of their many bold and desperate deeds, and the capture and death of Collins, Berry, Barnes, and Arkansas Johnson. With illustrations. Dallas, Texas, Dallas Commercial Steam print., 1878. Wrappers. Exceedingly rare.

110 [2] p. illus. 23 cm.

This exceedingly rare little book was reprinted with eighty-nine pages by John A. Norris, of Austin, Texas, in blue wrappers, and later reprinted by N. H. Gammel, of Austin, in tan wrappers. Neither reprint edition is illustrated. The most common one seen is the Norris reprint. Very few copies of the original edition seem to exist; I have only seen two copies in all my years of collecting. It is said to have been written by a Dallas newspaper reporter named Morrison. It is quite similar to one written by Thomas E. Hogg and published in Denton, Texas (see Item 1001).

163. ———

From ox-teams to eagles. A history of the Texas and Pacific railway. [Dallas, Texas, 1948.] Stiff pict. wrappers. OP.

2 p.l., 5–50 [2] p. front., illus. 26.7 cm.

A little book issued by the Texas and Pacific Railroad, now scarce. It contains some material on Sam Bass and his robberies of Texas and Pacific trains at Eagle Ford and Mesquite.

164. ———

True story of Sam Bass, the outlaw. Round Rock, Texas, written and published for the Sam Bass Café [1929]. Pamphlet. (Cover title.)

11 [1] p. front. 16 cm.

A pamphlet published by the Sam Bass Café of Round Rock, Texas, where Bass was killed. First issues of this pamphlet are scarce, but its publisher kept it in print for advertising purposes until he went out of business. This condensed history of Bass was based on the files of the adjutant general of Texas and written by the son of a Texas Ranger. The author merely hits the high spots of Bass's career and is in error in stating that the robbers seized $65,000 in the Union Pacific robbery, and also that the Eagle Ford robbery was the first in Texas by the Bass gang. The robbery of the Houston and Texas Central at Allen, Texas, was the gang's first Texas robbery. The Eagle Ford robbery of the Texas and Pacific was the third. There are many other errors.

165. Bassett, Samuel Clay

Buffalo County, Nebraska, and its people. A record of settlement, organization, progress and achievement, by Samuel Clay Bassett. Illustrated. Vol. I. Chicago, the S. J. Clarke publishing co., 1916. Three-quarter leather. Scarce.

xxi, 392 p. front. (port.), plates, ports., maps. 26.6 cm.

Has a long chapter on the murder of the two nesters Mitchell and Ketchum by I. P. Olive, and of the latter's trial and death.

166. Bate, W. N.

Frontier legend. Texas finale of Capt. William F. Drannan, pseudo frontier comrade of Kit Carson. Based on research, by W. N. Bate. Results of research on Capt. Drannan who published two books in which he made claims of association with Kit Carson for a period of at least twelve years. . . . New Bern, North Carolina, Owen G. Dunn co., publishers, 1954. Stiff wrappers.

5 p.l., [11]–68 [1] p. plates, ports, facsm. 22.7 cm.
Bibliography: p. [69]

A deserved debunking of Drannan's books. The author points out many examples of Drannan's false claims and distorted statements.

167. Bates, Mrs. D. B.

Incidents on land and water; or, four years on the Pacific coast. Being a narrative of the burning of the ships Nonantum, Humayoon and Fanchon, together with many startling and interesting adventures on sea and land, by Mrs. D. B. Bates. Boston, James French and co., 1857. Pict. cloth. Scarce.

5 p.l., [11]–336 p. front., 4 plates (incl. front.). 20.2 cm.

Contains a chapter on Murieta. The chapter is incorrectly numbered XVII; it should be numbered XIV, following XIII and preceding XV. The actual Chapter XVII is in the correct position. This book was evidently a popular one in its day, for it had four printings the year it was published and another in 1858.

168. Bates, Edmund Franklin

History and reminiscences of Denton county, by Ed. F. Bates. . . . Denton, Texas, McNitzky printing co., [1918]. Cloth. Scarce.

xi p., 2 l., 412 p. front., plates, ports., 2 fold. photographic scenes. 23.5 cm.
Index: p. 408–412.
Half title.

This book contains a chapter on Sam Bass, telling of his life in Denton, Texas, his start in crime, his career, and his death. The author's account of the capture of Joel Collins after the Union Pacific robbery is all wrong. Murphy did not break jail at Tyler, Texas, but skipped bond in a frame-up arranged with the officers so that he might betray his friend Sam Bass. Nor did the killing of Grimes at Round Rock occur in a saloon; it took place in Koppel's store, where Bass had gone to purchase tobacco.

169. Bates, J. C. (ed.)

History of the bench and bar of California. Edited by J. C. Bates. San Francisco, Bench and Bar publishing co., publishers, 1912. Leather. Scarce.

2 p.l., [5]–572 p. ports., 26.5 cm.

Obituary and biographical section double column.

Contains much on lawlessness and the early courts of California.

170. Beach, Goodwin B.

Petrus Sclopetarius (Pistol Pete). . . . A true story of the old west done in Latin by Goodwin B. Beach, Litt. D. [N.p., n.d.] Pict. wrappers. (Cover title.)

9 p. 21.5 cm.

A little pamphlet about Pistol Pete written in Latin for the professor's Latin classes. It was privately printed and is an unique little item, but one wonders why such an inaccurate book was chosen for translation when there are so many others with more reliable history.

171. Beadle, J. H.

Brigham's destroying angels; being the life, confessions and startling disclosures of the notorious Bill Hickman, the Danite chief of Utah. Written by himself, with explanatory notes by J. H. Beadle. Illustrated. New York, Geo. A. Crofutt, publisher, 1872. Pict. cloth. Scarce.

vii, [9]–219 [5] p. front. (port.), plates. 17.6 cm.

Last 5 p. adv.

Reprinted many times in wrappers.

172. Beal, M. D.

A history of southeastern Idaho. An intimate narrative of peaceful conquest by empire builders. The fruits of their labors along tortuous rivers and valleys now sparkle like pearls in the diadem that is Idaho, the gem of the mountains, by M. D. Beal. . . . Illustrated with photographs. Caldwell, Idaho, the Caxton printers, ltd., 1942. Cloth. OP.

11 p.l., [23]–443 p. front., plates, ports., map. 19.7 cm.

Bibliography: p. [385]–392; notes: p. [395]–432; index: p. [433]–443.

Half title.

Chapter 9 deals with road agents, outlaws, and rustlers of Idaho, with special attention to "Diamond Field" Jack Davis.

173. Beals, Carleton

American earth. The biography of a nation, [by] Carleton Beals. Philadelphia, New York, Toronto, J. B. Lippincott co. [1939]. Cloth. OP.

4 p.l., 9–500 p. 21.8 cm.

Bibliography: p. 472–475; index: p. 477–500.

At head of title: Carleton Beals.

Chapter XIII, entitled "Wars of Wyoming," deals with the Johnson County War and the sheep wars of that state, the hanging of Jim Averill and Cattle Kate Watson, and the siege of the Nate Champion cabin. There is also some information about the Hole-In-the-Wall country and its outlaws.

174. Beals, Frank Lee

Buffalo Bill, by Frank Lee Beals. . . . Illustrations by Jack Merryweather. Chicago, Wheeler publishing co. [1943]. Pict. cloth.

2 p.l., 252 p. illus. chapter headings. 18.8 cm.

Illus. end papers; American Adventure Series.

There is a chapter on Wild Bill Hickok, which the author spells Hickock. He also brings Slade into the picture.

175. Beattie, George William, and Helen Pruitt Beattie

Heritage of the valley; San Bernardino's first century, by George William Beattie and Helen Pruitt Beattie. With a foreword by Henry R. Wagner. Pasadena, Calif., San Pasqual press, 1939. Cloth. OP.

xxv, 459 p. plates, ports., maps (1 fold.), facsm. 25.4 cm.

List of references: p. 427–439; index: p. 449–459.

176. ———

Heritage of the valley; San Bernardino's first century, by George William Beattie and Helen Pruitt Beattie. Oakland, Calif., Biobooks, 1951. Cloth. OP.

xxix, 459 [1] p. plates, maps (all col.). 25.6 cm.

List of references: p. 427–439; index: p. 441–459.

Half title, "California Southeast"; illus. front end papers; map rear end papers; vignette.

Colophon "1000 copies printed by Lederer, Street and Zeus co., inc. Typography by Arthur G. Henry, art work by Wm. F. M. Kay."

Both the de luxe and the original editions have some minor material on Joaquín Murieta.

177. Beattie, Kim

Brother, here's a man! The saga of Klondike Boyle, by Kim Beattie. . . . With a foreword by her late majesty, Queen Marie of Russia. New York, the Macmillan co., 1940. Cloth. OP.

xiv p., 2 l., 309 p. front. (port. with signature in facsm.), plates, ports. 22 cm.
Half title; "First printing" on copyright p.

Contains quite a bit of material about Soapy Smith, as do most other books about the Klondike.

178. Beaumont, G. H.

G. H. Beaumont's railroad stories. Jesse James and the telegraph operator. Lord have mercy on a railroad man. . . . [Kansas City, printed by Seip printing co., 1912.] Pict. wrappers. Scarce.

4–80 p. illus. 18.5 cm.

Has some material about the James boys and Jesse's murder by Bob Ford. There is also a long poem about the author's personal encounter with Jesse when the former was a telegraph operator.

179. Bechdolt, Frederick Ritchie

Tales of the old-timers, by Frederick R. Bechdolt. . . . New York, and London, the Century co. [1924]. Pict. cloth. OP.

6 p.l., 3–367 p. front. 19.5 cm.
Half title; device.

Good writing but poor history. The book is full of errors. The author's account of the Lincoln County War is all wrong. He has "thirty odd" riders in the posse that shot Tunstall. In the episode in which Dick Brewer tries to persuade Tunstall to "make a run for it" before they leave the ranch, the author has the Englishman saying, "We'll ride to *London* and I'll accept service from Sheriff Brady and there won't be any fight." He evidently means Lincoln; this mistake could have been the printer's.

He has the capture of Baker and Morton wrong and says, "One of the prisoners edged his horse close to a posse-man named McCloskey and managed to steal his revolver." He then has the prisoners killing McCloskey, and, as they whip their horses to a run, "Billy the Kid had his Winchester out and in action before his companions really knew what was taking place." This version, of course, gives the Kid full credit for the killing of the two.

He intimates that Buckshot Roberts lived at Blazer's Mill and gives an erroneous account of the battle there. He says that Brewer's posse threatened to fire the building where Roberts had taken refuge after being shot but that the Indian agent told them that it was government property. Blazer's Mill was not government property, however; Bechdolt apparently had it confused with the Mescalero Indian Reservation nearby.

He gives a detailed account of the killing of Dick Brewer and certainly calls upon his imagination when he writes: "Within the room the face of Shot-gun [*sic*] shows, all twisted with pain as he raises his body, and his lips are white; the sweat drops are coursing down his forehead while the Winchester leaps to his shoulder." Who was in the room to see the white lips and sweat drops? And did not the author know that Roberts could not raise the Winchester to his shoulder because of old wounds that had given him the name Buckshot?

There are many other errors in every chapter, and many proper names are misspelled.

180. ———

When the west was young, by Frederick Bechdolt. . . . New York, the Century co., 1922. Cloth. OP.

6 p.l., 3–309 p. front. 19.3 cm.
Half title.

In this book the author perpetuated the Wild Bill Hickok fable of the ten men in the McCanles "fight" and says that when the fight took place "Hickok, who was scarcely more than a boy then, was alone in the little sod house and when the fight was over he had eleven bullet wounds and thirteen knife wounds." Later the author says: "How many men he killed is a mooted question. But it is universally acknowledged that he slew them fairly." It is too bad that such an able writer did not investigate his subject before passing it on as history.

He says that Hickok was town marshal of Abilene for several years, but actually Hickok served only for eight months, from April to December, 1871. The author makes Wild Bill a superman who could twist a man's arm until the bones snapped, although in the beginning his hero was "scarcely more than a boy."

He repeats the many fictitious legends about Joaquín Murieta and is mistaken in saying Bat Masterson was marshal of Dodge City and that Wyatt and Virgil Earp succeeded him. There are many other errors throughout.

181. Beck, Warren A.

New Mexico, a history of four centuries, by Warren A. Beck. Norman, University of Oklahoma press [1962]. Cloth.

xii p., 1 l., 3–363 p. plates, ports. maps. 24 cm.
Bibliography: p. 337–352; index: p. 353–363.
Half title; "First edition" on copyright p.

Contains a chapter on lawlessness in New Mexico, including the Lincoln County War. The author does not have the killing of Huston Chapman exactly correct, and he repeats the fable that four thousand bullet holes were found in the jacal in which Elfego Baca defended himself against a crowd of cowboys. Yet he writes that Baca was untouched. It is hard to believe that a man with such scant protection could have been missed if four thousand bullets had actually been fired at him.

182. Beckett, V. B.

Baca's battle, by V. B. Beckett. Elfego Baca's epic gunfight at 'Frisco Plaza, N.M., in 1884, as reported at the time. Together with Baca's own final account of the battle. Houston, Texas, Stagecoach press [n.d.]. Pict. wrappers.

6 p.l., 13–30 [1] p. 17.8 cm.
Half title; illus. double t.p.
Colophon: "This edition limited to 800 copies. . . ."

One part of this pamphlet is a reprint by the author from *The Black Range*, published in Chloride, New Mexico, in 1884; the other part is a reprint from Baca's own pamphlet, which he had printed while running for office (see Item 104).

183. Beebe, Lucius, and Charles Clegg

The American west, the pictorial epic of a continent, [by] Lucius Beebe and Charles Clegg, with title page in color by E. S. Hammack, and more than 1000 illustrations. New York, E. P. Dutton & co., inc., publishers, 1955. Cloth. OP.

5 p.l., 11–511 [1] p. illus., plates, map, facsms. 28.6 cm.
Bibliography: p. 508–511.
Half title; illus. end papers; double illus. t.p. (col.).

Primarily a picture book, the book does, however, have some text on such outlaws as Joaquín Murieta, Black Bart, the James boys, the Youngers, Belle Starr, and Bob Ford and such gunmen as Wild Bill Hickok and the Earps. Many of the authors' statements are incorrect, as, for example, the statement that Ed Jennings was killed by Temple Houston in the courtroom "in the presence of judge and jury." Jennings was killed in a saloon after a quarrel in the courtroom. The authors also seem to jeer at the fact that Jesse James was killed while standing on a chair straightening a picture on the wall. They call this episode the "idealized version still cherished by the soft headed to this day." If so, there are a lot of soft-headed historians.

The authors reprint a picture which they claim is of the James and Younger boys taken while on a spree in Kansas City. This picture appeared on the cover of the October, 1953, issue of *Great Guns*, a gun collector's magazine, and later on the cover of *True West*. Both magazines were swamped with letters denying that the pictured men were the James and Younger boys, some claiming to know the men and giving their names. The authors also say Belle Starr was a resident of Dodge City and repeat the legend that she robbed some gamblers after Blue Duck had lost two thousand dollars that belonged to her. The authors further say that Doc Holliday "lived for fifteen years after his Tombstone days," but actually he left Tombstone shortly after the O K Corral fight in 1881 and died in 1887.

184. ———, and ———

Hear the train blow. A pictorial epic of America in the railroad age, [by] Lucius Beebe and Charles Clegg. With ten original drawings by E. S. Hammack and 860 illustrations. New York, E. P. Dutton & co., inc., publisher, 1952. Pict. cloth.

4 p.l., 1 p., 10–409 [7] p. illus., plates, ports., facsms. 28.7 cm.

Half title; illus. double t.p. (col.); illus. end papers; "First edition" on copyright p.; last 7 p. unnumbered.

A chapter entitled "Car Robbers and Bindle Stiffs" deals largely with train robbers, such as the James boys and the Daltons.

185. ———, and ———

U.S. west, the saga of Wells Fargo, by Lucius Beebe and Charles Clegg. New York, E. P. Dutton & co., inc., publishers, 1949. Pict. cloth.

8 p.l., 17–320 p. illus., plates, ports., map, facsms. 26.3 cm.

Chronology: p. 304–310; bibliography: p. 311–313; index: p. 315–320 (triple column).

Half title; illus. double t.p. (col.); illus. end papers; "First edition" on copyright p.

The authors give a fairly accurate account of the trouble at Rock Creek Station, but they write that Wild Bill was quite surprised when he read Nichols' account of his Rock Creek "fight" with the McCanleses in *Harper's Magazine*, although Nichols said that it was written from a personal interview with Wild Bill.

"There is one item of photographic evidence in the McCanles shooting," say the authors, "a daguerreotype in the California State Library showing Dave McCanles on horseback with a bottle in his hand in front of the Rock Creek Pony Express Station. No less authority than Arthur Chapman says the bottle contained whisky. The inference is tenable that, when the time arrived for McCanles to draw and defend himself, his hand and aim were palsied from a low way of life. No other available moral seems to attach to the affair at Rock Creek." It is not possible that this picture was made at any time near the day of the "fight," and it was never proved that McCanles wore a gun. The book has a long chapter on the various robberies of Wells Fargo throughout the West.

186. Beers, George A.

Vásquez; or, the hunted bandits of San Joaquin. Containing thrilling scenes and incidents among the outlaws and desperadoes of southern California. With a full and accurate account of the capture, trial and execution of the noted bandit, by George A. Beers, esq. New York, Robert M. DeWitt, publisher [1875]. Pict. wrappers. Rare.

2 p.l., [7]–141 p. diagr. 23.5 cm.
Double column; 2 p. adv. at end; port. of Vásquez with facsm. of his signature on cover.

Before he wrote this book for the New York publishers, Beers, a young reporter with the *San Francisco Chronicle*, was with the posse that chased and captured Vásquez. Parts of his story are different from Truman's and Sawyer's and in the love themes he seems partial to fiction. Like many reporters of that day, he no doubt embellished his account here and there, but as a whole it is dependable. Although the book sold well at the time, the author realized only a pittance from it. Now it is rare and sells at a premium.

187. Belden, John J.

Life of David Belden, [by John J. Belden]. New York, and Toronto, Belden brothers, 1891. Cloth. Scarce.

vi p., 1 l., 9–472 p. front., ports. 25 cm.

Belden became one of the leading judges of early California. Among his collection of speeches is the one in which he sentences Tiburcio Vásquez, the notorious California outlaw.

188. Bell, Horace

On the old west coast; being further reminiscences of a ranger, [by] Major Horace Bell. Edited by Lanier Bartlett. New York, William Morrow & co., 1930. Cloth (label pasted on). Scarce.

xiv p., 1 l., 336 p. front., plates, ports., facsms. 24.3 cm.
Notes: p. 308–329; index: p. 330–336.
Illus. end papers (dif.); cattle brands at end of each chapter; pub. device.

The book is drawn from the wealth of unpublished material that Major Bell left at his death, containing much information that he did not wish to make public while his subjects were still alive. There is material on Murieta and other California outlaws.

189. ———

Reminiscences of a ranger; or, early times in southern California, by Major Horace Bell. Los Angeles, Yarnell, Caystile & Mathes, printers, 1881. Pict. cloth. Very scarce.

7 p.l., [17]–457 p. 23.5 cm.

This is said to be the first cloth-bound book printed, bound, and published in Los Angeles. Its scarcity is largely the result of the fact that the publishers had the only print shop in town, and, since this was the biggest job they had ever undertaken, they did not have sufficient type for the complete book. So, after printing the first half, they took the type down and reset it for the second half. The result was a small edition.

Reprinted in Santa Barbara by William Hebberd in 1927 and again in 1933. Foreword written by Arthur M. Ellis, with illustrations by James S. Bodrero.

8 p.l., 499 p. front., illus. 20 cm.

This later edition contains an index identifying many of the characters mentioned in the original edition. Both editions have much information on the lawlessness of early California.

190. Bell, John C.

The pilgrim and the pioneer. The social and material developments in the Rocky mountains, by John C. Bell. . . . Lincoln, Nebr., printed by the International publishing ass'n [1906]. Cloth. OP.

xii, 13–531 p. front., illus., plates. 20.8 cm.
Leaf of errata, 7th preliminary page.

Contains some information on Alferd Packer, his crime and trial. (Most writers spell his first name Alfred, but Packer himself signed his name Alferd.)

191. Bell, John T.

History of Washington County, Nebraska. Its early settlements, and present status, resources, advantages and future prospects, [by] John T. Bell. . . . Omaha, Nebr., printed at the Herald Steam Book and Job printing house, July, 1876. Wrappers. Rare.

[3]–64 [6] p. 21.6 cm.
Last 6 p. adv.

Has a chapter on crime, criminals, and horse thieves.

192. Bell, Katherine M.

Swinging the censer. Reminiscences of old Santa Barbara, by Katherine M. Bell. Compiled by Katherine Bell Cheney. . . . Santa Barbara, Calif., MCMXXXI. Dec. cloth. Scarce.

xx p., 3 l., 3–287 p. front. (port.), illus., plates, ports. 20 cm.
Half title; illus. end papers.

Contains some heretofore unrevealed information about Jack Powers and his gang of outlaws.

193. Belle, Frances P.

Life and adventures of the celebrated bandit Joaquín Murrieta [*sic*], his exploits in the state of California. Translated from the Spanish of Ireneo Paz by Frances P. Belle. Chicago, Reagan publishing corp., 1925. Cloth. OP.

x, 174 p. 21.2 cm.

Untrimmed.

Colophon (on copyright p.): "This first edition printed on London feather weight paper consists of 975 copies."

Republished in 1937 by the Charles T. Powner co., Chicago.

A translation from the Spanish of the fifth edition published in Los Angeles.

194. [Benders, the]

The five fiends; or, the Bender hotel horror in Kansas. This family of fiends have for a number of years been systematically murdering travelers who stopped at their hotel or store, by a most singular method, which has never been discovered until the killing of Dr. York, the brother of Senator York, of Kansas. This book contains full and startling details of their lives and awful crimes. . . . Philadelphia, Old Franklin publishing house, 1874. Pict. wrappers. Exceedingly rare.

1 p.l., 3–60 [1] p. illus., plates, plan. 23.2 cm.

Captions under plates in both English and German.

This rare book is crudely printed and illustrated. The first part gives some history of the Benders but soon switches to wild fiction told through another character, who claims that there were three identical Bender girls (operating at that time under the name of Liefens), who, with their husband (the same man married to all three sisters), were committing wholesale murders near Nagadotches [*sic*], Texas.

This book was reprinted in Chicago by Charles J. Heck with the exact title except that "singular" was misspelled "singulum." This printing also contains (pp. 71—96) "Lizzie Lee's Daughter; or, a Rich Father's Remorse."

195. Benedict, John D.

Muskogee and northeastern Oklahoma, including the counties of Muskogee, McIntosh, Wagoner, Cherokee, Sequoyah, Adair, Delaware, Mayes, Rogers, Washington, Nowata, Craig and Ottawa, by John D. Benedict. Chicago, the S. J. Clarke publishing co., 1922. Pub. in three volumes. Cloth. Scarce.

Vol. I, 9 p.l., 19–693 p. front. (port. with tissue), plates, ports. 27.7 cm.

Index: p. 687–693.

Vols. II and III, biographical.

Volume I contains a condensed history of Henry Starr.

196. Benedict, Omer K. (ed.)

The roundup, Dewey, Oklahoma, held annually week of July fourth. Published by Joe A. Bettles. Edited by Omer K. Benedict. Illustrated by Joe DeYong. [N.p.], 1916. Stiff pict. wrappers. 2-hole tie.

[32] p. (no pagination). illus., plates. 23.6 cm.

Has a section on "Boot Hill," in which the author mentions Wild Bill Hickok, Bat Masterson, Bill Tilghman, Wyatt Earp, Frank Canton, E. D. Nix, and others.

197. Benefield, Hattie Stone

For the good of the country. Por el bien del país, by Hattie Stone Benefield. Illustrations by Patricia Benefield Williams. Los Angeles, Lorrin L. Morrison, publisher, 1951. Pict. cloth. OP.

8 p.l., 138 p. front. (port.), illus., plates, ports., maps. 28 cm.

Foxen family tree: p. [87]–135; index: p. 136–138.

Half title; illus. end papers; double t.p. with map.

Colophon: "For the Good of the Country" is printed in a limited edition of 600 copies, 500 copies of which are numbered. This copy being number ——. (Signed).

This privately printed book has some material on Murieta and Vásquez.

198. Bennett, Edwin Lewis

Boom town boy in old Creede Colorado, by Edwin Lewis Bennett. Chicago, Sage Books [1966]. Cloth.

4 p.l., 11–213 p. plates, port. 21.6 cm.

Half title; pub. device.

An interesting account of the author's personal experiences in the wild mining town of Creede. There is an account of the killing of Bob Ford by Ed O. Kelly, whom the author calls Ed O'Kelly, as so many other writers do. He is mistaken when he writes that Kelly "was killed by a law officer in *Texas*." It happened in Oklahoma City. There is mention of Soapy Smith, Poker Alice, Calamity Jane, and Frank James.

199. Bennett, Estelline

Old Deadwood days, by Estelline Bennett. New York, J. H. Sears & co., inc., publishers [1928]. Pict. cloth. OP.

xi p., 1 l., 3–300 p. front. (port.), plates. 21 cm.

Half title; illus. t.p.; untrimmed.

Reprinted in 1929; republished by Charles Scribner's sons in 1935.

The author tells about Calamity Jane and quotes a Dr. Babcock as saying that her beauty was her greatest asset, but most people who knew her said that she was coarse and ugly. The author is also wrong in saying that Jane died on August 2, "the twenty-seventh anniversary of the murder of Wild Bill." She died on August 1.

200. Bennett, William P.

The first baby in camp. A full account of the scenes and adventures during the pioneer days of '49 . . ., by Wm. P. Bennett. . . . Salt Lake City, Utah, the Rancher publishing co., 1893. Wrappers. Scarce.

3 p.l., 9–68 p. fold. plates. 17 cm.

Pictures 22 x 28 cm. are supposed to accompany this book, but are seldom found. The book contains material on road agents and holdups.

201. Benscholter, George E.

Book of facts concerning the early settlements of Sherman county, descriptive of its present business and agricultural developments and natural advantages, by Geo. E. Benscholter. Loup City, Nebr., Loup City Northwestern print. [n.d., ca. 1897]. Wrappers. Rare.

2 p.l., 76 p. 18.4 cm.

Contains quite a bit of history about the Olives and the murder of Luther Mitchell and of Ami Ketchum and some information on Doc Middleton.

202. Benton, Jesse James

Cow by the tail, by Jesse James Benton, with an introduction by Richard Summers. Boston, Houghton Mifflin co., 1943. Cloth. OP.

xii p., 1 l., 225 p. 20.4 cm.
Half title; illus. double t.p.; signature in facsm. at end of text; headpieces; untrimmed; first edition, 1943 over imprint.

Here is another old-timer who claims he knew Billy the Kid well and that the Kid had come up the trail with a herd of cattle from a ranch in Uvalde County, Texas.

"The herd was bound for some point in Kansas," he writes. "Billy and Gus [White] quit at Fort Mobeetie in the Panhandle where I was working for Odem." One cannot help wondering why cattle would be driven hundreds of miles out of the way through the Panhandle from Uvalde County to get them to the markets then existing in Kansas. Further, if Mr. Benton had worked in Mobeetie, he should have known that it was not a fort, though it was near Fort Elliott.

Mr. Benton claims that the Kid went by the name of Billy LeRoy. The publisher's editor adds a footnote that Benton's account "does not always agree with other published versions" and informs the reader that "Billy the Kid was sometimes known as Billy LeRoy in Texas." Does this editor, like many others, believe what his writer says simply because he is writing of his own life? Perhaps both editor and author had read that fantastic novel, *Billy LeRoy*, published by the *Police Gazette* sixty years earlier.

The author also writes that Pat Garrett stepped into Pete Maxwell's bedroom from an adjoining room when he killed the Kid. There is also some material on the James boys, and the author says that he was named for Jesse James.

203. Berry, Gerald L.

The whoop-up trail (Alberta-Montana relationships), by Gerald L. Berry. . . . Edmonton, Alberta, published by Applied Art Products, ltd., 1953. Cloth.

3 p.l., 7–143 p. plates, ports., maps, plan. 23.3 cm.
Appendices: p. 133–136; bibliography: p. 137–139; index: p. 140–143.
Preface verso t.p.

Contains some material on the vigilantes of Montana and the later vigilantes of Granville Stuart's day.

204. Berton, Pierre

Klondike. The life and death of the last great gold rush, by Pierre Berton. London, W. H. Allen, 1960. Cloth.

8 p.l., 3–456, i–xix [2] p. plates, 4 maps (in front). 21.9 cm.
Coda: p. 417–438; notes on sources: p. 439–445; bibliography: p. 446–456; index: p. i–xix.
Half title; illus. end papers (dif.).

Has a long chapter on Soapy Smith and his gang, as well as scattered material.

205. ———

The Klondike fever. The life and death of the last gold rush, by Pierre Berton. New York, Alfred A. Knopf, 1958. Cloth. OP.

viii p., 1 l., 3–457, i–xix [2] p. 4 maps in front. 21.8 cm.
Notes on sources: p. 439–445; bibliography: p. 446–457; index: p. i–xix.
Half title; illus. end papers (dif.); "First edition" on copyright p.; pub. device; untrimmed.

In a long chapter on Soapy Smith the author makes the mistake of stating that Soapy got his start in Leadville, Colorado, "the stamping ground of Calamity Jane and Wild Bill Hickok." Neither statement is true. He also states that Ed O'Kelly [*sic*] "shot down Bob Ford on the main street of Creede." Ford was shot in his own tent saloon.

206. Beverly, Bob

Hobo of the rangeland, by Bob Beverly. Lovington, N.M. [n.d., ca. 1941]. Pict. wrappers. Scarce.

4 p.l., 5–87 [1] p. plates. 23.5 cm.

Has some material on Belle Starr and a mention of Bronco Bill.

207. Biggers, Don H.

German pioneers in Texas. A brief history of their hardships, struggles and achievements. Compiled for the Frederickburger Wochenblatt and Frederick Standard. By Don H. Biggers. [Fredericksburg], press of the Fredericksburg publishing co., 1925. Cloth. OP.

4 p.l., [3]–230 p. plates, ports. 22.2 cm.

Contains some information on Waldrip and his gang as well as other lawlessness in early Texas.

208. ———

Shackleford county sketches, [by] Don H. Biggers. Done into a book in the Albany News office, October, 1908. Boards. Rare.

[71] p. (no pagination). front. 26.5 cm.
Appendix (articles first published in the *Dallas News*): last 15 p.

This rare book contains material on the Millet Ranch outlaws and John Larn, of Fort Griffin, Texas.

209. Biles, J. Hugh

The early history of Ada, by J. Hugh Biles. Ada, Okla., published by the Oklahoma State Bank of Ada, Oklahoma, in commemoration of its fiftieth anniversary, 1954. Cloth. OP.

xv p., 2 l., 5–160 p. plates, ports. 23.5 cm.
Half title; device; "First edition" on copyright p.

Chapter 8 deals largely with the hanging of Jim Miller, Joe Allen, Jesse West, and B. B. Burrell.

210. Billings, Buck

The owlhoot trail, by Buck Billings. New York, Pyramid Books [1956]. Stiff pict. wrappers (col.).

2 p.l., 5–126 p. 16.2 cm.

This book has an unreliable account of Sam Bass. The author introduces some fictitious characters, whom he names Lloyd Frazier and Colonel Fairchild, and has Bass killed by Frazier.

211. [Billy the Kid]

Billy the Kid. Las Vegas newspaper accounts of his career, 1880–1881. Waco, Texas, published by W. M. Morrison [1958]. Stiff wrappers. Scarce.

2 p.l., 5–29 p. 23 cm.
"First edition: 1,000 copies" on copyright p.; litho-printed.

This is a little book of excerpts from the Las Vegas, New Mexico, papers, many of which were filled with false accounts of the Kid's activities even in his own day. For example, the *Las Vegas Daily Optic* of Friday, June 10, 1881, says that the Kid met four of Chisum's cowboys, killed three in cold blood, and sent the fourth back to Chisum with the news that he was killing the men for the debt owed him. This account is perhaps the origin of that fable.

212. ———

The cowboy's career; or, the daredevil deeds of "Billy the Kid," the most noted New Mexico desperado, by "one of the Kids." Chicago, St. Louis, Belford, Clarke & co., 1881. Pict. wrappers. Exceedingly rare.

2 p.l., [7]–140 p. 2 full p. plates. 19 cm.

The only complete copy of this book to my knowledge is in the library of my friend Jeff Dykes, who allowed me the pleasure of examining it.

213. Bingham, Helen

In Tamal land, by Helen Bingham. San Francisco, the Calkins publishing house [1906]. Pict. cloth. Scarce.

7 p.l., 141 p. front., plates, port. 23.2 cm.
Half title.

Contains some slight information on Three-Fingered Jack (Manuel) García and Joaquín Murieta.

214. Birney, Herman Hoffman

Vigilantes, by Hoffman Birney. A chronicle of the rise and fall of the Plummer gang of outlaws in and about Virginia City, Montana, in the early '60s; drawings by Charles Hargens. Philadelphia, the Penn publishing co., [1929]. Cloth. Scarce.

8 p.l., [17]–346 p. front., illus., plates, ports., facsm. map. 21 cm.
Half title; illus. end papers; vignette; untrimmed.
Colophon: "Two hundred and fifty copies of this edition have been specially bound and signed by the author. This is number ——."
Also published in a trade edition.

About a third of this book appeared in the *Saturday Evening Post* in short articles before publication in book form. There is little that is new about the Montana vigilantes.

215. Bishop, William Henry

Old Mexico and her lost provinces. A journey in Mexico, southern California, and Arizona by way of Cuba, by William Henry Bishop. . . . With illustrations. New York, Harper & brothers, 1883. Pict. cloth. Scarce.

x p., 1 l., 509 p. front. (map), plates, map. 20.5 cm.
Last 6 p. adv.

The last six pages list other books by the same publishers. Some copies of the book have only two pages of these advertisements. The book has some information about Tombstone, Arizona, Billy the Kid, Curly Bill Brocius, Wyatt Earp, Doc Holliday, the McLaurys, the Clantons, and the O K Corral fight.

216. Bivins, Mrs. J. K.

Memoirs, [by Mrs. J. K. Bivins, n.p., n.d.]. Cloth. Scarce.

2 p.l., 138 p. front., plates, ports. 23 cm.

A privately printed book with a chapter on Cullen Baker, an early Texas outlaw.

217. Black, A. P. (Ott)

The end of the long horn trail, by A. P. (Ott) Black. Selfridge, N.D., published by Selfridge Journal [n.d., ca. 1936]. Stiff wrappers. (Cover title.) OP.

4–59 p. front., illus., plates. 22.5 cm.
Blank leaf following each of the first 3 chapters.

The author tells about knowing Bill Powers when he was wagon boss of the Hashknife outfit and before he went to Oklahoma to join the Dalton gang. Writing of the Cherokee Strip, he calls it the "Chesakee Strip," but of course this might be an error of the printer; however, he misspells other names, such as Quantrell for Quantrill and John Loren for John Larn, and he misnames Bat Masterson as Bob Masterson.

He says that Bob Ford ran a honky-tonk in Cripple Creek, Colorado, instead of Creede, and he is entirely wrong in saying that George Scarborough (which he spells Scarbar) killed John Wesley Hardin. He makes the statement that "Hardin had killed thirty-one men and Scarbar [*sic*] had killed thirty-one when they met. Scarbar killed his thirty-second when he put Hardin away." As we know, Hardin was killed by John Selman. The author also declares that Calamity Jane was Hickok's wife and that she owned a ranch near New England, North Dakota.

218. Black, Jack

You can't win, by Jack Black, with a foreword by Robert Herrick. New York, the Macmillan co., 1926. Cloth. OP.

xi p., 1 l., 394 p. 19.5 cm.
Half title; untrimmed.

This story, about the author's own criminal career, touches upon Jesse and Frank

James and Bob Ford and tells about his contacts with Bat Masterson and Soapy Smith. He says that Masterson was marshal of Dodge and died "peacefully in bed." Both statements are incorrect. Masterson was sheriff of Ford County and died at his desk while a reporter for the *New York Journal American.*

219. Blacker, Erwin R. (ed.)

The old west in fact. Edited by Erwin R. Blacker. New York, Ivan Obolensky, inc. [1962]. Boards with cloth spine.

xxiv p., 1 l., [3]–446 [1] p. 24 cm.
Half title; "First printing" on copyright p.

Among other western subjects, this book has two chapters on outlaws, an excerpt from Garrett's book on Billy the Kid (Item 807) and one from Gillett's *Six Years with the Texas Rangers* (Item 829) on the killing of Sam Bass. In the editor's introductory remarks concerning the latter, he repeats some of the false statements made by Teddy Blue Abbott. In this chapter he, of course, makes the same mistakes Gillett made, such as having Frank Jackson returning to Denton and Jim Murphy committing suicide. In one chapter, entitled "The Cattlemen," he quotes the complete text of Charlie Siringo's first book, *A Texas Cowboy*, and perpetuates many mistakes about the life and death of Billy the Kid.

220. Blake, Herbert Cody

Blake's western stories. The truth about Buffalo Bill (William F. Cody), Wild Bill (J. B. Hickok), Dr. Carver, California Joe, Yellow Hand, Tall Bull, the pony express, the old .44 Colt, derailing of the Union Pacific train, reprisal on the Cheyennes under Turkey Leg. History and busted romances of the old frontier. Brooklyn, published by Herbert Cody Blake, 1929. Wrappers. (Cover title.) Scarce.

32 [1] p. plates, ports. 23 cm.

Most of this book is devoted to debunking Buffalo Bill and the claims about the marvelous shooting of Wild Bill Hickok. The author makes the strong statement that Buffalo Bill never killed an Indian in his life.

221. Blanchard, Leola Howard

Conquest of southwest Kansas, by Leola Howard Blanchard. A history and thrilling stories of frontier life in the state of Kansas. [Wichita, printed and bound by the Wichita Eagle press, 1931.] Pict. cloth. OP.

3 p.l., 7–355 p. illus., plates, ports. 20.3 cm.
Vignette; copyright notice on verso of flyleaf.

Material on Dodge City and on Henry Brown and Ben Wheeler in the robbing of the Medicine Lodge bank.

222. Bland, T. A.

Life of Albert B. Meacham. [by] T. A. Bland, together with his lecture, the tragedy of the lava beds. Washington, T. A. & M. C. Bland, publishers, 1883. Cloth. Scarce.

1 p.l., [3]-48 p. front. (port.), plates, port. 22.5 cm.

The latter half of this book is Meacham's lecture delivered at Park Street Church, Boston, Massachusetts, May 24, 1874, which contains much material on Captain Jack, the Modoc outlaw.

223. Blankenship, Russell

And there were men, [by] Russell Blankenship. New York, Alfred A. Knopf, 1942. Cloth. OP.

xi [1] p., 1 l., 3-300 [1] p., i-iii [1] p. 21.8 cm.

Glossary: p. 292-297; acknowledgments: p. 299-300 [1]; index: p. i-iii [1].

Half title; pub. device; untrimmed; "First edition" on copyright p.

This book has a long chapter on the vigilantes of Montana and the outlaws they exterminated, giving much information on Henry Plummer, Boone Helm, Fred Patterson, Jack Gallaher, Clubfoot George Lane, and many others.

224. Bliss, Frank E.

The life of Hon. William F. Cody known as Buffalo Bill, the famous hunter, scout and guide. An autobiography [by Frank E. Bliss]. Hartford, Conn., Frank E. Bliss [1879]. Pict. cloth. Rare.

xvi, 17-365 p. front. (port., signed in facsm. and with tissue), illus., plates, letter in facsm. 22 cm.

This rare book is the earliest authentic biography of Cody. It contains material on Wild Bill Hickok, but gives another false account of the McCanles "fight." At least it is different from the usual accounts. The author calls Wild Bill a pony-express rider and says that he arrived at Rock Creek Station just in time to save the stock tender's wife, who was being assaulted by five of the McCanles "desperadoes." Wild Bill succeeded in killing four of them; the fifth escaped. The author at least holds his odds within the bounds of reason and does not have Wild Bill wounded. "Wild Bill remained at the station," Bliss writes, "with the terrified woman until the stage came along, and then he consigned her to the care of the driver. Mounting his horse he at once galloped off, and soon disappeared in the distance, making up for lost time.

"This was the exploit that was on everybody's tongue and in every newspaper. It was one of the most remarkable and desperate hand to hand encounters that has ever taken place on the border." The book also has some information on Joseph Slade.

225. Block, Eugene B.

Great stagecoach robbers of the west, [by] Eugene B. Block. Garden City, N.Y., Doubleday & company, inc. [1962]. Cloth.

5 p.l., [11]–262 p. plates, ports., facsms. 21.5 cm.
Bibliography: p. [251]–252; index: p. [253]–262.
Half title; map on end papers; illus. t.p.; "First edition" on copyright p.

This book has chapters on such stage robbers as Tom Bell, Black Bart, Dick Fellows, Pearl Hart, Sam Bass, and Joaquín Murieta. There are many errors of fact.

226. ———

Great train robberies of the west, [by] Eugene B. Block. New York, Coward-McCann, inc. [1959]. Cloth.

6 p.l., 13–317 p. 22 cm.
Half title.

This book consists of short accounts of train robberies of the American West, but the word "great" seems to have little significance, for many of the better-known robberies are omitted. The book contains many misstatements. On page 46 the author says of the Union Pacific robbery at Big Springs, Nebraska, that "one robber went directly to the open safe, pulled out the treasure box, and dumped its contents, $60,000 in gold coin *and currency*, into his bag." In the first place, the safe was time-locked and the $60,000 in twenty-dollar gold pieces were not in this safe but in wooden boxes. He also states that Bass's first Texas train robbery was at Mesquite, but it was at Allen, and the Mesquite robbery was his last one. The author has the killing of Bass all wrong. He also has the killing of Pike Landusky wrong and says that Black Jack Ketchum "was hanged for the murder of a sheriff in New Mexico." He was hanged for train robbery. There are many other errors.

227. Blodgett, Rush Maxwell

Little dramas of old Bakersfield, as seen by a boy and told in after years, by Rush Maxwell Blodgett. Los Angeles, printed by Carl A. Bundy Quill & press, 1931. Cloth and boards. Scarce.

3 p.l., 9–222 p. vignettes. 21.3 cm.
Half title.

This privately printed little book contains a short sketch of McKinney the outlaw.

228. Bloss, Roy S.

Pony express—the great gamble, by Roy S. Bloss. Berkeley, Calif., Howell-North, 1939. Cloth. OP.

xi, 159 p. front., illus., plates, ports., facsms., maps (1 fold.). 23.6 cm.

Bibliography: p. 141–144; appendix: p. 145–153; index: p. 155–159.

Facsms. on end papers; illus. t.p.; headpieces.

Has some mention of Joseph Slade, whom the author calls an "experienced murderer and whisky drinker," and of Wild Bill Hickok, who he says "was an unknown stock-tender." But the author does correctly state that only three were killed in the Rock Creek Station affair.

229. Bloyd, Levi

Jefferson county history. Rock Creek station, the scene of the "Wild Bill" Hickok, McCanles killing. . . . Compiled by Levi Bloyd. 8 full pages of pictures. [Fairbury, Nebr., Holloway publishing co., n.d.] Pict. wrappers. (Cover title.) Scarce.

[20] p. (no pagination). illus., plates, ports., maps. 21.8 cm.

Gives a good account of the "fight" at Rock Creek Station and attempts to correct the fictitious reports of the affair. The first part of the book is made up of excerpts from the *Harper's Magazine* articles on Wild Bill, published in the February, 1867, issue, and of Ned Buntline's book entitled *Buffalo Bill and His Adventures in the West.* Then follow short biographies of Hickok and Dave McCanles and the true story of the Rock Creek Station trouble.

230. Blythe, T. Roger (ed.)

A pictorial souvenir and historical sketch of Tombstone, Arizona, "the town too tough to die. . . ." Compiled, sketched and edited by T. Roger Blythe. . . . [Tombstone, printed by Tombstone Epitaph, n.d.] Pict. wrappers.

[30] p. (no pagination). illus. (1 double p.). 15.2 x 22.5 cm. (Oblong.)

Contains drawings of many historical sites and buildings of Tombstone, together with the town's history. It is disappointing, however, that the editor repeats many of the false legends concerning Wyatt Earp, such as having him a deputy U.S. marshal when he arrived in Tombstone; having him the one who hit Curly Bill Brocius over the head and taking him to jail after the killing of White; and saying that it was Earp who held off the mob trying to lynch Johnny-behind-the-Deuce. All these statements are untrue.

231. Boatright, Mody, et al. (eds.)

Mesquite and willow, edited by Mody C. Boatright, Wilson M. Hudson, Allen Maxwell. Dallas, Texas, Southern Methodist University press [1957]. Pict. cloth. OP.

viii p., 1 l., 3–203 p. fold. table. 23.3 cm.

Contains a chapter on outlaws.

232. **Boethel, Paul C.**

The history of Lavaca county, by Paul C. Boethel. San Antonio, Texas, the Naylor co., 1936. Cloth.

5 p.l., 151 p. 23.5 cm.
Half title.

233. ———

Sand in your craw, by Paul C. Boethel. Austin, Texas, printed by Van Boeckmann-Jones [1959]. Pict. cloth. OP.

6 p.l., 3–134 p. 24.2 cm.
Index: p. 129–34.
Half title; double page t.p.

Has information on murders, feuds, cattle rustling, and other lawlessness in Lavaca County, Texas.

234. **Boggs, Mae Hélène Bacon**

My playhouse was a Concord coach. An anthology of newspaper clippings and documents relating to those who made California history during the years 1822–1888. Compiled by Mae Hélène Bacon Boggs. [Oakland, Calif., printed at the Howell-North press, 1942.] Cloth. Rare.

xvi, 763 [1] p. illus., plates, ports., maps (incl. 7 fold.), facsms. 32.5 cm.
Index: p. 749–763.
Half title; illus. end papers; illus. t.p.; double column.
Colophon: "My Playhouse Was a Concord Coach is not for sale, but is presented to ——."

This is practically a history of western stagecoaching as taken from contemporary newspapers and contains much information on road agents Black Bart, Tom Bell, and others.

235. **Boller, Henry A.**

Among the Indians. Eight years in the far west: 1858–1866, embracing sketches of Montana and Salt lake, by Henry A. Boller. Philadelphia, T. Ellwood Zell, 1868. Cloth. Rare.

xvi, 17–428 p. front. (fold. map). 19 cm.
Half title.

Has a short chapter on the vigilantes and outlaws of Montana and the hanging of Henry Plummer, but most of the book is devoted to the author's life with the Indians. Most of the existing copies of this rare book lack the map.

236. Bonney, Edward

Banditti of the prairies; or, the murderer's doom! A tale of the Mississippi valley, by Edward Bonney. Chicago, E. Bonney, 1850. Cloth. Rare.

2 p.l., [9]–196 p. plates, ports. 22 cm.

Imprint on cover: "Chicago, W. W. Davenport, 1850."

Republished by same publisher in 1853; by T. B. Peterson, of Philadelphia, in 1853 in an edition of 244 pages; by D. B. Cook and co., of Chicago, in 1858, and again in 1859. Published in Chicago by Belford, Clarke & co., in 1881, and by the Homewood publishing co., in 1890. A still later edition was published undated in Chicago on cheap paper and with poor printing, and a recent reprint has been issued by the University of Oklahoma press in the Western Frontier Library series.

The first edition is exceedingly rare and the book is somewhat a history of the Mormons during the Nauvoo period and contains much material on the outlaws of the early Middle West. It originally appeared as a newspaper serial.

237. Bonsal, Stephen

Edward Fitzgerald Beale, a pioneer in the path of empire, 1822–1903, by Stephen Bonsal, with 17 illustrations. New York and London, G. P. Putnam's sons, 1912. Cloth. OP.

xii p., 1 l., 312 p. front., plates, ports. 22.5 cm.

Index: p. 307–312.

T.p. in red and black; untrimmed.

Contains some material on Joaquín Murieta and Three-fingered Jack García. The author says that the head of Murieta and the hand of Three-Fingered Jack were brought to his camp "but a few hours after these scoundrels were shot."

238. Booker, Anton S.

Wildcats in petticoats. A garland of female desperadoes—Lizzie Merton, Zoe Wilkins, Flora Quick Mundis, Bonnie Parker, Katie Bender and Belle Starr, by Anton S. Booker. Girard, Kans., Haldeman-Julius publications [1945]. Wrappers.

3–24 p. 21.5 cm.

In his chapter on Belle Starr the author makes many errors about incidents, places, and ages. Many of his dates are wrong, and the book is of no historical consequence.

239. [Boot Hill]

World famous Boot hill. They buried them with their boots on. [Dodge City, Dodge City Junior Chamber of Commerce, n.d.] Leaflet.

[4] p. (no pagination). 15.3 cm.

240. Botkin, B. A. (ed.)

Folk-say, a regional miscellany, 1930, edited by B. A. Botkin. Norman, University of Oklahoma press, 1930. Pict. cloth. OP.

10 p.l., 21–473 [1] p. front., illus., music. 23.6 cm.
Notes: p. 429–439; contributors: p. 443–454; index: p. 457–473.
Half title; vignette.

The section entitled "Apocrypha of Billy the Kid," by Maurice G. Fulton, presents a story of the Kid's life as published in the *Las Vegas Optic* as a serial in the latter part of 1882. Fulton confesses that the first chapters are missing and begins the narrative with Chapter VII. Chapter VIII is also missing, but beginning with Chapter IX the account continues to the end. The whole thing is a wild piece of fiction written in the style of the dime novels of the day. It has the Kid doing the talking as he tells the story of his life.

The anonymous narrator makes a personal visit to the Kid at his rendezvous and learns from him what he wants to know by "investigating questions." The Kid likes his interviewer from the beginning, and invites him to join his band. The Kid tells him: "I was born in County Limerick, Ireland, about 1859. My father's name was William. He was a poor peasant, and like all poor classes of peasantry, suffered much and did not escape persecution." But what finally drove the Kid away from Ireland was the "ruin of my two sisters by a son of our landlord." This blow killed his father, and his mother took the children to Canada. From Montreal they went to Nova Scotia, where his mother married "an old reprobate named Antrim and soon afterward accompanied him to New Mexico." The rest of the account is just as ridiculous.

241. ———

Folk-say. A regional miscellany, 1931, edited by B. A. Botkin. Norman, University of Oklahoma press, 1931. Dec. cloth. OP.

5 p.l., [11]–254 p. 23.5 cm.
Half title.

This collection has a chapter on the Apache Kid.

242. ———

A treasury of American folklore. Stories, ballads, and traditions of the people. Edited by B. A. Botkin . . . with a foreword by Carl Sandburg. New York, Crown publishers [1944]. Pict. cloth. OP.

xxvii [2] p., 2–932 p. music. 22 cm.
Index: p. 919–932.
Half title; vignette.

Many pages are devoted to western outlaws and gunmen. The editor's section on Wild Bill Hickok is made up of quotations from George Ward Nichols' article in *Harper's Magazine*, and Frank J. Wilstache's *Wild Bill Hickok*. His material on Billy the Kid is largely from Burns's *Saga of Billy the Kid*, and chapters V to VII are from *The Cowboy's Career* and Charlie Siringo's *History of Billy the Kid*. It is too bad he did not choose more reliable books on both subjects. Most of the Jesse James material is from Love's *The Rise and Fall of Jesse James*, and his Sam Bass material is from Wayne Gard's *Sam Bass*. The latter two are trustworthy accounts.

243. ———

A treasury of Mississippi river folklore. Stories, ballads, traditions and folkways of the mid-American river country. Edited by B. A. Botkin. Foreword by Carl Cramer. New York, Crown publishers, inc. [1955]. Pict. cloth. OP.

xx, 620 p. illus., music. 22 cm.
Index to authors: p. 603–609; index to subjects: p. 611–620.
Half title; vignette.

Contains information on the Harpes and on John A. Murrell, early outlaws of the Mississippi Valley.

244. ———

A treasury of southern folklore. Stories, ballads, traditions, and folkways of the people of the south. Edited with an introduction by B. A. Botkin. With a foreword by Douglas Southall Freeman. . . . New York, Crown publishers [1949]. Pict. cloth. OP.

xxiv, 776 p. music. 22 cm.
Index: p. 763–776 (triple column).

Has some material on the Jameses, the Youngers, and John A. Murrell. The editor misspells Quantrill's name throughout.

245. ———

A treasury of western folklore, edited by B. A. Botkin. Foreword by Bernard DeVoto. . . . New York, Crown publishers, inc. [1951]. Pict. cloth. OP.

xxvi p., 3 l., 7–806 p. music. 21.6 cm.
Index: p. 793–806 (triple column).
Illus. p.
Published also in special Southwest, Rocky Mountain, and Pacific Coast editions. The Southwest edition has a special foreword by J. Frank Dobie (2 l. before t.p.).

In a long chapter entitled "Law and Order, Ltd.," the compiler quotes from various books on many of the western gunmen, such as Clay Allison, Joaquín

Murieta, Black Bart, Jesse James, Bill Doolin, Billy the Kid, Al Jennings, Tom Horn, the Apache Kid, Cherokee Bill, Belle Starr, Calamity Jane, Sam Bass, Harry Tracy, Elfego Baca, and Wild Bill Hickok. Nothing new is added.

246. ———, and Alvin F. Harlow (eds.).

A treasury of railroad folklore. The stories, tall tales, traditions, ballads and songs of the American railroad man. Edited by B. A. Botkin and Alvin F. Harlow. . . . New York, Crown publishers, inc. [1953]. Pict. cloth. OP.

xiv [3] p., 4–530 p. illus., music. 21.8 cm.
Appendix: p. 467–524; index: p. 525–530 (triple column).
Half title; illus. end papers; illus. chapter headings; vignette.

Has material on the train robberies of the Renos and the James gang, Rube Burrow's raids, and Evans and Sontag.

247. Boyd, William Harland, and Glendon J. Rodgers (eds.)

San Joaquin vignettes. The reminiscences of Captain John Barker. Edited by William Harland Boyd [and] Glendon J. Rodgers. Bakersfield, Calif., seventeenth annual publication of the Kern county historical society and the county of Kern through its museum, 1955. Pict. cloth. OP.

xi, 111 p. plates, ports. 23.8 cm.
Vignette.

Contains some information about the lawlessness of early California, with information on Jack Powers.

248. Boyer, Glenn G.

An illustrated life of Doc Holliday, by Glenn Boyer. [Glenwood Springs, Colo., Reminder publishing co., 1966.] Stiff. pict. wrappers.

2 p.l., 4–64 [1] p. plates, ports. (1 on t.p.). 21.7 cm.
Picture index: recto back wrapper.

249. ———

Suppressed murder of Wyatt Earp, by Glenn G. Boyer. San Antonio, Texas, the Naylor co., book publishers of the southwest [1967]. Cloth.

xix p., 2 l., 135 p. front. (port.), plates, ports. 21.6 cm.
Appendices: p. 69–116; notes and references: p. 117–125; index: p. 127–135.
Half title; pub. device.

It is rather a mystery where the author gets his title, and the publishers say that "many will learn for the first time about Wyatt's second wife, Mattie, who committed suicide after he abandoned her," but that has been pointed out in several sources, especially in Frank Waters' *The Earp Brothers of Tombstone.*

250. **[Boylan, John]**

The old Lincoln county courthouse, Lincoln, N.M. [N.p., n.d.] Pamphlet.

[6] p. (no pagination). maps. 13.6 x 19.8 cm. (Oblong.)

Double column; pict. front wrapper; map on back wrapper.

Gives some information on Billy the Kid, Tom O'Folliard, Pat Garrett, John Poe, and Kip McKinney.

251. **Boynton, Percy Holmes**

The rediscovery of the frontier, by Percy H. Boynton. Chicago, Illinois, University of Chicago press [1931]. Pict. cloth. OP.

ix, 184 [1] p. 18.7 cm.

Half title; pub. device; untrimmed.

Contains much material on Billy the Kid and Pat Garrett and some on the Daltons.

252. **Brace, Charles Loring**

The new west; or, California in 1867–1868, by Charles Loring Brace. . . . New York, G. P. Putnam and son . . ., 1869. Cloth. Scarce.

xii, [13]–373 p. 21 cm.

Contains a chapter on stage robbers, though the author names no names.

253. **Bracke, William B.**

Wheat country, by William B. Bracke. New York, Duell, Sloan and Pearce [1950]. Cloth. OP.

viii p., 1 l., 3–309 p. 22 cm.

American Folkway Series.

Index: p. 299–309.

Half title; map on end papers.

This book, edited by Erskine Caldwell, contains some information on Wild Bill Hickok and his death and has a brief account of the Dalton raid at Coffeyville, Kansas.

254. **Bradley, Glenn Danforth**

The story of the Santa Fe, by Glenn Danforth Bradley. . . . Boston, Richard G. Badger . . . [1920]. Cloth. OP.

7 p.l., 17–288 p. front., plates, ports. 20.5 cm.

Source material: p. 272–279; index: p. 281–288.

Map on end papers (dif.); thesis (Ph.D.), University of Michigan, 1915.

This book has a chapter on Dodge City, Kansas, in its wild days and gives some information on its gunmen.

255. Bradley, R. T.

The outlaws of the border; or, the lives of Frank and Jesse James, their exploits, adventures and escapes, down to the present time. Together with the achievements, robberies and final capture of the Younger brothers, by R. T. Bradley. . . . St. Louis, J. W. Marsh, publishers, 1880. Cloth. Rare.

ix, [3]–302 p. front., illus., ports. 20 cm.

The last half of this book is taken from Edwards' *Noted Guerrillas* (Item 664). Like most books of this period about the James boys, it is not very reliable. In 1882 it was republished under the following imprints: St. Louis, J. W. Marsh; Toledo, G. R. Barrow; Cincinnati, Cincinnati publishing co.; New Orleans, Southern publishing co.; Chicago, J. S. Goodman & co.; and Philadelphia, Wm. Flint.

256. Brady, Cyrus Townsend

Recollections of a missionary in the great west, by Rev. Cyrus Townsend Brady. . . . New York, Charles Scribner's sons, 1900. Cloth. Scarce.

6 p.l., 200 p. front. (port. with tissue). 19 cm.
Half title; gilt top; untrimmed.

Contains a chapter on train and bank robbers with some mention of the Dalton raid at Coffeyville, Kansas.

257. Brady, Jasper Ewing

Tales of the telegraph. The story of a telegrapher's life and adventures in railroad, commercial and military work, by Jasper Ewing Brady. . . . New York, Doubleday & McClure co., 1899. Dec. cloth. Scarce.

viii p., 1 l., 272 p. front., plates, facsm. 19.3 cm.
Half title; device.

Contains some minor material on train robbery.

258. Brady, William A.

Showman, [by] William A. Brady. Illustrated. New York, E. P. Dutton & co., inc., 1937. Cloth. OP.

5 p.l., 9–278 p. front., plates, ports. 22.5 cm.
Half title; untrimmed.

Has some ridiculous and erroneous material on the Earps.

259. Branch, E. Douglas

The cowboy and his interpreters, [by] Douglas Branch; illustrations by Will James, Joe DeYong, Charles M. Russell. New York, London, D. Appleton and co., 1926. Dec. cloth. Scarce.

ix [1] p., 1 l., 277 [1] p. front., illus. 21.3 cm.

Bibliography: p. 271–[278].

Half title; illus. end papers; pub. device; untrimmed; first edition: figure (1) at end of bibliography.

In a chapter on Sam Bass, the author says that the Union Pacific robbery netted the outlaws $5,000 from the passengers and that they made a haul of $115,000 in twenty-dollar gold pieces from the express car. He is confused about the amounts. They did not get near that amount from the passengers and got only $60,000 from the express car. There are many more mistakes, which have been taken up in my *Burs Under the Saddle* (Item 7).

260. ———

Westward. The romance of the American frontier, by E. Douglas Branch. Woodcuts by Lucina Smith Wakefield. New York and London, D. Appleton and co., 1930. Cloth. OP.

ix [1] p., 2 l., 3–626 [1] p. illus., maps (1 double p.). 23.2 cm.

Notes on material: p. 598–[609]; index: p. 611–[627].

Half title; map on end papers; illus. chapter headings; vignette; untrimmed; first edition: figure (1) at end of index.

Contains some material on the Lincoln County and Johnson County wars, with a slight mention of Billy the Kid and other outlaws.

261. Brayer, Herbert O.

Range murder: How the Red Sash gang dry-gulched Deputy United States Marshal George Wellman. A vignette of the Johnson county war in Wyoming, by Herbert O. Brayer. Evanston, Illinois, Branding Iron press, 1955. Stiff wrappers. (Cover title.) OP.

20 p. 19 cm.

"Limited number edition" No. ——.

262. Breakenridge, William M.

Helldorado. Bringing the law to the mesquite, by William M. Breakenridge. With illustrations. Boston and New York, Houghton Mifflin co., 1928. Cloth. OP.

xix, 256 p. front., plates, ports. 23.2 cm.

Half title; pub. device; First edition: 1928 under imprint.

A most interesting book about Tombstone, Arizona, in its wild days, told by one of the law officers of that period. Mr. Breakenridge is confused concerning Black Jack Ketchum. It is really Black Jack Christian he is writing about. He says that none of the Earps were ever elected to office in Cochise County, but some of them were appointed to office and thus had the law behind them. His account of the O K Corral fight shows the Earps in a very bad light.

263. Breihan, Carl W.

Badmen of frontier days, by Carl W. Breihan. New York, Robert M. McBride co. [1957]. Cloth.

11 p.l., 1 p., 12–315 p. plates, ports. 20.9 cm.

Half title; facsm. on front end papers; map on rear end papers; device.

There are chapters on Murrell, Plummer, King Fisher, the Reno brothers, Sam Bass, Rube Burrow, Billy the Kid, Harry Tracy, the Daltons, and Bill Doolin.

This book is so filled with errors of fact in every chapter that it would take many pages to enumerate them, as I have done in my *Burs Under the Saddle*. In addition the paper is of poor quality, the text full of typographical errors, and the list of illustrations is not in order with the illustrations themselves.

264. ———

The complete and authentic life of Jesse James, by Carl W. Breihan. With an introduction by Homer Croy. New York, Frederick Fell, inc., publishers [1953]. Cloth.

[49]–287 p. 31 p. plates, ports., facsms., 8 l. 21.8 cm.

Appendix: p. [273]–278; index: p. [281]–287.

This is Mr. Breihan's first book and contains many of the errors he repeats in his later books. However, in this one he uses fewer fictional devices, such as conversations and imaginary thoughts. The author errs in saying that Quantrill had an older brother killed in Kansas, and he, like so many others, misspells Ed O. Kelly's name as Ed O'Kelly. He also misspells other names, such as Bella Starr for Belle Starr, as in the *Police Gazette* novel; Jim Read for Jim Reed; and Jim Collins for Joel Collins.

265. ———

The day Jesse James was killed, [by] Carl W. Breihan. New York, Frederick Fell, inc., publishers [1961]. Cloth and boards.

xxvi p., 1 l., 3–235 p. plates, ports. 21 cm.

Index: p. 225–235.

Half title; illus. t.p.

To begin with, the title of this book is deceptive. One would expect it to deal with the day Jesse was killed, but it is a complete biography. The author's many errors begin with his foreword and end only with the end of the book. It does not seem possible that any person trying to write history could make so many errors of fact, dates, and statistics.

266. ———

Great gunfighters of the west, [by] Carl W. Breihan. London, John Long [1961]. Cloth.

5 p.l., 11–175 [1] p. illus. chapter headings. 21.5 cm.

This book has chapters on Wild Bill Hickok, Bill Longley, Cullen Baker, Bat Masterson, Henry Starr, Henry Brown, Ben Thompson, Clay Allison, and Frank Leslie. Like most of Mr. Breihan's books, this one is full of errors—far too numerous to list here. Many of them are pointed out in my *Burs Under the Saddle*—filling more than five pages of double column—not including such errors as the statement that Billy Dixon was killed at the battle of Adobe Walls. In his chapter on Henry Brown the author gives the date of the Adobe Walls fight two days after it actually took place. He has Hickok being invited by Ned Buntline to come east in 1874 and join his show *Scouts of the Prairie*. Hickok went east in 1873 and joined Buffalo Bill in a play called *Scouts of the Plains*, written by Fred G. Meador.

The author also states that Wild Bill's first publicizing was in *Harper's Weekly* by "Colonel Nicholas" [*sic*], but it was *Harper's New Monthly Magazine*, and the author was George Ward Nichols. He also says that Cherokee Bill was educated at Cherokee, Kansas, and at a Catholic Indian school at Carlisle, Pennsylvania; but Carlisle was a government school with no religious affiliation.

267. ———

Great lawmen of the west, [by] Carl W. Breihan. London, John Long [1963]. Cloth.

6 p.l., 13–191 [1] p. illus. headpieces. 21.5 cm.

Another of the many books Mr. Breihan has written about western outlaws and peace officers, and like the others, full of errors. Since this book was not included in my *Burs Under the Saddle*, it will be discussed in some detail here. On the dust jacket the publishers tell us that the author "lives in St. Louis, Missouri, the home of Jesse James." Jesse never lived in St. Louis, though he did live for a time in St. Joseph.

The book contains chapters on Wyatt Earp, Pat Garrett, Burton Mossman, Tom Smith, Commodore Perry Owens, Billy Breakenridge, Ranald Mackenzie (though why this army officer is classed with law officers is beyond me), Bill Tilghman, and Chris Madsen. The author is mistaken in saying that Doc Holliday went to Dodge City with Wyatt Earp. He says that Ed Masterson was killed instantly when shot by Jack Wagner, but Masterson walked across the street to Hoover's Saloon before dying.

Mr. Breihan is rather careless with his dates throughout. He says that Earp shot

George Hoy "in August, 1879," but he was shot July 26, 1878, and lived until August 21. Such minor errors as placing Nellie Cushman's Russ House at Sixth and Toughnut streets instead of Fifth and Toughnut are frequent. He writes of Doc Holliday telling Earp how he could capture Dave Rudabaugh who had escaped from the Las Vegas jail; but he is writing of 1877, and Rudabaugh did not escape from Las Vegas until 1881. He also tells of an incident I have never seen in print before when he says that Big Nose Kate "could be seen chasing Doc up the street [of Dodge], firing at his buttocks with a shotgun loaded with mustard seed and rice."

He names White as "the former sheriff of Tombstone," but White was town marshal. His spelling of Suppy for Sippy is doubtless a typographical error. He has Virgil Earp dying in Goldfield, Arizona, rather than Goldfield, Nevada. He says that the Benson stage was robbed on March 18, but it happened on March 15. He says that when Morgan Earp was killed, he was playing pool with his brother Wyatt, but he was playing with Hatch, the owner of the establishment. He has Wyatt "confronting" Stillwell just before he was killed, but Stillwell was more likely killed from ambush. Phin Clanton was sent to prison in 1887 and survived for several years after his release, but the author has him killed in 1882.

He writes that Billy the Kid was killed by Garrett "the night of July 13" instead of the fourteenth, and that Garrett himself was killed on February 28, 1908, instead of the twenty-ninth—more near misses.

He has Tom Smith running Ben Thompson out of town, but those two never had any trouble in Abilene. He has Calamity Jane riding into Abilene to try to get Smith's job for Wild Bill Hickok and is also in error in having Smith killing the son of the publisher of the *Abilene Chronicle*. Historians will wonder where he got this information. There seems to be no record of Smith killing anyone in Abilene. He has General Miles appointing Smith to the post of U.S. marshal and at one point has a detachment of troops from Fort Leavenworth coming to Abilene to keep the peace. According to the records, Smith alone was keeping the peace in good fashion.

He has Commodore Perry Owens and Old Mart Blevins shooting it out, Blevins being killed in March, 1887. But Blevins disappeared from his ranch, and his fate was never known. The author says that in a battle at the Tewksbury ranch "Hampton Blevins and a man named Duchet were the only two to escape with no injuries." He has Blevins killed by Owens a few pages further on. But Blevins was killed in the battle at the ranch.

Mr. Breihan says that Little Bill Raidler was sent to Ohio State Penitentiary, where he met O. Henry, "whose influence over Little Bill prevailed even in the young man's later life," and he has Raidler becoming a well-known writer, something no one else ever heard of. He tells many things Mrs. Tilghman did not seem to know about her husband, for she did not mention them in her splendid biography of him.

He has Mayor Dog Kelly wiring Wyatt Earp, then serving as an officer in Wichita, to come to Dodge and serve as marshal. All other accounts say that Mayor George Hoover (whom Mr. Breihan calls Major) sent the wire. The author says that Earp brought Neal Brown and Ed Masterson with him. He also incorrectly states that Bill Tilghman was with Bat Masterson when he caught the train robbers at Lovell's camp. He states that Tilghman married the widow Flora Robinson in 1877, but her name was Flora Kendall. He is also wrong in saying that the Kiowa renegades under Dull Knife invaded the area in 1881. They arrived in 1878. He states that "in the following year Pat Sughrue was elected sheriff," but Sughrue was not elected until November 6, 1883, and took office January 14, 1884. Mr. Breihan states that Tilghman "was called to run the marshal's office at Oklahoma City in 1911," but he was chief of police of that city.

His chapter on Chris Madsen is also full of errors. He states that Madsen took a posse after Kid Lewis and Crawford Foster and trailed them to Wichita Falls, Texas, where they were caught robbing a bank. They were not caught until later, about ten o'clock that night, and they were captured by Ranger Bill McDonald and Rangers McCauley and McClure. The author states that the president of the bank and the cashier were killed during the robbery, but many years later I knew the president, J. A. Kemp, personally. The cashier, Frank Dorsey, was killed, and the bookkeeper, H. H. Langford (whom I also knew), was wounded. The author says that an hour or two later after the capture Madsen and his posse started back for El Reno. But Madsen had nothing to do with the capture. He further states that when the posse got back to Wichita Falls a mob had lynched Lewis and Foster. They were lynched, all right, but after McDonald and his Rangers had turned them over to a guard of twenty-five men selected by the judge to protect the jail. There are many other errors.

268. ———

Outlaws of the old west, [by] Carl W. Breihan. London, John Long [1959]. Pict. cloth.

10 p.l., 19–224 p. facsms. 21.8 cm.

Half title; headpieces.

An English edition of the author's *Badmen of Frontier Days* (Item 263). The only difference in the two books is that in the American edition the first chapter is about John Murrell and in the English edition it deals with the James and Younger boys.

269. ———

Quantrill and his Civil War guerrillas, by Carl W. Breihan. Denver, Sage Books [1959]. Cloth.

5 p.l., 11–174 p. plates, ports., facsms. 23.5 cm.
Roster of guerrillas: p. 166–174.
Half title.

Like most of the author's other books, full of errors.

270. ———

Younger brothers, by Carl W. Breihan. San Antonio, Texas, the Naylor co. . . . [1961]. Pict. cloth.

xiii, 260 p. illus., plates, ports., facsm. 21.8 cm.
Half title; illus. end papers (dif.).

Much of this book is similar to the author's earlier volumes on Jesse James. He repeats the same errors and myths. As in most of his other books, he spells Jim Reed's last name as Read, but this time he does spell Belle Starr's first name correctly.

271. Brent, Rafer (ed.)

Great western heroes. Seven true stories of the men who tamed the west. Edited by Rafer Brent. New York, Bartholomew House, inc. [1957]. Stiff pict. wrappers.

4 p.l., [9]–191 p. 19.6 cm.
Half title; pub. device; "First printing" on copyright p.

It is typical for books of this quality to include the word "true" in the title. As usual, there is very little truth in it. These stories first appeared in men's magazines, and they are characteristic of that type of writing.

There are chapters on Henry Brown, Bat Masterson, Pat Garrett, Wyatt Earp, Sam Bass, John Slaughter, and Buffalo Bill Cody. In the chapter on Bat Masterson the author has the killing of Sergeant King wrong and repeats the legend about Clay Allison backing down before Wyatt Earp's bluff. I'm afraid that is Earp's version. There are similar mistakes in every chapter; seven pages of them are listed in my *Burs Under the Saddle* (Item 7).

272. Brent, William

The complete and factual life of Billy the Kid, [by] William Brent. New York, Frederick Fell, inc. [1964]. Boards.

7 p.l., 212 [1] p. illus., ports., facsms. 21.5 cm.
Half title; Bonney family tree: p. [213].

This book corrects many of the legends about Billy the Kid, but the author makes quite a few mistakes himself. He has Mrs. Antrim telling Ash Upson all the untrue information about the Kid's birth, their moving to Kansas in 1863, Billy having a younger brother, and the mother moving to Colorado, where she married Mr. Antrim. Although it has been proved that Henry Brown's name was spelled Hendry by some writers solely from a typographical error which once appeared, Mr. Brent says that "there is a *d* in Brown's first name, not Henry, as most writers erroneously call it."

He says that the Kid was the one who killed Morton and Baker, though others were also shooting. He does not have Peppin with Sheriff Brady and deputies Matthews and Hindman when they were ambushed by the Kid's gang. He is also mistaken when he says that the Kid admitted killing Beckwith during the battle at the McSween home. In writing about the Brown-Wheeler robbery of the bank at Medicine Lodge, Kansas, he is also mistaken when he says: "The robbers were pursued and overtaken by a posse. Two men in Brown's gang were killed, Hendry [*sic*] was captured, and hanged promptly from the nearest tree." All the members of Brown's gang were captured, and it was not until after they had been placed in jail that the mob took them out and hanged them. Brown was killed when he ran, and Wheeler was also shot trying to run away. After that they were all hanged.

The author is also wrong in saying that Chapman, Mrs. McSween's lawyer, was killed in a saloon where he had gone to have a drink. He was killed on the street. The author admits that there were three bullet holes in Carlyle's body, but he gives the Kid credit for killing him. He has Garrett both a sheriff and a U.S. marshal, and Bob Olinger (whose name he misspells) a deputy U.S. marshal. Neither had federal commissions.

Of the mob at Las Vegas, the author says that it broke up when the station agent went out and told the men that they would be in trouble for detaining the U.S. mail. "The train then slowly got under way," he writes, and "the mob danger was over." That is not the way it happened at all. The author also makes a statement, one I have not seen elsewhere, that the Kid amused his jailer, Bell, while they played cards by slipping his handcuffs on and off. He misspells Gauss' name as Geiss, as so many others do, and is mistaken in saying that after Bell and Olinger were killed "Geiss [*sic*] arrived with a heavy file, and the Kid ordered him to cut the chains between the two leg irons." Gauss merely tossed the Kid a small miner's pick to free himself.

Mr. Brent also has the Kid "shifting his knife to his left hand" and "drawing his gun as he stepped into the doorway" the night he was killed. But those who examined him after his death found no gun, though the author said that "his pistol was still clutched in his right hand, the butcher knife on the floor a few feet away," when he was examined after his death. On the next page he writes that "then they examined the Kid's revolver. Four live shells were in the cylinder, with the hammer down on an empty."

He gives Bonnie Parker the name Bonnie Baker. He also wants to give the Kid credit for killing Buckshot Roberts, though he says that "Charlie Bowdre is generally credited by fellow posse members as the man who gave Roberts his death wound." He gives the Kid credit for killing Bob Beckwith and Bernstein, and though he admits that there is some doubt about it, he says that the Kid "claimed Bernstein," which he did not. There are many other errors.

273. ———, and Milarde Brent

The hell hole, by William Brent and Milarde Brent. Yuma, Ariz., Southwest printers . . ., 1962. Pict. wrappers.

2 p.l., 61 p. front., plates, ports. 19 cm.

Tells something of the life and crimes of Buckskin Frank Leslie, Pearl Hart, and other Arizona outlaws. The authors' account of Frank Leslie's prison life is not accurate. Instead of trying to disprove some of the fiction written about him, they perpetuate it. They are certainly mistaken in having him released from prison in 1907. He was pardoned by Governor Benjamin J. Franklin on November 17, 1896.

274. Bridwell, J. W.

The life and adventures of Robert McKemie, alias "Little Reddy," from Texas. The dare-devil desperado of the Black Hills region, chief of the murderous gang of treasure coach robbers. Also, a full account of the robberies committed by him and his gang in Highland, Pike and Ross counties; with full particulars of Detective Norris' adventures while effecting the capture of members of the gang. Compiled from authentic sources by J. W. Bridwell. Hillsboro, O., printed and published at the Hillsboro Gazette office, December, 1878. Pict. wrappers. Rare.

[3]–56 p. ports. 22.6 cm.

Reprinted in facsimile in an edition of one hundred copies by the Frontier press, Houston, Texas, 1955. Stiff wrappers.

[3]–56 [4] p. illus., plates, ports. 21.4 cm.

Last 4 p. plates and ports.

The original edition is an exceedingly rare item about an outlaw of the Black Hills who made a specialty of robbing the treasure coaches of the Deadwood–Cheyenne run. McKemie is credited with the daring holdup at Cheyenne Crossing and South Pass City and with the murder of Johnny Slaughter, the well-known stage driver. He was a member of the Joel Collins–Sam Bass gang at the start of their criminal careers, but after his careless murder of Slaughter he was run out of the gang. I know of but three copies of this book, one of which I once owned.

275. Briggs, Harold E.

Frontiers of the northwest. A history of the upper Missouri valley, by Harold E. Briggs. . . . Illustrated. New York, London, D. Appleton-Century co., inc., 1940. Cloth. OP.

xiv p., 1 l., 3–629 p. front., plates (4 ports. on 1 plate), maps. 22.8 cm.

Bibliography: p. 595–612; index: p. 613–629.

Half title; map on end papers; pub. device; first edition: figure (1) at end of index.

In one section, entitled "The Calamity Jane Myth," some space is devoted to debunking this well-known character. In another, entitled "Justice in the Mining Camps," the author deals with the Vigilance Committee of Montana and with Henry Plummer's gang.

276. Briggs, L. Vernon

Arizona and New Mexico, 1882. California, 1886. Mexico, 1891, by L. Vernon Briggs. . . . Privately printed. Boston, 1932. Cloth. Scarce.

x, 282 p. front. (port.), plates, ports., facsms. 23.7 cm.

Untrimmed.

This contains some information on the killing of Jesse James by Bob Ford. The author criticizes Governor Crittenden for the manner in which he conspired with the Ford brothers for Jesse's death.

The author has a poor opinion of the Earps, which he spells Arps. "There has been much lawlessness and disorder in Cochise County," he writes, "which has arisen from the misconduct and criminal deeds of deputy U.S. Marshals. . . . It was during the time when the rule of these official desperadoes was at its height, when they were backed by a district judge, a postmaster and a newspaper, that the candidate for Governor visited Tombstone with a petition.

"One hears the story of the celebrated Arp family," he continues, "who, until recently, with the authority of the law to back them up, contaminated civil and criminal jurisprudence in the Territory. . . . Only a few months ago these men, officers of the law, slaughtered in cold blood unarmed and innocent citizens in the street. The Arps are said 'to have carried the commission of legally constituted authority in their pockets, refined knavery in their heads and hearts, blood in their eyes, shotguns and revolvers in their hands, and raped the law which they had sworn to execute.' "

277. Brininstool, Earl Alonzo

Fighting Red Cloud's warriors. True tales of Indian days when the west was young, by E. A. Brininstool. . . . Columbus, Ohio, the Hunter-Trader-Trapper co., 1926. Pict. cloth. OP.

7 p.l., 17–241 [1] p. front., plates, ports. 18.7 cm.

7 p. adv. at end.

"The Frontier Series," Vol. 2.

There is a long chapter on Calamity Jane in which the author quotes her autobiography in full, with a few additional pronouns and some reparagraphing. He also quotes extensively from Brown and Willard's *The Black Hills.* In his footnotes he has tried to correct some of the legends about Calamity, but, as so many others do he gives the day of her death as August 2: "It is a peculiar coincidence that the death of Calamity Jane should have occurred at almost the same hour of the same day of the same month, twenty-seven years later, as that of Wild Bill Hickok, one of her former friends, and near whom she was buried."

278. ———

Fighting Indian warriors. True tales of the wild frontiers, by E. A. Brininstool. Harrisburg, Pa., the Stackpole co., 1953. Pict. cloth. Scarce.

xiii, 353 p. front., plates, ports., map, facsm. 21.7 cm.

Half title.

An enlarged and expanded edition of the author's *Fighting Red Cloud's Warriors.* (see Item 277). Again there is a chapter on Calamity Jane in which he debunks the legend that Jane captured Jack McCall with meat cleaver.

279. Bristol, Rev. S.

The pioneer preacher. Incidents of interest and experiences in the author's life . . . , by Rev. S. Bristol. . . . Illustrated by Isabelle Blood. Chicago, New York, Fleming H. Revell [1887]. Cloth. Scarce.

viii, 9–330 p. front. (port.). 19.7 cm.

Has some material on outlawry and robbery.

280. Bristow, G. O.

Lost on Grand river, by G. O. Bristow. Nowater, I.T., Cherokee Air publishing co., 1900. Wrappers. Very rare.

131 p. 18.5 cm.

Has much on the outlaws of the Indian Territory, such as Cherokee Bill, Jim French, the Daltons, Bill Doolin, Henry Starr, and Bill Cook. The only copy I have seen is in the Library of Congress, and its pulp paper has almost disintegrated.

281. Bristow, Joseph Quayle

Tales of old Fort Gibson. Memories along the trail to yesterday of the Oklahoma, Indian territory and the old south, by Joseph Quayle Bristow. New York, Exposition Press [1961]. Cloth.

14 p.l., [29]–246 [1] p. 21 cm.
Appendices: p. [243–247].
Half title; pub. device; "First edition" on copyright p.

Has a chapter on Al Jennings, some information on Henry Starr, and some mention of Doc Holliday, Cherokee Bill, and others.

282. **Brome, Vincent**

Frank Harris, the life and loves of a scoundrel, by Vincent Brome. New York, London, Thomas Yoseloff [1959]. Cloth.

ix, 246 p. Front. (port.), plates, ports., facsms. 21.5 cm.
Bibliography: p. 234–240; index: p. 241–246.
Half title; vignette.

Throughout the pages dealing with Harris' *My Reminiscences as a Cowboy* the author is critical and doubtful about the truth of his statements, as well he might be. "Many details," the author writes, "of the story as Harris unfolded it were totally unconvincing. . . . Continuously in the last quarter of his life, when he was said to have written *On the Trail* (the English title of the above book), sheer poverty drove him to write and sponsor exaggerated books some of which he later regretted." He repeats some of Harris' stories about his experiences as a cattle rustler.

283. **Bronaugh, Warren Carter**

The Youngers' fight for freedom. A southern soldier's twenty years' campaign to open northern prison doors—with anecdotes of war days, by W. C. Bronaugh, . . . who spent the period from 1882 to 1902 to secure the release of Cole, Jim and Bob Younger from the Minnesota state penitentiary. . . . Columbia, Mo., printed for the author by E. W. Stephens publishing co., 1906. Cloth. Scarce.

6 p.l., 15–398 p. front. (port.), plates, ports. 21 cm.

A book different from all the others dealing with the James and Younger brothers, and reliable. The author spent twenty years of his life working to get the Youngers pardoned from the Minnesota penitentiary. From 1882 to 1902 he wrote letters, spent his own money and that raised from friends, traveled thousands of miles, and camped on the trail of governors, pardon boards, and wardens. He did not give up until the Youngers were released.

284. **Bronson, Edgar Beecher**

Red blooded, by Edgar Beecher Bronson. . . . Chicago, A. C. McClurg & co., 1910. Pict. cloth. OP.

viii, 3–341 [1] p. front., plates. 21 cm.

Partly reprinted from various publications. Republished by George H. Doran co., New York, with some changes in the title page.

An excellent piece of western Americana with a chapter on Clay Allison; one, entitled "Triggerfingeritis," tells about stagecoach robberies by Dunc Blackburn, shotgun messengers such as Boone May, and horse thieves such as Doc Middleton. A long chapter on "The Evolution of a Train Robber" relates the story of the robbing of the Southern Pacific by Kit Joy, Mitch Lee, Taggart, and George Cleveland.

285. ———

The vanguard, by Edgar Beecher Bronson. . . . New York, George H. Doran co. [1914]. Pict. cloth. OP.

5 p.l., 9–316 p. 19.6 cm.

Half title; illus. end papers (col.).

The author spells John Chisum's name as Chisholm. He tells of the hanging of Lame Johnny and gives some information on the Apache Kid.

286. Brooks, Juanita

John Doyle Lee, zealot-pioneer, builder-scapegoat, by Juanita Brooks. . . . Glendale, Calif., the Arthur H. Clark co., 1964. Cloth.

16 p.l., [17]–404 p. front. (port.), plates, ports., facsms., maps, charts. 24.5 cm.

Appendix: p. [379]–384; bibliographical notes: p. [385]–388; index: p. [389]–404.

Half title: Western Frontiersmen Series IX; pub. device.

287. ———

The Mountain Meadow massacre, by Juanita Brooks. Stanford, Calif., Stanford University press [1950]. Cloth. OP.

vii [1] p., 243 p. 23.5 cm.

Appendix: p. 169–223; bibliography: p. 225–237; index: p. 239–243.

Half title; map on end papers.

Contains much on John D. Lee and some material on Porter Rockwell.

288. Brophy, Frank Cullen

Arizona sketch book. Fifty historical sketches, by Frank Cullen Brophy. [Phoenix, Ariz., printed by Ampco press, Arizona-Messenger printing co., 1952.] Cloth.

xi, 310 p. plates. 21 cm.

Bibliography: p. 297–301; index: p. 303–310.

Half title; map on end papers.

Has a short chapter on the Apache Kid and some information on Wyatt Earp, John

Slaughter, Commodore Perry Owens, and others. The author makes quite a hero of Wyatt Earp and says that he "*tracked* Frank Stillwell to Tucson," though we know that Earp was in Tucson with the train carrying the body of his brother Morgan to California. When he saw Stillwell in the railroad yards, he and his party killed him from ambush. The author also has Earp killing Curly Bill Brocius, though most authorities deny it. He also says that the Clantons were waiting in the O K Corral to kill the Earps, but we know that the Earps were the aggressors in that fight.

289. Brosnan, Cornelius James

History of the state of Idaho, by C. J. Brosnan. . . . New York, Chicago, Boston, Charles Scribner's sons [1918]. Cloth. Scarce.

xiii p., 2 l., 237 p. front. (double p. col. map), illus., plates, ports., maps. 20 cm.
Supplement: p. 213–231; index: p. 233–237.

Contains some material on the vigilantes of Idaho.

290. Brothers, Mary Hudson

Billy the Kid. The most hated, the most loved outlaw New Mexico ever produced. Story by Bell Hudson. Written by Mary Hudson Brothers. [Farmington, N.M., Hustler press, 1949]. Stiff pict. wrappers with 2 hole tie.

5 p.l., 13–52 p. 2 ports. (incl. front.). 24.7 cm.
Half title.

This little book is largely taken from the author's *A Pecos Pioneer* (see Item 291), and contains the same mistakes. There are many misspelled proper names, as well as errors of fact.

291. ———

A Pecos pioneer, by Mary Hudson Brothers. Albuquerque, published by the University of New Mexico press, 1943. Cloth. Scarce.

vii p., 1 l., 169 p. front. (group port.). 23.5 cm.
Half title; device.

This book is based upon notes by the author's father, Bell Hudson, but she makes the mistake of crediting the Chisholm Trail to John Chisum, and I question her version of the manner in which J. W. Bell was killed when she says that the Kid ran up the steps (after Bell had taken him to an outside toilet) and "the farther he got the faster he went." How did he run so fast with leg irons on? She has the Kid breaking down the door of the armory, getting a gun and shooting Bell just as the latter fired at him. This is the first account in which Bell had shot at the Kid. She also gives Bell's first name as George, though his initials were J. W. There are many, many more mistakes.

292. Brown, Dee

The gentle tamers; women of the old west, [by] Dee Brown. New York, G. P. Putnam's sons [1958]. Cloth. OP.

5 p.l., 11–317 [1] p. plates, ports. 22 cm.
Notes: p. 299–310; index: p. 311–317; [acknowledgments: p. 318].
Half title; pub. device.

In his chapter on Belle Starr, the author is mistaken in writing that her brother was killed "while riding with Jim Lane's Red Leg bushwhackers." Her brother was a loyal southerner. He also says that Belle was sentenced to a six-month term in prison, but she was sentenced to nine months. He is also mistaken in calling Rose of Cimarron an outlaw.

293. ———, and Martin F. Schmitt

Trail driving days. Text by Dee Brown, picture research by Martin F. Schmitt. New York, Charles Scribner's sons; London, Charles Scribner's sons, ltd., 1952. Pict. cloth. OP.

xxii p., 1 l., 264 p. plates, ports., cattle brands, facsms. 30.5 cm.
Bibliography: p. 255–264.
Half title; errata leaf tipped in; vignette; first edition: letter "A" on copyright p.

This is mostly a picture book containing many familiar photographs of various outlaws, but it does contain a new picture which the authors say is of Billy the Kid, but about which there is some doubt. In the chapter on the Kid, the authors repeat all the old legends about the Kid's early life, the killing of the blacksmith who insulted his mother, his absence when Tunstall was killed, his swearing at Tunstall's grave to avenge him, and the judge's sentence of the Kid and his impudent answer, as well as the one about his being in a card game with Bell when he killed him. They also have the battle in Lincoln incorrect and seem to follow the Walter Noble Burns account (see Item 337).

294. Brown, F. Yeats (ed.)

Escape. A book of escapes of all kinds. Arranged and edited with introduction by F. Yeats Brown. . . . New York, the Macmillan co., 1933. Cloth. OP.

4 p.l., 9–212 p. 20.5 cm.
Half title; pub. device; untrimmed.

Contains a selection about Harvey Logan's escape from the Knoxville, Tennessee, prison, taken from *You Can Escape*, by Edward H. Smith. The editor fails to correct the misspelling of Tom Ketchum's name as Ketcham.

295. Brown, George Rothwell (ed.)

Reminiscences of Senator William M. Stewart, of Nevada. Edited by George

Rothwell Brown. New York and Washington, the Neale publishing co., 1908. Cloth. Scarce.

11 p.l., [21]–358 p. front. (port. with tissue). 22.5 cm.

The author tells about the killing of Van Sickle by Sam Brown and about stage holdups, and says he witnessed the O K Corral battle—from a distance. He must have been quite a distance away, for he claims that six of the Clantons were killed. Only two Clantons and two McLaury brothers took part in the fight, and only three men were killed. He spells Earp as Erp.

296. Brown, James Cabell

Calabaza; or, amusing recollections of an Arizona "city," by J. Cabell Brown. Illustrated with original drawings. San Francisco, published by Valleau & Peterson, printers and publishers [1892]. Wrappers. Rare.

5 p.l., [13]–251 p. front., illus. 18.4 cm.

Calabaza was a rugged camp in the Santa Cruz Valley of Arizona, just north of the Mexican border. It was the refuge of tough *hombres* from all parts of the West. The town was broken up by riots. What was left of it moved to Nogales, where it is said its citizens "could keep one foot on the bar rail and the other on the boundary line."

297. Brown, Jesse, and A. M. Willard

The Black Hills trails. A history of the struggles of the pioneers in the winning of the Black Hills, by Jesse Brown and A. M. Willard, edited by John T. Milek. Rapid City, S.D., Rapid City Journal co., 1924. Cloth. Scarce.

6 p.l., [17]–572 p. front., illus., plates, ports. 23.6 cm.

One of the standard histories of the Black Hills, this book contains much information on the outlaws of that section. The authors write that Dave McCanles was the leader of a band of outlaws and horse thieves, that when he started to draw his gun on Wild Bill Hickok the latter shot him dead, and that "the fall of the leader demoralized the rest of the gang who immediately fled, but Bill succeeded in bringing down two of them mortally wounded." We know that there was no gang, but only three men and McCanles' son, and that they were not outlaws. The authors also say that Kate Shell "seized a grub hoe and with it killed the wounded *robber* named Woods." This is also untrue. It was Wellman who wielded the hoe in a most cowardly manner. They say further that Wild Bill "killed many men in his time, but always in a manner as to be within the law and justified, usually being a fraction of a second too quick for the other fellow." They do correctly say, however, that A. C. Tipple was the bartender at Saloon No. 10 when Wild Bill was killed.

These authors claim that Wild Bill had been in Abilene only a short time before he "killed a number of desperate characters and so terrorized the other scoundrels that they moved to newer and safer ground." We know that he only killed two men in Abilene, one his deputy and friend. The authors also give some unreliable information on Calamity Jane.

298. Brown, John

Twenty-five years a parson in the wild west; being the experiences of Parson Ralph Riley, by Rev. John Brown. . . . Fall River, Mass., printed for the author, 1896. Cloth. Scarce.

4 p.l., 9–215 p. front. (port.). 18.7 cm.

Relates experiences with stagecoach robbers in Nevada and with train robbers in Texas.

299. Brown, Mark H.

The plainsmen of the Yellowstone. A history of the Yellowstone basin, by Mark H. Brown. New York, G. P. Putnam's sons [1961]. Cloth.

6 p.l., [13]–480 p. 7 maps (all double p. except 1). 24 cm.

Some interesting books: p. [464]–467; acknowledgments: p. [468]–470; index: p. [471]–480.

Half title; map on end papers; untrimmed; pub. device.

Has a long chapter on outlaws and lawlessness in Montana and Wyoming. There is information on the Johnson County War, the hanging of Jim Averill and Cattle Kate, as well as that of Flat Nose George Curry, and the crimes of the Wild Bunch.

300. ———, and W. R. Felton

Before barbed wire; L. A. Huffman, photographer on horseback, by Mark H. Brown and W. R. Felton. Illustrated with photographs. New York, Henry Holt and co., [1956]. Cloth. OP.

6 p.l., 13–256 p. plates, ports. 28.6 cm.

Notes on photographs: p. 215–223; notes on text: p. 225–236; bibliography: p. 237–240; acknowledgments: p. 241–243; index: p. 245–254.

Half title; map on end papers.

Contains a chapter on the vigilantes of Montana and some information on the Johnson County War of Wyoming.

301. ———, and ———

The frontier years. L. A. Huffman, photographer of the plains, by Mark H. Brown and W. R. Felton. New York, Henry Holt and co. [1955]. Cloth. OP.

6 p.l., 13–272 p. front. (port.), plates, ports. 28.5 cm.

Notes on text: p. 237–250; notes on photographs: p. 251–257; bibliography: p. 259–261; acknowledgments: p. 263–266; index: p. 267–272.

Half title; maps on end papers (dif.).

Has some new material on Calamity Jane and also on Big Nose George Parrott.

302. Brown, Robert L.

An empire of silver. A history of the San Juan silver rush, by Robert L. Brown. Illustrated with photographs. Caldwell, Idaho, the Caxton printers, ltd., 1965. Cloth.

13 p.l., [27]–328 p. plates, facsms. 21.5 cm.

Half title; map on end papers; pub. device.

In a chapter entitled "Crime and Justice" the author tells about the lynching of Billy LeRoy and his brother, who went under the name Frank Clark. He also tells of the stage robberies committed by Ike Stockton and the Charles Allison gang and of the lynching of Stockton. He gives an account of Bat Masterson's experiences as a peace officer at Silverton, Colorado, and of the McCarthy gang holding up the bank at Delta. He also tells about the Marlows and their troubles in Texas and devotes several pages to the crimes of Alferd Packer, whose first name he spells Alfred, as most other writers do.

303. ———

Ghost towns of the Colorado Rockies, by Robert L. Brown. Illustrated with photographs. Caldwell, Idaho, the Caxton printers, ltd., 1968. Cloth.

15 p.l., [31]–401 p. plates, port. 21.7 cm.

Index: p. [398]–401.

Half title; map on end papers; pub. device.

Has some material about Joseph Slade and his killing of Jules Reni, whose name the author spells Beni. Also has a mention of Bat Masterson, and Alferd Packer, whose name he spells Alfred.

304. Brown, Robert R. (ed.)

History of Kings county. Edited by Robert R. Brown . . ., J. E. Richmond, supervising editor . . ., Handford, Calif., A. H. Canoston, 1940. Fabrikoid. OP.

5 p.l., 13–385 p. front. (port.), plates, ports. 27.7 cm.

Index (in front of book): p. [6–8].

Contains material on Murieta and Vásquez.

305. Brown, Will C.

Sam Bass and company, by Will C. Brown. N.Y., published by the New American Library [1960]. Stiff pict. wrappers.

3 p.l., 7–144 p. 18 cm.

Acknowledgments: p. 143–144.

Like most books of its caliber, this one is full of errors and conversations that never took place but it appears that the author was merely writing a piece of fiction.

306. Brownlee, Richard S.

Gray ghosts of the Confederacy. Guerrilla warfare in the west, 1861–1865, [by] Richard S. Brownlee. Baton Rouge, Louisiana State University press [1958]. Cloth. OP.

xi p., 1 l., 3–274 p. plates, ports., maps. 22.2 cm.

Bibliography: p. 247–252; appendix: p. 253–261; index: p. 265–274.

Half title; map on end papers; illus. double t.p.

Has much on the James boys, the Youngers, and other outlaws of their gangs.

307. Bruffey, George A.

Eighty-one years in the west, by George A. Bruffey. Butte, Mont., the Butte Miner co., printers, 1925. Cloth. Scarce.

4 p.l., [11]–152 p. front. (port.). 20.2 cm.

Half title; device.

Material on the Montana vigilantes and outlaws, the hanging of Slade, and the Plummer gang.

308. Bryan, Jerry

An Illinois gold hunter in the Black Hills. The diary of Jerry Bryan, March 13 to August 20, 1876, with an introduction and notes by Clyde C. Watson. . . . Springfield, Ill., Illinois State Historical society, 1960. Stiff wrappers.

5 p.l., 11–40 p. 8 plates, 3 maps. 22.8 cm.

Has some material on the killing of Wild Bill Hickok.

309. Bryant, Will

Great American guns and frontier fighters. Written and illustrated by Will Bryant. NewYork, Grossett & Dunlap, publishers [1961]. Pict. cloth.

6 p.l., 11–160 p. illus., plates (mostly col.). 28 cm.

Glossary: p. 158–160.

Has some information on Bill Doolin, Red Buck, Bitter Creek Newcomb, Bill Tilghman, Heck Thomas, and others.

310. [Buchanan, James]

Message to the President of the United States. Washington, 1860. Sewn. (Caption title). Rare.

64 p. 22.5 cm.

36th Congress, 1st Session, Ex. Doc. No. 32.

Deals with J. D. Lee and the Mountain Meadow Massacre and other crimes.

311. Buckbee, Edna Bryan

Pioneer days of Angel's Camp, by Edna Bryan Buckbee. Angel's Camp, Calif., published by Calaveras Californian [1932]. Stiff pict. wrappers. OP.

3 p.l., 80 p. front., plates, ports. 19.4 cm.

Has some stories about Black Bart.

312. ———

The saga of old Tuolumne, by Edna Bryan Buckbee. Sixteen full-page illustrations from photographs. New York, the Press of the Pioneers, inc., 1935. Cloth. Scarce.

x p., 3 l., 526 p. front., plates. 23.5 cm.

Bibliography: p. [492]–500; pioneers of Tuolumne County: p. 501–521; towns and camps of Tuolumne region: p. 523–526.

Half title.

Contains some material on Murieta and other California outlaws.

313. Buel, James William

The border outlaws. An authentic and thrilling history of the most noted bandits of ancient and modern times, the Younger brothers, Jesse and Frank James, and their comrades in crime. Compiled from reliable sources only and containing the latest facts in regard to these celebrated outlaws, by J. W. Buel. . . . Illustrated with portraits and colored plates. St. Louis, Historical publishing co., 1881. Cloth. Rare.

4 p.l., [11]–252 p. front. (port. of 3 Youngers), illus., plates (8 col.), ports. 19.2 cm.

[Published with]

The border bandits. An authentic and thrilling history of the noted outlaws, Jesse and Frank James and their band of highwaymen. Compiled from reliable sources only and containing the latest facts in regard to these desperate freebooters, by J. W. Buel. . . . Illustrated with late portraits and colored plates. St. Louis, Historical publishing co., 1881.

4 p.l., [7]–48 [4] p. front. (port. of 2 James brothers), plates (4 col.), ports. 19.2 cm.

Republished by the same publishers in 1882, and in later years. Also published by Alvord and Speigh, Syracuse, N.Y., in 1883, and published several times in cheap editions, both together and separately by I. & M. Ottenheimer, of Baltimore.

Buel is unreliable in all his books, and his writings seem to border upon the sensational rather than to rely upon historical facts. For instance, he has the Muncie robbery taking place at night, though it occurred in the afternoon. Throughout he makes many unnecessary mistakes on matters easily verified by the newspapers.

314. ———

Heroes of the plains; or, lives and wonderful adventures of Wild Bill, Buffalo Bill . . . and other celebrated Indian fighters . . . including a true and thrilling history of Custer's "last fight" . . . also a sketch of the life of Sitting Bull and his account of the Custer massacre as related to the author in person, J. W. Buel. . . . St. Louis, Historical publishing co., 1881. Cloth. Scarce.

7 p.l., 21–548 p. front. (col.), illus., plates (col.), ports. 21 cm.

Republished under the same imprint in 1882, 1883, and 1884; published again in Philadelphia in 1886 and 1891.

This is no dime novel, though it reads like one. It is a thick book, and its size and large circulation caused readers to accept it as fact. Thus it was that legends about Wild Bill and Buffalo Bill were created and are still being perpetuated by careless writers.

This book retains the false story started by Nichols in *Harper's Magazine*. The author also claims to have come into possession of Hickok's diary, given him by his widow. Her son-in-law denies that Wild Bill kept a diary. Buel places Rock Creek Station in Kansas rather than Nebraska. He incorrectly claims that the McCanleses were horse thieves, saying that "they had long been a terror to the central part of Kansas, had killed more men and stolen a greater number of horses than any other two thieving cut-throats that ever figured in the annals of western outlawry." In the "fight" he has Wild Bill's skull fractured, three gashes in his breast, a forearm cut, one deep wound in the hip and two in the right leg, and his right cheek cut open, besides all the bullet wounds.

"This combat," says Buel, "of one man fairly whipping ten acknowledged desperadoes, has no parallel, I make bold to say, in any authentic history" (note the exact words in Item 668). Buel says that this "fight" occurred December 16, 1870, but the actual date was July 12, 1861.

After such a tale one naturally loses confidence in the writer, and, sure enough, there are similar exaggerations and false tales throughout the book, one notable example being Hickok's duel with four opponents at one time, in which he killed three men and wounded the fourth. The author calls Mike Williams, Hickok's own deputy at Abilene, Jim McWilliams, and like many other details in the book his version of the killing of Coe (which he spells Cole) and Williams is all wrong. To point out all the errors in the book would take many pages.

315. ———

Jesse and Frank James and their comrades in crime, the Younger brothers, the notorious border outlaws. An authentic account of the most daring bandits of modern times, the Younger brothers, also Jesse and Frank James and their comrades in crime. Compiled from the most reliable sources, and containing the latest facts, by J. W. Buel. Fully illustrated. Baltimore, I. & M. Ottenheimer [n.d.]. Pict. wrappers.

2 p.l., 7–188 p. front., illus. 19 cm.

A cheap reprint of the author's *Border Outlaws* (Item 313), with omissions.

316. ———

Life and marvelous adventures of Wild Bill, the scout. Being a true and exact history of all the sanguinary combats and hair-breadth escapes of the most famous scout and spy America ever produced, by J. W. Buel. . . . Illustrated. Chicago, Belford, Clarke & co., 1880. Pict. wrappers. Rare.

3 p.l., 7–92 [1] p. front. (port.), illus. 18 cm.

Republished in 1888, and published again in Chicago, by G. E. Wilson, in 1891 with same format.

The first and perhaps the rarest book written about Wild Bill Hickok. It is a continuation of the legend about the Hickok-McCanles "fight" and an example of highly imaginary and exaggerated sensationalism. In February, 1867, *Harper's Magazine* published a story about Hickok written by Colonel George Ward Nichols purportedly told by Hickok himself to the author. The tale was proved to be pure fabrication throughout, but most of the books on Wild Bill that followed Buel rehashed the wild tale. Emerson Hough probably used this book for his chapter on Hickok in his *Story of the Outlaw*. The criticisms of Buel's later books apply to this book as well.

317. ———

The true story of "Wild Bill" Hickok, by J. W. Buel. Edited by J. Brussel. . . . New York, Atomic Books, inc. [1946]. Stiff pict. wrappers.

3–96 p. 18.8 cm.

More or less a reprint of the *Life of Wild Bill* (Item 316), with a chapter devoted to the *Harper's Magazine* article, a chapter on Calamity Jane, and a chapter of notes correcting the false legends so long prevalent about Wild Bill. Yet in his chapter on Calamity Jane the editor repeats most of the incorrect legends about her, for example, that she was named Calamity by Captain Egan, that she captured McCall with a meat cleaver, and that she died on August 2, 1903.

318. **[Buffalo Bill]**

Buffalo Bill (Hon. Wm. F. Cody) and his wild west companions, including

Wild Bill, Texas Jack, California Joe, Captain Jack Crawford, and other famous scouts of the western plains. Chicago, George M. Hill co. [1893]. Pict. wrappers. Scarce.

2 p.l., 7–234 p. illus. 19 cm.
Device.

A laudatory, but undependable, "life" of Buffalo Bill by an anonymous writer. In his chapter on Wild Bill Hickok he quotes from the dime novelist Prentiss Ingraham, who was always unreliable.

319. Buffum, George Tower

On two frontiers, by George T. Buffum. . . . Frontispiece by Maynard Dixon, pen-and-ink illustrations by Frank T. Merrill. Boston, Lothrop, Lee & Shepard co. [1918]. Dec. cloth. Scarce.

vii p., 1 l., 3–375 p. front., illus. 19.7 cm.
Half title; illus. chapter headings; device; untrimmed.

This book has a chapter on Curly Bill Brocius and some of his exploits in Charleston, Arizona, one on the vigilantes of Bonanza Gulch, and one on Wild Bill Hickok. In the chapter on Wild Bill the author has the McCanles "fight" taking place at "Widow Waltman's cottage." He repeats the early false account of this "fight" and states that "when he [Hickok] had only six shots left, with nine opponents left [he had already killed Dave McCanles], he learned that he was thoroughly efficient with the bowie knife." Then follows some ridiculous dialogue.

320. ———

Smith of Bear City, and other frontier sketches, by George T. Buffum. Illustrated with six photogravures from original drawings by F. T. Wood. New York, the Grafton press, 1906. Dec. cloth. Scarce.

xii [1] p., 1 l., 248 [1] p. front., plates (with tissues). 21.4 cm.
Half title; device; untrimmed.

Contains several chapters on outlaws, such as Soapy Smith, Curly Bill Brocius, and Clay Allison, most of them highly fictitious. In the chapter on Clay Allison the author calls Chunk Colbert Chutt and says that Allison killed him with a *derringer* when they sat down together. Of Billy the Kid he says, ". . . at the age of twenty-six he had killed twenty-seven men," which is, as we know, incorrect. Further, he makes the statement that "when he [the Kid] was pursued after having killed his jailer he displayed the white flag, and when the posse came near to receive his surrender he shot the entire band." His account of the mob holding up the departure of the train at Las Vegas, on which the Kid was prisoner, is all wrong. It was Pat Garrett, not Stewart, as the author states, who had Billy the Kid under arrest, and Dave Rudabaugh was the man the mob was after.

321. Buntline, Ned (pseud. of Edward Zane Carrol Judson)

Buffalo Bill, by Ned Buntline. New York, American publishers, inc. [n.d.]. Pict. wrappers. Also published in cloth. Scarce.

[3]–314 p. front., illus. 19 cm.

One of the lurid early accounts of Buffalo Bill. Said to be the book that introduced Cody to the circus world. Contains more false history of Wild Bill Hickok.

322. ———

Buffalo Bill and his adventures in the west, by Ned Buntline. New York, J. S. Ogilvie publishing co., 1886. Pict. wrappers. Scarce.

[3]–314 [4] p. front., illus. 19.4 cm.
4 p. adv. at end.

This is the same book as Item 318 with a different title. Both contain the most brazen of all the falsehoods written about the Hickok-McCanles trouble. The author calls David McCanles "Jake" and wrongly spells his last name as McKandlas. He has McCanles kill Buffalo Bill's father before the eyes of his entire family, and the whole account is written in a sickening, cheap, theatrical style.

Buntline, thinking that he knew what the East expected of the West, took up his pen and dashed off his first Buffalo Bill story. It was read by Cody with the utmost amazement. It "told of deeds he had never done and could never hope to match, of talents he did not possess, and noble sentiments which he did not boast."

Buffalo Bill himself signed fabulous ghost-written tales and let them be published under his own name. He once wrote his publishers: "I am sorry to have to lie so outrageously in this yarn. My hero has killed more Indians on one war trail than I have killed all my life. But I understand this is what is expected of border tales. If you think the revolver and bowie knife are used too freely, you may cut out a fatal shot or stab whenever you deem it wise."

323. Burch, John P.

Charles W. Quantrell [*sic*], a true history of his guerrilla warfare on the Missouri and Kansas border during the Civil War of 1861 to 1865, by John P. Burch. Illustrated. As told by Captain Harrison Trow, one who followed Quantrell through his whole course. [Vega, Texas, 1923.] Dec. cloth. OP.

7 p.l., 15–266 p. front. (port.), illus., plates. 20.2 cm.

Somehow one loses confidence in a biographer who does not know how to spell his subject's name correctly. His name was spelled Quantrill and his Christian names were William Clarke, not Charles W. The text of the book is just as unreliable. It has some material on Cole Younger and Jesse James as guerrillas.

324. Burdick, Usher Lloyd

Jim Johnson, pioneer. A brief history of the Mouse river loop country, by Usher L. Burdick. [Williston, N.D., privately printed, 1941.] Wrappers. OP.

2 p.l., 7–32 [1] p. front. (port.). 22.8 cm.
"Edition limited to 300 copies."

Contains a good account of the vigilantes and some bad men of North Dakota.

325. ———

Life and exploits of John Goodall, by Usher L. Burdick. . . . Watford City, N.D., published by the McKenzie County Farmer, 1931. Wrappers. OP.

3 p.l., [7]–29 p. front., ports. 22.7 cm.
Copyright notice and "First edition" on t.p.

Contains some information on the Montana vigilantes organized by Granville Stuart to rid the country of horse thieves.

326. ———

Tales from buffalo land. The story of George "W." Newton . . ., by Usher L. Burdick. Baltimore, Wirth brothers, 1939. Wrappers. OP.

3 p.l., 9–26 [1] p. front. (port.), plates. 22.8 cm.
Vignette.
Reprinted same year.

More material on horse thieves and the Montana vigilantes.

327. ———

Tales from buffalo land. The story of Fort Buford, by Usher L. Burdick. Baltimore, Wirth brothers, 1940. Cloth. OP.

3 p.l., [7]–215 p. front. (port.), plates, ports., fold. letter in facsm. 20.6 cm.
Untrimmed.

Although this book has practically the same title as the preceding one, it is an entirely different item. It has some information on horse thieves and the Montana vigilantes, as do the author's other books.

328. Burgess, Opie Rundle

Bisbee not so long ago, by Opie Rundle Burgess. San Antonio, Texas, the Naylor co., book publishers of the southwest [1967]. Pict. cloth.

xi p., 4 l., 179 p. plates, ports. 21.7 cm.
Half title; pub. device.

Tells of the early days of Bisbee, Arizona, with a chapter on the robbery of the

Goldwater and Castaneda store by the Heath gang and the hanging of Dan Dowd, Dan Kelly, Tex Howard, and Red Sample and the lynching of Heath. There is mention of the killing of Morgan Earp at Tombstone and the chase of the Apache Kid by John Slaughter.

329. Burk, Mrs. Clinton (Calamity Jane)

Life and adventures of Calamity Jane, by herself. [N.p, n.d. ca. 1896.] Pict. wrappers. (Cover title.) Rare.

7 p. 16.5 cm.

Reprinted later in Livingston, Montana, by Post print. [n.d.].

8 p. 16.5 cm.

Modern reprints have been made available within the last few years.

Calamity Jane wandered about the country selling these little pamphlets for an income during her declining years. It is said to have been ghost-written by another woman at Calamity's dictation, but she had a propensity for romancing and seeking notoriety. Calamity brags a lot about what she accomplished in life, and it is said by historians that about the only true statement in this pamphlet is the first paragraph, in which she tells of her birth.

On page 2 she says she "joined Custer as a scout at Fort Russell, in 1870, and started for Arizona for the Indian campaign." Custer never was at Fort Russell, nor did he ever set foot in Arizona. In 1870, the year Jane says she scouted for him, Custer was in Fort Leavenworth, Kansas.

On page 3 she writes: "We were afterwards ordered to Fort Custer, where Custer City now stands, where we arrived in the spring of 1874; remained around Fort Custer all summer and were ordered to Fort Russell in the fall of 1874, where we remained until the spring of 1875." Fort Custer was not built until 1878.

There are many stories about how Jane acquired the prefix Calamity, but the most popular version, and the one she gives in her autobiography, is that while Captain Egan and she were on an expedition to quell an Indian uprising in Wyoming, the captain was shot. Calamity, in advance of the column, heard the shot and looked around in time to see Egan reeling in his saddle. She hastened back in time to catch the wounded officer before he fell. Upon recovering, the captain told her, "I name you Calamity Jane, the heroine of the plains."

The truth of the matter is that when Egan heard that a woman dressed in men's clothing was consorting with his soldiers he sought her out and booted her from camp. He made the statement that he had never seen her before and never wanted to see her again.

Errors are plentiful throughout the book, too many to list here, and though the original of this rare little pamphlet is valuable as a collector's item, it is worthless historically.

330. Burke, John M.

"Buffalo Bill" from prairie to palace. An authentic history of the wild west, with sketches, stories of adventure, and anecdotes of "Buffalo Bill," the hero of the plains. Compiled by John M. Burke ("Arizona John") with authority of General W. F. Cody ("Buffalo Bill"). Chicago and New York, Rand McNally & co., 1893. Pict. cloth. Scarce.

6 p.l., 13–275 [1] p. front. (port. with signature in facsm.), illus., plates, ports., facsm. 20 cm.

Half title; 1 p. adv. at end.

The author does not repeat here the often-told tale of the Hickok-McCanles trouble but does dwell at length on Wild Bill's bravery. He spells Jack McCall's name McCaul and, in telling of Slade's killing Jules Reni, misspells the Frenchman's name Jules Bevi.

331. Burks, A. L.

The Mayberry murder mystery of Bonita City, [by A. L. Burks, Alamogordo, N.M., Alamogordo News, n.d.]. Stiff wrappers. (Cover title.)

2 p.l., 12 p. plates, ports. 17 cm.

332. Burlingame, Merrill G.

The Montana frontier, by Merrill G. Burlingame. . . . End plates and maps by George A. Balzhiser. Helena, Mont., State publishing co. [1942]. Cloth. Scarce.

xiii p., 1 l., 418 p. front. (relief map), illus., plates, ports., maps, diagr., tables. 22.2 cm.

Footnotes: p. 357–381; appendix (chronological outline): p. 385–390; bibliography: p. 391–397; index: p. 399–418.

Map of Montana, 1863 (front end papers); map of Montana, 1890 (back end papers); vignette.

Contains a chapter on the vigilantes and the Henry Plummer gang of road agents.

333. Burnham, Frederick Russell

Scouting on two continents, by Major Frederick Russell Burnham. . . . Elicited and arranged by Mary Nixon Everett. Garden City, N.Y., Doubleday, Page & co., 1926. Cloth. OP.

xxii p., 1 l., 370 p. front., illus., plates, ports., maps, facsms. 23.5 cm.

Glossary: p. 369–370.

Half title; t.p. in red and black; device; "First edition" on copyright p.

Reprinted in 1927.

Contains some material on the Tonto Basin War, and also tells of the capture of

Vásquez and the author's interview with him. It has some information about Soapy Smith as well.

334. ———

Taking chances, by Major Frederick Russell Burnham. . . . Elicited and arranged by Mary Nixon Everett. Los Angeles, Calif., Haynes corp., publishers, 1944. Cloth. Scarce.

xxix p., 1 l., 293 p. plates, ports., facsm. 23.5 cm.
Half title.

This book was privately printed in a small edition and is now quite scarce. It has a chapter on Quantrill's guerrillas, mentioning, among others, the James boys and the Youngers.

335. Burns, Robert Homer, Andrew Springs Gillespie, and Willing Gay Richardson

Wyoming pioneer ranches, by three native sons of the Laramie plains, Robert Homer "Bob" Burns, Andrew Springs "Bud" Gillespie [and] Willing Gay Richardson. Laramie, Wyoming. . . . Top-of-the-World press . . ., 1955. Cloth. OP.

vii p., 1 l., 3–752 p. plates, ports., maps, facsms., cattle brands. 26 cm.
Bibliography: p. 705–715; index to text: p. 716–740; index to pictures: p. 741–746; addenda: p. 747–752.
Double column.

Some material on Tom Horn and the Johnson County Invasion.

336. Burns, Walter Noble

The Robin Hood of El Dorado; the saga of Joaquin Murrieta [*sic*], the famous outlaw of California's age of gold, by Walter Noble Burns. New York, published by Coward-McCann, inc. [1932]. Cloth. OP.

5 p.l., 304 p. front. (facsm.). 21 cm.
Half title; untrimmed; first edition: "C M" in device at bottom of copyright p.

This book has become the most widely read account of Murieta's life, perhaps because it is modern and written in a charming style. The motion picture based on it also made it popular. It is, more or less, a gathering together and rewriting by an able writer of material in other, earlier books about Murieta. The author combines the Ridge and *Police Gazette* versions, the former using the name Rosita for Joaquín's sweetheart and the latter, Carmela. Burns combines the two and calls her Rosita Carmen, but he follows the fictitious account created by Ridge. This book is said to be a "biography," but should be classed as fiction just as his *Saga of Billy the Kid* (Item 337) should be.

337. ———

The saga of Billy the Kid, by Walter Noble Burns. . . . Garden City, N.Y., Doubleday, Page & co., 1926. Pict. cloth.

5 p.l., 322 p. 21.3 cm.

Half title; illus. end papers (col.); vignette; untrimmed; "First edition" on copyright p.

Reprinted many times and still available.

Burns was honest enough to call his work a "saga," and I doubt that he expected his readers to take it as history; otherwise he would not have included such a quantity of imaginary dialogue. He gives few dates and cites no sources, and although the book is highly entertaining, it reads more like folklore than biography.

He follows all the legends about the Kid's birth, the move to Coffeyville in 1862, his mother's marriage in Colorado, and all the other legends created by Ash Upson. He repeats the story that the Kid killed the blacksmith who insulted his mother and that he killed twenty-one men during his short career. Most of the incidents he writes about the Kid are incorrect, and he perpetuates the fable about Mrs. McSween playing her piano while her home burned.

This romantic piece of folklore has been mistaken for fact by many and has remained so popular that it has been kept in print in both this country and in England. Many librarians keep the book in the fiction section of their shelves, where it should be.

338. ———

Tombstone, an Iliad of the southwest, by Walter Noble Burns. Garden City, N.Y., Doubleday, Page & co., 1927. Cloth.

ix p., 1 l., 388 p. 21.4 cm.

"Sources": p. vii–ix.

Half title; t.p. in red and black; vignette; untrimmed; "First edition" on copyright p.

Reprinted in 1929 with added material and illustrated by Will James, and reprinted many times since.

Like the author's *Saga of Billy the Kid* (Item 337), this book is written more as entertaining fiction than as historical fact. The author makes the turbulent old town of Tombstone live vividly, but again I wonder who recorded all the conversations. He is very much in favor of the Earps and paints them in glowing colors as men who could do no wrong. The truth is somewhat less extravagant.

339. Burroughs, Burt E.

Tales of an old "border town," and along the Kankakee. A collection of historical facts and intimate personal sketches of the days of the pioneers in Momence, Illinois, and the hunting grounds of the Kankakee marsh and "Bogue island." By Burt E. Burroughs. . . . Fowler, Ind., the Benton Review shop [1925]. Cloth. Scarce.

x, 314 p. front. (port.), plates, ports., facsm. 20.2 cm.

Contains a chapter on old Shafer, an outlaw of the early west.

340. Burroughs, John Rolfe

Where the old west stayed young, by John Rolfe Burroughs. The remarkable history of Brown's park for the first time, together with an account of the rise and fall of the range-cattle business in northwestern Colorado and southwestern Wyoming, and much about cattle barons, sheep and sheepmen, forest rangers, range wars, long riders, paid killers, and other bad men. New York, William Morrow and co., 1962. Pict. boards and cloth.

viii p., 1 l., 3–376 p. front. (col.), illus., plates, ports., facsms., cattle brands. 28.5 cm.

Index: p. 364–376.

Half title; cattle brands on end papers; text double column.

There are several chapters on the bad men of Brown's Park and Robbers' Roost, such as the Wild Bunch, the Ketchums, Matt Warner, Tom Horn, Harry Tracy, and some of the earlier ones.

341. [Burrow, Rube]

Complete official history of Rube Burrows [*sic*], and his celebrated gang. A story of his life and exploits, without a parallel in crime and adventure. Birmingham, Ala., Lyman & Stone, publishers and stationers [n.d.]. Wrappers. (Cover title.) Rare.

2 p.l., [5]–144 p. front., illus., ports. 16.8 cm.

3 p. adv. at end.

This is perhaps the rarest of the books on Rube Burrow and gives a fairly accurate account of his operations.

342. ———

Rube Burrow's raids. Historic highwayman. Night riders of the Ozarks; or, the Bald Knobbers of Missouri. . . . New York, published by Richard K. Fox, 1891. Pict. wrappers. Rare.

2 p.l., [5]–42 [8] p. illus. 24.4 cm.

Last 8 p. adv.; double column.

Two books bound in one, both examples of the *Police Gazette's* pieces of sensational fiction, but a collector's item.

343. Burt, Maxwell Struthers

The diary of a dude-wrangler, by Struthers Burt. New York, London, Charles Scribner's sons, 1924. Pict. cloth. OP.

viii p., 2 l., 3–331 p. front. (with tissue). 21 cm.

Half title; vignette; untrimmed.

Reprinted in 1938 with "List of Ranches": p. 333–343.

The author here touches upon the Johnson County War, but he makes a mistake in stating that two freighters escaped from the besieged house of Nate Champion and spread the alarm. The "two freighters" were actually two trappers, Bill Walker and Ben Jones, and they did not escape. When they went to the river for water, they were captured and held prisoners by the attacking party. Jack Flagg, a neighboring ranchman, was the man who spread the alarm.

344. ———

Powder River; let 'er buck, by Struthers Burt. Illustrated by Ross Santee. New York, Toronto, Farrar & Rinehart, inc. [1938]. Cloth. OP.

xi p., 1 l., 3–389 [11] p. front. (map), illus. 20.8 cm.

[Rivers of America series.]

Bibliography: p. 377–380; index: p. 381–389.

Half title; t.p. in red and black; vignette; first edition: "F R" in device on copyright p.

Last 11 pages "Rivers and American Folk" by Constance Lindsay Skinner.

Reprinted several times.

Quite a bit of space is devoted to the Johnson County War, and the author corrects the error he made in his *Diary of a Dude-Wrangler* about Walker and Jones. He tells of the Hole-In-the-Wall gang and Tom Horn. This excellent writer has written one of the best books of the Rivers of America series.

345. Burt, Olive Woolley (ed.)

American murder ballads and their stories, collected and edited by Olive Woolley Burt. New York, Oxford University press, 1958. Pict. boards.

xiii p., 1 l., 3–272 p. front., music. 22 cm.

Index: p. 263–272.

Half title; pub. device.

Has some material on Sam Bass, Billy the Kid, the Evans-Sontag robbers, Wild Bill Hickok, Jesse James, Murieta, the Plummer gang, the Reno gang, and the Johnson County War. Of Sam Bass the editor writes: "For a number of years before his death he had ridden about the country robbing banks, stealing horses and shooting down anyone who stood in his way." But Bass never robbed a bank, nor did he shoot anyone until the day he was mortally wounded himself.

She also writes: "The contemptible Billy the Kid . . . killed a number of men in New Mexico with the excuse that an *unknown* ruffian had insulted his mother on the streets of Silver City." On a later page she writes that "Billy was a buck-toothed, unkempt, illiterate villain who went about shooting folks for the fun of it," and adds that "his killing aroused the whole countryside against the sheriff, ruined his career as a lawman, and, his friends have told me, his disposition."

She repeats some of the legends about Murieta and admits that historians today claim that this "popular bandit-hero never lived," but says she has found "many contemporary newspaper references to him." She admits that most of the stories told about Jesse James are legends. The book is an interesting collection of folk songs, but the editor's comments are unreliable.

346. Burton, Jeff

Black Jack Christian: outlaw. Being a true and exciting account of the life and death of William Christian, the first outlaw in New Mexico to be known as Black Jack. Containing also his early life and crimes in Texas and Oklahoma, his robberies and murders in New Mexico, his hold-ups and death in Arizona; and his mistaken identification with a later desperado named Thomas E. Ketchum, who was also known as "Black Jack," by Jeff Burton. Time: 1871–1947. [Santa Fe, N.M., the Press of the Territorian, 1967.] Cloth. Also pub. in wrappers.

42 p. 22.5 cm.
Appendix and sources: p. 35–42.

This book, Number 14 of a series of western Americana, deals with the lesser known of the "Black Jacks," starting with his young career in Texas and Oklahoma and telling of his robberies and murders throughout the Southwest.

347. Burton, Richard Francis

The city of the saints, and across the Rocky mountains to California. By Richard F. Burton. . . . London, Longman, Green, Longman and Roberts, 1861. Cloth. Scarce.

x p., 1 l., 707 p. front., illus., plates (part with tissues), 2 fold. maps. 22 cm.
Appendices: p. 609–686; index: p. [687]–707.
Half title.
Reprinted in New York by Harper and brothers, 1862.
xii p., 2 l., 547 p. front., illus., fold. map, fold. plan. 23.5 cm.

The original edition is now quite scarce, but it was reprinted by the Long Book Company in 1951. It contains material on road agents and Joseph Slade.

348. Bush, I. J.

Gringo doctor, by Dr. I. J. Bush. Foreword by Eugene Cunningham. Illustrated by James Wallis. Caldwell, Idaho, the Caxton printers, ltd., 1939. Pict. cloth. OP.

8 p.l., [17]–262 p. front., illus. 23.6 cm.
Half title; illus. end papers; pub. device.

Has some minor material on John Wesley Hardin, John Selman and Jim Miller.

349. Bushick, Frank H.

Glamorous days, by Frank H. Bushick. San Antonio, Texas, the Naylor co., 1934. Cloth. OP.

vi, 308 p. front. (port.), plates, ports. 23.8 cm.
Appendix: p. 305–308.
Half title; device; "First edition" on copyright p.

Touches upon many western outlaws, with chapters on King Fisher, Ben Thompson, and John Wesley Hardin. The author claims that his account of the killing of Ben Thompson and King Fisher is related for the first time. "The actual facts were not made public at the time," he writes, "nor for many years afterward, for reasons that can be readily understood." He then proceeds to name McLaughin, a bartender; Canada Bill, a gambler; and Harry Tremaines, an English variety actor, as the men who shot Thompson and Fisher from a nearby box in the theater. The killers immediately left town. The author gives a fairly accurate account of the robbery of the Union Pacific and the death of Bass at Round Rock, except that he has Arkansas Johnson with Bass at Round Rock, though that character was killed earlier in a battle with the Rangers.

350. Butcher, Solomon D.

Pioneer history of Custer county and short sketches of early days of Nebraska, [by S. D. Butcher]. Broken Bow, Nebr., [privately printed at Denver, by the Merchants publishing co.], 1901. Cloth. Scarce.

4 p.l., [7]–403 [5] p. front. (tissue), plates, ports. 24 cm.
5 p. adv. at end; leaf of errata.

Has a long chapter on the lynching of Kid Wade, the horse thief, one on the exploits of Dick Milton, and material on I. P. Olive and the burning of Mitchell, and his companion Ketchum.

351. Byers, Major S. H. M.

With fire and sword, by Major S. H. M. Byers. . . . New York, the Neale publishing co., 1911. Cloth. OP.

5 p.l., [11]–203 p. front. 19 cm.
Half title.

Has some mention of the James boys as guerrillas.

352. Byrne, W. E. R.

Tale of the elk, by W. E. R. Byrne. Charleston, W. Va., West Virginia publishing co. [1940]. Cloth. Scarce.

8 p.l., [17]–455 p. front. (port.), plates. 23.5 cm.

Half title.

Chapter XLII tells about Al Jennings in West Virginia before he became an outlaw. It contains material I have not seen elsewhere.

353. Byrum, E. E.

Behind prison bars. A reminder of our duties toward those who have been so unfortunate as to be cast into prison. By E. E. Byrum. . . . Moundsville, W.Va., Gospel Trumpet publishing co., 1901. Pict. cloth. Scarce.

3 p.l., [9]–150 p. plates, ports. 18.2 cm.

Has some information on the prison life of the Younger brothers.

C

354. [Cahuengas Valley]

In the valley of the Cahuengas. The story of Hollywood. Written by the publicity department, Hollywood branch, Security Trust & Savings Bank. Hollywood, published by Hollywood Branch of the Security Trust & Savings Bank [n.d.]. Pict. wrappers. OP.

48 p. plates (1 double p.), ports., map at end. 19.8 cm.

Has a section on Tiburcio Vásquez.

355. Cain, Ella M.

The story of Bodie, by Ella M. Cain, with introduction by Donald I. Segerstrom. San Francisco, Calif., Fearsom publishers, in co-operation with Donald I. Segerstrom. Sonora, Calif., Mother Lode press [1956]. Cloth. OP.

xi, 196 p. plates, ports., facsms. 23.6 cm.

Index: p. 191–196.

Half title.

Has much on outlaws, such as Three-Fingered Jack García and Piocher Kelly, and the vigilantes.

356. [Calamity Jane]

Copies of Calamity Jane's diary and letters. Taken from the originals now on exhibit at the Wonderland Museum, Billings, Montana. [Billings, Mont., published by Don C. Foote, 1951.] Wrappers. (Cover title.)

[28] p. (no pagination). 15 cm.

In letters to her daughter, Jane twice wrote that she was no kin to Bell [*sic*] Starr, yet in her final affidavit she confessed that Belle was her sister and said that she had been raised by Ben Waddell and his wife, who were killed in Oklahoma. She also says that Belle married William Hickok, a cousin of her own daughter's father, James Butler Hickok. Though she was nearing the end of her life, she still seemed to have a weakness for telling tall tales. None of her statements are true. Many of these letters were included in Mumey's *Calamity Jane* (Item 1565). The very first sentence in this little pamphlet is wrong: ". . . Calamity Jane died, August 2, 1903. . . ." She died August 1.

357. [California]

California's age of terror. Murieta and Vásquez (general cover title). Crimes and career of Tiburcio Vásquez. The bandit of San Benito county and notorious early California outlaw. Compiled from newspaper accounts of the period and first hand information from some of those who played a part in this story. Hollister, Calif., published by the Evening Free Lance, copyright 1927 by M. F. Hoyle.

5–26 p. front. (port.).

[Published with]

The history of Joaquín Murieta, the king of California outlaws whose band ravaged the state in the early fifties, by John R. Ridge. Revised edition. . . . Pict. wrappers. Scarce.

3–83 [1] p. 22.5 cm.

A later reprint of the 1874 edition published by Fred'k MacCrellish and co. (see Item 1855).

358. ———

Fresno county centennial almanac. A compendium of interesting and useful historical facts & old tales gathered to mark the 100th anniversary of the founding of Fresno county. . . . Fresno, Calif., published by Fresno county centennial committee, April, 1956. Pict. wrappers. OP.

2 p.l., 5–184 p. plates, ports., map. 25.4 cm.

Has a section on train robberies by Chris Evans and John Sontag.

359. ———

Historic facts and fancies. Historic and landmark section of California federated women's clubs. . . . [San Francisco, 1907.] Wrappers. Scarce.

148 [4] p. plates, ports. 26 x 17.2 cm.

Contains a story about Tom Bell.

360. ———

History of Alameda county, California, including its geology, topography, soil and production; together with a full and particular record of the Spanish grants. . . . Illustrated. Oakland, M. W. Wood, publisher, 1883. Cloth. Scarce.

vii p., 1 l., [9]–1001 p. front. (port. with tissue), ports. 26.3 cm.

Has a long chapter on crime and such outlaws as Vásquez, Procopio, Juan Soto and others.

361. ———

History of Tuolumne county, California, compiled from the most authentic records. San Francisco, published by B. F. Alley, 1882. Calf. Rare.

xi, 509 [48] p. ports. 21.4 cm.

Has a chapter on stage robbers and other criminals, such as Murieta and Tom Bell.

362. ———

Illustrated history of Plumas, Lassen & Sierra counties, with California from 1513 to 1850. San Francisco, Fariss & Smith, 1882. Cloth. Rare.

5 p.l., [9]–507 p. front., plates, ports., map (col.). 28 cm.

Has a chapter on lynching and outlawry.

363. ———

Journal of the assembly, California. 1853. Vol. II [N.p., 1853.] Cloth and calf. Rare.

722 p. 23.4 cm.

At the assembly meeting of March 26, 1853, a joint resolution was introduced to offer a reward for the capture of Murieta. In the appendix, Document No. 49 contains an argument against offering this reward. The chairman of the committee says in part: "To set a price upon the head of any individual who has not been examined and convicted by due process of law, is to proceed upon an assumption of his guilt. . . . Unless the said Joaquín be endowed with supernatural qualities, he could not have been seen at the same time in several places, widely separated from each other. The offer of such a reward would be likely to stimulate cupidity, to magnify fanciful resemblance, and dozens of heads similar in some respect to that of Joaquín might be presented for identification." Murieta's sister denied that the head later brought in was that of her brother, and many old-timers still think it was that of "just another Mexican."

364. ———

The mysteries and miseries of San Francisco, by a Californian. Showing up all the various characters and notabilities (both in high and low life) that have figured in San Francisco since its settlement. New York, Garrett & co., publishers [1853]. Wrappers. Exceedingly rare.

[7]–208 p. 22 cm.
Double column.

This is perhaps the earliest book dealing with Joaquín Murieta since it first appeared the year before Ridge's book. Though fiction, it is included in this work because of its early mention of this outlaw. This author names Joaquín's sweetheart Carmencitto.

365. Callison, John J.

Bill Jones of Paradise valley, Oklahoma. His life and adventures for over forty years in the great southwest. He was a pioneer in the days of the buffalo, the wild Indian, the Oklahoma boomer, the cowboy and the outlaw. Copiously illustrated from photographs and drawings from real life, by John J. Callison. . . . [Chicago, printed by M. A. Donohue & co., 1914.] Cloth. Scarce.

6 p.l., 13–328 p. front., illus., plates. 19.5 cm.

This privately printed book was written in a humorous vein, and contains some material on the Dodge City gunmen and Billy the Kid. Like one or two other writers, the author says that the Kid had killed twenty-three men when he was himself killed at the age of twenty-three. He also says that the Kid worked on a ranch owned by Jesse James, Cole Younger, and three more of their gang and that the Kid stole some cattle from them, whereupon they chased his gang of rustlers and killed all of them except Billy and one other. I corresponded with this old-timer before his death and bought all the remaining copies of his book. It was a very scarce item until I began releasing the remainder, and it is still scarce.

366. Callon, Milton W.

Las Vegas, New Mexico, the town that wouldn't gamble, by Milton W. Callon. Las Vegas, N.M., published by Las Vegas Daily Optic . . ., 1962. Cloth.

xiv p., 1 l., 352 p. plates. 23.5 cm.
Index: p. 341–352.
Half title; map on end papers.
Colophon: "First edition limited to 1500 copies. No. ——," on half title page.

A local history of Las Vegas in its early days with some material on Billy the Kid and his gang as well as Bob Ford and the James boys. He is mistaken, however, in saying that the Kid was captured at Stinking Springs "on the afternoon of December 24, 1880." He was captured on the morning of December 23.

367. Calvin, Ross

Sky determines. An interpretation of the southwest, by Ross Calvin. New York, the Macmillan co., 1934. Dec. cloth. OP.

xii p., 1 l., 354 p. front., plates. 20.2 cm.
Bibliography: p. 343–346; index: p. 347–354.
Half title; untrimmed.
Republished in a revised and enlarged edition in 1948 by the University of New Mexico press, Albuquerque.

Has a chapter containing information about the robbery of the Southern Pacific by Mitch Lee, Kit Joy, and Frank Taggart and their capture and death. The author also debunks Billy the Kid as the Robin Hood he is pictured to be by some writers.

368. Campbell, W. P.

Oklahoma, the mecca for the men of mystery. John Wilkes Booth, escape and wanderings until final ending of the trail by suicide at Enid, Oklahoma, January 12, 1903, [by W. P. Campbell. Oklahoma City, 1922]. Wrappers. Scarce.

3 p.l., 1 p., 2–142 p. illus., ports., diagr., map. 19.6 cm.
Illus. t.p.; some copies have a leaf (p. 143–144) added.

Contains some information on Temple Houston and his killing of one of the Jennings boys and the subsequent outlawry of Al and Ed Jennings.

369. Campbell, William C.

From the quarries of Last Chance gulch. A "news history" of Helena and its Masonic lodge. Compiled from the files of Helena newspapers; the Helena Herald, the Helena Independent, and the Montana Radiator, plus some personal research. By William C. Campbell. . . . Helena, privately printed by the author. The Montana Record publishing co. [1951]. Pict. cloth. Scarce.

x p., 1 l., 3–253 p. front. (port.), illus., plates, ports., facsms. 23.5 cm.
Half title; illus. end papers; "First edition" on copyright p.

Contains some material on the Montana vigilantes.

370. Cannon, Miles

Toward the setting sun, by Miles Cannon. Portland, Oreg., printed by Columbian press, inc. [1953]. Stiff wrappers. OP.

3 p.l., 7–157 p. 22.8 cm.

Has some unreliable information on Henry Plummer and his outlaws, and a mention of Billy the Kid.

371. Canton, Frank M.

Frontier trails. The autobiography of Frank M. Canton, edited by Edward Everett Dale. With illustrations. Boston and New York, Houghton Mifflin co., 1930. Cloth. Scarce.

xvii p., 1 l., [3]–236 [1] p. front., ports. 21.3 cm.
Half title; pub. device; first edition: 1930 under imprint.

This autobiography of Frank Canton, written shortly before his death and edited from the manuscript he left, tells of his experiences during the Johnson County War and of his later experiences with the outlaws of Oklahoma. Canton was hired by the large cattle interests to fight the smaller owners and so-called rustlers in the Johnson County War, and naturally he tells their side of the story. The group picture following page 110 is erroneously labeled "the Dalton Brothers and their sister." It is a picture of the Youngers and their sister. Much of the book is devoted to the better-known outlaws of Oklahoma and the time Canton was peace officer there. But much of his information is wrong, especially the killing of Bill Doolin, who he says was killed by Bill Dunn after Doolin had got up from a sickbed. The author also gives a long account of Ben Cravens.

Mrs. Huckaby, in her *Ninety-Four Years In Jack County* (Item 1059) says that Canton's real name was Joe Horner. Dr. Dale, editor of Canton's book, states in his introduction: ". . . it seems well to state that the author's real name was not Frank Canton. In his youth he became involved in a difficulty that caused him to leave his Texas home and disappear into the farther depths of the American wilderness." An old-time resident of Jack County recently wrote me that Canton, known to him as Jack Horner, was really a bad man.

During his days in Texas he was charged several times with cattle theft. On October 10, 1874, he killed a Negro soldier and wounded another in a saloon at Jacksboro, and at one time he was jailed for robbing a bank in Comanche, Texas, in 1877, but escaped and left Texas in 1878.

It is understandable why he left a gap of seven years in his autobiography, omitting those years of questionable morals and criminal acts.

372. Cantonwine, Alexander

Star forty-six, Oklahoma. [Oklahoma City, printed by Pythian Times publishing co.], 1911. Cloth. Scarce.

334 p. front. (port.), illus. 24 cm.

Contains some material on the Daltons and other Oklahoma outlaws.

373. [Captain Jack]

Captain Jack, the chief of the Modocs. A thrilling work, complete in itself, giving a full description of the blood-thirsty murderer of General Canby. . . . New York, Orum & company, publishers [n.d.]. Pict. wrappers (col.). Rare.

[7]–96 [4] p. illus. 16.2 cm.
No. 29 of the ten cent popular novels.

374. Carey, Henry L. (ed.)

The thrilling story of famous Boot Hill and modern Dodge City . . ., edited by Henry L. Carey, publisher. Dodge City, Kans., Herbert Etrick, printers, 1937. Pict. wrappers. (Cover title.) OP.

[25] p. (no pagination). illus., plates, ports. 19.5 cm.
Last 7 p. adv.

Tells of the founding of Dodge City, its gun marshals, and Boot Hill.

375. Carlisle, William L.

Bill Carlisle, lone bandit. An autobiography; illustrations by Charles M. Russell; introduction by J. R. Williams; end papers by Clarence Ellsworth. Pasadena, Calif., Trail's End publishing co., inc. [1946]. Cloth. OP.

4 p.l., [9]–220 p. front., plates, ports., facsm. 21 cm.
Map and legend on end papers; pub. device.
Republished in a de luxe limited and signed edition, bound in morocco.

This is the honest autobiography of the last of the lone train robbers, a man who allowed himself to be captured rather than take a human life.

376. Carmer, Carl

Stars fell on Alabama, [by] Carl Carmer. Illustrated by Cyrus LeRoy Baldridge. New York, Farrar & Rinehart, inc., 1934. Cloth. OP.

xiv p., 1 l., 3–294 p. front. (col. map), illus., plates (part col.). 22 cm.
Half title; illus. end papers; last 20 p. (plus 2 l.) on yellow paper.

Has a chapter on Rube Burrow, his capture and death.

377. Carpenter, Frank G.

Canada and New Foundland, by Frank G. Carpenter. . . . With 116 illustrations from original photographs. Garden City, N.Y., Doubleday, Page & co., 1924. Pict. cloth. OP.

xiv p., 1 l., 311 p. front., plates. 23.5 cm.
Index: p. 303–311.
Half title: "Carpenter's World Travels;" map on end papers; pub. device; t.p. in red and black; "First edition" on copyright p.

Chapter XXXVIII, entitled "The Royal Canadian Mounted Police," deals with lawlessness and touches upon Soapy Smith.

378. Carr, Harry

Los Angeles, city of dreams, by Harry Carr; illustrations by E. H. Suydam. New York, London, D. Appleton-Century co., inc., 1935. Cloth. OP.

ix [1] p., 1 l., 3–403 p. front. (col., with tissue), illus., plates. 23.5 cm.
Index: p. 393–403.

Half title; illus. end papers; headpieces; vignette; first edition: figure (1) at end of index.

Devotes some space to the outlaws of southern California, such as Murieta, Vásquez, and Jack Powers.

379. ———

The west is still wild. Romance of the present and the past, by Harry Carr, with illustrations by Charles H. Owens. Boston and New York, Houghton Mifflin co., 1932. Cloth. OP.

iv p., 1 l., [3]–257 p. front., illus., maps. 21.2 cm.

Col. map on front end papers; vignette; title label pasted on; first edition: 1932 under imprint.

Chapter XXI, entitled "Bandits and the Church," tells of Vásquez. Earlier in the book there is some information on the Apache Kid, Billy the Kid, and the O K Corral fight. The author makes the statement that Billy the Kid "fought his way out of jail," but there was no fight, just a couple of murders.

380. Carr, John

Pioneer days in California, by John Carr. Historical and personal sketches. Eureka, Calif., Times publishing co., Book and Job printing, 1891. Dec. cloth. Scarce.

13 p.l., [33]–452 p. front. (port.). 22.5 cm.

Has much on the lawlessness of the period.

381. Carson, John

Doc Middleton, the unwickedest outlaw, by John Carson. [Santa Fe, N.M., 1966.] Stiff wrappers.

2 p.l., 5–34 [1] p. port. 22.8 cm.

References: p. 34 [1].

No. 9 of the Press of the Territorian series.

Has a good account of Doc Middleton, the notorious horse thief. Also has some mention of Kid Wade, Luke Short, Print Olive, and Boone Helm.

382. Carter, Hodding

Lower Mississippi, by Hodding Carter. Illustrated by John McGrady. New York, Toronto, Farrar & Rinehart, inc. [1942]. Cloth. OP.

x p., 1 l., 3–467 p. front. (map), plates (2 double p.), music. 21 cm.

[Rivers of America series.]

Selected bibliography: p. 443–451; index: p. 453–467.

Half title; illus. end papers; double illus. t.p.; first edition: "F R" in device on copyright p.

One of the Rivers of America series, edited by Stephen Vincent Benét and Carl Carmer, it has a chapter on outlaws dealing with Amanda Bannoris, John Murrell, the Harpes, and other river bandits.

383. Carter, Capt. Robert Goldthwaite

The old sergeant's story. Winning the west from the Indians and bad men in 1870 to 1876, by Captain Robert G. Carter. . . . New York, Frederick H. Hitchcock, publisher, MCMXXVI. Cloth. Scarce.

8 p.l., 17–220 p. front., plates, ports. 23.5 cm.
Half title; pub. device.

The author devotes a chapter to the outlaw Red McLaughlin and calls the Earps "the most desperate criminals Arizona ever knew." He is wrong, however, in saying that Virgil Earp was killed in Willcox when a bartender hit him over the head with a whisky bottle. Much of his information on Wild Bill Hickok is incorrect. He states that he was in Deadwood when Wild Bill was killed and that he was killed in Al Swiner's [*sic*] Dance Hall. There seems to be much confusion among writers about the place where Hickok was killed. Colonel Wheeler, in his *Frontier Trail,* places the killing at Nuttall and Mann's Saloon; Wilstach says that it took place in the Bella Union; and Harry Young says the Sixty-Six Saloon. But most authors concede that it happened in the No. 10 Saloon. The author also states that Jack McCall was rearrested in Omaha. He was captured in Laramie, Wyoming.

384. Carter, W. A.

McCurtain county and southeast Oklahoma. History, biography, statistics. A complete church, lodge, profession, business and trade directory of the county. By W. A. Carter. Idabel, Okla. 1923. Cloth. Scarce.

3 p.l., 9–381 p. front., plates, ports. 22.5 cm.

Has a chapter on the Carpenter gang, noted outlaws of eastern Oklahoma.

385. Carter, W. N.

Harry Tracy, the desperate outlaw. A fascinating account of the famous bandit's stupendous adventures and daring deeds. The most thrilling man-hunt on record . . ., by W. N. Carter. Chicago, Laird & Lee, publishers [1902]. Wrappers. Scarce.

7 p.l., [9]–296 [4] p. front., illus., plates, ports., maps, plan. 18.8 cm.
4 p. adv. at end.

386. ———

Harry Tracy, the desperate western outlaw. . . . The most thrilling man-hunt on record. . . . Melodramatic scenes and tragic death, by W. N. Carter. Over

90 half-tones and text etchings. Chicago, Laird & Lee, publishers [1902]. Pict. wrappers. Scarce.

8 p.l., [9]–295 p. front., plates, ports., map. 18.5 cm.
4 p. adv. at end.

This is practically the same book as Item 385, except for the change in title.

387. Caruthers, William

Loafing along Death Valley trails, by William Caruthers. A personal narrative of people and places. . . . Ontorio, Calif., published by Death Valley publishing co., 1951. Pict. cloth. OP.

4 p.l., [11]–191 p. plates, ports., map. 23.3 cm.
Index: p. [189]–191.

A chapter entitled "Genial Crooks" contains some material on Joaquín Murieta, Tiburcio Vásquez, Three-Fingered Jack García, and others. It also tells of the burial of Tillie Younger, who the author claims was a member of the Jesse James gang, but this is the first time I have seen this name mentioned.

388. Case, Lee

Lee's official guide book to the Black Hills and the Badlands, by Lee Case. Sturgis, S.D., the Black Hills and Badlands association, 1952. Stiff pict. wrappers. OP.

2 p.l., 5–112 p. maps (4 double p.). 21.5 cm.

Contains material on Wild Bill Hickok, Jack McCall, and Calamity Jane.

389. Case, Nelson

History of Labette county, Kansas, from the first settlement to the close of 1892. By Nelson Case. Topeka, Kansas, Crane & Co., publishers, 1893. Cloth. Scarce.

7 p.l., 13–372 p. front., plates, tables. 19.7 cm.

Contains a chapter on crime and the Bloody Benders.

390. Case, Theodore S. (ed.)

History of Kansas City, Missouri, with illustrations and biographical sketches of some of its prominent men and pioneers, edited by Theodore S. Case. Syracuse, N.Y., Mason & co., publishers, 1880. Leather. Scarce.

5 p.l., [13]–726 p. front., ports. (all with tissues, incl. front.). 26 cm.

Gives some information on the robbery of the fair at Kansas City by Jesse James and his gang.

391. Casey, Robert J.

The Black Hills and their incredible characters. A chronicle and a guide, by Robert J. Casey. Indianapolis, New York, the Bobbs-Merrill co., inc., publishers [1949]. Cloth.

5 p.l., 11–383 p. front., plates, ports., 31 p. guide in pocket at end. 22 cm.
Appendix: p. 345–371; index: p. 372–383.
Half title; map on end papers; "First edition" on copyright p.

In his chapter on Hickok the author relates the corrected version of the McCanles affair, but writes as though he does not believe it. He writes: "It is an established fact that Hickok was seriously wounded. He was thought to be dying when the stage line finally got him to a St. Louis hospital, and he was in bed for several weeks." He does not cite any sources for this statement, and Hickok did not receive a scratch since his victims were unarmed. Buel, Hough, and other writers stated that Hickok was gravely wounded, but all their accounts have been proved false. This book also contains a chapter on Calamity Jane (who he says was born in 1850), Jack McCall, Fly-Speck Billy, and others. He also has the date of Jane's death wrong. He says she died "twenty-seven years to the day after the death of Wild Bill on August 2, 1903."

Writing of the Collins gang in Dakota, he calls one of them William Reddy. It was actually Reddy McKemie. He includes Frank Towle and a Jack Farrell in the gang and refers to Berry as Jim Perry, though that could be a typographical error. He quotes one Doc Peirce in describing the killing of Joel Collins, but the account is all wrong.

392. ———

The Texas border, and some borderliners. A chronical and a guide, by Robert J. Casey. Indianapolis, New York, the Bobbs-Merrill co., inc., publishers [1950]. Cloth. OP.

6 p.l., 13–440 p. front., plates, ports., guide in pocket at end. 22 cm.
Appendix: p. 397–417; bibliography: p. 418–425; index: p. 427–440.
Half title; map on end papers; untrimmed; "First edition" on copyright p.
Also published in a special "Lone Star Edition" signed and tipped in.

The author takes in some large territory and covers practically all the outlaws in the Southwest, including those involved in the Lincoln County War. In his account of the Kid's killing of Bell, he uses the Burns version. His chapter on Sam Bass is full of flaws, and he has the Union Pacific "jackpot" at $75,000 instead of $60,000.

He says that Billy the Kid's mother was married in Denver "to a man named Antrim whose first name *has been forgotten*." He says that the Kid "killed a man who made some uncouth remarks to *Mrs. Bonney*. His mother financed his way out of town and thereafter is lost to sight." He follows many of the legends created by Ash Upson, such as having the Kid ride eighty miles to release his friend Segura from a Texas jail. He says that Buckshot Roberts was a former Texas Ranger who had been crippled in service.

He credits the Kid with killing Bernstein "one night when the gang were running off some horses" without any reason "except, maybe, for target practice." He has the date of the Kid's death as July 13. It should be July 14. His account as a whole is very unreliable. The book also has some information on John Wesley Hardin, John Selman, Clay Allison, George Scarborough, and others.

393. Castel, Albert

A frontier state at war; Kansas, 1861–1865, by Albert Castel. Ithaca, N.Y., published by the American Historical association, Cornell University press [1958]. Cloth. OP.

xi, 251 [1] p. plates, ports. 23.3 cm.
Bibliography: p. 233–245; index: p. 247–251.

Has some mention of the James and Younger brothers during their guerrilla days.

394. ———

William Clarke Quantrill: his life and times, by Albert Castel. New York, Frederick Fell, inc., publishers [1962]. Cloth.

3 p.l., 250 p. plates, ports., maps. 21 cm.
Notes: p. [233]–244; index: p. [245]–250.
Half title; double t.p.

A fairly correct history of Quantrill and his times, including the James and Younger outlaws. The one doubtful statement I find is the author's claim that when Jesse was murdered by Bob Ford Mrs. James was pregnant. I have never seen this statement before, nor did she bear any children after Jesse's death.

395. Castleman, Harvey N.

The bald knobbers. The story of the lawless night-riders who ruled southern Missouri in the 80's, by Harvey N. Castleman. Girard, Kans., Haldeman-Julius publications [1944]. Wrappers.

2 p.l., 5–29 p. 21.5 cm.

Deals with outlawry immediately after the Civil War in Missouri.

396. ———

Sam Bass, the train robber. The life of Texas' most popular bandit, [by] Harvey N. Castleman. Girard, Kans., Haldeman-Julius publications, 1944. Wrappers.

[2]–24 p. 21.5 cm.

A fairly accurate account, but the author does say that the butcher boy on the train being robbed at Mesquite, Texas, was seen with a revolver, but went back into the coach without firing a shot when Sam Bass said to him, "We don't need any peanuts." All other accounts I have seen report that he did shoot a couple of robbers with his little "peashooter," though he did no more damage than break the skin. The author is also wrong in stating that Jim Murphy "died of poison administered by his own hand."

397. ———

The Texas rangers. The story of an organization that is unique, like nothing else in America, [by] Harvey N. Castleman. Girard, Kans., Haldeman-Julius publication, 1944. Wrappers.

24 p. 21.5 cm.

Includes the story of the killing of Sam Bass and the treachery of Jim Murphy.

398. [Catalogue]

Catalogue [of] Wells, Fargo and company historical exhibit, etc., at the World's Columbian Exposition, Chicago, 1893. [San Francisco, printed by H. S. Crocker co., 1893.] Wrappers. (Cover title.) Scarce.

1 p.l., 3–32 p. 19.5 cm.

A listing of 175 exhibits, including material concerning the California stage and train robbers.

399. Cattermole, E. G.

Famous frontiersmen, pioneers and scouts; the vanguards of American civilization. Two centuries of the romance of American history . . ., by E. G. Cattermole. Elegantly illustrated. Chicago, the Coburn & Newman publishing co., 1883. Pict. cloth. Scarce.

xvi p., 1 l., 19–540 p. front. (with tissue), plates. 19.7 cm.

Republished by Donohue & Henneberry, Chicago, with same format in 1886, 1890, and again in 1926.

Has a chapter on Hickok, but the author does not mention his troubles with McCanles.

400. Caughey, John Walton

History of the Pacific coast, by John Walton Caughey. . . . Los Angeles, privately published by the author, 1933. Cloth. (Label pasted on spine.) Scarce.

xii, 429 p. illus., ports., maps. 25 cm.

Index: p. 407–429.

Half title; map on end papers.

Has some material on Joaquín Murieta and Juan Flores.

401. ———

Their majesties the mob, [by] John W. Caughey. [Chicago], University of Chicago press [1960]. Cloth.

6 p.l., 214 p. 22.2 cm.
Bibliography: p. [206]–208; acknowledgments: p. [209]; index: p. [211]–214.
Half title.

The story of the vigilantes, including those of California and Montana. Also tells of the hanging of Henry Plummer and some of his gang.

402. Chafetz, Henry

Play the devil. A history of gambling in the United States from 1492 to 1955, by Henry Chafetz, Illustrated by Christopher Simon. New York, Clarkson N. Potter, inc., publishers [1960]. Cloth.

7 p.l., 3–475 p. plates, headpieces. 24 cm.
Notes about sources: p. [455]; bibliography: p. 457–461; index: p. 463–475.
Half title; pub. device.

Has some information on Wyatt Earp, Doc Holliday, Wild Bill Hickok, the James boys, Bob Ford, Bat Masterson, John Murrell, Soapy Smith, Ben Thompson, and others.

403. Chaffin, Lorah B.

Sons of the west; biographical account of early-day Wyoming, [by] Lorah B. Chaffin. Illustrated with photographs. Caldwell, Idaho, the Caxton printers, ltd., 1941. Pict. cloth. OP.

10 p.l., [21]–284 p. plates, ports. 23.5 cm.
Bibliography: p. [277]–279; appendix: [280]–284.
Half title; pub. device.

Touches upon the Johnson County War and the killing of Nate Champion and Nick Ray.

404. Chalfant, Willie Arthur

Gold, guns & ghost towns, by W. A. Chalfant. Stanford, Calif., Stanford University press [1947]. Pict. cloth. OP.

xi, 175 p. 26 cm.
Half title; illus. end papers (col.); illus. double t.p. (col.); pub. device.

Has much on lawlessness of the early mining camps.

405. ———

Outposts of civilization, by W. A. Chalfant. Boston, the Christopher publishing house [1928]. Cloth. Scarce.

3 p.l., 9–193 p. 20.5 cm.
Pub. device.

Has a chapter on the gunmen and vigilantes of Nevada and one on the bandits of California. His account of Murieta follows the Ridge version, repeating the legend about the reward notice.

406. ———

The story of Inyo, by W. A. Chalfant. [Chicago, W. B. Conkey co.], published by the author, 1922. Cloth. Scarce.

xviii, 358 p. front. (fold. map). 19.6 cm.
Appendices: p. 334–358.
Leaf of errata pasted inside back cover.

Republished [Los Angeles, Citizen's print shop, inc., 1933].

6 p.l., 13–430, vii p. front. (fold. map). 23.4 cm.

Both books contain a chapter on lawlessness and quite a bit of material on Tiburcio Vásquez.

407. Chamberlain, Newell D.

The call of gold. True tales on the gold road to Yosemite, by Newell D. Chamberlain. Illustrated. [Mariposa, Calif., Gazette press, 1936.] Cloth. OP.

xii p., 1 l., 183 p. front., plates, ports., maps, facsm. 20 cm.
"First edition" on copyright p.

Tells of the killing of Murieta and follows the Ridge version that his wife was "mistreated and killed before his eyes."

408. Chambers, Homer S.

The enduring rock. History and reminiscences of Blackwell, Okla., and the Cherokee strip . . ., by Homer S. Chambers. . . . Blackwell, Oklahoma, Blackwell publications, inc., publisher, 1954. Fabrikoid.

3 p.l., 120 p. front., plates, ports. 23.6 cm.
Partly double column.

Has some material on the killing of Ben Cravens and Dynamite Dick, the Oklahoma outlaws.

409. Chapel, Charles Edward

Guns of the old west, by Charles Edward Chapel. New York, Coward-McCann, inc. [1961]. Pict. cloth.

6 p.l., 5–306 p. illus., plates, facsm. 26 cm.

Bibliography: p. 293–298; index: p. 299–306.

Half title; illus. double t.p.

In a chapter entitled "When the Colt Was King," the author mentions several outlaws of the Southwest. In dealing with Sam Bass, he makes many errors, such as having him working for Sheriff Everheart in his first job in Texas. Bass never did work for Everheart, but for Sheriff Egan, though the latter was not sheriff when Bass went to work for him. The author says that Bass arrived in Texas "in the late sixties," but he did not arrive until the summer of 1870. He says that Joel Collins was a cattle man, but he was a bartender when Bass met him. He dates the Union Pacific robbery at Big Springs as April 18, but it took place on September 18. His information about the robbery is unreliable, and he has the killing of Collins and Heffridge all wrong. His account of Bass's Texas robberies is also wrong, as well as his end at Round Rock. The author is also wrong in saying that Murphy committed suicide "while in prison."

410. ———

Levi's gallery of long guns and western riflemen, by Charles Edward Chapel. [San Francisco, Levi Strauss & co., n.d.] Pict. folder (col.). Scarce.

[8] p. (no pagination). illus. 14.8 cm.

Has material on Joaquín Murieta, John X. Beidler, and Henry Plummer.

411. ———

Levi's gallery of western guns and gunfighters, by Charles Edward Chapel. [San Francisco, Levi Strauss & co., n.d.] Pict. folder (col.).

[8] p. (no pagination). illus., plates, ports. 14.8 cm.

Has material on Billy the Kid, Wild Bill Hickok, and Butch Cassidy's Wild Bunch.

412. Chapman, Arthur

The pony express. The record of a romantic adventure in business, by Arthur Chapman. Illustrated with contemporary prints and photographs. New York and London, G. P. Putnam's sons, 1932. Cloth. Scarce.

6 p.l., 13–319 p. front., plates, ports., facsm. 23 cm.

Bibliography: p. 311–314; index: p. 317–319.

Half title; map on end papers; untrimmed.

Another effort to correct the wild legend of the Hickok-McCanles trouble at Rock Creek Station. The author also devotes a chapter to Joseph Slade.

413. Chapman, Berlin Basil

The founding of Stillwater. A case study in Oklahoma history, by Berlin

Basil Chapman. . . . [Oklahoma City, Okla., published by the Times-Journal publishing co., 1948.] Cloth Scarce.

xxi, 245 p. front., plates, ports., map, facsm., plan. 23.8 cm.
Appendices: p. 160–230; bibliography: p. 231–233; index: p. 234–245.

The author says that Marshal Hueston was killed in the fight at Ingalls "by the Starr and Doolin gang," but Starr was not in the Doolin gang.

414. Charles, Mrs. Tom

More tales of Tularosa, by Mrs. Tom Charles. Alamogordo, N.M., Bennett printing co., 1961. Cloth.

4 p.l., 9–58 [1] p. front., plates, ports. 23.7 cm.

This little book is an addition to the author's earlier *Tales of the Tularosa* (Item 415). In her chapter on George Coe she makes several mistakes. She says that the Lincoln County War started when Billy the Kid killed Sheriff Brady. It had already started with the murder of J. H. Tunstall. She is mistaken in having the Kid foreman of Tunstall's ranch. The foreman was Dick Brewer. She also has the murder of Tunstall and the murder of Sheriff Brady all wrong, as well as the battle at Blazer's Mill, which she says was the "first battle of the Lincoln County War." There are many other errors.

415. ———

Tales of the Tularosa, by Mrs. Tom Charles. Alamogordo, N.M., 1963. Cloth. OP.

3 p.l., 69 p. front., plates, ports., map (1 double p.). 24 cm.
Illus. t.p.
Colophon: "Two thousand copies of this book have been printed at the Pass to the North by Carl Hertzog."

Contains a chapter on the Apache Kid.

416. Chatterton, Fenimore C.

Yesterday's Wyoming. The intimate memoirs of Fenimore Chatterton, territorial citizen, governor and statesman. An autobiography. [Aurora, Colorado], published by Powder River publishers & booksellers, 1957. Cloth. OP.

7 p.l., [15]–133 p. plates, ports. (1 tipped in). 23.6 cm.
Index: p. [126]–133.
Half title.
Colophon: "Edition limited to 1000 copies of which this is No. ——."

Contains a chapter on Tom Horn and his trial, and some mention of Cattle Kate, Jim Averill, and Calamity Jane.

417. Cheek, W. Raymond

The story of an American pioneer family. The frontier trail, by W. Raymond Cheek. New York, Exposition press [1960]. Cloth.

6 p.l., [13]–124 p. 21 cm.
Half title; pub. device; "First edition" on copyright p.

Contains a chapter on the outlaws of the Indian Territory, such as the Daltons, the Barkers, and others.

418. Chilton, Charles

The book of the west. An epic of America's wild frontier and the men who created its legends, [by] Charles Chilton, with a preface by Professor Oscar Cargill. . . . Illustrated by Eric Tansley. Indianapolis, New York, the Bobbs-Merrill co., inc., . . . publishers [1962]. Boards and cloth.

4 p.l., 9–320 p. illus., 2 maps (both double p.). 26 cm.
Half title; map on end papers (col.); "First edition" on copyright p.

In his section on outlaws and gunmen the author makes many mistakes, misspells proper names and gives some wrong dates. He follows the well-known legends concerning Billy the Kid, has Jesse James in the Liberty State bank robbery, and says that the train robbery near Council Bluffs was the first "large scale train robbery in the United States." He has five men in the Union Pacific robbery, though there were six. He says that the Allen Station robbery took place on February 23. It occurred on the twenty-second. He is another writer who has L. G. Murphy dying a few days before the battle of the McSween home. He died several months afterward. There are many other errors.

419. Chisholm, Joe

Brewery gulch. Frontier days in old Arizona—last outpost of the great southwest, by Joe Chisholm. San Antonio, Texas, the Naylor Co. [1949]. Cloth. Scarce.

xi, 180 p. front. 21.7 cm.
Index: p. 177–180.
Half title.

This most interesting book, assembled from Chisholm's earlier writings, was published twelve years after his death. It deals with most of the better-known outlaws of Arizona, and the writer's opinion of the Earps is not a favorable one. He seems to think that it was the Earp clique who robbed the stages and that it was Doc Holliday who killed Philpot, and he says that Holliday "was a vicious killer if there ever was one in the Southwest." Of the O K Corral fight, he says that the Earps knew the Clantons were unarmed and leaving town and that when they threw up their hands at Virgil Earp's command the Earps commenced shooting. He claims the Clantons were "deliberately assassinated."

420. Chrisman, Harry E.

The ladder of rivers. The story of I. P. (Print) Olive, [by] Harry E. Chrisman. Denver, Sage books [1962]. Cloth.

10 p.l., 21–426 p. plates, ports., facsms., map, cattle brands, ear-marks. 22.3 cm.

Notes and sources: p. 372–403; appendix: p. 404–407; bibliography: p. 408–414; index: p. 415–426.

Half title; pub. device.

A well-written biography of one of cattle land's unique characters, revealing many things heretofore unrecorded.

421. ———

Lost trails of the Cimarron, [by] Harry E. Chrisman. Denver, Sage books [1961]. Cloth.

7 p.l., 15–304 p. plates, ports., maps, facsm., cattle brands. 22.4 cm.

Appendix: p. 287–293; index: p. 294–304.

Half title; map on end papers; pub. device.

Has material on Dodge City, the Coe outlaws, Wyatt Earp, Bat Masterson, and others.

422. [City Directory]

City directory of Abilene, Kansas, 1904–05. [N.p.], American Directory co. [1905]. Stiff wrappers. Scarce.

2 p.l., [5]–156 [20] p. illus. 20.8 cm.

19-p. telephone directory at end; adv. scattered throughout.

Contains some information on Wild Bill Hickok while he was marshal at Abilene.

423. Clairmonte, Glenn

Calamity Jane was her name, [by] Glenn Clairmonte. Denver, Sage books [1959]. Cloth.

5 p.l., 11–215 p. plates, ports. 22.3 cm.

Half title; pub. device.

Also published in pict. wrappers.

The author says on page 1 that Calamity Jane was born May 1, 1852, yet on page 25 she says that Jane's birth date was May 1, 1886, thirty-four years later. This, of course, could be a typographical error. She has Jane riding off to Arizona with Custer to scout for him against the Apaches, but Custer never campaigned in Arizona, and Jane never scouted there. The author says that Hickok named her Calamity.

She says that Calamity married Hickok in 1870 when they met a preacher on the prairie between Hays City and Abilene. It seems that Hickok had killed three men in Hays City whom Calamity had warned him against and that they were on their way to Abilene. Though most historians hold that Jane never married Hickok and that he was too much of a dandy to marry one of her coarse nature, this author makes such a marriage quite convincing. She has Jane riding two hundred miles to the battleground of the Little Big Horn, where Custer and his men had been annihilated, finding the dismembered body of her brother, and burying it. She writes that when Jane heard of Wild Bill's murder by McCall, she went to Mann's saloon to see his body but "stumbled out through the press of curious people without speaking." She admits that Jane made up the tale about cornering McCall in Shurdy's butcher shop.

In this book the Belle Starr to whom Jane was introduced as the daughter of Major Waddell turns out to be her own half-sister, an illegitimate older daughter of her own mother, not the Belle Starr of Oklahoma fame.

424. Clampitt, John Wesley

Echoes from the Rocky mountains. Reminiscences and thrilling incidents of the romantic and golden age of the great west; with graphic accounts of its discovery, settlement and grand development, by John W. Clampitt. . . . Elaborately illustrated. Chicago, New York, Philadelphia, and San Francisco, Belford, Clarke & co., 1888. Pict. cloth. Scarce.

xvi, 19–671 p. front. (port. with tissue), illus., plates. 24.7 cm.

Republished with same imprint and collation in 1889 and 1890.

Has a chapter on outlaws and the vigilantes, with information on Plummer, Ives, Yeager, Stinson, Gallaher, Ray, Slade, and Zachary.

425. Clappe, Mrs. Louise Amelia Knapp Smith

The Shirley letters from California mines in 1851–52. Being a series of twenty-three letters from Dame Shirley . . . to her sister in Massachusetts and now reprinted from the *Pioneer Magazine* of 1854–55, with synopsis of the letters and emendations by Thomas C. Russell, together with "an appreciation by Mrs. M. T. V. Lawrence." Illustrated. San Francisco, printed by Thomas C. Russell at his private press . . ., 1922. Boards and cloth. Scarce.

1 p., 2 l., 3–350 p. front., 8 plates (all col. incl. front., with tissues). 24 cm.

Limited to 450 copies; also published in special issues, one of 50 and another of 200 copies.

The letters first appeared serially in the *Pioneer Magazine* under the pseudonym of "Dame Shirley" during 1854 and 1855. The book was republished by Grabhorn Press of San Francisco in two volumes in 1933, in an edition of five hundred copies (141 and 144 pages). It was republished again in 1949 with an introduction by Carl Wheat, New York, Alfred A. Knopf. Dec. cloth.

xix p., 1 l., 3–216 p. plates (col.). 21.7 cm.
Half title; map on end papers; pub. device.

All have some material on Joaquín Murieta.

426. Clark, Barzilla W.

Bonneville county in the making, by Barzilla W. Clark. Idaho Falls, Idaho, published by the author, 1941. Pict. cloth. OP.

6 p.l., 140 p. front., ports., map (incl. front.). 23.5 cm.
Addenda: p. 136–140.
Half title; vignette.

Has a chapter on the vigilantes and another on stage robbers, the hanging of Plummer, Slade, and the rest of the road agents.

427. Clark, Henry W.

History of Alaska, by Henry W. Clark. New York, the Macmillan co., 1930. Cloth. OP.

x p., 3 l., 208 p. plates, maps (1 double p.). 22.6 cm.
Index: p. 193–208.
Half title.

Contains some material on Soapy Smith.

428. Clark, Ira G.

Then came the railroads. The century from steam to diesel in the southwest, by Ira G. Clark. Norman, University of Oklahoma press [1958]. Cloth.

xv p., 1 l., 3–336 p. plates, ports., maps (1 double p.). 23.6 cm.
Bibliography: p. 318–324; index: p. 325–336.
Half title; double t.p.; "First edition" on copyright p.

Much space is devoted to train robbery, including those of the James and Younger boys, Sam Bass, the Daltons, and the Doolin and Jennings gangs.

429. Clark, O. S.

Clay Allison of the Washita, first a cow man then an extinguisher of bad men. Recollections of Colorado, New Mexico and the Texas panhandle. Reminiscences of a '79er, [by O. S. Clark, Attica, Ind., G. M. Williams], 1920. Stiff wrappers. Exceedingly rare.

1 p.l., 38 p. 24.5 x 13.2 cm.

Three loose-leaf inserts, seldom found in copies of the book.

This little book was privately printed for friends. Part of the final insert reads: "And finally when the curiosity and novelty has worn off and the little thing [the book] is scuffed about, trampled on, battered around, and shoved behind the clock, and from there to the old garret, where all the old literary gems are often stored, then eventually it will reach the woodhouse ready for the junk pile." Perhaps the prophecy of the author came true, as it is almost impossible to find a copy today. The author tells of his experiences in meeting Clay Allison on the trail and of some of Allison's subsequent killings. He also quotes a long story about Allison from Alfred Henry Lewis' *Sunset Trail.*

Reprinted in Houston, Texas, by the Frontier press of Texas, in 1954.

2 p.l., [5]–31 [1] p. front., plates, ports. 21.3 cm.

430. ———

Clay Allison of the Washita. First a cowman and then an extinguisher of bad men. Recollections of Colorado, New Mexico and the Texas panhandle. Reminiscences of a '79er. [Attica, Ind., 1922.] Stiff wrappers. Scarce.

4 p.l., 9–135 p. front., plates, ports., map. 24 cm.

Although this book has the same title as the 1920 edition (Item 429), it contains much added material by other writers, as well as illustrations and a map not included in the 1920 edition. This edition has also become rather scarce and is the only one known to many bibliophiles. It contains an introduction not included in the first edition, and the author also names his two trail companions, which he failed to do in the first edition. Paragraphing and wording of material from the 1920 edition are identical. The book has some material on the big fight at Tascosa, Texas.

431. Clarke, Donald Henderson

The autobiography of Frank Tarbeaux, as told to Donald Henderson Clarke. . . . New York, the Vanguard press, MCMXXX. Boards and cloth. Scarce.

ix [1] p., 3 l., 3–386 [1] p. 21.3 cm.

Half title; illus. end papers; pub. device; untrimmed.

The subject of this autobiography claims that he and his father opened the Chisholm Trail in 1863. He says that the herds were divided into "bands" of five thousand each and that with each "band" were a mess wagon and ten or fifteen cowboys. According to the cowman's standards this would be a rather unwieldy herd for fifteen cowboys. When a cowman speaks of a "band" he means horses; he uses "herd" when referring to cattle. The author speaks rather disparagingly of Buffalo

Bill and says that "all his history is pure fiction." He makes the strong statement that "Buffalo Bill never killed an Indian in his life, and those people who say they saw him do it are suffering from hallucinations." He has Wild Bill Hickok marshal of Dodge City and further states that he had just left a poker game in Deadwood when Wild Bill was killed and that Hickok was killed by "one of the McCoys, and was sent to do the job by Johnny Varnes who had it in for Bill." He has the killing take place in Mann and Manning's saloon. There are many other unreliable statements; for example, he says that Calamity Jane was first heard of in Deadwood, where she was just an ordinary dance-hall girl. He also claims to have been a close friend of Wild Bill, the James boys, and many other western outlaws. He claims to have shot Bob Ford through the lungs in a fracas in southern Colorado.

432. Clarke, Mary Whatley

The Palo Pinto story, by Mary Whatley Clarke. Fort Worth, Texas, printed and bound by the Manney co. . . . [1956]. Cloth.

x, 172 p. plates, ports. 22 cm.
Index: p. 171–172.
Half title.

Has a chapter on Sam Bass, giving some new material.

433. Claussen, W. Edmunds

Cimarron—"last of the frontier." Pictures and story by W. Edmunds Claussen. . . . [N.p.], 1948. Stiff pict. wrappers. OP.

[24] p. (no pagination). plates. 22.6 cm.
Device.

Contains some material on Black Jack Ketchum and several pages on Clay Allison.

434. Clay, John

My life on the range, by John Clay. Chicago, privately printed [1924]. Cloth. Rare.

4 p.l., 365 [1] p. front. (port., signature in facsm.), plates, ports. 23.5 cm.
Half title; device; gilt top; untrimmed.
Republished by Antiquarian press, New York, in 1961, with an introduction by E. E. Dale and again by the University of Oklahoma press in 1962 with an introduction by Donald R. Ornduff.

This well-written book about the author's ranch experiences has become scarce in the first edition, and is one of the much-sought-after cattle books. It is said that Clay kept copies on his desk in Chicago, and friends helped themselves until the supply became exhausted. He was one of the better-known ranch owners of the

Northwest and a well-educated Scotchman. His picture of ranch life is authentic. He relates many incidents of the Johnson County War and tells about Tom Horn.

435. ———

The tragedy of Squaw Mountain, by John Clay. [Chicago, designed and printed by Maders printing co., n.d.] Stiff wrappers. Rare.

19 [1] p. ports. 22 cm.

Top of each page decorated with colored drawings.

Contains a story about Tom Horn.

436. Cleaveland, Agnes Morley

No life for a lady, by Agnes Morley Cleaveland. Illustrations by Edward Borein. Boston, Houghton Mifflin co., 1941. Cloth.

ix p., 1 l., [3]–356 p. illus. 23.5 cm.

Life in America series.

Half title; map on end papers; illus. chapter headings; device; first edition: 1941 under imprint.

Reprinted many times.

One of the really good western books, it contains some information on Clay Allison and a few other New Mexico outlaws.

437. ———

Satan's paradise, from Lucien Maxwell to Fred Lambert, by Agnes Morley Cleaveland. With decorations by Fred Lambert. Boston, Houghton Mifflin co., 1952. Cloth. OP.

viii p., 1 l., 274 p. 21.4 cm.

Half title; tailpieces; vignette; first edition: 1952 over imprint.

A well-written book, largely about a peace officer named Fred Lambert, with chapters on the Black Jack gang, Clay Allison, and other gunmen of New Mexico. The author is mistaken in saying that Ketchum was hanged for murder. He was hanged for train robbery, which had been made a hanging offense in New Mexico.

438. Cleland, Robert Glass

California pageant, the story of four centuries, by Robert Glass Cleland. Illustrated by Raymond Lufkin. New York, Albert A. Knopf, 1946. Dec. cloth. OP.

x p., 1 l., 257 p. front. (col.), illus. (col.). 21.7 cm.

Index: p. 247–257.

Illus. chapter headings (part col.).

Gives a brief account of Murieta.

439. ———

The cattle on a thousand hills; Southern California, 1850–1870, by Robert Glass Cleland. San Marino, Calif., the Huntington library, 1941. Cloth. OP.

xvi p., 1 l., [3]–327 p. facsm., map, cattle brands. 23.3 cm.
Appendix: p. [277]–315; index: p. [319]–327.
Half title; Huntington Library Publication; vignette.

Republished with addition in 1951.

xvi p., 1 l., 3–365 p. plates, ports., map, facsms. 23.3 cm.
Appendices: p. 235–279; notes: p. 281–338; bibliography: p. 339–349; index: p. 351–365.
Half title; vignette.

Has much on Murieta and Vásquez. Although the second edition has the same chapters as the first, there are some changes in the text, paragraphing, maps, and illustrations, a long section of notes and a bibliography have been added. A new Section V in the appendix is devoted to Tiburcio Vásquez—an interview by the *Los Angeles Star* in 1874. The first edition Appendix III has a lengthy account of Juan Flores, his activities, and his execution.

440. ———

History of California: the American period, by Robert Glass Cleland. New York, the Macmillan co., 1922. Cloth. OP.

xiii p., 1 l., 512 p. front. (fold. map), plates, map, facsm. 22.6 cm.
Appendices: p. 469–502; index: p. 503–512.
Half title.

Has some material on Murieta and other California outlaws.

441. ———

The Irvine ranch of Orange county, 1810–1950, by Robert Glass Cleland. San Marino, Calif., the Huntington library, 1952. Cloth. OP.

vii p., 1 l., 3–163 p. plates, ports., map. 23.5 cm.
Index: p. 155–163.
Half title.

Chapter VI deals with the outlaws of Orange County, the killing of Sheriff Barton, and the hanging of Juan Flores.

442. Clemens, Samuel Langhorne (Mark Twain, pseud.)

Life on the Mississippi, by Mark Twain. . . . With more than 300 illustrations. Sold by subscription only. Boston, James R. Osgood and co., 1883. Dec. cloth. Scarce.

9 p.l., [21]–624 p. illus., plates. 23 cm.
Few copies with gilt edge.

The English edition was published in London and issued about five days before the American edition. A portion of the book was printed and published in Toronto. The author tells of the death of Jesse James and gives some information about Murrell.

443. ———

Roughing it, by Mark Twain (Samuel L. Clemens), fully illustrated by eminent artists. . . . Hartford, Conn., American publishing co.; Chicago, F. G. Gilmer and co. . . ., 1872. Pict. cloth. Scarce.

xviii, [19]–591 p. front. (double p. with tissue), illus., plates. 22 cm.
Appendix: p. [572]–591.

The English edition was actually the first edition, since it was issued a week before the American edition. The English edition was published in London in two volumes, Volume I being *Roughing It* and Volume II being *Innocents at Home*. Later editions show a battered *M* in the first line of the contents and broken *y* in "My," the first word of Chapter I, and on page 242 words are missing from the twentieth and twenty-first lines. The American edition was reissued in 1886, 1888, 1891, 1895, 1899, 1903, 1913, 1924, and many other years.

Contains some material on road agents, Joseph Slade, and other bad men of the West.

444. Clover, Samuel Travers

On special assignment; being the further adventures of Paul Travers; showing how he succeeded as a newspaper reporter, by Samuel Travers Clover. . . . Illustrated by H. G. Laskey. Boston, Lothrop publishing co. [1903]. Pict. cloth. Scarce.

5 p.l., 11–307 [4] p. front., illus. 18.3 cm.
4 p. adv. at end; device.
Republished in New York in 1965.

The author was a reporter sent out by a Chicago paper to cover the Johnson County War. Although written in the form of fiction, the book calls actual names and relates factual incidents as the author witnessed them.

445. Clum, John P.

It all happened in Tombstone, by John Clum. Reprinted from the *Arizona Historical Review,* October 1929, with a foreword and annotations by John D. Gilchriese. Flagstaff, Ariz., Northland press, 1965. Pict. cloth.

vii, 45 p. 26 cm.

Appendix: p. 37–45.

Half title.

Colophon: "Two hundred copies of this special, limited edition were printed. This is Number ——," on half-title page.

Also published in a trade edition.

This book was written by Clum as a tribute to his close friend Wyatt Earp. The original publication in the *Arizona Historical Review* has been very scarce, and this beautiful little book is indeed a welcome addition to the history of Tombstone. It is fully annotated on the margins by John Gilchriese, the acknowledged authority on the Earps. On the margin of page 31 the date of Warren Earp's birth is given as March 9, 1885, instead of 1855. This is a typographical error on the part of the printer, and Mr. Gilchriese called my attention to it before I read the book.

446. Clum, Woodworth

Apache agent. The story of John P. Clum, by Woodworth Clum. With illustrations. Boston, New York, Houghton Mifflin co., 1936. Cloth. Scarce.

xiv p., 2 l., 3–296 [1] p. front. (col.), plates, ports. 21.7 cm.

Index: p. 295–[297].

Half title; pub. device; first edition: 1936 under imprint.

There was also a very small special edition of this book bound in blue leather and autographed by Mrs. Clum and the author. It has a new title page, and on the next page is the following note: "For those whom John P. Clum, and whose friendship he cherished, I have printed a few copies of this book. It is made up of the Houghton Mifflin edition of *Apache Agent,* to which has been added an epilogue. . . . W. C."

The epilogue consists of eleven unnumbered pages between the original text and the index.

Deals with life in Tombstone and the outlaws and gunmen of that period, such as the Earps, Johnny Behan, Doc Holliday, Luke Short, and Billy Breakenridge. It gives an account of the O K Corral fight.

As mayor of Tombstone and publisher of the *Epitaph,* with the Earps on his police force, Clum was understandably partial to the Earps, who, he writes, "did their duty and did it well." He says that Stuart Lake wrote the best account of the O K Corral fight, but today few who know the details of the fight would agree with him.

447. Coates, Robert M.

The outlaw years. The history of the land pirates of the Natchez trace, by Robert Coates. New York, the Literary Guild of America, 1930. Pict. Cloth.

7 p.l., 3–308 p. front., plates, facsm. 21.2 cm.

Bibliography: p. 303–308.

Half title; map on end papers; vignette; untrimmed.

Here we have short histories of the Harpes, the Murrells, Joseph Hare, and Samuel Mason, the land pirates of the Mississippi.

448. Coblentz, Stanton Arthur

Villains and vigilantes. The story of James King of William, and pioneer justice in California, by Stanton A. Coblentz. Illustrated from contemporary prints and portraits. New York, Wilson-Erickson, inc., 1936. Cloth. OP.

vii p., 1 l., 261 p. front., plates, ports. 23.5 cm.

Principal authorities consulted: p. 255–256; index: p. 257–261.

Half title.

Republished with same collation by Thomas Yoseloff in 1937.

"New material in this edition," on copyright p.

The author's account of Murieta follows the Ridge version.

449. Coburn, Walt

Stirrup high, by Walt Coburn. Decorations by Ross Santee. Foreword by Fred Gipson. New York, Julian Messner, inc. [1957]. Cloth.

4 p.l., 9–190 p. front., illus. 21.5 cm.

Half title; illus. t.p.

The story of the author's boyhood days on his father's ranch, with a chapter on Butch Cassidy and the Wild Bunch.

450. Cochran, John S.

Bonnie Belmont. A historical romance of the days of slavery and the Civil War, by Judge John S. Cochran. [Wheeling, W.Va., press of Wheeling News, 1907.] Cloth. Scarce.

3 p.l., 7–291 p. plates (1 fold.), ports. 23.6 cm.

This privately printed book was limited to one thousand copies. The author says in his preface that the book is true though the names of some of the characters have been changed. There is a chapter on the James and Younger brothers which is reliable except for a few minor details. The author says that Mrs. James's second husband, Mr. Samuel, found his home so "uncongenial that he left and was never heard of afterward." Mr. James, the first husband, not Mr. Samuel (the third husband) went to California during the gold rush and died there before he could return home. Dr. Samuel lived with Jesse's mother until he died. He also claims that Jesse was bloodthirsty and loved to kill.

451. Cody, Louisa Frederici

Memories of Buffalo Bill, by his wife Louisa Frederici Cody, in collaboration with Courtney Ryley Cooper. New York, London, D. Appleton and co., MCMXIX. Cloth. Scarce.

3 p.l., 325 [1] p. front. (port.). 21 cm.
Half title; pub. device; first edition: figure (1) at end of text.

Has some information on Wild Bill Hickok.

452. Cody, William Frederick

An autobiography of Buffalo Bill (Colonel W. F. Cody). Illustrated by W. C. Wyeth. New York, Cosmopolitan book corp., 1920.

4 p.l., 328 p. front. (port.), plates. 20.4 cm.
Lettered on cover: "Buffalo Bill's Own Life Story."

453. ———

Buffalo Bill's own story of his life and deeds. This autobiography tells in his own graphic words the wonderful story of his heroic deeds. . . . His autobiography is brought up to date including a full account of his death and burial written by his boyhood chum and life-long friend William Lightfoot Visscher. . . . Illustrated with rare engravings and photographs. [Chicago, John R. Stanton, 1917.] Cloth. [Memorial edition.] Scarce.

xii, 15–352 p. front. (port.), illus., plates, ports. 21.4 cm.
"The End of the Trail," by Col. William Lightfoot Visscher; p. 338–352; port. of Cody pasted on cover with facsm. of signature below.

454. ———

Life and adventures of "Buffalo Bill," Colonel William F. Cody. This thrilling autobiography tells in Col. Cody's own graphic language the wonderful story of his long eventful and heroic career, and is supplemented with a chapter by a loving, life-long friend covering his last days, death and burial. . . . The whole work comprising an authentic history of many events inseparably interwoven with the exploration, settlement and development of our great western plains. Illustrated with many rare engravings. Chicago, John R. Stanton co., publishers, [1917]. Cloth. Scarce.

xiii [1], 5–352 [1] p. illus., plates. 20 cm.
"The End of the Trail," by Col. William Lightfoot Visscher: p. 338–342; port. of Cody on cover; initials.

Republished, New York, Wiley book co. [1927]; republished again Lookout Mountain, Golden, Colo., Mrs. Johnny Baker [1939]. Cloth. Scarce.

xiii [1] p., 15–352 p. front. (port.), illus., plates. 20.5 cm.

Gives an account of Wild Bill's duel with Dave Tutt.

455. ———

Story of wild west and camp-fire chats, by Buffalo Bill (Hon. W. F. Cody). A full and complete history of the renowned pioneer quartet, Boone, Crockett, Carson and Buffalo Bill's conquest of England with wild west exhibition. . . . Richmond, Va., B. F. Johnson and co. [1888]. Cloth. Scarce.

xvi, 17–766 p. front. (col.), illus., plate (col.), ports. 20 cm.
Illus. t.p.; t.p. in red and black.

This book has less Wild Bill material than most of Cody's other books and does not repeat that threadbare account of his "fight" with the McCanles group.

456. ———

True tales of the plains, by Buffalo Bill (William F. Cody), frontiersman and late chief of scouts, U. S. Army. New York, Empire book co., 1908. Cloth. (port. pasted on.) Scarce.

2 p.l., 259 p. front. (port. with signature in facsm.), illus., plates, ports. 19.2 cm.
Issued in New York, with same date and collation by Cupples & Leon, with 6 p. adv. at end, and with headpieces and device.

Most of Cody's books were ghost-written and contain chapters on Wild Bill Hickok which follow the pattern established by Buel. The author also places Rock Creek Station in Kansas instead of Nebraska, has ten men in the McCanles "gang," and calls David McCanles Jacob—all of which illustrates how closely the author followed another writer's material, without checking its accuracy, despite Buffalo Bill's claim that Hickok described the fight to him personally. Cody numbers Wild Bill's wounds as three bullet wounds, eleven buckshot wounds, and thirteen knife wounds. He also says that Hickok killed four men in Abilene. He killed only two, one of them his own deputy and friend.

457. Coe, Charles H.

Juggling a rope; lariat roping and spinning, knots and splices; also the truth about Tom Horn, "king of the cowboys," by Charles H. Coe. . . . Pendleton, Oreg., Hamley & co., 1927. Cloth. Scarce.

4 p.l., 9–114 p. front., plates, ports. 19.7 cm.
Index: p. third prelim. leaf.

Part V is devoted entirely to the defense of Tom Horn.

458. Coe, George Washington

Frontier fighter, the autobiography of George W. Coe, who fought and rode with Billy the Kid. As related to Nan Hillary Harrison. Boston and New York, Houghton Mifflin co., 1934. Pict. cloth. Scarce.

xiv p., 1 l., 220 p. front. (port.), plates, ports.. facsm. 21.2 cm.

Half title; pub. device; first edition: 1934 under imprint.

Republished in 1951 by University of New Mexico press, Albuquerque. Cloth. OP.

Though a good friend of Billy the Kid, the author was never considered an outlaw. As a participant in the Lincoln County War, he gives, I believe, a fairly accurate account of the affair and the Kid's activities. But, like most old-timers, he is inaccurate about dates. For instance, on page 157 he gives 1904 as the year of Garrett's death. It should be 1908. The reprint by the University of New Mexico Press failed to correct such errors, and Glenn Shirley, in his *Toughest of Them All* (page 14) repeats the erroneous date. The author perpetuates the old legends that the Kid's parents moved to Coffeyville, Kansas, in 1862 and that his mother remarried in Colorado. Coe says: "His mother's marriage to Antrim was perhaps the tragic turning-point in the Kid's life" and that "his little soul became warped with hatred for his step-father."

The author also has the Kid, at the age of twelve, killing a blacksmith with a penknife. He says that Billy and Brewer were on the trail with Tunstall when he was killed. He does not mention Widenmann or Middleton on this venture but does say that Tunstall never carried a gun. We know that to be incorrect because in letters Tunstall wrote to his parents he stated that he carried a gun. The author writes that Mr. Shields performed the last rites for Tunstall. It was Dr. Ealy who performed the service. He also says that the Kid and he carried the coffin to the grave. The records show that the Kid was under arrest by the Murphy crowd at the time.

The author has only five men "behind the adobe wall" when Brady was killed —the Kid, Henry Brown, Fred Waite, John Middleton, and Jim French. He also makes the statement that the bullets fanned the skirts of Mrs. McSween as she went back and forth from her burning house to Colonel Dudley's camp. That is also incorrect. All shooting stopped when she made her appearance.

He says that Colonel Dudley was tried for his actions during the battle of the McSween home and was "court martialled and thrown out of the United States Army" and that the trial "cost the Government between forty and fifty thousand dollars." Dudley was tried, but he was found not guilty. The author is also mistaken in saying that the Kid's trial for killing Sheriff Brady was held in Las Cruces. It was held in Mesilla. The author repeats the card-game and dropped-card version of the killing of Bell. He, too, has the Kid killing twenty-one men by the age of twenty-one, when he himself was killed. He misspells McCloskey's name as McLoskie and says that John Silman (Selman) came from Port (Fort) Griffin, Texas.

459. Coe, Urling C.

Frontier doctor, by Urling C. Coe, M.D. New York, the Macmillan co., 1939. Cloth. OP.

ix p., 1 l., 264 p. 20.9 cm.
Half title; tail pieces.

One chapter, entitled "Horse Thieves and Rustlers," relates the author's experiences in doctoring shot-up rustlers.

460. Coe, Wilbur

Ranch on the Ruidoso. The story of a pioneer family in New Mexico, 1871–1968, by Wilbur Coe, with an introduction by Peter Hurd. New York, Alfred A. Knopf, 1968. Pict. cloth.

xviii p., 2 l., 5–279 p. front. (col.), plates, ports. (2 col.), maps. 23.5 cm.
Pub. device; "First edition" on copyright p.

The author of this book, the son of Frank Coe, tells of his life as a successful rancher. The early chapters deal with his troubles during the Lincoln County War and his friendship with Billy the Kid. He mistakenly gives Olinger credit for firing the first shot that killed Tunstall. He is also mistaken in saying that Murphy died before the battle at the McSween home. He died several months later. The author spells Gauss's name as Goss and says that he chopped off Billy the Kid's leg irons. But Gauss merely tossed a miner's pick to Billy. All these events, of course, took place before the author's birth, and most of his information about them is secondhand. On the whole the book is most interesting.

461. Colburn, J. G. W.

The life of Sile Doty, the most noted thief and daring burglar of his time. The leader of a gang of counterfeiters, horse thieves, and burglars of the New England, middle and western states. The terror of Mexico during 1849. Illustrated. Compiled by J. G. W. Colburn. Toledo, Ohio, Blade printing & paper co., 1880. Cloth. Rare.

2 p.l., 5–269 p. front., illus. 22.8 cm.
Also issued in yellow pictorial wrappers.

I hesitated for some time to include this book in a bibliography of western outlaws, but Doty did operate to some extent in the middle and southwestern states. Although he cannot be considered a western outlaw in the usual sense, he was a notorious lawbreaker in his day. This is a rather scarce book owing to the fact that the subject's family succeeded in destroying many copies of it.

462. ———

The life of Sile Doty, 1800–1876. A forgotten autobiography. The most noted thief and daring burglar of his time. A foreword by Randolph G. Adams. [Detroit], Alved of Detroit, inc., 1948. Cloth. Scarce.

x p., 2 l., 288 p. front., illus. 21.7 cm.
Half title.

A modern reprint of the rare first edition.

463. Cole, Cornelius

Memoirs of Cornelius Cole, ex-senator of the United States from California, [by Cornelius Cole]. New York, McLoughlin brothers, 1908. Cloth. Scarce.

x, 354 p. front. (port.). 24.5 cm.
Device; untrimmed.

Contains some material on the arrest of Vásquez, the California outlaw.

464. Cole, Philip G.

Montana in miniature. The pictorial history of Montana from early exploration to early statehood, by Philip G. Cole. Illustrated by Olaf C. Seltzer. Edited by Van Kirk Nelson, M.D., Cato K. Butler. Kalispell, Mont., O'Neill printers, 1966. Pict. cloth.

vii, 2–216 [1] p. front. (col.), plates (part col.). 28.2 cm.
Half title; pub. device.

Has a short text on the verso of one page with a full-page illustration on the facing recto page. Among other events of Montana's history, it deals with the Montana vigilantes, Henry Plummer, the hanging of George Ives, and Kid Curry and his killing of Pike Landusky.

465. Coleman, Max M.

From mustanger to lawyer, by Max M. Coleman. . . . Book One, Part A, from 1890 to 1910. . . . [San Antonio, Texas, printed in the United States of America by the Carleton printing co., 1952.] Cloth. OP.

13 p.l., [29]–156 p. illus., plates. ports. 23.6 cm.
Colophon (verso third prelim. leaf): "This limited first edition of Part A From Mustanger to Lawyer consists of 500 copies signed by the author of which this is number ——."

In one chapter the author tells of the arrest of Bill Cook and Skeeter Baldwin, the Oklahoma outlaws. A typographical error on page 130 names Pat Garrett as Barrett. The table of contents is labeled "index" and appears before the title page. (The following year the author published Part B of this same title, but since it contains no material on outlaws it is omitted here.)

The author makes the statement that wearing a gun on the left side with the stock turned to the front "was a relic from the Lincoln County War of New Mexico, that style being instituted by the notorious Billy the Kid." I fail to understand the reason for this assertion unless the author was referring to the picture of the Kid that was printed backward.

466. Collier, William Ross, and Edwin Victor Westrate

Dave Cook of the Rockies, frontier general, fighting sheriff and leader of men, by William Ross Collier and Edwin Victor Westrate. . . . Illustrated from contemporary photographs by Joseph Collier. New York, Rufus Rockwell Wilson, inc., 1936. Cloth. OP.

xv, 224 p. front. (port.), plates, ports. 23.5 cm.
Half title.

A history of this famous Colorado detective, with an extended account of the capture of Musgrove and his gang, as well as other outlaws.

467. ———, and ———

The reign of Soapy Smith, monarch of misrule in the last days of the old west and the Klondike gold rush, by William Ross Collier and Edwin Victor Westrate. Illustrated from photographs. Garden City, New York, Doubleday, Doran & co., inc., 1935. Cloth. OP.

vi p., 2 l., 299 p. front. (port.), plates. 20.6 cm.
Half title; illus. end papers; untrimmed; "First edition" on copyright p.

In a chapter on the life and death of Bob Ford the authors give his killer's name as Ed O'Kelly. His name was Ed O. Kelly. This mistake has been made by many other writers.

468. Collins, Dabney Otis

Great western rides, [by] Dabney Otis Collins. Illustrated by Nick Eggenhofer. Denver, Sage books [1961]. Pict. cloth.

9 p.l., 19–277 p. front., illus., plates. 22.2 cm.
Index: p. 273–277.
Half title; illus. end papers; pub. device; bibliography at end of each chapter.

Has chapters on the Wild Bunch, the Johnson County War, and Joseph Slade.

469. ———

The hanging of bad Jack Slade, by Dabney Otis Collins. Illustrated by Paul Busch. Denver, Colorado, Golden Bell press [1963]. Pict. wrappers (col.).

48 p. illus., plates, ports. 21.7 cm.

Gives a full account of the hanging of Joseph Slade by the vigilantes.

470. Collins, Dennis

The Indians' last fight; or, the Dull Knife raid, by Dennis Collins. [Girard, Kans., press of the Appeal to Reason, 1915.] Cloth. Scarce.

3 p.l., [9]–326 p. front., plates, ports. 23.7 cm.

In telling about western outlaws, the author claims that one of the principal reasons for their development was the publication of wild West fiction and dime novels which created false impressions of the West and inflamed the imaginations and corrupted the minds of the younger generation.

471. Collins, Hubert Edwin

Warpath & cattle trail, by Hubert E. Collins; with a foreword by Hamlin Garland. Illustrated by Paul Brown. New York, William Morrow & co., 1928. Cloth. Scarce.

xix p., 1 l., 296 p. front., illus., plates. 24 cm.
Notes: p. 289–296.
Half title; illus. front end papers; map on rear end papers; tailpieces; vignette; untrimmed.

This volume contains a chapter on Cherokee Bill, telling about the outlaw's life before he started upon his career of crime. The author claims to have known him as a young man, but Cherokee Bill was hanged in 1894 at about the age of twenty and so would have been a small boy at the time the author claims to have known him. There are other mistakes.

472. Collison, Frank

Life in the saddle, by Frank Collison. Edited and arranged by Mary Whatley Clarke. With drawings by Harold D. Bugbee. Norman, University of Oklahoma press [1963]. Boards.

xvi p., 1 l., 3–243 p. illus. 19.6 cm.
Half title.

This is Volume 21 of the University of Oklahoma Press Western Frontier Library Series and is the second book in the series published from the original manuscript. It has some information about the Lincoln County War, the killing of Tunstall, and Billy the Kid.

473. Colter, Eli

The adventures of Hawke Travis. Episodes in the life of a gunman, by Eli Colter. New York, the Macmillan co., 1931. Pict. cloth. OP.

4 p.l., 220 p. 19.3 cm.
Half title.

474. Combs, Joseph F.

Gunsmoke in the Redlands, by Joseph F. Combs. San Antonio, Texas, the Naylor co. . . . [1968]. Pict. cloth.

xii p., 2 l., 121 [1] p. plate, ports. 21.7 cm.
Plat on front end papers; map and plan on rear end papers.
Half title; pub. device.

A story about the Wall-Border feud of east Texas.

475. Compendious History

of Ellsworth county, Kansas, from its early settlement to the present time. Embracing the executive and educational departments, population, sketches of prominent men, general character of the land, and condition of the people. . . . Ellsworth, Kans., printed at the Recorder office, 1879. Wrappers. Rare.

2 p.l., 5–59 p. 17.7 cm.
3 p. business cards at end; "First edition" on t.p.

This exceedingly rare little book contains some material on Wild Bill Hickok.

476. Conard, Howard L. (ed.)

Encyclopedia of the history of Missouri. A compendium of history and biography for ready reference. Edited by Howard L. Conard. New York, Louisville, St. Louis, the Southern History co., 1901. Three-quarter leather. Rare.

Vol. I, 4 p.l., 632 p. plates, ports., (with tissues). 27.5 cm.
Double column.

Tells of the James boys, the Youngers, and Bob and Charlie Ford.

477. Conn, William

Cow-boys and colonels. Narrative of a journey across the prairie and over the Black Hills of Dakota. From "*Dans les montagnes rocheuses*" of Baron E. de Mandat-Grancey, with additional notes not contained in the original edition, by William Conn. London, Griffith, Farran, Okeden & Welsh . . ., 1887. Cloth. Scarce.

xi, 352 p. front., plates. 22 cm.
Pub. device.

Republished in 1888. An American edition of 364 pages was published in New York in 1887. Reprinted again by J. B. Lippincott in 1963 in both cloth and wrappers.

A translation of the French of Mandat-Grancey, with the addition of a few unimportant notes. As in the original, there is a most ridiculous account of the killing of Wild Bill Hickok. See Item 1436.

478. Connell, Robert, Sr.

Arkansas, by Robert Connell, Sr. New York, the Paebar co., publishers, 1947. Cloth. OP.

ix, 9–128 [2] p. front., plates, ports. 21 cm.

This book has nothing to do with the state of Arkansas but tells about a character who went by that name. The author writes about some of his western experiences and has some information about Bucky O'Neal.

479. Connelley, William Elsey

Quantrill and the border wars, by William Elsey Connelley. . . . Cedar Rapids, Iowa, the Torch press, publishers, 1909. Cloth. Scarce.

9 p.l., [17]–542 p. front. (port.), illus., fold. map, diagrs. 24 cm.
Index: p. [485]–539; errata: p. [541]–542.
Half title; device; untrimmed.
Republished with an introduction by Homer Croy in 1956.

A thoroughly annotated book relating many of the exploits of the guerrillas, with some mention of the lives of the James and Younger boys while they were with Quantrill. Mr. Connelley's account is a most prejudiced one, and he seems to have ferocious loathing and contempt for his subject. It is filled with the author's too positive opinions and much confusing secondary matter. There are also many errors.

480. ———

Wild Bill and his era. The life & adventures of James Butler Hickok, by William Elsey Connelley . . ., with introduction by Charles Morceau Harger. New York, the press of the Pioneers, 1933. Pict. cloth. Scarce.

xii p., 1 l., 229 p. front. (port.), plates, ports. 24.3 cm.
Notes: p. 215–221; index: p. 223–229.
Half title; untrimmed.

The author here shows marked partiality for his subject. He says that McCanles' followers were "wild and reckless men, many of them outlaws" and claims that they were armed when they went to Rock Creek Station, and that they went there to create a disturbance. If this is true, it seems strange that McCanles would take his young son with him. Also, one wonders why, if they were armed, none of them used guns in their own defense. The author seems to place a great deal of trust in

Wilstach's interview with Sarah Shull, who said that "she had heard McCanles say he was going to clean up on the people at the station." The author does admit, however, that Hickok fired the shot that killed McCanles from behind a curtain and that he then killed both Woods and Gordon.

"When Wild Bill was shot," he writes, "at the old Bella Union saloon in Deadwood [it was actually in Saloon No. 10], Calamity Jane was among the first to reach the spot. While the men hesitated to pursue the assassin, fearful for their lives, Jane started into raging, fiery-hearted action. Her mingled grief and fury left no room in her heart for fear. In her hurry she left her weapon behind and was completely unarmed. But that did not deter her. She went after her man, just the same, defiant and unafraid of his guns, *still smoking from the murder*. She found him in a butcher shop, and seizing a cleaver from a rack, flew at him like a wildcat. Alone, she subdued and held him until her more timid associates came and secured him." All that is very romantic, but Calamity was nowhere near when the killing took place. The cleaver business is one of the lies she told in her autobiography.

The author also repeats the legend that Calamity got her nickname when she rescued Captain Egan from the Indians. As so many others do, he gives the date of her death as August 2, though she died at 5 o'clock on August 1. (It is believed that writers gave her death as August 2 because Wild Bill's death had occurred on that date twenty-seven years earlier and it would sound more romantic to have her die on the anniversary of his death.) He also makes the error of saying that Calamity Jane was the first white woman to enter the Black Hills. He repeats many legends as truth about Wild Bill's fantastic shooting.

481. Connolly, Christopher P.

The devil learns to vote. The story of Montana, [by] Christopher P. Connolly. New York, Covici Friede, publishers [1938]. Cloth. OP.

5 p.l., 13–310 p. front. (port.), plates, ports. 21 cm.

The first few chapters deal with the outlaws, road agents, and vigilantes of Montana, giving a good account of Henry Plummer and his gang.

482. Convict Life

at the Minnesota state prison, Stillwater, Minnesota. Profusely illustrated. St. Paul, Minn., published by W. C. Heilbron [1909]. Wrappers. Scarce.

3 p.l., [7]–155 [3] p. front., plates, ports., facsm. 19.5 cm.
Device.

One chapter, entitled "Real Facts about the Northfield, Minnesota, Bank Robbery," is related by Cole Younger.

483. Cook, David J.

Hands up; or, twenty years of detective life in the mountains and on the plains. Reminiscences of Gen. D. J. Cook, superintendent of the Rocky Mountain Detective Association. A condensed criminal record of the far west. Denver, Republican print, 1882. Wrappers. Exceedingly rare.

285 p. front. (port.), plates. 23 cm.

Illus. half title.

This rare book was originally published to be sold on trains by newsboys. It was reprinted the same year bound in cloth. When the cloth edition was first issued, there was a picture of two upraised hands with a scalping knife on the cover. The knife was said to have formerly belonged to Wild Bill Hickok and to have been given to Cook. The design was made from a photograph of Wild Bill's hands and his scalping knife. It is said that the book was largely written by Thomas Fulton Dawson, a prolific writer and editor. The scarcity of the first edition is claimed by some to be the result of using its pages for gun wadding during an Indian scare.

The book was reprinted to cover thirty-five years in 1897, Denver, W. F. Robinson Printing co., in cloth. Now also scarce.

7 p.l., [13]–442 p. front. (port. with signature in facsm.), illus., plates, ports. 23.5 cm.

It was reprinted again in 1958 by the University of Oklahoma press as one of their Western Frontier Library series with an introduction by Everett L. DeGolyer, Jr. Boards.

xvi p., 1 l., 3–319 p. plates. 19.8 cm.

484. Cook, James Henry

Fifty years on the old frontier, as cowboy, hunter, guide, scout and ranchman, by James H. Cook; with an introduction by Brigadier-General Charles King, U.S.V. . . . New Haven, Yale University press . . ., MDCCCCXXIII. Cloth. OP.

xix p., 1 l., 3–291 p. front., plates (1 col., 2 fold.), ports. 24 cm.

Index: p. 283–291.

Half title; pub. device.

Reprinted in several editions, including one by the Lakeside press of Chicago. Republished again by the University of Oklahoma press in 1957 with an introduction by J. Frank Dobie.

An outstanding western book with much on outlawry and a good firsthand account of the battle between the cowboys and Elfego Baca, a fight in which the author participated. He states that Billy the Kid was a New York City tough and that "doubtless he read some yellow back novels about the bandits of the West before he started on his career of crime in New Mexico." Evidently Mr. Cook did not know that the Kid left New York while he was still a baby.

485. ———

Longhorn cowboy, by James H. Cook, edited and with an introduction by Howard R. Driggs, and with drawings by Herbert Stoops. New York, G. P. Putnam's sons [1942]. Pict. cloth. OP.

xi p., 1 l., 241 p. front., illus. (double p.). 20.5 cm.

Half title; illus. end papers; headpieces.

This book is a juvenile edition of Item 484.

486. Cook, Jim (Lane)

Lane of the Llano, being the story of Jim (Lane) Cook as told to T. M. Pearce; illustrated by Walter J. Heffron. Boston, Little, Brown and co., 1936. Pict. cloth. OP.

xiv p., 1 l., [3]–269 p. front. (port.), illus. 21.3 cm.

Half title; pict. map on end papers; vignette.

The author at one time assumed the name Jim Lane (see pages 144 and 188). This book is supposedly an autobiography, but it is unreliable, for the author placed too much trust in a faulty memory or was exercising his imagination. He claims to have been in the burning McSween home with Billy the Kid during the Lincoln County War, but his name is not mentioned in any other account. Unlike some other writers, he says that Mrs. McSween was not in the house while it was burning but that the boys played the piano and sang while the bullets poured into the house.

"Eventually," he writes, "the soldiers set fire to the roof, and about twilight the Kid decided to make a break. There was a long adobe wall which ran to the house and down to the creek. We broke out along this wall—Billy, Tom O'Folliard and myself and some others. The Negro soldiers had placed themselves around two sides of the wall, and they couldn't fire at us without shooting each other. When Billy started out he said, 'Don't shoot any of the soldiers if you can help it. We don't want to have any more government murders to account for. Shoot your guns in the air to scare them niggers.'" The account is absurd. Men fighting for their lives would have had no compunction in shooting a soldier if it meant the difference between life and death. Moreover, the battle was not between the Kid's crowd and the soldiers but between the McSween faction and the Murphy followers.

487. Cook, John R.

The border and the buffalo. An untold story of the southwest plains. The bloody border of Missouri and Kansas. The story of the slaughter of the buffalo. Westward among the big game and wild tribes. A story of mountain and plain, by John R. Cook. Topeka, Kans., monotyped and printed by Crane & co., 1907. Pict. cloth. Scarce.

xii, 351 [1] p. front. (port.), plates, ports. 23.5 cm.

Republished as a Lakeside Classic in Chicago by R. R. Donnelley and sons co., in 1938. Edited with a historical introduction by M. M. Quaife.

Contains some information about the Benders of Kansas, and the reprint has an added footnote on Billy the Kid. A friend told the author that fifteen men followed the Benders when they tried to escape in a wagon and that they killed the entire family where they were camped on the Verdigris River, dividing their money and swearing one another to secrecy. I have not seen this statement elsewhere.

488. Coolidge, Dane

Arizona cowboys, by Dane Coolidge, with photographs by the author. New York, E. P. Dutton and co., inc., 1938. Pict. cloth. OP.

5 p.l., 13–160 p. front., plates. 20.8 cm.

Half title; "First edition" on copyright p.

Contains a chapter on the Pleasant Valley War between the Grahams and the Tewksburys.

489. ———

Fighting men of the west, by Dane Coolidge; with an introduction by the author; illustrated with halftones. New York, E. P. Dutton & co., inc., publishers [1932]. Cloth. OP.

7 p.l., 13–343 p. front., plates, ports. 22.2 cm.

Index: p. 339–343.

Half title; vignette; "First edition" on copyright p.

This author incorrectly states that after Billy the Kid killed his guards, Bell and Olinger, Pat Garrett lost his nerve, and John Poe was put in Garrett's place. Garrett stayed on the job until the Kid was killed. Coolidge also makes the preposterous statement that the Kid "was not satisfied to have a woman in every placita, but cast his ruthless eyes on one of a different class, who met his advances with scorn. *It was to save her that Billy the Kid was killed.* And, to protect her good name, Poe himself built up a fictitious account of the event." His account of the Kid's death is different, too. He says that the Kid went to Maxwell's to cut off a slab of bacon to take with him to the sheep camp where he was hiding out.

He has Poe and McKinney near the gate instead of on the porch. In fact, he says that McKinney was sitting on the edge of the board walk because one of his spurs was hung under the plank and he could not move.

He says that Clay Allison's specialty "was killing sheriffs and town marshals and officers of the law." He repeats all the many legends about Allison and tells of his visit to Dodge City to kill Bat Masterson, who he says was the city marshal. Bat was never city marshal of Dodge. He was sheriff of Ford County. The caption under the portrait of Masterson reads: "Bat Masterson the fighting town marshal of Dodge City who absented himself when Clay Allison came."

In typical fashion, his account of Tom Horn is full of errors. He has Horn killing a boy named Yaples. The boy's name was Willie Nickells. Strangely enough, a year after this book was published Stookie Allen repeated all this misinformation, illustrating how false history is handed down (see Item 25).

490. ———

Gringo gold; a story of Joaquín Murieta, the bandit, by Dane Coolidge. New York, E. P. Dutton & co., inc., 1939. Cloth. OP.

5 p.l., 13–249 p. 19.6 cm.
Half title; untrimmed.

The story of Murieta told in fiction form. As history it is unreliable.

491. Cooper, Courtney Ryley

High country, the Rockies yesterday and to-day, by Courtney Ryley Cooper. Illustrated. Boston, Little, Brown and co., 1926. Pict. cloth. OP.

6 p.l., [3]–294 p. front., plates. 21.2 cm.
Half title; device.

The last chapter deals with the psychology of the gunman and contains material on Wild Bill Hickok and the killing of Bob Ford. There is also some information about Henry Starr.

492. Cooper, Frank C.

Stirring lives of Buffalo Bill, Colonel Wm. F. Cody, last of the great scouts, and Pawnee Bill, Major Gordon W. Lillie, white chief of the Pawnees . . ., by Frank Cooper. [New York, Parsons and co., inc., 1912.] Dec. cloth. (Col. label pasted on.) OP.

5 p.l., 11–223 [1] p. double front. (ports. tissues between), plates, ports. 18.8 cm.

Although this book was published in 1912, four years after Cody's *True Tales of the Plains,* the author uses Cody's account practically verbatim and continues to hand down the same false information about Hickok begun by Nichols. On page 65 the author has nine men in the party of the McCanles "gang," though on page 66 he has Wild Bill killing ten men. He states that Hickok was "wounded by three bullets, eleven buckshot, and cut in thirteen places." The truth is that he did not receive a single injury. The author adds that it took Wild Bill six months to recover (Emerson Hough claimed that it took a year). Of the fight he says in part:

"Although wounded with buckshot and bullet, he [Wild Bill] fought on. The cabin was filled with smoke. Everyone he struck was an enemy; with his faithful bowie knife he never faltered, until all were calm and still. Bleeding from everywhere, he felt around the walls to steady himself at the door, then crawled to the well, and drank from a bucket of water which had been freshly drawn on his arrival; then he fell in a faint."

493. Corbin, Charles R.

Why news is news, by Charles R. Corbin. . . . New York, the Roland Press co. [1928]. Cloth. OP.

v p., 1 l., 3–191 p. front. (facsm.). 22 cm.
Appendix: p. 177–185; index: p. 187–191.
Pub. device.

Contains a chapter on Jesse James and repeats the old legend about Jesse giving a woman money for the landlord and then holding up the landlord to recover it. In the book a character named John T. (Texas Jack) Tyler tells some wild tales about Jesse, among them one about the murder of Jesse by Bob Ford, which he concludes by saying, "Twenty minutes later [after Jesse was killed] that dirty Ford was full of bullet holes." Ford was not killed until several years later.

494. Corle, Edwin

Desert country, by Edwin Corle. Edited by Erskine Caldwell. New York, Duell, Sloan & Pearce [1941]. Cloth. OP.

viii p., 1 l., 3–357 p. 22.2 cm.
American Folkways series.
Index: p. 349–357.
Half title; map on end papers; "First edition" on copyright p.

Tells about the O K Corral fight between the Earps and the Clantons and also has some minor material about Billy the Kid.

495. ———

The Gila river of the southwest, by Edwin Corle. Illustrated by Ross Santee. New York, Toronto, Rinehart & co., inc. [1951). Cloth. OP.

9 p.l., 5–402 p. front. (double p. map), illus. 21 cm.
Bibliography: p. 377–386; index: p. 387–402.
Half title; illus. t.p.; first edition: Letter "R" in device on copyright p.

The author is confused in his facts about Pearl Hart. He says she robbed a train in 1899. Her only robbery was of a stagecoach in 1898.

496. ———

Mojave; a book of stories, by Edwin Corle. New York, Liveright publishing corp. [1934]. Pict. cloth. OP.

5 p.l., 11–272 p. 19.5 cm.
Half title; device; untrimmed.

A chapter entitled "The Ghost of Billy the Kid" is a well-written piece of fiction which has been reprinted in many anthologies since its first appearance.

497. ———

The royal highway (El Camino Real), by Edwin Corle. Indianapolis, New York, the Bobbs-Merrill co., inc. [1949]. Pict. cloth. OP.

6 p.l., 13–351 p. plates, ports., maps. 22.2 cm.
Appendix: p. 331–334; bibliography: p. 335–339; index: p. 341–351.
Half title; map on end papers; untrimmed; "First edition" on copyright p.

In a chapter entitled "Your Money or Your Life," the author gives an account of Murieta, and makes some mention of Vásquez. Here is another author who repeats the legend about Murieta increasing the reward money on a wanted poster.

498. Corner, William (ed.)

San Antonio de Bexar. A guide and history. Compiled and edited by William Corner. Illustrated. San Antonio, Texas, Bainbridge & Corner, Christmas, 1890. Cloth. Scarce.

vi p., 2 l., 166 p. illus., plates (part col.), plans, facsms. 26.5 cm.
Illus. front end papers; plan on rear end papers; leaf of errata page [viii], 27 unnumbered p. adv. at end.

Has some mention of the killing of Ben Thompson and King Fisher by Joe Foster, whose name he misspells Forster. There is also mention of other desperadoes of early San Antonio.

499. Cossley-Batt, Jill Lillie Emma

The last of the California rangers, by Jill L. Cossley-Batt. New York and London, Funk & Wagnalls co., 1928. Cloth. Scarce.

xix, 299 p. front., illus., plates, ports., facsm. 21.4 cm.
Index: p. 295–299.
Half title; illus. end papers; untrimmed.

This English author devotes several chapters to Murieta and other California outlaws. She continues to rehash Ridge's account of Murieta. She claims that Murieta divided his gang into five different squads, each one having as its leader one of the numerous Joaquíns, thus allowing Murieta seemingly to commit crimes in widely separated sections.

500. Coursey, O. W.

Beautiful Black Hills; a comprehensive treatise on the Black Hills of South Dakota . . ., for popular readings, by O. W. Coursey. . . . Mitchell, S.D., published by the Educator supply co. [1926]. Cloth. Scarce.

4 p.l., [11]–265 [3] p. plates, ports. 19.4 cm.

3 p. adv. at end; "References": fourth prelim. leaf.

Contains chapters on Wild Bill Hickok and Calamity Jane The author is mistaken in saying that Hickok built the cabin at Rock Creek where the McCanles "fight" took place. He also says that "McCanles and his gang surrounded the place, and in a few minutes the fight was on. After it was over *Harper's Magazine* sent a reporter out to the field to get the facts, and he reported eight men killed by Bill single handed and alone. This number has been accepted as quite accurate." The author adds, however, that "the other side claims only three men were killed by Bill—Dave McCanles, the leader of the gang; James Wood, his cousin; and James Gordon, an employee."

There are other errors. Of Calamity Jane the author erroneously says that she died "August 2, the twenty-seventh anniversary of the assassination of her old-time idol, Wild Bill Hickok." This is a very common mistake.

501. ———

Wild Bill (James Butler Hickok), by O. W. Coursey. . . . Mitchell, S. D., published by the Educator supply co. [1924]. Cloth. Scarce.

4 p.l., [9]–80 p. illus., ports. 18.8 cm.

"Reprinted from the Sioux Falls Daily Argus-Leader."

Only a few of these little books were printed. The author tames down the McCanles-Hickok affair somewhat. While some writers have claimed the fight was the result of McCanles' horse stealing and others have stated that he was trying to collect a debt, this author says that the trouble started over the woman Kate Shull. But he makes quite a to-do over the marvelous shooting of his hero: "Wild Bill was a sure shot. He never missed! He could shoot backward and forward at the same time; and he is undoubtedly one of the few men who ever lived that could."

According to this biographer, Wild Bill brought his marksmanship into play one day in North Platte, Nebraska: "Wild Bill, facing the desperate character who entered the front door, had shot him with a revolver in his left hand, while with his right hand he had thrown the other gun back over his shoulder and shot the man coming from the rear. History does not record a more dare-devil act, a more astute piece of gun work, or a cleaner fight."

And so the legends of Hickok's shooting march on. The only trouble is, there is not one shred of evidence that this event ever took place.

502. Court of Appeals

at Tyler, Texas, October term, 1882. Ex parte Ben Thompson for bail. [N.p., no t.p.] Pamphlet. Rare.

17 p. 21 cm.

503. Cowan, Robert Ellsworth (Bud)

Range rider, by Bud Cowan; an introduction by B. M. Bower; illustrated by Ross Santee. Garden City, N.Y., Doubleday, Doran & co., inc., 1930. Pict. cloth. OP.

x p., 1 l., 289 p. front., plates. 21.2 cm.
Half title; device; untrimmed.
Reprinted same year under Sun Dial press imprint.

This book has a chapter on Big Nose George Parrott and gives some information about his capture and lynching. The author was the third husband of B. M. Bower (Mrs. Bertha M. Sinclair-Bower), who wrote the introduction, and she is the better writer of the two. There is also a chapter on the Hole-in-the-Wall and its bunch of outlaws.

504. Cowling, Mary Jo

Geography of Denton county, by Mary Jo Cowling. . . . Dallas, Banks Upshaw and co., 1936. Cloth. Scarce.

xii, 132 p. front. (cattle brands), plates, ports., map, tables. 22.3 cm.
Bibliography: p. 126–130; index: p. [131]–132.
Map on end papers; vignette.

A condensed account of the highlights in the life of Sam Bass.

505. Cox, William R.

Luke Short and his era, [by] William R. Cox. Garden City, N.Y., Doubleday and co., inc., 1961. Cloth.

4 p.l., [9]–214 p. 21.3 cm.
Acknowledgments: p. [188]–189; bibliography: p. [190]–192; notes: p. [193]–203; index: p. [205]–214.
Half title.

Contains many errors of fact and some wrong dates.

506. Crabb, Richard

Empire on the Platte, by Richard Crabb. Illustrated by Ernest L. Reedstrom. Cleveland and New York, the World publishing co. [1967]. Pict. cloth.

x, 273 p. illus., plates, ports., facsms. 21.6 cm.

Index: p. 363–373.

Half title; illus. t.p.; illus. map on end papers; "First edition" on copyright p.

One of the most nearly complete histories of the feud between the Olives and Luther Mitchell and Ami Ketchum, with some material on Doc Middleton, Jesse James, and Johnny Ringo.

507. Craig, Newton N. (Nute)

Thrills 1861 to 1887, by Nute Craig. [Oakland, Calif., published by N. N. Craig, 1931.] Morocco. Scarce.

5 p.l., [7]–62 [1] p. front., plates, facsm. of letter from Thomas A. Edison. 20 cm.

508. Craighead, Erwin

Mobile: fact and tradition. Noteworthy people and events, by Erwin Craighead. . . . Mobile, Ala., the Powers printing co., MCMXXX. Cloth. Scarce.

4 p.l., 9–373 p. illus. 19.6 cm.

Index: p. 369–373.

Contains some material on the John Copeland gang.

509. Crawford, Lewis Ferandus

Rekindling camp fires. The exploits of Ben Arnold (Conner) (Wa-si-cu-Tam-a-he-ca). An authentic narrative of sixty years in the old west as Indian fighter, gold miner, cowboy, hunter and army scout. Map, illustrations, bibliography, index and notes by Lewis F. Crawford. . . . Bismarck, N.D., Capital book co. [1926]. Cloth. Scarce.

8 p.l., 15–324 p. front. (port.), plates, map. 22.4 cm.

Bibliography: p. 311–313; index: p. 315–324.

Illus. half title; untrimmed.

Also published in a de luxe edition of 100 signed and numbered copies, three-quarter leather, boxed.

Colophon: "This edition is limited to one hundred copies of which this is No. ——."

This author claims that Calamity Jane's real name was Jane Somers, that she was born in Princeton, Missouri, in 1851, and that she died August 2, 1903. He says that the stories that she served as a scout and guide are the invention of people who never knew her. The book contains a chapter on Joseph Slade and some stories about Doc Middleton.

510. Crawford, Thomas Edgar

The west of the Texas Kid, 1881–1910. Recollections of Thomas Edgar

Crawford, cowboy, gun fighter, rancher, hunter, miner. Edited and with an introduction by Jeff C. Dykes. With original drawings by Nick Eggenhofer. Norman, University of Oklahoma press [1962]. Boards.

xviii p., 1 l., 3–202 p. illus. 19.8 cm.

Half title; double illus. t.p.; "First edition" on copyright p.

This is Volume 20 of the University of Oklahoma Press Western Frontier Library Series. Unlike most of the other books in the series it is a first printing, not a reprint of earlier editions. This little book is interesting but filled with mistakes. The author claims that Henry Starr was his companion on the cattle trails. Starr never drove cattle up any trail. He also claims to have met Belle Starr in a dance hall in Laredo, Texas, where she was working as a dance-hall girl. There is no evidence that Belle ever went that far south or worked as a dance-hall girl.

He further states that Henry Starr gave Belle expensive gifts. Belle was twenty-five years old when Henry was born, and he was only sixteen when Belle was murdered in 1889. The author is confused in his geography when he writes that Belle's "ranch" was "forty or fifty miles west of what is now Oklahoma City." Her property, Younger's Bend, was in the eastern part of the old Indian Territory, a long way east of Oklahoma City.

The author also makes a great many errors about Calamity Jane. He has her serving as a dance-hall girl, a vigilante, and a soldier all at the same time. She never was a vigilante, or a soldier, though she was what might be called a camp follower. Nor was she ever a cowpuncher, dressed in "chaps and six-shooters," as he says. As a whole the book is very unreliable.

511. **Crichton, Kyle S.**

Law and order, ltd. The rousing life of Elfego Baca of New Mexico, by Kyle S. Crichton. Santa Fé, New Mexico publishing corp., 1928. Cloth. Scarce.

viii p., 1 l., [3]–219 p. plates, ports. 22.2 cm.

Pub. device.

Also published in a limited, numbered and signed de luxe edition of 375 copies.

Colophon: "Three hundred and seventy-five copies of this first edition of two thousand copies have been inscribed by Mr. Baca and the author. Of the three hundred and fifty autographed copies which are for sale, this is copy No. ——."

The first book devoted entirely to this noted gunman, it includes much information about the now famous fight at Frisco, New Mexico, his association with Billy the Kid, and two chapters on Joel Fowler. Some of the stories about Billy the Kid have been heretofore untold, but the author errs in placing the Kid's trial at Lincoln instead of at Mesilla. He repeats the legend about the judge's sentence and the Kid's answer, but he does give a slightly different version of it.

512. Crites, Arthur S.

Pioneer days in Kern county, by Arthur S. Crites. Los Angeles, the Ward Ritchie press, 1951. Pict. cloth. OP.

viii p., 1 l., 3–279 p. plates, ports., maps. 23.5 cm.
Half title; vignette.

Chapter 31 deals with James McKinney, an outlaw.

513. Crittenden, Henry Huston

The Crittenden memoirs, compiled by H. H. Crittenden. Fully illustrated. New York, G. P. Putnam's sons, 1936. Cloth. Scarce.

xv, 17–542 p. front., plates, ports., facsm., fold. general. table, coat of arms. 24.2 cm.
Addenda: p. [515]–529; index: p. 531–542.
Half title; pub. device.
Also published on rag paper, bound in cloth and boards in an edition of 100 signed and numbered copies.

A large portion of this book is devoted to the life of the James brothers and the trial of Frank James. Governor Crittenden offered the reward which ultimately led to Jesse's death. In a letter from Frank Dalton there is an account of the killing of Ed O. Kelly which is all wrong.

514. Crockett, George Louis

Two centuries in east Texas. A history of San Augustine county and surrounding territory, from 1685 to the present time, by George Louis Crockett. . . . Dallas, Texas, the Southwest press [1932]. Cloth. Very scarce.

xi, 372 p. 23.8 cm.
Bibliography: p. 355–357; corrigenda *et* addenda: p. 359–364; index: p. 365–372.

This book contains a history of the feud between the Moderators and the Regulators and the rampant lawlessness of that time.

515. Croft-Cook, Rupert, and W. S. Meadmore

Buffalo Bill, the legend, the man of action, the showman, by Rupert Croft-Cook and W. S. Meadmore. London, Sidwick and Jackson, ltd. [1952]. Boards.

4 p.l., 9–239 p. front. (port.), plates, ports., facsm. 21.8 cm.
Bibliography: p. 235–239.
Half title.

Tells some incidents in the early life of Wild Bill Hickok, his experiences as an actor, and his murder by Jack McCall. Also tells about Slade's hiring Buffalo Bill as a pony-express rider.

516. Crosthwait, William L., and Ernest G. Fisher

The last stitch, by William L. Crosthwait, M.D., and Ernest G. Fisher. Philadelphia and New York, J. B. Lippincott co. [1956]. Cloth and boards. OP.

7 p.l., 15–250 p. 21 cm.
Half title.

Has some information on the Al Jennings gang and the Wall-Border feud in East Texas.

517. Crouch, Carrie J.

A history of Young county, Texas, by Carrie J. Crouch. Austin, Texas, Texas state historical association, 1956. Pict. cloth. OP.

xiv p., 1 l., 3–326 p. plates, ports., cattle brands. 24 cm.
Volume II of Texas county and Local History series.
Bibliography: p. 295; index: p. 297–326.
Half title; map on end papers; device.

Tells the story of the Marlow brothers and their desperate fight with a mob.

518. ———

Young county, history and biography, by Carrie J. Crouch. Dallas, Texas, Dealey and Lowe, 1937. Fabrikoid. Scarce.

8 p.l., 339 [3] p. front., plates, ports., cattle brands, diagr. 22.3 cm.
Bibliography and index on unnumbered pages at end.
Map on end papers; pub. device; "First edition" on copyright p.

In a chapter entitled "Young County Trials" the author gives a brief history of the Marlow brothers.

519. Crowe, Pat

Pat Crowe, his story, confession and reformation. New York, G. W. Dillingham [1906]. Pict. wrappers. Scarce.

4 p.l., 9–252 p. front., 5 plates (incl. front.). 19.5 cm.

A good account of this outlaw and his crimes.

520. ———

Spreading evil. Pat Crowe's autobiography. New York, the Branwell co. [1927]. Cloth. Scarce.

xvi, 3–331 [1] p. 19.4 cm.
Half title.

521. **Croy, Homer**

Corn country, by Homer Croy. Edited by Erskine Caldwell. New York, Duell, Sloan & Pearce [1947]. Cloth. OP.

vi p., 2 l., 3–325 p. 21.8 cm.
Index: p. 319–325.
Half title; map on end papers; "First edition" on copyright p.

Gives a brief account of Lame Johnny and mentions Jesse James.

522. ———

He hanged them high. An authentic account of the fanatical judge who hanged eighty-eight men, by Homer Croy. New York, Duell, Sloan and Pearce; Boston, Little, Brown and co. [1952]. Cloth.

viii p., 1 l., [3]–278 p. front. (port.), plates, ports. 21 cm.
Sources: p. [239]–271; index: p. [273]–278.
Half title; "First edition" on copyright p.

A well-written book, not without humor, which gives some information on Judge Parker's background and boyhood which Harrington did not include in his *Hanging Judge*. A typographical error on page 83, Forth Smith for Fort Smith, is likely to identify the first edition. The author makes one statement about Belle Starr that I do not think he intended to make: ". . . one item in her attire was a holster which she wore becomingly at her waist. It contained two revolvers." No one wore two guns in one holster.

523. ———

Jesse James was my neighbor, by Homer Croy. New York, Duell, Sloan and Pearce [1949]. Cloth. OP.

xii p., 2 l., 3–313 p. 21 cm.
Sources, including a necrology of the bandits and a note on the James family today: p. 265–307; index: p. 309–313.
Half title.

To me this is a most refreshing book on Jesse James. The author's notes and sources cast much new light on the subject. One of the first things I do with a new book by Mr. Croy is read the index, which is invariably full of humor. In his account of Bob Ford's killing he spells Ed O. Kelly's name correctly, not as Ed O'Kelly, as so many other writers do.

524. ———

Last of the great outlaws. The story of Cole Younger, by Homer Croy. New York, Duell, Sloan and Pearce [1956]. Cloth.

x p., 1 l., 3–242 p. illus., plates, ports. 21 cm.
Sources: p. 214–235; index: p. 237–242.
Half title; "First edition" on copyright p.

Much on the Youngers, the Jameses, Belle Starr, and many of the other outlaws of that period. He has Cole Younger the father of Belle Starr's daughter, Pearl, but Cole denied it.

525. ———

Trigger marshal. The story of Chris Madsen, by Homer Croy. New York, Duell, Sloan and Pearce [1958]. Cloth.

x p., 1 l., 3–267 p. plates, ports., facsms. 21 cm.
Time clock (chronology): p. 243–245; sources: p. 246–260; index: p. 263–267.
Half title; "First edition" on copyright p.

Based upon a manuscript written by Chris Madsen himself, the book has much material on the Oklahoma outlaws, including Arkansas Tom, Ben Cravens, the Daltons, Al Jennings, Little Dick, Red Buck, Tulsa Jack, Zip Wyatt, and Marshals Heck Thomas and Bill Tilghman. He pretty well covers all the Oklahoma outlaws and calls the Jennings gang rank amateurs, which is about the same opinion most other historians have of them.

526. Crumbine, Samuel J.

Frontier doctor, by Samuel J. Crumbine, M.D. The autobiography of a pioneer on the frontier of public health. Philadelphia, Dorrance & co. [1948]. Cloth. OP.

ix, 11–284 p. 20.5 cm.
Pub. device.

The author not only did much for the public health of later Dodge City but also doctored some of the early marshals. He tells about Boot Hill.

527. Culley, John Henry (Jack)

Cattle, horses & men of the western range, by John H. (Jack) Culley. Illustrations by Katherine Field. Los Angeles, Calif., the Ward Ritchie press [1940]. Cloth. Scarce.

xvi p., 1 l., [3]–337 p. front. (port.), illus., plates. 23.5 cm.
Index: p. [333]–337.
Half title; illus. t.p.

This excellent book was written by a well-educated Englishman who came to the United States and became manager of the large Bell Ranch of New Mexico. The author devotes some space to the various gunmen of that state. Among them are

Clay Allison and Black Jack Ketchum (two chapters), and there is some information on Joel Fowler and William McGinnis. The author makes the mistake of calling Chunk Colbert by the name Chunk Cooper.

528. Cummins, Jim [James R.]

Jim Cummins' book, written by himself. The life story of the James and Younger gang and their comrades, including the operations of Quantrell's [*sic*] guerrillas, by one who rode with them. A true but terrible tale of outlawry. Illustrated. Denver, Colorado, the Reed publishing co., 1903. Pict. cloth. Very rare.

xv [1] p., [17]–191 p. front. (port.), plates, ports., facsm. 20 cm.

An exceedingly rare book giving previously untold information about the Missouri outlaws. In his old age Jim Cummins' memory was bad. I corresponded with him while he was an inmate of the Old Soldiers' Home at Higginsville, Missouri. On September 29, 1926, he wrote me that he did not remember ever having written such a book. Yet in the next sentence he wrote "The book I sent you [Burch's *Quantrell*, Item 323] was copied off my original book with about one-third of this present book added."

Cummins had been written about so exaggeratedly in wild West fiction, and in real life he was such a meek-looking man, that when he tried to give himself up after the James gang was disbanded no one would believe he was Cummins. He was never brought to trial.

529. Cunningham, Eugene

Famous in the west, by Eugene Cunningham. . . . Cover design and decorations by Forrest Wood. El Paso, Texas, Hicks-Haywood co., 1926. Pict. wrappers (col.). Exceedingly rare.

3 p.l., 25 p. front., illus. 20.5 cm.

Reprinted in a limited and numbered facsimile edition in Dallas, 1958.

This rare little pamphlet was originally published as an advertisement to be distributed by a firm dealing in cowboy-style clothes. It is said to have been published in an edition of sixty thousand copies, but when the dealer discovered how much postage it would take to distribute them, he gave up the idea and destroyed most of the copies. The author tells about the Texas Rangers and outlaws of the Southwest. The author has Billy the Kid born a "Bonney" and repeats the early legends, such as the one that his mother married in Colorado, and the one that the Kid killed the blacksmith who insulted her. The author makes the statement that Colonel Dudley declared he would not interfere in the battle at the McSween home "unless the women were fired on." According to Mrs. McSween, Dudley had little respect for women.

The author says that McSween was "too shaken" to carry a weapon, but it is a well-known fact that McSween never carried a gun because of religious scruples. The author repeats the usual legends about the Kid's escape from Lincoln and about his death, and ends by saying, "Today, so utterly has all trace of the very graves [the Kid's, Bowdre's, and O'Folliard's] vanished, that there are those who say that the Kid has never been killed."

530. ———

Triggernometry, a gallery of gunfighters. With technical notes on leather slapping as a fine art, gathered from many a loose holstered expert over the years, by Eugene Cunningham. Foreword by Eugene Manlove Rhodes. Illustrations from the Rose Collection, San Antonio. New York, the press of the Pioneers, inc., 1934. Pict. cloth. Scarce in 1st edition.

xvii p., 1 l., 441 p. illus., plates, ports. 23.5 cm.

Bibliography: p. 440–441.

Half title.

Republished, Caldwell, Idaho, the Caxton printers, ltd., in 1941, 1947 and 1952. These publishers have kept it in print to date, but the first edition is hard to come by.

This book has become a standard work and is reliable on most points. The author also corrects the legend about Wild Bill Hickok's "fight" with McCanles. He is mistaken, however, in saying that Calamity Jane captured Jack McCall with a meat cleaver in a butcher shop after he had murdered Wild Bill. It has been proved that Calamity Jane was nowhere near at the time. That was merely one of her own claims.

The author closely follows Upson's account of Billy the Kid, having him born as William H. Bonney; his parents moving to Coffeyville, Kansas, in 1862 (before that town was founded); and his mother remarrying in Colorado. He also has the Kid, at the age of twelve, killing a man who had attacked Moulton, a friend. He also follows the Upson legends about the Kid's fighting Indians and going to Mexico and to Arizona, where he killed a drunken blacksmith. He credits the Kid with killing Morton and Baker, but admits that the whole gang was shooting at Carlyle when he tried to escape. He only credits the Kid with killing eight men. He continues to misspell Tom O'Folliard's name as O'Phalliard. He agrees that Wyatt Earp never arrested Ben Thompson in Ellsworth and says that in all his research he has never found any evidence for it. Neither have I, except in Lake's account, and in those of writers who have since followed Lake blindly.

531. Cunningham, James Charles

The truth about Murietta [*sic*]; anecdotes and facts related by those who knew him and disbelieve his capture, by J. C. Cunningham. Los Angeles, Calif., Wetzel publishing co., inc. [1938]. Cloth. OP.

9 p.l., 13–286 p. 4 l. plates and ports. at front. 19.2 cm.

Gives quite a controversial version of the death of Murieta, and as proof the author records the testimony of old-timers.

532. Cunningham, Robert E.

Trial by mob, by Robert E. Cunningham. . . . Stillwater, Okla., Redland press, 1957. Stiff wrappers.

2 p.l., 24 p. 21 cm.

The lawless activities of the White Caps of early Oklahoma and their cruelties.

533. Curran, J. J.

Mr. Foley, of Salmon. A story of life in a California village. By J. J. Curran. San Jose, Calif., published by the author, printed by Melvin, Hillis & Black, 1907. Dec. cloth. Scarce.

1 p.l., 5–186 p. 17.7 cm.

Has some mention of Black Bart and the Ruggles brothers, stage robbers.

534. [Curry, Mrs. Bell]

Parsons, Labette county, Kansas. Years from 1869 to 1895. Story of the "Benders." [Parsons, Kans., Bell Bookcraft Shop, n.d.] Cloth. Scarce.

2 p.l., 117 [7] p. 22 cm.

Contains a chapter on the Benders.

535. Curtis, Albert

Fabulous San Antonio, by Albert Curtis. San Antonio, Texas, the Naylor co. [1955]. Cloth.

ix p., 8 l., 298 [1] p. plates. 21.6 cm.

Tells of the killing of Ben Thompson and King Fisher.

536. Cushing, Marshall

The story of our post office, the greatest department in all its phases. By Marshall Cushing. Illustrated with over four hundred and fifty fine engravings. Boston, Mass., A. N. Thayer & co., publishers, 1893. Pict. cloth. Scarce.

2 p.l., 1034 p. front. (port.), illus., plates, ports., facsms. 24.3 cm.

Has material on Rube Burrow, Ed Reeves, Black Bart, Ham White, and Big Jack Davis.

537. Cushman, Dan

The great North trail. America's route of the ages, by Dan Cushman. New York, Toronto, London, Sydney, McGraw-Hill book co. [1966]. Pict. cloth.

3 p.l., 383 [1] p. maps. 23.5 cm.
Sources: p. 369–374; index: p. 375–383.
Half title; "First edition" on copyright p.

There is a very good chapter on Henry Plummer and his gang of road agents, and their end by the vigilantes. The author tells something of Wild Bill Hickok's days as marshal at Abilene and has quite a bit of material on the Lincoln County War. He claims the Kid was named William H. Bonney and calls Buckshot Roberts by the name Buckshot Williams. He also misspells Hindman's name as Hindeman, and gives the Kid credit for killing Beckwith. He has Sheriff Brady with the posse which killed Tunstall. Brady was not present. He also gives the Kid credit for killing Morton and Baker and says that the Coe boys were of "desperate fame."

There is some material on the Johnson County War. The author has a Wyoming rancher, during a severe winter storm, say: "Thank God, the tally books won't freeze." The famous exhortation, "Cheer up, boys, whatever happens, the books won't freeze," is credited to a saloon keeper named Luke Murrin. He tells of the hanging of Jim Averill and Cattle Kate Watson and the killing of Nate Champion and Nick Ray. There is some mention of Wyatt Earp, Doc Holliday, Print Olive, and Soapy Smith.

D

538. Dacus, Joseph A.

Life and adventures of Frank and Jesse James, the noted western outlaws, by Hon. J. A. Dacus, Ph.D. . . . Illustrated. St. Louis, N. D. Thompson & co., publishers. . . . Chicago, J. S. Goodman . . ., 1880.

5 p.l., [11]–383 [1] p. front., illus., ports. 19 cm.
Also published in Indianapolis the same year.

539. ———

Illustrated lives and adventures of Frank and Jesse James, and the Younger brothers, the noted western outlaws, by Hon. Joseph A. Dacus. . . . New edition. Enlarged and improved with history complete to 1881. St. Louis, N. D. Thompson and co., 1881. Cloth. Scarce.

8 p.l., [13]–458 [1] p. front., illus., ports., facsm. 19 cm.

An enlarged edition with biographies of the Youngers.

540. ———

Illustrated lives and adventures of Frank and Jesse James, and the Younger brothers, the noted western outlaws, by Hon. Joseph A. Dacus. . . . Illustrated with portraits from life and numerous engravings made expressly for this book. New edition enlarged and improved with history complete to 1882, including the death and funeral of Jesse James. St. Louis, N. D. Thompson and co., 1882. Cloth. Scarce.

2 p.l., 498 p. front., illus., ports., facsm. 19 cm.

Also published in New York and Cincinnati same year.

This edition has forty-two pages on the Youngers not included in the 1880 edition and has different portraits and illustrations. All these books are more sensational than reliable. The Cincinnati edition has 498 pages; the New York edition, 520 pages; and the St. Louis edition, 458 pages. There were many more editions of this book.

541. [**Daggett, Thomas F.**]

Billy LeRoy, the Colorado bandit; or, the king of American highwaymen. A complete and authentic history of this famous young desperado. His crimes and adventures. New York, published by Richard K. Fox, Police Gazette [1881]. Pict. wrappers (col.). Rare.

2 p.l., 7–66 [10] p. front., illus. 23.8 cm.

10 p. adv. at end.

Later the same year a revised edition appeared under the title *The Life and Deeds of Billy LeRoy, Alias the Kid,* with the same imprint. It was reprinted with the original title restored in 1883.

Another of the *Police Gazette* series on criminals printed on the familiar pink paper. Purporting to be the life of Billy the Kid, it is nothing but the fruits of a vivid imagination of a hack writer, with just enough half-truths to make it confusing. The author lays the scene in Colorado instead of New Mexico; he makes his hero an actor impersonating a female character. The author has invented a brother Sam to join the Kid (in one place he calls him Arthur). Although the author calls no names, he has the killing of Bell and Olinger all wrong, and he repeats the fable about the Kid's shooting the cowboys who worked for Chisum. The book ends with a preposterous account of Billy and his brother being hanged in Del Norte, Colorado. Though a scarce collector's item, it is worthless historically.

In the early 1880's there really was a noted highwayman named Arthur Pond who used the alias Billy LeRoy. He operated in the San Juan section of Colorado, and in 1881 was sentenced to ten years in the Detroit prison. It is possible that the author of the above book had heard of this character and took the name for his story, but he leaves the impression that he was attempting to write about Billy the Kid.

542. ———

The outlaw brothers, Frank and Jesse James. Lives and adventures of the two scourges of the plains. . . . [New York], published by Richard K. Fox, proprietor of Police Gazette [1881]. Pict. wrappers. Rare.

2 p.l., 7–67 [7] p. front., illus., plan. 24.5 cm.

7 p. adv. at end; adv. verso front wrapper; adv. recto and verso back wrapper.

Later published in a revised edition with new illustrations.

Another example of the *Police Gazette's* historically worthless outlaw series, which have now become rare collector's items.

543. Dale, Edward Everett

Cow country, by Edward Everett Dale. Norman, University of Oklahoma press, 1942. Cloth.

ix p., 2 l., [3]–265 p. illus. 21 cm.

Index: p. [259]–265.

Half title; headpieces; vignette; "First edition" on copyright p.

Contains minor mention of certain outlaws and the Johnson County War.

544. Dale, Henry

Adventures and exploits of the Younger brothers, Missouri's most daring outlaws, and companions of the James boys, by Henry Dale. . . . New York, Street & Smith, 1890. Wrappers. Scarce.

[5]–191 p. front. 19 cm.

Secret Service series, No. 32.

16 p. adv. at end.

For the most part unreliable. The author says that Belle Starr's maiden name was Starr and that she married Cole Younger. The whole account is written in the sensational dime-novel style.

545. [Dalton Brothers]

The Dalton brothers and their astounding career of crime, by an eyewitness. With numerous illustrations reproduced from photographs taken on the spot. . . . Chicago, Laird & Lee, publishers, 1892. Pict. wrappers. Rare.

3 p.l., 9–220 [4] p. front., illus., facsm., plan. 19.3 cm.

Pinkerton Detective series, No. 6, 1892.

Also published in cloth. Republished by J. S. Ogilvie, New York, and reprinted again by W. F. Kelleher, Cliffside Park, N.J., in 1951.

546. ———

The Dalton brothers and their astounding career of crime, by an eye-witness. Introduction by Burton Rascoe. New York, Frederick Fell, inc., publishers, 1954. Cloth.

17 p.l., 35–251 p. illus., plates, ports. 20.9 cm.
Half title; plates and ports. inside both front and rear covers, and flyleaves.

A later reprint of Item 545. In his introduction Mr. Rascoe says that this is the "first authenticated and only exact account of what occurred on the fifth day of October, 1892, in Coffeyville, Kansas," but I think he would find that the little book by David Stewart Elliott (Item 671) is also quite correct and was written by a local editor immediately after the fight. Mr. Rascoe also disbelieves that any of the Daltons were ever in California or that they ever committed a train robbery there. But court records show that they were arrested there and placed in jail, from which they escaped. "Nearly all fictionalized stories of outlaws, including those of the Jim Reed gang, Sam Bass and the James boys, have the gimmick about an apprenticeship in California." I have never seen any account, fictional or factual, which claimed that Sam Bass was in California. When Jim Reed went there, he had no gang with him, only his wife Belle Starr. Mr. Rascoe also says that he can find no record to substantiate that Frank Dalton was ever a U.S. deputy marshal. He has just failed to look in the right places.

547. ———

The Dalton gang, the famous gang of outlaws. [Racine, Wisc., Whitman publishing co., n.d.] Pict. wrappers (col.). Scarce.

3–182 [9] p. 17.2 cm.
Last 9 p. adv.

548. Dalton, Emmett

Beyond the law, by Emmett Dalton, only survivor of the famous Dalton gang. New York, J. S. Ogilvie publishing co., 1918. Wrappers. Scarce. Also pub. in cloth.

vi, iii, 5–190 p. front., illus. 18.3 cm.
Copyright notice on t.p.

549. ———

When the Daltons rode, by Emmett Dalton, in collaboration with Jack Jungmeyer. Garden City, N.Y., Doubleday, Doran & co., inc., 1931. Pict. cloth. Scarce.

viii, 313 p. front. (port.), plates, ports. 21.5 cm.
Half title; illus. end papers; vignette; untrimmed; "First edition" on copyright p.
Republished in 1937 under the imprint of Sun Dial press.

550. Dalton, Kit

Under the black flag, by Captain Kit Dalton, a Confederate soldier. A guerrilla captain under the fearless leader Quantrell [*sic*] and a border outlaw for seventeen years following the surrender of the Confederacy. Associated with the most noted band of free booters the world has ever known. [Memphis, Tenn., Lockhart publishing co., 1914.] Stiff pict. wrappers. Scarce.

2–252 p. front., illus., plates, ports. 19.6 cm.
Text starts on verso of t.p.

One cannot understand why a writer like this one, supposedly writing about his own life, could possibly make the statements he does, unless in his dotage his memory has turned to fantastic hallucinations. Not only does he say that Belle Starr was a half-blood Cherokee and was educated in the Carlisle Indian School, but also he claims to have served as marshal with Wild Bill Hickok at Deadwood, Colorado (!), and later in the same capacity at Cheyenne. "I know nothing," he writes, "of William [*sic*] Hickok's career after we parted in Cheyenne except that he was assassinated several years later in Tombstone, Arizona." Hickok was not named William, he was never marshal of either Deadwood or Cheyenne, and he was not killed in Tombstone.

The author states that Bob Ford was shot through a window supposedly by "some luckless fellow who had lost his pile in Bob's infamous joint," and adds, "but I had no hand in the killing." And though he claims to have fought with Quantrill, he does not even know Quantrill's given name, but calls him Charles William. There are many, many other mistakes which have been enumerated in my *Burs Under the Saddle*.

551. Dalton, Rev. William J.

The life of Father Bernard Donnelly, with historical sketches of Kansas City, St. Louis and Independence, Missouri, by Rev. William J. Dalton. Kansas City, Mo., published by Grimes-Joyce printing co., 1921. Cloth. Scarce.

8 p.l., [19]–197 p. plates. 19.5 cm.

Tells the story about Jesse James saving the life of Father Kennedy who had once befriended him.

552. Dana, Rocky, and Marie Harrington

The blonde ranchero. Memories of Juan Francisco Dana as told to Rocky

Dana and Marie Harrington. Los Angeles, Calif., Dawson's book shop [1960]. Cloth. Scarce.

ix, 11–133 p. front. (port.), illus., plates, ports., facsms. 21.7 cm.

Half title; pub. device.

Printed in an edition of five hundred copies, this little book has a chapter on the vigilantes and outlaws of California such as Murieta, Jack Powers, Juan Soto, Joaquín Valenzuela, and Solomon Pico.

553. Dane, G. Ezra

Ghost town. Wherein is told much that is wonderful, laughable, and tragic, and some that is hard to believe, about life during the gold rush and later in the town of Columbia on California's mother lode, as remembered by the oldest inhabitants and here for the first time set down, [by] G. Ezra Dane, in collaboration with Beatrice J. Dane. Illustrated by Fred Ludekens. . . . New York, Tudor publishing co. [1941]. Pict. cloth. Scarce.

xx p., 1 l., 311 p. illus. (full p. plates). 22.3 cm.

Half title; headpieces.

A chapter on Murieta and Vásquez and another on Black Bart. The author follows most of the old legends about Murieta, does not give Vásquez much space, but devotes a whole chapter to Black Bart.

554. Daniels, Jonathan

The devil's backbone. The story of the Natchez trace, by Jonathan Daniels, with map and headpieces by the Dillons. New York, Toronto, London, McGraw-Hill Book co., inc. [1962]. Cloth.

4 p.l., 3–278 [1] p. illus. (headpieces), map (front end papers). 23.4 cm.

Sources and acknowledgments: p. 259–267; index: p. 269–278.

Illus. t.p.

Deals with the bandits of the Natchez Trace, such as Joseph Hare, the Harpes, the Mason gang, and John A. Murrell.

555. Darby, Ada Claire

"Show me" Missouri, by Ada Claire Darby. . . . Illustrated by Ellen Word Carter. Kansas City, Missouri, Burton publishing co., publishers [1938]. Buckram. OP.

2 p.l., 9–142 p. front., illus. 20.5 cm.

Map on end papers; map on cover.

In a chapter on St. Joseph, Missouri, the author tells of the death of Jesse James.

556. Darley, Rev. George M.

Pioneering in the San Juan. Personal reminiscences of work done in southwestern Colorado during the "Great San Juan Excitement." By Rev. George M. Darley. . . . Chicago, New York, Toronto, Fleming H. Revell co., 1899. Pict. cloth. Scarce.

5 p.l., 15–225 [1] p. front. (port with tissue), plates. 19.8 cm.

Contains a chapter on lawlessness.

557. David, Robert Beebe

Malcolm Campbell, sheriff, by Robert B. David. The reminiscences of the greatest frontier sheriff in the history of the Platte valley, and the famous Johnson county invasion of 1892. Caspar, Wyo., Wyomingana, inc. [1932]. Cloth. Scarce.

4 p.l., [7]–361 [5] p. front., plates, ports., maps, facsms., plan. 20.2 cm.
Half title; chronological table of contents at end.

A good account of the Johnson County War, and some material on Alferd Packer.

558. Davidson, Levette J., and Forrester Blake (eds.)

Rocky mountain tales. Edited by Levette J. Davidson and Forrester Blake, with drawings by Skelly. Norman, University of Oklahoma press, 1947. Cloth. OP.

xiv p., 1 l., 3–302 p. illus. 22 cm.
Index: p. 293–302.
Half title; "First edition" on copyright p.

Has some information on John Reynolds and Joseph Slade.

559. Davidson, Lorenzo D.

Down through the years. A collection of random observations on the life and times of these last past and most thrilling eight decades, from the pen of one who has enjoyed them thoroughly, by Lorenzo D. Davidson. Hopkins, Minn., published by the Hennepin County Review, 1938. Cloth. Scarce.

5 p.l., 149 p. 19.8 cm.

Has a chapter on the James boys and Polk Wells. The author is mistaken in saying that Polk Wells died in prison.

560. Davie, John L.

My own story, by John L. Davie, mayor emeritus of the city of Oakland, California. Oakland, the Post-Enquirer publishing co., 1931. Stiff wrappers. Scarce.

4 p.l., 1 p., [14]–174 p. front., plates, ports. 23.3 cm.
Double column.

Has some scattered material on outlaws.

561. Davis, Clyde Brion

The Arkansas, by Clyde Brion Davis; illustrated by Donald McKay. New York, Toronto, Farrar & Rinehart, inc. [1940]. Cloth. OP.

x p., 1 l., 3–340 p. front. (map). 20.9 cm.
Rivers of America series.
Acknowledgments: p. 328–330; index: p. 331–340.
Half title; illus. end papers; illus. t.p.; first edition: "F R" in pub. device on copyright p.

The author gives an accurate sketch of Judge Parker's court and tells about the bad men and peace officers of Dodge City, such as Bill Tilghman and Bat Masterson.

562. Davis, George Wesley

Sketches of Butte (from vigilante days to prohibition), by George Wesley Davis. Boston, the Cornhill co. [1921]. Cloth. Scarce.

vi p., 3 l., 3–179 p. plates, ports. 19.3 cm.
Half title; pub. device.

Contains a chapter on the Montana vigilantes and outlaws.

563. Davis, Jean

Shallow diggin's. Tales from Montana's ghost towns. Compiled by Jean Davis. Illustrated with photographs. Caldwell, Idaho, the Caxton printers, ltd., 1963. Cloth.

8 p.l., [17]–375 [2] p. plates. 21.6 cm.
Bibliography: p. [376]; index: p. [377].

Contains information about the Plummer gang, the Montana vigilantes, the hanging of Slade, the killing of Jules Reni, the killing of Pike Landusky by Kid Curry, and the hanging of Plummer and his followers.

564. Davis, Mary Lee

Sourdough gold. The log of a Yukon adventure, by Mary Lee Davis. . . . With maps by the author and illustrated by photographs. Boston, W. A. Wilde co., publishers [1933]. Cloth. OP.

9 p.l., 17–351 p. front., plates, ports., maps (1 large fold. at end). 22.2 cm.
Half title; pub. device.

Tells of the many rackets Soapy Smith worked while in Skagway, and of his death and the breaking up of his gang.

565. ———

Uncle Sam's attic. The intimate story of Alaska, by Mary Lee Davis. Illustrated by author's photographs. Boston, Mass., W. A. Wilder co. [1930]. Cloth. OP.

xvi p., 402 p. front. (port.), plates, ports., map. 22 cm.
Pub. device.

Has a chapter on Soapy Smith and his death.

566. Davis, Richard Harding

The west from a car window, by Richard Harding Davis. . . . Illustrated. New York, Harper & brothers . . ., 1892. Pict. cloth. Scarce.

5 p.l., 3–242 [1] p. front., illus., plates. 19 cm.
Pub. device.

In a chapter on Creede, Colorado, the author tells of Soapy Smith and Bob Ford. Of Ford's killing of Jesse James he writes "Ford never quite recovered from the fright he received when he found out who it was he killed." That is rather preposterous, for Ford knew Jesse well and had planned the killing for some time. In the last chapter the author tells of some of Ben Thompson's exploits and of his killing. He spells Bat Masterson's name Masterden.

567. Davis, Robert H., and Arthur B. Maurice

The calif of Bagdad, being Arabian night flashes of the life, letters and work of O. Henry, William Sydney Porter, [by] Robert H. Davis and Arthur B. Maurice. New York, London, D. Appleton and co., MCMXXXI. Cloth. Scarce.

xi p., 1 l., 3–411 p. front. (port.), illus., plates (1 col.), ports., facsms. 22.4 cm.
Index: p. 403–411.
Half title; pub. device; untrimmed; first edition: figure (1) at end of index.

Has much on Al Jennings' association with O. Henry.

568. Davis, Sam P. (ed.)

The history of Nevada. Edited by Sam P. Davis. . . . Illustrated. Reno, Nev., Los Angeles, Calif., published by the Elms publishing co., 1913. Cloth. Pub. in two volumes. Scarce.

Vol. I, 3 p.l., [11]–646 p. front. (ports. with tissue), plate, ports., (part with tissues). 24.3 cm.
Vol. II, 647–1279, i–xxiii p. front. (with tissue), plates, ports., (part with tissues). 24.3 cm.
Index (Vol. II): p. i-xxiii.

Has a chapter on lawlessness and such bad men as Jack Davis, Sam Langford, and Farmer Peel.

569. Dawley, T. R.

Mercedes; or, the outlaw's child. An original tale of California, the scenes of which are laid at the time mobs, riots and lawless men were as plenty in San Francisco as golden slugs. New York, 1866. Pict. wrappers. Rare.

67 p. 17.5 cm.

An early example of the dime novel about western outlaws.

570. Dawson, Charles

Pioneer tales of the Oregon trail and of Jefferson county, by Charles Dawson. Topeka, Kans., Crane & co., 1912. Pict. cloth. Scarce.

xv, 488 p. front. (port.), ports., maps (1 col.), tables. 23.4 cm.

This book is one of the first in which the author tried to publish a correct account of the Hickok-McCanles trouble and to show "the wide variance between the truth and fiction as told by Emerson Hough" (Item 1038). He was also the first to claim that Wild Bill shot McCanles from behind a curtain and ambushed Woods and Gordon from an unseen shelter.

"Emerson Hough's account of this affair," he writes, "is given [and he quotes nearly two pages from Hough's *Story of the Outlaw*] to show the wide variance between truth and fiction. Hough wrote this story some forty years ago, securing the data many times at second-hand without personal investigation. It is indeed unfortunate that Hough gave to the world such an erroneous history of this affair." He does not seem to know that Hough copied his misinformation from Buel.

571. Day, B. F.

Gene Rhodes, cowboy (Eugene Manlove Rhodes), by B. F. Day. Illustrated by Lorance F. Bjorklund. New York, Julian Messner, inc. [1954]. Cloth.

6 p.l., 13–192 p. illus. 21.5 cm.
Books [and other writings] by Rhodes: p. 185–187; index: p. 189–192.
Half title; illus. t.p.; illus. chapter headings.

Contains some material about the Apache Kid, Billy the Kid, Bill Doolin, and the Dalton gang.

572. Day, Donald

Big country: Texas, by Donald Day. Edited by Erskine Caldwell. New York, Duell, Sloan & Pearce [1947]. Cloth. OP.

x p., 1 l., 3–6 p., 1 l., 9–326 p. 21.7 cm.
[American Folkways series.]
Index: p. 316–326.

Half title.

The author makes the statement that the Alamo Saloon, in Abilene, Kansas, was presided over by Wild Bill Hickok. It is true that he did a lot of gambling there, but he never worked in it or owned it.

573. Day, Jack Hays

The Sutton-Taylor feud, by Jack Hays Day. Authentic. [San Antonio, produced by the presses of Sid Murray & son, printers, n.d.] Stiff wrappers. Scarce.

6 p.l., 9–40 p. front., plates, ports. 21.5 cm.

This scarce little book tells some of the inside facts of the feud from the Taylor side by one of the participants and a kinsman of the Taylors.

574. DeBarth, Joe

The life and adventures of Frank Grouard, chief of scouts, U. S. A., by Joe DeBarth. Illustrated. St. Joseph, Mo., Combe printing co. [1894]. Pict. cloth. Rare.

xii p., 6 l., [21]–545 p. front. (port.), plates, ports. 22.8 cm.

Contains a chapter on Frank and Jesse James.

575. Debo, Angie

Prairie city, the story of an American community, by Angie Debo. New York, Alfred A. Knopf, 1944. Cloth. OP.

xiv p., 1 l., 3–245, i–viii p. plates. 21.8 cm.
Index: p. i–viii.
Half title; vignette; untrimmed.

Has a mention of Dick Yeager and Isaac Black, Oklahoma outlaws.

576. ———

Tulsa; from Creek town to oil capital. By Angie Debo. Norman, University of Oklahoma press, MCMXLIII. Cloth. OP.

xii p., 1 l., 3–123 p. plates, map. 20.5 cm.
Index: p. 119–123.
Half title.

Has some information on the various outlaws of Oklahoma, such as the Cook gang, the Glass gang, and the Dalton gang.

577. ——— (ed.)

The cowman's southwest, being the reminiscences of Oliver Nelson, freighter, camp cook, cowboy, frontiersman in Kansas, Indian territory, Texas and Oklahoma, 1878–1893. Edited by Angie Debo. . . . Glendale, Calif., the Arthur H. Clark co., 1953. Cloth.

9 p.l., [19]–343 p. front. (map), plates, cattle brands, map. 24 cm.
Index: p. [333]–343.
Half title: "Western Frontiersman Series IV"; pub. device; untrimmed.

A most interesting book of reminiscences, with some material on many of the outlaws of Oklahoma and Texas, telling, among other things, of the Dalton raid at Coffeyville and the Henry Brown raid on the bank at Medicine Lodge. Has much information on Billy the Kid and some on John Wesley Hardin.

578. Defenders

and offenders. New York, D. Buchner & co. [1888]. Dec. cloth. Rare.

[124] p. (no pagination). ports. (col.). 23.6 cm.

Has portraits of criminals, many of them western outlaws, with a short sketch of each one on the facing page. Includes Jim Burrow, Charles Parker, Frederick Witrock, Edward Kinney, and Tom Price (The last three were members of the Jim Cummings gang).

579. Delay, Peter J.

History of Yuba and Sutter counties, California, with biographical sketches of the leading men and women of the counties who have been identified with their growth and development from the early days to the present. History by Peter J. Delay. Illustrated. . . . Los Angeles, Calif., Historic Record co., 1924. Three-quarter leather. Scarce.

11 p.l., [39]–1328 p. plates, ports. 27.5 cm.

Contains much material on Tom Bell and some minor information on Joaquín Murieta.

580. Delony, Lewis S.

40 years a peace officer. A true story of lawlessness and adventure in the early days in southwest Texas, by Lewis S. Delony. [N.p., n.d.] Stiff pict. wrappers. (Cover title.) Scarce.

2 p.l., 61 p. 21.8 cm.
First 8 p. unnumbered.
Double column; stapled.

This interesting and little-known book contains material on the Taylor-Sutton feud, the hanging of Bill Longley, and the capture and killing of John Wesley Hardin, as well as many other crimes in Texas. The author errs, however, in saying that John Selman killed Sam Bass.

581. DeMilt, A. P.

Story of an old town, with reminiscences of early Nebraska and biographies of pioneers, by A. P. DeMilt. A narrative of truth describing the birth of Nebraska and its progress, of its oldest towns, and its first settlers. Omaha, Nebr., published by Douglas printing co., 1902. Pict. cloth. Scarce.

2 p.l., [7]–173 p. illus., plates, ports. 22.2 cm.

In Chapter IV the author tells about the James boys' mother as a schoolteacher in the town of which he writes—Decatur, Nebraska. He tells also about her losing an arm in the explosion of the bomb, but he has all his facts wrong. "This cruel and blood-thirsty act was perpetuated by the villainous Quantrell [*sic*] and his rebel outlaws, venting their terrible spleen upon an innocent mother and child for the spite and hatred they held for her sons, Jesse and Frank." He claims that the Quantrill men also waylaid and murdered the father and that "the latter atrocious act was what incited Frank and Jesse to become outlaws, and over the dead body of their murdered father they registered an oath in heaven that neither would rest until the last member of Quantrell's band bit the dust of death with their boots on." We know, of course, that the James boys were members of Quantrill's forces and not his enemies and that Pinkerton detectives threw the bomb. The author claims that the James boys succeeded in hounding Quantrill and his entire gang to their deaths. He states that Charlie Ford was killed and that Bob Ford committed suicide—just the opposite of what really happened. The book is filled with misspelled words and poor grammar, such as "he learnt" for "he taught." Line 6 on page 7 should be "topography" instead of "typography." He also mentions the hanging of Henry Plummer.

582. Denison, Merrill

Klondike Mike. An Alaskan odyssey, by Merrill Denison. New York, Morrow & co., 1943. Cloth. OP.

xi p., 10 l., 3–393 p. plates, ports., map, facsms. 21 cm.
Half title; device; 8 p. plates and ports. before text.
Republished in Seattle, Wash., by Leslie O. Johnson in 1948.

This well-written story of the Far North gives some new and interesting material on Soapy Smith during his stay in Skagway, where he met his death.

583. Denton, B. E. (Cyclone)

A two-gun cyclone. A true story, by B. E. (Cyclone) Denton. Illustrated by Jack Patton. Dallas, Texas, B. E. Denton . . . [1927]. Pict. cloth. Scarce.

viii p., 2 l., 145 p. front. (port.), plates (1 col.). 19.4 cm.
Half title.

A little book of reminiscences written by an old-timer after he had reached his late seventies. He was a typical old-time Texas cowboy, uneducated and bighearted. I knew him well, and he could have told a much better story if he had tried.

584. De Veny, William

The establishment of law and order on western plains, by William De Veny. Portland, Oreg., Optimist print . . ., 1915. Wrappers. Exceedingly rare.

4 p.l., 9–120 p. illus., plates, port. (group). 17 cm.

The author states in his preface that it was his intention "of having about one hundred copies printed to be used by my family and myself for gifts to a few personal friends." There is no auction record of this book, and, according to all the information I was able to unearth, there was only one copy known to authorities, that one being locked in a vault of the Oregon Historical Society. However, William F. Kelleher, a book dealer in New Jersey, succeeded in finding another copy, which soon rested upon a shelf in my personal library.

The book deals largely with lawlessness in the various Kansas county-seat fights and has some material on Dodge City, where the author lived in its early days. He writes of Wyatt Earp, Mysterious Dave Mathers, Luke Short, and others.

585. Devil Anse;

or, the Hatfield-McCoy outlaws. A full and complete history of the deadly feud existing between the Hatfield and McCoy clans. Thrillingly narrated and graphically illustrated.

[Published with]

Trujillo; or, Bob Montclair, the terror of El Dorado. A truthful portrayal of the life and adventures of this noted bandit and desperado. Profusely illustrated. New York, Richard K. Fox, publisher, 1889. Pict. wrappers. Rare.

Part I, [Devil Anse] 2 p.l., [5]–32 p. front., illus.
Part II, [Trujillo] 2 p.l., [5]–28 p. front., illus. 21.8 cm.
Double column.

Another of those familiar pink-paper *Police Gazette* publications of no historical value, but now a collector's item. Though it is claimed that the latter section is a "truthful" account of a "noted" bandit, the character has been created out of whole cloth.

586. Dewey, Frederick H.

Spanish Jack, the mountain bandit; or, the pledge of life. New York, Beadle and Adams, 1873. Pict. wrappers. Rare.

100 p. 16.5 cm.

The story of an outlaw who appeared between San Francisco and San Diego—in the author's mind. Another example of the early Beadle novels, this one from Starr's American Novel series.

587. DeWolf, J. H.

Pawnee Bill (Major Gordon W. Lillie), his experiences and adventures on the western plains; or, from the saddle of a "cowboy and ranger" to the chair of a "bank president," by J. H. DeWolf. [N.p.], published by Pawnee Bill's Historic Wild West co., 1902. Col. pict. boards. Rare.

> 4 p.l., 13–108 p. illus., front., plates, ports. 23.7 cm.
> Vignette.

Contains some information on the James brothers.

588. Dibble, Roy Floyd

Strenuous Americans, [by] R. F. Dibble. . . . New York, Boni and Liveright, publishers [1923]. Cloth. Scarce.

> 9 p.l., 15–370 p. front. (port. with signature in facsm.), ports. 22.4 cm.
> Short bibliography after each chapter.
> Half title; pub. device; untrimmed.

Chapter I is about Jesse James.

589. Dick, Everett

The sod-house frontier, 1854–1890. A social history of the northern plains from the creation of Kansas & Nebraska to the admission of the Dakotas, by Everett Dick. . . . Illustrated. New York, London, D. Appleton-Century co., inc., 1937. Pict. cloth. OP.

> xviii p., 1 l., 550 p. illus., plates. 22.8 cm.
> Bibliography: p. 519–528; index: p. 529–550.
> Half title; pub. device; untrimmed; first edition: figure (1) at end of index.
> Reprinted in 1938 with same imprint and then 15 years later [1953] by Johnson publishing co., of Lincoln, Nebr.

A scholarly book which covers life on the frontier thoroughly. Contains a chapter on lawlessness and the vigilantes and another on the homesteader-cattleman war of the early frontier.

590. ———

Vanguards of the frontier. A social history of the northern plains and the Rocky mountains from the earliest white contacts to the coming of the homesteader, by Everett Dick. . . . Illustrated. New York, London, D. Appleton-Century co., inc., 1941. Pict. cloth. OP.

> xvi p., 1 l., 574 p. front., plates. 23 cm.
> Bibliography: p. 519–545; index: p. 547–574.

Half title; map on end papers; pub. device; untrimmed; first edition: figure (1) at end of index.

Another extensive work by this author touching upon, among many other subjects, vigilantes and the Johnson County War.

591. Dickson, Arthur Jerome (ed.)

Covered wagon days. A journey across the plains in the sixties, and pioneer days in the northwest. From the private journals of Albert Jerome Dickson, edited by Arthur Jerome Dickson. Cleveland, the Arthur H. Clark co., 1929. Cloth. Scarce.

8 p.l., [19]–287 p. front., plates, ports. (with tissues), fold. map at end. 24.6 cm.
Index: p. [281]–287.
Half title; pub. device; untrimmed; gilt top.

An excellent history based on the journals of a man who went west in the early days. He gives some firsthand information about such outlaws as Henry Plummer and Joseph Slade and about the vigilantes of Virginia City.

592. Dickson, Samuel

San Francisco is your home, by Samuel Dickson. Stanford, Calif., Stanford University press [1947]. Pict. boards. OP.

viii p., 1 l., 3–262 p. illus. 22.2 cm.
Acknowledgments: p. 256–258; index: p. 259–262.
Half title; end papers same as covers; illus. t.p.

Contains a long chapter on Black Bart.

593. ———

Tales of San Francisco. Comprising San Francisco Is Your Home, San Francisco Kaleidoscope and the Streets of San Francisco, [by] Samuel Dickson. Stanford, Calif., Stanford University press, 1957. Pict. cloth. OP.

viii p., 1 l., 3–711 p. 22.5 cm.
Acknowledgments: p. 699; index: p. 703–711.
Half title; double illus. t.p.

Has a chapter on Black Bart and material on Murieta.

594. Dillon, Richard H. (ed.)

California trail herd. The 1850 Missouri-to-California journal of Cyrus C. Loveland. Edited and annotated by Richard H. Dillon. Los Gatos, Calif., the Talisman press, 1961. Cloth.

4 p.l., 13–137 [1] p. front. 23.7 cm.
Appendix: p. 125–126; index: p. 128–137.

Half title; illus. t.p.; map on end papers.

Has some mention of Murieta, Vásquez, and Jack Powers.

595. Dils, Lenore

Horny Toad man, by Lenore Dils. [El Paso, Texas], Boots and Saddle press [1966]. Pict. cloth.

4 p.l., 190 p. front., plates, ports., facsms. 23.5 cm.

Acknowledgments: p. 182–183; bibliography: p. 183; index: p. 184–190.

Illus. map on end papers; illus. t.p.; colophon: Boots and Saddle press [No. ——] and signed by author; headpieces.

The history of the early-day Horny Toad Division of the Santa Fe Railroad in New Mexico. There is mention of such gunmen and outlaws as Pat Garrett, Bat Masterson, George Scarborough, Dallas Stoudenmire, Jeff Milton, J. B. Gillett, Billy the Kid, Bass Outlaw, and John Wesley Hardin, as well as some new material on Burt Mossman. The author is mistaken in saying that Bat Masterson was sheriff of Dodge. He was sheriff of Ford County.

596. Dimsdale, Thomas Josiah

The vigilantes of Montana; or, popular justice in the Rocky mountains. Being a correct and impartial narrative of the chase, trial, capture and execution of Henry Plummer's road agent band, together with accounts of the lives and crimes of many of the robbers and desperadoes, the whole being interspersed with sketches of life in the mining camps of the "Far West"; forming the only reliable work on the subject ever offered the public, by Prof. Thos. J. Dimsdale. Virginia City, M.T., Montana Post press, D. W. Tilton & co., book and job printers, 1866. Pict. wrappers. Exceedingly rare.

iv, [5]–228 [2] p. 16 cm.

2 p. adv. at end; adv. verso front wrapper; adv. recto and verso back wrapper.

Republished in 1882, 1915, and later, all editions being issued by different publishers except the second. The third edition in 1915 was issued by Al Noyes, with footnotes and illustrations and with an appended history of Southern Montana.

4 p.l., [9]–290 p. front., plates, ports., facsms. 24 cm.

Table of contents labeled "index" and placed at end.

There have been many subsequent reprints, including one by the University of Oklahoma Press as the first of the Western Frontier Library Series.

xii p., 1 l., 2–268 p. 19.6 cm. Boards.

Half title.

The original edition is said to be the first book produced by a printing press in

Montana. Perhaps no book excells Dimsdale's in presenting the picture of the lawless conditions that characterized the mining camps of the Rocky Mountain country. The author was editor of the Virginia City *Montana Post* and a participant in the extraordinary campaign against lawlessness. The book ran serially in the *Post* before being published in book form.

597. Dixey, Harry (pseud.)

The Collis express robbers [or hunting down two desperate criminals, by Harry Dixey]. New York, Street and Smith co., Oct. 20, 1897. Pict. wrappers. Rare.

31 p. 21.3 cm.
No. 449 of the Old Log Cabin series.
Double column.

A dime-novel version of the activities of the Evans-Sontag "gang," including its California train robberies.

598. Dixon, William Hepworth

White conquest, by William Hepworth Dixon. In two volumes. London, Chatto and Windus, Piccadilly, 1876. Cloth. Rare.

Vol. I, viii, 356 [12] p. 23 cm.
Half title; vignette; 12 p. adv. at end.
Vol. II, vi, 373 p. 23 cm.
Half title; vignette.

Volume I has four chapters on Vásquez, giving a fairly comprehensive history of this outlaw. The book was translated into French, and most of it appeared in a French weekly the same year. The name of the weekly was *Le Tour du Monde nouveau Journal des Voyages*. Publié sous la Direction de M. Edouard Charton. . . . Librarie Hachette et cie. . . . Paris . . . ., 1876. The translation, entitled "La Conquête Blanch," is by William Hepworth Dixon, and appeared in the February 19, 1876, issue, No. 789 in the sixteenth year of publication.

599. Dobie, J. Frank

Apache gold & Yaqui silver, by J. Frank Dobie. Illustrated by Tom Lea. Boston, Little, Brown and co., 1939. Cloth.

xvii p., 1 l., 3–366 p. front. (col.), illus., plates (col.), plan. 22.5 cm.
Appendix: p. 357–366.
Half title; vignette.
Colophon: "Two hundred and sixty-five numbered copies of this Sierra Madre edition have been printed . . . and autographed by the author and . . . artist. This is No. ——." Also published in a trade edition.

This fascinating book on lost mines contains some interesting material on the Apache Kid.

600. ———

Coronado's children. Tales of the lost mines and buried treasures of the southwest, by J. Frank Dobie. Illustrated by Ben Carlton Mead. Dallas, Texas, the Southwest press [1930]. Pict. cloth.

xv, 367 p. front., illus., plates, map, charts. 24 cm.
Notes: p. 343–359; glossary: p. 361–367.
Map on end papers; tailpieces; device; untrimmed.

Republished many times, but the first state can be identified by the dedication. The original manuscript read in part: " . . . to the memory of my father R. J. Dobie, a clean cowman of the Texas soil." The publishers deleted the word "clean," an act which displeased the author, and the word was restored in subsequent editions. This is another book on lost mines. In the chapter entitled "*Los Muertos No Hablan*" there is some information on Zwing Hunt and Russian Bill.

601. ———

Cow people, [by] J. Frank Dobie, with photos. Boston, Toronto, Little, Brown and co. [1964]. Fabrikoid.

x p., 2 l., 3–305 p. illus., plates, ports., facsm. 21.5 cm.
Index: p. 301–305.
Half title; pub. device; "First edition" on copyright p.

Contains some information on Billy the Kid and Henry Brown. This is the last book Mr. Dobie wrote before his death. He had just received an advance copy and had read a few chapters before lying down to take an afternoon nap from which he never awoke. Some enterprising bookman had a few copies bound in leather, and they immediately brought an exorbitant price.

602. ———

The flavor of Texas, by J. Frank Dobie, with illustrations by Alexander Hogue. Dallas, Dealey and Lowe, 1936. Cloth.

6 p.l., 287 p. front., illus. 22.5 cm.
Index: p. [285]–287.

Has some information on Clay Allison and other gunmen.

603. ———

Guide to life and literature of the southwest, with a few observations, by J. Frank Dobie. Illustrated. Austin, University of Texas press, 1943. Wrappers. Also published in cloth.

2 p.l., [7]–111 p. front., illus., plates, music. 22.8 cm.

This work, originally mimeographed for distribution to the author's students, was later printed in wrappers, with a few bound in cloth. It was not for sale, but for free distribution, although a few copies did reach the shelves of booksellers. The same plates were loaned to Southern Methodist University Press, and a run was made under that imprint. The book is not a true bibliography but an excellent check list with comments on many western books, some of which deal with outlaws.

604. ———

Guide to life and literature of the southwest. Revised and enlarged in both knowledge and wisdom, [by] J. Frank Dobie. Dallas, Southern Methodist University press, 1952. Cloth.

viii, 222 p. illus., music. 23.6 cm.
Index: p. 197–222.
Half title; double t.p.; facsm. of signature on cover.

A greatly enlarged edition of the original. In writing about Pat Garrett's book on Billy the Kid, the author misspells Ash Upson's name as Upton. At first I thought this might be a typographical error, but the same mistake occurs in the index.

605. ———

Tales of old-time Texas, [by] J. Frank Dobie. Illustrated by Barbara Latham. Boston, Toronto, Little, Brown and co. [1955]. Cloth and boards.

xvi p., 1 l., [3]–336 p. front., illus., plates. 21.5 cm.
Notes and credits: p. [313]–327; index: p. [329]–336.
Half title; pub. device; "First edition" on copyright p.

Contains a chapter on Sam Bass.

606. ———

A vaquero of the brush country, by J. Frank Dobie, partly from the reminiscences of John Young. Illustrated by Justin C. Gruelle. Dallas, Texas, the Southwest press, 1929. Cloth and boards (imt. rattlesnake skin).

xv, 314 p. front. (col.), illus., plates, facsm. 24 cm.
Appendix: p. 299–303; index: p. 305–314.
Map on end papers; pub. device; untrimmed.

This is Mr. Dobie's first book, and the first edition may be identified by the word "river" after "Río Grande" on the map on the end papers. The author told me "I have always had a particular dislike for the redundance of 'river' in conjunction with 'Rio.' When I found this idiotic redundancy in my own book I was not happy. I had not seen the proof of these end papers. I immediately had 'river' taken out and also made other corrections." A few copies of the second edition came out before the change was made.

The plates of the original book were destroyed, and when the Southwest Press went out of business it turned the copyright back to the author. Grosset & Dunlap then reset the book in 1934, but later ceased printing it and turned the plates back to the author. He then let Little, Brown and Company have them, and that publisher has subsequently kept the book in print. In fact most of Mr. Dobie's books are kept in print, many having been reprinted since his death.

This book contains some sidelights on such gunmen as King Fisher, Ben Thompson, and Billy the Kid.

607. ——— (ed.)

Southwestern lore, edited by J. Frank Dobie. Publications of the Texas Folk-lore Society, No. IX, 1931. . . . Dallas, the Southwest press [1931]. Fabrikoid.

v, 198 [1] p. illus., music. 23.4 cm.
Index: p. 193–198.

In a chapter on folklore shooting there is much debunking of the marvelous shooting of such gunmen and outlaws as Wild Bill Hickok and Billy the Kid.

608. Doctor, Joseph E.

Shotguns on Sunday, by Joseph E. Doctor. Los Angeles, Westernlore press [1958]. Pict. cloth.

5 p.l., 11–230 p. plates, port. 21 cm.
Half title; headpieces.

The life of Jim McKinney, one of the West's last bad men. Also has material on other outlaws, such as the Daltons, the Jameses, Evans, and Sontag and on the O K Corral fight and other western battles. The author claims that McKinney was not well known because he did not have a "press agent," as so many others did. "The power of press agentry," the author writes, "in sustaining an outlaw's reputation is well demonstrated by the fact that one of the West's best known desperadoes, Joaquín Murietta [*sic*] did not exist at all except in the imagination of a learned Cherokee who made him up in a fictional pot-boiler that ultimately passed as truth."

609. [Dodge City]

"Howdy," this is your official Dodge City greeter and guide, cowboy capital of the world. . . . Dodge City, Kans., [Strange & Hetzell publishing co., 1954]. Stiff pict. wrappers. Scarce.

3 p.l., 5–70 p. plates, ports., fold. map at end. 22.6 cm.
Adv. scattered throughout.

Has chapters on Wyatt Earp and Boot Hill. Mentions most of the Dodge City gunmen.

610. ———

World famous Boot Hill. They buried them with their boots on. [N.p., n.d.] Leaflet.

4 p. 15.2 cm.

Issued by the Junior Chamber of Commerce of Dodge City, the leaflet has some information on Bat Masterson, Ed Masterson, Wyatt Earp, and others.

611. Donaghey, George Washington

Autobiographical sketch of George W. Donaghey. The first three stages in the drama of life . . ., [by George W. Donaghey. N.p. [Little Rock], 1924]. Pict. wrappers. (Cover title.) Scarce.

[5]–31 [1] p. front. (port.). 26 cm.
Double column.

The author, onetime governor of Arkansas, tells of his early experiences as a cowboy in Texas. He makes some mention of Bill Longley and Sam Bass.

612. Donald, Jay

Outlaws of the border. A complete and authentic history of the lives of Frank and Jesse James, the Younger brothers, and their robber companions, including Quantrell [*sic*] and his noted guerrillas, the greatest bandits the world has ever known. A wonderful record of crime and its consequences, drawn with great care from reliable sources. A thrilling narrative, vividly written by Jay Donald. Fully illustrated. Chicago, Coburn & Newman publishing co. . . ., 1882. Pict. cloth. Scarce.

ix, 11–520 p. front., plates, ports. 19.7 cm.
Republished the same year in both Philadelphia and Cincinnati.

One of the better early histories of the Jameses and the Youngers. Like so many other writers on the James boys, this author seems determined to bring the Jameses into the Big Springs holdup of the Union Pacific, which was engineered by Joel Collins and Sam Bass. Like many others, too, he is wrong about the amount of money obtained in the robbery, stating that they got $62,000 from the express car and enough from the passengers to bring the total to near $100,000. He has Sam Bass and Bill Longley in the James gang and calls Bill Chadwell a Minnesota horse thief and outlaw who joined the James gang when they went north to rob the bank at Northfield, Minnesota.

613. Donaldson, Thomas Corwin

Idaho of yesterday, by Thomas Donaldson. Introduction by Thomas B. Donaldson. Illustrated by photographs. Caldwell, Idaho, the Caxton printers, ltd., 1941. Cloth. OP.

9 p.l., [19]–406 p. front. (port.), plates, ports., facsms. 23.5 cm.
Index: p. [403]–406.
Half title; pub. device.

Contains a chapter on lawlessness and the vigilantes of early Idaho.

614. Donoho, Milford Hill

Circle dot, a true story of cowboy life forty years ago, by M. H. Donoho. Topeka, Kans., monotyped and printed by Crane & co., 1907. Cloth. Very scarce.

3 p.l., 7–256 p. front. 20 cm.

Includes material on some of the outlaws of the Indian Territory, and the gunmen of Dodge City. The author tells about the killing of Phil Coe by Hickok, but has the time and place wrong.

615. Donovan, J. W.

Skill in trials; containing a variety of civil and criminal cases won by the art of advocates, with some of the skill of Webster, Choate, Beach, Butler, Curtis, Davis, Fountain and others. Gives a sketch of their work and trial stories with hints on speeches and new selections of western eloquence, by J. W. Donovan. . . . Rochester, N.Y., Williamson Law Book co., 1899. Cloth. Scarce.

2 p.l., 173 p. 19.2 cm.
3 p. adv. at end.

Among other trials discussed is the one of Bronco Sue, of Socorro, New Mexico, who was defended by A. J. Fountain.

616. Doughitt, Katherine Christian (Mrs. J. W.)

Romance and dim trails. A history of Clay county [Texas], [by] Katherine Christian Doughitt (Mrs. J. W.), editor-in-chief. Dallas, Texas, William T. Tardy, published, 1938. Fabrikoid. Scarce.

7 p.l., 280 p. front., plates, ports. 23.2 cm.
Cattle brands: p. 269–280.
Map on end papers; leaf of errata tipped in; device.

In one chapter the author writes that the James and Younger brothers visited Clay County, where a sister of the Jameses lived for a time. She also tells of a man who came there in 1936 claiming to be the real Jesse James, and says he was quite convincing. Such impersonations went on for years.

617. Douglas, Clarence Brown

The history of Tulsa, Oklahoma, a city with a personality. Together with a glimpse down the corridors of the past into old Indian territory, the five civilized tribes, the Creek nation, Tulsa recording district and Tulsa county. How Oklahoma was created and something of the builders of a commonwealth. . . . Chicago-Tulsa, the S. J. Clarke publishing co., 1921. Cloth. Pub. in three volumes.

Vol. I, 6 p.l., 15–695 p. front. (port. with tissue), plates (part with tissues). 27.8 cm.
Device.
Vols. II and III, biographical.

Tells about some of the Oklahoma outlaws, such as Texas Jack, Bill Doolin, Bill Cook, Cherokee Bill, Henry Starr, and the Daltons, and officers Heck Thomas and Chris Madsen.

618. ———

Territory tales. Oklahoma in the making from the twin territories, by a pioneer editor who was there, Col. Clarence B. Douglas. El Reno, published by El Reno American, 1951. Stiff wrappers. OP.

3–50 p. 1 port. 22.8 cm.
Double column.

Has a chapter on Heck Thomas which tells about the killing of Jim and Pink Lee, a chapter on Bud Ledbetter and his capture of Al Jennings, and a chapter on Bill Dalton. The author's account of the killing of Dalton is inaccurate, as are other statements. He writes that "soon after the battle at Ingalls, Bill Dalton returned to California, there not being room in any bandit gang for both him and Doolin." That is incorrect. Dalton was in Doolin's gang, and he never returned to California until he was carried there in a coffin. He says Dalton formed a new gang and "soon became the most famous outlaw of his time." That, too, is incorrect. He also gives some information on such outlaws as Grat Dalton, Emmett Dalton, Bill Doolin, Bill Powers, and Dick Broadwell.

619. Douglas, Claude Leroy

Cattle kings of Texas, by C. L. Douglas. Dallas, Texas, published by Cecil Baugh [1939]. Cloth. Scarce.

xiv p., 1 l., 376 p. front., illus., plates, ports., map. 22.5 cm.
Half title; illus. end papers; device.

A few copies were bound in cowhide with the hair left on. This work first appeared serially in *The Cattleman Magazine.* The author says that Billy the Kid often "likkered up" at the bars of Tascosa, but Dr. Hoyt, who knew the Kid well, says that he never took a drink while he was there.

620. ———

Famous Texas feuds, [by] C. L. Douglas. . . . Dallas, Texas, the Turner co. . . . [1936]. Pict. cloth and leather. Scarce.

v p., 1 l., 173 p. front. (port.), ports. 20.4 cm.

Tells about many of the bloody feuds of Texas.

621. ———

The gentlemen in white hats; dramatic episodes in the history of the Texas rangers, by C. L. Douglas. Dallas, Texas, South-west press . . . [1934]. Cloth. Scarce.

vii, 205 p. front., illus., plates, ports. 22.5 cm.
Pub. device.

There is little that is new in this book. In the chapter on John Wesley Hardin some of the tales are merely legend. The author has Mrs. Hardin on the train with her husband when he was captured in Florida, but she was in Texas at the time.

622. Douglas, Ford

The cattle rustlers of Wyoming; or, Thorpe, of the Hole-in-the-Wall country. A story of Wyoming and the cattle country, written around one of the most thrilling and dramatic incidents in the history of the west—the "Rustlers' War" of 1892, by Ford Douglas. New York, J. S. Ogilvie publishing co., 1916. Stiff pict. wrappers (col.). Rare.

3–190 p. 18.8 cm.
12 p. adv. at end.

Published with "Ten Secret Service Stories," totaling fifty-six pages. The book is fiction but follows closely the history of the war.

623. Douglas, Marjory Stoneman

The Everglades; river of grass, by Marjory Stoneman Douglas. Illustrated by Robert Fink. New York, Toronto, Rinehart & co., inc. [1947]. Cloth. OP.

7 p.l., 5–406 p. illus., 2 maps. 21 cm.
Acknowledgments: p. 386–390; bibliography: p. 391–398; index: p. 399–406.
Half title; illus. t.p.; illus. end papers; illus. chapter headings.

Has material on the Ashley gang and several pages on Edgar Watson, the man some credit with killing Belle Starr.

624. Drago, Harry Sinclair

Great American cattle trails. The story of the old cow paths of the east and the longhorn highways of the plains, by Harry Sinclair Drago. Illustrated with photographs and maps. New York, Dodd, Mead & co. [1965]. Cloth.

xii p., 1 l., 274 p. plates, ports., maps (1 double p.). 23.2 cm.
Notes: p. 253–260; bibliography: p. 261–262; index: p. 263–274.
Half title; illus. end papers.

Has a chapter on Wild Bill Hickok and material on other gunmen, such as Billy the Kid, the Earps, John Wesley Hardin, Doc Holliday, Bat Masterson, Ben and Bill Thompson, and the Talbot gang.

625. ———

Lost bonanzas. Tales of the legendary lost mines of the American west, by Harry Sinclair Drago. New York, Dodd, Mead & co. [1966]. Cloth.

xii p., 1 l., 3–276 p. 23.2 cm.
Bibliography: p. 263–265; index: p. 267–276.
Half title; maps on end papers.

Has two chapters on the Reynolds brothers, outlaws of Colorado.

626. ———

Outlaws on horseback. The history of the organized bands of bank and train robbers who terrorized the prairie towns of Missouri, Kansas, Indian territory and Oklahoma for half a century, by Harry Sinclair Drago. Illustrated with photographs and a map. Endpaper drawings by Lorence F. Bjorklund. New York, Dodd, Mead & co. [1964]. Cloth.

xxiii, 320 p. plates, ports., map (double p.). 23.3 cm.
Notes: p. 301–306; bibliography: p. 307–308; index: p. 309–320.
Half title; illus. end papers; double t.p.
Also published in a de luxe edition of 150 signed copies, bound in crimson leather with gold stamping, gilt top, and in a slip case.

I am glad to see more and more writers, this author among them, correcting some of the false legends that have been plaguing historians for many years. Yet on page 2 he has the Youngers cousins of the James boys, though he later denies it.

I think he is wrong in having Jesse James in the Liberty Bank robbery; it has been proved that he was in bed with a lung wound at the time. I also think he is mistaken when he says that Preston Shirley had preceded his father to Sycene. Preston settled in Collin County, near McKinney. I also disagree with him when he says that Shirley sold out his business in Carthage and moved to Texas. He lost his inn when the town burned.

Though Cole Younger denied that he fathered Belle Starr's first child and Jim Reed apparently accepted her as his own, Mr. Drago claims that it was Cole's "beyond reasonable doubt." Otherwise, he has given good accounts of his characters and has spiked many common legends such as the legend about Rose of Cimarron that has been handed down for so long.

627. ———

Red river valley. The mainstream of frontier history from the Louisiana bayous to the Texas panhandle, by Harry Sinclair Drago. New York, Clarkson N. Potter, inc., publishers [1962]. Imt. cloth and boards.

5 p.l., [11]–328 p. 21.5 cm.
Notes: p. [307]–314; bibliography: p. [315]–319; index: p. 320–328.
Half title; map on end papers; pub. device.

The author is mistaken in his statement that "when the law put Cole [Younger] away, she [Belle Starr] became attached to another bandit, Jim Reed, a savage brute." Cole was not "put away" for the Northfield robbery until 1876. Reed was killed in 1874, and Belle had been living with him for several years at that time. He intimates that Belle married Sam Starr to get Reed's share of the Grayson robbery, but that is untrue. He is also mistaken in saying that Belle was sentenced to the House of Correction in Detroit in 1882. She was sentenced on March 8, 1883.

The author writes as though Jim July had been killed before Belle's death. He says that Jim was "arrested for horse stealing, he jumped bail, was shot by a deputy marshal, and died of his wounds while awaiting trial." But Belle was murdered February 3, 1889, and Jim July was killed January 26, 1890, more than a year later. He was killed by Marshal Heck Thomas while resisting arrest on a robbery charge after he had jumped bail. I also think the author is mistaken when he says that Bill Doolin was once a deputy who rode for Parker's court. I have never seen that statement before. Doolin went into outlawry straight from his days as a cowboy on the Halsell ranch.

628. ———

Roads to empire. The dramatic conquest of the American west, by Harry Sinclair Drago. Illustrated with photographs and a map. New York, Dodd, Mead & co. [1968]. Cloth.

xii p., 3 l., 270 p. plates, ports., facsms., map (double p.). 23.5 cm.
Notes: p. 247–257; bibliography: p. 259–262; index: p. 263–270.
Half title.

Chapter XXI, entitled "Vigilante Justice," deals with Henry Plummer's gang and the vigilantes of Montana.

629. ———

Wild, woolly & wicked. The history of the Kansas cow towns and the Texas cattle trade, by Harry Sinclair Drago. New York, Clarkson N. Potter, inc., publisher [1960]. Cloth.

viii p., 1 l., 354 p. 21.5 cm.

Notes: p. 343–349; bibliography: p. 351–354.

Half title; map on end papers; "First printing" on copyright p.

Also published in a de luxe edition of 250 copies bound in leather.

This book does much to debunk some of the nonsense written about the Earps. The author is mistaken, however, when he closes his information about Sam Bass with the statement that "Texas Rangers brought Bass's ill-starred career to a gory end at Round Rock, Denton County, on the tenth of July, 1878." Round Rock is in Williamson County, far south of Denton County, and Bass was shot on July 19 and died from his wounds on the twenty-first.

The author says that when a wandering evangelist came to Dodge and held services at Rowdy Kate's place, Prairie Dog Dave Morrow got tired of listening and shot the place up. This event took place in the Gay Lady Dancehall, and it was Mysterious Dave Mather who did the shooting.

The author is also mistaken when he writes that Wyatt Earp "had found the money to buy an interest in the immensely profitable Oriental Saloon and gambling establishment." Lou Rickabaugh, the owner of the Oriental, gave Earp an interest in the gambling concession for protection. The author is also in error when he refers to George Bolds as Bowles, and in giving George Hoy the name Ed Hoyt.

630. Drannan, Capt. William F.

Thirty-one years on the plains and in the mountains; or, the last voice from the plains. An authentic record of a life time of hunting, trapping, scouting and Indian fighting in the far west, by Capt. William F. Drannan. . . . Copiously illustrated by H. S. DeLay, and many reproductions from photographs. Chicago, Rhodes & McClure publishing co., 1899. Dec. cloth. Scarce.

6 p.l., 17–586 [9] p. front. (port. signed in facsm.), plates, ports. 20.2 cm.

9 p. adv. at end.

Republished with same imprint and collation in 1900; republished by Thomas W. Jackson publishing co., Chicago, 1900, and later.

This book deals largely with the Montana vigilantes, tells of the death of Henry Plummer, gives some information on Captain Jack, the Modoc Indian outlaw, and gives other events in the life of a braggart.

The author claims that he was a close friend of Kit Carson, but that is doubtful, and he has never been mentioned in any book about Carson. He states in one place that he first met Carson in St. Louis in 1847 and in another place that he attended Carson's wedding to Josefa Jaramillo, but the wedding took place four years earlier, in 1843. The author also claims that he, Carson, and Jim Hughes left St. Louis in 1847 and went up the Neosho River and west to Fort Bent, when in reality Carson stopped in Howard County, Missouri, to visit relatives and then went up the Missouri River by steamboat to Fort Leavenworth, where he was to act as guide in escorting some raw recruits through the Comanche country to New Mexico.

The author tells about a duel he had with a man named Shewman in 1853. In Carson's own book he tells about a duel he had with a man he calls Shumer in 1835, twelve years before Drannan said that he met Carson. The part the author claims to have played in the Modoc War has never been mentioned by other historians. His claims of service in the various campaigns are refuted by the National Archives in Washington; his name is not to be found in their records.

His dates are so mixed that in his second book, *Capt. Wm. F. Drannan, Chief of Scouts*, he has himself in two different places at the same time. It is said that he was uneducated and that his wife wrote *Thirty-one Years on the Plains* to provide an income for them. It is also said that one hundred editions were issued in the first ten years after publication, and that may well be true, for Drannan and his wife traveled throughout the country selling them, and they must have sold a great many, for it was a popular book in its day. The book is filled with misstatements, but perhaps Drannan was not so much to blame, since like a great many other old-timers he loved to be in the public eye, and his wife, being an apt reader of other histories saw her chance to make him a hero and make his narrative entertaining enough to sell well.

631. Draper, William R.

A cub reporter in the old Indian territory, by Wm. R. Draper. Girard, Kans., Haldeman-Julius publications [1946]. Wrappers.

3–32 p. 21.5 cm.

Notes and comments: p. 25–32 (double column).

Tells of the capture of Cherokee Bill and other Oklahoma outlaws.

632. ———

Exciting adventures along the Indian frontier. A reporter's experiences in the red man's territory and in the old Cherokee strip during the '90s, by Wm. R. Draper. Girard, Kans., Haldeman-Julius publications [1946]. Wrappers.

2 p.l., 5–32 p. 21.5 cm.

Notes and comments: p. 30–32 (double column).

633. ———, and Mabel Draper

Old grubstake days in Joplin. The story of the pioneers who discovered the largest and richest lead and zinc mining field in the world. By Wm. R. Draper and Mabel Draper. Girard, Kans., Haldeman-Julius publications [1946]. Wrappers.

3–32 p. 21.5 cm.

Has some mention of Jesse James in Joplin.

634. Dresser, Albert

California's pioneer mountaineer of Rabbit gulch. John Thomas Mason's meanderings in the out of the way places of the western wilds. A short sketch of his ancestry, starting with the famous French explorer, La Salle, who was in the Great lakes territory of America in 1669. Mason crossed the plains in 1851, and, to the present time, has spent 79 years in the Rabbit creek region and Sierra county. Together with facts—curious, furious, funny and fine—of this rough and rich country in early days which have been little heard of or else forgotten, [by Albert Dresser]. San Francisco, Albert Dresser, 1930. Cloth. Scarce.

6 p.l., 13–72 [1] p. illus., plates (1 col.), facsms. 25 cm.

Half title.

Colophon: "A limited, numbered edition of Five Hundred and Twenty-five copies, privately published by Albert Dresser, in the month of November, and the year Nineteen Thirty, of which this is No. ——."

Has material on some of the earlier outlaws of California, especially on one White-headed Ross.

635. Driggs, Benjamin Woodbury

History of Teton valley, Idaho, by B. W. Driggs. Caldwell, Idaho, the Caxton printers, ltd., MCMXXVI. Boards. Scarce.

6 p.l., [13]–227 p. front., plates. 23.5 cm.

Has a chapter on outlawry.

636. Driggs, Howard Roscoe

Westward America, by Howard R. Driggs. With reproductions of forty water color paintings by William H. Jackson. Trails edition. New York, G. P. Putnam's sons [1942]. Cloth. OP.

x p., 1 l., 312 p. 40 col. plates (incl. front.). 29.3 cm.

Bibliography: p. 301–302; index: p. 305–312.

Half title.

Also published in trade edition.

A chapter entitled "Rock Creek" contains a true account of the Hickok-McCanles "fight."

637. Driscoll, R. E.

Seventy years of banking in the Black hills, by R. E. Driscoll. First National Bank of the Black hills, 1876–1946. [Rapid City, S. D., the Gate City Guide, publishers, 1948.] Stiff pict. wrappers. Scarce.

4 p.l., 11–87 p. front. (port.). 23 cm.

In writing about the various banks of the Black Hills, the author gives some information on a bank robbery in which Tom O'Day was involved.

638. Drumheller, Daniel

"Uncle Dan" Drumheller tells thrills of the western trails in 1854, by "Uncle Dan" Drumheller. Spokane, Wash., Inland-American printing co., 1925. Raised leather. Scarce.

xi, 131 p. 2 ports. (incl. front. with tissue). 19.5 cm.

Half title; chapter and divisions printed in red; foreword before t.p.

The author writes of his long experiences in the West as a miner, pony-express rider, cattleman, and rancher. He tells about some of the outlaws, including Boone Helm and Brocky Jack.

639. Drury, Aubrey

California, an intimate guide, by Aubrey Drury. New York, London, Harper & brothers, publishers, 1935. Cloth. Pict. label pasted on. OP.

xvi p., 1 l., 592 p. plates, maps. 22.2 cm.

Acknowledgments: p. 559–561; index: p. 563–592.

Half title; pub. device; t.p. in red and black.

Contains a little information on Vásquez and Black Bart.

640. ———

John A. Hooper and California's robust youth, by Aubrey Drury. Together with a foreword by Arthur W. Hooper. San Francisco, Calif., [Lawton Kennedy, printers], 1952. Cloth. OP.

3 p.l., 85 p. front. (port.), plates, ports. 27 cm.

Vignette; t.p. in red and black.

Contains slight, but new, material on Murieta.

641. Drury, Rev. P. Shelden (ed.)

The startling and thrilling narrative of the dark and terrible deeds of Henry Madison, and his associate and accomplice, Miss Ellen Stevens. . . . Edited by Rev. P. Shelden Drury. Cincinnati, published by Barclay & co. [1857]. Pict. wrappers. Rare.

9–36 p. front., plates. 25 cm.
Vignette.

A good example of the many sensational books on the early outlaws written or edited by ministers.

642. Drury, Wells

An editor on the Comstock lode, by Wells Drury. Foreword by Ella Bishop Drury. Illustrated with photographs. New York, Toronto, Farrar & Rinehart, inc. [1936]. Cloth. Scarce.

xx p., 1 l., 3–343 p. front., illus., plates, ports., map, diagr. 23.5 cm.
Appendix: p. 297–330; index: p. 331–343.
Half title; first edition: "F R" in device on copyright p.

Republished by Pacific Books, Palo Alto, Calif., in 1948.

xx p., 1 l., 3–307 p. plates, ports., map. 23.5 cm.
Index: p. 295–307.

Both books have material on road agents, such as Henry Plummer and Boone Helm, devote a whole chapter to Milton Sharp, and tell about Farmer Peel, Jack Davis, and the vigilantes.

643. Dudley, J. H.

The climax in crime of the 19th century, being an authentic history of the trial, conviction and execution of Stephen Morris Ballew for the murder of James P. Golden, in Collin county, Texas, on the 21st day of October, 1870, with a short sketch of the early life of the murderer, by J. H. Dudley. Quincy, Feb. 28, 1872. Wrappers. Exceedingly rare.

208 p. front. (port.). 20.8 cm.

644. Du Fran, Dora (D. Dee, pseud.)

Low down on Calamity Jane, by D. Dee. Rapid City, S.D. [1932]. Pict. Wrappers. (Cover title.) Rare.

12 p. 22 cm.
Foreword on verso of front cover; port. on cover.

This little pamphlet was written by a woman who claimed to have known Calamity Jane, and it is said that she was in a position to know the "seamy side of [Jane's] character" since she was quite a character herself. But, she is unreliable. Established historical facts make many of the statements in her book highly improbable.

Although other writers are just as unreliable regarding Jane's birthplace and the date of her birth, this author makes the claim that Jane was born in Fort Laramie, Wyoming, giving the date as 1860. Jane herself says that she was born in Princeton,

Missouri, May 1, 1852. The author also says that Jane was "often called Mary Jane Canary [*sic*], but this was nothing but a nickname. She liked to sing, but her voice was anything but musical, so they called her Canary after the mules, which were also called Rocky Mountain canaries."

645. Duke, Thomas S.

Celebrated criminal cases in America, by Thomas S. Duke, captain of police, San Francisco. Published with approval of the Honorable Board of Police Commissioners of San Francisco. San Francisco, Calif., the James H. Barry co., 1910. Cloth. Scarce.

xii p., 3 l., [3]–567 p. front., plates, ports. 23.5 cm.
Tipped-in slip on p. 14; tissues between double p. ports.

This work deals with outlaws and murderers, crime and criminals over the whole nation. The chapters on the Pacific Coast outlaws treat of Murieta, Vásquez, Black Bart, the Evans-Sontag gang, and Harry Tracy. Chapters on the Middle West discuss Alferd G. Packer, the Daltons, the Benders, and the James-Younger gang. The chapter on Murieta is taken from the Ridge book, and the one on Vásquez is taken from the Sawyer account.

646. Duncan, L. Wallace (ed.)

History of Montgomery county, Kansas, by its own people. Illustrated. . . . Published by L. Wallace Duncan. Iola, Kans., press of Iola Register, 1903. Cloth. Scarce.

2 p.l., [5]–852 p. plates, ports. (with tissues). 26 cm.
Index (table of contents): p. [833]–837; personal references and biographies: p. 838–852.

Contains a chapter on the Dalton raid at Coffeyville.

647. Duncan, Lee

Over the wall, by Lee Duncan, ex-convict No. 9256, Oregon state prison. Frontispiece. New York, E. P. Dutton & co., inc. [1936]. Pict. cloth. Scarce.

4 p.l., 9–368 p. front. 21 cm.
Half title; "First edition" on copyright p.

Contains some material on Harry Tracy and Dave Merrill.

648. Dunham, Dick, and Vivian Dunham

Our strip of land. A history of Daggett county, Utah, by Dick and Vivian Dunham. [Manila, Utah, published by Daggett county Lions club, 1947.] Stiff pict. wrappers.

vi, 106 p. 22.8 cm.

A history of Brown's Hole with a great deal of material on the outlaws of that section and the activities of Butch Cassidy's Wild Bunch and others. Also tells about some of the exploits of Tom Horn.

649. Dunlop, Richard

Doctors of the American frontier, by Richard Dunlop. Garden City, N.Y., Doubleday & co., 1965. Pict. cloth.

viii p., 2 l., 228 p. illus., plates, ports. 21.5 cm.
Bibliography: p. [210]–221; index: p. [222]–228.
Half title; illus. t.p.; untrimmed; "First edition" on copyright p.

A most interesting book about the early frontier doctors, their hardships and successes with so few surgical instruments. One of the doctors was Dr. Thomas D. Hodges, who later became Tom Bell, the stagecoach bandit. There is material on the O K Corral fight, the wounding of Virgil Earp, and the killing of Morgan Earp and some mention of Calamity Jane and Doc Holliday. There is also some material on Jesse James and Billy the Kid.

650. Dunn, J. B. (Red) John

Perilous trails of Texas, by J. B. (Red) John Dunn. (Edited by Lillith Lorraine.) Dallas, Texas, published for the author by the Southwest press, publishers [1952]. Cloth. Scarce.

ix, 163 p. front. (port.), illus., plates, ports. 21.6 cm.
Untrimmed; errata slip.

Deals with lawlessness on the Mexican border.

651. Dunning, Harold Marion

The life of Rocky Mountain Jim (James Nugent), by Harold Marion Dunning. Boulder, Colorado, Johnson publishing co., 1967. Stiff pict. wrappers.

2 p.l., 1 p., 4–48 [1] p. plates, ports., map on recto of back wrapper. 22.7 cm.
Copyright notice on t.p.

652. Durham, George

Taming the Neuces strip. The story of McNelly's rangers, by George Durham as told to Clyde Wantland. Foreword by Walter Prescott Webb. Austin, University of Texas press [1962]. Cloth.

xx p., 1 l., [3]–178 p. illus., ports., map. 21.9 cm.
Half title; illus. t.p.; illus. headpieces.

Gives one of the best accounts of the life and work of McNelly and his Rangers and corrects some of the errors made by N. A. Jennings. The work was originally published serially in one of the western magazines quite a few years before publication in book form. The author is incorrect in dealing with the circumstances of the killing of Ben Thompson and King Fisher.

653. Durham, Philip, and Everett L. Jones

The Negro cowboys, by Philip Durham and Everett L. Jones. Illustrated. New York, Dodd, Mead & co. [1965]. Cloth.

x, 278 p. illus., plates, ports., 4 maps. 20.8 cm.
Notes: p. 231–253; bibliography: p. 254–270; index: p. 271–278.
Half title.

This book is unique in that it is the first one written about the Negro as a cowboy, and it is regrettable that the authors omitted one of the most noted of Texas Negro bronc busters and cowboys, Bone Hooks of Amarillo. There is some material on various outlaws and gunmen, such as Clay Allison, Sam Bass, Calamity Jane, Wyatt Earp, John Wesley Hardin, Wild Bill Hickok, and Bat Masterson, as well as on the Lincoln and Johnson county wars. The authors err in calling Buckshot Roberts by the name Rogers and in stating that Tom Horn was hanged in Laramie. He was hanged in Cheyenne.

654. Dyer, T. J.

First white settlement in Oklahoma. A story of the first white settlement in what is now the state of Oklahoma, then known as Indian territory and other stories. By T. J. Dyer. Alva, Okla. [1930]. Cloth. Rare.

2 p.l., [5]–37 p. 3 ports. 19 cm.

655. Dykes, Jefferson C.

Billy the Kid, the bibliography of a legend, [by] J. C. Dykes. Albuquerque, University of New Mexico press, 1952. Wrappers.

5 p.l., 11–186 p. front. 22.8 cm.
Index: p. 179–186.
Device.
Head of title: "University of New Mexico Publication in Language and Literature, No. 7."

A total of 500 copies of this book were published, 470 copies in wrappers and 30 in cloth. The thirty cloth copies were numbered and signed for friends. The publication department of the university paid for the first printing, though it bears the imprint of the University of New Mexico Press. Then the press took over and issued the "First edition, second printing" with minor corrections. This edition totaled 1,000 copies, 500 in wrappers and 500 in cloth.

The book is more a check list than a true bibliography, but each entry contains much information on the content of the book listed, and the author points out many false and inaccurate statements made by the various authors. It is the first complete list of materials on this young outlaw and includes songs, plays, motion pictures, phonograph records, and magazine articles.

656. Dykstra, Robert R.

The cattle towns, [by] Robert R. Dykstra. New York, Alfred A. Knopf, 1968. Cloth.

7 p.l., [3]–386 p. plates, ports., maps (1 double p.). 22 cm.

Appendices: p. [371]–383; acknowledgments: p. [385]–386; index: p. [i]–x.

Half title; pub. device; untrimmed; "First edition" on copyright p.

The author treats the Kansas cow towns from a different angle from that used by most writers dealing with this subject. He concentrates on their growth, economic condition, and decline rather than upon the lawlessness so often emphasized. The book is heavily annotated, and the author uses a distinctive method of numbering the footnotes, proceeding from 1 to 9 and then starting over with 1, even in the same chapter. In all the copies I have examined I find in the index the figures *vi*, *v*, and *iv* following the figure *iii* in that order.

He mentions some of the gunmen of the cow towns, but they seem to be of secondary interest to him. I was glad to note that he does not claim that Wyatt Earp was in Ellsworth at the time Billy Thompson killed Sheriff Whitney. He repeats the legend about John Wesley Hardin shooting through a wall of an adjoining room in the hotel and killing a man because he was snoring. He writes that Bat Masterson "killed no one in or around Dodge, where he lived for several years." While he was sheriff of Ford County, Masterson killed Al Wagner, and he came back later to kill Al Updegraff.

E

657. Ealy, Ruth R.

Water in a thirsty land, [by] Ruth R. Ealy. N.p., 1955. Fabrikoid. Rare.

6 p.l., 1 p., 8–243 p. plates, ports., plan, facsm. 22.4 cm.

A collection of private papers and the diary of a missionary doctor sent to Lincoln, New Mexico, by his church. He arrived during the Lincoln County War and soon afterward preached Tunstall's funeral. The book gives information on the burning of McSween's home and new material on Billy the Kid. The book was published in a small edition, being prepared mostly for family and friends. It is an important addition for collectors of Billy the Kid material.

658. Earle, J. P.

History of Clay county and northwest Texas, by J. P. Earle. [Henrietta, Texas, 1897.] Wrappers. Rare.

64 p. front., ports. 22.4 cm.

Reprinted in 1963 by the Red Brick book shop of Austin, Texas. Limited to 300 copies.

Has some material on the Jameses and the Youngers, as well as the Jesse Brown gang.

659. Eaton, Frank

Pistol Pete, veteran of the old west, by Frank Eaton. With illustrations. Boston, Little, Brown and co., 1952. Cloth.

x p., 1 l., [3]–278 p. plates, ports. 21 cm.

Half title; pub. device; "First edition" on copyright p.; facsm. of author's signature at end of text.

A wild tale of a man who trained himself, as he grew up, to be able to kill all the men who took part in the murder of his father. The writer tells of having a horse race with Belle Starr and losing his Winchester to her. He says that when Belle refused to let Edgar Watson take her home from a dance, he hid out on her trail home and shot her, though Watson was never convicted of the crime. Yet Eaton declares that he and his friends heard the shot and chased Watson for a hundred miles and killed his horse in the gun battle which followed, and that Belle's friends hanged Watson with Belle's lariat—a most preposterous tale for we know that Watson was killed in Florida much later. The writer tells about killing the last man on his "wanted list" in Albuquerque, New Mexico, with Pat Garrett looking on and with Garrett's sanction. The book reads like wild West fiction and is filled with doubtful statements. The author turns out to be a regular one-man army, and though just a boy when he started on his chase, he matched his skill against a number of hardened killers. He also gives his version of how the Benders were killed. One reviewer wrote that "books like this one are a distinct menace to western history."

660. Eaton, Jeannette

Bucky O'Neill of Arizona, by Jeannette Eaton. Illustrated by Edward Shenton. New York, William Morrow and co., 1949. Pict. cloth. OP.

6 p.l., 13–219 p. illus., plate (double p.). 20.8 cm.

Half title; illus. chapter headings; illus. double t.p.

A story about the Arizona peace officer for young readers. It also tells about Wyatt Earp, Buckskin Frank Leslie, and others.

661. [Edinburgh Lady, an]

A rapid run to the wild west, by an Edinburgh lady. Edinburgh, privately printed by R. & R. Clark, 1884. Stiff wrappers. Rare.

2 p.l., [5]–35 p. 17.5 cm.
Half title; untrimmed.

Has some information on the holdups of the West.

662. Edwards, J. B.

Early days in Abilene, by J. B. Edwards. Edited and published by C. W. Wheeler, printed in the *Abilene Chronicle*, 1896; reprinted in *Abilene Daily Chronicle*, 1938, with added material from the papers of J. B. Edwards. [N.p., n.d.] Pict. wrappers. (Caption title.) Rare.

16 p. illus., plates, ports. 30.5 x 23.5 cm.
Triple column; tissues inside front and back wrappers.

The author relates some events of early Abilene and writes of Wild Bill Hickok and Jack McCall. He lived in Abilene from its founding and knew its history first-hand. The last letter I received from him was at the time he autographed a copy of this book for me. He was 102 years old then and died shortly afterward.

663. Edwards, Jennie (Mrs. John N. Edwards)

John N. Edwards, biography, memoirs, reminiscences, and recollections. His brilliant career as soldier, author, journalist. Choice collection of his most notable and interesting newspaper articles, together with some unpublished poems and many private letters. Also a reprint of Shelby's expedition to Mexico, an unwritten leaf of the war. Compiled by his wife, Jennie Edwards. Kansas City, Mo., Jennie Edwards, publisher, 1889. Cloth. Rare.

3 p.l., 9–428 p. front. (port.). 19.2 cm.
Also published in a limited edition of 100 copies, numbered and signed.

Contains a chapter on the killing of Jesse James reprinted from the *Sedalia Democrat*, April, 1882, which became a classic.

664. Edwards, John N.

Noted guerrillas; or, the warfare of the border. Being a history of the lives and adventures of Quantrell [*sic*], Bill Anderson, George Todd, Dave Poole, Fletcher Taylor, Peyton Long, Oll Shepherd, Arch Clements, John Maupin, Tuck and Woot Hill, Wm. Gregg, Thomas Maupin, the James brothers, the Younger brothers, Arthur McCoy and numerous other well known guerrillas of the west, by John N. Edwards. . . . Illustrated. St. Louis, Mo., Bryan, Brand & co., Chicago, Ill., Thompson & Wakefield; San Francisco, Calif., A. L. Bancroft & co., 1877. Cloth. Scarce.

xi, [13]–488 [2] p. front. (port.), plates, ports. 21.8 cm.
2 p. adv. at end.
Reprinted in 1879 and later.

This book is not considered reliable. The author was an honest man and believed what he wrote, but he obtained most of his information, which proved to be false, from Frank and Jesse James while they were hiding out. The book went through several editions, but has since been discredited. The author seems to strive to glorify outlaws and outlawry, perhaps because he was a loyal southerner.

665. [Eighty-Niners, the]

Oklahoma, the beautiful land, by the 89ers. Oklahoma City, Okla., published by the Times-Journal publishing co. [1943]. Pict. cloth. OP.

3 p.l., 352 p. plates, ports., map. 24 cm.

Has some information about the Daltons, Bill Doolin, Charlie Bryant, Bill Powers, Bitter Creek Newcomb, Charlie Pierce, Al Jennings, and the Oklahoma marshals.

666. Eikemeyer, Carl

Over the great Navajo trail, by Carl Eikemeyer. . . . Illustrated with photographs taken by the author. New York, [press of J. J. Little & co.]. 1900. Pict. cloth. Scarce.

9 p.l., 21–170 p. front. (port. with tissue), plates (1 col. with tissue). 21.5 cm.

Has material on cattle thieves and the Button gang of New Mexico.

667. Eisele, Mrs. Fannie L.

A history of Noble county, Oklahoma. Written by Mrs. Fannie L. Eisele. Covington, Okla. [1958]. Pict. wrappers. OP.

159 p. plates, ports. 17 cm.

Has some mention of the Dalton gang, Ben Cravens, Bill Doolin, Cattle Annie, and Little Britches (whom the author calls Little Bridges). She misspells Doolin's name as Dulin, and Red Buck as Red Nach.

668. Eisele, Wilbert E. (Ross Lyndon)

The real Wild Bill Hickok, famous scout and knight chivalric of the plains —a true story of pioneer life in the far west, by Wilbert E. Eisele (Ross Lyndon). . . . Denver, Colo., William H. Andre, publisher, 1931. Pict. cloth. OP.

8 p.l., 15–364 p. front. (port.), illus. 20 cm.
Half title; vignette; port. of author on verso of dedication p.; first edition: "Collector's edition" on copyright p.

The author claims that the McCanleses were desperate horse thieves who were overrunning the country. He closely follows preceding false accounts, names the McCanleses Jim and Jack, and states that "Jim was the biggest cutthroat of them all." He follows Buel in placing the fight in a dugout, and has the usual ten men in the McCanles party. Using the Buel and Nichols accounts as patterns, he makes even stronger statements than they, such as that "the bowie in Bill's hands now did desperate work, plunging from one heart to another, and drawing great fountains of blood which spurted about until the floor was fairly flooded; but his own life current assisted largely to swell the bright red streams, for his body was punctured by bullet holes and knife thrusts, yet the inner recesses of his life had not been touched and his strong arm continued to do its deadly work." The author brings in Captain Kingsbury, as Buel did, and uses Buel's own words (written in 1883) without quotation marks in saying: "This combat, of one man fairly whipping ten acknowledged desperadoes, has no parallel, I make bold to say, in any authentic history" (p. 52) (see Item 314).

This writer gets not only his facts but also his dates wrong, when he states that this "fight" took place on December 16, 1860. Seeking to justify his erroneous and fantastic tale, he adds the following note at the bottom of his chapter on the event:

"NOTE—In recent years it has been much the fashion among a certain clique of writers to give an entirely different version of this celebrated border fight. However, the present writer is of the opinion that this latter version, in which but three men were reported to have been killed by Wild Bill, is wholly incorrect and a distortion of the real facts. It appears to have had its animus among a group of Southern sympathizers, who never forgave Bill for the terrible execution he wrought later upon the Confederate soldiers while acting as a Union scout and spy during Civil War days; consequently, they seized every opportunity to villify him and minimize his exploits. It is to be noted that no such detractions were made during Wild Bill's lifetime.

"The account as given in the preceding paragraphs of this chapter has been accepted as authentic for many years, as is set forth in the writings of such authors as Col. George Ward Nichols, noted Civil War historian, in 1867 [*sic*]; later by Buffalo Bill in his Autobiography, 1879; still later by J. W. Buel, in 1881, in his "Heroes of the Plains"; by Emerson Hough in "North of 36"; and by John Hays Hammond in an article written for Scribner's some years ago. . . . Bill never denied it."

I do not know where he could have found five more unreliable historians than the ones he mentions. Most of his quotations are from unreliable sources, among them Sutton's *Hands Up*, a most untrustworthy book. This author also says that Wild Bill was reburied at Mt. Moriah on August 3, 1877, but John McCormick, who helped with the reburial, says that it was carried out on September 1, 1879.

669. El Comancho (pseud. of Walter Shelley Phillips)

The old timer's tale, by El Comancho. Chicago, the Canterbury press, 1929. Pict. boards. Scarce.

5 p.l., 114 p. front. (port.), plates. 20.3 cm.
Half title; pub. device.
Two errata slips inserted, the first one reading: "Page 15, line 7 should be line 6;" the second reading: "Page 47, line 5 should follow line 24."

The author mentions Wild Bill Hickok, Joseph Slade, Bat Masterson, and others. He says that Calamity Jane was "born under the family name of Carney" and that she was buried in "Boothill Cemetery." She was buried in Mt. Moriah, in Deadwood.

670. Elkins, Capt. John M.

Life on the Texas frontier, by Capt. John M. Elkins. Beaumont, Texas, press of the Greer print, 1908. Cloth. Rare.

1 p.l., [3]–108 p. 1 port. 23.5 cm.

The author tells about the Redding gang of rustlers in Texas. The copy I examined was filled with penciled corrections.

671. Elliott, David Stewart

Last raid of the Daltons. A reliable recital of the battle with the bandits in Coffeyville, Kansas, October 5, 1892, by David Stewart Elliott. . . . First edition. Illustrated by E. A. Filleau. Coffeyville, Kans., Coffeyville Journal print, 1892. Pict. wrappers. Rare.

5 p.l., [13]–71 [1] p. front. (port.), illus., ports., plan at end. 19.2 cm.
"First edition" on t.p.

Reprinted in facsimile in 1954 in an edition of sixty pages. The illustrations are on different pages from those in the original, and the facsimile ends with Chapter X, omitting the last two chapters of the original and the plan at the end. The author was editor of the *Coffeyville Journal* and was an eyewitness to the battle of the citizens and the Dalton gang. It is said that he was the first man to reach the wounded Emmett Dalton. He wrote this little book to give an account of what he saw and published it in a limited edition. It is now very rare and a collector's item.

672. Ellis, Amanda M.

Bonanza towns; Leadville and Cripple creek, by Amanda M. Ellis. [Colorado Springs, Colo., the Dentan printing co., 1954.] Stiff wrappers.

2–48 [1] p. plates, ports. (4 full p.). 21.5 cm.

"First edition" on verso front cover; imprint and copyright p. on verso front cover; bibliography and acknowledgments recto back wrapper.

Much on lawlessness and an account of Soapy Smith.

673. ———

Pioneers, by Amanda M. Ellis. [Colorado Springs, Colo., printed by the Dentan printing co., 1955.] Stiff wrappers.

2 p.l., [1] 6–52 p. plates, ports., facsm. 21.5 cm.

Has a chapter on Soapy Smith.

674. Elman, Robert

Fired in anger. The personal handguns of American heroes and villains, by Robert Elman. Introduction by Harold L. Peterson. Garden City, N.Y., Doubleday & company, inc., 1968. Cloth.

9 p.l., 19–480 p. illus., plates, ports., facsms., map. 26.5 cm.
Index: p. 476–480.
Half title; "First edition" on copyright p.

The story of personal handguns and their descriptions, beginning with the weapons of Columbus and extending down through the ages to those of modern gangsters and gunmen. Among the western outlaws there are sections on the James gang, Belle Starr, Cherokee Bill, Henry Starr, Wild Bill Hickok, Heck Thomas, and Bat Masterson.

The author is mistaken in saying that Belle Starr and Emma Jones burned down a store in an Arkansas village and that a stockman named Patterson obtained her release from jail. That event occurred in Dallas, Texas. He repeats the old legend about Blue Duck losing two thousand dollars of Belle's money in a poker game at Dodge and Belle holding up the house to get the money back.

The author writes that "Wild Bill's career in Abilene was bloody, beginning with two killings on the day he became marshal and marked by continual gunplay until the local authorities dismissed him a year later for resorting to violence more often than seemed necessary." Hickok killed no one the day he became marshal, and he did not last a year as marshal. The only two men he killed during his entire stay were Phil Coe and, by mistake, his deputy and friend, Mike Williams.

The author is also mistaken in saying that Hickok "spent most of 1872 as marshal of Hays again, where he had somehow made his peace with the officers of the Army post." He is also mistaken when he says that after Jack McCall killed Wild Bill he "tried to shoot the bartender Harry Young but the Colt misfired." Harry Young was not the bartender at Saloon No. 10, where the killing took place.

In his section on Heck Thomas, the author has Jim Thomas, Heck's brother, as express messenger on the train that was robbed by the Bass gang and says that the robbery took place on February 22, 1876, and netted $2,000. That robbery took place on February 22, 1878, and the loot amounted to $1,280. After the robbery, the author says, "they pulled four more robberies," but the Bass gang only robbed four trains altogether. He has both Thomases chasing Bass and says that when they were joined by "a small detachment of Texas Rangers" they killed several of the gang and captured several others. The only one they killed was Arkansas Johnson, in a battle on Salt Creek, and the only ones they captured were Jim Murphy and his father, who were not really members of the Bass gang at the time.

Perhaps the most serious mistake he makes is when he writes that "on that date [July 19], the streets of Austin became a battleground as the gang decided to make a stand right in the middle of town." The battle occurred in Round Rock, some miles north of Austin. "It was not Heck," he writes, "but one of the Rangers who fired the shot that killed Bass." Heck Thomas was not in Round Rock.

"No one kept track of whose bullets felled at least three other badmen," he continues. Only two outlaws were killed, Bass and Barnes. Though there were only two others in the gang, Jackson and Murphy, the author writes: "The gang numbered about a dozen at this time. Several threw down their arms and surrendered; a few got away, but they were finished as a train-robbing outfit."

In his section on Bat Masterson he says that Bat, the Earps, and Bill Tilghman "killed or captured so many rustlers, horse thieves, murderers, train and bank robbers that no authority had been able to estimate the total." He is also mistaken in having Ben Thompson in Sweetwater, Texas, when Bat was shot by Sergeant King. In his autobiography Thompson does not mention being there; nor do his biographers. The author is also mistaken in having Wyatt Earp the city marshal of Dodge City, and in having Masterson a deputy in Tombstone. While he was in Arizona Masterson was merely a gambler. The author repeats the legend about Earp and Masterson running Clay Allison out of Dodge. Altogether, however, there is much to interest and enlighten gun buffs.

675. Elmhirst, Captain Pennell

Fox-hound, forest and prairie, by Captain Pennell Elmhirst. Illustrated by J. P. Sturgess and J. Marshman. . . . London, Glascow, Manchester and New York, George Routledge and sons, ltd., 1892. Pict. cloth. Scarce.

xv [1] 584 p. illus., plates. 23 cm.
Half title; 2 p. adv. in front.

Tells something about Virginia City and the hanging of George Ives.

676. Elzner, Jonnie Ross

Lamplights of Lampasas county, Texas, by Jonnie Elzner. Austin, Texas, Form Foundation publishing house [1951]. Pict. cloth. OP.

ii, [5]–219 p. plates, maps. 23.7 cm.
Appendices: p. 187–219.

Has material on the Horrell-Higgins feud and other lawlessness.

677. Emery, J. Gladston

Court of the damned. Being a factual story of the court of Judge Isaac C. Parker and the life and times of the Indian territory and old Fort Smith, by J. Gladston Emery. New York, Comet press books [1959]. Cloth.

8 p.l., 3–194 p. illus. 20.9 cm.

Gives some early history of Fort Smith and Judge Parker's court, but, like those of so many other writers, his accounts of the various outlaws are untrustworthy. He states that a Dr. Stewart was a member of the Sam Bass gang "operating in the state of Texas mainly, but headquartering in the Choctaw Nation." He further states that Stewart was executed largely because "he was connected directly with Sam Bass and his unholy crew of desperate train robbers who had committed many wanton killings." Sam Bass never operated or headquartered in Oklahoma, nor did anyone named Stewart join his band, and the band certainly did not "commit" many killings.

The author's account of the killing of Belle Starr is incorrect and he says of the gun buried with her: "The pistol was once the property of the outlaw Cole Younger, her first husband's brother." She was never married to a Younger, though some claim that she was married to Cole and that her daughter, Pearl, was fathered by him.

His account of the Daltons robbing two banks at Coffeyville, Kansas, also contains some errors. He gives Bill Powers' first name as Tim and Dick Broadwell's first name as Chip, and he greatly exaggerates the amount taken from the banks. He is also in error in saying that Emmett was killed and that Bob was wounded in the arm and left hip and "quietly spirited out of town to be lodged in jail at Independence." Emmett lived to serve a prison term and after his release lived in California for many years. Bob was killed during the battle at Coffeyville.

678. Emmett, Chris

Shanghai Pierce, a fair likeness, by Chris Emmett, with drawings by Nick Eggenhofer. Norman, University of Oklahoma press [1953]. Cloth.

xiii p., 1 l., 3–326 p. illus., plates, ports., maps. 24 cm.
Bibliography: p. 313–319; index: p. 321–326.

Half title; illus. double t.p.; illus. chapter headings; "First edition" on copyright p.

An interesting book about one of Texas' most colorful cowmen. There is some material on the Taylor-Sutton feud and on John Wesley Hardin, Jack Helm, Ben Thompson, Wild Bill Hickok, and other gunmen. I cannot agree with the author, however, when he says that two pistols were a "necessary part of his [the cowboy's] accoutrement . . . he would have felt too light on his feet if not wearing two six-shooters, or out of balance at the hips were he wearing only one." I also think he exaggerates Hardin's disarming of Wild Bill Hickok.

679. Emrich, Duncan

It's an old wild west custom, [by] Duncan Emrich. New York, the Vanguard press, inc. [1949]. Pict. cloth. OP.

xiv p., 1 l., 3–313 p. illus., cattle brands. 21.3 cm.
Half title; illus. t.p.; illus. chapter headings.

Has a chapter on bad men, but tells nothing new.

680. Enfield, Dr. J. E.

The man from Packsaddle, by Dr. J. E. Enfield. Hollywood, House-Warven publishers, 1951. Cloth. OP.

3 p.l., 5–186 p. 23.5 cm.
Device.

The autobiography of a man who rode the outlaw trail, though he does not give the reason for his start as a hunted man. He uses fictitious names for his characters and thus damages the historical value of the book, although he does save some embarrassment and perhaps avoids charges of libel.

681. Erskine, Mrs. Gladys (Shaw)

Broncho Charlie; a saga of the saddle, by Gladys Shaw Erskine. The life story of Broncho Charlie Miller, the last of the pony express riders. New York, Thomas Y. Crowell co., publishers [1934]. Cloth. Scarce.

xiv p., 1 l., 316 p. front. (port.), plates, ports., maps (1 fold.), facsm. 22.5 cm.
Half title; map on end papers; vignette; untrimmed.
Also published in England without date.

Contains information on some Dodge City gunmen whom Broncho knew there.

682. Erwin, Allen A.

The southwest of John H. Slaughter, 1841–1922. Pioneer cattleman and trail driver of Texas, the Pecos, and Arizona and sheriff of Tombstone, by Allen A. Erwin. Glendale, Calif., the Arthur H. Clark co., 1965. Cloth.

14 p.l., [27]–368 p. front. (port.), plates, ports., map (fold.), facsms. 24.5 cm.
Bibliography: p. [341]–348; index: p. [351]–368.
Half title: "Western Frontiersmen Series x"; pub. device; untrimmed.

Contains a foreword on the book by William MacLeod Raine (perhaps the last writing he completed before his death), and a foreword on the author by Ramon F. Adams. It is the first, and a long-needed, book on the famous John Slaughter and shows much research. It is well annotated. However, in a footnote on page 178, the author is mistaken in saying that Tom Horn was hanged in Colorado. He was hanged in Cheyenne. He is also mistaken in saying that Stillwell was killed by Wyatt Earp and Doc Holliday while they were taking Morgan Earp's body to California. Virgil Earp and his wife were escorting the body. Wyatt had gone to Tucson to see them off when he ambushed Stillwell. The book deals with many incidents in the life of Tombstone and tells about many of the outlaws and gunmen, such as Clay Allison, Burt Alvord, the Apache Kid, Sam Bass, Jim Berry, Billy the Kid, Charlie Bowdre, Henry Brown, Augustin Chacon, Billy Claiborne, Curly Bill Brocius, the Earps, the Clantons, Doc Holliday, Pat Garrett, John Wesley Hardin, John Heath, Tom Horn, the Ketchums, Sandy King, Bill Longley, Bob Olinger, John Ringo, John Selman, Luke Short, and Billy Stiles, and recounts the O K Corral fight.

683. Erwin, Carol, and Floyd Miller

The orderly disorderly house, by Carol Erwin and Floyd Miller. Garden City, N.Y., Doubleday & co., inc., 1960. Cloth.

3 p.l., [7]–284 p. 21.5 cm.
Half title.

Has some new material on Matt Kimes, the Oklahoma outlaw.

684. Estes, George

The stagecoach, by George Estes. . . . Cedarwood, P.O. Trousdale, Oreg., published by George Estes' publishers [1925]. Three-quarter leather. Rare.

xvi, 409 p. front. (port.), plates (1 fold., 1 col.), facsms. 24.5 cm.
Half title; in a chapter with information about the Cow Parsnip Trail is tipped in a small envelope of parsnip seeds.
Colophon: "The Stagecoach inscription panel Six-Horses Limited Edition only one thousand autographed copies. [No.] ——, inscribed to ——, who helped pull the Stagecoach through by paying for this number the sum of Ten Pinches of Gold Dust. [Signed] Geo. Estes, author."

This scarce and unusual privately printed book has several chapters dealing with stage holdups and other lawlessness.

685. Evans, Clyde (ed.)

Adventures of the great crime-busters, edited by Clyde Evans. New York, New Power publications [1943]. Cloth. OP.

5 p.l., 11–256 p. 21 cm.
Half title.

A chapter on Jesse James gives an account of the Northfield Bank raid. A chapter on Billy the Kid is a reprint of part of a chapter from Pat Garrett's book. Nothing of value is added to the many books on outlaws except to make the list longer.

686. Evans, James W., and A. Wendell Keith

Autobiography of Samuel S. Hildebrand, the renowned Missouri "bush-whacker" and inconquerable Rob Roy of America; being his complete confession recently made to the writers, and carefully compiled by James W. Evans and A. Wendell Keith, M.D., of St. Francois county, Mo., together with all the facts connected with his early history. Jefferson City, Mo., State Times book and job printing house, 1870. Wrappers. Rare.

13 p.l., [25]–312 p. front., illus., plates. 19 cm.

A rare and readable account of this notorious outlaw's activities.

687. Evans, Max

Long John Dunn of Taos, by Max Evans. Los Angeles, Calif., Westernlore press, 1959. Pict. cloth.

xi p., 1 l., 15–174 [2] p. plates, ports., facsm. 21.2 cm.
Half title; headpieces.

The author repeats the false stories that Billy the Kid killed the man who insulted his mother when he was a boy of twelve and that he killed a total of twenty-one men. He also tells about Black Jack Ketchum's robberies and hanging.

688. Every, Edward Van

Sins of America as "exposed" by the *Police Gazette*, by Edward Van Every. . . . With an introduction by Thomas Beer. With 206 reproductions of the original woodcut illustrations. New York, Frederick A. Stokes co., MCMXXXI. Cloth. Scarce.

xx p., 1 l., 297 p. front., illus., plates. 32 cm.
Half title; illus. t.p.

This unique book contains accounts of some of the early sensational crimes of America founded upon some of the cases reported by the *Police Gazette* and includes many of the woodcuts first used in that journal. The first half of the book is printed on white paper, and the last half on the familiar pink paper of the

Police Gazette. It also contains a fantastic account of the Benders and has them starting their criminal career in Illinois.

689. ———

Sins of New York as "exposed" by the *Police Gazette,* by Edward Van Every. . . . With an introduction by Franklin P. Adams. . . . With 120 reproductions of the original woodcut illustrations. New York, Frederick A. Stokes co., MCMXXX. Cloth. Scarce.

xvi p., 2 l., 3–299 p. illus., plates, facsm. 32 cm.
Half title; illus. t.p.

The last half of this book is printed on the pink paper of the *Gazette.* It has some material about Jesse James and a facsimile of a letter purportedly written by him.

F

690. Fable, Edmund, Jr.

Billy the Kid, the New Mexican outlaw; or, the bold bandit of the west! A true and impartial history of the greatest of American outlaws. His adventures and crimes committed in the west. The history of an outlaw who killed a man for every year of his life. . . . Denver, Colo., published by the Denver publishing company [1881]. Pict. wrappers (col.). Exceedingly rare.

4 p.l., [9]–83 p. plates, ports. 22.6 cm.
Western Border series, No. 1.
Adv. on verso of back wrapper.

A most amazing distortion of facts. Although the author states in the title that it is a "true and impartial history," there is scarcely a sentence from beginning to end which contains a grain of truth. The foreword is dated July 15, 1881, the day after Billy the Kid was killed. Either the author was an extraordinarily fast writer, or he had the book completed except for the last chapter when the Kid was killed. Most of the proper names are misspelled, and all the facts are wrong. He makes John Chisom [*sic*] the head of a band of cattle thieves, and his account of the killing of Bell and Olinger is just the reverse of the truth. He records the innermost thoughts of the Kid and has him coming to the West in adulthood.

His description of the Kid's clothes will bring a smile to anyone who knows the West. "His dress," he writes, "was arranged with a view to attract attention. He wore a blue dragoon jacket of the finest broadcloth, heavily loaded down with gold embroidery, buckskin pants, dyed a jet black with small tinkling bells sewed down the sides. . . . Underneath this garment were his drawers of fine scarlet broadcloth, extending clear down to the ankle and over his feet, encasing them like stockings. But his hat was the most gorgeous and the crowning feature of his getup. . . . And this whole structure of a hat was covered with gold and jewels until it sparkled and shone in a dazzling and blinding manner when one looked upon it. There was a gold cord around the crown as large as a man's thumb, and a great bright rosette at the left side set it off in all its glory. The *shoes* worn by this young prince of the plains were *low quartered* with patent silver spurs fixed *in the heels,* which took the place of the common clumsy arrangements that ordinary equestrians use" [italics added].

I would love to have seen anyone attempt to dress in this theatrical fashion in the old West and live to enjoy his glory. This description gives one an idea of the absurdity of the whole book. No wonder Pat Garrett complained bitterly about the inaccuracy of the several books (of which this was one) preceding his own account.

J. C. Dykes, in his excellent bibliography of Billy the Kid, asks doubtfully, "Was this item ever printed?" I succeeded in finding only one copy, in the Boston Athenaeum, which is said to be the only copy extant. I have a photostat copy in my library.

691. Fairfield, Asa Merrill

Fairfield's pioneer history of Lassen county, California; containing everything that can be learned about it from the beginning of the world to the year of our Lord, 1870. The chronicles of a border county settled without law, harassed by savages, and infested by outlaws . . ., by Asa Merrill Fairfield. San Francisco, published for the author by H. S. Crocker co. [1916]. Pict. cloth. Scarce.

xxii p., 1 l., 3–506 p. front. (port.), plates, fold. map at end. 22.3 cm.
Half title.

A scarce, privately printed history of early California and some of its lawlessness.

692. Fairfield, Ula King

Pioneer lawyer. A story of the western slope of Colorado, by Ula King Fairfield. [Denver, Colo., W. H. Kistler stationery co.], 1946. Cloth. OP.

x p., 1 l., 156 p. front., plates, ports., facsm. 22.2 cm.
Half title; device.
"Only 300 copies printed in private edition."

Has some material on bank robbery and feuds.

693. Fallwell, Gene

The Texas rangers. A factual illustrated account of the nation's oldest and most famous state law enforcement officers since 1823 . . ., [by Gene Fallwell]. . . . Connell printing co., 1959. Pict. wrappers.

2 p.l., 3–28 p. illus., plates, ports. 21.6 cm.

Many Texas Rangers are mentioned in this brief history of the force, among them Major J. B. Jones, Captain Tom Hickman, Frank Hamner, John R. Hughes, and my personal friend Captain M. T. (Lone Wolf) Gonzaullas. In a little section about Sam Bass the author leaves the impression that Bass was killed on July 19, 1878, "thus," he writes, "ending the ten-month outlaw career of Bass on his twenty-seventh birthday." He was shot on the nineteenth but did not die until the twenty-first, which was his birthday.

694. Fanning, Peter

Great crimes of the west. Pete Fanning, author, for thirty-seven years a San Francisco police officer. [San Francisco, printed by Ed Barry co., 1929.] Cloth. Scarce.

4 p.l., 9–292 p. 19.5 cm.

Author's port. on t.p.; copyright notice on verso of flyleaf.

The author has brought together a number of stories on crime and outlaws. Only two chapters fit this book's purpose: the one on Black Bart and the one on the Daltons. Neither is accurate. The author names the participants of the Coffeyville raid as Bob, Gratt, and Emmett Dalton; Tom Evans; "Texas Jack" Moore; and Ollie Ogee. The last three are incorrect.

695. Farber, James

Texans with guns, by James Farber. Illustrations by R. L. McCollister. San Antonio, Texas, the Naylor co. [1950]. Cloth.

xi p., 1 l., 3–195 p. illus. 21.6 cm.

Index: p. 191–196.

Half title; vignette.

Covers most of the Texas gunmen. In his introduction the author makes this modest statement: " 'Texans With Guns' makes claim to great accuracy. You may possibly nail me on a date or so, but you'll probably find these stories the most accurate versions ever written." Before reading many pages, I found the statement that John Selman of Fort Griffin was not to be connected with the John Selman who killed John Wesley Hardin in El Paso. They were one and the same man. His description of Clay Allison's killing of Chunk Colbert is all wrong. He repeats the legend about Wyatt Earp arresting Ben Thompson in Ellsworth, Kansas, and makes many, many more mistakes.

696. ———

Those Texans, by James Farber. Illustrations by John H. McClelland. San Antonio, Texas, the Naylor co. [1945]. Cloth. OP.

xi p., 1 l., 3–171 p. front., illus., plates. 21 cm.
Index: p. 167–171.
Half title.

Has a chapter on gunplay in which the author gives short sketches of many of the outlaws of the Southwest. He says that the Younger brothers were "as dastardly a collection of murdering cutthroats as the American scene has ever beheld," and he claims that Belle Starr got her name by marrying Jim Starr. He makes the statement that Clay Allison "killed for the sheer delight of seeing men fall and didn't always like to kill them outright, or instantly, for that would have left his sadistic mind unsatisfied." Nearly all of his information on gunmen is unreliable.

697. Farquhar, Franklin S.

History of Livingston, California. Narrative and biography, by Franklin S. Farquhar. Livingston, Calif., published by the Chronicle, 1945. Stiff wrappers. Scarce.

7 p.l., 168 [1] p. front. (port.). 21.3 cm.
Errata slip.

In Chapter VI there are two pages on the Dalton gang, almost one full page being devoted to Bill Dalton's death, which it is claimed, happened in Ardmore, Texas. It happened near Ardmore, Oklahoma. The author has Dalton married to Jane Bliven and hiding in the Bliven mansion, but he also has him being elected to the California state legislature from Paso Robles.

698. Farrow, Marion Humphreys

Troublesome times in Texas, by Marion Humphreys Farrow. [San Antonio, Texas, the Glegg co., 1957.] Cloth. Also pub. in pict. stiff wrappers.

v, 78 p. ports. 22.8 cm.
Bibliography: p. 75–78.

The author intimates that Sam Bass and Sebe Barnes were killed at Round Rock by Ranger John B. Jones, which is incorrect. He also touches upon the Taylor-Sutton feud and other lawlessness in Texas.

699. ———

Troublesome times in Texas, by Marion Humphreys Farrow. [San Antonio, Texas, the Naylor co. . . ., 1959.] Cloth.

ix, 106 p. plates, ports. 21.8 cm.

Bibliography: p. 97–102; index: p. 103–106.
Half title; illus. t.p.

This edition has an added index, a different arrangement of plates and portraits and more notes (see Item 698). It has material on the Texas Rangers and on cattle thieves, Sam Bass, John Wesley Hardin, the Taylor-Sutton feud, the Kingfisher gang, and other lawlessness.

700. Fast, Howard Melvin

The last frontier, [by] Howard Fast. . . . New York, Duell, Sloan and Pearce [1942]. Cloth. OP.

xii p., 1 l., 3–307 p. 22 cm.
Half title; illus. map on end papers; "First edition" on copyright p.

Contains a chapter on Dodge City and some of its gunmen.

701. Faulkner, Virginia

Roundup: a Nebraska reader, compiled and edited by Virginia Faulkner. Line drawings by Elmer Jacobs. Lincoln, University of Nebraska press, 1957. Pict. cloth.

xv p., 1 l., 493 p. illus. (col.). 23.7 cm.
Sources: p. 491–493.
Half title; map and illus. on end papers; double illus. t.p.

A chapter entitled "The Myth of Wild Bill Hickok" debunks the old legend about the McCanles "fight," as well as some others about Wild Bill. Another chapter deals with the Mitchell-Ketchum tragedy, and there is one on the lynching of Kid Wade. There is also some material on Pat Crowe.

702. Feder, Sid

Longhorns and short tales of Victoria and the Gulf coast, by Sid Feder. Victoria, Texas, Victoria Advocate publishing co., 1958. Stiff wrappers.

4 p.l., 9–128 [1] p. illus., plates, ports., facsms. 23 cm.
Index: p. 121–128.

Has some material on the Taylor-Sutton feud.

703. Feitz, Leland

Myers avenue. A quick history of Cripple Creek's red-light district, by Leland Feitz. With photos. Colorado Springs, Colo., printed by Dentan-Berkeland printing co., inc., 1967. Stiff pict. wrappers.

4 p.l., 5–27 p. plates (3 full p.). 21.5 cm.

704. Fellows, Dexter, and Andrew A. Freeman

This way to the big show. The life of Dexter Fellows, by Dexter Fellows and Andrew A. Freeman. New York, Halcyon House [1936]. Cloth. Scarce.

7 p.l., [3]–361 p. front. (port.), plates, ports. 26 cm.

Appendix: p. [343]–352; index: p. [353]–362.

The authors tell about Wild Bill Hickok's life as a showman and about his murder by Jack McCall. Mr. Fellows tells about registering in a hotel in Topeka where Emmett Dalton was night clerk and about meeting Cole Younger when he was with a wild West show. He quotes one of the show programs that told the old legend that Calamity Jane "once saved" [a] coach when the driver was killed by bandits by seizing the lines and whipping the horses to a run, safely bringing the coach to its destination." This is one of her own tales which never happened.

705. Fenley, Florence

Grandad and I. A story of a grand old man and other pioneers in Texas and the Dakotas, as told by John Leakey to Florence Fenley. [Leakey, Texas John Leakey, publisher, 1951.] Cloth. Rare.

4 p.l., 9–179 p. front., plates, ports. 21.2 cm.

Last 18 pages plates and ports.; "First printing" on copyright p.

Contains a chapter on King Fisher, relating some of his escapades not found in other books. The author says in several places that King Fisher was killed in 1882. He was killed in 1884.

706. Fenwick, Robert W.

Alfred [*sic*] Packer. The true story of Colorado's man-eater, by Robert W. Fenwick. [Denver, Denver Post, 1963.] Stiff pict. wrapper (col.).

1 p.l., 3–40 p. illus., plates, ports., maps (1 double p.), facsm. 27 cm.

Double column.

Perhaps the most complete history of this sanguinary man and his trials. The author, like most writers, spells his subject's first name Alfred. Packer signed his name Alferd.

707. Ferguson, Charles D.

The experiences of a forty-niner during thirty-four years' residence in California and Australia. By Charles D. Ferguson. Edited by Frederick T. Wallace. Cleveland, Ohio, the Williams publishing co., 1888. Cloth. Scarce.

xviii p., 1 l., 9–507 p. front. (double p. port.), plates. 22.6 cm.

Cover title: "A Third of a Century in the Gold Fields."

Has much on lawlessness.

708. Ferguson, Mrs. Tom B.

They carried the torch. The story of Oklahoma's pioneer newspapers, by Mrs. Tom B. Ferguson. Illustrated by Benton Ferguson. Introduction by Edith Johnson. Kansas City, Mo., Burton publishing co., publishers [1937]. Pict. cloth. Scarce.

5 p.l., 16–132 p. front., illus. 20.5 cm.

Has some scattered material on the Oklahoma outlaws, such as Dick Yeager.

709. Fergusson, Erna

Erna Fergusson's Albuquerque. Drawings by Li Brown. Albuquerque, N.M., Merle Armitage editions [1947]. Cloth. OP.

5 p.l., 87 [1] p. front., illus., plates. 23.5 cm.
Double t.p. in red and black; pub. device.

Contains some short, but new, stories about Elfego Baca.

710. ———

Murder & mystery in New Mexico, [by] Erna Fergusson. Frontispiece by Peter Hurd. Albuquerque, N.M., Merle Armitage editions [1948]. Cloth. OP.

6 p.l., 15–192 [1] p., 5 l. plates, ports. at end. 23.5 cm.
Half title; double t.p. in red and black; map on front end papers; headpieces in silhouette; pub. device; "First edition" on copyright p.

A well-written book with chapters on several of the New Mexico outlaws, such as Vicente Silva, Billy the Kid, and Tom Ketchum. The author follows Upson's account of Billy the Kid's early life as regards his birth, the early move to Kansas, and the mother's marriage in Colorado. The stories about the Kid's stabbing of the blacksmith who insulted his mother, his fights with Indians, and his rescue of Segura are much the same as Upson's, except that in her version the stabbed man lives, though the Kid thinks he has killed him and runs away. She makes the common mistake of having the Kid going to Maxwell's to see his sweetheart when he is killed. Her chapters on Vicente Silva and Tom Ketchum are more reliable, but fewer legends have been invented about those two outlaws.

711. ———

Our southwest, by Erna Fergusson; photographs by Ruth Frank and others. New York & London, Alfred A. Knopf, 1940. Cloth. OP.

7 p.l., 3–376, vi p., 1 l. front., plates, 2 fold. maps, 1 double p. map (col.). 22.5 cm.
Index: p. i–vi.
Half title; map on end papers; pub. device; untrimmed; "First edition" on copyright p.

The author says that Billy the Kid was killed by Pat Garrett when he went to Pete Maxwell's to visit his sweetheart. That story, which has been repeated by many writers, is incorrect.

712. Fergusson, Harvey

Rio Grande, by Harvey Fergusson. New York, Alfred A. Knopf, 1933. Pict. cloth.

x p., 1 l., 3–296, i–viii p. 15 p. plates at end. 22.4 cm.
Bibliography: p. 292–296; index: p. i–viii.
Half title; pub. device; vignette; untrimmed; "First edition" on copyright p.

Has quite a bit of material on Elfego Baca, as well as some on Billy the Kid, Joel Fowler, and others. The author says that Billy the Kid briefly ruled a region "as large as France because he was faster on the draw than any other man in it," but he has his towns mixed when he says that Ben Thompson dominated Houston in similar fashion. He speaks of Wild Bill Hayward as a famous gunman. Perhaps he means Wild Bill Hickok.

713. Fetherstonhaugh, R. C.

The royal Canadian mounted police, [by] R. C. Fetherstonhaugh. New York, Carrick & Evans, inc. [1938]. Cloth. OP.

xii p., 1 l., 3–322 p. plates, maps (3 fold.). 24 cm.

Contains some material on Soapy Smith.

714. Field, Henry M.

Our western archipelago, by Henry M. Field. With illustrations. New York, Charles Scribner's sons, 1895. Dec. cloth. Scarce.

6 p.l., 250 p. front. (with tissue), plates, map (col.). 21.3 cm.
Half title.

Has a chapter on the Montana vigilantes, though the author calls no names.

715. Fielder, Mildred

Wild Bill and Deadwood, by Mildred Fielder. Seattle, Superior publishing co. [1965]. Cloth.

5 p.l., 11–160 p. front. (port.), plates, ports., facsms. 27.5 cm.
Bibliography: p. 146–149.
Half title; "First edition" on copyright p.

This is largely a book of early, and interesting, pictures. In her text the author tells nothing new, though she makes some errors, such as referring to Rock Creek as Rock Springs. She has Texas Jack Omohundro killed in 1876, but he died of pneumonia on June 28, 1880. She is also mistaken in having a Con Stapleton a member of the poker game in which Hickok was killed. The man was Charlie Rich.

716. Fierman, Floyd D. and Dr. John O. West (eds.)

Billy the Kid, the cowboy outlaw; an incident as recalled by Flora Spiegelberg. Edited by Dr. Floyd S. Fierman and Dr. John O. West. [Philadelphia, press of Maurice Jacobs, inc.] Reprinted from *American Jewish Historical Quarterly*, Vol. LV, No. 1 (September, 1965). Stiff wrappers.

98–106 p. 22.8 cm.

The tale Flora Spiegelberg tells is the substance of which legends are created. She has Billy the Kid robbing stagecoaches and doing other things he never did. She closes her story by saying, "Trying to escape he was shot and killed by the sheriff," a statement known to be incorrect.

717. Filcher, J. A.

Untold tales of California. Short stories illustrating phases of life peculiar to the early days of the west. Embalmed in book that they may remain when the actors are gone, by J. A. Filcher. [N.p., published by the author], 1903. Cloth. Rare.

3 p.l., [9]–161 p. 3 plates. 17.6 cm.

Has a chapter on stage holdups.

718. Finger, Charles Joseph

Adventures under sapphire skies, by Charles J. Finger, with sketches made en route by Helen Finger. New York, William Morrow & co., 1931. Cloth. Scarce.

viii p., 2 l., 3–293 p. illus., maps. 18.8 cm.

Index: p. 289–293.

Half title; untrimmed.

Tells of the Lincoln County War and Billy the Kid. The author has the Kid killed at Pete Maxwell's house, but places the killing at Fort Stanton instead of Fort Sumner.

719. ———

The distant prize. A book about rovers, rangers and rascals, by Charles J. Finger. Decorations by Henry Pitz. New York, London, D. Appleton-Century co., inc., 1935. Cloth. Scarce.

ix, 330 p. 21 cm.

Index: p. 325–330.

Half title; illus. end papers; illus. chapter headings; untrimmed; first edition: figure (1) at end of index.

Has some mention of such outlaws as Billy the Kid, Jesse James, Bob Ford, and Sam Bass. The author repeats the legend about Murieta reading the wanted poster offering a reward for him and writing an additional reward on the sign.

720. ———

Foot-loose in the west. Being an account of a journey to Colorado and California and other western states, by Charles J. Finger. With sketches made en route by Helen Finger. New York, William Morrow and co., 1932. Cloth. Scarce.

viii p., 2 l., 302 p. illus., plates, maps. 18.8 cm.

Index: p. 295–302.

Half title; vignette; untrimmed.

Has material on Captain Jack, the Modoc outlaw and some slight mention of the Jameses and Daltons, as well as the California outlaws Vásquez, Murieta, and Black Bart.

721. Fisher, Anne B.

The Salinas, upside-down river, by Anne B. Fisher. Illustrated by Walter K. Fisher. New York, Toronto, Farrar & Rinehart, inc. [1945]. Cloth. OP.

xviii p., 2 l., 5–316 p. illus., map (double p.). 21 cm.

Acknowledgments: p. 303–304; bibliography: p. 305–308; note by illustrator: p. 309–310; index: p. 311–316.

Half title; illus. end papers; illus. t.p.; first edition: "F R" in device on copyright p.

Contains much information on Vásquez, his loves, and his capture.

722. Fisher, O. C.

It occurred in Kimble, by O. C. Fisher; illustrations by Lonnie Rees, cover design by Hal Jones. Houston, Texas, the Anson Jones press, MCMXXXVII. Pict. cloth. Scarce.

13 p.l., [29]–237 [3] p. front., illus., ports. 23.6 cm.

"Printed sources consulted": p. [239].

Half title; on cover: "The Story of a Texas County."

Colophon: "Of this first edition . . . 500 copies have been printed of which this is ——."

Two chapters, "The Big Outlaw Roundup of '77," and "Outlaws and Trigger-pulling," are devoted to the outlaws of Kimble County, Texas.

723. ———

The Texas heritage of the Fishers and the Clarks, by O. C. Fisher. . . . Illustrated. Salado, Texas, the Anson Jones press, MCMLXIII. Pict. cloth.

xx p., [21]–241 [1] p. front. (port.), illus., plates, ports., map. 27.4 cm.

Appendix: p. [195]–[236]; index: p. [237]–[242].
Half title; illus. end papers.
Limited edition in slip case.

Has a section on John King Fisher and gives some new information on his early life.

724. ———, and Jeff C. Dykes

King Fisher, his life and times, by O. C. Fisher and J. C. Dykes. Norman, University of Oklahoma press [1966]. Boards.

xvii p., 1 l., 3–157 p. 19.6 cm.
Western Frontier Library series.
Bibliography: p. 149–153; list of publications of this series: p. 155–157.
Half title; illus. t.p.

One of the few original publications in the Western Frontier Library Series. Has material on King Fisher, Ben Thompson, Bat Masterson, the Taylor-Sutton feud, and the Texas Rangers.

725. Fisher, Vardis, [and] Opal Laurel Holmes

Gold rushes and mining camps of the early American west, by Vardis Fisher [and] Opal Laurel Holmes. Illustrated with photographs. Caldwell, Idaho, the Caxton printers, ltd., 1968. Pict. cloth.

xiii p., 1 l., 466 p. plates, ports., facsms. 28.6 cm.
Notes: p. 448–450; illustrations: p. 451–455; selected bibliography: p. 456–458; index: p. 459–466 (triple column).
Half title; illus. double t.p.; text double column.

The most complete treatise of early mining in the West that I have examined. Like a good historian he corrects some of the false history that has been written about this subject. He deals with such California outlaws as Tom Bell, Joaquín Murieta, Tiburcio Vásquez, Black Bart, Three-Fingered Jack García, and Jack Powers. He has some material on the Montana vigilantes, as well as those of California, including material on Henry Plummer, Boone Helm, Joseph Slade, and others. He also touches upon Billy the Kid, Wild Bill Hickok, Soapy Smith, Bob Ford, Jack McCall, and Jesse James. Among the noted females he includes are Calamity Jane, Cattle Kate Watson, and many of the better-known prostitutes of the West. He goes to some length to correct some of the drivel that has been written about Wyatt Earp. This is a large, heavy book, but well worth the effort and strength to read it through.

726. Fisher, Walter M.

The Californians, by Walter M. Fisher. . . . London, the Macmillan co., 1876. Cloth. Rare.

x, 236 p. 19.2 cm.
Half title; 31 p. adv. at end, numbered [1] to 28 [3].

Contains a chapter on lawlessness, including the activities of Vásquez and Chávez.

727. Fishwick, Marshall W.

American heroes, myth and reality, by Marshall W. Fishwick. Introduction by Carl Carmer. Washington, D.C., Public Affairs press [1954]. Cloth.

viii p., 3 l., 3–242 p. 23.5 cm.
Sources: p. 234–238; bibliographical notes: p. 239; index: p. 240–242.
Half title.

Has a chapter on Billy the Kid in which the author does some debunking of the legends and writers about the Kid. Yet he repeats the old tale about the judge condemning the Kid to be "hanged by the neck until you are dead, dead, dead," and the Kid's answer, "And you go to hell, hell, hell." The book also has some material on the James boys, the Daltons, Bob Ford, and others.

728. Fitzgerald, John D.

Papa married a Mormon, [by] John D. Fitzgerald. Englewood Cliffs, [N.J.], Prentice-Hall, inc. [1955]. Cloth. OP.

x, 298 p. plates, ports. 21.3 cm.
Half title.

Contains a chapter on the killing of the outlaw Laredo Kid.

729. Fitzpatrick, George (ed.)

This is New Mexico, edited by George Fitzpatrick. Sketches by Wilfred Stedman. Santa Fe, the Rydal press [1948]. Cloth. OP.

x p., 2 l., 2–328 p. 23.5 cm.
Half title; map on end papers; vignette.

A collection of articles from the *New Mexico Magazine*. It contains a story about Billy the Kid, by Eugene Cunningham; and one about Clay Allison, by J. Frank Dobie. Cunningham repeats all the old legends about the Kid's life, his "wanderings" in Old Mexico and Arizona; his eighty-one-mile ride to free his friend Segura; the marriage of his mother to Antrim in Colorado, and others. He is mistaken in having Bowdre in the burning McSween home. He has the Kid arrested (with his consent, it seems) for the murder of Brady and Hindman, but pleading "not guilty" and walking out of jail. He also has the Kid killed on July 13, rather than on the fourteenth.

730. ———

This is New Mexico, edited by George Fitzpatrick. Albuquerque, N.M., Horn & Wallace, publishers [1962]. Cloth.

ix, 324 [1] p. front. (col. and tipped in). 23.7 cm.
Acknowledgments: p. 323–324.
Half title; map on end papers.

This edition omits some of the articles that appear in the first edition (Item 729), including the one by Cunningham, and adds some about Elfego Baca and Billy the Kid. Thirty-one articles of the first edition are retained, and nineteen new ones are added.

731. [**Fitzsimmons, Joseph**]

An appeal to the people of the state of Texas, of the territory between the Nueces river and the Rio grande, prepared by certain civil authorities of that district, and addressed through the Hon. Secretary of State of the United States to the President, to Congress, and to the country for protection against incursions of the savages of the state of Coahuila, Mexico. . . . Corpus Christi, Texas, Free press print, 1878. Wrappers. (Cover title.) Rare.

40 p. 19.4 cm.

A speech and a collection of affidavits dealing with crimes committed by Mexican outlaws against Texas citizens.

732. Flannery, L. G. (Pat) (ed.)

John Hunton's diary, 1876–'77. Vol. 2, by L. G. (Pat) Flannery. [Lingle, Wyo., printed by Guide-Review, 1958.] Imt. suede.

2 p.l., 289 [2] p. plates, ports., 2 maps at end. 15.2 cm.
Index to names: p. 270–289.
Colophon: "This is number —— of 1500 copies (signed), Fort Laramie, Wyoming."

Has some material on Sam Bass, Joel Collins, Calamity Jane, Wild Bill Hickok, Reddy McKemie, and Jack McCall. The author misspells McCall's name as McCaul, and Hickok's as Hicock as well, also giving Hickok the initials J. J. Of Calamity Jane he writes: "Her achievements have been greatly magnified by every writer I have ever read for she was the commonest of her class." He says that Wild Bill "was assassinated by a stage driver, Jack McCaul [*sic*] who was lynched for the deed by a mob, reputedly led by Calamity Jane." He has the Big Spring robbery of the Union Pacific on the night of September 18, 1878, rather than 1877, and he says that the amount of the loot was $70,000 and that the gang was ultimately captured by U.S. Marshal Leach, of Ogallala. Leach was not a U.S. marshal, but a clerk in a store. Nor was the gang captured. Three were killed, and the rest escaped. (Volume I of the work has no material on outlaws.) See also Items 733 to 735.

733. ———

John Hunton's diary, 1878–'79. Vol. 3, by L. G. (Pat) Flannery. [Lingle, Wyo., printed by Guide-Review, 1960.] Imt. suede.

7 p.l., [1] p., 12–228 [2] p. plates, ports., 2 maps. 15.4 cm.
Name index: p. 207–228.

Has some material on Jim Berry before and during the time he was with Sam Bass and Joel Collins.

734. ———

John Hunton's diary, Vol. 4, 1880–'81–'82. Lingle, Wyo., printed by Guide-Review [1963]. Imt. suede.

7 p.l., 15–245 [2] p. plates, ports., maps. 15.4 cm.
Index: p. 247–259.
Colophon: "This is number —— of 1500 copies."

Has some material on Calamity Jane.

735. ———

John Hunton's diary, Vol. 5, 1883–'84. Lingle, Wyo., printed by Guide-Review [1964]. Imt. suede.

8 p.l., 16–259 [2] p. plates, ports., maps. 15.4 cm.
Index: p. 247–259.
Colophon: "This is number —— of 1500 copies."

Has some mention of Calamity Jane, the Johnson County War, Nate Champion, Nick Ray, and Bill Thompson.

736. Fletcher, Baylis John

Up the trail in '79, by Baylis John Fletcher. Edited and with an introduction by Wayne Gard. Norman, University of Oklahoma press, [1968]. Boards.

xxiii p., 1 l., 3–118 p. 2 plates, 2 ports. 19.8 cm.
Western Frontier Library series, No. 37.
Bibliography: p. 114–115; list of other books in this series: p. 116–118.
Pub. device; "First printing" on copyright p.

Contains a chapter devoted to the Big Spring robbery of the Union Pacific by Joel Collins and his gang. The author calls M. F. Leach by the name Billy Lynch. He also tells a different story about Leach's pursuit of the robbers. He gives Jim Thompson the name Thomas and has the killing of Collins and Heffridge in the wrong locale. The author also says that Jim Berry was killed "while resisting arrest." He was shot by Sheriff Glascock while running away. He has Frank Jackson wanting to kill Jim Murphy because he was reported to be a traitor. It was

Jackson who defended Murphy from the other members of the gang. He has Dick Ware giving Bass his fatal wound. No one knows for certain who shot Bass.

737. Fletcher, Ernest M.

The wayward horseman, [by] Ernest M. Fletcher. Edited by Forbes Parkhill. Denver, Sage books [1958]. Cloth.

5 p.l., 11–217 p. plates, ports. 22.3 cm.
Index: p. 215–217.
Half title; pub. device.

The author says that his group joined a Texas outfit who were "also delivering cattle to an agency" and that they later learned that the Texas outfit was really Sam Bass and his gang, who, on their way home, robbed the Union Pacific. Bass and his gang were not driving cattle just before this robbery. The author also says that they "buried the loot, fled to Ogallala and separated." He also incorrectly states that a prostitute named Polka Dot was responsible for the killing of Bob Ford.

738. Florin, Lambert

Boot Hill. Historic graves of the old west, by Lambert Florin. . . . Seattle, Superior publishing co. [1966]. Cloth.

5 p.l., [11]–192 p. front., plates, facsms. 27.5 cm.
Half title; illus. end papers; "First edition" on copyright p.

Tells about the Earp-Clanton fight and the killing of Billy the Kid. The author also gives an account of Henry Plummer, but he is mistaken in saying that the girl Plummer married was Eliza Bryan. Her name was Electra. Many of the outlaws of Arizona and New Mexico are mentioned.

739. ———

Ghost town album, by Lambert Florin. Maps and drawings by David C. Mason. Seattle, Wash., Superior publishing co. [1962]. Pict. cloth.

6 p.l., 15–184 p. front., illus., plates, maps. 27.3 cm.
Illus. end papers; double column; "First edition" on copyright p.

Deals with the ghost towns of most of the western states, and has material on such gunmen as Alferd Packer, Bob Ford, Ed O. Kelly, (whom the author calls Ed O'Kelly), Soapy Smith, Dave Rudabaugh, Joaquín Murieta, Black Bart, and others. He repeats many of the legends about Murieta and writes that Russian Bill was hanged because the population was "fed up" with his pranks, the climax being that he had shot off a finger of a gambler trying to show off his marksmanship. That was not the reason Russian Bill was hanged. He was a horse thief.

740. Fogarty, Kate Hammond

The story of Montana. By Kate Hammond Fogarty. New York and Chicago, the A. S. Barnes co. [1916]. Cloth. Scarce.

x, 302 p. front., plates, map. 18.7 cm.

Index: p. [293]–302.

Has a chapter on road agents and vigilantes in which the author deals with the Plummer gang.

741. Foght, Harold Waldstein

The trail of the Loup; being a history of the Loup river region, with some chapters on the state, [by] H. W. Foght. [Ord, Nebr.], 1906. Cloth. Scarce.

8 p.l., [17]–296 p. front. (port.), illus., plates (1 fold.), ports., maps, plans. 26 cm.

Has some information on cattle stealing; I. P. Olive and his feud with Mitchell and Ketchum.

742. Foote, Stella Adelyne

Letters from Buffalo Bill. Taken from the originals now on exhibit at the Wonderland museum, Billings, Montana . . ., by Stella Adelyne Foote. . . . Billings, Mont., Foote publishing co., museum ed., 1954.

3 p.l., [4]–80 p. plates, ports., facsms. 23.5 cm.

Has some mention of Wild Bill Hickok.

743. Ford, Tirey L.

Dawn and the dons. The romance of Monterey, by Tirey L. Ford. With vignettes and sketches by Jo Moro. San Francisco, A. M. Robertson, MCMXXVI. Pict. boards. Scarce.

xiii p., 1 l., 236 p. illus., facsms. 23.5 cm.

Index: p. 233–236.

Map on end papers; headpieces; tailpieces; vignette.

In Chapter XVIII, devoted entirely to Murieta, the author gives a romantic account of his young love and repeats the legend about him scrawling beneath the reward notice. It is strange how people seized upon this romantic piece of fiction and treasured it as real history.

744. Foreman, Grant

A history of Oklahoma, [by] Grant Foreman. Norman, University of Oklahoma press, MCMXLII. Cloth. Scarce.

xiv p., 1 l., 3–384 p. front., plates, ports., maps (1 fold.), facsms. 23.5 cm.
Bibliography: p. 362–366; index: p. 367–384.
Half title.

Has some mention of the Dalton gang, the Doolin and Jennings gangs, the Buck gang, Dutch Henry's band, and others.

745. ———

Muskogee, the biography of an Oklahoma town, by Grant Foreman. Norman, University of Oklahoma press [1943]. Cloth. OP.

xi p., 2 l., 3–169 p. plates, ports., fold. map. 19.5 cm.
Enlarged and privately printed by the author in a later edition.

Contains material on some of the outlaws of Oklahoma, especially the Cook gang.

746. Forest, Col. Cris

Hildebrand, the outlaw; or, the terror of Missouri, by Col. Cris Forest. . . . New York, Robert M. DeWitt, publishers . . ., 1869. Pict. wrappers. Rare.

[9]–100 p. front. 16 cm.
1 p. adv. on verso t.p.

A dime thriller which has become rare and worth a much higher price.

747. Forrest, Earle Robert

Arizona's dark and bloody ground, by Earle R. Forrest; with introduction by William MacLeod Raine. Caldwell, Idaho, the Caxton printers, ltd., 1936. Cloth.

10 p.l., [21]–370 p. illus., plates, ports. 19.5 cm.
Notes: p. [310]–339; acknowledgments: p. [340]–341; bibliography: p. [342]–343; principal characters: p. [344]–352; index: p. [353]–370.
Half title; map on end papers; pub. device.
Reprinted in 1948 with additions and changes.

Perhaps the best and most complete history of the Graham-Tewksbury feud, this book reveals intelligent research. It has some accounts of the Apache Kid, Billy the Kid, Tom Pickett, and the killing of Andy Copper by Commodore Owens.

748. ———, and Edwin B. Hill

Lone war trail of Apache Kid, by Earle R. Forrest and Edwin B. Hill. Illustrations by Charles M. Russell. Pasadena, Calif., Trail's End publishing co., inc. [1947]. Cloth. OP.

12 p.l., 27–143 p. [1]. plates (1 col.), ports. 23.6 cm.
Notes: p. 115–132; bibliography: p. 133–136; index: p. 137–143.
Half title; legend and map on end papers; pub. device.
Also published in a de luxe edition of 250 copies, signed and bound in morocco.

A well-written history, and up to the time of its publication the most nearly complete work on this notorious Arizona Indian outlaw.

749. Forsee, Peter A.

Five years of crime in California; or, the life and confession of G. W. Strong, alias G. W. Clark, who was tried, convicted, and hung, August 31st, 1866, at Ukiah City, Mendocino county, California, for the murder of Frances Holmes. A truthful record of this most extraordinary man . . . together with evidence . . . legal proceedings . . . rulings of the courts before whom he was tried. . . . Compiled and arranged by deputy sheriff and one of his prison guards, George Washinton [*sic*] Thompson. Ukiah City, Mendocino county, California, published by Peter A. Forsee, January 25th, 1867. Wrappers. Rare.

46 p. 23.3 cm.

750. Fortson, John

Pott county and what has come of it. A history of Pottawatomie county, by John Fortson. [Shawnee, Okla., Herald printing co.] Published under the auspices Pottawatomie county historical society, 1936. Stiff wrappers. (Caption title.) Scarce.

1 p.l., 5–90 p. plates, ports. 23.5 cm.

Has some information on some of the outlaws of Oklahoma, such as Bob and Bill Christian, Red Buck George Thorne, George (Hookie) Miller, and Al Jennings. The author gives an account of the lynching of Jim Miller and his companions for the murder of Angus Bobbitt.

751. Foster-Harris

The look of the old west, by Foster-Harris, with illustrations by Evelyn Curro. New York, the Viking press, 1955. Pict. cloth and boards.

x p., 1 l., [3]–316 p. illus., maps (1 double p.). 27.7 cm.
Bibliography: p. [303]–305; index: p. [307]–316.
Half title; illus. t.p.

Has some information on many of the outlaws of the West, such as Billy the Kid, Butch Cassidy, Bill Carver, Jim Courtright, King Fisher, John Wesley Hardin, the James boys, Harvey Logan, Harry Longabaugh, Bill Longley, Jack McCall, and Ben Thompson, and such gunmen as Wyatt Earp, Bat Masterson, Luke Short, and Dallas Stoudenmire.

752. Fouts, Burnett W. (Bob)

The gunfight of the age in verse form, by Burnett W. "Bob" Fouts. The story of the famous Earp-Clanton feud which culminated in the historical gunfight at the "O. K." Corral in Tombstone, Arizona, October 26, 1881. [Tombstone], 1946. Stiff pict. wrappers. OP.

8 p. 19.7 x 8.2 cm.

753. Fowler, Gene

Timber line; a story of Bonfils and Tammen, by Gene Fowler. New York, Covici, Friede, publishers, MCMXXXIII. Cloth. Scarce.

8 p.l., 13–480 p. front. (2 ports.). 21.8 cm.
Half title; t.p. in black and green; facsm. of signature on cover; untrimmed.

This book has been republished several times, but the first edition has become quite scarce. It contains a long chapter on the life and execution of Tom Horn.

754. Foy, Eddie, and Alvin F. Harlow

Clowning through life, by Eddie Foy and Alvin F. Harlow. Illustrated. New York, E. P. Dutton & co. [1928]. Cloth. Scarce.

4 p.l., 3–331 p. front. (port.), plates, ports. 23 cm.
Half title; device; untrimmed.

The author tells of his experiences in Dodge City, Kansas, and Tombstone, Arizona, as an early-day actor among the gunmen of those wild towns. In Dodge he became a close friend of Bat Masterson.

755. Frackelton, Will

Sagebrush dentist, as told by Dr. Will Frackelton to Herman Gastrell Seely. Chicago, A. C. McClurg & co. [1941]. Cloth. Scarce.

3 p.l., 9–246 p. 22.3 cm.
Half title.

Reprinted with added material (publisher's preface, introduction, and a chapter on Buffalo Bill's divorce suit) in 1947 by Trail's End publishing co., Pasadena, Calif.

6 p.l., 13–258 p. front. (port.). 22 cm.
Half title; pub. device.

The author spins an interesting yarn, and among other things tells of his experiences with Butch Cassidy, Harry Longabaugh, Tom O'Day, and the rest of the Wild Bunch in their own lair. He gives some new material on both Calamity Jane and Soapy Smith.

756. France, George W.

The struggles of life and home in the north-west. By a pioneer homebuilder. Life, 1865–1889, [by] Geo. W. France. New York, I. Goldman, steam printer, 1890. Stiff wrappers. Rare.

11 p.l., 23–607 p. front. (port.), plates, facsms. 22.6 cm.

Title on cover: "Pilgrimage to Hell." Filled with crime, robbery, murder, prison life of the author, and vigilantes, covering the states of Utah, Arizona, California, Nevada, Idaho, Montana, Washington, Oregon and Alaska.

757. Francis, Francis, Jr.,

Saddle and moccasin, by Francis Francis, Jr. London, Chapman and Hall ltd., 1887. Cloth. Scarce.

xi, 322 p. 20.3 cm.

Makes some mention of Curly Bill Brocius, Russian Bill, and others.

758. Franke, Paul

They plowed up hell in old Cochise, by Paul Franke. Douglas, Ariz., Douglas Climate club, 1950. Stiff wrappers. OP.

2 p.l., 5–58 [2] p. front., illus., plates, ports., map. 19.7 cm.

Half title; map inside each cover; t.p. on verso of contents; headpieces.

Has much material on the outlaws of Arizona. The author tells of the hanging of John Heath, the O K Corral fight, and other explosive events in Arizona. The author is partial to the Earps and says that Sheriff Behan "had the backbone of a jellyfish."

759. Franks, J. M.

Seventy years in Texas; memories of the pioneer days, Indian depredations and the northwest cattle trail, by J. M. Franks. Gatesville, Texas, 1924. Wrappers. Scarce.

2 p.l., [5]–133 [1] p. front. (port.). 23.5 cm.

The author says that Wild Bill Hickok was killed in 1880. He was killed in 1876. The author also tells of the killing of Phil Coe by Wild Bill, but calls him Phil Cole, a mistake often made by others. He also has Wild Bill's middle initial as "H."

760. Frantz, Joe B., and Julian Ernest Choate, Jr.,

The American cowboy; the myth and the reality, [by] Joe B. Frantz and Julian Ernest Choate, Jr. Norman, University of Oklahoma press, [1955]. Cloth.

xiii [1] p., 1 l., 3–232 p. plates. 22 cm.

Bibliography: p. 203–222; index: p. 223–232.

Half title; pub. device; "First edition" on copyright p.

Has some information on Billy the Kid, the Johnson County War, the Tonto Basin War, Cattle Kate Watson, Ben Thompson, Sam Bass, Wild Bill Hickok, and others. The authors repeat the legends about the Kid going to Pete Maxwell's "to be comforted by his *querida*," and they further say that "the Kid was at Maxwell's in another room," and "sensing the presence of a stranger in the dark house, the Kid came quietly into Maxwell's bedroom, where Garrett sat on the edge of the bed." When the Kid said, "*Quién es?*" they write, "Garrett fired twice at the direction from which the sound came, and that was all." They say that Collins robbed the Union Pacific to repay his friends for money he had received from the sale of a herd and had gambled away.

They write, "Debts to one's friends must be paid—that is good; but to get the money, a robbery is staged—that is bad."

761. Fraser, Mrs. Hugh, and Hugh C. Fraser

Seven years on the Pacific slope, by Mrs. Hugh Fraser and Hugh C. Fraser. With illustrations. New York, Dodd, Mead and co., 1914. Cloth. Scarce.

xii p., 1 l., 391 p. front., plates. 23.6 cm.
Half title; vignette; untrimmed.

This contains a chapter on Billy the Kid, though his name is not mentioned. The story the authors tell is most ridiculous and a good example of the tales garrulous old-timers tell about the Kid.

762. Frederick, James Vincent

Ben Holladay, the stagecoach king. A chapter in the development of transcontinental transportation, by J. V. Frederick. . . . Glendale, Calif., the Arthur H. Clark co., 1940. Cloth.

8 p.l., [19]–334 p. front. (with tissue), plates, fold. map, facsm. 24.3 cm.
Appendix: p. 281–303; bibliography: p. [307]–313; index: p. [319]–334.
Half title; pub. device; untrimmed.

Tells of some of the early stagecoach robberies, and has material on Joseph Slade and Broncho Jack.

763. Freeman, George D.

Midnight and noonday; or, dark deeds unraveled. Giving twenty years experience on the frontier; also the murder of Pat Hennesey [*sic*] and the hanging of Tom Smith, at Ryland's Ford, and the facts concerning the Talbot raid on Caldwell. Also the death dealing career of McCarty and incidents happening in and around Caldwell, Kansas, from 1871 until 1890, by G. D. Freeman. Caldwell, Kans. [printed by the author], 1890. Boards. Exceedingly rare.

4 p.l., 9–405 p. front. (port.). 20 cm.

Reprinted in 1892, bound in cloth and with the same text but with the addition of a certificate, signed by seven old-time pioneers attesting to the truth of the narrative, which appears on page 406. The pioneers, in turn, are vouched for by the editor of the *Caldwell News*. The second printing is bound in red cloth, and the first edition is so rare that some collectors think that the 1892 edition was the only one published. The book contains much material on the gunmen and their gun battle in Caldwell, and tells of the Medicine Lodge bank robbery by Henry Brown and Ben Wheeler.

764. Freeman, James W. (ed.)

Prose and poetry of the live stock industry of the United States, with outlines of the origin and ancient history of our live stock animals. . . . Illustrated. Prepared by authority of the National Live Stock association, Denver and Kansas City. [Franklin Hudson publishing co., 1905.] Dec. leather. Vol. I (only vol. published). Very rare.

11 p.l., 25–757 p. illus., plates, ports. (part with tissues). 27.8 cm.
Double column; gilt top.

One of the most important and most sought-after books on the cattle industry. In all my years of book collecting, I have only once seen it listed in a dealer's catalogue. When a dealer does find a copy, he always has a waiting list. All copies of the book, bound in leather, were issued to members of the National Livestock Association, each with the name of the individual member stamped in gold on the cover and a certificate with seal bound in. It is said that the publication of this one volume bankrupted one printing company and almost bankrupted the association. Three volumes had originally been planned; but after the expense of the first volume, the project was abandoned.

The book was republished in facsimile by the Antiquarian Press, New York, in 1960, with a new introduction by Ramon F. Adams. This edition is limited to five hundred and is in a slip case.

The book is said to have been written by Charles F. Martin, the secretary of the association. The chapter entitled "The Range Rustler" contains material on the Johnson County and Lincoln County wars. The writer calls Billy the Kid an "infamous cutthroat" and says that he "died a violent death at the ripe age of twenty-three and at that time had killed twenty-three men—one for each year of his horrible life—having committed his first murder when he was but fourteen years old." That information is all wrong.

765. Freeman, Lewis Ransome

Down the Yellowstone, by Lewis R. Freeman. . . . With illustrations. New York, Dodd, Mead and co., 1922. Cloth. OP.

12 p.l., 282 p. front., plates, ports. 22.6 cm.
Half title; t.p. in red and black; device; untrimmed.

Republished in London by William Heineman, ltd., in 1923.

Contains much new information on Calamity Jane.

766. French, Chauncey Del

Railroadman, by Chauncey Del French. New York, the Macmillan co., 1938. Cloth. OP.

vi p., 2 l., 292 p. plates, ports., facsm. 22 cm.
Half title.

Has a chapter on Dodge City and some of its gunfighters, including Bat Masterson, and much on bank robberies of the Northwest. The author is mistaken in saying that Bat Masterson succeeded his brother Ed as city marshal of Dodge. He also has Wyatt Earp marshal of Dodge, but Earp never held that office.

767. French, George (ed.)

Indianola scrap book. Fiftieth anniversary of the storm of August 20, 1886. History of a city that once was the gateway of commerce for this entire section. Victoria, Texas, compiled and published by the Victoria Advocate, 1936. Cloth. Scarce.

3–198 p. plates, ports., map, facsm. 23.5 cm.

Contains some material on the Taylor-Sutton feud and the killing of Bill Sutton by Jim Taylor.

768. French, Joseph Lewis (ed.)

A gallery of old rogues, edited by Joseph Lewis French. New York, Alfred H. King, inc. [1931]. Cloth. OP.

vi p., 2 l., 11–285 p. 23 cm.
Half title.

An anthology concerning outlaws, some from the American West, such as Billy the Kid, Al Jennings, and Joseph Slade. The chapter on Billy the Kid is from Burns's *Saga of Billy the Kid*, and there are two chapters by Al Jennings, both from his *Beating Back*. On the cover the editor's middle name is incorrectly spelled Louis.

769. ———

Gray shadows, compiled by Joseph Lewis French. Illustrated with woodcuts by Roger Buck. New York, the Century co. [1931]. Pict. cloth. OP.

xi p., 1 l., 3–376 p. front., illus., plates. 21.4 cm.
Half title; vignette; illus. chapter headings; "First edition" on copyright p.

Chapter VII is about the Al Jennings gang and taken from Jennings' *Beating Back*. Chapter IX is about Ed Morrell and taken from Morrell's *The Twenty-fifth Man.*

770. ———

The pioneer west. Narratives of the westward march of empire. Selected and edited by Joseph Lewis French, with a foreword by Hamlin Garland. Illustrations in color by Remington Schuyler. Boston, Little, Brown and co., 1923. Pict. cloth. OP.

xiv p., 1 l., 386 p. front. (col.), plates (col.). 21 cm.
Republished in 1924.

An anthology of the West containing, among other subjects, a chapter on Alder Gulch from Nathaniel Langford's *Vigilante Days and Ways* and one on Joseph Slade from Mark Twain's *Roughing It.*

771. French, Wild James (Wild Jim)

Wild Jim, Capt. W. J. French, Texas ranger, the Texas cowboy and saddle king. [Chicago, M. A. Donohue & co., printers, n.d.] Pict. wrappers. (Cover title.) Rare.

15 p. ports. on front and back wrappers. 22.2 cm.

This little pamphlet is a sampling of the larger book that followed (Item 772) and was distributed to help the sale of the latter.

772. ———

Wild Jim, the Texas cowboy and saddle king, by Capt. W. J. French. Illustrated. Antioch, Lake co., Capt. W. J. French, publishers, 1890. Pict. wrappers. Exceedingly rare.

76 p. front. (port.), illus. 23.2 cm.

Among other things the author tells about the "fight" between Wild Bill and the McCanles "gang," as "Wild Bill told it to me." Like others, he repeats that "Jim and Jack McCandal [*sic*] were horse thieves and murderers, and had killed more than thirty men, women and children." His description of the "fight" is typical of those preceding it: ". . . when the door gave way, the old trusty rifle belched forth, and the leader of the gang, Jim McCandal fell with a bullet-hole through his heart as big as a hen egg. Then the battle of nine to one began in earnest. Bill killed three more with his forty-five Colts pistol before they could reach him, cutting the number down to six to one, and, by this time, Bill was fighting like a lion. Then Jack McCandal, a big, strong, burly man, brother of the first outlaw shot, sprang at Wild Bill like a panther, with a big knife in his hand, threatening to cut his throat, but Wild Bill, at the first stroke of his knife, completely disembowled his antagonist. Six of their number had now been killed dead, and two lay on the floor with mortal wounds. The only two who had not been either killed or wounded, mounted their saddles and rode away as fast as their horses could carry them, one saying to the other, 'Pard, we run against the devil this time.' "

The author has Wild Bill wounded with bullet holes, cuts, and a broken skull as other writers before him do. He also says that he was in Deadwood when Hickok was killed and gives an equally unreliable account of that killing and McCall's trial.

773. French, William

Some recollections of a western ranchman. New Mexico, 1883-1899, by Hon. William French. London, Methuen & co., ltd. [1927]. Cloth. Scarce.

vi p., 1 l., 283 [8] p. 22.7 cm.
8 p. adv. at end.
Republished by Frederick A. Stokes co., New York, 1928, 283 p. (no advertising at the end).

One of the really good, though obscure, books on the West, containing information previously unknown about many of the western outlaws, such as the Wild Bunch, Joel Fowler, and Black Jack Ketchum. Most of these outlaws worked for the author on his ranch. Since he was a participant, he gives a good account of the fight at Frisco, New Mexico, between the cowboys and Elfego Baca. This volume represents only half of the author's original manuscript (see Item 774).

774. ———

Some recollections of a western ranchman. New Mexico, 1883–1899, by the Hon. William French. New York, Argosy-Antiquarian, ltd., 1965. Pict. buckram. Pub. in 2 volumes.

Vol. I, vi p., 1 l., 283 p. 24.2 cm.
Half title.

Further recollections of a western ranchman, New Mexico, 1883–1899, being Volume II of some recollections of a western ranchman by Captain William French. Edited and with an introduction by Jeff C. Dykes from the complete original manuscript hitherto unpublished. New York, Argosy-Antiquarian, ltd., 1965. Pict. buckram.

Vol. II, xx p., 1 l., 285–527 p. front. (port.). 24.2 cm.
Index: p. 517–527.
Half title.
Limited to 750 two-volume sets in slip case.

The second volume was published through the co-operation of Captain French's daughter who retained that part of the original manuscript which the English publishers omitted because of the length and high cost. It is a welcome addition to the preservation of the author's interesting life's story.

775. [Fridge, Ike]

History of the Chisum war; or, life of Ike Fridge. Stirring events of cowboy life on the frontier [as told to Jodie D. Smith. Electra, Texas, J. D. Smith, 1927.] Stiff pict. wrappers. Rare.

70 [1] p. illus. front. 22 cm.

For some years this little book was so rare that J. Frank Dobie, in his introduction to his *Life and Literature of the Southwest* (1943 edition), said that it was unobtainable. As a book collector, I found my interest aroused by this statement, and after much diligent research, I finally located and bought the small remainder which had been stored in a country print shop. Since then I have scattered a few copies among other collectors and dealers, and the book has become better known, although it is still considered comparatively rare and the edition is now exhausted.

Like most of the old-timers who have written books, Fridge seems to have had a bad memory and little knowledge of his characters before his association with them. He says Billy the Kid's father died when the Kid was sixteen and that he began to drift when his mother married again. According to the author's account, the Kid killed his first man when he entered a deserted sheep camp and prepared himself a meal. The Mexican sheepherder came back and began abusing him; then he ran at him with a knife, and Billy shot him.

Fridge relates that once the outlaw returned home to find the house surrounded. In his escape he was wounded, and, the author says, "the faithful mother made trips to his mountain rendezvous daily and nursed her outlaw son back to health." I have never seen that statement elsewhere.

Fridge states that the Kid fell in love with a girl who did not return his love but, instead, helped Pat Garrett trap him. As he tells the story, Garrett went to Maxwell's house, holed up out of sight, and finally received a signal from the girl that Billy was in her parlor, the room next to Maxwell's. Maxwell left the house, purposely making a lot of noise so that the Kid would think the guest was leaving. Billy had heard them talking, but the girl had convinced him that the voices were those of Maxwell and a friend. The Kid, thinking Maxwell had remained in the room, went in to talk with him.

"As he came through the door," reports Fridge, "Pat Garrett had him covered. Just as soon as the Kid discovered the *marshal* he went for his *guns*. But Garrett had only to pull the trigger and the most dangerous outlaw ever on the western Texas and New Mexico ranges was no more." Fridge also says that Garrett was a United States marshal and that after the Kid was killed he "asked the government for troops to aid in running down the rest of the bunch and when the U.S. soldiers interfered the outlaws were without a leader." All that is absurd.

This book was indirectly the cause of the author's death. It was printed for him by Jodie D. Smith at Electra, Texas, and the author, an old man, left with two large suitcases filled with copies to sell to his friends in the Seymour, Texas, country. He had to change trains at Wichita Falls and carry the two heavy cases of books from one train to another. The effort tore loose some adhesions from an old bullet wound he had received in his abdomen years earlier. He died a few days later in a Wichita Falls hospital, and no one knows what became of the books.

776. Frink, Maurice

Cow country cavalcade. Eighty years of the Wyoming stock growers' association, by Maurice Frink. Denver, Colo., the Old West publishing co., Fred A. Rosenstock, 1954. Cloth. OP.

xvi p., 1 l., 3–243 p. plates, ports., map, facsms., earmarks, cattle brands. 23.5 cm.

Appendix: p. 237–238; sources: p. 239–240; index: p. 241–243.

Half title.

Has a long chapter on the Johnson County War. The author speaks disparagingly of Frank Canton and calls him the "Jekyll and Hyde of the Plains." More than one writer claims that he went under an assumed name and left Texas under a cloud.

777. ———, W. Turrentine Jackson, and Agnes Wright Spring

When grass was king. Contributions to the western range cattle industry, [by] Maurice Frink . . ., W. Turrentine Jackson . . ., [and] Agnes Wright Spring. . . . Boulder, University of Colorado press, 1956. Cloth. OP.

xv [2], 5–465 p. illus., plates, ports., tables. 23.7 cm.

Bibliography after each author's section; index: p. 452–465.

Half title; map on end papers.

Has material on both the Johnson County and the Lincoln County wars.

778. Fritz, Percy Stanley

Colorado, the centennial state, by Percy Stanley Fritz. . . . New York, Prentice-Hall, inc., 1941. Cloth. OP.

xii p., 2 l., 3–518 p. front. (double p. col. map), illus., plates, maps, facsms., music. 23.5 cm.

Bibliography after each chapter; appendix: p. 493–495; index: p. 497–518.

Half title.

Gives a short history of Alferd Packer, who is referred to as Alfred.

779. Fry, Eugene

Historical episodes of Denton, [by] Eugene Fry. [Denton, Texas, Wm. H. McNitzy, master printer, n.d.] Wrappers. (Cover title.) Rare.

1 p.l., [3]–23 p. 19.6 cm.

This little pamphlet devotes two pages to Sam Bass's life in Denton and his start in outlawry.

780. Fulcher, Walter

The way I heard it. Tales of the Big Bend, by Walter Fulcher. Edited with introduction and notes by Elton Miles. Austin, University of Texas press [1959]. Cloth. OP.

xxvi p., 1 l., [3]–87 p. front. (port.), plates. 22 cm.
Half title; illus. end papers; pub. device.

A chapter entitled "Outlaws and Bandidos" deals with members of the Black Jack Ketchum gang and tells about the robbery of the Southern Pacific at Dryden, in which Ben Kilpatrick and Ole Beck were killed, and about some of the Mexican bandits of the Big Bend country.

781. Fuller, George W.

A history of the Pacific northwest, by George W. Fuller. . . . New York, Alfred A. Knopf, 1931. Dec. cloth. Scarce.

xvi p., 1 l., [3]–383 [15] p. front., plates, ports., maps (1 fold.). 24.2 cm.
Notes: p. [341]–383; index: p. [385]–[399].
Half title; device.

Contains some material on Henry Plummer which is found in the author's *The Inland Empire of the Pacific Northwest*, published three years earlier (see Item 782).

782. ———

The inland empire of the Pacific northwest. A history, by George W. Fuller. . . . Spokane, Denver, H. G. Linderman, 1928. Cloth. Pub. in 3 vols. Scarce.

Vol. I, xiii p., 1 l., 240 p. plates, ports., maps (1 fold.). 23.5 cm.
Half title.
Vol. II, vii, 258 p. plates, ports., maps (1 fold.). 23.5 cm.
Half title.
Vol. III, vii, 259 p. plates, ports., maps. 23.5 cm.
Index: p. 241–259.
Half title.

Volume III contains some new material on the life of Henry Plummer before he went to Montana Territory.

783. **Fuller, Henry Clay**

Adventures of Bill Longley. Captured by Sheriff Milton Mast and Deputy Bill Burrows, near Keatchie, Louisiana, in 1877, and was executed at Giddings, Texas, 1878, by Henry C. Fuller. Nacogdoches, Texas [Baker printing co., n.d.]. Stiff pict. wrappers. Scarce.

4 p.l., [68] p. (no pagination). front. (port.). 21.8 cm.
Double column; illus. t.p. on verso flyleaf; business cards scattered throughout.

A complete story of the life of one of Texas' most notorious outlaws. It is said he had his picture made standing between his heavily bearded captors so that the world would know he was not captured by "kids."

784. ———

"A Texas sheriff"; a vivid and accurate account of some of the most notorious murder cases and feuds in the history of east Texas, and the officers who relentlessly pursued the criminals till they were brought to justice and paid the full penalty of the law. Also many illustrations of the most prominent characters, by Henry C. Fuller. . . . Nacogdoches, Texas, Baker printing co., 1931. Pict. wrappers. Scarce.

6 p.l., 11–80 p. front., illus., ports. 22 cm.
Double column.
"Short biography of A. J. Spradley" (before title page): 3–8.

Tells about many Texas murders, including the one by Bill Mitchell of James Truitt, the result of one of Texas' many feuds. The author also touches upon the Border-Wall-Broocks feud.

785. ———

"A Texas sheriff." A. J. Spradley, sheriff of Nacogdoches county, Texas, thirty years. Unusual and thrilling incidents. Henry C. Fuller, author. Nacogdoches, Texas, 1931. Cloth. Rare.

5 p.l., 11–80 p. front. (port. with tissue), plates, ports. 22.2 cm.
Double column.

The frontispiece in this edition is the same as the picture on the wrapper of the paper-bound edition (Item 784). It has a different title page, which in the paper edition appears after page 8 and is repeated in the cloth edition. Except for these variations the two editions are the same.

786. **Fulton, Maurice Garland**

Maurice Garland Fulton's history of the Lincoln county war. Edited by Robert N. Mullin. Tucson, Ariz., University of Arizona press [1968]. Cloth.

9 p.l., 13–433 p. front. (port.), plates, ports., map. 23.6 cm.
Index: p. 423–433.
Half title; map on end papers; pub. device.

This long-awaited book represents a lifetime of research by a meticulous historian whose tireless pursuit of detail prevented him from finishing the book before his death. His personal friend and fellow historian, Robert N. Mullin, completed the task, for which all those interested in the history of the West are grateful. This book, together with William A. Kelleher's *Violence in Lincoln*, are the last word on the history of this turbulent section of the West. The author mentions all the participants in the war and includes many newspaper excerpts never before reprinted. The book is well documented and a definitive contribution to western history.

787. ———

Roswell in its early years, [by] Maurice G. Fulton. [Roswell, N.M., Hall-Poobaugh Press, inc., n.d., ca. 1963.] Pict. wrappers.

5 p.l., 11–44 p. plates, ports. 22.8 cm.

Contains some good material on the Horrell raid, the Beckwiths, the Lincoln County troubles; the killing of Morton, Baker, and McCloskey; the killing of Brady and Hindman and the battle of the McSween home; and the killing of Billy the Kid.

788. **———, and Paul Horgan (eds.)**

New Mexico's own chronicle. Three races in the writings of four hundred years. Adapted and edited by Maurice Garland Fulton and Paul Horgan. Dallas, Banks Upshaw and co. [1937]. Cloth. Scarce.

xxviii p., 1 l., 3–155 p., i–xxiv [2], 159–372 p. illus., ports., maps (1 double p.), facsms. 23 cm.
Notes: p. 351–364; index: p. 367–371.
Half title; t.p. in brown and black.

Contains excerpts from books on New Mexico history and has some information about the outlaws of that territory. There are two articles on Billy the Kid: one from R. B. Townshend's *The Tenderfoot in New Mexico*, and an article by Alfred E. Hyde, illustrated by J. N. Marchand from *Century Magazine*, entitled "The Old Regime in the Southwest: The Reign of the Revolver in New Mexico." There is also an article about Joel Fowler from William French's *Some Recollections of a Western Ranchman.*

789. Fultz, Hollis B.

Famous northwest manhunts and murder mysteries, by Hollis B. Fultz. [Elma, Wash., printed on the press of the Elma Chronicle, 1955.] Cloth. OP.

4 p.l., 229 [1] p. plates, ports. 21.5 cm.
T.p. in red and black; copyright notice on dedication p.

Contains considerable material on Harry Tracy, Dave Merrill, Henry Plummer, Boone Helm, Roy Gardner, and others.

790. Furlong, Thomas

Fifty years a detective, by Thomas Furlong. . . . 35 real detective stories. Hitherto unpublished facts connected with some of Mr. Furlong's greatest cases. . . . Illustrated. . . . St. Louis, C. E. Barnett . . . [1912]. Pict. cloth. Scarce.

2 p.l., 5–352 [2] p. illus., plates, ports. 19.5 cm.
Copyright notice on flyleaf preceding t.p.; table of contents at end.

Much of this book is about crimes which are not concerned with western outlaws, but there are several chapters on various train robberies in the West.

G

791. Gage, Jack R.

The Johnson county war is a pack of lies, by Jack R. Gage. The Barons' side, with The Johnson county war ain't a pack of lies, by Jack R. Gage. The rustlers' side. [Cheyenne, Wyo., Flintlock publishing co., 1967.] Cloth.

xvi, 79 p. plates, ports. 26 cm.

This unique book gives both sides of the Johnson County War and is printed one in reverse to the other.

792. ———

Tensleep and no rest, by Jack Gage. A historical account of the range war of the Big Horns in Wyoming. Casper, Wyo., Prairie publishing co. [1958]. Cloth. OP.

3 p.l., 222 [4] p. plates, map, facsms. 23.5 cm.
Last 4 p., "appendage."

An account of the war between the sheepmen and the cattlemen in Wyoming.

793. Gamel, Thomas W.

Life of Thomas W. Gamel. [N.p., n.d., ca. 1932.] Wrappers. (Caption title.) Rare.

32 p. 22.5 cm.

A little-known book containing some material on the Mason County War and Scott Cooley.

794. Gann, Walter

Tread of the longhorns, by Walter Gann. Illustrations by R. L. McCollister. San Antonio, Texas, the Naylor co. [1949]. Cloth.

ix, 188 p. 21.5 cm.
Index: p. 187–188.
Half title; illus. chapter headings.

Contains a chapter on cattle thieves and range wars, including the Lincoln County and Johnson County wars. The author says that Billy the Kid had "more individual killings to his credit than any other living man," which we know is untrue. He also says that the Kid was finally stopped by Pat Garrett, "who bored a hole through his right side in a Mexican 'dobe house."

795. Gantt, Paul H.

The case of Alfred [*sic*] Packer, the man-eater, [by] Paul H. Gantt. [Denver], University of Denver press [1952]. Cloth. OP.

6 p.l., 13–157 p. plates, ports., facsms. 22.2 cm.
Appendix: p. 115–127; bibliography: p. 128–129; notes and references: p. 130–153; index: p. 154–157.
Half title; illus. map on end papers; vignette.

A complete history of this character, well annotated and reliable except that like nearly all writers, the author misspells Alferd's name.

796. Ganzhorn, Jack

I've killed men, by Jack Ganzhorn. Illustrated. London, Robert Hale, ltd. [1940]. Cloth. OP.

ix, 11–288 p. front. (port.), plates, ports. 22 cm.
Half title.
Republished by Devin-Adair Company, New York, in 1959, the first American edition; published as a reprint in Devin-Adair's Western Americana series, with 32 fewer pages.

A little-known book which gives an account of the Earp-Clanton feud and the O K

Corral fight. The author was reared in Tombstone and has a low opinion of the Earps. He says that when he was a boy taking a stagecoach trip with his stepmother, Doc Holliday started to hold up the stage and then recognized his stepmother and rode off with his followers.

797. Gard, Wayne

The Chisholm trail, by Wayne Gard, with drawings by Nick Eggenhofer. Norman, University of Oklahoma press [1954]. Cloth.

xi p., 1 l., 3–296 p. illus., plates, ports., maps. 24 cm.
Bibliography: p. 165–280; index: p. 281–296.
Half title; double illus. t.p.; illus. chapter headings.

Has material on many of the outlaws and gunmen of the trail-driving days, such as John Wesley Hardin, Ben Thompson, Henry Brown, Wild Bill Hickok, and Bat Masterson.

798. ———

Fabulous quarter horse; Steel Dust. The true account of the most celebrated Texas stallion, by Wayne Gard. With illustrations by Nick Eggenhofer. New York, Duell, Sloan and Pearce [1958]. Pict. cloth.

6 p.l., 13–64 p. illus. (3 double p.). 28.7 cm.
Bibliography: p. 57–60; index: p. 61–64.
Half title; vignette.

Has some material on Sam Bass, mostly about his race horse, the Denton Mare.

799. ———

The fence cutters, [by] Wayne Gard. Reprinted from the *Southwestern Historical Quarterly*, Vol. LI, No. 1 (July, 1947). Wrappers. (Cover title.) OP.

15 p. 24 cm.

A chapter from the author's *Frontier Justice*, read as a paper before the Texas State Historical Society. This reprint deals with the lawlessness of wire cutting in the range country.

800. ———

Frontier justice, by Wayne Gard. Norman, University of Oklahoma press, 1949. Cloth.

xi p., 1 l., 3–324 p. illus., plates, ports., map, facsms. 22 cm.
Bibliography: p. 291–308; index: p. 309–324.
Half title; vignette; "First edition" on copyright p.

Deals with western feuds, the vigilantes, cattle rustlers, such outlaws and gunmen as Sam Bass, Billy the Kid, the Earps, John Wesley Hardin, Wild Bill Hickok, and Ben Thompson, and the Lincoln County and Johnson County wars.

801. ———

The great buffalo hunt, by Wayne Gard, with drawings by Nick Eggenhofer. New York, Alfred A. Knopf, 1959. Pict. cloth.

xii p., 1 l., [3]–324 [i–xii] 1 l. illus. (1 double p.), plates. 21 cm.
Bibliography: p. [309]–324; index: p. [1]–xii.
Half title; illus. t.p.; pub. device.

Has some mention of Wild Bill Hickok, Bat Masterson, William Tilghman, and John Poe.

802. ———

Rawhide Texas, by Wayne Gard. Norman, University of Oklahoma press [1965]. Cloth.

xi p., 1 l., 3–236 p. plates. 23.5 cm.
Selected bibliography: p. 216–224; index: p. 225–236.
Half title; pub. device; "First edition" on copyright p.

In a chapter entitled "Men of the Law," the author tells about the lawmen and the Texas Rangers, the killing of Sam Bass, the capture of John Wesley Hardin, and the death of Ben Thompson and mentions Jim Courtright and other Texas bad men.

803. ———

Sam Bass, by Wayne Gard. With illustrations. Boston and New York, Houghton Mifflin co., 1936. Cloth. Scarce.

vi p., 2 l., 262 p. front., plates, ports., facsms. 21.2 cm.
Bibliography: p. [249]–251; index: p. [253]–262.
Map on end papers; pub. device; first edition: 1936 under imprint.

The most complete and reliable work on Sam Bass to date. The author is the only biographer to trace Bass's ancestry. Republished in stiff wrappers by the University of Nebraska Press in 1969.

804. Gardiner, Charles Fox

Doctor at Timberline, by Charles Fox Gardiner, M.D. Illustrated by R. H. Hall. Caldwell, Idaho, the Caxton printers, ltd., 1939. Cloth. OP.

8 p.l., [17]–315 p. front., illus., plates. 23.5 cm.
Half titles (on recto of front.); pub. device; vignette.

Chapter 19, entitled "Lawless Justice," deals with the Black gang of outlaws and the end of Black Jack.

805. Gardner, Raymond Hatfield (Arizona Bill)

The old wild west. Adventures of Arizona Bill, by Raymond Hatfield Gardner (Arizona Bill), in collaboration with B. H. Monroe; illustrated by Grady Sowell. San Antonio, Texas, the Naylor co., 1944. Cloth.

4 p.l., 315 p. front. (port.). 21 cm.
Index: p. 309–315.
Half title; illus. end papers; illus. chapter headings.

Occasionally we find an author who claims a personal acquaintance with all the old outlaws of the West, as Gardner does in this book. He says that he often met Wild Bill Hickok in Tombstone, Arizona, but Hickok was never in Arizona. He repeats that old legend about Hickok fighting ten men in the McCanles "gang," with all its sanguinary results.

There are mistakes on every page, and it would take many pages to point them out, as illustrated in my *Burs Under the Saddle* (Item 7). The author has the robbery of the Union Pacific at Big Springs, Texas, instead of Nebraska; repeats the story about Calamity Jane capturing Jack McCall with a meat cleaver; has Hickok an officer at Dodge; has Bass robbing his first train in Texas; and makes hundreds of other errors that are so ridiculous they are amusing.

806. Gardner, Roy

Hellcatraz, by Roy Gardner. . . . [N.p., n.d.] Stiff pict. wrappers. Scarce.

4 p.l., 9–109 p. plates, ports. 19.5 cm.

These little books on life in Alcatraz were sold by the author while he was serving as a guide at the Golden Gate Exposition. He was a latter-day train robber.

807. Garrett, Patrick Floyd

The authentic life of Billy, the Kid, the noted desperado of the southwest, whose deeds of daring and blood made his name a terror in New Mexico, Arizona and northern Mexico, by Pat F. Garrett, sheriff of Lincoln county, N.M., by whom he was finally hunted down and captured by killing him. A faithful and interesting narrative. Santa Fe, N.M., New Mexican printing and publishing co., 1882. Pict. wrappers. Exceedingly rare.

3 p.l., [7]–137 p. front. (port.), plates, port. 21.6 cm.
Leaf of errata tipped in.

Page 121 should read 113, and from that page to the end of the book the pagination is wrong. The same portrait appears on the verso of the back wrapper and on the frontispiece. Recto of back wrapper is a page of advertising.

Because of the widespread criticism of the way he killed the Kid, Garrett wanted the world to have his version of the killing, which appears in this book. Although

Garrett gave his name to the book, it is said to have been written by his friend Ash Upson, with whom he lived. Upson, a newspaperman who could write with a flourish, gave Garrett the best of the controversy and painted the young outlaw in dark colors; the more he built up the Kid as a super bad man, the more credit his friend Garrett received. The author, whatever his identity, makes the mistake of spelling Tom O'Folliard's name as Tom O. Folliard.

Upson knew very little about the Kid's early life. Although he claimed to have boarded with the Kid's mother in both Santa Fe and Silver City, he seems to have gained very little information about the Kid's life before the Lincoln County War. His imagination supplied incidents from the Kid's boyhood which one finds hard to believe yet difficult to disprove.

The author created many legends about the Kid which have lived to the present time, such as having the family moving from New York to Coffeyville, Kansas, in 1862 (though that town was not yet in existence in that year); having Billy's widowed mother moving to Colorado and there marrying William Antrim (when in fact she was married in Santa Fe, New Mexico); and having them moving to Silver City (again, before that town had been founded). The tales about Billy killing a blacksmith who had insulted his mother, killing Indians, and rescuing wagon trains, as well as his escapades in Old Mexico, his eighty-one-mile ride to rescue his friend Segura from a Texas jail—all these episodes, together with the claim that the Kid was born a Bonney instead of a McCarty, are false. The author has many of the Kid's killings all wrong; in fact, the whole book can be picked to pieces from beginning to end.

The book was reprinted in 1953 by the Frontier Press of Houston, Texas, with some extra illustrations from the Rose Collection. It was reprinted again in 1954 by the University of Oklahoma Press, with an introduction by J. C. Dykes, as Number 3 in the Western Frontier Library Series.

808. ———

Pat F. Garrett's authentic life of Billy the Kid, edited by Maurice Garland Fulton. New York, the Macmillan co., 1927. Cloth. Paper label pasted on; paper title on back strip. Scarce.

xxviii p., 2 l., 233 p. front. (col.), plates, ports., map, facsm., plan. 22.2 cm.
Half title.

The facsimile of the original title page shown in this volume is not the same as that of the originals I have examined and owned, neither in size of type nor in position (see Item 807). The illustrations, too, are different. The original is illustrated by a few drawings; the reprint, by many photographs. This edition has been well edited, much of the paragraphing having been changed, and has been well annotated by an editor who made a thorough study of Billy the Kid. This edition is therefore much more valuable historically than the original edition. It is strange that forty-five years elapsed between the first and second printings.

809. ———

Authentic life of Billy the Kid, by Pat F. Garrett, greatest sheriff of the old southwest. Foreword by John M. Scanland, and eye witness reports. Edited by J. Brussel. New York, Atomic books, inc., 1946. Pict. wrappers. OP.

5 p.l., 11–128 p. 18.5 cm.

A cheap reprint of Item 807, with a new foreword and occasional editing. Some new material has been added, including an analysis of Billy's handwriting.

810. ———

Pat F. Garrett, the authentic life of Billy the Kid, with a biographical foreword by Jarvis P. Garrett. Albuquerque, Horn & Wallace, publishers, inc., 1964. Cloth.

27 p.l., [7]–139 [11] p. front. (port.), illus., plates, ports., facsms. 23.7 cm.

This edition contains a forty-three-page foreword by Garrett's son Jarvis and includes some facts, taken from the family papers, never before revealed. It is a splendid edition. In the foreword the editor tells about the murder of A. J. Fountain and his son, about Garrett's attempt to arrest Oliver Lee and James Gilliland, and about Garrett's murder.

811. Garst, Doris Shannon

The story of Wyoming and its constitution and government, by Doris Shannon Garst. [Douglas, Wyo.], printed by Douglas Enterprise [1938]. Cloth. OP.

3 p.l., 179 p. front. (col. flag), ports., map. 19 cm.
Index: p. 173–179.
Questions and references after each chapter.

Treats of the Johnson County War.

812. ———

When the west was young, by Shannon Garst. Drawings by F. C. Reed. Douglas, Wyo., Enterprise publishing co., 1942. Cloth. OP.

6 p.l., [13]–248 [1] p. front., illus. 23.4 cm.
Illus. half title; illus. end papers.

Contains a chapter on the Johnson County War.

813. **———, with Warren Garst**

Wild Bill Hickok, [by] Shannon Garst with Warren Garst. New York, Julian Messner, inc. [1952]. Cloth. OP.

viii, 183 p. front. 21.8 cm.

Chronology: p. 178; bibliography: p. 179–180; index: p. 181–183.

Half title; headpieces.

The authors have written this book for young readers. They do not follow the old legend of the McCanles "fight," but they do describe a scene in which "Woods was found dead at the rear of the house, and later Gordon's body was found near the creek. For several minutes Bill stared at the corpses in silence. The sight made him ill."

I very much doubt that this scene took place. In the first place, Hickok was used to blood-letting and would have no sympathy for an enemy. In the second place, it would have been quite a feat to have gazed at both dead men at once, since Gordon died some distance from the house. The authors have Calamity Jane capturing McCall after Hickok's murder, though she was nowhere near the scene.

814. Garwood, Darrell

Crossroads of America. The story of Kansas City, [by] Darrell Garwood. New York, W. W. Norton & co., inc. [1948]. Cloth. OP.

6 p.l., 13–331 p., 1 l. plates, ports. 21.7 cm.

Sources and acknowledgments: p. 323–326; index: p. 327–331.

Half title; map on end papers; pub. device; "First edition" on copyright p.

Contains a chapter on Jesse James and information on the Youngers and the Northfield Bank robbery. The author gives William Clarke Quantrill's first name as Charley.

815. Gautier, George R.

Harder than death. The life of George R. Gautier, an old Texan living at the Confederate home, Austin, Texas. Written by himself. [N.p.], 1902. Wrappers. Rare.

62 p. 3 plates, 1 port. 21.3 cm.

Tells about the author's lawlessness and about life in the penitentiary.

816. Gay, Antoinette G.

Calle de Alvarado, by Antoinette G. Gay. Monterey, Calif., the Monterey trade press [1936]. Pict. imt. suede. Scarce.

3 p.l., 3–91 p. illus. 20.2 cm.

"First edition" on verso of last p.

Has a chapter on Tiburcio Vásquez.

817. Gay, Beatrice Grady

"Into the setting sun." A history of Coleman county, by Beatrice Grady Gay. Drawings by Mollie Grady Kelley. . . . [N.p., n.d.] Pict. cloth. Scarce.

x, 193 p. front., illus., plates, ports., maps. 20.4 cm.

In one chapter an old-timer tells about his experiences as a Ranger and sheriff, his capture of John Wesley Hardin, his part in capturing Sam Bass near Round Rock after Bass was shot, and his roles in capturing lesser-known outlaws.

818. Gay, Felix M.

History of Nowata county, by Felix M. Gay. Stillwater, Okla., Redlands press, 1957. Stiff wrappers.

3–36 p. 21 cm.
Bibliography: p. 35–36.

Has a section on the Dalton gang. The author is careless with his proper names. The first name of the Dalton boys' father was Lewis, not Louis. The first name of the older brother who was a U.S. marshal was Frank, not Fred.

819. Gaylord, Chic

Handgunner's guide, including the art of the quick-draw and combat shooting, by Chic Gaylord. New York, Hastings House, publishers [1960]. Pict. cloth.

8 p.l., 17–176 p. illus., plates, ports. 25.5 cm.
Index: p. 171–176.
Half title.

Contains short biographies of Wyatt Earp, Doc Holliday, Harvey Logan, Wild Bill Hickok, John Wesley Hardin, Billy the Kid, Ben Thompson, Bat Masterson, Luke Short, Johnny Ringo, William Tilghman, and Clay Allison.

820. [Gelz, Jacob]

Uncle Sam's life in Montana. [Butte City, Mont., 1905.] Stiff wrappers. Scarce.

[3]–118 [2] p. front. 19.2 cm.

Has some material on the lawlessness in Montana.

821. George, Andrew L.

The Texas convict. Thrilling and terrible experiences of a Texas boy, by A. L. George, Brownwood, Texas. Austin, Texas, Ben C. Jones & co., 1893. Cloth. Scarce.

xvi, 232 [12] p. 20.8 cm.

822. ———

A Texas prisoner, by Andrew L. George. Sketches of the penitentiary, convict farms and railroads, together with poems and illustrations. [Charlotte, N.C.], 1895. Pamphlet. Scarce.

32 p. illus., plates. 17 cm.

The author mentions John Wesley Hardin, who was in prison with him.

823. George, Todd Menzies

Just memories and twelve years with Cole Younger, by Todd Menzies George. [N.p.], 1959. Leather.

ii, [3]–99 p. 1 plate, 2 ports. 21.5 cm.

A chapter on Cole Younger deals with his life after his release from prison. The author was a sympathetic friend.

824. Gibbons, Rev. James Joseph

In the San Juan, Colorado. Sketches, by Rev. J. J. Gibbons. [Chicago, press of Calumet book & engraving co., 1898.] Pict. cloth. Scarce.

3 p.l., 7–194 p. plates. 18.2 cm.

Also published under the title "Notes of a Missionary Priest in the Rocky Mountains," New York, by the Christian press association publishing co., 1898.

825. Gibbs, Josiah F.

The Mountain meadow massacre, by Josiah F. Gibbs. Illustrated by nine full-page and five half-page engravings from photographs taken on the ground. Salt Lake City, Salt Lake Tribune publishing co., 1910. Pict. wrappers. Scarce.

2 p.l., 5–59 p. plates, map. 22.5 cm.

826. Gibson, A. M.

The life and death of Colonel Albert Jennings Fountain, by A. M. Gibson. Norman, University of Oklahoma press [1965]. Cloth.

xi [1] p., 1 l., 3–301 p. plates, ports., map. 23.5 cm.

Bibliography: p. 289–293; index: p. 294–301.

Half title; "First edition" on copyright p.

A well-written and long-needed book about one of the leading characters in New Mexico. It contains much on the lawlessness of that state and tells about Oliver Lee, Jim Gilliland, Pat Garrett, and others, with a mention of Billy the Kid.

827. Gilchriese, John D.

The street fight [by] John D. Gilchriese. [N.p., n.d.]

1 sheet. diagr., double column. 39.4 x 22.3 cm.

A diagram accompanying a colored print, 13½ x 22 inches, reproduced from an oil painting by the noted western artist Don Percival. The artist was commissioned by Mr. Gilchriese to do the painting for the Wyatt Earp Museum of Tombstone, Arizona, after Mr. Gilchriese had spent some twenty-odd years researching the subject.

The item is listed here because it is the first time the location of this famous fight has been correctly identified. Nearly all historians have called it the "O. K. Corral Fight," but it actually took place on Fremont Street near the corner of Third Street. The painting gives the exact location of each contestant and where those who were shot fell. The fight started in a vacant lot, but six seconds later the antagonists had backed into Fremont Street. Only five hundred copies of the print were made, each numbered and signed by the artist. I regret that Mr. Gilchriese's definitive book on Wyatt Earp has not been published so that I might have included it in this bibliography.

828. Gilfillan, Archer B.

A goat's eye view of the Black Hills, by Arthur B. Gilfillan. Illustrated by Cec Carroll. [Rapid City, S.D., Dean & Dean, publishers, 1953.] Stiff pict. wrappers. OP.

5 p.l., 9–106 p. illus. 21.2 cm.

Contains a chapter on Calamity Jane and a mention of Wild Bill Hickok, mostly concerning the motion picture of his life.

829. Gillett, James B.

Six years with the Texas rangers, 1875 to 1881, by James B. Gillett. . . . Austin, Texas, von Boeckmann-Jones co., publishers [1921]. Cloth. Scarce.

5 p.l., 11–332 [1] p. front., ports. 19.2 cm.
Device; front. tissue.

Published in a small edition by the author and sold personally by him; republished by Yale University Press in 1925, edited by Milo M. Quaife. This edition, in turn, was republished by the Lakeside Press of Chicago, in 1943. It was also published under the title *The Texas Ranger*, in collaboration with Howard Driggs, by the World Book Co., Yonkers-on-Hudson, N.Y., 1927.

Though considered one of the better Ranger books, the author makes many mistakes, especially in his chapter on Sam Bass.

830. Gilliland, Maude T.

Rincon. (Remote dwelling place.) A story of life on a South Texas ranch at the turn of the century. Written and illustrated by Maude T. Gilliland. [Brownsville, Texas, Springman-King lithograph co., n.d.] Cloth.

xvi, 105 [1] p. front. (port.), illus., plates, ports., maps, facsm. 23.5 cm.
Bibliography: p. [107].

Has a chapter on the bandit raids of southwestern Texas, mostly by Mexican outlaws.

831. Gillis, O. J.

To hell and back again, its discovery, description, and experiences; or, life in the penitentiary of Texas and Kansas. By O. J. Gillis. [Little Rock, Ark., Democrat printing and lithographing co., 1906.] Wrappers. Scarce.

vii, 9–112 [1] p. 19 cm.

The author mentions Emmett Dalton, who was in prison with him.

832. [Gimlett, F. E.]

Over trails of yesterday. Stories of colorful characters that lived, labored, loved, fought and died in the gold and silver west. Abner Villa via Salida, Colo., published by the Hermot [of Arbor-Villa, 1941]. Stiff wrappers. (Cover title.) Scarce.

2 p.l., [1] p., 6–47 p. plates. 21 cm.

Tells about the robbing of the Delta Bank in 1893 by the McCarthy gang.

833. Ginty, E. B.

Missouri legend, a comedy, by E. B. Ginty. New York, Random House [1938]. Cloth. OP.

4 p.l., 3–180 p. 21.2 cm.
Half title; vignette; untrimmed.

A play about the James boys and the killing of Jesse by Bob Ford.

834. ———

Missouri legend. Acting edition. Comedy in three acts, by E. B. Ginty. [New York], Dramatists play service, inc. [1940]. Stiff wrappers. OP.

2 p.l., 5–76 p. 19 cm.

835. Gipson, Fred

Fabulous empire; Colonel Zack Miller's story, by Fred Gipson, with an introduction by Donald Day. Boston, Houghton Mifflin co., 1946. Cloth. OP.

ix p., 1 l., 411 p. 21 cm.
Half title; first edition, 1946, under imprint.

Contains some information on Henry Starr.

836. Gish, Anthony

American bandits. A biographical history of the nation's outlaws—from the days of the James boys, the Youngers, the Jennings, the Dalton gang and Billy the Kid, down to the modern bandits of our own day, including Dillinger, "Pretty Boy" Floyd, and others, by Anthony Gish. Girard, Kans., Haldeman-Julius publications [1938]. Stiff wrappers.

2 p.l., [5]–101 [1] p. 21.5 cm.
11 p. adv. at end.

A cheap rehash of many stories about western outlaws, as well as some about modern city gangsters. The author says that, though Billy the Kid was one of the worst desperadoes of the Southwest, he "does not properly belong in a history of bandits. So he will be mentioned only briefly. He was a killer, who rustled cattle and went in for petty thievery as a sideline." Only four short paragraphs are devoted to this best-known outlaw, who he says, "early became a blacksmith's apprentice" and later became angry and "shot the blacksmith." The author also makes many mistakes about Belle Starr and has many of his dates wrong.

837. Glasscock, Carl Burgess

Bandits of the Southern Pacific, by C. B. Glasscock. New York, Frederick A. Stokes co., MCMXXIX. Cloth. OP.

5 p.l., 294 p. front., ports. 19.8 cm.
Pub. device; illus. end papers; untrimmed.

This book is mostly about the train robbers of California. In a chapter on the Daltons the author discusses their raid on the banks of Coffeyville, Kansas. In the few pages he devotes to this final exploit of the Dalton gang, he makes many errors in detail. He has two members of the gang named Tom Heddy and Allie Agers. The correct names of the two members of the gang he had in mind were Dick Broadwell and Bill Powers. He has the battle of Coffeyville all wrong and says that "Emmett, weak from loss of blood, was unable to mount. . . . Hasty examination convinced the others that he was dead." As we know, Emmett was the only survivor, but in this book the survivor is the man the author calls Allie Agers.

838. ———

Big Bonanza. The story of the Comstock lode, by C. B. Glasscock. Indianapolis, Bobbs-Merrill co., publishers, 1931. Cloth. OP.

4 p.l., 13–368 p. front. (port.), plates. 22 cm.
Bibliography: p. 359; index: p. 363–368.
Map on end papers.

Has some information on the vigilantes of Virginia City.

839. ———

Gold in them hills. The story of the west's last wild mining days, by C. B. Glasscock. . . . Illustrated. Indianapolis, Bobbs-Merrill co., publishers [1932]. Cloth. OP.

xiii p., 1 l., 17–330 p. front. (port.), plates, ports. 22.5 cm.
Index: p. 325–330.
Half title; map on end papers; untrimmed; "First edition" on copyright p.

Contains some new information on Wyatt Earp. It is said that the mention of Earp's name in Tonopah made claim jumpers move on to other claims.

840. ———

A golden highway. Scenes of history's greatest gold rush yesterday and today, by C. B. Glasscock. . . . Illustrated. Indianapolis, the Bobbs-Merrill co., publishers [1934]. Cloth. OP.

8 p.l., 13–333 p. front., plates, ports. 22.5 cm.
Bibliography: p. 317–321; index: p. 325–333.
Half title; map on end papers; untrimmed; "First edition" on copyright p.

Contains some material on Black Bart and Murieta. The author tells a story about Murieta which he says has never been read in any other book. "It seems," he writes, "that when the bullets began to fly too frequently in Joaquín's direction a Frenchman sought out the bandit and offered to have a shirt of mail made for him, for one thousand dollars in gold. When the armor arrived from France, Murrietta [*sic*] ordered the Frenchman to put it on. Then he stood at a distance and emptied his revolver into the armor, while the salesman fainted from fright. When the victim was revived and found unwounded, however, Joaquín promptly paid over the thousand dollars in gold." I am afraid that is just another of the many sensational stories about the outlaw.

841. ———

Then came oil. The story of the last frontier, by C. B. Glasscock. Indianapolis, New York, the Bobbs-Merrill co., publishers [1938]. Cloth. OP.

6 p.l., 11–349 p. front., plates, ports. 22.3 cm.
Bibliography: p. 327–329; index: p. 333–349.
Half title; map on end papers; "First edition" on copyright p.

This book has several chapters on Oklahoma outlaws, but tells nothing new. There is a rehash of Belle Starr's life, and some well-known facts about Cherokee Bill and the Daltons are repeated. The author is mistaken in saying that Belle "was a woman of breeding, culture and education." Later he continues along this line when he writes: "From time to time she revolted at the coarseness around her.

Then she packed her bags with silks and furs and silver toilet articles and made her way to Eastern cities or resorts where she lived at the best hotels, spent money lavishly, enjoyed the theatres and stocked up with books for her return to the wilds."

842. ———

The war of the copper kings; builders of Butte and wolves of Wall Street, by C. B. Glasscock. . . . Indianapolis and New York, the Bobbs-Merrill co., publishers [1935]. Cloth. OP.

ix p., 3 l., 17–314 p. front., plates, ports. 22.3 cm.
Half title; untrimmed; "First edition" on copyright p.

The second chapter deals with the Montana vigilantes and the Plummer gang of road agents.

843. **Goethe, C. M.**

"What's in a name?" (Tales, historical or fictitious about 111 California Gold Belt place names). By C. M. Goethe. . . . [Sacramento, Calif., the Keystone press, 1949.] Cloth. OP.

xxii, 202 p. illus., plates, facsm. 23.5 cm.

Has some material on Black Bart.

844. **Gollomb, Joseph**

Master highwaymen, [by] Joseph Gollomb. New York, the Macaulay co. [1927]. Cloth. Scarce.

5 p.l., 11–312 [1] p. 22.5 cm.
Half title; untrimmed.

Contains a long chapter on the life of Murieta. Based on the *California Police Gazette* version, it adds many preposterous situations, such as having Murieta a bodyguard of Santa Anna, though Murieta could have been but a boy in Santa Anna's time. The author also portrays Murieta as having a passion for reading the classics.

845. **Good, Milton**

Twelve years in a Texas prison, by Milt Good, as told to W. E. Lockhart. (Illustrations drawn by Isabel Robinson). . . . Amarillo, Texas, printed by Russell stationery co., 1935. Stiff pict. wrappers. Scarce.

3 p.l., 7–88 p. front. (port.), illus., ports. 24 cm.

The story of a somewhat well-known cattle rustler of recent years.

846. Goodrich, Mary

On the old Calaveras road, by Mary Goodrich. [Angel's Camp, Calif., 1929.] Pict. wrappers. Scarce.

2 p.l., 5–17 p. plates. 22.4 cm.

Has some material on Joaquín Murieta.

847. Goodwin, Nat C.

Nat Goodwin's book, by Nat C. Goodwin. Illustrated. Boston, Richard G. Badger, the Gorham press . . . [1914]. Dec. cloth. Scarce.

xv p., 1 l., 17–366 p. plates, ports. 24.6 cm.
Index: p. [359]–366.
Half title; pub. device; untrimmed.

In a chapter entitled "Robert Ford" the author tells about a talk he had with Bob Ford immediately after Ford killed Jesse James. "We chatted for two hours—agreeably," he writes. "After a bit he told me all about his life with Jesse James—how he had been befriended by the bandit. Casually he described the killing and laughed as if it were a great joke that he had to wait eighteen months for James to turn his back toward him!"

Later on the author writes "Not excepting even Benedict Arnold this boy [Ford] was the most universally despised individual this country ever produced. He drifted farther west after the murder and became one of the most desperate characters those lawless days ever knew. He met his end in a bar room in Cripple Creek. That time he tried to shoot a man whose back was not turned!" It was in Creede, not in Cripple Creek, that Kelly killed Ford.

848. Gordon, Mike

I arrested Pearl Starr, and other stories of adventure as a policeman in Fort Smith, Arkansas, for 40 years. By Mike Gordon. [Fort Smith, Press-Atgus, printers, n.d., ca. 1958.] Stiff wrappers.

[3]–32 p. port. 22.8 cm.

This book tells about Pearl, Belle's daughter, running a house "on the line" and has some material about Henry Starr. My copy has the following four lines typed and taped in at the end of the text: "David Lockhart, Lee Sutton and Henry Starr was robbing the bank at Harrison, Arkansas, when Henry Starr was killed. This information was given me by Frank Carlton."

849. Gordon, S.

Recollections of old Milestown, by S. Gordon. Miles City, Mont. [Independent printing co.], 1918. Thin cloth. Scarce.

2 p.l., 3–42 [3] p. front., plates, ports. 23.2 cm.

A scarce book containing material on the vigilantes of Miles City.

850. Gordon, Welche

Jesse James and his band of notorious outlaws, by Welche Gordon. Chicago, Laird & Lee, publishers, 1890. Pict. wrappers (col.). Rare.

2 p.l., [7]–238 [4] p. front., illus., plates, ports. 18.8 cm.
Pinkerton Detective series, No. 42.
4 p. adv. at end.
Device.

Another example of the cheap literature of the period. Like many others, it is not very reliable. The author misspells Quantrill's name as Charles W. Quantrell and gives Dick Liddill's last name as Little.

851. Gorman, Harry M.

My memories of the Comstock, by Harry M. Gorman. Illustrated by John & Marie Gorman. . . . Los Angeles, San Francisco, New York, Sutton-House, publishers [1939]. Pict. cloth. OP.

7 p.l., 15–222 p. illus. 22.2 cm.
Half title; illus. chapter headings; pict. map on end papers.

Contains some information on stagecoach robberies and Milton Sharp.

852. Goss, Helen Rocca

Highwaymen in the quicksilver mining region, by Helen Rocca Goss. [N.p.]. Reprinted from Historical Society of Southern California *Quarterly*, September, 1955. Stiff wrappers. (Cover title.) OP.

20 p. 25.4 cm.
Notes: p. 18–20.

Has much on stagecoach robberies and other outlawry.

853. ———

The life and death of a quicksilver mine, by Helen Rocca Goss. Los Angeles, Calif., published by the Historical Society of Southern California . . ., 1958. Cloth. OP.

xv p., 1 l., 3–150 p. front. (2 ports.), plates, ports. 26.2 cm.
Reference notes: p. 129–139; index: p. 143–150.
Half title; map on end papers (col.).

In a chapter entitled "Rustlers and Road Agents" the author deals with stagecoach robberies of the late eighties.

854. Gradet, Roger

Images du far-west. 250 illustrations et textes de Roger Gradet. [N.p., Achevé d'imprimer . . . . de la Presse Jurassienne à Dole, 1936.] Stiff pict. wrappers (col.).

5 p.l., 15–172 p. illus. 27.6 cm.
Index: p. 171–173.

A book about the West written in French. Has some sections on Wild Bill Hickok, Belle Starr, Bill Tilghman, and others. The author has Bat Masterson sheriff of Dodge City, though he was sheriff of Ford County, and he also has Henry Brown sheriff of Caldwell, Texas, rather than marshal of Caldwell, Kansas.

855. Graham, Jean

Tales of the Ozark river country, by Jean Graham. [Clinton, Mo., press of Martin printing co., 1929]. Pict. wrappers. Scarce.

2 p.l., 5–43 p. plates. 19.4 cm.

Has some information on the Youngers and tells about the death of John Younger.

856. Grant, Bruce

The cowboy encyclopedia. The old and the new west from the open range to the dude ranch, by Bruce Grant. Illustrated by Jackie & Fiore Mastri. New York, Chicago, San Francisco, Rand McNally & co. [1951]. Pict. cloth. OP.

6 p.l., 13–160 [2] p. front. (col.), illus. 13 full p. (3 col.), maps, cattle brands. 26 cm.
Bibliography: p. [161–162].
Illus. half title; illus. t.p.

For some reason the author has short biographical sketches of Billy the Kid, Sam Bass, Wild Bill Hickok, and some others, although they do not belong in a book of this nature. The sketches contain factual errors and the author repeats old legends which have been proved false.

857. Grant, Jack

Trail dust and gun smoke. Factual stories of a cowboy's life, by Jack Grant. New York, Washington, Hollywood, Vantage press [1965]. Cloth.

5 p.l., 9–122 p. 20.7 cm.
Cowboy lingo: p. 120–122.
Half title; "First edition" on copyright p.

858. Graphic Tale

of the most daring and successful train robbery in the history of the northwest. Capture of the desperadoes and their incarceration in the Helena jail, together with only truthful narrative ever published giving details of escape on the day set for trial. Great moral lesson for benefit of rising generation. Illustrated. Helena, Mont., State publishing co., publishers, 1909. Wrappers. Rare.

3 p.l., 7–52 p. ports. 23.5 cm.

Tells about the robbery of the Oriental Limited on the Great Northern, near Rondo, Montana, September, 1909, by George Frankhouser and Charles McDonald.

859. Graves, Richard S.

Oklahoma outlaws. A graphic history of the early days in Oklahoma; the bandits who terrorized the first settlers and the marshals who fought them to extinction; covering a period of twenty-five years, by Richard S. Graves. . . . [Oklahoma City, State printing and publishing co., 1915.] Pict. wrappers. Scarce.

3 p.l., [3]–131 p. front., plates, ports. 17.5 cm.
Republished in Fort Davis, Texas, in 1968.

Touches upon most of the better-known Oklahoma outlaws and marshals. In 1914–1915 a group of old officers of Oklahoma, including Nix, Madsen, and Tilghman, organized a company and made a motion picture entitled *The Passing of the Oklahoma Outlaw*. It was to be a true presentation of history, and Mr. Tilghman was chosen director. Mr. Graves was paid to write this little book from material given him by Mr. Tilghman, and the latter had it printed in a local print shop. It was published to be sold at the theaters where the picture was exhibited.

It contains some statements that I strongly doubt, such as the one that Heck Thomas helped break up the Sam Bass gang and that in one robbery of a train, "between Galveston and Denison," he kept $22,000 from the Bass gang by hiding it in a stove and giving the robbers a bundle of worthless paper in its place.

The serious student or researcher may wish to make a detailed comparison of this book with Zoe A. Tilghman's *Outlaw Days* (Item 2212). Further comparison of the two with J. A. Newsom's *The Life and Practice of the Wild and Modern Indian* (Item 1609) may also prove rewarding.

860. [Graves, S. H.]

On the "White Pass" pay-roll, by the president of the White Pass & Yukon route. Chicago [the Lakeside press] 1908. Pict. cloth. Rare.

vii p., 3 l., 15–258 p. front., plates. 20.2 cm.
Appendix: p. [251]–258.
Half title; device; untrimmed.

This rare, privately printed book contains a chapter of firsthand information on Soapy Smith.

861. Graves, W. W.

Life and letters of Rev. Father John Shoemaker, S.J., apostle to the Osages, by W. W. Graves. St. Paul, Kans., Parsons, Kans., published by the Commercial publishers [1928]. Cloth. Scarce.

5–144 [4] p. front., plates. 19.3 cm.

Has some mention of Wild Bill Hickok.

862. Gray, Arthur Amos

Men who built the west, by Arthur Amos Gray. Illustrated by photographs. Caldwell, Idaho, the Caxton printers, ltd., 1945. Pict. cloth. OP.

7 p.l., [15]–220 p. front., plates, ports., maps, facsms. 23.5 cm.
Index: p. [217]–220.
Half title; pub. device.

This book devotes a chapter to stagecoach robbery and such road agents as Black Bart and Henry Plummer and his gang, and tells of the criminal activities of Joseph Slade.

863. Gray, Frank S.

Pioneering in southwest Texas. True stories of early day experiences in Edwards and adjoining counties, by Frank S. Gray. Edited by J. Marvin Hunter. [Austin, Texas, printed and bound . . . by the Steck co., 1949.] Cloth. OP.

vii, 247 p. plates, ports., facsm. 23 cm.
Map on flyleaf.

Has some chapters on train robbery by Bud Newman, Bill and Jeff Taylor, and Pierre Keaton.

864. Great American Parade, The

Garden City, New York, Doubleday, Doran & co., inc., 1935. Cloth. Scarce.

xiv p., 1 l., 611 p. 21 cm.
Half title.

An anthology containing a chapter on Billy the Kid taken from Walter Noble Burns's *The Saga of Billy the Kid.*

865. Greene, Capt. Jonathan H.

A desperado in Arizona, 1858–1860; or, life, trial, death, and confession of Samuel H. Calhoun, the soldier-murderer, by Capt. Jonathan H. Greene. Santa Fe, Stagecoach press, 1964. Cloth.

xvi p., 1 l., 19–89 p. front. (port.), plate, facsm. 17.7 cm.
Half title.

A reprint of the original edition published in Cincinnati by the author in 1862 (not seen). It is the story of an outlaw who started his career early in life, getting his start from a man named Caldwell. Though his activities ranged over much of the Southwest, most of them were concentrated in Arizona.

866. ———

Secret band of brothers. A full and true exposition of all the various crimes, villainies and misdeeds of the powerful organization in the United States, by the "reformed gambler," . . . with illustrative engravings. . . . Philadelphia, T. B. Peterson and brothers [1858]. Cloth. Rare.

4 p.l., 9–302 p. front. 19 cm.

Deals with the early outlaws of the Mississippi Valley.

867. Greene, Laurence

America goes to press. The news of yesterday, by Laurence Greene. Indianapolis, New York, the Bobbs-Merrill co., publishers [1936]. Cloth. OP.

7 p.l., 15–375 p. 22.3 cm.
Half title; untrimmed; "First edition" on copyright p.

Contains newspaper accounts of the killing of Jesse James and the Daltons' end at Coffeyville, Kansas.

868. Greenwood, Robert

The California outlaw, Tiburcio Vásquez. Compiled by Robert Greenwood, including the rare contemporary account by George Beers, with numerous photographs and excerpts from contemporary newspapers. Los Gatos, Calif., the Talisman press, 1960. Pict. cloth and boards.

3 p.l., 11–296 p. front. (port.), plates, ports., facsms. 23.5 cm.
Half title; map on end papers; t.p. in three colors.

A fifty-nine-page history of this noted outlaw, followed by the complete reprint of the book about Vásquez by George A. Beers published in 1875 (see Item 186). At the time Beers was a reporter for the *San Francisco Chronicle* and a member of the posse hunting Vásquez.

869. Greer, James Kimmins

Bois d'arc to barb'd wire; Ken Carey: southwestern frontier born, by James K. Greer. Dallas, Texas, Dealey and Lowe, 1936. Pict. cloth. OP.

7 p.l., 428 p. plates, maps. 22.5 cm.
Bibliographical notes: p. [411]–423; index: p. [425]–428.
Illus. double t.p.; maps on end papers (dif.).

870. ———

Grand prairie, by James K. Greer. Dallas, Texas, Tardy publishing co. [1935]. Cloth. Rare.

4 p.l., 284 p. plates, maps. 19.7 cm.
Notes: p. 235–264; index: p. 265–284.

This book has become exceedingly scarce. It contains a great deal of information about various outlaws of Texas. On page 169, however, the author erroneously states that John Selman killed John Wesley Hardin in 1865. The killing actually took place in 1895, thirty years later. That could be a typographical error, but the author has other incorrect dates, such as that of Garrett's murder, which took place in 1908, not 1907. There are other errors.

871. Greever, William S.

The bonanza west. The story of the western mining rushes, 1848–1900, by William S. Greever. Norman, University of Oklahoma press [1963]. Cloth.

xiv p., 1 l., 3–430 p. plates, ports., maps. 23.5 cm.
Bibliography: p. 391–404; index: p. 405–430.
Half title; "First edition" on copyright p.

Has some material on Wild Bill Hickok and Calamity Jane. The author says that Jane was born "about 1851." She was born in 1852. I think the author is also in error when he says that Jack McCall lost a bag of gold dust to Hickok in a poker game. Where would a saloon bum get a sack of gold dust? He also says that McCall bragged about killing Hickok in Cheyenne, but most historians claim that the killing took place in Laramie.

872. Gregg, Jacob Ray

Pioneer days in Malheur county. Perpetuating the memory of prominent pioneers and preserving authentic history of the county as told to Jacob Ray Gregg. . . . Los Angeles, privately printed by Lorrin L. Morrison, printing and publishing, 1950. Cloth. OP.

7 p.l., 5–442 p. front. (port.), plates, ports. 23.5 cm.
Half title (recto front.); map on end papers.

Has some material on the vigilantes of eastern Oregon and Idaho.

873. Gregory, Lester

True wild west stories, [by] Lester Gregory. The Viscount series. London, Andrew Dakers, ltd. [n.d.]. Cloth. OP.

3 p.l., 7–219 p. front. (col.), illus. (full p. plates). 20.5 cm.
Half title; pub. device.

Although the author has "true" in his title, there is very little truth in his text. As so many other writers claim, he says repeatedly that the James and Younger boys were cousins. They were not related. He says that Jesse was older than Frank, repeats the old, old story about Jesse giving the widow money to pay off her mortgage, and quotes Jesse using modern slang. The author is mistaken in saying that Slade was hired by the merchants of Julesburg to clean up the town, and he has Slade's killing of Jules Reni all wrong.

He says that Wyatt Earp's reputation began in Wichita, Kansas, where he was marshal, hired especially to get Mannen Clements, whose first name he spells Manning. Earp was never marshal of Wichita. He also has Earp a U.S. marshal when he went to Tombstone, and he says that the Clantons sent word to the Earps from the O K Corral that they were waiting for a showdown. He is also mistaken in saying that Billy Claiborne took part in the fight and did quite a bit of shooting but made tracks when he saw the Earps coming. He even says that Doc Holliday "downed Claiborne with a couple of shots." He is also wrong in saying that Ike Clanton spent many years in jail for this affair.

He has the McCanles group a gang of outlaws who had been holding up stages and terrifying inhabitants and says that they were all "wanted men and known killers." He claims that they were waiting at Rock Creek Station to rob the stage and that Hickok "was a green kid" driving the stage. He also repeats some of the legends about Hickok's marvelous shooting stunts. He has McCall shooting Hickok in the back. Hickok was shot in the back of the head.

The author evidently thinks that Billy the Kid was much older than he was when he left New York. He says that the Kid had to fight and demonstrate pugilistic ability to hold his own there. He repeats the legend about the Kid killing a man at the age of twelve. He misnames John Tunstall as Mr. Turnbull and says that it was a battle when Sheriff Brady and Deputy Hindman were killed. According to this author, when Garrett captured him, the Kid had 21 notches on his gun, and he was placed in jail at Mesilla. He was jailed in Lincoln after his trial. He also has the Kid killing his jailers "by a ruse, luring them one at a time into his cell." He is also mistaken when he says that the Kid was killed on July 15 "before the sun set." Billy was killed near midnight on July 14. There are other errors too numerous to enumerate. Why do writers select subjects about which they know so little?

874. Grey, Frederick W.

Seeking a fortune in America, by F. W. Grey. With a frontispiece. London, Smith, Elder & co. . . ., 1912. Cloth. Scarce.

xiv, 307 [4] p. front. (port. with tissue). 20.8 cm.
Half title; 4 p. adv. at end.

This author, an Englishman, erroneously states that Billy the Kid was a half-blood Indian. He also says that when Pat Garrett discovered the house of the Kid's sweetheart, "after tying and gagging her," he lay in wait there for the Kid. When the outlaw appeared, Garrett shot him from behind a sofa. The author claims that he heard the story from Kip McKinney, with whom he worked on a mining venture; but if McKinney told him that story, he was only jobbing him. He further states that the Kid killed men "just for the sport of it." He also gives some minor information about Luke Short and an incorrect account of the killing of Ben Thompson.

875. Griffis, Joseph K.

Tahan. Out of savagery into civilization. An autobiography, by Joseph K. Griffis. New York, George H. Doran co. [1915]. Cloth. Scarce.

8 p.l., 17–263 p. front. (port.), plates, ports. 19.7 cm.
Half title.

In a chapter entitled "With a Gang of Outlaws" the author tells of Tom Starr and of his meeting with Jesse James.

876. Griggs, George

History of Mesilla valley; or, the Gadsden purchase, known in Mexico as the Treaty of Mesilla . . ., by George Griggs. . . . [Las Cruces, N.M., Bronson printing co.], 1930. Stiff wrappers. Rare.

7 p.l., [3]–128 p. illus., maps. 22.6 cm.
Index: p. 125–128.
Map on t.p.

A local history containing some information on Billy the Kid and Pat Garrett. The author credits the Kid with killing twenty-seven men. His account differs from most others in that he says the Kid's first victim was a miner who had run off with his sister. The Kid had no sister. Like the authors of several other accounts, he states that the Kid killed Chisum's riders to get even with Chisum. He also says that Garrett killed the Kid with a rifle and that the Kid was twenty-six years old when he was killed. He tells about Billy's father, whom he calls Frank Bonney, being killed by the Apaches in Arizona. He is also mistaken about the circumstances of the killing of Bell and in stating that Billy killed Olinger with a Winchester instead of a shotgun.

877. Grisham, Noel

Tame the reckless wind. The life and legends of Sam Bass, by Noel Grisham. Illustrations by Col. Gene Fallwell. Austin, Texas, San Felipe press, 1968. Pict. cloth.

xiv p., 1 l., [3]–100 p. illus., map, music. 22.4 cm.
Appendix: p. 93–96; bibliography: p. 97; index: p. 99–100.
Half title.

Though the author says that this book "contains new details," there is not much new except a lot of conversation which no one recorded at the time. The author writes that at Doan's Store near Red River one could "get all the ingredients necessary for that trail delicacy 'son-of-a-gun stew.'" One did not buy those ingredients at a store but got them from a fresh-killed calf. Nor was the stew a trail delicacy. There was no time to prepare a dish when traveling on the trail. The author talks about tumbleweeds blowing about Doan's Crossing, but I am afraid he would find no such vegetation at that point.

He has Joel Collins selling a herd of cattle in Deadwood. The herd was sold in Kansas. He writes that "other Deadwood contemporaries with Bass and Collins were Kitty LeRoy, and Mary Jane Canary [*sic*]," but Calamity Jane did not arrive in Deadwood until just before Wild Bill Hickok was killed in August, 1876. At that time Bass and Collins were gathering a herd of cattle to take north.

I think that the author is mistaken when he says "Collins and Heffridge (after the U. P. robbery) rode toward Texas by way of Leadville, Denver and Albuquerque." Going by way of the last-named town would certainly be far out of the way. On page 42 the author says that "it was on September 26 that Collins and his two companions had gone into Buffalo Station." Collins went to Buffalo Station on September 25, and he had only one companion—Heffridge.

The author scores another near miss when he says that Tom Spottswood "had joined the gang by February 23, 1878." He was in the robbery at Allen, Texas, on February 22 of that year. The author has Jackson a medical student. He was a tinner's apprentice. The author says that Collins owned a saloon in San Antonio, but he was only a bartender. The author also says that Collins owned a ranch near San Antonio—also incorrect. Henry Koppel's name is spelled Kopperal, and there are other mistakes.

878. Griswold, Don L., and Jean Harvey Griswold

The carbonate camp called Leadville, [by] Don L. Griswold and Jean Harvey Griswold. [Denver], University of Denver press, 1951. Cloth. OP.

viii p., 3 l., 282 p. illus., plates, ports. 23.2 cm.
Bibliography p. 276–277; index: p. 278–282.
Half title; maps on end papers (dif.).

Scattered throughout the book are accounts of crimes and holdups.

879. Guerin, Mrs. E. J.

An autobiography. Mountain Charley; or, the adventures of Mrs. E. J.

Guerin who was thirteen years in male attire. An autobiography comprising of a period of thirteen years' life in the states, California and Pike's peak. Dubuque, privately printed, 1861. Wrappers. Exceedingly rare.

2 p.l., 5–45 p. 22 cm.

The story of a woman who dressed as a man, worked on riverboats and as a brakeman on railroads and found other masculine employment as she wandered the country looking for the man who had murdered her husband. In 1858 she worked in the mines of Colorado and then opened a bakery and saloon near Denver, where she was dubbed "Mountain Charley." She finally shot the man who had killed her husband, wounding him severely. She married her bartender, H. L. Guerin, in 1860. The only copy of the original edition known to me is in the DeGolyer Foundation Library at Southern Methodist University.

From this copy a reprint was issued by the University of Oklahoma Press in 1968, with an introduction by Fred W. Mazzulla and William Kostka, as No. 40 of the Western Frontier Library Series.

xv p., 1 l., 3–112 p. 19.6 cm.
Half title: "The Western Frontier Library."

880. Guernsey, Charles Arthur

Wyoming cowboy days. An account of the experiences of Charles Arthur Guernsey, in which he tells in his own way of the early territorial cattle days and political strifes, and deals with many of the state's and nation's famous characters. . . . True to life, but not autobiographical. Romantic, but not fiction. Facts, but not history. Profusely illustrated. New York, G. P. Putnam's sons, 1936. Cloth. Scarce.

x p., 1 l., 13–288 p. front., plates, ports., facsms. 24.3 cm.

Contains some material on the Johnson County War.

881. Guinn, J. M.

A history of California, and an extended history of its southern coast counties; also containing biographies of well-known citizens of the past and present, by J. M. Guinn. Illustrated. Complete in two volumes. Los Angeles, Historic Record co., 1907. Three-quarter leather. Very scarce.

Vol. I, 19 p.l., [33]–1074 p. front. (port. with tissue), ports. (part with tissues). 29.5 cm.
Index: p. [i]–ix (in front).
Double column; gilt edges.
Vol. II, biographical.

In Chapter XXVII, entitled "Crime, Criminals and Vigilance Committees," the author tells of the hanging of Jenkins and the careers of Murieta and Vásquez.

882. ———

Historical and biographical record of southern California, containing a history of southern California from its earliest settlement to the opening year of the twentieth century, by J. M. Guinn. . . . Chicago, Chapman publishing co., 1902. Leather. Scarce.

11 p.l., [33]–1019 p. plates, ports. 28.8 cm.
Gilt edges.

Some material on the Flores and Vásquez gangs, the Solomon Pico gang, and Jack Powers.

883. ———

History of the state of California and biographical record of the Sacramento valley, California. An historical story of the state's marvelous growth from its earliest settlement to the present time, by J. M. Guinn. . . . Chicago, the Chapman publishing co., 1906. Leather. Very scarce.

12 p.l., [33]–1712 p. ports. 29.7 cm.
Double column; gilt edges.

In a chapter on crime and criminals, the author gives accounts of Murieta and Vásquez.

884. ———

History of the state of California and biographical record of San Joaquin county, containing biographies of well-known citizens of the past and present. State history by J. M. Guinn. . . . History of San Joaquin county, by George H. Tinkham. Illustrated. Los Angeles, Calif., Historic Record co., 1909. Pub. in two volumes. Three-quarter leather. Very scarce.

Vol. I, 9 p.l., [33]–303 p. 1 port. (with tissue). 29.4 cm.
Double column; gilt edges.
Vol. II, biographical.

In the chapter on crime and criminals the author's account of Murieta and Vásquez is virtually the same as that in his other books.

885. Guyer, James S.

Pioneer life in west Texas . . ., by James S. Guyer. . . . Brownwood, Texas . . ., 1938. Pict. cloth. Scarce

xi p., 1 l., 3–185 [2] p. illus., plates, ports. 23.4 cm.
Port. of author on t.p.

The author's chapter on Billy the Kid is full of inaccurate statements. He says that he first met Billy on the trail to Dodge City with a herd of cattle. The Kid never drove cattle on the Dodge City trail. He says that Garrett was with Murphy, which is incorrect, and that after the battle at the McSween home both sides met and decided "to let bygones be bygones." He says that Pat Garrett and two deputies waited in ambush at the Maxwell house for Billy the Kid to meet his sweetheart. "About ten o'clock . . . Billy walked slowly into the Maxwell yard, on to the porch, and stepping lightly down the hallway called softly, 'Lucia! Lucia!' Bang! A flash from a small table in the hall snuffed out the life of William B. Bonney" [*sic*].

H

886. Hadfield, R. L.

Picturesque rogues. A chronicle of the lives and adventures of a diversity of rogues in which will be found something of the saving grace of honor, by R. L. Hadfield. London, H. F. & G. Witherby [1931]. Cloth. Scarce.

5 p.l., 11–207 p. 22.7 cm.
Index: p. 203–207.
Half title.

Most of the chapters deal with foreign outlaws, but there are two on American bad men, Henry Plummer and Billy the Kid. The author's chapter on Plummer is unreliable and tells nothing new. He tells all the legends of the Kid's birth and early years, just as Upson did. He has the killing of Brady wrong, as well as that of Grant, and has the Kid stealing horses to drive to Leadville, Colorado. He has Pete Maxwell living in Bosque Grande and sick when the Kid goes to visit him. He has the Kid slipping into the sick room and firing but getting shot in the heart himself.

887. Hafen, LeRoy R., and Carl Coke Rister

Western America. The exploration, settlement, and development of the region beyond the Mississippi, by LeRoy R. Hafen . . . and Carl Coke Rister. . . . New York, Prentice-Hall, inc., 1941. Cloth. OP.

xxiv p., 1 l., 698 p. front. (col. map), illus., maps (2 col. incl. front.), facsm. 23.5 cm.
Bibliography after each chapter; index: p. 669–698.
Half title.

Deals with the vigilantes and outlaws throughout the entire West.

888. ———, and Francis Marion Young

Fort Laramie and the pageant of the west, 1834–1890, by LeRoy R. Hafen and Francis Marion Young. Glendale, Calif., the Arthur H. Clark co., 1938. Cloth. OP.

6 p.l., [17]–429 p. front., illus., diagrs., fold. map. 24 cm.
Half title; pub. device; untrimmed.

Has some material on road agents, stage holdups, and a mention of Sam Bass.

889. Hagan, William T.

Indian police and judges. Experiences in acculturation and control, by William T. Hagen. New Haven and London, Yale University press, 1966. Cloth.

7 p.l., 194 [12] p. last 12 p. plates and ports. 20.9 cm.
Bibliography: p. [177]–183; index: p. [185]–194.
Half title; "Yale Western Americana Series, 13."

The author says that Bob and Emmett Dalton were United States deputy marshals but lost their positions when they were exposed as bootleggers. They were stealing horses, not bootlegging. He also tells some things about the Cook gang, and has a mention of Belle Starr, Blue Duck and Captain Jack, the Modoc outlaw.

890. Haley, J. Evetts

Charles Goodnight, cowman & plainsman; with illustrations by Harold Bugbee, [by] J. Evetts Haley. Boston, New York, Houghton Mifflin co., 1936. Cloth. Scarce in first edition.

xiii p., 1 l., 485 p. front. (port., signature in facsm.), illus., map (double p.), facsm. 22 cm.
"A note of bibliography": p. [469]–472; index: p. [475]–485.
Half title; vignette; first edition: 1936 under imprint.
Republished by the University of Oklahoma press in 1949 with some changes.

A distinguished biography of an outstanding cattleman, this book contains references, scattered but mostly reliable, to certain outlaws of the Southwest. The author does say, however, that Billy the Kid was killed in the spring of 1881, but I fear that July is not considered a spring month.

891. ———

George W. Littlefield, Texan, by J. Evetts Haley. Drawings by Harold D. Bugbee. Norman, University of Oklahoma press, MCMXLIII. Cloth. OP.

xiv p., 1 l., 3–287 p. front., illus., ports., maps. 22 cm.
Index: p. 283–287.
Half title; vignette; "First edition" on copyright p.

Another good biography of a well-known Texas cattleman with information on various outlaws and on Billy the Kid's visit to the Texas Panhandle. The author, however, in quoting M. H. Dowell, fails to correct this statement "Phil Coe . . . was himself killed by Wild Bill Hickok while trailing a herd to Kansas."

892. ———

Jeff Milton, a good man with a gun, by J. Evetts Haley, with drawings by Harold D. Bugbee. Norman, University of Oklahoma press, 1948. Cloth. OP.

xiii p., 1 l., 3–430 p. illus., plates, ports., map. 23.8 cm.
Index: p. 417–430.
Half title; illus. t.p.; "First edition" on copyright p.

An excellent biography of one of the famous law-enforcement officers of the Southwest, detailing his activities among its outlaws and gunmen, such as John Wesley Hardin, Black Jack Ketchum, John Selman, George Scarborough, Burt Alvord, and Billy Stiles. Part of the first printing of this book is distinguished by the index line "Greenway, John Campbell: 366, 411" (page 421) upside down and out of alphabetical order.

893. ———

Jim East, trail hand and cowboy, [by] J. Evetts Haley. [Canyon, Texas], 1931. Wrappers. (Caption title.) Rare.

[23] p. (no pagination). 23.3 cm.

A reprint from the *Panhandle-Plains Historical Review* for 1931, containing some material on Billy the Kid.

894. ———

The XIT ranch of Texas, and the early days on the Llano Estacado, by J. Evetts Haley. . . . Chicago, the Lakeside press, 1929. Cloth. Rare in the first edition.

xvi, 261 p. front. (map), plates, ports. maps (1 fold.), facsms. 23.6 cm.
Appendix: p. 235–250; bibliography: p. 251–255; index p. 257–261.
Vignette.

Owing to a threatened lawsuit, which forced it off the market, the first edition has become rare. In 1953 it was reprinted, with some changes and omissions, by the University of Oklahoma Press. It contains some material on outlaws, brand blotters, and cattle rustlers.

895. **[Haley, John A.]**

A history of Lincoln county post offices. Folklore and tales about people and postmasters in early southwestern New Mexico, [by John A. Haley]. Stiff wrappers.

32 p. illus. 21.6 cm.

Taken from the 1913 *Lincoln County Yearbook*, by John A. Haley. There is some information about Pat Garrett, Ash Upson, and Alexander McSween, and the book lists the postmasters of the towns and villages in Lincoln County.

896. Hall, Angelo

Forty-one thieves. A tale of California, [by] Angelo Hall. Boston, the Cornhill co., [1919]. Pict. cloth. Scarce.

4 p.l., 133 p. 19.2 cm.
Half title; pub. device.

An account of the holdup of the Graniteville stage near Nevada City in 1879, the murder of William F. Cummins, and the pursuit of the criminals by Bed-bug Brown and others.

897. Hall, Bert L.

Experiences of John Edmund Boland, early day river character. Chamberlain, S.D., published by Bert L. Hall [n.d.]. Pict. wrappers. (Cover title.) Scarce.

[13] p. (no pagination). 22.9 cm.

Has some material on Calamity Jane.

898. Hall, Frank

History of the state of Colorado, embracing accounts of the prehistoric races and their remains; the earliest Spanish, French, and American explorations . . ., the first American settlements founded; the Rocky mountains, the development of cities and towns, with the various phases of industrial and political transition from 1858 to 1890 . . ., by Frank Hall, for the Rocky Mountain Historical co., Chicago, the Blakeley printing co., 1889–95. Pub. in four volumes. Dec. cloth. Scarce.

Vol. I, xvi p., 1 l., 17–564 p. front. (port.), plates, ports. 26.8 cm.
Index: p. 554–564.
Vol. II (pub. in 1890), xiv p., 1 l., 17–574 p. front. (port.), ports., maps. 26.8 cm.
Vols. III and IV, biographical.

Volume I contains some material on the Espinosas and Musgrove, the Colorado outlaws, and Volume II has more information on the Espinosa brothers. The author also gives a lengthy account of Billy the Kid, most of it inaccurate. He continues to uphold the legends about the Kid's early life and about his killing Chisum's cowboys for a debt Chisum owed him. He says the Kid went to Maxwell's place to see his sweetheart and that Garrett followed him with a posse. Garrett, according to Hall, entered Maxwell's room through a window, and when the Kid rushed in *with a rifle,* Garrett cut him down, ending the Kid's life at the age of *twenty-six.* Why the story of the Kid's life should appear in a history of Colorado is a mystery. A second edition brings the history to a later date, 1890 to 1897.

899. [Hall, Frank O., and Lindsey H. Whitten]

Jesse James rides again, [by Frank O. Hall and Lindsey H. Whitten]. Lawton, Okla., published by LaHoma publishing co. [1948]. Pict. wrappers. OP.

3 p.l., 7–48 p. front., plates, ports. 27.8 cm.
Double column.

A story of J. Frank Dalton, who claimed to be the real Jesse James, written by two reporters of the *Lawton Constitution* from interviews with this aged character. The authors try hard to convince the reader with the truth of their assertions, but I still believe that poor old Jesse was laid in his grave in 1882. The book is filled with preposterous statements.

900. Hall, Frederic

The history of San Jose, and surroundings, with biographical sketches of early settlers. By Frederic Hall. . . . Illustrated with map and engravings in stone. San Francisco, printing house of A. L. Bancroft and co., 1871. Cloth. Rare.

xv, 537 p. front., plates, large fold. map at end. 23.5 cm.

Has several chapters on crime and outlaws.

901. Hall, Gordon Langley

The two lives of Baby Doe, by Gordon Langley Hall. Illustrated with photographs. Philadelphia, Macrae Smith co. [1962]. Cloth.

7 p.l., 15–252 p. plates, ports. 21.2 cm.
Epilogue: p. 239–243; postscript: p. 247–252.
Half title; illus. t.p.; untrimmed.

The author describes the James boys and the Ford brothers as doing some mining in California Gulch, a detail I have never seen before. Also mentioned is Bat Masterson's gambling hall, where Tabor sometimes gambled.

902. Hall, J. M.

The beginnings of Tulsa, by J. M. Hall. . . . [N.p., n.d.] Suede on thin boards. Scarce.

2 p.l., 1 p., 6–100 p. plates, ports. 23 cm.
Double column.

Has some material on the early marshals, including Heck Thomas, Grat Dalton, and Bud Ledbetter. Also has a mention of the shooting of Texas Jack.

903. Hall, James

The Harpe's head. A legend of Kentucky, by James Hall. . . . Philadelphia, Key & Biddle . . ., 1833. Wrappers. Rare.

2 p.l., [9]–256 p. 16 cm.
36 p. adv. at end.

Reprinted in London by A. K. Newman and Co. in 1834 in two volumes, under the title *Kentucky: A Tale,* and without the preface which appeared in the 1833 edition.

Vol. I, 2 p.l., 230 [2] p. 18 cm.
Vol. II, [3]–242 p. 18 cm.

Tells the story of Harpe and his head.

904. ———

Legends of the west, by James Hall. . . . Cincinnati, Applegate and co., publishers, 1857. Cloth. Rare.

xvi, [17]–435 [16] p. 19.5 cm.
16 p. adv. at end.

Also tells the story of Harpe and his head.

905. Hall, Trowbridge

California trails, intimate guide to the old missions. The story of the California missions, by Trowbridge Hall. New York, the Macmillan co., 1920. Cloth. OP.

8 p.l., 3–243 p. front., plates. 21.5 cm.
Half title.

The author repeats the legend about Joaquín Murieta being horsewhipped by the Americans and his swearing to kill ten Americans for every lash he had received.

906. Hall-Quest, Olga W.

Wyatt Earp, marshal of the old west, by Olga W. Hall-Quest. New York, Ariel Books, Farrar, Straus and Cudahay [1956]. Cloth. OP.

viii p., 1 l., 3–177 p. 21.5 cm.
Half title.

A juvenile book on the life of Wyatt Earp. The author follows Stuart Lake's account very closely and repeats the tale about Earp disarming Ben Thompson at Ellsworth. That never happened; nor did the killing of Sheriff Whitney occur as she and Lake describe it. Bill Thompson did not say, "I'll get me a sheriff if I can't get anybody else," and deliberately shoot Whitney. The sheriff was a friend of the Thompsons, and his killing was a drunken accident. She tells the tale of Earp's meeting with Clay Allison just as Lake told it. Her account of the O K Corral fight is also similar to Lake's.

907. Hamilton, James McClellan

From wilderness to statehood. A history of Montana, 1805–1900, by James McClellan Hamilton. . . . Pen sketches by Betty G. Ryan. . . . Portland, Oreg., Binsford & Mort, publishers [1957]. Cloth. OP.

xv, 620 p. illus. 24.2 cm.
Index: p. 602–620.
Map on end papers; pub. device.

Has a chapter on the Montana vigilantes, the hanging of George Ives, and Henry Plummer, Bill Bunton, Whisky Bill Graves, Jack Gallaher, Club-foot George Lane, and other road agents of that period.

908. Hamilton, Thomas Marion

The young pioneer. When Captain Tom was a boy. Thrilling tales of a real boy's frontier adventures among Indians, pioneers, scouts, cowboys and bandits, by Thomas Marion Hamilton. Washington, D.C., the Library press [1932]. Fabrikoid. Scarce.

6 p.l., [15]–284 p. 1 plate. 20 cm.
Half title; vignette.

Unless this book was intended to be a collection of tall tales, I feel safe in saying that it is one of the most ridiculous books ever written. The author says that Billy the Kid was captured by Pat Garrett in Tombstone, Arizona, and jailed there. The Kid's sweetheart then came to Tombstone and secured a job as cook in the hotel across the street from the jail and proceeded to put sleeping drugs in the food sent to the jail guards so that Billy could escape.

Albert J. Fountain and his little son were murdered in the White Sands of New Mexico on January 31, 1896, and neither the killers nor the victims were ever found. In spite of the fact that Billy the Kid was killed in 1881, this author states that the Kid warned Fountain about his impending murder as he started on his journey. The records show that at this time the Kid had been officially dead for fifteen years; yet Mr. Hamilton says that Billy followed Fountain and saw him murdered by the Tate gang. According to this account, Billy caught up with this gang, gave them a lecture on their dastardly deed, and, as time passed, killed them one by one. The author claims that Billy told him this story personally.

The account of the Kid's killing by Pat Garrett is also preposterous. According to the author, the Kid's sweetheart had persuaded him to give himself up on the basis of a promise made her by Garrett; but when the Kid arrived at her home, Garrett shot him with a rifle while hiding in a peach orchard. The author not only disregards facts but also seems indifferent to the correct spelling of proper names.

He spells O'Folliard's name as O'Foulard and Bowdre's as Bowder and says that Garrett was killed by Wayne Bonzell (Brazil).

909. Hamilton, Winifred Oldham

Wagon days on Red river, by Winifred Oldham Hamilton. [Raton, N.M., Daily Range print], 1947. Stiff pict. wrappers. (Cover title.)

3-35 [1] p. front., plates. 23.4 cm.

The book seems to be told by an old-timer named Uncle George Oldham (doubtless related to the compiler), who tells some new incidents in the lives of Black Jack and Sam Ketchum. He has Dee Harkey saying that Black Jack had held up a train in Trinidad, Colorado. Ketchum never held up a train there. The author also gives some information about Soapy Smith and his gang.

910. Hamlin, Lloyd, and Rose Hamlin

Hamlin's Tombstone picture gallery. . . . Glendale, Calif., published by Western Americana press of Glendale, 1960. Stiff pict. Wrappers. (Cover title.)

22 [2] p. front. (col.), illus., plates, ports., col. illus. both sides of back cover. 27.8 x 27.8 cm.

Index: information about the book and the authors on the page ordinarily used for title page; "First edition" on same p.

A collection of excellent photos of Tombstone and some of its inhabitants. There is also an excellent text, telling about the Earps, Doc Holliday, Sheriff Johnny Behan, the Clantons, the McLaurys, and the O K Corral fight. All the authors' information is reliable.

911. Hamlin, William Lee

The true story of Billy the Kid. A tale of the Lincoln county war, by William Lee Hamlin. Illustrated with photographs. Caldwell, Idaho, the Caxton printers, ltd., 1959. Cloth.

xviii p., 1 l., 364 [16] p. front., plates, ports., map, facsms., plans. 21.6 cm.

Appendix and commentary: p. [335]-347; notes: p. [348]-364.

Half title; pub. device; last 16 p. facsms.

The many mistakes this author has made about Billy the Kid and the Lincoln County War are covered in my *Burs Under the Saddle* (Item 7).

912. Hammond, Isaac B.

Reminiscences of frontier life. Compliments of I. B. Hammond. Portland, Oreg., 1904. Wrappers. Rare.

4 p.l., [9]-134 [1] p. illus., ports. 21 cm.

Privately printed for friends. The author died while the book was in press. The printer, no doubt believing that he would not recover his printing costs, scrapped almost the entire edition, only a few copies escaping; hence its rarity. It contains material on some outlaws of the frontier and tells about the hangings by the vigilantes and about the last of Laramie road agents.

913. Hammond, John Hays

The autobiography of John Hays Hammond. Illustrated with photographs. New York, Farrar & Rinehart, inc. [1935]. Cloth. Pub. in two volumes. (Boxed.) OP.

Vol. I, xiii p., 1 l., 3–383 p. front. (port.), plates, ports., map. 23.2 cm.
Half title.
Vol. II, 4 p.l., 382–813 p. front., plates, ports. 23.2 cm.
Bibliography: p. 779–782; index: p. 785–813.
Half title; paged continuously.

In Volume I, Mr. Hammond, who was in Tombstone, Arizona, in 1879, tells about Wyatt Earp, for whom he has nothing but praise. He says that he later met Earp again in Tonopah, Nevada, and hired him to take care of the claim jumpers.

914. Hamner, Laura V.

Light 'n hitch. A collection of historical writings depicting life on the high plains, by Laura V. Hamner, with paintings by Dord Titz. Dallas, Texas, American Guild press [1958]. Pict. cloth. OP.

x p., 2 l., [15]–349 [1] p. illus., plates, ports., maps, plan. 23.3 cm.
Appendix A: [319]–334; Appendix B: p. [335]–337; index of illustrations and maps: p. [338]; index of first lines: p. [339]; general index: p. [340]–349; errata: p. [350].
Half title; map on front flyleaf; cattle brands on rear flyleaf.
Also published in a de luxe edition with slip case.
Colophon (pasted on half-title p.): "This is Book No. —— of an autographed limited edition of one thousand copies. Signed ——."

The book has some material on Bat Masterson and a mention of Sam Bass.

915. ——

The no-gun man of Texas. A century of achievement, 1835–1929, by Laura V. Hamner. Illustrated by Ben Carlton Mead and Terry Stowe. [Amarillo, Texas, privately printed], by Laura V. Hamner, 1935. Pict. cloth. Scarce.

viii p., 1 l., 3–256 p. front. (port.), map (on first front flyleaf). 20 cm.
Appendix: p. 251–254; glossary: p. 255–256.
Half title.

In this story of the life of Charles Goodnight there is a chapter on Dutch Henry, the noted horse thief.

916. ——

Short grass & longhorns, by Laura V. Hamner. Norman, University of Oklahoma press, 1943. Cloth. Scarce.

5 p.l., 3–269 p. plates, maps. 22 cm.

A bog rider's bibliography: p. 253–254; index: p. 255–269.

Copies of the first issue of this book (an edition of thirty copies published in 1942 in an effort to secure its adoption as a supplementary reading book in the Texas public schools) are very rare and have become collector's items. Published without illustrations, the first issue has no index and is 254 pages long. The trade edition was printed in August, 1943, and again in January, 1945. It contains material on Billy the Kid and his stay in Tascosa.

917. Hanes, Colonel Bailey C.

Bill Doolin: Outlaw O. T., [by] Colonel Bailey C. Hanes. With an introduction by Ramon F. Adams. Norman, University of Oklahoma press [1968]. Boards.

xxiii p., 1 l., 3–207 p. plates, ports. 19.6 cm.

No. 41 of the Western Frontier Library series.

Bibliography: p. 201–207.

Half title; illus. double t.p.; "First edition" on copyright p.

The first and only book devoted entirely to Bill Doolin. The author did some genuine research and clears up some erroneous statements made by others.

918. Hansen, Harvey J., and Jeanne Thurlow Miller

Wild oat in Eden. Sonoma county in the 19th century, by Harvey J. Hansen and Jeanne Thurlow Miller. Foreword by Gaye Lebaron. Photographs by Ansel Adams, John Lebaron & Beth Winter. Santa Rosa, Calif., MCMLXII. Pict. cloth. Scarce.

4 p.l., 147 p. front., plates, ports., facsms., maps. 26.8 cm.

Sources: p. 140–142; index: p. 143–147.

Untrimmed.

Contains a chapter entitled "Land of the Highwayman" which contains material on Black Bart and the "Big Foot Gang."

919. Hardin, John Wesley

The life of John Wesley Hardin, from the original manuscript as written by himself. Seguin, Texas, published by Smith & Moore, 1896. Wrappers. Scarce.

2 p.l., [5]–144 p. front. (port.), illus., ports. 18.8 cm.

Republished by Frontier Times of Bandera, Texas, in 1926.

Republished in 1961 by the University of Oklahoma press as No. 16 of the Western Frontier Library series, with an introduction by Robert G. McCubbin.

In the first copies of the original edition released by the printers the portrait of Joe Hardin, John's brother, is mislabeled John W. Hardin. The book is carefully written; in fact, so well written that some claim that it came from the pen of someone more literate than Hardin. On the other hand, Hardin was not as illiterate as many believed; he taught a frontier school as a young man, and his study of law while he was in prison no doubt improved his education. Newspapers reported that he was trying to finish his manuscript in El Paso just before he was killed. Whoever the writer was, he was careful of names and dates. He tells about his life up to his death, and this latter is discussed in an appendix, with a quotation from the *El Paso Herald* of August 20, 1895.

920. Hardy, Allison

Kate Bender, the Kansas murderess. The horrible history of an arch killer, [by] Allison Hardy. Girard, Kans., Haldeman-Julius publications, 1944. Wrappers.

[2]–24 p. 21.4 cm.

A history of the Bender family, concluding with various theories and hearsay about their end, but no details of their deaths have ever been verified.

921. ———

Wild Bill Hickok, king of gun-fighters, by Allison Hardy. Girard, Kans., Haldeman-Julius publications [1943]. Wrappers.

1 p.l., [3]–23 p. 21.3 cm.

A small book on a large subject, but a fairly accurate one. The author debunks some of the earlier accounts, such as those by Buel and Hough.

922. Harkey, Dee

Mean as hell, by Dee Harkey. Line drawings by Gene Roberts. [Albuquerque, N.M.], University of New Mexico press, 1948. Cloth.

xvi, 223 [1] p. illus., plates, ports. 20.2 cm.

Index: p. 219–223.

Half title.

Illus. t.p.; map on end papers.

A most interesting account of lawlessness in New Mexico. Soon after the book was released to dealers, the publishers recalled all unsold copies, or asked the dealers to black out the word "outlaw" after the name of Lee Dow in the index on page 220, and they also added an errata slip on preliminary page xv, correcting the name Ace Christmas on pages 110, 116, and 219 to U. S. Christmas. There was no new edition printed for this purpose. In the next printing, however, these corrections were made in the text. The first printing may be identified by these errors.

The author had personal experience with many of the outlaws as a peace officer, and he records some facts not found elsewhere. He has a chapter on the Dalton gang in New Mexico, but the Daltons themselves did not go to New Mexico, though some of the remnants of their gang got there. In a chapter on John Wesley Hardin the author says after Hardin was released from prison "he was active in all kinds of outlawry in and around El Paso until his death." He also has a chapter on the Lee-Garrett feud.

923. Harlow, Alvin F.

Murders not quite solved, [by] Alvin F. Harlow. New York, Julian Messner, inc., publishers [1938]. Cloth. OP.

vi p., 1 l., 3–368 p. 22.4 cm.
Half title; untrimmed.

Contains a chapter on the Benders.

924. ———

Old waybills, the romance of the express companies, by Alvin F. Harlow. New York, London, D. Appleton-Century co., inc., 1934. Cloth.

xii p., 1 l., 503 [1] p. front., illus., plates, ports., facsms. 22.5 cm.
Bibliography: p. 489–[497]; index: p. 499–[504].
Half title; pub. device; untrimmed; first edition: figure (1) at end of index.
Republished in 1937.

About half of this book deals with train and stagecoach robberies, with information on the Jameses and Youngers, Sam Bass, Black Bart, Evans, Sontag, and others.

925. ———

"Weep no more my lady," [by] Alvin F. Harlow. New York, London, Whittlesey House, McGraw-Hill book co., inc. [1942]. Cloth. OP.

x p., 1 l., 3–455 p. front., illus., plates, music. 23.5 cm.
Acknowledgments: p. 441–443; index: p. 445–455.

The author devotes a long chapter to the activities of Quantrill and the James boys in Kentucky and contends that the James boys' stepfather, Dr. Samuel, spelled his name thus, while the Kentucky branch of the same family spelled the name Samuels, adding the *s*.

926. Harlow, Victor Emmanuel

The most picturesque personality in Oklahoma, Al Jennings, by Victor E. Harlow. Oklahoma City, Harlow publishing co., 1912. Wrappers. Rare.

12 p. port. 20.5 cm.

A short sketch of Al Jennings and his activities. This little pamphlet has become very rare.

927. Harman, Samuel W.

Belle Starr, the female desperado, by S. W. Harman. Houston, Texas, Frontier press of Texas, 1954. Stiff wrappers.

2 p.l., [5]–59 [5] p. front., plates, ports. 21.3 cm.
Last 5 pages plates and ports. from the Rose collection.

A separate reprint of a chapter taken from the author's *Hell on the Border* (Item 929) and, like the original, full of errors.

928. ———

Cherokee Bill, the Oklahoma outlaw, by S. W. Harman. Houston, Texas, Frontier press of Texas, 1954. Stiff wrappers.

2 p.l., [5]–56 [7] p. front. (port.), plates, ports. 21.3 cm.
Last 7 pages plates and ports. from the Rose collection.

A separate reprint of a chapter taken from the author's *Hell on the Border* (Item 929).

929. ———

Hell on the border; he hanged eighty-eight men. A history of the great United States criminal court at Fort Smith, Arkansas, and of crime and criminals in the Indian territory, and the trial and punishment thereof before . . . Judge Isaac C. Parker . . . and by the courts of said territory, embracing the leading sentences and charges to grand and petit juries delivered by the world famous jurist—his acknowledged masterpieces, besides much other legal lore. . . . Illustrated with over fifty fine half-tones. By S. W. Harman, compiled by C. P. Sterns. Fort Smith, Ark., the Phoenix publishing co. [1898]. Stiff green wrappers. Exceedingly rare.

xiii, 720 p. front. (port.), illus., plates, ports., map, tables. 21.8 cm.

Later published in an abridged edition.

ix, [1]–9, 10–320 p. plates, ports. 19.5 cm.

Published again in 1953 with some changes.

xiii, 303 p. plates, ports. 19.7 cm.

The rare original has become a collector's item and is the chief source of practically every book and feature story on the old court and Oklahoma outlaws. It originated from an idea of J. Warren Reed, the criminal lawyer who was such a thorn in Judge Parker's side. Although Reed's name does not appear, he financed its publication. He had Samuel W. Harman, a professional juryman, write it, and it appears under his name. The book was printed in an edition of only one thousand copies; and, though largely statistical and dry, the first edition was soon exhausted because of the reputation of Judge Parker's court.

A second edition was issued in the print shop of Kendall College, but was abridged and had four hundred fewer pages, some of the dull part being left out. It, too, has become very scarce. Most of the transcripts from the court records and biographical sketches in the original edition are said to have been compiled by C. P. Sterns, and are not too trustworthy. The book contains much material on the outlaws of the Indian Territory who were tried and condemned in Parker's court, but some of the material not dealing directly with the court is unreliable, especially that about Belle Starr.

930. Harriman, Alice

Pacific history stories. Montana edition, by Alice Harriman. . . . San Francisco, the Whitaker & Ray co., inc., 1903. Pict. cloth. Scarce.

6 p.l., 11–198 [1] p. front. (col.), illus., plates, ports., facsm. 17.3 cm.
Pub. device.
Western Series of Readers, edited by Han Wagner.

Has a chapter on the Montana vigilantes.

931. Harrington, Fred Harvey

Hanging judge, by Fred Harvey Harrington. Illustrations from photographs. Caldwell, Idaho, the Caxton printers, ltd., 1951. Cloth.

8 p.l., 17–204 p. front. (port.), plates, ports., facsm. 23.6 cm.
Notes on sources: p. 195–199; index: p. 200–204.
Half title; map on end papers; headpieces; pub. device; vignette.

Any book about Judge Parker is of necessity full of material about outlaws. This one contains chapters on the Daltons, Belle Starr, and many others. The author is mistaken when he says that Bill Doolin "and two others had been dropped from the Dalton gang just before the disastrous invasion of Coffeyville." Doolin did not like the idea of such a rash act and refused to take part. He also makes the statement that Jim Reed, Belle Starr's husband, was "slaughtered in a Texas gunfight." He was treacherously murdered by a deputy seeking the reward.

932. Harris, Edward

Outlaws of the Black Hills of Dakota and Wyoming, by Edward Harris. London, 1890. Excessively rare.

I have never been able to locate a copy of this book, though I have searched diligently for it over a period of many years.

933. Harris, Frank

My reminiscences as a cowboy, [by] Frank Harris; illustrations by William Gropper. New York, Charles Boni . . ., 1930. Stiff pict. wrappers. OP.

7 p.l., 15–217 [2] p. plates. 18.6 cm.
Half title; illus. end papers; vignette.

934. ———

On the trail. My reminiscences as a cowboy, by Frank Harris. London, John Lane, the Bodley Head, ltd. [1930]. Cloth. Scarce.

8 p.l., 9–247 [8] p. 19.2 cm.
Half title; 8 p. adv. at end.

The English edition of Item 933. Although the introductions to both editions have the same heading, "From Ireland to Texas," they are entirely different. The American edition was written by H. M. Kallen, and the London edition was written by the author, Frank Harris. The American edition is in wrappers and is illustrated; the London edition is in cloth and without illustrations. Chapter X in the American edition is entitled "Camp Knockouts" and in the London edition is entitled "An Indian Blockade." Chapter XI of the American edition, "Buffalo Hunting," does not appear in the English edition, and the London edition has some chapters that do not appear in the American edition. The American edition has sixteen chapters; the London edition, fourteen.

Both books are full of inaccuracies and are mostly wildly imaginary. They are included in this work because of the author's preposterous account of Wild Bill Hickok. The author says that Hickok was elected marshal of Wichita, or Dodge (he "forgot which"—and both are wrong), and soon after being "elected" (he was appointed) he was called to a saloon where a row was going on and killed three of the most quarrelsome participants. When Hickok came out of the saloon, according to this tale, he killed a well-liked railroad man. The dead man's friends ran Hickok out of town, and he went as meekly as a lamb.

The author, who claims to have become an intimate friend of Hickok, says that Wild Bill was brought up in Missouri. He says that Hickok's first killing was the result of a quarrel over a watch and that the man he quarreled with was a Ned Tomlin, the son of a banker (this tale I think is confused with the story of Dave Tutt, though the author places the event in Pleasant Hill, where the author was reared, not in Springfield, where Hickok killed Tutt). The author claims that he was with Hickok in Taos, New Mexico, and he tells of their riding the Chisholm Trail together and of their raids into Old Mexico to steal cattle. Hickok never had any interest in cattle, nor did he ever drive them up the trail. Altogether it is a most ridiculous fabrication.

935. Harris, Judge Frank

History of Washington county and Adams county, by Judge Frank Harris. [N.p., n.d.] Stiff pict. wrappers. (Cover title.) OP.

3 p.l., 7–74 p. front. (port.). 22.2 cm.
Pioneer honor roll: p. 71–74; double column.

Has much on lawlessness and Rattlesnake Jack Slade.

936. Harris, Phil

This is Three Forks country, by Phil Harris. . . . [Muskogee, Oklahoma, Hoffman printing co., 1965.] Stiff wrappers.

4 p.l., [11]–74 p. plates, ports. 22.8 cm.
Map on front cover; "First edition" on copyright p.

Contains a chapter on Belle Starr. The author is in error when he says that Belle's husband, Sam Starr, was the son of "Old Sam Starr." He was the son of Tom Starr. He also says Cole Younger was her "former husband." He intimates that the Youngers were in prison in Minnesota when Belle acquired her home at Younger's Bend, but the Youngers and the Jameses visited her there before they went to Minnesota.

937. Harrison, Benjamin S.

Fortune favors the brave. The life and times of Horace Bell, pioneer Californian, by Benjamin S. Harrison. Los Angeles, the Ward Ritchie press, 1953. Cloth. OP.

xvi p., 1 l., 3–307 p. plates, ports., facsms. 24 cm.
Notes on sources: p. 279–290; bibliography: p. 291–294; index: p. 295–307.
Half title.

A well-written story of the life of Major Bell as an early-day Californian. It also contains some material on Murieta.

938. Harrison, Fred

Hell holes and hangings, by Fred Harrison. Clarendon, Texas, Clarendon press, 1968. Cloth.

ix p., 2 l., 170 p. front., plates, ports. 22.3 cm.
Bibliography: p. 169–170.

In his chapter on New Mexico the author states that Sheriff Brady led the posse that killed Tunstall, but this is not true. He is also wrong in saying that Governor Sheldon replaced Governor Axtell. He gives Billy the Kid credit for killing Sheriff Brady, and is mistaken in saying that McSween "gathered 41 gunmen and barricaded them within his home near the edge of the village." McSween's "gunfighters" were scattered through several houses in Lincoln. He tells about Buckskin Frank Leslie and his killing of Claiborne (which the author spells Claybourn).

939. Hart, Herbert M.

Old forts of the southwest, by Herbert M. Hart. Drawings by Paul J. Hartle. Seattle, Superior publishing co. [1964]. Cloth.

4 p.l., [1] p., 10–192 p. plates, ports., plans, maps, facsm. 17.3 cm.
Acknowledgments: p. 182; directory of military forts: p. 183–190; index: p. 191–192.
Half title; illus. map on end papers; "First edition" on copyright p.

In his chapter on Fort Hays the author tells about Wild Bill Hickok's troubles with the soldiers, but is mistaken in saying that he was a U.S. marshal. He mentions Bat Masterson and Wyatt Earp in Dodge, and later in Ellsworth, where he was supposed to have arrested Ben Thompson. The author does correct this error later, however, when he writes: "Although Earp later claimed his fame began at Ellsworth, it appears this is based more on hindsight than on facts."

940. Hart, William Surrey

My life east and west, by William S. Hart. With illustrations. Boston and New York, Houghton Mifflin co., 1929. Cloth. Scarce.

vii [1] p., 1 l., 3–362 [1] p. front. (col.), plates, ports. 22 cm.
Index: p. 355–[363].
Half title; pub. device; untrimmed; first edition: 1929 under imprint.

Contains some material on Wild Bill Hickok, Bat Masterson, and Wyatt Earp. In a reprint of a talk given in April, 1925, before the Lamb's Club in New York, the author says that the bad element of Abilene, Kansas, imported Phil Coe (whom he calls Cole) from Texas to kill Hickok. He tells how Coe "learned that Wild Bill was fond of animals; how at midnight, knowing Hickok was in the Bull's Head Saloon, he went to a corral and stole a shepherd dog, and took him in front of the saloon and tied him to the door, then hid behind a post and shot the dog, knowing Hickok would come to succor the poor animal; how the plot worked—how Hickok did come—a-running—but with a gun in each hand; how Phil Cole [*sic*] lay stretched staring upward with a dying dog trying to lick—the wrong man's hands; how the bad element, in darkness across the street, were quickly mustered; how they must get Hickok at once, or leave town, whipped and beaten, their power gone forever; how they watched Hickok re-enter the saloon—but eight gun-men, bad men followed—there was no back door; how Hickok stood with his back to them, yet such was the instinct and courage of this wonderful man that one of the eight men made his first move . . . and then Hickok's two guns came from nowhere and leaped into life. . . . How when his twelve shots had been fired and the smoke had cleared away, eight men were dead or dying on the floor of the Bull's Head Saloon, at Abilene, Kansas, in 1869. . . ." All this was told to a believing audience, and yet there was not one word of truth in it from beginning to end. Hickok only killed two men while in Abilene, one Phil Coe and the other his own friend and deputy.

Incidentally, the author is also wrong in saying that Charlie Russell, the famous cowboy artist, was born in Burlington, New Jersey. He was born in St. Louis, Missouri. He attended a military school in Burlington for a very short time.

941. ———

William S. Hart in Wild Bill Hickok. Los Angeles, privately printed by Will A. Kistler co., printers, 1923. Pict. wrappers. Rare.

36 p. 20.7 cm.

Evidently taken from the motion picture Mr. Hart made about Hickok. Like most motion pictures, it is anything but history. He has the McCanles "fight" at what he calls Point of Rocks instead of Rock Creek. He repeats the tale about eight men fighting Hickok and has them all killed instead of letting two escape, as most other writers tell it. He says that Hickok had to spend a year in the hospital in Kansas City and that he was a flute player. I have never read those details before. He has him killing twelve men at Hays City, twenty-five in Abilene, and nine in Ellsworth.

He claims that when a young girl from Boston got off the train at Dodge City, Wild Bill fell in love with her and that she was the only love of his life. Mr. Hart has Hickok killing seven soldiers, after which he promised General Custer he would never carry a gun again. He has him sending money to McCanles' son (whom he calls Lawrence instead of Monroe) each month after killing the father. He has both Calamity Jane and Jack McCall in Dodge and Wild Bill a gambler there. None of these characters were in Dodge City. He says that Calamity Jane was an illegitimate child and that Hickok was deeply in love with her—this after saying that the girl on the train was the only love of his life. The whole book is a piece of poorly written fiction in the guise of history.

942. **Haskell, Henry C. and Richard B. Fowler**

City of the future. A narrative history of Kansas City, 1850–1950, by Henry C. Haskell [and] Richard B. Fowler. Foreword by Robert A. Roberts. Illustrated by Frank H. Miller. Kansas City, Mo., Frank Glenn publishing company, inc. [1950]. Cloth. OP.

10 p.l., 19–193 p. illus., full p. plates. 22.6 cm.
Acknowledgments and bibliography: p. 181–185; index: p. 187–193.
Half title; map on end papers; double t.p.

Gives some material on Wyatt Earp, Wild Bill Hickok and Jesse James.

943. **Hattich, William**

Pioneer magic, by William Hattich. New York, Washington, Hollywood, Vantage Press [1964]. Cloth.

6 p.l., 13–73 p. illus., 7 full p. plates. 20.7 cm.
Half title; "First edition" on copyright p.

In a chapter entitled "The Holdup Industry," the author tells of stagecoach robberies in California and around Tombstone, Arizona, and makes mention of the O K Corral battle.

944. **Havighurst, Walter**

Annie Oakley of the wild west, by Walter Havighurst. New York, the Macmillan co., 1954. Cloth.

viii p., 1 l., 246 p. plates, ports., facsms. 21.6 cm.
Acknowledgments: p. 234–236; index: p. 237–246.
Half title; illus. map on front end papers; illus. rear end papers; "First printing" on copyright p.

Has some material on Doc Middleton, both as an outlaw and as a showman with Buffalo Bill.

945. **Havins, T. R.**

Something about Brown. (A history of Brown county, Texas), by T. R. Havins. Brownwood, Texas, Banner printing co. [1958]. Cloth.

4 p.l., 208 p. 8 plates. 22.3 cm.
Appendix: p. 179–203; index: p. 204–208.
Half title.

Contains several pages devoted to John Wesley Hardin.

946. **Hawes, Harry B.**

Frank and Jesse James in review for the Missouri society. Address by

Harry B. Hawes. Washington, D. C., February 25, 1939. Pamphlet. (Cover title.) Scarce.

28 [1] p. 23 cm.

A pamphlet giving some of the highlights of the James boys' careers.

947. Hawkeye, Harry (pseud.)

Rube Burrows [*sic*], the outlaw. A book of thrilling adventures and desperate deeds, narrating actual facts as obtained from principals and eye-witnesses, by Harry Hawkeye. Illustrated. Baltimore, Md., I. & M. Ottenheimer, publishers, 1908. Pict. wrappers (col.). Scarce.

2 p.l., 7–172 [20] p. illus. 18.5 cm.
Last 20 p. adv.

Another of those cheap and inaccurate books common in the early twentieth century.

948. ———

Tracy, the outlaw, king of bandits. A narrative of the thrilling adventures of the most daring and resourceful bandit ever recorded in the criminal annals of the world, by Harry Hawkeye. Illustrated. Baltimore, Md., I. & M. Ottenheimer, publisher, 1908. Pict. wrappers. Scarce.

2 p.l., [9]–184 p. front., illus. 18.5 cm.
4 l. adv. at end.

Another of those unreliable paper-backed books so popular at the beginning of the century.

949. Hawley, James H. (ed.)

History of Idaho, the gem of the mountains. James H. Hawley, editor. Illustrated. Chicago, the S. J. Clarke publishing co., 1920. Pub. in three volumes. Cloth. Scarce.

Vol. I, 8 p.l., 19–895 p. front. (port.), plates, ports. 28.5 cm.
Vols. II and III, biographical.

Has a chapter on lawlessness and the professional bad man and contains material on the vigilantes, Henry Plummer, Cherokee Bob, Boone Helm, Farmer Peel, George Ives, Bob Zachary, and others.

950. Haydon, Arthur Lincoln

The riders of the plains. Adventure and romance with the north-west mounted police, 1873–1910, by A. L. Haydon. Illustrated with photographs, maps and diagrams. Chicago, A. C. McClure & co.; London, Andrew Melrose, 1910. Cloth. Scarce.

xvi, 385 p. front. (with tissue), plates, ports., maps (1 fold.), diagrs. (1 fold.). 23.3 cm.

Appendix: p. 355–[380]; index: p. 381–385.

Half title; pub. device; t.p. in red and black.

Embodies some material on Soapy Smith, his life and death in the Yukon.

951. Hayes, Augustus Allen, Jr.

New Colorado and the Santa Fe trail, by A. A. Hayes, Jr. . . . . Illustrated. New York, Harper and brothers, 1880. Dec. cloth. Scarce.

7 p.l., [17]–200 p. front. (map), illus. 23.2 cm.

A collection of articles from *Harper's Magazine* and the *International Review*. Contains some material on road agents and stagecoach robberies.

952. Hayes, Benjamin

Pioneer notes from the diaries of Judge Benjamin Hayes, 1849–1875. Los Angeles, privately printed [McBride printing co.], 1929. [Edited and published by Marjorie Tisdale Walcott.] Cloth. Scarce.

ix, 13–307 p. front. (port.), plates, ports., map, facsms. 23.4 cm.

Index: p. 303–307.

Half title.

Has some slight mention of Joaquín Murieta and tells about bringing in dead two of the Murieta gang. It also has much information on various other acts of lawlessness in California.

953. Hayes, Jeff W.

Paradise on earth. By Jeff W. Hayes. . . . Portland, Oreg., F. W. Bates and co., publishers, 1913. Pict. French wrappers. OP.

5 p.l., 112 p. front. (port. with signature in facsm.) 21 cm.

In a chapter entitled "The Bad Man From Bodie," the author tells about Jim Slack, an outlaw of the period.

954. Hayes, Jess G.

Apache vengeance. Illustrations by Horace T. Pierce. Albuquerque, University of New Mexico press, 1954. Pict. cloth. OP.

xviii p., 1 l., 185 p. illus. 19.6 cm.

Appendices: p. 165–185.

Half title; illus. t.p.

(At head of title: "True Story of Apache Kid. Jess G. Hayes.")

One of the best and most thorough books written about Apache Kid, the notorious Indian outlaw.

955. ——

Boots and bullets. The life and times of John W. Wentworth, by Jess G. Hayes [Tucson, Ariz.], University of Arizona press [1967]. Cloth.

xiv p., 1 l., 139 p. plate, port. 19.7 cm.
Half title; double illus. t.p.; pub. device.

The author tells of the famous robbery of a Porter and Hall pack train by Cicero Grime, his brother Lafayette, and Curtis B. Hawley. There is a chapter on the Pleasant Valley War between the Tewksburys and the Grahams and the killing of Andy and Sam Blevins by Sheriff Commodore Perry Owens. There is also a short chapter on Pearl Hart and her companion robber, Joe Boot.

956. ——

Sheriff Thompson's day—turbulence in the Arizona territory, [by] Jess G. Hayes. Tucson, Ariz., University of Arizona press [1968]. Cloth.

8 p.l., 190 p. plates, ports. 19.7 cm.
Index: p. 185–190.
Half title: pub. device.

The story of crime and the regime of one of Arizona's outstanding sheriffs. There is some information on the Apache Kid and Ike and Phineas Clanton and the killing of Ike by Commodore Perry Owens.

957. Hayes, William Edward

Iron road to empire. The history of 100 years of progress and achievements of the Rock Island lines, [by] William Edward Hayes. [New York, Simmons-Boardman publishing corp., 1953.] Cloth. OP.

xiii p., 1 l., 3–306 p. plates, ports., map. 23.5 cm.
Bibliography: p. 297–298; index: p. 299–306.
Half title; double t.p.

Chapter 16 deals with the robbery of the Rock Island at Adair, Iowa, by the James gang.

958. [Hays City]

"It pays to live in Hays because ——." [N.p., n.d.] Wrappers. Rare.

[36] p. (no pagination). plates. 14.7 x 22 cm.

The early-history section tells about the exploits of Wild Bill Hickok when he was marshal at Hays City.

959. Hazard, Lucy Lockwood

In search of America, by Lucy Lockwood Hazard. . . . New York, Thomas Y. Crowell co. [1930]. Cloth. Scarce.

xxv p., 4 l., 7–586 p. 22 cm.

Bibliography after each chapter; index: p. 583–586.

An anthology containing some outlaw material.

960. Hearn, Walter

Killing of Apache Kid, [by] Walter Hearn. [N.p., n.d.] Stiff pict. wrappers. (Cover title.) Scarce.

32 p. 18 cm.

A story of the killing of Apache Kid by one of those who killed him.

961. Hebard, Grace Raymond

The pathbreakers from river to ocean. The story of the great west from the time of Coronado to the present, [by] Grace Raymond Hebard. . . . Four maps and numerous illustrations. Chicago, the Lakeside press, 1911. Cloth. Scarce.

x p., 1 l., 263 p. front., illus., 4 maps. 19 cm.

Bibliography: p. 255–257; index: p. 259–263.

Device.

Republished by Arthur H. Clark, Glendale, Calif., 1932, 1940, with the addition of pronouncing vocabulary and different illustrations.

Although the author was teacher of political science in the University of Wyoming until her death, and was considered an able historian, in this book she perpetuated the Hickok-McCanles legend.

"Members of the McCanlass [*sic*] gang," she writes, "once leagued together to put him out of the way, . . . and at one time a roomful attacked Wild Bill alone. When the smoke cleared away it was found that ten men had been killed." The author evidently followed the legend created by Nichols and Buel.

962. Hebert, Frank

40 years prospecting and mining in the Black Hills of South Dakota, by Frank Hebert. . . . [Rapid City, S. D., Rapid City Daily Journal, 1921.] Cloth. Scarce.

5 p.l., 199 p. front. (port.), illus., plates, ports. 21 cm.

The author gives information on road agents and on the deaths of Lame Johnny Bradley and Fly-Specked Billy.

963. Heckman, Capt. William L.

Steamboating sixty-five years on Missouri's waters. The historical story of developing the waterway traffic on the rivers of the middle west, by Captain William L. Heckman, "Steamboat Bill." Illustarted [*sic*] from photographs. . . . Kansas City, Burton publishing co., publishers [1950]. Pict. cloth. OP.

16 p.l., 33–284 p. front., plates. 20.2 cm.
Half title; illus. end papers.

Tells of Frank James's job as bouncer at the Standard Theater and gives other information about the James boys.

964. Heermans, Forbes

Thirteen stories of the far west, by Forbes Heermans. Syracuse, N.Y., C. W. Bardeen, publisher, 1887. Cloth. Scarce.

4 p.l., [9]–263 p. 18.4 cm.

In his foreword the author states that these stories "are reports of actual experiences, written up from his note-book, with such changes in names, places and minor incidents as his personal safety seems to require." Judging from Chapter VII, entitled "The Wedding At Puerta de Luna," however, his stories are wild fiction. In this chapter he has a preposterous story of Billy the Kid holding up a wedding dance, killing his own father, and losing his own life in the quicksands of the Pecos River while trying to escape from his holdup victims.

965. Heilbron, W. C.

Convict life at the Minnesota state prison, Stillwater, Minnesota. Profusely illustrated. St. Paul, Minn., published by W. C. Heilbron [1909]. Wrappers. Scarce.

3 p.l., [7]–155 [3] p. front., plates, ports., facsm. 19.5 cm.
Device.

One chapter, entitled "Real Facts about the Northfield, Minnesota, Bank Robbery," is related by Cole Younger. This book has been reprinted several times.

966. Hemphill, Vivia

Down the mother lode, by Vivia Hemphill. Sacramento, Calif., Purnell's, 1922. Boards. Scarce.

4 p.l., [9]–91 p. 19 cm.

Has chapters on Tom Bell and Rattlesnake Dick.

967. Henderson, George C.

Keys to crookdom, by George C. Henderson, with an introduction by

August Vollmen. . . . New York, London, D. Appleton and co., MCMXXIV. Pict. cloth. OP.

xix, 429 p. plates, ports., facsms. 21 cm.

Appendix: p. 391–422; index: p. 423–429.

Half title; device; first edition: figure (1) at end of index.

In a chapter entitled "Robbers," the author deals with Roy Gardner, and in one entitled "Bandits," he has information on Murieta, Vásquez, Black Bart, Harry Tracy, and the James and Younger brothers.

968. Henderson, Jeff S. (ed.)

100 years in Montague county, Texas. Edited by Lieutenant Colonel Jeff S. Henderson. . . . Cover by Mrs. Mabel Goodwin. . . . Saint Jo, Texas, printed by Ipta printers [n.d., ca. 1958]. Stiff pict. wrappers.

[104] p. (no pagination). plates, ports., map (double p.). 28 cm.

Adv. scattered throughout.

Has a small section on outlaws, mentioning the James boys, Wes Hardin, Al Jennings, Belle Starr, and Sam Bass. The book states that Bass had a hideout in Montague county, where he spent some time after each "job," but the statement that he was killed in "an attempted train robbery at Round Rock, Texas," is a mistake. He went to Round Rock to rob a bank, but was killed before attempting it.

969. Hendricks, George David

The bad man of the west, by George D. Hendricks; drawings by Frank Anthony Stanush. San Antonio, Texas, the Naylor co., publishers, 1941. Cloth.

xv, 310 p. front., plates, ports., facsm. 23.5 cm.

Appendix: p. 271–291; bibliography: p. 295–298; index: p. 301–310.

Half title; illus. end papers; vignette.

The author makes an attempt to analyze the bad man from the psychological point of view and describes each man's hair, eyes, and characteristics. He tells nothing new, though he does approach his subject from a new angle. His work represents some research in many books on his subject, but he repeats many false legends.

He says that Hickok's reputation started at the Rock Creek Station, where he was "just a flunky handling mules and horses" and that he "took it upon himself to defend Mrs. Wellman while her husband was away, from a vicious station operator named McCanles, for whom Hickok had formerly worked and to whom Wellman owed money." Hickok was not defending Mrs. Wellman, and her husband was not away but was at the station at the time. Nor did Wellman owe McCanles money, though the Overland Stage Company for which Wellman worked did owe McCanles for the purchase of the station.

The author admits that there were only three men in the "gang" and says that only two of them were killed but that the killing "spread from mouth to mouth and increased in leaps and bounds until the 'vicious McCanles gang' mounted to eight vile ruffians, bent upon murder!" It was the *Harper's Magazine* article that started this tale, not word from "mouth to mouth," and in later years it was Buel, Hough, and many other writers who tried to make it more than a legend. The author also tells some tall tales about Wild Bill's shooting, and of the killing of Phil Coe he writes: "One day he shot unsuspecting Phil through the back as Phil started out through a door—and that was the end of the Wild Bill Hickok–Phil Coe feud." We know this to be far from the truth. In another place he writes: "While [Hickok] was sheriff in Kansas, he murdered Phil Coe in a rage of jealous hate." Hickok was city marshal at Abilene when the killing took place, not a sheriff. He also writes that "a mob hanged Jack McCall for shooting Wild Bill Hickok in the back." McCall was legally hanged in Yankton, not lynched by a mob.

Most of the author's information on the characters in his book is unreliable. He says that Billy the Kid "blamed cruel treatment by his stepfather Antrim for his always wanting to 'get even' with just anybody who trod on his small toes." He follows the old legend about the Kid killing the man who insulted his mother when he was twelve and continues the myth that he killed twenty-one men—as many writers put it: "a man for each year of his life." He says that the mob at Las Vegas threatened to lynch the Kid, but it was Dave Rudabaugh they wanted.

There are so many mistakes in this book that it would take many pages to enumerate them. See a fuller discussion in my *Burs Under the Saddle* (Item 7).

970. Hendrix, John M.

If I can do it on horseback. A cow-country sketchbook, by John Hendrix. Introduction by Wayne Gard. Illustrations by Malcolm Thurgood. Austin, University of Texas press [1964]. Cloth.

xv p., [1] p., [3]–355 p. illus. headpieces, map (double p.). 23.6 cm.
Index: p. [315]–355.
Half title; pub. device.

Mr. Hendrix was a very good friend of mine whom I visited many times and with whom I used to attend the Texas Cowboy Reunion at Stamford. He was my favorite contributor to the *Cattleman's Magazine*, and many of his articles from that publication appear in this book. There is some mention of the killing of Sam Bass and of Billy the Kid, William Morton, and Tom O'Folliard, though he misspells the last name as O'Fallard.

971. Hendron, J. W.

The story of Billy the Kid, New Mexico's number one desperado, by J. W.

Hendron. [Santa Fe, N.M., printed by the Rydal press, inc., 1948.] Pict. wrappers. Scarce.

3–31 p. plate, port., plan. 22.7 cm.

This little book was apparently published without being proofread, to judge by the many misspelled words. The author claims that the Kid's mother was born in New Orleans of French extraction. Other biographers say that she was Irish. He claims that the Kid ran away from his New York home and in 1871 landed in Kansas City, where he loafed around the stockyards. The author is also in error in the statement that the Kid went to New Mexico with John Chisum's foreman, whom he met at the stockyards. He tells a most fantastic tale about the Kid's escape from the Lincoln jail and about someone slipping him a knife and a piece of wood while he was incarcerated. These were hidden in "a *tortita,* a little sweet cake about the size of a biscuit." He states that the Kid kept the knife concealed in his rectum and at every opportunity whittled on the piece of wood to form a key to fit his handcuffs.

972. Hening, H. B. (ed.)

George Curry, 1861–1947. An autobiography. Edited by H. B. Hening. Illustrated with photographs and a portrait and sketches by Sam Smith. [Albuquerque, New Mexico], University of New Mexico press [1958]. Cloth.

xv, 336 p. front. (col. port. tipped in), illus., plates, ports. 24.2 cm.
Index: p. 319–336.
Half title.

Has much material on the Lincoln County War, Billy the Kid, and the troubles of Oliver Lee and has some information on Elfego Baca and other characters of New Mexico.

973. Hennessy, W. B.

Tracy, the bandit; or, the romantic life and crimes of a twentieth century desperado, by W. B. Hennessy. Twenty-five full page pictures by C. D. Rhodes. Chicago, M. A. Donohue & co. [1902]. Cloth. Port. pasted on. Scarce.

6 p.l., 13–336 p. front. (port.), plates. 19 cm.
Also published in wrappers.

Another unreliable book about this outlaw.

974. Henry, Stuart Oliver

Conquering our great American plains. A historical development, by Stuart Henry. . . . Illustrated. New York, E. P. Dutton & co., inc. [1930]. Cloth. Scarce.

xvi p., 1 l., 3–395 p. front. (map), plates, ports., plan. 21.5 cm.

Appendix: p. 353–381; index: p. 383–395.
Half title; untrimmed.

In the early twenties the author stirred up quite a controversy throughout the nation by criticizing Emerson Hough's novel *North of 36*. Most critics excused Hough on the ground of artistic license. In studying Hough's nonfiction, I find him to be just as inaccurate in dates and events. The author devotes the latter part of this book to his side of this controversy and demonstrates that he is a conscientious historian. Most of the book concerns Abilene, Kansas, in its wild days, and the author gives Wild Bill Hickok considerable attention.

Most of Hickok's biographers glorify him, but Mr. Henry sees him in a different light, and especially his career in Abilene, Mr. Henry's home town. Henry gives the opinions most Abilene residents held of Hickok. It was their opinion that Wild Bill consorted with the criminal element too much, and they tended to regard him as a desperado who spent most of his time at the gaming tables rather than patrolling the streets in search of lawbreakers. He was also thought to invite too many personal feuds. Hickok's reign as officer in Abilene lasted only eight months, from April 15 to December 13, 1871. The two men he shot were killed near the end of his career there, not at the beginning. One killing was brought on mostly by personal jealousy and enmity, and the other was a mistake.

975. Hertzog, Peter

A directory of New Mexico desperadoes, compiled by Peter Hertzog. [Santa Fe, N.M., the press of the Territorian, 1965.] Stiff wrappers.

1 p.l., 3–44 [4] p. 23 cm.
Western Americana series, No. 5.
4 p. adv. at end.

Lists alphabetically nearly six hundred outlaws and gunmen, among them Clay Allison, Henry Brown, Butch Cassidy, the Clantons, Bill Doolin, Jesse Evans, Joel Fowler, Kit Joy, Black Jack Ketchum, John Kinney, the McLaureys, Billy the Kid, John Ringo, Dave Rudabaugh, and Ike Stockton.

976. ———

Legal hangings, by Peter Hertzog. Illustrated by Storm D. Townsend. Scene: New Mexico. Time: 1861–1923. [Santa Fe, N.M., the press of the Territorian, 1966.] Stiff wrappers.

1 p.l., 3–39 p. illus. 23 cm.
Western Americana series, No. 10.

An edition limited to nine hundred copies. It gives good accounts of several hangings in New Mexico, among them the hanging of Black Jack Ketchum.

977. ———

Little known facts about Billy the Kid, by Peter Hertzog. Illustrated by William Ford. . . . [Santa Fe, N.M., the press of the Territorian, 1963.] Wrappers.

1 p.l., 3–32 p. illus., plates, facsms. 22.8 cm.

Copyright and "First edition" on verso of front wrapper.

This little pamphlet tells about the marriage of Billy the Kid's mother to Mr. Antrim and gives a facsimile of the marriage record. There are also facsimiles of letters written by Charlie Bowdre and J. C. Lee, as well as of some of the current newspaper reports of that day.

978. ———

Old town Albuquerque, by Peter Hertzog. Drawings by Walter Dawley. . . . [Portales, N.M., printed by Bishop printing & litho co., for the press of the Territorian. . . . Santa Fe, N.M., 1962.] Wrappers. (Cover title.)

28 [1] p. illus., plates, port., plan (double p.). 22.8 cm.

At head of title: The Press of the Territorian presents Number 1 of a series; "First edition" verso of t.p.

Mentions Billy the Kid, Pat Garrett, and Elfego Baca.

979. Hess, Joseph F.

The autobiography of Joseph F. Hess, the converted prize-fighter. A book of thrilling experiences and timely warnings to young men. . . . Rochester, N.Y., E. R. Andrews, printer, 1886. Pict. wrappers. Rare.

iv p., 1 l., [3]–140 p. 21 cm.

980. Hickman, Dr. Warren Edwin

An echo from the past. A first-hand narration of events of the early history of the Arkansas valley of Colorado, by Dr. Warren Edwin Hickman. Denver, Colo., printed by the Western Newspaper Union, 1914. Stiff wrappers. Scarce.

3 p.l., 7–179 p. front. (port.). 19.5 cm.

The story of Colorado during its outlaw days. The author uses fictitious names for his characters, although he states that they "can be readily recognized by people familiar with those times."

981. Hickman, William

Brigham's destroying angels; being the life, confession and startling disclosures of the notorious Bill Hickman, the Dante chief of Utah. Written by himself, with explanatory notes by J. H. Beadle. . . . Illustrated. Salt Lake City, Utah, Shepard publishing co., publishers . . ., 1904. Pict. cloth. Scarce. Also pub. in wrappers.

3 p.l., [9]–221 p. front. (port.), plates, ports. 17.5 cm.
5 p. adv. at end.

982. **Hicks, Edwin P.**

Belle Starr and her Pearl, by Edwin P. Hicks, with a foreword by Homer Croy. Little Rock, Ark. [Pioneer press], 1963. Cloth.

xxiv p., 1 l., 183 p. plates, ports., facsms. 23.5 cm.
Index: p. 179–183.
Half title; map on end papers.

The author intimates that Cole Younger was in Liberty, Missouri, during the bank robbery there, but he was not. He also says that Preston Shirley had moved to Scyene, Texas, before the Civil War. He went to McKinney, Texas. He has Belle running off with Cole and becoming pregnant by him. He is mistaken in having Cole the leader of the gang and "committing the first bank robbery in America." All through the book the author has Cole constantly reading his Bible. I do not think he was that religious.

He says that both of Belle's brothers were shot down, which is true, but the killings took place at different times and places. Hicks also has the James boys and the Youngers robbing stages in California, but I do not believe that is correct. He says that Belle dashed through Dallas filling the air with lead and that the local lawmen made no attempt to stop her. I find no record of that event. He also repeats the legend about Belle setting fire to a store, and a Mr. Patterson giving her twenty-five hundred dollars to get her out of trouble.

The author also has Belle sending Cole all the money she could raise for his defense after the Northfield bank robbery, and also repeats that old legend about Blue Duck losing two thousand dollars he had borrowed from Belle and Belle holding up the gambling hall to get the money back.

The author is mistaken in identifying the John Middleton who was Belle's lover as the same John Middleton who rode with Billy the Kid. When the latter Middleton left the Kid in Tascosa, Texas, he was a middle-aged man, and the John Middleton of the Indian Territory was still a young man when killed. The author is also mistaken in saying that Middleton left the Kid's gang in 1880. He left the Kid at the same time Henry Brown and Wayte left, in the fall of 1878. On the whole, however, this is a fairly well-done history of Belle Starr and devotes more space to her daughter, Pearl, than any other book to date.

983. **Hicks, John Edward**

Adventures of a tramp printer, 1880–1890, by John Edward Hicks. Kansas City, Mo., Mid-Americana press [1950]. Cloth. Title label pasted on. OP.

5 p.l., 11–285 p. 23.6 cm.

Bibliography: p. 283–285.
Half title; "First edition" on copyright p.

The author tells about his subject's wanderings over the country as a tramp printer. He was in St. Joseph, Missouri, when Jesse James was killed there, and he tells something of that event.

984. [Hidalgo County, New Mexico]

Service record of men and women of Hidalgo county. Sponsored by V. F. W. Post No. 3099. Assisted by the Lordsburg, New Mexico, & community businessmen. [Lordsburg, N.M., n.d.] Fabrikoid. Scarce.

6 p.l., 11–144 [12] p. plates, ports., map. 27.4 cm.
Last 12 p. full-page adv.
Photo-litho printed.

The first twenty-nine pages of the book comprise a list of servicemen from Hidalgo County. Beginning on page 32 there are contributions by various writers, and beginning on page 119 there is much material on Curly Bill Brocius, Johnny Ringo, the hanging of Russian Bill, and Sandy King. Most of the stories are not found elsewhere. Only four hundred copies of this book are said to have been issued.

985. Hildebrand, C. D.

Eighteen years behind the bars. An outline sketch of the prison life of the once famous outlaw, C. D. Hildebrand. Written by himself. Fort Wayne, Ind., Gazette co., printers, 1881. Wrappers. Rare.

4 p.l., [8]–157 p. illus., port. 19.8 cm.

986. Hill, J. L.

The end of the cattle trail, by J. L. Hill. Long Beach, Calif., George W. Moyle publishing co. [n.d.]. Wrappers. Scarce.

2 p.l., 5–120 p. front., plates. 22 cm.

The author has written a splendid little book as far as the cattle trails are concerned; but, like most old-timers, he has written some of it by hearsay. He states that the Lincoln County War originated between sheepmen and cowmen and that the first man Billy the Kid killed was Black Smith (evidently he had heard that the Kid killed a blacksmith early in his career). He says that John Chisum, which he spells Chisholm, wanted the man put out of the way.

Referring to the killing of the Kid, the author says that Billy was to stay at Maxwell's "ranch" on a certain night and sleep with "one of the boys." Garrett and two deputies went to the "ranch" before the Kid arrived. The deputies "lay down flat on the ground a little way from the trail that led into the house," and

Garrett went to bed with the "boy the Kid was to sleep with." When the Kid arrived, Garrett rose up and shot him. His information on the James and Younger gang is a little more accurate.

987. Hill, John Alexander

Stories of the railroad, by John A. Hill. New York, Doubleday & McClure co., 1899. Cloth. Scarce.

5 p.l., 7–297 p. front., plates, facsm. 19.2 cm.
Half title; pub. device.

Has a chapter on Mormon Joe (Hogg), the robber.

988. Hill, Richard C.

A great white Indian chief. Thrilling and romantic story of the remarkable career, extraordinary experiences hunting, scouting and Indian adventures of Col. Fred Cummins "Chief La-Ko-Ta," told by Richard C. Hill. . . . [N.p., 1912.] Pict. wrappers. Scarce.

1 p.l., 3–24 p. front., plates, ports. 23.5 cm.
Illus. front and back wrappers, inside and out.

Has some material on Calamity Jane.

989. Hill, Rita

Then and now, here and around Shakespeare, by Rita Hill. [N.p.], 1963. Pict. wrappers.

1 l., 1 p., 4–51 p. plates. 23 cm.

A history of the town of Shakespeare, New Mexico, containing material on some of its outlaws, such as Curly Bill Brocius, the Clantons, Billy Grounds, and Zwing Hunt and telling about the hanging of Russian Bill and Sandy King.

990. Hill, W. A.

Historic Hays . . . ., by W. A. Hill. [Hays, Kans., printed by the News publishing co., 1938.] Pict. wrappers. Scarce.

2 p.l., 7–81 [1] p. plates, ports. 22.7 cm.

In his chapter on Wild Bill Hickok the author says that David McCanles tried to shoot Bill "but was too slow and was killed." He has but seven men in the "gang" and has Hickok kill one as he comes in the front door and another as he comes in the back door. Then he says, "the other four members of the bunch fled." He states that Hickok killed five men in Hays and that "up to the time he went to Abilene he had killed forty-nine men besides a large number of Indians and men he had killed in the Civil War." Of Hickok's death, the author writes: "While in Deadwood, South Dakota, he was shot in the back by James [*sic*] McCall, who was evidently in the employ of the grafters."

991. ———

Rome, the predecessor of Hays. Founded by "Buffalo Bill" Cody, by W. A. Hill. [Hays, Kans., n.d.] Stiff wrappers. Rare.

[11] p. (no pagination). front. (port.). 15.2 cm.
Adv. on front and back wrappers.

Has some unreliable material on Wild Bill Hickok.

992. Hinton, Arthur Cherry, and Philip H. Godsell

The Yukon, [by] A. Cherry Hinton . . . in collaboration with Philip H. Godsell. . . . Member Explorers club, New York. Philadelphia, Macrae Smith co. [1955]. Cloth. OP.

xiv, 184 p. plates. 20.3 cm.
Appendix: p. 177–179; index: p. 181–184.
Half title; pub. device.

Contains two chapters on Soapy Smith, telling about his activities in Skagway and his death.

993. [History of Buchanan County]

The Daily News' history of Buchanan county and St. Joseph, Mo., from the time of the Platte purchase to the end of the year 1898. Preceded by a short history of Missouri. Supplemented by biographical sketches of noted citizens, living and dead. St. Joseph, by the St. Joseph publishing co., press of Lon Hardman [n.d.] Cloth. Scarce.

2 p.l., 569 p. front. (port.), plates, ports. 23.5 cm.
Errata: p. 333–334; index: p. [562]–569.

Gives an account of the murder of Jesse James.

994. Hitchcock, Frank

A true account of the capture of Frank Rande, "the noted outlaw," by the late Frank Hitchcock, sheriff of Peoria county, Ill., for twelve years. Edited by John W. Kimsey. . . . Peoria, Ill., J. W. Franks & sons, printers and binders, 1897. Pict. boards. Scarce.

3 p.l., 9–156 [2] p. front. (port.), plates. 18.5 cm.

One of the few books written about this outlaw.

995. Hitchcock, Mary E.

Two women in the Klondike. The story of a journey to the gold-fields of

Alaska, by Mary E. Hitchcock, with 105 illustrations and map. New York and London, G. P. Putnam's sons, 1899. Pict. cloth. Scarce.

> xiv p., 1 l., 485 [2] p. front. (with tissue), illus., plates, large fold. map in pocket at end. 22.7 cm.
>
> Index: p. 477–485.
>
> T.p. in red and black; 2 p. adv. at end; untrimmed.

Contains some material on Soapy Smith.

996. Hittell, Theodore H.

History of California, by Theodore H. Hittell. San Francisco, N. J. Stone and co., 1898. Pub. in four volumes. Calf. Scarce.

> Vol. I, xxxvi, 27–799 p. 23.5 cm.
>
> Vol. II, xli, 43–823 p. 23.5 cm.
>
> Vol. III, xli, 43–981 p. 23.5 cm.
>
> Vol. IV, xli, 43–858 p. 23.5 cm.
>
> Vols. I and II published by Pacific Press publishing house, and Occidental publishing co.
>
> Vols. III and IV published by N. J. Stone and co.

Book X, Chapter IV, deals entirely with Joaquín Murieta. This account is taken largely from the 1871 edition of the John Rollin Ridge's book. Unlike Bancroft, this author credits Ridge as his authority but admits that his source is unreliable. However, the inclusion of the legend in history by such a reputable historian strengthened people's belief in it.

997. Hobbs, James

Wild life in the far west; personal adventures of a border mountain man. Comprising hunting and trapping adventures with Kit Carson and others; captivity and life among the Comanches; services under Doniphan in the war with Mexico, and in the Mexican war against the French; desperate combats with Apaches, grizzly bears . . ., by Capt. James Hobbs. . . . Illustrated with numerous engravings. Published by subscription only. Hartford, Conn., Wiley, Waterman & Eaton, 1872. Cloth. Scarce.

> 8 p.l., [17]–488 p. front. (col. with tissue), illus., plates, ports. 21.6 cm.
>
> Republished in 1873, 1874, and 1875.

Contains a chapter on Joaquín Murieta.

998. Hobbs, Richard Gear

Glamorland—the Ozarks. Third of a glamor series, by Richard Gear Hobbs. First edition. Cover design by Mrs. Annie Hobbs Woodcock. [Manhattan, Kans., 1944.] Stiff pict. wrappers. OP.

2 p.l., [1] p. 6–76 [40] p. plates, ports. 22.8 cm.
Last 40 p. plates.

Has some new material on Wild Bill Hickok in the days when he was in Springfield, Missouri. The author, like many others, spells Quantrill's name Quantrell.

999. Hogan, Ray

The life and death of Clay Allison, by Ray Hogan. [New York], published by the New American Library [1961]. Stiff pict. wrappers.

vi, 7–160 p. 18 cm.

A typical example of the newsstand paper-backed books, written as history but filled with fictitious events.

1000. ———

The life and death of Johnny Ringo, by Ray Hogan. [New York], published by the New American Library [1963]. Stiff pict. wrappers.

vii p., 2 l., 11–128 p. 2 maps (both double p.). 18 cm.

Acknowledgments: p. 127–128.

Similar to other Signet books, mostly fiction based upon the life of an actual character, but written as actual history.

1001. [Hogg, Thomas E.]

Authentic history of Sam Bass and his gang, by a citizen of Denton county, Texas. Denton, Texas, printed at the Monitor job office, 1878. Wrappers. Exceedingly rare.

1 p.l., [5]–143 p. 22.5 cm.
1 p. adv. and adv. on both sides of back wrapper.

Republished in Bandera, Texas, by the Frontier Times, 1926. Wrappers. (Cover title.) OP.

56 p. 25.9 cm.
Double column.

Also published by Frontier Times in 1932 in a "Museum Edition," with eleven pages added by the publisher.

3 p.l., 7–192 p. 18.8 cm.

The original edition is exceedingly rare. It is one of the first books written about Sam Bass. The author was a member of the posse that chased Bass all over Denton County. There are the usual number of errors in the original edition, and both reprints are filled with typographical errors.

1002. Holbrook, Stewart H.

Let them live, by Stewart H. Holbrook. New York, the Macmillan co., 1938. Cloth. OP.

4 p.l., 178 p. 20.7 cm.
Index: p. 173–178.
Half title; "First printing" on copyright p.

Has some material on Jesse James and Black Bart.

1003. ———

Little Annie Oakley & other rugged people, by Stewart H. Holbrook. New York, the Macmillan co., 1948. Pict. cloth. OP.

x p., 1 l., 238 p. 21.5 cm.
Half title; "First printing" on copyright p.

Contains material on Calamity Jane and the James boys and also has some unreliable information on Luke Short. As so many other writers do, the author gives the date of Calamity Jane's death as August 2, but he does correct many other legends about her. The author also says that Calamity Jane lived openly with Charley Utter and that only after Wild Bill was murdered did she claim him as a sweetheart, seizing upon his notoriety.

1004. ———

Murder out yonder. An informal study of certain classic crimes in backcountry America, by Stewart H. Holbrook. New York, the Macmillan co., 1941. Cloth. OP.

5 p.l., 255 p. 24.3 cm.
Index: p. 249–255.
Half title; "First printing" on copyright p.

1005. ———

The Rocky mountain revolution, by Stewart H. Holbrook. New York, Henry Holt and co. [1956]. Cloth. OP.

9 p.l., 19–318 p. 21.4 cm.
Acknowledgments: 305–306; bibliography: p. 307–309; index: p. 313–318.
Half title; maps on end papers.

Contains some information on Butch Cassidy.

1006. ———

The story of American railroads, by Stewart H. Holbrook. New York, Crown publishers [1947]. Cloth. OP.

x, 468 p. illus., plates, ports., facsms. 23.5 cm.
Bibliography: p. 453–457; index: p. 459–468.
Half title; vignette.

Deals to some extent with train robberies and with such outlaws as the Renos, the Jameses, the Youngers, Sam Bass, and the Evans-Sontag gang.

1007. ———

Wild Bill Hickok tames the west, by Stewart H. Holbrook. Illustrated by Ernest Richardson. New York, Random House [1952]. Dec. cloth. OP.

6 p.l., 3–179 p. illus., plates (col.). 21.8 cm.
Bibliography: p. 179.
Half title; illus. end papers (col.); pub. device; illustrated chapter headings (col.); "First edition" on copyright p.

Written for juvenile readers, this book tames down the McCanles "fight" somewhat. The author has McCanles "strapping two revolvers on" as he prepares to go to Rock Creek Station and even has McCanles' twelve-year-old son arming himself. It seems to me that writers of historical juvenile books should be especially careful about their facts, because the impressions that people receive in their youth are enduring ones.

1008. ——— (ed.)

Promised land. A collection of northwest writings. Edited by Stewart H. Holbrook. New York, London, Whittlesey House, McGraw-Hill book co., inc. [1945]. Cloth. OP.

xviii p., 1 l., 408 p. 23 cm.
Half title; untrimmed.

Contains a chapter, entitled "The Last of Harry Tracy," from William MacLeod Raine's *Famous Sheriffs and Western Outlaws.*

1009. Holcombe, R. I. (comp.)

History of Marion county, Missouri, written and compiled from the most authentic official and private sources. Including a history of its townships, towns and villages. . . . Illustrated. St. Louis, E. F. Parkins, 1884. Leather. Rare.

x p., 1003 p. front. (port.), illus., plates, ports. 24.5 cm.

Gives an account of the murders of Jesse James and Bob Ford.

1010. Holland, Gustavus Adolphus

"The double log cabin," being a brief symposium of the early history of Parker county, together with short biographical sketches of early settlers and their trials. . . . Compiled and written by G. A. Holland. [Weatherford, Texas], 1931. Wrappers. Scarce.

1 p.l., [9]–83 p. illus., plates, ports., facsm. 23 cm.

A privately printed little history of a Texas frontier county, containing, among other material, information on the Texas Rangers and on lawlessness, as well as on Sam Bass and Arkansas Johnson.

1011. ———

History of Parker county and the double log cabin; being a brief symposium of the early history of Parker county, together with short biographical sketches of early settlers and their trials, by G. A. Holland, assisted by Violet M. Roberts. Weatherford, Texas, the Herald publishing co., 1937. Cloth. Scarce.

4 p.l., 11–296 p. front., plates, ports., facsm. 23.6 cm.
Index: p. 281–296.

A revised and enlarged edition of the 1931 publication (Item 1010) with much added material.

1012. ———

The man and his monument. The man was J. R. Couts, his monument the Citizens National Bank. Written and compiled by G. A. Holland. . . . [Weatherford, Texas], press of the Herald publishing co., November, 1924. Wrappers. Scarce.

[32] p. (no pagination). front. (fold. scene). 20.5 cm.
Device.

In Chapter IV there is some information on Sam Bass.

1013. Hollon, W. Eugene

The southwest; old and new, by W. Eugene Hollon. New York, Alfred A. Knopf, 1961. Two-tone cloth.

xiv p., 3 l., 3–485, i–[xviii] p., 1 l. plates, ports. 24.3 cm.
Bibliographical notes: p. 465–[487]; index: p. i–[xix].
Half title; "First edition" on copyright p.; untrimmed.

Has some mention of Wild Bill Hickok, Billy the Kid, Bat Masterson, Wyatt Earp, and other gunmen.

1014. Holloway, Carroll C.

Texas gun lore, by Carroll C. Holloway. San Antonio, Texas, the Naylor co. [1951]. Cloth. Scarce.

xii p., 7 l. (port., plates), 3–238 p. 21.6 cm.

Index to 800 notorious gun fighters: p. 182–227; bibliography: p. 229–232; index: p. 233–238.

Half title.

A history of guns from flintlocks down to present-day arms. This work also contains much material on outlaws and gunmen, but most of his information is wrong. His index of eight hundred gunfighters is also full of errors.

1015. Holloway, W. L. (ed.)

Wild life on the plains and horrors of Indian warfare, by a corps of competent authors and artists, being a complete history of Indian life, warfare and adventure in America. . . . Superbly illustrated. St. Louis, Mo., published by Royal publishing co. [1891]. Pict. cloth. Rare.

6 p.l., 13–592 p. front., illus., plates. 23.5 cm.

Much of this book is the same as Custer's *My Life On the Plains.* It also contains a chapter on Hickok. The fictional Nichols article from *Harper's* is quoted at length.

1016. Homsher, Lola M. (ed.)

South pass, 1868. James Chisholm's journal of the Wyoming gold rush. Introduction and edited by Lola M. Homsher. . . . [Lincoln, Nebr.], University of Nebraska press, 1960. Pict. boards.

vi p., 1 l., 3–244 [1] p. illus., maps. 24 cm.

Supplementary notes: p. 203–235; bibliography: p. 236–239; list of original headings: p. 241–242; acknowledgments: p. 243–244.

Illus. t.p.

Contains some information on the Wyoming vigilantes and some of their hangings.

1017. Hooker, William Francis

The prairie schooner, by William Francis Hooker. Chicago, Saul brothers, 1918. Pict. cloth. Scarce.

7 p.l., [17]–156 p. front. (col.), illus., plates. 18.3 cm.

Half title; device.

The author devotes only five pages to Wild Bill Hickok and calls him "just a plain gambler and not a very good one." Nor does he praise Hickok's courage. He writes that "an undersized little California buccaro challenged him to walk into the street and fight a duel at twenty paces" and that "Bill laid down, saying his eyes had gone back on him and that his shooting days were over."

1018. Hoole, W. Stanley

The James boys rode south; a thrilling and authentic new episode in the fabulous lives of the most dashing desperadoes of modern times, Frank and Jesse James, and their comrades in crime. The real story, based largely on newspaper accounts and witnesses' testimonials, of the only foray of the James gang into the deep south and the subsequent trial of Frank James in the United States circuit court in Huntsville, Alabama, for the robbery of a government paymaster at Muscle Shoals, March 11, 1881, by W. Stanley Hoole. Illustrated with an original drawing by Charles Brooks. Tuscaloosa, Ala., privately printed for the author, March, 1955. Stiff pict. wrappers. OP.

12 p.l., 25–52 p. illus. 20.6 cm.
Bibliography: p. 49–52.
Half title.
Colophon: "This edition limited to five hundred and twenty-five signed copies of which twenty-five are reserved for private circulation. Number ——."

Deals mostly with the robbery of the paymaster at Muscle Shoals and the trial of Frank James as a participant.

1019. Hoover, H. A.

Early days in the Mogollons (Muggy-Yones), by H. A. Hoover. Tales from the bloated goat. Notes and introduction by Francis L. Fugate. El Paso, Texas, Western press, 1958. Stiff pict. wrappers.

6 p.l., 13–61 [3] p. plates, map, facsm., diagr. 23.8 cm.
Half title.

Has some material on the Wild Bunch, Butch Cassidy, Elza Lay, William H. Antrim, Billy the Kid's stepfather, and stage robberies.

1020. Hoover, Mildred Brooks

Historic spots in California. Counties of the coast range, [by] Mildred Brooks Hoover. With an introduction by Robert Glass Cleland. . . . Stanford University, Calif., Stanford University press; London, Humphrey Milford, Oxford University press [1937]. Cloth. Scarce.

xxiii, 718 p. front. (map). 20.7 cm.
Index: p. 687–718 (triple column).
Half title.

Contains some material on Murieta and Vásquez and their hide-outs.

1021. Hopper, W. L. (Bill)

Famous Texas landmarks. By W. L. (Bill) Hopper. . . . Dallas, Texas, the Arrow press, 1966. Cloth.

2 p.l., 5–107 p. 2 plates. 20.5 cm.

Mentions Doc Holliday, Wyatt Earp, Pat Garrett, and Billy the Kid, as well as many Texas Rangers. In a chapter on Tascosa the author has some information on Temple Houston and Bat Masterson and mentions the big fight there.

1022. Hopping, Richard C.

A sheriff-ranger in chuckwagon days, [by] R. G. Hopping. [New York], Pageant press [1952]. Cloth. OP.

5 p.l., 246 p. plates, ports. 20.9 cm.
Half title; "First edition" on copyright p.

As the sheriff of a West Texas county, the author naturally came in contact with some of the outlaws of his day. During the run in Oklahoma he slept one night in a large gambling tent in which several beds had been set up in a corner. When asked by a cowboy the next morning how he had slept he answered that he had slept soundly.

The cowboy commented, " 'You might not have slept so good had I told you who that cowpuncher was in that bed next to you. That was Emmett Dalton. It's rumored that he's on the dodge because of the Coffeyville bank robbery.' "

Of course, we know that Emmett Dalton was severely wounded at Coffeyville, arrested, tried, and sent to prison for many years and was not on the dodge at the time.

1023. Horan, J. W.

On the side of the law. Biography of J. D. Nicholson . . ., by J. W. Horan. . . . Drawings by James Bicoll. Edmonton, Alberta, Canada, published by the Institute of Applied Arts, ltd., Educational publishers, 1944. Cloth. OP.

6 p.l., 7–275 [4] p. illus., ports., maps. 21.7 cm.
Index to characters: p. [276]–[279].

The exploits of the Royal Northwest Mounted Police and their battles with the cattle rustlers and outlaws of Canada.

1024. Horan, James D.

Across the Cimarron, by James D. Horan. New York, Crown publishers, inc. [1956]. Boards. OP.

xvi p., 1 l., 3–301 p. front. (port.), plates, ports. 21.6 cm.
Half title.

Has much material on Dodge City and some of its characters, such as Bat Masterson, Wyatt Earp, Doc Holliday, and Bill Tilghman.

1025. ———

Desperate men. Revelations from sealed Pinkerton files, by James D. Horan. New York, G. P. Putnam's sons [1949]. Pict. cloth.

xx p., 1 l., 3–296 p. plates, ports., facsm. 22.2 cm.
Index: p. 293–296.
Half title; map on end papers; untrimmed.

Mr. Horan is quite mistaken when he writes that "on August 16, Sam's brother, Black Jack [Ketchum], made a foolhardy attempt to hold up a train near Folsom singlehanded, supposedly *in revenge against the railroad for his brother's death.* The conductor and express messenger wounded him in the right arm [only Conductor Harrington wounded him], but like Jim Younger at Northfield, Black Jack was an ambidextrous gunman. *He swung his rifle to his left shoulder and continued firing, wounding the two trainmen.*" (Italics added.)

Ketchum's right arm was shattered with buckshot, and he certainly did not shift a gun to his left shoulder. He was using a six-gun, not a rifle, and he dropped it immediately to crawl under the train and make his way into the brush and darkness. He certainly did not "continue firing," and the two trainmen he wounded were the express messenger whom he shot in the jaw earlier, and Conductor Harrington, whom he shot in the neck at almost the same instant Harrington wounded him.

On page 12 the misspelling of Dacus as Bacus, is probably a typographical error. The first half of the book deals with the James-Younger gang; the last half, with Butch Cassidy's Wild Bunch.

1026. ———

Desperate men. Revelations from sealed Pinkerton files, by James D. Horan. Newly revised and enlarged. Garden City, N.Y., Doubleday & co., inc., 1962. Pict. cloth.

9 p.l., [3]–391 p. illus., plates, ports., facsms. 24 cm.
Index: p. [383]–391.
Half title.

A greatly enlarged edition of the original (Item 1025), containing seventeen more chapters and has all the same errors and more.

1027. ———

Desperate women, by James D. Horan. New York, G. P. Putnam's sons [1952]. Pict. cloth. OP.

xi [1] p., 2 l., 3–336 p. plates, ports., facsms. 22 cm.
Bibliography: p. 323–330; index: p. 331–336.

Half title.

A companion volume to the author's *Desperate Men* (Items 1025 and 1026), this is an entertaining book. Book I deals with women spies of the Civil War, and Book II tells about the desperate women of the West, though some of them were not really so "desperate." Nothing new has been added to the stories about Calamity Jane and Belle Starr, although the author does debunk some of the legends about them. He has some new material on Cattle Kate, Pearl Hart, and Rose of Cimarron.

In his chapter on Belle Starr he refers to the book entitled *Frank James, the Only True History of the Life of Frank James, Written by Himself*, stating that he is convinced the book was really written by Frank James. How he determined that is beyond me. "Frank's book was published eleven years after his death," he writes. "No ghost writer would have permitted such an illiterate, maudlin piece of trash to be published. There is little doubt that the book was written, as the title claimed, by James himself. He knew Belle quite well. . . ." The author states that "Jesse James led his brother Frank and the Youngers into Liberty to hold up the Clay County Savings Association Bank—the first robbery of its kind in the nation's history." Jesse was bedridden with a lung wound when the Liberty bank was robbed. As for the Frank James book, see my comments under this item (Item 1144). There are many other mistakes and several typographical errors as well.

1028. ———

The great American west. A pictorial history from Coronado to the last frontier, by James D. Horan. New York, Crown publishers, inc. [1959]. Cloth. OP.

5 p.l., 11–288 p. plates (part col.), ports., maps, facsms. 31 cm.

Bibliography: p. 281–283; picture credits: p. 284; index: p. 285–288.

Half title; illus. t.p.; double column.

Has a chapter dealing with most of the better-known western outlaws, as well as the famous O K Corral fight. In his account the author says that the Clantons were waiting for the Earps. They were almost certainly leaving town to avoid a fight, or they would have been better prepared. The author has Jesse James robbing the Liberty bank and says that Henry Starr was a nephew of Belle Starr, which is incorrect. Belle got the last name Starr through marriage. There are other errors.

1029. ———

The Wild Bunch, [by] James D. Horan. [New York], a Signet book, published by the New American library [1958]. Stiff pict. wrappers.

xi p., 13–190 [2] p. 18 cm.

A paper-backed book about Butch Cassidy and his gang.

1030. ———, and Howard Swiggett

The Pinkerton story, by James D. Horan and Howard Swiggett. New York, G. P. Putnam's sons [1951]. Cloth. OP.

xiii p., 1 l., 3–366 p. front., plates, ports., facsms. 22 cm.
Appendix: p. 349–358; index: p. 359–366.
Half title; pub. device.

Written from the confidential files of the Pinkerton Detective Agency, the book contains chapters on many of the train robbers, such as the Renos, Rube Burrow, and the Evans-Sontag gang.

1031. ———, and Paul Sann

Pictorial history of the wild west. A true account of the bad men, desperadoes, rustlers and outlaws of the old west—and the men who fought them to establish law and order, by James D. Horan and Paul Sann. New York, Crown publishers, inc. [1954]. Pict. boards. OP.

4 p.l., 1 p., 10–254 p. front., illus., plates, ports., facsms. 31 cm.
Picture credits: p. 247; bibliography: p. 248–250; index: p. 251–254.
Half title; double column.

On page 66 there is a picture of a woman on horseback with the caption "Sallie Chisum, daughter of John Chisum." Sallie was Chisum's niece, not his daughter; Chisum never married. On page 241 the upper picture of Augustine Chacon and the Mexican outlaw Chaves is mislabeled "Black Jack in irons, linked with Chacon, another outlaw." Much of the text is also unreliable. Although the authors rightly debunk many of the old legends about western outlaws, they still follow those created by Ash Upson about Billy the Kid, such as the move to Coffeyville, Kansas, in 1862, the mother marrying in Colorado, and Billy's killing of the blacksmith for insulting his mother. They repeat the Lake story about Wyatt Earp disarming Ben Thompson in Ellsworth when Sheriff Whitney was killed. That event never took place.

They leave the impression that the Clantons went to the O K Corral for a fight when they write: "The outlaws were lined up along the 'dobe wall of the Assay office backing on the corral, spread out so they wouldn't make a bunched target when it came time to fight." They are among those who say that the outlaws "fired seventeen shots, only three scoring." The men did not have that many guns and had no time to reload. Besides, who would be counting the shots during that exciting time?

1032. Horn, Calvin

New Mexico's troubled years. The story of the early territorial governors, by Calvin Horn. With a foreword by John F. Kennedy. Albuquerque, Horn & Wallace, publishers [1963]. Cloth.

10 p. l., [21]–239 [1] p. front. (port.), ports. 23.6 cm.
Bibliography: p. 223–231; index: p. 233–239.
Half title; illus. end papers; notes after each chapter.

Has quite a bit of material on the Lincoln County War, Billy the Kid, and other lawlessness in New Mexico.

1033. Horn, Tom

Life of Tom Horn, government scout and interpreter. Written by himself, together with his letters and statements by his friends. A vindication. Thirteen full page illustrations. Denver, Colo., published (for John C. Coble) by the Louthan book co. [1904]. Cloth. Scarce.

7 p.l., [17]–317 p. front., plates, ports. 18.8 cm.
Pub. device.
Also published in wrappers, less scarce than the cloth-bound issue.

Republished in 1964 by the University of Oklahoma press as No. 26 in the Western Frontier Library Series, with an introduction by Dean Krakel.

xviii p., 1 l., 3–277 p. 19.6 cm.

The authorship of this book is variously attributed to Horn himself; his friend and employer, rancher John C. Coble; and Hattie Louthan, of the family which owned the Louthan Book Company, publisher of the book. It is an attempt to vindicate the crimes of Horn, and much of it is about his scouting days in Arizona.

1034. Horrible and Awful Developments

from the confession of William Morrison, the Rocky mountain trapper; giving a true and faithful account of his murders and depredations on the plains and his escape from the Indians after killing the son of their chief; which is a true history of his life up to the time of his execution at Springfield, Illinois, for murder. . . . Philadelphia, published by E. E. Barclay, 1852. Pict. wrappers. Rare.

[5]–31 [1] p. illus. 21.8 cm.
Illus. t.p.

Republished in 1853 with front. and without illus. t.p.

32 p. illus. 23 cm.

Published in two parts, Part II being a narrative of his wife, whom he treated barbarously.

1035. Horton, Thomas F.

History of Jack county. Being accounts of pioneer times, excerpts from county court records, Indian stories, biographical sketches and interesting events, written and compiled by Thomas F. Horton. Jacksboro [Texas], Gazette print [n.d., ca. 1932]. Stiff wrappers. Scarce.

2 p.l., 166 p. 23 cm.

This little book, which contains some material on Sam Bass and his gang, is quite rare because most of the edition was burned. It tells of Joe Horner's battle with Negro soldiers before he left Texas and assumed the name Frank Canton.

1036. Hosmer, Hezekiah L.

Montana, an address delivered by Chief-Justice H. L. Hosmer before the Traveler's club, New York city, Jan., 1866. Published by request. New York, printed by the New York printing co., 1866.

23 p. 22.8 cm.

Hosmer was the first chief justice of Montana and brought with him into the territory the first semblance of organized law and order. This work, among the earliest books to give authentic information on the region, includes material on the vigilantes, robbers, road agents, and stage lines.

1037. Hough, Emerson

The story of the cowboy, by E. Hough. Illustrated by William L. Wells and C. M. Russell. New York, D. Appleton and co., 1897. Dec. cloth. OP.

xii, 349 [6] p. front., plates. 19.5 cm.
Addenda: p. 345–349.
Half title: "The Story of the West Series, edited by R. Hitchcock." 6 p. adv. at end.

Reprinted many times through the years, on one occasion published in two volumes, under the general title *Builders of the Nation*, by the Brampton society, New York. The original edition is quite scarce.

In a chapter entitled "Wars of the Range" the author gives an unreliable history of Billy the Kid. He claims that the Lincoln County War was the bloodiest of all range wars and makes the exaggerated statement that two or three hundred men were killed in the conflict. After studying all his books on the West, I have found Mr. Hough careless and unreliable as a historian. He misspells John Chisum's last name as Chisholm and says that Billy the Kid was killed at the age of twenty-three after he had killed twenty-three men. He says that the Kid killed seven Mexicans "just to see them kick," that he paraded on the platform before the courthouse in Lincoln for half an hour after he had killed his two jailers, and that he took a horse from a passer-by when he decided to leave town.

According to Hough, the whole country was an armed camp, and "the wayfarer who saw a body of men approaching was obliged to guess, and guess quickly, which side he favored. If he guessed wrong, the coyotes had another meal." Pat Garrett "finally got track of the little ruffian just as he was about to leave the country for Mexico." Garrett, the author says, learned that Billy was to call at night at a "certain ranch" to tell his Mexican sweetheart good-by. As the Kid entered the house, he passed two of Garrett's deputies outside. "He apparently was about to repent of having violated his customary rule of shooting first and inquiring afterward, and had pulled his gun from the scabbard [no westerner calls a six-gun holster a scabbard], and was looking out at the men as he came backing into the door, with his boots in one hand."

Garrett recognized the Kid and shot him immediately. The author says that Garrett was "none too quick, for Billy heard him as he *rose from behind the bed, holding the scared ranchman down with one arm as he fired*." He then says "Billy turned quickly about and made a quick but ineffectual shot, for he was dead even as he fired." Although the account of the Johnson County War is more accurate, it too can be shot full of holes.

1038. ———

The story of the outlaw. A study of the western desperado, with historical narratives of famous outlaws; the stories of noted border wars; vigilante movements and armed conflicts on the frontier, by Emerson Hough. New York, the Outing publishing co., 1907. Boards. Very scarce in the original edition.

xiv p., 1 l., 401 p. front., plates, ports., cattle brands. 19 cm.

Half title; t.p. in red and black; pub. device; first state has printer's rule at the top of page v.

A writer of Hough's ability, with a following of readers who believed in the authenticity of his accounts, should certainly have made an independent investigation of his subjects and not merely repeated the earlier fables, even to incorrect names. In this book he repeats the Buel legend about the Hickok-McCanles "fight," and, to make it more sensational, he places the fight in the dark interior of a dugout instead of the log house from which Wild Bill did the shooting. Although Hickok was just a stable hand, Hough makes him agent of the station.

Nichols said that his information came from an interview with Hickok; and it is possible that Wild Bill, wishing to make himself a hero and having a penchant natural to westerners for "loading" easterners, may have made such statements. Later historians who took the trouble to dig into the records found that Hickok and Wellman had murdered three men in cold blood and had attempted to murder Monroe McCanles, a twelve-year-old boy. David McCanles never pulled a gun.

Hough also fixes the date of the "fight" as December 18, 1861, five months later than the correct date, and errs to the extent of placing Rock Creek Station in Kansas instead of Nebraska. His reputation as a writer gave this misleading account great prestige, even though all the details, such as the number of participants, the use of knives, the time, and the place, are wrong. He states that Hickok was alone when he was attacked by *ten* men and that he killed eight of them. Such a conglomeration of misinformation and error is unforgivable in a writer of Hough's reputation and ability.

In 1901, six years before this book was published, Mr. Hough wrote an article on Billy the Kid for *Everybody's Magazine*, in which he made just as many preposterous statements about the Kid as he does here about Wild Bill. Before writing this book, however, he visited New Mexico again and looked up Pat Garrett. It is said that they traveled over the Billy the Kid country, and Garrett must have enlightened him considerably, because his account of the Kid in this book is entirely different from that of his magazine article and in his *Story of the Cowboy*, written nine years earlier. He corrects the spelling of Chisum's name, gives the correct age of the Kid, and tells a more accurate story of the Kid's death.

However, he claims that Buckshot Roberts was neutral in the Lincoln County War and had closed out his affairs to leave the country. I believe Mr. Hough was the first writer to have Brewer and Roberts buried together, but many have followed him. He said that he was told this by a John Patten, but Dr. Blazer's son, who was present, denies it.

He says that Sam Bass had "not a few murders" to his credit, but unless he killed the deputies at Round Rock, he never killed a man during his entire short career. Of Bass's death at Round Rock, the author writes "The citizens got wind of his coming one day, just before he rode into Round Rock for a little raid. The city marshal and several others opened fire on Bass and his party and killed them to a man." We know all this to be incorrect. There are many other errors throughout the book.

1039. House, Boyce

City of flaming adventure. The chronicle of San Antonio, by Boyce House. Illustrations by Melvin D. Jordan. San Antonio, Texas, the Naylor co. [1949]. Cloth.

ix, 214 p. front., illus. 21.6 cm.

Acknowledgments and bibliography: p. 201–206; index: p. 209–214.

Half title; illus. end papers; first printing in a "Fiesta Edition."

Has some material on Wild Bill Hickok, Ben Thompson, King Fisher, John Wesley Hardin, Sam Bass, and Jesse James, but contains nothing new.

1040. ———

Cowtown columnist, by Boyce House. San Antonio, Texas, the Naylor co., publishers [1946]. Cloth.

xii p., 1 l., [3]–275 p. 20.8 cm.
Index: p. [273]–275.
Half title.

Includes chapters on Billy the Kid, Sam Bass, Ben Thompson, Belle Starr, and El Paso, the last chapter dealing with such gunmen as John Wesley Hardin, John Selman, and George Scarborough. In his chapter on Billy the Kid the author repeats the legend about the Kid playing a game of cards with Bell, dropping a card, having Bell pick it up, and, as Bell is doing so, jerking his gun from its holster and killing him. The author says that Olinger, the last man the Kid killed, was his twenty-first victim. He also repeats the false story about Belle Starr refusing to identify her husband, Jim Reed, after his murder in order to prevent the killer from collecting the reward offered for Reed's capture dead or alive.

1041. ———

Oil field fury, by Boyce House. San Antonio, Texas, the Naylor co. [1954]. Cloth.

vii p., 2 l., 142 p. plates, ports. 21.5 cm.
Index: p. 141–142.
Half title.

In a chapter entitled "Picturesque Citizens," there is some material on such gunmen as John Wesley Hardin, John Selman, George Scarborough, and Pat Garrett.

1042. ———

Texas treasure chest, by Boyce House. San Antonio, Texas, the Naylor co. [1956]. Pict. cloth.

ix p., 1 l., 3–187 p. 28 cm.
Acknowledgments: p. 187.
Half title; vignette.

Has a chapter on outlaws and gunmen, such as John Wesley Hardin, Sam Bass, Bill Longley, and Bat Masterson.

1043. House, Edward Mandell

Riding for Texas. The true adventures of Captain Bill McDonald of the Texas rangers, as told by Colonel Edward M. House to Tyler Mason. With a foreword by Colonel House. New York, a John Day book, Reynal & Hitchcock [1936]. Pict. cloth. OP.

xii p., 1 l., 229 p. 19.6 cm.
Half title; untrimmed.

Like most books about the Texas Rangers, this one also deals with some of the outlaws of Texas.

1044. Houts, Marshall

From gun to gavel. The courtroom recollections of James Mathers of Oklahoma, as told to Marshall Houts. New York, William Morrow & co., 1954. Cloth. OP.

x, 246 p. 22 cm.
Half title; map on end papers.

The author touches upon some of the early outlaws of Oklahoma, among them Bill Dalton and Henry Starr, but the book is primarily about murder trials in which the author took part and which did not involve the real outlaws.

1045. Howard, H. R.

The history of Virgil A. Stewart, and his adventures in capturing and exposing the great "western land pirate" and his gang, in connexion with the evidence; also of the trials, confessions, and execution of a number of Murrell's associates in the state of Mississippi during the summer of 1835, and the execution of five professional gamblers by the citizens of Vicksburg, on the 6th of July, 1835 . . ., compiled by H. R. Howard. New York, Harper & brothers . . ., 1836. Dec. cloth. Rare.

vi, [7]–273 p. 19.5 cm.
36 p. adv. numbered [1] to 36 of other books by the publishers at the end.
Label pasted on.

Reprinted in 1837 and in 1847 with illustrations. Another edition, under the title "Pictorial Life and Adventures of John A. Murrell," was published in Philadelphia in 1847 with 126 pages.

The earliest account of a detective's experiences in bringing to justice the Murrell gang of outlaws.

1046. ———

The life and adventures of Joseph T. Hare, the bold robber and highwayman. With 16 engravings. New York, Hillong and brother, 1847. Wrappers. Rare.

107 p. illus. 23.4 cm.

On cover: "By the author of the 'Life of John Murrell.' "
Reprinted in 1849.

Another example of the early books on outlaws.

1047. Howard, Helen Addison

Northwest trail blazers, by Helen Addison Howard. Illustrated with photographs. Caldwell, Idaho, the Caxton printers, ltd., 1963. Cloth.

xviii p., 1 l., 418 p. front. (col.), illus., plates, ports. 21.5 cm.
Bibliography: p. [397]–408; index: p. [409]–418.
Half title; pub. device.

Has much material on the Plummer gang and the Montana vigilantes.

1048. Howard, James W. (Doc)

"Doc" Howard's memoirs, written by Sergeant "Doc" Howard, member of Company B, 5th U.S. cavalry under General Carr, 1867–1872. [n.p., n.d., (ca. 1931).] Stiff wrappers. (Cover title.) Rare.

24 p. 23.2 cm.
Double column.

This rare little book is said to have been printed in an edition of only thirty copies. It tells about Cheyenne in its wild days and contains some information on Wild Bill Hickok and Calamity Jane. The author refers to Deadwood as Dead Wood's.

1049. Howard, Joseph Kinsey

Montana, high, wide and handsome, by Joseph Kinsey Howard. New Haven, Yale University press . . ., 1943. Cloth. OP.

vi p., [4] l., [8]–347 p. 21 cm.
Acknowledgments and bibliography: p. [330]–339; index: p. [341]–347.
Map on end papers.

A well-written book giving some history of Montana, its vigilantes, and some of its latter-day outlaws. In a chapter entitled "Nine Holes in Rattlesnake Jake," the author tells about horse thieves, the vigilantes, and the killing of Rattlesnake Jake Fallon and his partner, Long-Haired Owens.

1050. ——— (ed.)

Montana margins. A state anthology, edited by Joseph Kinsey Howard. . . . New Haven, Yale University press . . ., 1946. Cloth. OP.

xviii, 527 p. 24 cm.
Appendix: p. 517–521; index to authors and acknowledgments: p. 522–527.

Contains a chapter on Joseph Slade from Dimsdale's *Vigilantes of Montana*, and another on cattle rustlers and the latter-day vigilantes from Granville Stuart's *Forty Years on the Frontier*.

1051. Howard, Robert West (ed.)

This is the west. Edited by Robert West Howard. Illustrated. New York, Chicago, San Francisco, Rand McNally & co. [1957]. Cloth. OP.

4 p.l., 248 p. illus., plates, map. 24.2 cm.

Appendix: p. 221–248.
Half title.

First published as a Signet paper-back book without illustrations. It has chapters on gunmen and lawmen, dealing with Butch Cassidy and his Wild Bunch, the Johnson County War, and the Texas Rangers.

1052. Howe, Charles E.

Dramatic play entitled "Joaquín Murieta de Castillo, the celebrated bandit." In five acts. San Francisco, Commercial book and job steam printing establishment, 1858. Wrappers. Rare.

42 p. 22.2 cm.

An attempt to dramatize the John Ridge version of Joaquín Murieta's life. There are some changes in names, but the play did much to renew and perpetuate the legends about Murieta. It also helped perpetuate that legend that the state offered a $5,000 reward and that Murieta scrawled under the wanted poster that he would give $10,000.

1053. Howe, Charles Willis

Timberleg of the Diamond Tail and other frontier anecdotes, by Charles Willis Howe. Illustrated by R. L. McCollister. San Antonio, Texas, the Naylor co. [1949]. Pict. cloth.

ix, 153 p. 21.6 cm.
Half title; illus. chapter headings.

Has a chapter on bad men and the law, dealing with some of the better-known Oklahoma and New Mexico outlaws. The author says that Hickok "accounted for the liquidation of eighty-seven men not including Indians during his reign as peace officer," a statement which is pure exaggeration of course. He repeats the legend about Billy the Kid having killed twenty-one men by the time he was twenty-one years of age.

1054. Howe, Elvon L. (ed.)

Rocky mountain empire. Revealing glimpses of the west in transition from old to new, from the pages of the Rocky Mountain Empire Magazine of the Denver Post, edited by Elvon L. Howe. With a foreword by Palmer Hoyt. Garden City, N.Y., Doubleday & co., inc. [1950]. Cloth. OP.

xiv p., 1 l., 272 p. 21 cm.
Half title; map on end papers; illus. chapter headings; pub. device; untrimmed; "First edition" on copyright p.

Contains a chapter on Bill Carlisle, the lone train robber of Wyoming.

1055. Hoyt, Henry Franklin

A frontier doctor, by Henry F. Hoyt; with an introduction by Frank B. Kellogg, and with illustrations. Boston, and New York, Houghton Mifflin co., 1929. Cloth. Scarce.

xv, 260 p. front. (port.), plates, ports., facsms. 21.3 cm.

Half title; pub. device; untrimmed; first edition: 1929 under imprint.

A well-written and interesting book with some material on Billy the Kid and life in old Tascosa. The author's information on Billy the Kid is correct. He also gives some new material on Jesse James, but makes an error in stating that the big fight in Tascosa took place on March 23, 1886. The correct date was March 21. He also confuses the LX Ranch with the LS Ranch. He is mistaken in saying that after Jack McCall killed Hickok he was captured "about a week later near Fort Pierre and hanged." McCall was captured at Laramie.

1056. Hubbard, Freeman H.

Railroad avenue. Great stories and legends of American railroading, by Freeman H. Hubbard. New York, London, Whittlesey House, McGraw-Hill book co., inc. [1945]. Cloth. Scarce.

x, 374 p. front., illus., plates, ports., map. 23 cm.

Vocabulary and railroad lingo: p. 331–367; acknowledgments: p. 368; index: p. 369–374.

Half title; vignette; "First printing" on copyright p.

Contains a chapter on the James gang and their train-robbing activities.

1057. Hubbard, Harry D.

Building the heart of an empire, by Harry D. Hubbard. Edited by James A. Metcalf. . . . Boston, Meador publishing co., MCMXXXVII. Cloth. Scarce.

7 p.l., 17–318 p. front. (port.), illus., plates, ports., fold. map. 21 cm.

Bibliography: p. 317–318.

Half title; pub. device.

In Chapter V the author tells about Black Bart's last holdup and his capture.

1058. Hubbs, Barney

Robert Clay Allison, gentleman gunfighter, 1840–1887. "He never killed a man that didn't need killing." Compiled in 1966, under the supervision of Barney Hubbs. . . . [Pecos, Texas, 1966.] Stiff pict. wrappers.

2 p.l. front. (port.), illus., plates, ports. 26.8 cm.

Cover title: "Shadows Along the Pecos."

A short but fairly well-done biography of Clay Allison with some previously unpublished photographs and plates. The last half of the book (including sixteen pages of plates) tells about W. D. Johnson, a Pecos rancher and businessman.

1059. Huckaby, Ida Lasater

Ninety-four years in Jack county, 1854–1948, written and compiled by Ida Lasater Huckaby. [Austin, Texas, the Steck co., 1949.] Cloth. OP.

xvi p., 1 l., [3]–513 [1] p. plates, ports., fold. map, tables. 23.5 cm.

In her chapter "Law and Lawlessness on the Frontier," the author deals with outlaws and robberies of West Texas and makes the statement that a man named Joe Horner, of Jacksboro, got into trouble and went to the Northwest, where he took the name Frank Canton and became a well-known peace officer. In his autobiography Canton himself says nothing about having been Joe Horner (see Item 371).

1060. Hudson, Wilson M.

Andy Adams, his life and writings, [by] Wilson M. Hudson. Dallas, Southern Methodist University press, 1964. Two-tone cloth.

xv p., 1 l., 3–274 p. plates, ports. 23.5 cm.
Notes: p. 227–258; bibliography: p. 259–265; index: p. 267–274.
Half title; illus. t.p.; pict. end papers.

Has some mention of Sam Bass, King Fisher, Wild Bill Hickok, Tom Horn, Bat Masterson, Ben Thompson, and the Johnson County War.

1061. ———, and Allen Maxwell (eds.)

The sunny slopes of long ago. Edited by Wilson M. Hudson [and] Allen Maxwell. Dallas, Southern Methodist University press [1966]. Cloth.

viii p., 6 l., 3–204 p. front. (port.), plates, ports. 23.5 cm.
Notes after each chapter; contributors: p. 198–200; index: p. 201–204.
Half title: "Publication of Texas Folklore Society Number XXXIII."

Contains a chapter on Billy the Kid and the Lincoln County War.

1062. Hueston, Ethel (Mrs. Powelson)

Calamity Jane of Deadwood Gulch, by Ethel Hueston. Indianapolis, New York, Bobbs-Merrill co., publishers [1937]. Cloth. OP.

3 p.l., 7–306 p. 20.7 cm.
Half title; untrimmed; "First edition" on copyright p.

Republished by Grossett and Dunlap with frontispiece and illustrations, but without a date.

Although written in a factual style, this book is strictly fiction.

1063. Hughes, Dan de Lara

South from Tombstone. A life story, by Dan de Lara Hughes. London, Methuen & co., ltd. [1938]. Cloth. Scarce.

v p., 1 l., 311 [1] p. 20.3 cm.

A scarce book with some material on the Heath gang in Arizona. The author spells Doc Holliday's name as Halliday. He tells about many of the Arizona outlaws, such as Billy Stiles, Burt Alvord, and Augustine Chacon.

1064. [Hughes, John R.]

The killing of Bass Outlaw. Austin, Texas, Brick Row book shop, 1963. Stiff wrappers. Scarce.

2 p.l., [5] p. (no pagination). one side of paper. 27.7 cm.
Edition limited to 250 copies.

A facsimile of a letter and telegram sent by Captain Hughes to General W. H. Mabry, telling him about the killing of Ranger Joe McKidrict by Bass Outlaw and about the killing of Outlaw by John Selman. The editor makes some mistakes in his foreword, such as having Selman killed by John Scarborough. Scarborough's first name was George. He also has Scarborough killed by Kid Curry on April 6. Scarborough was fatally wounded by parties unknown and died on April 5. The editor refers to the killing of Outlaw as occurring on April 6, but the letter from Hughes is dated April 5.

1065. Hughes, Marion

Oklahoma Charley, by Marion Hughes. . . . Oklahoma Charley . . . miner, cowboy, corndoctor, Indian scout, invalid, prospector, polygamist, horse trader . . . snakecharmer, book-agent . . . and booze fighter. . . . St. Louis, John P. Wagner & co. [1910]. Pict. wrappers. Rare.

2 p.l., [7]–159 p. front., illus. 18.8 cm.

The author presents, among other drivel, a most preposterous tale about Billy the Kid. He relates that the Kid was born in Illinois and was named Billy LeRoy (the author may have been a *Police Gazette* fan; the whole account shows the influence of the *Police Gazette's Billy LeRoy*). Among other things, he has the Kid hold up a stagecoach with a corncob on a stick to prove his bravery to a gang of road agents he wanted to join. The corncob incident was probably suggested by an incident in the *Gazette* novel, where it was related that when Billy LeRoy's guards wondered at his using a gun as small as a .32, LeRoy answered: "A corncob is just as good as a pistol to hold up a stage with." There was a Billy LeRoy who operated in Colorado, but this author has most of his incidents fitting the Kid's life in New Mexico.

1066. Hughes, Richard B.

Pioneer years in the Black Hills, by Richard B. Hughes, prospector, miner, cattleman, frontier printer, surveyor-general, real estate developer, and pioneer newspaper reporter. Edited by Agnes Wright Spring. . . . Glendale, Calif., the Arthur H. Clark co., 1957. Cloth.

8 p.l., [19]–366 p. front. (port.), plates, ports., facsms. 24.7 cm.
Appendices: p. [323]–353; index: p. [357]–366.
Half title: "Western Frontiersman Series VI"; pub. device; untrimmed.

Has material dealing with Calamity Jane, the death of Wild Bill Hickok, and the trial of Jack McCall and has a chapter on the early-day road agents. The author is mistaken, however, in saying that Hickok killed several soldiers while he was marshal of Abilene. He also tells of his "killing or seriously crippling ten well armed men" of the McCanles "gang," but qualifies the statement with, "It was related of him [Wild Bill]."

1067. Hullah, John

The train robber's career. A life of Sam Bass, the notorious desperado of the southwest, with some account of his followers, by John Hullah, of the Chicago Press. Chicago, Belford, Clarke & co.; St. Louis, Belford, Clarke publishing co., 1881. Pict. wrappers. Very rare.

2 p.l., [17]–178 p. front., 4 plates (incl. front.). 17.6 cm.

The author is mistaken when he writes that, when the stage driver (Johnny Slaughter) was killed, "Collins and Heffridge fired at him with Winchester rifles and killed him instantly." This killing was done by Reddy McKemie. He is also mistaken in saying that Allen Station, where the Bass gang held up their first train in Texas, was "six miles north of McKinney and twenty-four miles north of Dallas." McKinney is thirty-two miles north of Dallas, and Allen is eight miles south of McKinney. The author also says that the gang seized between twenty-five hundred and three thousand dollars in this robbery, but they failed to gain that much from all four of their Texas train robberies. The author incorrectly states that Captain Peak was a recorder of Dallas and had been induced by the Texas Express Company to resign his position and enter its employment as a detective. Peak belonged to the Texas Rangers. The author says nothing about Murphy's death, but gives full descriptions of some of the members of Bass's gang. On the whole, this is one of the more reliable books about Bass. The only copy known to me was owned by my late friend Martin Ismert, of Kansas City, Missouri.

1068. Hultz, Fred S.

Range beef production in the seventeen western states, by Fred S. Hultz.

New York, John Wiley and sons, inc.; London, Chapman and Hall, ltd., 1930. Cloth. OP.

xv, 208 p. front., plates, ports., maps, charts, diagrs., tables. 21 cm.
Index: p. 201–208.
Half title.

Although primarily a book on livestock, there is a chapter on the Johnson County War of Wyoming.

1069. Hume, James B., and John N. Thacker

Report of Jas. B. Hume and Jno. N. Thacker, special officers, Wells, Fargo & co.'s express, covering a period of fourteen years, giving losses by train robbers, stage robbers and burglaries, and a full description and record of all noted criminals convicted of offenses against Wells, Fargo & company since November 5th, 1870. San Francisco, H.S. Crocker & co., stationers and printers . . ., 1885. Wrappers. Rare.

3 p.l., [7]–91 p. 23.5 cm.

This rare report gives the birthplace, age, occupation, physical description, and prison sentences of more than two hundred outlaws who had robbed shipments of Wells, Fargo and Company.

1070. Humphrey, Seth King

Following the prairie frontier, [by] Seth K. Humphrey. [Minneapolis], University of Minnesota press [1931]. Cloth. OP.

5 p.l., 264 p. front. 21.2 cm.
Half title.

The author gives some information on the Benders, the James-Younger gang, and the Northfield Bank robbery. He is in error, however, when he writes, "And when Jesse James was finally shot by one of his own gang, the state of Missouri virtually sent the fellow to prison for life."

1071. Humphreys, J. R.

The lost towns and roads of America, [by] J. R. Humphreys. Photographs by the author. Garden City, N.Y., Doubleday & co., inc. [1961]. Cloth.

6 p.l., 13–194 p. plates. 21.7 cm.
Index: p. 191–194.
Half title; map on end papers.

Contains some material on the Harpes and the Robbers Roost gang of Utah.

1072. Hungerford, Edward

Wells Fargo. Advancing the American frontier, by Edward Hungerford. New York, Random House [1949]. Pict. cloth. OP.

xvi p., 1 l., 2–374 p. plates, ports., 2 maps (1 double p.), tables. 23.5 cm.
Bibliography: p. 259–262; index: p. 263–274.
Half title; illus. double t.p.; headpieces; "First printing" on copyright p.

Deals with stage robbers of California, such as Tom Bell, Black Bart, and Rattlesnake Dick.

1073. Hunt, Frazier

Cap Mossman, last of the great cowmen, by Frazier Hunt. With sixteen illustrations by Ross Santee. New York, Hastings House, publishers [1951]. Pict. cloth. OP.

5 p.l., 3–277 p. illus. 21 cm.
Half title; illus. end papers (each dif.); vignette.

During his lifetime the subject of this book was an Arizona Ranger, and he had many interesting experiences with the outlaws of that state. On page 171 there is a misplaced word in the line reading, "Cap had no picture of good Smith," which, I am sure, should read, "Cap had no good picture of Smith." There are several other typographical errors, such as Sam Carlos for San Carlos and Toscosa for Tascosa. There is some mention of the Graham-Tewksbury feud and of Tom Pickett, onetime member of Billy the Kid's gang. There is also a chapter on Augustine Chacon, Burt Alvord, Billy Stiles, and Bob Downing.

1074. ———

The long trail from Texas; the story of Ad Spaugh, cattleman, by Frazier Hunt. New York, Doubleday, Doran & co., inc., 1940. Cloth. OP.

5 p.l., 300 p. front. (port.). 20.6 cm.
Half title; vignette; untrimmed; "First edition" on copyright p.
1st prelim. p.: "This story was published serially under the title 'The Last Frontier.' "

Has some minor information about Wild Bill Hickok and Calamity Jane and material on Doc Middleton and his gang of horse thieves.

1075. ———

The tragic days of Billy the Kid, by Frazier Hunt. Maps by Robert N. Mullin. New York, Hastings House, publishers [1956]. Pict. cloth. OP.

6 p.l., 316 p. maps (3 double p.), plans. 21 cm.
Half title; maps on end papers.

Has much new material on Billy the Kid. It is perhaps the account nearest the truth to date. The author was fortunate in having the benefit of the studious research of such men as the late Maurice Fulton, Robert Mullin, and Phil Rasch. Altogether it is a reliable book, though there are a few minor errors, such as naming McNab Charlie instead of Frank in one place and getting Tunstall's name wrong.

1076. Hunt, Inez, and Wanetta W. Draper

To Colorado's restless ghosts, [by] Inez Hunt and Wanetta W. Draper. [Denver, Colo.], Sage books [1960]. Cloth.

6 p.l., 13–330 p. plates, ports., facsms. 23.5 cm.
Half title; pub. device.

Has a chapter on Soapy Smith with a mention of the killing of Bob Ford and some material on Alferd Packer, whose first name he spells Alfred, though Packer himself signed his name Alferd.

1077. Hunt, Lenoir

Bluebonnets and blood. The romance of "Tejas," by Lenoir Hunt. . . . Illustrated with drawings, photographs and maps. Houston, Texas, Texas books, inc. [1938]. Thin boards (Imt. cloth). Scarce.

xv p., 1 l., 3–433 p. front., plates, ports., maps, facsm. 23.3 cm.
Bibliography: p. 407–409; [notes]: p. 413–433.
Vignette.
Colophon (pasted on inside front cover): "Each of five hundred copies of the Founders' De Luxe edition of Bluebonnets and Blood is numbered and autographed by the author."

In a chapter on the Texas Rangers the author mentions such outlaws as John Wesley Hardin and Sam Bass.

1078. Hunt, Rockwell D.

California ghost towns live again. By Rockwell D. Hunt. . . . Foreword by Robert E. Burns. . . . Stockton, Calif., published by the College of the Pacific, 1948. Pict. wrappers. OP.

2 p.l., 7–69 [2] p. plates, map. 20.2 cm.
Suggestions for further reading: p. [71].
Publication of the California History Foundation, Number 1, March, 1948.

Has some short material on Joaquín Murieta.

1079. ———

California's stately hall of fame, by Rockwell D. Hunt. . . . Stockton, Calif., published by the College of the Pacific [1950]. Cloth. OP.

xxi p., 1 l., 675 p. front., plates, ports. 23.5 cm.
Selected references for further reading (bibliography): p. [601]–665; index: p. [667]–675.
Half title.

Contains a chapter on Joaquín Murieta.

1080. ———, and Nellie Van De Grift Sanchez

A short history of California, by Rockwell D. Hunt . . . and Nellie Van de Grift Sanchez. . . . New York, Thomas Y. Crowell co., publishers [1929]. Cloth. Scarce.

xiii p., 2 l., 3–671 p. plates, maps (2 fold.). 22.3 cm.
Appendices: p. 637–647; index: p. 649–671.
Half title; references for further reading at end of each chapter.

Devotes some space to California's outlaws—Murieta, Vásquez, and Juan Flores.

1081. Hunter, Col. George

Reminiscences of an old-timer. A recital of the actual events, incidents, trials, hardships, vicissitudes, adventures, perils, and escapes of a pioneer, hunter, miner, and scout of the Pacific northwest, together with his later experiences in official and business capacities, and a brief description of the resources, beauties and advantages of the new northwest; the several Indian wars, anecdotes etc., by Colonel George Hunter. San Francisco, H. S. Crocker and co., stationers and printers, 1887. Pict. cloth. Rare.

xxv, 454 p. front. (port.), illus., plates. 20.4 cm.
Half title; leaf of errata tipped in.

Reprinted the same year with an appendix; again reprinted, Battle Creek, Mich., Review and Herald, 1888 and 1889.

Contains some information on vigilantes and road agents.

1082. Hunter, John Marvin

Peregrinations of a pioneer printer. An autobiography, by J. Marvin Hunter, Sr. . . . Grand Prairie, Texas, printed in the U.S.A. by Frontier Times publishing house, 1954. Pict. cloth. OP.

2 p.l., 244 [3] p. plates, ports. 22.8 cm.
"Index to contents": p. [245–247].
Leaf of errata laid in.

Makes some mention of Scott Cooley, Thurman Skeeter Baldwin, John Wesley Hardin, George Scarborough, and Jeff Ake.

1083. ———

The story of Lottie Deno, her life and times, by J. Marvin Hunter. The story of the mysterious aristocrat who became a lady gambler and female daredevil of frontier days. [Bandera, Texas, published by the 4 Hunters, 1959.] Cloth.

vii, 199 p. plates, ports. 23.2 cm.

Has much on the history of Fort Griffin, Texas, and its shady citizens. Has material on Doc Holliday, John Selman, the killing of Scarborough, and other characters and events. The book largely comprises quotations from other books and reprints all of the little pamphlet credited to Calamity Jane. His chapter on Doc Holliday is an excerpt from Walter Noble Burns's *Tombstone.*

1084. ——— **(ed.)**

The trail drivers of Texas. Interesting sketches of early cowboys and their experiences on the range and on the trail during the days that tried men's souls. True narratives related by real cow-punchers and men who fathered the cattle industry of Texas. Published under the direction of George W. Saunders, president of the Old Time Trail Drivers' Association. Compiled and edited by J. Marvin Hunter. [San Antonio, Texas, Jackson printing co., 1920–1923.] Pub. in two volumes. Pict. cloth. Original edition rare.

Vol. I, [3]–498 p. ports. 23.3 cm.
Vol. II, 2 p.l., 3–496 [1] p. front., plates, ports. 22 cm.
Vol. I published in 1920; Vol. II, in 1923.
Crudely bound and printed.

The first volume was exhausted before the second volume was published; therefore, the first volume was reprinted in 1924 with some revisions and additions in an edition of 500 copies with a "second edition" imprint. [San Antonio, Globe printing co., 1924.] Pict. cloth. Scarce.

[5]–494 p. plates, ports. 22.8 cm.

Republished in one volume by Cokesbury press, Nashville, 1925.

xvi, 1044 p. front., plates, ports. 23.5 cm.

Republished again by Argosy-Antiquarian, ltd., of New York in 1963 in two volumes, a de luxe edition (in slip case), with a new introduction by Harry Sinclair Drago, and indexed. Pict. buckram. This edition limited to 750 copies.

Vol. I, xxviii, 549 p. front. (port.), plates, ports. 23.5 cm.
Vol. II, [549]–1070 p. plates, ports. 23.5 cm.
Paged continuously.

These books are mostly about cattle and, as such, are valuable contributions because they record heretofore untold history. They are listed here because they contain an (unreliable) article entitled "The Killing of Billy the Kid," by Fred Sutton. The writer says that the Kid killed a companion in New York at the age of twelve, then escaped to Kansas, where he worked on a farm for a year and a half before going to New Mexico. The Kid became an outlaw because he killed a rancher for whom he worked, or so says the writer. He also claims to have entered Greathouse's house with Jimmy Carlisle and Sheriff William Brady (whom he calls Bradley) when they were killed. But Brady was killed in Lincoln according to all other records, and Sutton has never been mentioned as a member of any posse sent after the Kid. The writer also says that Garrett killed the Kid in 1882. The killing occurred in 1881. There are many more errors, and the whole account is absurd.

1085. ———, and Noah H. Rose

The album of gun-fighters, by J. Marvin Hunter and Noah H. Rose. Decorated and designed by Warren Hunter. [Bandera, Texas, 1951.] Pict. cloth (in col.). Scarce.

xi p., 1 l., 236 p. plates, ports. 31 cm.

Half title; illus. end papers; illus. double t.p.; leaf of errata laid in.

Reprinted in 1955 with same collation, but without the errata slip and with corrections made.

Published in a limited edition, this volume contains portraits and short sketches of most of the outlaws and gunmen of the West. Rose's pictures have appeared in many western books, but this publication places a valuable gallery of western gunmen under one cover.

There are many mistakes in the text. The authors say that Bill Raidler was in prison with Al Jennings and when released became a nationally known story writer. They are evidently confusing Raidler with William Sidney Porter (O. Henry). They give the date of Calamity Jane's death as August 5, 1908, but she died on August 1, 1903. In telling about Sam Bass, they say that the Rangers, "under June Peak," were sent to Round Rock to prevent the bank robbery. Peak was not with the Rangers on that occasion. He was unsuccessfully trying to catch Bass in Denton County.

They are mistaken, too, in saying that John Selman took part in the Lincoln County War as a pal of Billy the Kid. He had his own gang during that period. They have the Kid killing a man for insulting his mother, and his mother marrying Antrim in Colorado, though they do correct the statement that Billy killed twenty-one men. There are many other errors of facts and dates.

1086. Hunter, Lillie Mae

The moving finger, by Lillie Mae Hunter, with illustrations by Bill Hacker. Borger, Texas, Plains printing co., 1956. Cloth. OP.

4 p.l., 2 l., 171 p. illus. 22.3 cm.

This little privately printed book is mostly about life in the cattle country of West Texas, but it does have some slight material on Sam Bass that I have never seen before. In writing of Ira Aten, the Texas Ranger, the author says that the event that influenced him to become a Ranger was his presence at the death of Bass when the good citizens of Round Rock sent for Aten's father, a minister, to come to pray for him.

1087. Huntington, George

Robber and hero, the story of the raid on the First National Bank of Northfield, Minnesota, by the James-Younger band of robbers in 1876. . . . Portraits, illustrations and biographical sketches. Compiled from original and authentic sources, by George Huntington. Northfield, Minn., the Christian Way co., 1895. Cloth. Scarce.

v [1] p., 1 l., 119 p. front. (port.), plates, ports., plan. 19.7 cm.

Reprinted in 1962 with an added seven-page bibliography.

A carefully written book based upon contemporary newspaper accounts and considered accurate.

1088. Huntington, William (Bill)

Bill Huntington's both feet in the stirrups. Illustrated by J. K. Ralston. [Billings, Mont. . . . Western Livestock Reporter press, 1959.] Cloth. OP.

3 p.l., [7]–408 p. illus. 21 cm.

"First printing" on copyright p.

In Chapter 9, entitled "Rustlers and Killers," there is some information on Tom O'Day, Butch Cassidy and his Wild Bunch, and others of the Hole-In-the-Wall country. There is also some mention of Calamity Jane.

1089. ———

Bill Huntington's good men and salty cusses. Illustrated by J. K. Ralston. [Billings, Mont., Western Livestock Reporter press, 1952.] Cloth. OP.

3 p.l., 207 p. illus. 21 cm.

Colophon (pasted on verso of flyleaf): "This is copy number —— of the limited first edition of 2,000 imprints."

Contains some material on Doc Middleton, Tom O'Day, and a few other outlaws of the Northwest, as well as a mention of Calamity Jane.

1090. Hurd, C. W.

Boggsville. Cradle of the Colorado cattle industry, by C. W. Hurd. [Boggsville, Bent County Democrat, 1957.] Stiff pict. wrappers. (Cover title.) OP.

2 p.l., 89 [3] p. plates, ports., map. 22.8 cm.
Index: p. [90–92].

Devotes a page to Jesse James and mentions Soapy Smith.

1091. Huson, Hobart

Refugio. A comprehensive history of Refugio county from aboriginal times to 1953. By Hobart Huson. . . . Refugio, Texas. . . . Aboriginal to 1861. Woodsboro, Texas, the Rooke Foundation, inc., 1933. Cloth. Pub. in two volumes.

Vol. I, xvi p., 1 l., 596 [20] p. plates, ports. 23.8 cm.
Half title; last 20 p. plates and ports.
Vol. II, 1 l., 633 [1] p. ports., facsms. 23.8 cm.
Appendix: p. 447–499; bibliography: p. 501–536; index: p. (for both volumes) 539–633.

Volume II contains a chapter on lawlessness and the Taylor-Sutton feud and deals with John Wesley Hardin, King Fisher, Ben and Bill Thompson.

1092. Hutchens, John K.

One man's Montana. An informal portrait of a state, by John K. Hutchens. Philadelphia and New York, J. B. Lippincott co. [1964]. Boards.

6 p.l., 13–221 p. 20.8 cm.

An interesting book by a newspaperman containing chapters on Henry Plummer, his gang, and their hangings; the hanging of Slade; and Calamity Jane. The author is mistaken when he writes that "maybe it really was true that she [Jane] cornered his [Wild Bill's] cowardly murderer, Jack McCall, with a butcher knife. . . ." The author also says that he met Emmett Dalton after Dalton's prison term but is mistaken when he says that during the Coffeyville raid Emmett "was saved from lynching only by a quick-thinking coroner who told the townfolk that Emmett, too, had died."

1093. Hutchinson, W. H.

Another notebook of the old west, by W. H. Hutchinson. Companion volume to a notebook of the old west. Chico, Calif., designed and printed . . . by Hurst & Yount [1954]. Pict. wrappers.

4 p.l., 88 p. 23.3 cm.
Vignette; 6 chapters with tailpieces, 6 without.

Includes a chapter on the killing of Nate Champion and one on Tiburcio Vásquez, the California bandit.

1094. ———

Another verdict for Oliver Lee, by W. H. Hutchinson. Pen sketches by H. D. Bugbee and Oliver Vandruff Bugbee. Clarendon, Texas, Clarendon press, 1965. Cloth.

ix p., 1 l., 22 [1] p. front., illus., plates, ports., marginal illus. (col.). 26 cm.
Colophon: "Another Verdict for Oliver Lee" has been set in Meloir of Herman Zapf, and six hundred and fifty copies have been printed on Nekoosa Fantasy paper at Clarendon Press, Clarendon, Texas."

Has some material on Oliver Lee, Pat Garrett, Jim Gilliland, and the Fountain murder, but it mostly quotes from Eugene Cunningham and is largely about him.

1095. ———

The life & personal writings of Eugene Manlove Rhodes, a Bar Cross man, [by] W. H. Hutchinson. Norman, University of Oklahoma press [1956]. Cloth.

xix p., 2 l., 3–432 [1] p. illus., plates, ports., map, facsm. 23.5 cm.
Check list of Eugene Manlove Rhodes's writing: p. 392–407.
Half title; illus. t.p.; "First edition" on copyright p.

Has material on such western outlaws and gunmen as the Apache Kid, Elfego Baca, Sam Bass, Billy the Kid, Dick Broadwell, Butch Cassidy, Black Jack Ketchum, Black Jack Christian, Billy and Ike Clanton, Curly Bill Brocius, Kid Curry, Bill Doolin, Wyatt Earp, James East, Joel Fowler, Pat Garrett, Tom Horn, Wild Bill Hickok, Jesse James, Bat Masterson, Ben Thompson, and others. The author comments at length on some of the mistakes Stuart Lake made in his book about Wyatt Earp.

1096. ———

A notebook of the old west, by W. H. Hutchinson. Designed and printed at Chico, Calif., by Bob Hurst for the author [Chico, Calif., 1947]. Stiff wrappers. OP.

4 p.l., 11–122 p. illus. 23.3 cm.
Vignette.

In a chapter on Wild Bill Hickok the author writes: "Women and gunsmoke followed Wild Bill like his reputation. The famous McCanles, or McCandless fight in which Wild Bill, at the age of 24, is reputed to have laid about him with knife and pistol until a baker's dozen lay weltering about him, had behind it a comely buxom figure of Sarah Shull." He goes on to enumerate other women who fell for Hickok, including Calamity Jane. He speaks of the McCanles "fight" as being "reputed," as though he had some doubt about it. One wonders why he did not therefore investigate the accuracy of the tale and correct it.

Of the death of Wild Bill and the capture of McCall, he writes: "The epilogue of this brief encounter with the last is speedily made. McCall was captured, tried and duly hung." That sequence of events took place upon McCall's second capture.

1097. ——— (ed.)

The Rhodes reader. Stories of virgins, villains and varmints, by Eugene Manlove Rhodes. Selected by W. H. Hutchinson. Norman, University of Oklahoma press [1957]. Cloth.

xxvii p., 1 l., 3–316 p. 23.6 cm.

Half title; illus. map on front end paper; illus. double t.p.; "First edition" on copyright p.

The final chapter, entitled "In Defense of Pat Garrett," deals with Billy the Kid, Pat Garrett, and some of the participants in the Lincoln County War. Its chief object seems to be a criticism of Burns's *Saga of Billy the Kid*. But Rhodes himself seems to have been under the impression that the Kid killed both Jimmy Carlisle and Joe Bernstein. He thinks, as I do, that Colonel Dudley played the "shabbiest chapter in this heartbreaking history."

1098. ———, and R. N. Mullin

Whiskey Jim and a kid named Billy, by W. H. Hutchinson and R. N. Mullin. Clarendon, Texas, Clarendon press, 1967. Cloth.

xi, 41 p. front., illus. 23.7 cm.

Half title; illus. t.p.; colophon: "This book has been set in Meloir type by Jaggars-Chiles-Stovall, inc., of Dallas, and 600 copies printed at the Clarendon Press, Clarendon, Texas."

The story of Jim Greathouse and some of his cattle-rustling experiences, his association with Billy the Kid, and his murder by Joel Fowler.

1099. Hutto, Nelson A.

The Dallas story, from buckskins to top hat. Written by Nelson A. Hutto. Cartoon by Bill McClanahan. . . . [Dallas, Texas, printed by William S. Henson, inc., 1953.] Pict. wrappers. OP.

2 p.l., 5–72 p. illus. 26.2 cm.

Double column.

Has some material on both Sam Bass and Belle Starr.

1100. Hyde, Albert E.

Billy the Kid and the old regime in the southwest, by Albert E. Hyde. An eye-witness account with the capture & defiance of a mob by that notorious desperado Dave Rudabaugh. Ruidoso, N.M., Frontier book co., 1961. Wrappers.

2 p.l., 5–31 p. plates. 21.7 cm.

An account that first appeared in *Century Magazine* in March, 1902, a fact which should have been noted by the publisher of this book. The author makes many mistakes. In the second paragraph he has Governor Wallace telling him that Billy the Kid "killed inoffensive people just to see them kick." He says that the Lincoln County War was a war between cattlemen and thieves. He has Sheriff Garrett bringing the prisoners captured at Stinking Springs into Las Vegas "in a cloud of dust." These prisoners were captured just before Christmas during a snowstorm. He has a Dr. Sutfin maintaining that "Billy the Kid was a Chicago bootblack whose mind had become inflamed by reading dime novels." He also says that Billy went to New Mexico at the age of sixteen, soon afterward running off with his employer's cattle and killing his employees. He joins many other writers in having the Kid killing twenty-one men before he died at the age of twenty-one, and he closes his account by having Billy killed "near Las Cruces" and saying that to "only one living soul in all the world did Garrett's fatal shot carry sorrow that moonlit night on the Bonita; the poor Mexican girl, his faithful sweetheart, to see whom for the last time he risked and forfeited his life, alone mourned him."

1101. Hyenne, Robert

El bandido Chileno. Joaquín Murieta en California, por Robert Hyenne. Edición illustrada. Barcelona [and] Mexico [n.d.]. Wrappers. Rare.

123 p. plates. 18.6 cm.

This book is supposed to have been translated from the French account, which, in turn, was received from Spain. In this version the author makes Murieta a *Chileno.* The Hyenne edition was pirated, and translated into Spanish, and issued as *El Caballero Chileno,* by "Professor" Acigar (See Item 1103).

1102. ———

El bandido Chileno. Joaquín Murieta en California, por Robert Hyenne. Traducido del francés por C. M. Edición illustrada. Santiago, Centro editorial 'La Prensa,' 1906. Wrappers. Rare.

2 p.l., [5]–123 [1] p. plates. 18.5 cm.
Index: p. [124].
4 p. adv. at end; Carlos Morla translation.

1103. ———

El caballero Chileno. Bandido en California. Unica y verdadero historia de Joaquín Murrieta [*sic*], por el Professor Acigar. Barcelona (España), Biblioteca Hercules [n.d.]. Wrappers. Rare.

206 p. 18.6 cm.

Pirated from the Hyenne edition (see Item 1101).

1104. Hyer, Julien

The land of beginning again. The romance of the Brazos, by Julien Hyer. Illustrated by Merritt Mauzy. Atlanta, Tupper & Love, inc. [1952]. Pict. Cloth. OP.

xi p., 1 l., 3–394 p. illus. 21.5 cm.
Half title; illus. t.p.; map on end papers.

Chapter IX deals with some of the Texas outlaws and gunmen, such as Sam Bass and John Wesley Hardin and tells about the big fight at Tascosa. Chapter XIII also deals with some of the outlaws of the Southwest. The author says that Billy the Kid was born William Bonner, and throughout the book he spells Chisum's name as Chisholm. Most of his information on outlaws is wrong.

I

1105. [Idaho]

Idaho, a guide in word and picture. Prepared by the Federal Writers' Project of the Works Progress Administration. The library edition. Caldwell, Idaho, the Caxton printers, ltd., 1937. Pict. cloth.

8 p.l., [17]–431 p. front., plates, maps. 23.6 cm.
Selected bibliography: p. [415]–418; acknowledgments: p. [419]–421; index: p. [423]–431.
Half title.

Has some information about Henry Plummer.

1106. Illustrated History

of New Mexico . . . from the earliest period to the present time, together with . . . biographical mention of many of its pioneers and prominent citizens of today. . . . Chicago, the Lewis publishing co., 1895. Cloth. Scarce.

671 [1] p. plates, ports. 30 x 23.5 cm.

Contains an account of the Lincoln County War in the chapter on that county's history, and in it there is much material on Billy the Kid, most of it inaccurate.

1107. Indian Territory

Descriptive, biographical and genealogical, including the landed estates, country [*sic*] seats etc., with a general history of the territory. In one volume. Illustrated. New York and Chicago, the Lewis publishing co., 1901. Fabrikoid. Scarce.

xvi, 956 p. plates, ports. (some with tissues). 27.2 cm.
Gilt edges.

Has a long section on all the outlaws of the Indian Territory, including the Dalton gang and the Cook gang. The author is mistaken in saying that Belle Starr's brother Ed was her twin, and he repeats all the early and false legends about her.

1108. Informe

de la comisión pesquisidora de la frontera del norte al ejecutivo de la unión en cumplimiento del artículo 3^0 de la ley de 30 de Setiembre de 1872. Monterey, Mayo 15 de 1873. Méjico, imprenta de Díaz de León y White, calle de Lerdo numero 2, 1874. Wrappers. Rare.

[3]–124 p. 28.7 cm.
Device.

This rare book, in Spanish, is a report of the commission investigating cattle stealing on the Texas-Mexico border.

1109. Ingham, George Thomas

Digging gold among the Rockies; or, exciting adventures of wild camp life in Leadville, Black Hills and the Gunnison country . . ., by G. Thomas Ingham. Philadelphia, Hubbard brothers [1880]. Cloth. Scarce.

xiii p., 1 l., 17–508 p. front., illus. 20 cm.

Republished [n.p.], Edgewood publishing co. [1882].

xiii p., 1 l., 17–452 p. front., plates. 19.5 cm.

Again reissued by Hubbard brothers, Philadelphia, in 1888.

Has some material on the road agents of the Black Hills.

1110. Ingraham, Col. Prentiss

Wild Bill, the pistol dead shot; or, Dagger Dan's double, by Col. Prentiss Ingraham. New York, Beadle and Adams, publishers, 1882. Pict. col. wrappers. (Cover title.) Rare.

22 p. 31.7 cm.
Triple column.

Wild Bill was a favorite with nearly all the early dime novelists, and Ingraham, like the rest, made him a superman engaging in exploits with no semblance of truth in them.

1111. ———

Wild Bill, the pistol prince, from early boyhood to his tragic death, by Colonel Prentiss Ingraham. New York, Beadle and Adams, 1884. Pict. col. wrappers. (Cover title.) Rare.

30 p. 21 cm.
Double column.

The author repeats the false story of the Rock Creek Station "fight" and closes his description of it with: "For this desperate affray, in which one man whipped ten desperadoes, killing eight of them, the title 'Wild Bill' was bestowed upon the famous borderman, who was unfitted for service for twelve long months. But few other men could have survived such fearful injuries as he received, or come out of an encounter so deadly." The author refers to Coe as Cole and says that McCall escaped after killing Wild Bill but finally surrendered. The account is filled with the inventions characteristic of the early dime novels.

1112. ———

Wild Bill, the pistol prince, by Colonel Prentiss Ingraham. New York, M. J. Ivers & co., publishers, 1899. Wrappers. Rare.

20 p. 21.6 cm.
Double column.

Another of those preposterous tales of Hickok's prowess. The author has the McCanles "fight" in a dugout and says that there were four McCanles (which he spells McCandless) brothers, all desperadoes, who came to steal the horses and attacked Wild Bill in his dugout.

As the author tells it: "The elder McCandless, the leader, sprung into the cabin first, a revolver in his hand, and fell dead on the threshold. . . . Bill seized his revolvers, and before his assailants could reach him laid three more of them dead before him. The remaining six now rushed *en masse* upon him, and instantly the fiercest fight of a single man against overwhelming numbers on record began." Thus he continues with such fables to the end.

1113. ———

Wild Bill's gold trail; or, the desperado dozen. A thrilling romance of Buffalo Bill's old pard, by Colonel Prentiss Ingraham. New York, Beadle and Adams, publishers, 1882. Pict. col. wrappers. (Cover title.) Rare.

28 [1] p. 31.2 cm.

Triple column.

Another wild tale typical of the Beadle and Adams novels.

1114. Inman, Henry

The great Salt Lake trail, by Colonel Henry Inman . . . and Colonel William F. Cody. . . . New York, the Macmillan co.; London, Macmillan and co., ltd., 1898. Pict. cloth. Scarce.

xiii, 529 p. front. (port. with tissue), illus., plates (part with tissues with letterpress), ports., fold. map. 22.5 cm.

Index: p. 525–529.

Republished in 1899. The first printing was bound in blue cloth, the second in brown. Reprinted again in 1914.

Contains some material on Joseph A. Slade.

1115. Isely, Bliss, and W. M. Richards

Four centuries in Kansas. Unit studies, by Bliss Isely and W. M. Richards. Wichita, Kans., the McCormick-Mathers co. [1936]. Pict. cloth. Scarce.

viii p., 1 l., 3–344 p. front., illus., ports., maps. 20.2 cm.

Bibliography: p. 332–338; index: p. 339–344.

Illus. end papers; vignette; suggestions for further reading and references at end of each unit except Unit XII.

Tells about the famous Kansas cow towns and has some material on Wild Bill Hickok.

1116. Isman, Felix

Webber and Fields, their tribulations, triumphs and their associates, by Felix Isman. New York, Boni and Liveright, publishers, MCMXXIV. Cloth. Scarce.

xii p., 1 l., 15–345 p. front., illus., plates, ports., facsm., music. 22.8 cm.

Half title; illus. end papers.

Has some material on Frank James when he served as doorkeeper for the Butler's Standard Theatre in St. Louis.

1117. Issler, Anne Roller

Stevenson at Silverado, by Anne Roller Issler. Caldwell, Idaho, the Caxton printers, ltd., 1939. Cloth. OP.

8 p.l., 17–247 p. front. (port.), plates, 2 ports. (incl. front.). 23.5 cm.

Half title; illus. end papers; pub. device.

The author devotes a chapter to stage robbing and Black Bart.

J

1118. Jaastad, Ben

Man of the west. Reminiscences of George Washington Oaks, 1840–1917. Recorded by Ben Jaastad. Edited and annotated by Arthur Woodward. [Tucson, Ariz., Arizona Pioneers' Historical society, 1956.] Stiff wrappers. Scarce.

9 p.l., 17–65 p. front. (port.), plate. 21.8 cm.
Notes: p. 49–65.
Untrimmed.
Colophon: "400 copies designed and printed by Lawton Kennedy."

Contains some new material on Bat Masterson, the Earps, Doc Holliday, the O K Corral fight, the Clantons, and other Tombstone characters. In a footnote the author says: "I never knew a Tombstone old-timer who had any use for the Earps."

1119. Jackson, Joseph Henry

Anybody's gold, the story of California's mining towns, by Joseph Henry Jackson. Illustrated by E. H. Suydam. New York, London, D. Appleton-Century co., inc. [1941]. Cloth. Scarce.

xiv p., 1 l., 3–467 [1] p. front., illus., plates. 23.2 cm.
"Reading list": p. 447–453; index: p. 455–[466].
Half title; illus. end papers; illus. chapter headings; untrimmed; first edition: figure (1) at end of index.

Reprinted several times.

Like most of this author's books, this one does much to convince the reader that most of the stories about the early California outlaw Murieta are pure fiction. The author touches upon practically all the California outlaws except Vásquez.

1120. ———

Bad company. The story of California's legendary and actual stage-robbers, bandits, highwaymen and outlaws from the fifties to the eighties, [by] Joseph Henry Jackson. New York, Harcourt, Brace and co. [1949]. Pict. cloth. OP.

xx p., 1 l., 3–346 p. plates, ports., relief map, facsms. (all in one section). 22 cm.
Notes on sources: p. 327–330; appendix: p. 331–335; index: p. 337–346.
Half title; "First edition" on copyright p.

One of the best books on California outlaws, this volume shows scholarly research. Many accounts of such outlaws as Murieta are revealed as legendary. It also contains good accounts of other California outlaws, such as Tom Bell, Rattlesnake Dick, Black Bart, Dick Fellows, and Tiburcio Vásquez.

1121. ———

The creation of Joaquín Murieta, [by] Joseph Henry Jackson. Stiff wrappers. (Cover title.) OP.

176–181 p. 23 cm.
Double column.
Reprinted from the *Pacific Spectator,* Volume II, No. 2, Spring, 1948.

Deals largely with the legends which have been created about Murieta.

1122. ———

Tintypes in gold; four studies in robbery, [by] Joseph Henry Jackson. Decorations by Giacomo Patri. New York, the Macmillan co., 1939. Cloth. Scarce.

5 p.l., 191 p. 20.8 cm.
Half title; illus. end papers; headpieces; vignette; "First edition" on copyright p.

Contains thorough studies of four celebrated California outlaws—Black Bart, Rattlesnake Dick, Dick Fellows, and Tom Bell—later incorporated into the author's *Bad Company* (Item 1120).

1123. Jackson, Mary E.

The life of Nellie C. Bailey; or, a Romance of the west, written by Mary E. Jackson. . . . Topeka, Kans., R. E. Martin & co., printers and binders, 1885. Dec. cloth. Very scarce.

4 p.l., [7]–399 p. front. (port.), plates, ports. 19 cm.

Primarily about a strange murder case which created a sensation in the early West, the book also gives an account of the hanging of Ben Wheeler and Henry Brown for the robbery of the Medicine Lodge bank.

1124. Jackson, Orich

The white conquest of Arizona. History of the pioneers, by Orich Jackson. Los Angeles, Calif., the Grafton co. (inc.), published by the West Coast magazine [1908]. Wrappers. Scarce.

2 p.l., [9]–52 p. plates, ports. 21.4 cm.

Has a chapter on early bad men of Arizona and the Montana gang.

1125. Jackson, Ralph Semmes

Home on Double bayou. Memories of an east Texas ranch, by Ralph Semmes Jackson. Illustrated by Bubi Kessen. Introduction by J. Frank Dobie. Austin, University of Texas press [1961]. Pict. cloth.

11 p.l., 3–136 p. illus. (headpieces), 2 ports., 2 maps. 23.5 cm.

Contains a chapter, entitled "Law and Order on Double Bayou," about an outlaw family in Chambers County, Texas.

1126. Jahns, Pat

The frontier world of Doc Holliday, faro dealer from Dallas to Deadwood, by Pat Jahns. New York, Hastings House, publishers [1957]. Cloth and boards.

xii p., 1 l., 3–305 p. 21.6 cm.
Bibliography: p. 287–293; index: p. 295–305.
Half title; footnotes after each chapter.

Perhaps the best biography of Doc Holliday thus far. It gives much information about Dodge City, Fort Griffin, and Tombstone; the Earps, the Clantons, the O K Corral fight; and Bat Masterson, Luke Short, and many other western gunmen.

1127. [James Boys]

Bank and train robbers of the West, James boys, Younger boys, etc. [N.p., n.d.] Cloth. (Cover title.) Scarce.

5 p.l., 9–287 p. front., illus., plates. 20 cm.

1128. ———

Centennial, 1856–1956, Kearney, Missouri. [Kearney, Mo., 1956.] Stiff pict. wrappers. (Cover title.) Ring hinged.

112 [1] p. plates, ports., plat. 28 cm.
Adv. scattered throughout.

Issued in celebration of Kearney's centennial, at which the robbing of the bank by the James boys was re-enacted. Contains a section on the James boys and tells about the bombing of the Samuel home near Kearney.

1129. ———

Die wilden Grenzrauber. Die furchtbare Geschichte der Thaten und Abenteuer von Frank und Jesse James. . . . Chicago, Ill. [n.d.]. Pict. wrappers. Rare.

1 p.l., [3]–96 p. plates, ports. 22.4 cm.

The story of the James boys in German.

1130. ———

Frank James and his brother Jesse, the daring border bandits. Baltimore, I. & M. Ottenheimer, publishers [1915]. Pict. wrappers. Scarce.

3 p.l., 7–186 [6] p. illus. 18.7 cm.
6 p. adv. at end.

One of the many cheap and sensational outlaw books issued by these publishers, none of which are of any historical value.

1131. ———

The James boys. A complete and accurate recital of the daredevil criminal career of the famous bandit brothers Frank and Jesse James, and their noted band of bank plunderers. . . . Chicago, the Henneberry co. [n.d.]. Cloth. Scarce.

x, 11–249 p. illus. 19 cm.

6 p. adv. at end.

Also published with same title by M. A. Donohue & co., Chicago, without date, in pictorial wrappers and with 8 p. adv. at end.

The two editions are exactly alike in both text and illustrations. Both bestow on Quantrill the given names Charles William and repeat the false story that his brother was killed in Kansas.

1132. ———

James Brödern eller, Missouris mest ryktbara röfvare öch mördare, Frank öch Jesse James. Minneapolis, Minn., J. Leachman & son, Forlaggare [n.d.]. Wrappers. Rare.

3–128 p. illus. 18.7 cm.

The story of the James boys in Norwegian.

1133. ———

Lives, adventures and exploits of Frank and Jesse James, with an account of the tragic death of Jesse James, April 3rd, 1882. The last daring feats of the James confederacy in the robbery and murder on the Rock Island train, July 14th, 1881; and at Glendale, Mo., September 17, 1881. [N.p., n.d.] Pict. wrappers. (Cover title.) Scarce.

[3]–96 p. front., illus. 22 cm.

Another book was published under this same title ca. 1892, with entirely different text and illustrations.

[125] p. (no pagination). front., illus. 18.7 cm.

Both books are worthless historically. The first book has a chapter on the robbery of the Union Pacific by Joel Collins and Sam Bass in order to bring Jesse James into the picture. The author claims that one of the robbers in this holdup was unknown but declares that it was Jesse. He also places the value of the loot at $100,000 instead of the $60,000, which the records show was the correct amount. Both books contain conversation that no one could have reliably recorded.

1134. ———

The Northfield raid. Fiftieth anniversary finds interest undimmed in the oft-told tale of repulse of the James-Younger gang. Wrappers. (Cover title.) Scarce.

22 p. plates, ports., facsm. 21.2 cm.
Double column.

Reprinted from the *Northfield News* of August 17 and September 3, 10, and 17, 1926.

1135. ———

The notorious outlaw, Jesse James, shot down by his pal. New York, John W. Morrison, publisher [n.d.]. Pict. wrappers. (Cover title.) Rare.

13 p. illus. 29.3 cm.
Double column.

Tells of the killing of Jesse James and has material on the Youngers.

1136. ———

A thrilling story of the adventures and exploits of Frank and Jesse James, containing a complete sketch of the romance of guerrilla warfare. . . . A graphic account of the tragic end of Jesse James. . . . [N.p., n.d., ca. 1892.] Pict. wrappers. Scarce.

[125] p. (no pagination). front. (port.), plate. 18.7 cm.

As in several other such books, Dick Liddill's last name is erroneously spelled Little.

1137. ———

Train and bank robbers of the west. A romantic but faithful story of bloodshed and plunder, perpetrated by Missouri's daring outlaws. A thrilling story of adventure and exploits of Frank and Jesse James, Missouri's twin wraiths of robbery and murder, containing a complete sketch of the romance of guerrilla warfare. Together with a graphic and detailed account of the robberies and murders of twenty years; and the last daring feats of the James' confederacy in the robbery and murder on the Rock Island train, July 14th, 1881, and at Glendale, Mo., Sept. 17th, 1881; to which is added an account of the tragic end of Jesse James, shot by a confederate, April 3d, 1882. Together with a record of the wild and reckless career of the Younger brothers now incarcerated in the penitentiary at Stillwater, Minn. . . . Chicago, Belford, Clarke & co.; St. Louis, Belford & Clarke publishing co. MDCCCLXXXII. Cloth. Rare.

Part I, 6 p. l., [9]–358 p. front., plates. 19.8 cm.
Part II, [9]–287 p. plates. 19.8 cm.

Part II is the same as Appler's *Guerrillas of the West*, 1876 edition (Item 68). Note the similarity of nearly all these books about the James brothers.

1138. ———

The wild bandits of the border. A thrilling story of the adventures and exploits of Frank and Jesse James, Missouri's twin wraiths of robbery and murder. . . . Chicago, Belford, Clarke & co.; St. Louis, Belford & Clarke publishing co. [1881]. Pict. wrappers. Scarce.

4 p.l., 9–313 p. 19.5 cm.

Published also by Laird and Lee of Chicago in several editions. Also published in Chicago by Donohue, Henneberry & co. [1891]. Pict. wrappers. Scarce.

5 p.l., 9–367 p. plates, ports. 19.3 cm.
Pinkerton Detective series, No. 8.

Most of these cheap books about the James boys were copied from the preceding books.

1139. James, Edgar

The Allen outlaws. A complete history of their lives and exploits, concluding with the Hillsville courthouse tragedy, by Edgar James. Profusely illustrated. Baltimore, published by Phoenix publishing co. [1912]. Pict. wrappers. Scarce.

5 p.l., 13–191 p. front., ports. 19 cm.

1140. ———

James boys; deeds and daring. A complete record of their lives and death. . . . Baltimore, I. & M. Ottenheimer [1911]. Pict. wrappers. Scarce.

182 p. front., illus. 19.5 cm.

1141. ———

The lives and adventures, daring holdups, train and bank robberies of the world's most desperate bandits and highwaymen, the notorious James brothers. The latest and most complete story of the daring crimes of these famous desperadoes ever published. Containing many sensational escapades never before made public, by Edgar James. Baltimore, I. & M. Ottenheimer, publishers [1913]. Pict. wrappers. OP.

3 p.l., 9–192 p. front., illus. 19.6 cm.

1142. [**James, Frank**]

Frank James and his brother Jesse. The daring border bandits. Baltimore, I. & M. Ottenheimer, publishers [1915]. Pict. wrappers. Scarce.

2 p.l., 7–186 p. front., illus. 18.5 cm.
6 p. adv. at end.

1143. ———

Life and trial of Frank James. [New York, Frank Tousey, 1883.] Pict. wrappers. (Cover title.) Scarce.

2–28 [4] p. 28.4 cm.

4 p. adv. at end; double column.

Republished in facsimile in 1952 except for the omission of the second story, "The Clink of Gold," pages 21 to 28 in the original edition, and a change of advertisements.

1144. ———

The only true history of the life of Frank James, written by himself. [Pine Bluff, Ark., Norton printing co., 1926.] Wrappers. (Cover title.) Rare.

4 p.l., 7–134 p. plates, ports. 15.2 cm.

This is one of the most brazen bits of writing it has been my experience to read. The author claims to be Frank James, although he says that his mother's name was Agnes Collins and that his father's last name was Nelson. Then, in the latter part of the book, he says that his father was Ed Reed, a brother of Jim Reed, and that he "was a base begotten child."

The real Frank James was pardoned and restored to full citizenship; yet this claimant to the name lived in Newton County, Arkansas, for forty years under the name Joe Vaughn, trying, he says, to hide his identity. According to his account, most of his life was spent among the Indians of Indian Territory.

Among other unbelievable things, he writes: "Readers, I know it will be hard to make people believe that I am the only Frank James that ever existed, and there never was a real Frank James, that the boy Frank James was none other than Edd Reed." He further states that "the world thinks that Robert Ford killed Jesse James, but I will say right here that the James boys were never captured."

The real Frank James died on the Samuel farm near Kearney, Missouri, on February 18, 1915. It is a well-known fact that after his pardon he worked as a shoe salesman in Missouri and Dallas, Texas; that he was employed in St. Louis as a doorkeeper at the Standard Theatre; and that at various times he acted as starter at the fairgrounds in St. Louis. He did not have to hide out on a farm in Arkansas afraid to reveal his identity.

The author says that his book was finished on December 10, 1925, ten years and ten months after the death of the real Frank James. (The author died February 14, 1926.) This worthless little book was published by his daughter, Sarah E. Snow, who upholds her father's claims. It is full of typographical errors, misspelled proper names, and confused geography. He says that "a short time after Jim Reed died Bell [*sic*] married Henry Starr. Henry Starr was killed in a pistol duel with a United States Marshal." Both statements are false.

Burton Rascoe, in his *Belle Starr, the Bandit Queen*, says that this book "is maudlin, illiterate, vague, confused, pathetic." Yet a few paragraphs later he says, "It is quite probable that, when he was on his uppers, he [Frank James] wrote this story of his life as it was published eleven years after his death. . . . There is something so pathetic about its general style and information that I have a deep suspicion that Frank James may actually have written it and that no 'ghost' or collaborator helped him out in the least."

I fail to see how Rascoe could possibly have arrived at this conclusion. Certainly, Frank James, as has been pointed out, did not hide out, nor did he need to. Much trash has been written about the James boys, but both Frank and Jesse would turn in their graves if they knew about this one.

1145. [James, Jesse]

Good-bye, Jesse! [Kansas City, Mo., published by the Kansas City Posse of the Westerners, 1959.] Pamphlet. (Cover title.) Pict. wrappers. OP.

20 p. 23 cm.

Introduction by Martin E. Ismert; double column.

Colophon: "This publication, by the Kansas City Posse of the Westerners, is limited to 500 copies of which this is No. ——."

A facsimile of the account of Jesse James's murder and some of his activities as appeared in the *Kansas City Daily Journal* of April 4, 1882.

1146. ——

Good bye Jesse James. A reprinting of six of the best news stories concerning the career and death of America's most famous outlaw, first printed in the *Kansas City Daily Journal* in 1882. Compiled and published by the Jesse James Bank Museum. Liberty, Missouri [n.d.]. Stiff pict. wrappers.

vii, 160 p. 21.2 cm.

Excerpts from the *Kansas City Daily Journal* dealing mostly with Jesse's death.

1147. ——

The inspiring story of a remarkable pioneer—Joseph Robidoux—who built the city—St. Joseph, Missouri. [N.p., n.d.] Pict. wrappers. (Cover title.) Scarce.

15 p. plates. 22.9 x 12 cm.

Tells of the murder of Jesse James by Bob Ford.

1148. ——

Jesse James: the life and daring adventures of this bold highwayman and bank robber and his no less celebrated brother, Frank James. Together with the thrilling exploits of the Younger boys. Written by xxx (one who dare not now disclose his identity.) The only book containing the romantic life of Jesse James and his pretty wife who clung to him to the last! Philadelphia, Pa., published by Barclay & co. . . . [1882]. Pict. wrappers. Rare.

19–96 p. illus., plates, ports. 23.5 cm.

Cover title: "The Life and Tragic Death of Jesse James, the Western desperado."

Port. of Jesse on front cover; port. of Jesse's father on back cover. (Neither correct.)

Republished in 1883 and 1886, and again in 1915, in facsimile, by William F. Kelleher, Cliffside Park, N.J. Cloth. OP.

1 p.l., 19–96 p. illus., ports. 22 cm.

Published in facsimile again by the Steck-Vaughn co., of Austin, Texas, in 1966. Pict. cloth. In slip case.

vii p., 2 l., 19–96 p. front., illus., plates, ports. 24.2 cm.

1149. ———

The St. Joseph Daily Gazette supplement. St. Joseph, Mo., April 9, 1882. (Newspaper.) Exceedingly rare.

4 p. ports., plan. Six columns to the page.

This practically unprocurable ephemera is a separate issue of the newspaper devoted entirely to the life, death, and burial of Jesse James. Printed less than a week after Jesse's murder, it is the primary source for many of the books on the James boys which followed. It is the only newspaper item included in this work, but I feel its importance justifies a place here.

1150. James, Jesse, Jr.

Jesse James, my father, written by Jesse James, Jr. . . . The first and only true story of his adventures ever written. Published and distributed by Jesse James, Jr. . . . Independence, Mo., the Sentinel printing co., 1899. Pict. wrappers. Rare.

2 p.l., [5]–194 p. ports. 19.6 cm.

Reprinted in Cleveland, Ohio, Arthur Westbrook co., ca. 1906. Wrappers. Scarce.

2 p.l., [15]–189 p. front., ports. 18.7 cm.

3 p. adv. at end.

Reprinted again in Dayton, Ohio, 1934.

2 p.l., [5]–194 p. 18.5 cm.

And again in Cleveland by the Buckeye publishing co.

Jesse James, Jr., says that he wrote this little book "to correct false impressions that the public have about the character of my father." In the latter part of the book he tells about his own life and the accusations that he was a train robber himself.

1151. ———

The facsimile edition of Jesse James, my father. The first and only true story of his adventures ever written, by Jesse James, Jr. With a foreword by William F. Kelleher. New York, Frederick Fell, inc., publishers [1957]. Cloth. OP.

7 p.l., [5]–198 [1] p. 4 ports. 18.4 cm.

1152. James, Jesse Lee, III

Jesse James and the lost cause, by Jesse Lee James III. New York, Pageant press [1961]. Cloth.

5 p.l., 11–183 p. 20.7 cm.
Appendix: p. 171–183.
Half title.

Another of those books claiming that Jesse James lived until 1951 under the name J. Frank Dalton. It is so full of ridiculous errors that it took seventeen pages to skim over them lightly in my *Burs Under the Saddle* (Item 7).

1153. James, John

My experience with Indians, by John James. Austin, Texas, Gammel's book store [1925]. Cloth. Scarce.

5 p.l., 13–147 p. front. (port.), plates, ports. 19.7 cm.
Half title.

Gives some false history about Belle Starr (whose name the author spells Bell Star), saying that her father was a U.S. Army officer and that she was a half-blood Cherokee.

1154. James, John Towers

The Benders of Kansas, by John T. James, attorney for the defense in the trial of the "Bender woman" at Oswego, Labette county, in 1889–1890. The complete story; facts, not fiction. Wichita, Kans., published by the Kan-Okla publishing co. [1913]. Cloth. Pict. label pasted on. Rare.

4 p.l., [11]–173 p. illus., ports., plan. 20.7 cm.

A full history of those unparalleled killers, related by their defense lawyer, who must have known the facts. There are several typographical errors, as well as some misspellings.

1155. James, Marquis

The Cherokee strip; a tale of an Oklahoma boyhood, [by] Marquis James. New York, the Viking press, 1945. Pict. cloth. OP.

6 p.l., 3–294 p. 21.8 cm.

Half title; map on end papers; vignette.

Also published in a de luxe signed edition, and in several trade editions thereafter.

In his youth the author was much impressed by the outlaw Dick Yeager and devotes a chapter to him in this book.

1156. ———

They had their hour, by Marquis James.... Indianapolis, the Bobbs-Merrill co., publishers [1934]. Cloth. OP.

5 p.l., 11–324 p. 23.7 cm.

Notes: p. 301–302; index: p. 305–324.

Half title; "First edition" on copyright p.

As in the previous book, Dick Yeager comes in for much attention, as does the Jennings gang. The author is mistaken in saying that Charlie Pearce was nicknamed Tulsa Jack. The real name of the latter was Blake. He also spells Buck Weightman's last name Wateman. I have never before seen it spelled other than Weightman or Waightman.

1157. James, Vinton Lee

Frontier and pioneer recollections of early days in San Antonio and West Texas, by Vinton Lee James. San Antonio, Texas, published by the author, Press Artes Graficas, 1938. Cloth. Rare.

7 p.l., 15–210 p. plates, ports. 23.9 cm.

Half title.

The author tells about King Fisher and his death and makes some mention of Billy the Kid, but says the Kid was from Arizona.

1158. James, William F., and George H. McMurray

History of San Jose, California. Narrative and biographical, by William F. James and George H. McMurray. Paul Gordon Trall, biographical editor. San Jose, Calif., A. S. Cawston, publisher, 1933. Cloth. Scarce.

2 p.l., [3]–243 [1] p. front., plates, ports. 26.5 cm.

Biographical sketches: p. [169]–239; index: p. [240]–243.

Contains some minor information on Joaquín Murieta and Tiburcio Vásquez.

1159. Jameson, Henry B.

Heroes by the dozen . . ., by Henry B. Jameson. First (Kansas centennial) edition. . . . Abilene, Kans., printed and bound . . . by Shadinger-Wilson printers, inc., 1961. . . . Pict. cloth.

3 p.l., 203 p. plates, ports., maps. 23.5 cm.

Copyright notice on t.p.

This author repeats some of the false legends about Wild Bill Hickok, has an inaccurate account of the killing of Phil Coe, and is wrong in saying that Dave Tutt was the first man Hickok killed. He is also mistaken in saying that Hickok "nipped a raid" in Kansas City when Jesse James was trying to rob the Fair of 1872. That robbery was successful, and Wild Bill was not present. The author also has Hickok in the Bella Union Saloon instead of the No. 10 Saloon when he was killed, and is wrong in saying that Jack McCall had been hunting Hickok "all the way from Texas to collect Mrs. Coe's reward." There are many other errors.

1160. ———

Miracle of the Chisholm trail, by Henry B. Jameson. [N.p., published by the Tri-State Chisholm Trail Centennial Commission . . ., n.d., ca. 1967.] Stiff wrappers.

2 p.l., 52 p. front. (map), plates, ports. 23 cm.

Contains chapters on Tom Smith and one on Wild Bill Hickok. In his chapter on Hickok the author says that "many of the stories about his escapades in Abilene and elsewhere are grossly exaggerated or were pure fabrications in the first place" yet he follows old legends in saying that Hickok "wiped out the McCanles gang of robbers at Rock Creek, Nebraska, stage coach station in 1861." The author also has Hickok making "a deal with the famous Jesse James to lay off the rich Abilene payrolls and cattle receipts in turn for 'protection' from the law at intervals when the James gang needed hiding, rest and supplies."

He also repeats the fable that after Hickok shot Phil Coe he sent for a preacher to pray for him, and also the one that Coe's mother offered $10,000 to anyone who would bring Hickok's head to her. The author says that Hickok later showed up in Deadwood, South Dakota, with his "old girl friend," Calamity Jane, and he is mistaken in having Hickok killed in the Bell [*sic*] Union Saloon. He is also wrong in saying that Jack McCall was from Texas. Most writers seem to credit Texas with all the outlaws. He writes, "McCall was tried, convicted and hanged," as though this happened immediately after Hickok's murder, but he was first tried in Deadwood and released. His conviction and hanging came later at Yankton as the result of a second trial.

1161. Jaramillo, Cleofas M.

Shadows of the past (Sombras del pasado), by Cleofas M. Jaramillo. Illustrated by the author. Santa Fe, Seton Village press [1941]. Pict. boards. Scarce.

3 p.l., 11–115 [1] p. front., illus. 23.5 cm.
Half title.

Contains a chapter on bandits, among them being Miguel Maes and Vicente Silva.

1162. [Jebb, Mrs. John Gladwyn]

A strange career. Life and adventures of John Gladwyn Jebb, by his widow. With an introduction by H. Rider Haggard. With portraits. Edinburgh and London, William Blackwood and sons, MDCCCXCV. Pict. cloth. Scarce.

xxv, 335 [32] p. front. (port. with tissue). 21 cm.
Half title; 32 numbered pages of adv. at end.

Some western experiences with the lawless.

1163. Jelinek, George

Ellsworth, Kansas, 1867–1947, by George Jelinek. Salina, [Kans.], published by Consolidated [1947]. Stiff wrappers. OP.

2 p.l., 5–32 p. plates, ports., facsm. 21.5 cm.
Vignette.

This little book tells about Ellsworth as a cow town and relates the story of the killing of Sheriff Whitney by Bill Thompson. The author is mistaken, however, in having Wyatt Earp arrest Ben Thompson at this time. Though Earp took credit for it, he was not in Ellsworth at the time.

1164. ———

90 years of Ellsworth and Ellsworth county history, by George Jelinek. Published in conjunction with Ellsworth's 90th anniversary observation, August, 1957. [Ellsworth, Kans., the Messenger press, 1957.] Stiff pict. wrappers. OP.

[69] p. (no pagination). 17.2 cm.
Double column.

Has material on Wyatt Earp, Ben Thompson, Bat Masterson, and the wild days of Ellsworth. The author repeats the tale that Earp arrested Ben Thompson when Sheriff Whitney was killed. Earp was not in Ellsworth at the time.

1165. Jenkins, A. O.

Olive's last roundup, by A. O. Jenkins. [Loup City, Nebr., the Sherman County Times, n.d.] Wrappers. Rare.

[98] p. (no pagination). front. (port.), plates, ports. 16.8 cm.
Last 17 p. adv.

This rare little book is the story of I. P. Olive and his lynching and burning of Luther Mitchell and Ami Ketchum. There is also some information on Doc Middleton.

1166. Jenkinson, Michael

Ghost towns of New Mexico. Playthings of the wind, by Michael Jenkinson, with photographs by Karl Kernberger. [Albuquerque, N.M.], University of New Mexico press, 1967. Cloth.

6 p.l., 156 p. plates, map. 21.8 x 26 cm. (oblong).
Bibliography: p. 155.
Half title; double illus. t.p.

Some of these ghost towns were the hangouts of the southwestern outlaws, such as Black Jack Ketchum, the Apache Kid, Sandy King, Russian Bill, Zwing Hunt, and Billy the Kid. As late as 1967 we find the author still repeating the old legends about Billy the Kid killing twenty-one men by the time he was twenty-one years old. The author has the Kid conferring with Governor Wallace at a hotel in White Oaks, but it is a well-known fact that the Kid met the governor at the home of Squire John B. Wilson in Lincoln.

The author is mistaken in saying that the Kid's gang was stealing cattle from the Mescalero Apache reservation and that "when the Indian agent objected, the Kid shot him." The author is also mistaken in saying that the Kid and his gang were captured at Stinking Springs on Christmas Eve of 1880. They were captured December 23. He also says that this capture was accomplished "after a prolonged battle," but there was no battle. Charlie Bowdre was killed when he attempted to come out to feed the horses, and sometime after that the others surrendered. Finally, on the night of the Kid's murder, the author says that Garrett shot three times—"perhaps the most celebrated shots in the annals of Western history"—but the records show that Garrett shot only twice, his second shot missing the Kid entirely.

1167. Jennewein, J. Leonard

Calamity Jane of the western trails, by J. Leonard Jennewein. Huron, S.D. Dakota books [1953]. Stiff pict. wrappers. Scarce.

2 p.l., 5–47 p. plates, ports., facsms. 22.5 cm.
Bibliography: p. 39–46.

Published in an edition of three thousand copies, this little book gives some new material on Calamity Jane and debunks some of the old legends.

1168. ———, and Jane Boorman (eds.)

Dakota panorama. Edited by J. Leonard Jennewein and Jane Boorman. [Sioux Falls, S.D., Midwest-Beach printing co.], 1961. Pict. cloth.

vii, 468 p. front., illus., plates, ports., maps, facsms., cattle brands. 26 cm.
South Dakota reading list: p. 400–442; index: p. 443–463; picture credits: p. 465.
Half title.

Gives an account of the killing of Wild Bill Hickok and the trial and hanging of Jack McCall.

1169. Jennings, Alphonso J.

Beating back, by A. Jennings and Will Irwin. Illustrated by Charles M. Russell. New York and London, D. Appleton and co., 1914. Cloth. Scarce.

5 p.l., 354 [1] p. front., plates, ports. 20 cm.
Half title; pub. device; first edition: figure (1) at end of text.

An autobiography of Al Jennings, edited and with an introduction by Will Irwin. Jennings tells about his start in outlawry, his life in prison, and his comeback after his release. This account was originally published serially in the *Saturday Evening Post* in seven installments, September–November, 1913, and was accompanied by eight illustrations by Charles M. Russell. The book carries eight illustrations, but only three of them by Russell. Jennings was not considered much of an outlaw.

1170. ———

Hors la loi! . . . La vie d'un outlaw Américain racontés par lui-même; traduction et adaptation de l'Américain et du slang par Blaise Cendrars. Paris, B. Grasset [1936]. Wrappers. Scarce.

332 p., 1 l. front. (port.). 19 cm.
At head of title: Al Jennings.

A French version of the life and crimes of Al Jennings.

1171. ———

Number 30664, by Number 31539. A sketch of the lives of William Sidney Porter (O. Henry) and Al Jennings, the bandit, by Al Jennings. Hollywood, Calif., the Pioneer press [1941]. Stiff wrappers. Rare.

4 p.l., 11–32 p. front. (port.), 2 additional ports. 21.3 cm.

A story of the prison life of O. Henry and Al Jennings.

1172. ———

Through the shadows with O. Henry, by Al Jennings. . . . Illustrated. New York, the H. K. Fly co., publishers [1921]. Pict. cloth. Scarce.

6 p.l., [11]–320 p. front., plates, ports. 21 cm.
Half title; pub. device.

This book deals mostly with Jennings' prison life and his friendship with O. Henry, who was confined in the same prison. As an Oklahoma outlaw familiar with the officers of that state, the author should have known better than call E. D. Nix by the name "Ed Nicks."

1173. Jennings, Napoleon Augustus

A Texas ranger, by N. A. Jennings. New York, Charles Scribner's sons, 1899. Col. pict. cloth. Very scarce.

x p., 1 l., 321 p. 19 cm.

Reprinted by Southwest press, Dallas, in 1930, with a foreword by J. Frank Dobie.

xv, 287 p. 24 cm.
Untrimmed.

Reprinted again in facsimile by the Steck co., Austin, Texas, 1959. Pict. cloth. In slip case.

Reprinted again by the Frontier Book co., Ruidoso, N.M., 1960. Cloth.

The first edition is exceedingly scarce, and the reprints are also becoming scarce. The book contains much material on Texas gunmen, such as John Wesley Hardin and King Fisher, and the Taylor-Sutton feud and other border troubles. The author is mistaken when he says that Sam Bass was killed "by Lee Hall and others of the Rangers." He is also mistaken when he says that Ben Thompson and King Fisher had gone to the Variety Theatre in San Antonio "for the express purpose of cleaning it out" when they were killed there.

1174. Jensen, Ann (ed.)

Texas ranger's diary and scrapbook, edited by Ann Jensen. Dallas, Texas, the Kaleidograph press [1936]. Cloth. Scarce.

6 p.l., 13–81 p. front., illus. 19.8 cm.

This small book is composed of short sketches about various subjects, among them one on Bass Outlaw and another on the killing of John Selman.

1175. Jerrett, Herman Daniel

California's El Dorado yesterday and today, [by] Herman Daniel Jerrett. Sacramento, Calif., press of Jo Anderson, 1915. Pict. cloth. OP.

6 p.l., 13–141 p. illus., plates, ports. 19.6 cm.
Half title.

Has a chapter on stage robbers.

1176. Jocknick, Sidney

Early days on the western slope of Colorado, and campfire chats with Otto Mears, the pathfinder, from 1870 to 1883, inclusive, by Sidney Jocknick. Denver, Colo., the Carson-Harper co., MCMXIII. Cloth. Scarce.

4 p.l., [9]–384 p. front. (port., signature in facsm.), plates, ports., map. 20.2 cm.
Appendix: p. [341]–384.

One chapter treats of Alferd Packer and his terrible crimes of murder and cannibalism, and another deals with George Howard, the highwayman.

1177. Johnson, Barry C. (ed.)

The English Westerners' 10th anniversary publication, 1964. A collection of original papers on American frontier history, contributed by members of the English Westerners' Society, edited by Barry C. Johnson. London, published by the English Westerners' Society, 1964.

1 p.l., 3–67 [1] p. illus., plates, maps. 24.2 cm.
Double column; "First printing of 500 copies."

Contains a chapter on the life of Tom Pickett, a companion of Billy the Kid, and one on the hanging of Jack McCall. All the chapters are well documented.

1178. Johnson, Dorothy M.

Famous lawmen of the old west, by Dorothy M. Johnson. Illustrated with photographs. New York, Dodd, Mead & co., 1963. Pict. cloth.

9 p.l., 15–151 p. ports. 21.5 cm.
Bibliography: p. 143–147; index: p. 149–151; short biography of author at end.
Half title; pub. device; untrimmed.

The author has Wild Bill Hickok elected sheriff of Hays City and says that at the end of his term he was re-elected. Hickok was not elected sheriff but was appointed city marshal. She is also mistaken in having McCall going to Cheyenne after he killed Hickok and there boasting of his deed. She repeats the fable about Wyatt Earp arresting Ben Thompson in Ellsworth after the killing of Sheriff Whitney. Her account of the fight at the O K Corral is also inaccurate. In fact, the whole book is full of errors, too many to list here.

1179. ———

Some went west, [by] Dorothy M. Johnson. Illustrated with photographs. New York, Dodd, Mead & co. [1965]. Cloth.

xii, 180 p. illus., plates, ports. 20.7 cm.
Bibliography: p. 175–177; index: p. 178–180.
Half title; vignette.

The author devotes several pages to Joseph Slade and his hanging. There are also some pages on Henry Plummer, Jack Cleveland, and the hanging of George Ives.

1180. Johnson, Francis

Big Goliath; or, the terror of the mines, by the author of steel arm; or, the robbers and regulators of California. . . . New York, Dick and Fitzgerald, publishers [1862]. Pict. wrappers. Rare.

19–107 p. 22 cm.

1181. ———

Steel arm; or robbers and regulators of California. . . . New York, Dick and Fitzgerald, publishers [1862]. Pict. wrappers. Rare.

19–111 p. 22 cm.

This item and Item 1180 constitute two more examples of the early dime novel which are of no historical value but are collectors' items.

1182. Johnson, (Mrs.) Grover C.

Wagon yard, by Mrs. Grover C. Johnson. Illustrated by Jerry Bywaters. Dallas, William T. Tardy [1938]. Cloth. Scarce.

3 p.l., 201 p. front., illus. 23.5 cm.

This book contains some minor and unreliable information about Billy the Kid. The author spells Quantrill's name as Quantrail and makes the statement that a Kansas jayhawker killed the father of the James boys and shot off one of their mother's arms. She says that Kid Lewis and Foster Crawford robbed a bank in Wichita Falls, Texas, but is mistaken in calling them members of the Al Jennings gang. Her information on Jim Murphy is confused; she claims that he was "imported" to trap Sam Bass. She also repeats the old fable about Jesse James and the widow whose mortgage was about to be foreclosed by the cruel landlord, whom Jesse paid off and then robbed to get the money back. Variations of this legend have been told since the days of Robin Hood.

1183. Johnson, W. F.

History of Cooper county, Missouri, [by] W. F. Johnson. Illustrated. Topeka, Cleveland, Historical publishing co., 1919. Three-quarter leather. Scarce.

10 p.l., [33]–1166 p. front. (port.), plates, ports. 27.7 cm.

Contains an account of the Otterville train robbery by the James and Younger boys.

1184. [Johnson County War]

The cattle baron's rebellion against law and order. A true history of the Johnson county invasion by an armed band of assassins. As published in the *Buffalo Bulletin*. Dedicated to the "Rustlers" of Johnson and other counties who rustled at the risk of their lives to defend their homes, their lives and their constitutional rights. [N.p., n.d., ca. Buffalo, 1892.] Folder. (Cover title.) Excessively rare.

[5] p. (no pagination). 30 cm.
Triple column.

This pamphlet, rare in the original edition, makes many serious accusations and calls names, listing some of Wyoming's most prominent cattlemen. Every effort was made to destroy all the copies and was so successful that only a few copies are known to exist. It originally appeared in the *Buffalo Bulletin* and ten days later was issued in folder form.

In 1955 the Branding Iron Press of Evanston, Illinois, reprinted it in a limited edition of one thousand copies. The text is placed in a half-pocket of a stiff pictorial wrapper on the inside of which is an introduction giving the details about the origin of the pamphlet and the history of the period. The editor makes the statement that this printing was made from the only known copy, but I examined another copy in the Library of the American Antiquarian Society, of Worcester, Massachusetts.

1185. Johnston, Alva

The legendary Mizners, by Alva Johnston. N.Y., Farrar, Straus and Young [1953]. Cloth and boards. OP.

5 p.l., 3–304 p. illus. 21.5 cm.
Half title; illus. double t.p.

Has a long chapter on Soapy Smith, with whom the Mizners had some association in the Klondike.

1186. Johnston, Charles Haven Ladd

Famous scouts, including trappers, pioneers, and soldiers of the frontier. Their hazardous and exciting adventures in the mighty drama of the white conquest of the American continent, by Charles H. L. Johnston. . . . Illustrated. Boston, L. C. Page & co. [1910]. Pict. cloth. Scarce.

ix p., 2 l., 340 [14] p. front., plates, ports. 20.5 cm.
Last 14 p. adv.

Republished in May, and again in September, 1911.

xi, 2 l., 348 p. front., ports. 20.5 cm.
20 p. adv. at end.

The author starts his chapter about Hickok by describing him as lying on the floor of a dugout bleeding "from many deep and dangerous wounds." This scene supposedly takes place after the "fight" at Rock Creek Station, which the author erroneously places in Kansas instead of Nebraska.

Mr. Eisele (Item 668) seems to have drawn heavily from this book, both in incorrect dates and in wording. The author continues the misspelling of McCanles' name and has them named Jack and Jim, as so many before him have done. Continuing to slander their character, he has them "killing more innocent men and running off more horses than any ranchers in this here country." He gives the same version of the Rock Creek affair as Buel and Hough do and claims that that version is the true one because it is "from Wild Bill's own recital of the fight as reported by James William Buel." The rest of the book is just as unreliable.

1187. Johnston, Harry V.

The last roundup, by H. V. Johnston. [Minneapolis, Minn., published by H. V. Johnston publishing co., n.d.] Cloth. OP.

6 p.l., 336 p. front., illus., plates. 22.3 cm.
Half title.

Has some material on the gunfighters of Dodge City and of Wyatt Earp and Curly Bill Brocius of Tombstone, and tells of the killing of Wild Bill Hickok.

1188. ———

My home on the range. Frontier life in the Bad Lands, by Harry V. Johnston. St. Paul, Minn., printed by the Webb publishing co. [1942]. Pict. cloth. OP.

6 p.l., 313 p. front. (port.), illus., plates, ports., cattle brands. 23.5 cm.
Vignette.

A book of reminiscences which contains some minor information on Wild Bill Hickok and Calamity Jane, as well as unreliable statements about Bill Dalton. The author says that Bill Dalton, "brother of the famous Daltons in the South," after planning to hold up the Northern Pacific, failed to show up, and his partners later found that he had killed himself. Of course, we know that Bill Dalton was killed in Oklahoma.

1189. Johnston, James A.

Alcatraz Island prison and the men who live there, by Warden James A. Johnston. New York, Charles Scribner's sons; London, Charles Scribner's sons, ltd., 1949. Cloth. OP.

v p., 2 l., 276 p. plates, ports., plan (double p.). 21.6 cm.
Index: p. 269–276.
Half title; first edition: letter "A" on copyright p.

Tells of many criminals, among them one fitting the particular subject of this work, Roy Gardner, a latter-day train robber. A chapter on this character tells of his life and suicide.

1190. Johnston, Philip

Lost and living cities of the California gold rush. A motoring and historical guide to the principal early mining camps first issued at Coloma, California, Jan. 24, 1948, on the centenary of the discovery of gold at Sutter's Mill, by Philip Johnston. Introduction by Phil Townsend Hanna. [Los Angeles, printed by Pacific press, inc.] Published by the Touring Bureau of the Automobile Club of Southern California [1948]. Wrappers. OP.

vi, 61 [1] p. 3 maps (1 double p.). 22.6 cm.
Index: p. 59–61.
Double column.

Contains material on Joaquín Murieta and Rattlesnake Dick.

1191. Jones, C. N.

Early days in Cooke county, 1848–1873, compiled by C. N. Jones. Gainesville, Texas [n.d., ca. 1936]. Stiff wrappers. Rare.

3 p.l., 5–88 p. front., ports. 23.8 cm.

Though a comparatively recent book, this volume seems to have become rare. It contains some material on outlawry. The author reverses the usual error by spelling Jesse Chisholm's name as Chisum.

1192. Jones, Horace

The story of Rice county, by Horace Jones. [Wichita, Kans. Wichita Eagle], 1928. Cloth. Scarce.

5 p.l., 9–135 p. illus. 19.5 cm.

Has some information about Wild Bill Hickok, Hurricane Bill, Fort Griffin, Texas, and other persons and places.

1193. [Jones, J. Elbert]

A review of famous crimes solved by St. Louis policemen, [by J. Elbert Jones]. St. Louis [n.d.]. Pict. cloth. (Cover title.) Scarce.

10 p.l., 21–300 p. plates, ports. 22.4 cm.

The author gives a short sketch of Pat Crowe's life; tells about the Glencoe robbery of which Jesse James, Jr., was suspected; and tells about the capture of Ben Kilpatrick and Laura Bullion, his paramour. The author is in error when he says that David Trousdale (which he spells Trusdale), the express messenger, killed Kilpatrick and his former cellmate, Ole Beck, near St. Louis during a train robbery. This event took place in the Big Bend country of Texas, near Sanderson.

1194. Jones, John P. (Slim)

Borger, the little Oklahoma, by John P. (Slim) Jones. . . . [N.p., n.d.] Pict. wrappers. (Cover title.) Rare.

171 p. 7 plates, 2 in front. 21.7 cm.

A story of outlawry in Texas during the modern oil-boom days, with some information about Matthew Kimes.

1195. ———

Borger, the little Oklahoma, by John P. (Slim) Jones. Read it and weep. . . . Vol. 2. . . . [N.p., n.d.] Pict. wrappers. (Cover title.) Rare.

7 p.l., 88 p. plates, ports. 22.2 cm.
Port. on front cover; 8 p. plates and ports. in front.

A companion piece to the author's first book in which he continues to reveal the rotten conditions of the Texas oil fields. His language is so plain and his accusations so pointed that both books were suppressed; hence their rarity.

1196. Jones, Lloyd

Life and adventure of Harry Tracy, "The modern Dick Turpin," by Lloyd Jones. Chicago, Jewett & Lindrooth, publishers, 1902. Cloth. Rare.

4 p.l., 9–219 [4] p. front. (port.), plate, port. 20.3 cm.
The table of contents is mislabeled "index" and placed at the back of the book. Lloyd is spelled Loyd on copyright p.

The author says that Bat Masterson was "a celebrated gambler, confidence man and crook." There is quite a bit of false information about Soapy Smith, with whom he claims Harry Tracy spent a lot of time, even to going to Alaska with him. He writes that Soapy "was in every way a quiet religious man" and "always prayed for success just before he was after the other fellow's wealth." He has Soapy killing ten men in one fight, a feat I have never seen recorded before.

He has Soapy killed in a fight which took place in a saloon and in which sixty-six men were killed and eighteen wounded. None of this is true. He mentions Pat Crowe and says that Tracy had him kidnap Cudahy's child, but does not mention Cudahy as being of the Cudahy Packing Company, but just as a man who had been trying to make love to Tracy's wife. He says that Tracy's wife's name was Florence, but most historians identify her as Merrill's sister Rose. He has Harry Longabaugh and Butch Cassidy with Tracy in Oregon, which I greatly doubt, and he also has the killing of Merrill by Tracy all wrong. He writes as a newspaper reporter and a close friend of Tracy and one whom he trusted and often secretly met for interviews.

1197. Jones, Mat Ennis

Fiddlefooted, by Mat Ennis Jones, with the assistance of Morice E. Jones. Denver, Colo., Sage books [1966]. Cloth.

5 p.l., 11–304 p. plates, ports., maps. 22 cm.
Cattle brands: p. 284–288; index: p. 289–304.
Half title; pub. device.

Has a mention of Bill Doolin (which the author spells Doolan) and his gang and names Bill Cook as a member of the gang, though he was not.

1198. Jones, Oliver F. (Derby)

Fifteen years in a living hell. A true story, by Oliver F. (Derby) Jones. [N.p., 1944.] Cloth. Scarce.

4 p.l., 9–131 p. 1 plate. 23.5 cm.

1199. Jones, Virgil Carrington

The Hatfields and the McCoys, [by] Virgil Carrington Jones. Chapel Hill, University of North Carolina press [1948]. Cloth. OP.

xii p., 2 l., 293 p. illus., plates, ports., facsms. 23.6 cm.
Appendix: p. 253–271; annotations: p. 272–280; index: p. 283–293.
Half title.

In giving the history of the famous Kentucky feud between the Hatfields and the McCoys, the author also tells something about the James boys' robbery of the bank at Huntington, West Virginia.

1200. [Jones, W. F.]

The experiences of a deputy U.S. marshal of the Indian territory, [by W. F. Jones. Tulsa, Okla., 1937]. Wrappers. (Cover title). Scarce.

40 p. front. (port.), 1 plate. 23 cm.

Has much material on Oklahoma outlaws, such as the Daltons, Bill Doolin, Al Jennings, the Buck gang, Ned Christie, and others, as well as an account of the Ingalls fight.

1201. Jordin, John F.

Memories, by John F. Jordin. Being a story of early times in Davis county, Missouri. Character sketches of some of the men who helped to develop its latent resources. Gallatin, Mo., published from the North Missourian press [1904]. Cloth. Scarce.

4 p.l., [186] p. (no pagination). 23 cm.

Has some information on the James boys and their robberies.

1202. Journal, The

of American history relating life stories of men and events that have entered into building the western continent. Reproductions from rare prints and works of art (American). . . . [New Haven, Conn.], Associated Publishers of American Records [1907]. Stiff col. wrappers. Scarce.

3 p.l., [9]–190 p. plates (part with tissues), ports., flags (col. and with tissues). 27.7 cm.
Double column; untrimmed.

In a long chapter, entitled "Reminiscences of a Montana Judge," by Judge Lyman E. Munson, the writer deals at length with the Montana vigilantes.

1203. Joyce, John A.

A checkered life, by Col. John A. Joyce. . . . Chicago, S. P. Rounds, Jr., 1883. Cloth. Rare.

6 p.l., 17–318 p. front. (port. with tissue), facsms. 20.4 cm.
Head and tail pieces.

Contains material on the author's life in prison, where he knew such men as Jack Reno and other criminals.

1204. Juan, Don (pseud. of John P. Buschlen)

Señor Plummer. The life and laughter of an old Californian, by Don Juan. Los Angeles, Times-Mirror, 1942. Cloth. Scarce.

6 p.l., 242 p. plates, ports. 19.5 cm.
Half title; illus. double t.p.

Interesting reminiscences of an early Californian who lived to a ripe old age. He gives much first-hand information on Vásquez and Murieta and, like many other early Spanish Californians, does not believe that the head which was pickled for exhibition was Murieta's.

1205. Judson, Katherine Berry

Montana. "The land of shining mountains," by Katherine Berry Judson. With twenty-four illustrations and a map. Chicago, A. C. McClurg & co., 1909. Pict. cloth. Scarce.

vii, [4] p., 1 l., 15–244 p. front., plates, ports., fold. map in front. 19 cm.
Appendix: p. 179–236; index: p. 239–244.

Contains a chapter on the vigilantes of Montana and the Plummer gang of outlaws.

K

1206. Kalbfus, Joseph H.

Dr. Kalbfus' book. A sportsman's experiences and impressions in east and west, by Dr. Joseph H. Kalbfus. . . . With a preface by his friend and successor, Seth E. Gordon. . . . [Altoona, Pa., the Times Tribune co., 1926.] Cloth. Scarce.

4 p.l., 342 p. front. (port.), 1 port. 21.4 cm.

The author tells about Slade's killing of Jules Reni and his subsequent hanging by the vigilantes.

1207. Kane, Larry

100 years ago with the law and the outlaw. In memory. Compiled and written by Larry Kane for John F. Courtney, owner, "100 Years Ago" exhibition. [N.p., n.d.] Wrappers. Scarce.

[52] p. (no pagination). 21.6 cm.

Contains short chapters on the Jameses, Youngers, Hickok, the Daltons, Wyatt Earp, Bat Masterson, Calamity Jane, Billy the Kid, and Belle Starr. The author makes mistakes in every chapter. He says that Charlie Ford fired the shot that killed Jesse James, but we know that the killer was Charlie's brother, Bob. He has Hickok born in 1827 instead of 1837 and has Hickok's family moving to the outskirts of Hays City, Kansas, in 1855. We know that Boone Helm, a member of the Plummer gang, was hanged in 1864; yet the author has him hoping to shoot Hickok in Kansas in 1867.

The author says that Hickok "was sent to Deadwood, S.D., where he enforced the law at the point of a gun, and on one particular occasion shooting and killing two outlaws who approached him from different directions." He has all this happening in 1874, but Hickok did not go to Deadwood until 1876, and he did not kill anyone there. He is another author who has McCall captured in a butcher shop by Calamity Jane, and he has him recaptured in Hays City. The mistakes he makes in other chapters are too numerous to list here.

1208. [Kansas]

Parsons, Labette county, Kansas. Years from 1869 to 1893. Story of "The Benders." [Parsons, Kans., Bell bookcraft shop, n.d.] Cloth. Scarce.

2 p.l., 117 [6] p. 22 cm.
Index: p. [119–123].

Has a chapter on the Bender family of murderers.

1209. ———

The story of the early life at Fort Hays and of Hays City. . . . [Hays, Kans., Hays Daily News.] Published by the Old Fort Hays Historical Association, inc., 1959. Pict. wrappers. OP.

44 p. illus., plates, ports., facsms. 27.7 cm.

Tells of the lawlessness of Hays City and of Wild Bill Hickok's reign as marshal there, and of his troubles with Tom Custer, when he had "to escape by night, never to return." Jim Curry, another Hays City bad man, is also mentioned.

1210. Karolevitz, Robert F.

Newspapering in the old west. A pictorial history of journalism and printing on the frontier, by Robert F. Karolevitz. Seattle, Wash., Superior publishing co. [1965]. Cloth.

6 p.l., 11–191 [1] p. plates, ports., map, facsms. 27.4 cm.
Index: p. 185–191.
Pict. map on end papers.

Has some mention of Bat Masterson and Wild Bill Hickok, as well as some material on Henry Plummer and the Montana vigilantes.

1211. Keatinge, Charles Wilbur (Montana Charlie, pseud.)

Gold miners of Hard Luck; or, Three-Fingered Jack, by Charles Wilbur Keatinge (Montana Charlie). . . . Cleveland, Ohio, published by the Arthur Westbrook co., 1927. Pict. wrappers. Scarce.

2 p.l., [7]–203 p. 18 cm.
Western Life series, No. 1.
20 p. of sample novel at end.

A fictitious account of Joaquín Murieta and Three-Fingered Jack García.

1212. Keith, Elmer

Sixguns by Keith. The standard reference work, [by] Elmer Keith. Harrisburg, Pa., the Stackpole co. [1955]. Two-tone cloth.

7 p.l., 308 p. front. (col.), illus., plates, ports. 28.7 cm.
Half title; double column.

In a chapter entitled "Gunfighting," the author gives some information on Soapy Smith, Billy the Kid, and other gunfighters.

1213. Keithley, Ralph

Bucky O'Neill, he stayed with 'em while he lasted, by Ralph Keithley. Caldwell, Idaho, the Caxton printers, ltd., 1949. Cloth. OP.

8 p.l., [17]–247 p. front. (port.), plates, ports., maps. 23.5 cm.
Index: p. [245]–247.
Half title; pub. device.

A biography of a noted Arizona peace officer, with an account of his chase and capture of four of the outlaws who robbed the Atlantic and Pacific train in 1889. The book also gives some information on the Earp-Clanton feud.

1214. Keleher, William A.

The fabulous frontier; twelve New Mexico items, by William A. Keleher. Santa Fe, N.M., the Rydal press [1945]. Cloth. Scarce.

ix p., 3 l., 3–317 p. illus., plates, ports. 23.5 cm.

Some sources of references: p. 283–286; index: p. 287–317.

Half title; map on end papers.

Printed in a limited edition of 500 copies. Republished by the University of New Mexico press, Albuquerque, 1962, in a revised and enlarged edition of 352 pages.

A scholarly and dependable book which can be safely used as a source for material on Billy the Kid, Pat Garrett, Jim Miller, and other New Mexico gunmen. The author is a thorough historian of that state.

1215. ———

Maxwell land grant, a New Mexico item, by William A. Keleher. Santa Fe, N.M., the Rydal press [1942]. Pict. cloth. Rare in first ed.

xiii p., 1 l., 3–168 p. front. (port.), plates, ports. 23.5 cm.

Sources: p. 155–156; index: p. 157–168.

Half title.

Republished in New York in 1964.

Although published comparatively recently, this book has become rare. It deals mostly with Lucien B. Maxwell and the huge land grant that became known by his name, but it does contain some material on Clay Allison, the vigilantes of New Mexico, and Billy the Kid.

1216. ———

Violence in Lincoln county, 1869–1881. A New Mexico item, by William A. Keleher. Frontispiece by Ernest L. Blumenchein. Albuquerque, N.M., University of New Mexico press [1957]. Cloth.

xvi p., 1 l., 3–390 p. front., plates, ports., facsms. 21.8 cm.

Index: p. 373–390.

One of the best histories of Lincoln County and its troubles, as well as of the life of Billy the Kid. It has many citations to newspapers and court records, and is well annotated. It is most trustworthy.

1217. Kelley, George H. (comp.)

Legislative history, Arizona 1864–1912, compiled by George H. Kelley, state historian. [Phoenix, Ariz., the Manufacturing stationers, inc., 1926. Cloth. Rare.

xiv p., 1 l., 399 p. front., ports., 11 fold. maps. 21.4 cm.

Index: p. [381]–399.

Reprints of messages of the various governors of the territory and state, some containing reports on outlaws and lawlessness.

1218. Kelley, Joseph (Bunco)

Thirteen years in the Oregon penitentiary, by Joseph (Bunco) Kelley. Portland, Oreg., 1908. Stiff wrappers. Scarce.

4 p.l., [1] p., 10–142 p. front., illus., plates, ports. 21.2 cm.
Vignette.

Contains some material on Harry Tracy and Dave Merrill, with whom the author was in prison.

1219. Kelley, Thomas P.

The Black Donnellys, by Thomas P. Kelley. [New York, Signet books, 1955.] Stiff col. wrappers.

4 p.l., 9–127 [1] p. 18 cm.

1220. ———

Jesse James, by Thomas P. Kelley. . . . [Toronto, London, New York, Export publishing enterprises, ltd., 1950.] Pict. col. wrappers. OP.

3 p.l., 7–158 p. 17.5 cm.

Another example of the wild fiction written about Jesse James. The author also brings Belle Starr into the picture and repeats some of the legends about her.

1221. Kelly, Charles

The outlaw trail. A history of Butch Cassidy and his Wild Bunch, Hole-in-the-Wall, Brown's Hole, Robber's Roost, by Charles Kelly. With decorations by Bill Fleming. Salt Lake City, Utah, published by the author, 1938. Pict. levant. Rare.

3 p.l., [9]–337 [1] p. front. (port.), illus., plates, ports. 23.5 cm.
Bibliography included in acknowledgments.
Illus. t.p.; map on end papers; headpieces; vignettes; 7 blank leaves at end; "First edition" on copyright p.

This privately printed book, limited to one thousand copies, is now quite scarce. It is an excellent history of the lives and exploits of the better-known outlaws of the Northwest. It was republished by Devin-Adair in 1959 with several new chapters, a postscript, and an index (see Item 1222).

1222. ———

The outlaw trail. A history of Butch Cassidy and his Wild Bunch, [by] Charles Kelly. New York, Devin-Adair co., 1959. Pict. cloth.

x p., 1 l., 3–374 p. illus., plates, ports. 21 cm.
Index: p. 362–374.
Half title; vignette; illus. t.p.; maps on end papers (dif.).

A reprint of the 1938 edition (see Item 1221), with two added chapters, a postscript, and an index.

1223. ———, and Hoffman Birney

Holy murder. The story of Porter Rockwell, by Charles Kelly and Hoffman Birney. New York, Minton, Balch & co. [1934]. Cloth. OP.

ix [1] p., 2 l., 3–313 p. front. (port.), plates, ports. 22.2 cm.
Acknowledgments: p. 299; bibliography: p. 301–306; index: p. 307–313.
Half title; pub. device.

Has much on John D. Lee and Orrin Porter Rockwell and their crimes, the "Destroying Angels," and the Mountain Meadow massacre.

1224. Kelly, Fannie

Narrative of my captivity among the Sioux Indians. By Fannie Kelly, with a brief account of General Sully's Indian expedition in 1864, bearing upon the events occurring in my captivity. Hartford, Conn., Mutual publishing co.; Philadelphia, Pa., Quaker City publishing house, 1871. Pict. cloth. Rare.

x p., 1 l., 11–285 p. front. (port.), illus., plates. 19.7 cm.

Has a mention of Wild Bill Hickok.

1225. Kelly, Florence Finch

Flowing stream. The story of fifty-six years in American newspaper life, by Florence Finch Kelly. . . . New York, E. P. Dutton & co., inc., 1939. Pict. cloth. OP.

xvi p., 1 l., 3–571 p. front. (port.). 24.2 cm.
Index: p. 561–571.
Half title; untrimmed.

In a chapter on New Mexico the author has some things to say about Billy the Kid.

1226. Kelly, H.B.

No man's land; an address delivered before the Kansas State Historical society in Topeka, February 11, 1889, by H. B. Kelly, of McPherson, Kansas. Topeka, Kans., Kansas publishing house; Clifford C. Baker, state printer, 1889. Wrappers. Rare.

[3]–15 p. 18.8 cm

Deals with much of the outlawry of the period.

1227. Kelly, Robin A.

The sky was their roof, [by] Robin A. Kelly, with many rare photographs, drawings, and four maps. London, Andrew Melrose, Stratford place [1955]. Cloth. OP.

xii, 252 p. illus., plates, ports., maps. 21.8 cm.

Notes: p. 217–228; bibliography: p. 229–231; glossary: p. 233–235; main Plains Indian tribes: p. 237–239; index: p. 243–252.

Half title; device on t.p.

Has some chapters on western gunmen and outlaws, including Sam Bass, Billy the Kid, Calamity Jane, Dutch Henry, Wyatt Earp, Pat Garrett, John Wesley Hardin, Boone Helm, Henry Plummer, and the James boys.

1228. Kelsey, D. M.

History of our wild west and stories of pioneer life. . . . A complete story of the settlement and conquest of the western frontier, relating the exciting experiences, daring deeds and marvelous achievements of men made famous by their heroic deeds . . ., by D. M. Kelsey. . . . Chicago, Thompson & Thomas [1901]. Pict. cloth. Scarce.

x [3] p., [15]–542 p. front. (col.), illus., plates, ports. 21.8 cm.

Contains a long chapter on Wild Bill Hickok in which the author repeats the old legends of the McCanles "fight" but says that the fight took place on December 16, five months after the trouble actually occurred. He misspells McCanles' name, calls David by the name Jim, and goes into gory details about the killing of six men and the wounding of two others, although he does let two escape. This author follows Buel's wild tale closely, and much of the information on Wild Bill is about as fantastic. He also follows the legend about Wild Bill's benevolent nature and his contributing to the support of Mrs. McCanles, "whom her husband left destitute," until her death.

1229. Kemp, Ben W., with J.C. Dykes

Cow dust and saddle leather, by Ben W. Kemp with J.C. Dykes. Norman, University of Oklahoma press [1968]. Cloth.

xvii p., 1 l., 3–300 p. plates, ports. 23.7 cm.

Appendix: p. 290–294; index: p. 295–300.

Half title; "First edition" on copyright p.

This biography of the author's father is interesting but contains many errors. In the foreword the co-author writes that "it would be a miracle if some minor errors in dates and in the spelling of names of places and some of the characters who appear briefly in the story did not appear. Benny and your editor have done the best we could to eliminate such errors, but we know we didn't find them all." Yet they should have discovered such glaring errors as the one on page 58, where they state that Dick Ware "was in the fight at Round Rock on July 20, 1889, when Sam Bass was killed." This fight occurred on Friday, July 19, 1878, but Bass, severely wounded, did not die until the following Sunday, the twenty-first.

In the chapter on Black Jack Ketchum there are many errors. The author states that "Black Jack and two of his gang tried to rob a Santa Fe passenger train near Clayton, New Mexico. Just as they were about to succeed, a porter on the train eased open a door at Black Jack's back and shot him through the arm, shattering the bone." Black Jack was alone on this attempted robbery, and it was a Colorado & Southern train, not the Santa Fe. Conductor Harrington was the person who shot Black Jack.

The author says further that Ketchum tried to reach "an isolated ranch," but "was so weak from loss of blood that he fainted and fell off his horse a hundred yards short of the house." Black Jack had not mounted any horse after being shot but had made his way to a tree on the edge of the railroad right of way and had crawled onto the tender of the train at Folsom. Again the author has a posse following Ketchum to this isolated ranch, where the men "saw him sitting with his back against a tree." He actually gave himself up to the train crew of a freight train. The author also says that Ketchum was rushed to Clayton, where a surgeon had to amputate his arm to have his life. Most other accounts have the amputation taking place in Trinidad.

Many varying accounts have been written about the death of the Apache Kid, but this author relates an entirely different one. He has the Apache Kid killed by Bill Keene, Sebe Sorrels, and Mike Sullivan after he and a companion stole a band of horses. Earle R. Forrest, in his *Arizona's Dark and Bloody Ground*, has the Kid killed by Walapai Clark "about 1893 or 1894." Later, in his *Lone War Trail of Apache Kid*, in which he collaborated with Edwin B. Hill, Forrest admitted his mistake and acknowledged that the Kid was only wounded and vanished completely.

Joe Chisholm, in his *Brewery Gulch*, has the Kid killed in Mexico by John Slaughter and Captain Benton "sometime in 1897 or 1898." William Sparks, in his *The Apache Kid, a Bear Fight and Other True Stories of the Old West*, claims that the Kid died of consumption in Old Mexico; and Jess G. Hayes, in his *Apache Vengeance*, claims that the circumstances of the Kid's death are unknown. Scores of other tales have been told about the Kid's death, but none has been officially accepted and certainly no rewards were ever paid for his capture or slaying.

1230. Kennedy, Captain

Jesse James' mysterious warning; or, the raid that almost failed, by Captain Kennedy. Baltimore, Md., I. & M. Ottenheimer [1915]. Stiff col. wrappers.

2 p.l., 7–170 p. 17.8 cm.

1231. ———

Jesse James' thrilling raid; or the daylight robbery of the Harkness bank, by Captain Kennedy. Baltimore, Md., I. & M. Ottenheimer [1913]. Stiff pict. col. wrappers.

2 p.l., 7–170 p. 17.8 cm.

1232. ———

Jesse James' wild leap; or, the hold-up of the through express, by Captain Kennedy. Baltimore, Md., I. & M. Ottenheimer [1915]. Stiff pict. col. wrappers.

1 p.l., 1–172 p. 17.8 cm.

1233. Kennedy, Michael S. (ed.)

Cowboys and cattlemen. A roundup from Montana, the magazine of western history. Selected and edited by Michael S. Kennedy. New York, Hastings house, publishers [1964]. Cloth.

xii p., 1 l., 3–364 p. front., illus., plates, ports., facsms. 25.5 cm.
Index: p. 356–364; notes after each chapter.
Half title; illus. end papers.

Has a chapter dealing with the rustlers and vigilantes of Montana and such outlaws as Rattlesnake Jake Fallon and Charles Longhair Owens. Also has a chapter on the Hole-in-the-Wall gang.

1234. Kent, William

Reminiscences of outdoor life, by William Kent, with a foreword by Stewart Edward White. Illustrated. San Francisco, Calif., A. M. Robertson, MCMXXIX. Boards and cloth. OP.

xii p., 1 l., 3–304 [1] p. front. (tissue with letterpress), plates. 20.7 cm.
Title label pasted on spine; untrimmed.

In his chapter on the Apaches, the author devotes several pages to the Apache Kid. In his chapter on New Mexico his information on the Lincoln County War and Billy the Kid is unreliable. He spells John Chisum's last name Chisholm and states that the war was fought between cattlemen and sheepmen. He repeats the old legend about the Kid threatening to kill Chisum and his cowboys.

Of the death of Billy the Kid he gives this inaccurate account: "After being arrested and escaping, he was finally hunted down and shot by Sheriff Pat Garrett, who crawled in his stocking feet into the room where he was sleeping and walked around in the dark feeling for the bed, with a drawn six-shooter. Billy heard the noise and got out of bed with his gun, and the two men were crawling around in the dark looking for each other. Finally the strain was too great and Billy spoke up and queried '*Quién es?*' (who is it?), whereupon Garrett shot and Billy's objectionable career was at an end."

1235. King, Dick

Ghost towns of Texas, by Dick King. San Antonio, Texas, the Naylor co. [1953]. Imt. leather. Scarce.

xiii p., 7 l., 3–140 p. plates. 21.6 cm.
Bibliography: p. 127–129; index: p. 133–140.
Half title.
Reprinted in 1955 and 1956.

Has some mention of Gregorio Cortez, a Texas outlaw, and his capture, and Jack Helm's killing by John Wesley Hardin. Also has a mention of the James and Younger boys.

1236. King, Ernest L.

Main line. Fifty years of railroading with the Southern Pacific, by Ernest L. King as told to Robert E. Mahaffay. Garden City, N.Y., Doubleday & co., inc., 1948. Pict. cloth. OP.

5 p.l., 11–271 p. 22 cm.
Index: p. 265–271.
Half title; illus. double t.p.; "First edition" on copyright p.

Like several other railroad books, this one has a chapter on train robberies. It deals with the De Autrement brothers, Burt Alvord, Grant Wheeler, the Daltons, Sontag, Evans, and others.

1237. King, Frank M.

Mavericks. The salty comments of an old-time cowpuncher, by Frank M. King. Illustration by Charles M. Russell. Introduction by Ramon F. Adams. Pasadena, the Trail's End publishing co., inc. [1947]. Cloth. OP.

xii p., 2 l., [5]–275 p. front. (col.). 21.5 cm.
Index: p. [273]–275.
Illus. end papers; illus. chapter divisions; pub. device.
Also published in a de luxe edition of 350 copies, numbered, signed, and bound in morocco.

Frank King knew many of the outlaws of the Southwest personally, and his book contains many references to them. The comments are selected from his column "Mavericks," which ran for years, until his death, in the *Western Livestock Journal* of Los Angeles. He was my personal friend, and he always deplored the fact that modern writers do not keep the records of the old outlaws straight; yet he sometimes got his facts wrong, too, as when he claimed that Sam Bass got $150,000 in twenty-dollar gold pieces in the Union Pacific robbery.

The author debunks some of the legends about Billy the Kid. He does not have much use for the Earp clan and does not recommend Lake's book, who he says "wants everybody to believe what he wrote about the 'Lion of Tombstone' is all true, which it ain't."

1238. ———

Pioneer western empire builders. A true story of the men and women of pioneer days, by Frank M. King. Profusely illustrated, including an original illustration by Charles M. Russell. . . . [Pasadena, Calif., the Trail's End publishing co., inc., 1946.] Cloth. Scarce.

8 p.l., [21]–383 p. front., plates, ports., map, facsm. 22 cm.

Also published in a de luxe edition, signed, numbered, and bound in morocco.

Contains some information on Billy the Kid and other outlaws of the Southwest. The author repeats the legend about the Kid's mother marrying Antrim in Colorado.

1239. ———

Wranglin' the past; being the reminiscences of Frank M. King. Illustrated. [Los Angeles], this first edition privately published for his friends by the author. [Printed by Haynes corp.], 1935. Fabrikoid. Scarce.

xi [1] p., 13–244 p. front. (port.), illus., plates, ports. 23.5 cm.

Illus. t.p.

Colophon: "This autographed first edition is limited to 300 copies to be sold at five dollars the copy, of which this is No. ——."

500 copies of the book were printed, 300 of them with the above colophon and 200 without. All copies had the statement "This first edition privately published for friends by the author, 1935" on the title page.

Republished in 1946 by Trail's End publishing co., Pasadena, Calif., with a preface by H. E. Britzman and an illustration by Charles M. Russell. "First revised edition" appears on the title page. This edition contains 284 pages.

Both editions contain considerable material on gunmen such as Johnny Ringo, Billy the Kid, and the Earps. The author also tells of the Tonto Basin War. He has only the Kid and Brewer on the trail with Tunstall when the latter was killed and says that the Kid was at the funeral and repeats the fable about his swearing to kill every man who had anything to do with Tunstall's death. There is a long account of the killing of O'Folliard and the mob at Las Vegas after the Kid's capture at

Stinking Springs. The date of the Kid's death is incorrect. The author does not have a very favorable opinion of Wyatt Earp, and his version of the O K Corral fight does the Earps no credit.

1240. King, Leonard

From cattle rustler to pulpit, by Leonard King. San Antonio, Texas, the Naylor co. 1943. Cloth. OP.

x, 216 p. front. (port.), illus. 21 cm.

Half title.

Taught cattle rustling by his father, this author became an expert and followed the outlaw trail until he was converted to religion and became a minister of the gospel.

1241. Kingston, Charles

Remarkable rogues, the careers of some notable criminals of Europe and America, by Charles Kingston, with eight illustrations. London, John Lane, the Bodley Head, ltd.; New York, John Lane co., MCMXXI. Cloth. Scarce.

x p., 1 l., 290 p. front., plates, ports. 22.5 cm.

Index: p. 287–290.

Half title; untrimmed.

Chapter 3, dealing with Belle Starr, is a most preposterous tale. The author has Belle's father, spelled Star, ignorant of the fact that his name was Shirley, and instead of portraying him as the respected tavern owner he was, the author has him an outlaw teaching his daughter the fine points of outlawry. He has Belle, at the age of fifteen, killing a man by choking him to death "with her small white hands." He says that her father, "the terror of Texas," was shot down in a running fight and that Belle "succeeded to the vacant leadership." He has her robbing a bank at Galveston, Texas, a town she never visited, and says that hundreds of farmers paid her weekly tribute to avoid being robbed by her gang. In the end he has her killed in a battle with a whole regiment of soldiers. From beginning to end this is a most fantastic tale.

1242. Kinyon, Edmund

The northern mines. Factual narratives of the counties of Nevada, Placer, Sierra, Yuba, and portions of Plumas and Butte, by Edmund Kinyon. Grass Valley-Nevada City, Calif., the Union publishing co. [1949]. Pict. cloth. OP.

6 p.l., 167 [2] p. illus., plates, ports., fold. map at end. 23.7 cm.

Acknowledgments: p. [168]; index: p. [169].

Has a chapter on Henry Plummer and chapters on various aspects of lawlessness.

1243. Kirsch, Robert, and William S. Murphy

West of the west. The story of California from the conquistadores to the great earthquake, as described by the men and women who were there. By Robert Kirsch and William S. Murphy. New York, E. P. Dutton & co., inc., 1967. Cloth.

xvi p., 1 l., [3]–526 p. illus., plates, ports., maps. 24 cm.
Bibliography: p. [507]–517; index: p. [519]–526.
Half title; "First edition" on copyright p.

Has some material on Captain Jack, the Modoc outlaw, and the hanging of James Gilbert Jenkins and has much material on Tiburcio Vásquez, mostly taken from *Vásquez, or the Hunted Bandits of the Joaquin*, by George Beers.

1244. Klein, Alexander (ed.)

Grand deception. The world's most spectacular and successful hoaxes, impostures, ruses and frauds. Collected and edited by Alexander Klein. Philadelphia, New York, J. B. Lippincott co. [1955]. Cloth.

7 p.l., 1 p., 16–382 p. 22 cm.
Half title; untrimmed.

Contains a chapter on Soapy Smith taken from *The Legendary Mizners*, by Alva Johnston. (see Item 1185).

1245. Klette, Ernest

The crimson trail of Joaquín Murieta, by Ernest Klette. Los Angeles, Wetzel publishing co. [1928]. Cloth. Scarce.

4 p.l., 11–215 [1] p. front. 20.2 cm.
Vignette; pub. device.

Though the publishers claim that this is a biography, it is merely a piece of romance based upon some of the legends preceding it.

1246. Knapp, Mrs. A. E. (ed.)

Pioneers of the San Juan country, by Sarah Platt Decker chapter N.S.D.A.R., Vol. III. Durango, Colo., Durango printing co. [1952]. Wrappers. OP.

8 p.l., 175 p. plates, ports., maps. 19.7 cm.

Has a chapter on the lynching of Bert Wilkinson and material on the Ike Stockton gang of outlaws.

1247. Kneedler, H. S.

Through storyland to sunset seas. What four people saw on a journey through the southwest to the Pacific coast, by H. S. Kneedler. With illustrations. Chicago, Knight, Leonard & co., printers, 1895. Stiff pict. wrappers. Scarce.

4 p.l., 7–205 p. illus., plates, ports. 22.6 cm.

Contains some information on train robberies and other lawlessness in the Southwest.

1248. Knight, Edward

Wild Bill Hickok. The contemporary portrait of a Civil War hero, [by] Edward Knight. Franklin, New Hampshire, the Hillside press, 1959. Cloth.

4 p.l., 9–61 p. 22.2 cm.
Bibliography: p. 60–61.
Half title.

This little book adds nothing new to the already exhaustive literature about Wild Bill. The author has Hickok killed in the "Bell-Union" Saloon, but the Belle Union was a theater, and he was killed in the No. 10 Saloon. There are other mistakes.

1249. Knight, Oliver

Fort Worth, outpost on the Trinity, by Oliver Knight. Norman, University of Oklahoma press [1953]. Pict. Cloth.

xiii p., 1 l., 3–302 p. plates, ports., plan, map. 22 cm.
Appendices: p. 231–277; bibliography: p. 279–282; index: p. 283–302.
Half title; "First edition" on copyright p.

Has a long chapter devoted to Jim Courtright and his death at the hands of Luke Short.

1250. Knowles, Horace (ed.)

Gentlemen, scholars and scoundrels. A treasury of the best of *Harper's Magazine* from 1850 to the present. Edited by Horace Knowles. New York, Harper & brothers [1959]. Cloth.

xix p., 2 l., 5–694 p. 23.8 cm.
Index to authors: p. 695–696.
Half title; illus. t.p.; pub. device.

Contains the purported interview of George Ward Nichols with Wild Bill Hickok as it appeared in the February, 1867, issue of *Harper's Magazine*.

1251. Koenigberg, M.

King news, an autobiography, [by] M. Koenigberg. Philadelphia, New York, F. A. Stokes co. [1941]. Cloth. OP.

3 p.l., 7–511 p. 22 cm.
Index: p. 503–511.

Half title; untrimmed.

Chapter I deals with the killing of King Fisher and Ben Thompson and also has some material on train robberies.

1252. Koller, Larry

The fireside book of guns, by Larry Koller. Harold I. Peterson, historian. Herb Glass, gun consultant. New York, Simon and Schuster, a Ridge press book [1959]. Cloth. OP.

5 p.l., [1] p., 16–284 p. illus., plates (many double p. and mostly col.), ports. 28.7 cm.

Bibliography: p. 279; index: p. 280–284.

Half title; illus. end papers (col. and dif.); illus. double p. t.p. (col.).

In Chapter 6, entitled "Bad Men and Peace Officers," the author says that Wyatt Earp was brought to Tombstone from Dodge City in 1879 "with a deputy Federal Marshal's badge to enforce law and order." He says that Wild Bill Hickok was perhaps the first of the famous "two-gun men" and that he fired "with deadly accuracy with both hands at the same time." He does not seem to know which story of the Rock Creek affair to accept or whether Wild Bill killed six or three, and he is mistaken in saying that Jack McCall killed Hickok "after an argument over a card game."

1253. ——— (ed.)

The American gun, Vol. I, Number 3, summer, 1961. New York, Madison books, 1961. Col. pict. cloth.

3 p.l., [4]–96 p. illus., plates, (part col.), map (col.). 34.4 cm.

Double and triple column.

Has a chapter on the shotgun, by Joseph E. Doctor, in which there are many errors. Of the O K Corral fight the writer says that all the Clantons fought back except Tom McLaury (which he spells McLowery), but some members of the Clanton crowd were not armed. He gives the card-game version of Billy the Kid's escape from the Lincoln jail and misspells Gauss's name as Geiss. He also spells Ed O. Kelly's name as Ed O'Kelly. He repeats the fable about Wyatt Earp standing off a crowd in Tombstone. He is also mistaken in saying that Heck Thomas killed Bill Doolin while the latter was attempting to rendezvous with his wife, and he is certainly mistaken when he claims that Buckshot Roberts, during the battle at Blazer's Mill, stood off "eight well-armed men during one of the Texas feuds, even after he had suffered a mortal wound." As everyone should know, this event was not a part of a Texas feud but was a battle in New Mexico. There are many other errors.

1254. Koop, W. E.

Billy the Kid. The trail of a Kansas legend, by W. E. Koop. [Kansas City, Mo., published by the Kansas City Posse of Westerners, 1965.] Cloth. Also published in wrappers.

xii, 16 p. front., illus., plates, ports., panorama, map (double p.). 23.8 cm.
Notes: p. 16.
Half title.
Colophon: "Book Number —— [Signed] ——. Limited to two hundred and fifty autographed copies."

First published as Vol. IX, No. 3, of the Kansas City Westerners' quarterly in September, 1964. It quickly became a collector's item. The author unearthed some new, hitherto unpublished, details about the Kid's days in Wichita, Kansas. He shows for the first time that Mr. Antrim and the Kid's mother were old acquaintances when they married and that they had adjoining town lots in Wichita.

1255. [Kopler, Philip W.]

The bell-wether thief of Missouri City, [by Philip W. Kopler.] Sewn. (Caption title.) Excessively rare.

[8] p. (no pagination). 24 cm.
Double column.

I examined the only known copy of this book in the library of my late friend Martin E. Ismert, of Kansas City, Missouri. It tells about the James boys and about the bombing of their home when Mrs. Samuel lost her arm.

1256. Krakel, Dean F.

The saga of Tom Horn. The story of a cattleman's war, with personal narratives, newspaper accounts and official documents and testimonials. Illustrated with the pageant of personalities, by Dean F. Krakel. [Laramie, Wyo., manufactured. . . . by the Laramie printing co.] [Laramie, Wyo., for the Powder River publishers, 1954.] Cloth. Scarce.

ix p., 1 l., [3]–277 p. illus., plates, ports. 23.6 cm.
Bibliography: p. 268–269; index: p. 272–277.

A thorough study of the trial and execution of Tom Horn. More than half of the book is about his trial, including the questions of the attorneys and the answers of the witnesses as the case progressed. A threatened law suit required the author and publisher to rewrite and replace seven pages of the illustrations and text after the volume had been printed and bound but before it was released. These changes were made by cutting out the deletions and tipping in new sheets. The text on pages 13 and 54 was changed, as well as several of the illustrations.

1257. Kroll, Harry Harrison

Rogue's company. A novel of John Murrell, by Harry Harrison Kroll. Indianapolis, New York, the Bobbs-Merrill co., publishers [1943]. Cloth. Scarce.

5 p.l., 11–412 p. 22.5 cm.

Half title; untrimmed; "First edition" on copyright p.

I have included very few works of outright fiction in this bibliography, but this novel seems to merit inclusion because it is a collector's item with a central character about whom little has been written.

1258. Krumrey, Kate Warner

Saga of Sawlog, [by] Kate Warner Krumrey. Denver, Colo., Big Mountain press [1965]. Cloth.

6 p.l., 13–417 p. plates, ports. 22.2 cm.

Index: p. 413–417.

Half title; maps on end papers (dif.).

A splendid history of life around Dodge City, Kansas, in its early days. The author mentions most of the peace officers of Dodge except Wyatt Earp. She gives an account of the robbery of the Spearville, Kansas, bank by Bill Doolin, Bitter Creek Newcomb, and Sam Yountis and the killing of Yountis.

1259. Kuykendall, Ivan Lee

Ghost riders of the Mogollon, by Ivan Lee Kuykendall. San Antonio, Texas, the Naylor co. [1954]. Cloth. Rare.

viii, 158 p. 19.7 cm.

Half title.

The story of the Tewksbury-Graham feud in Arizona, on which the author says he spent thirty years in research and five years in the writing. No sooner had the book been released when the publishers were sued by some of the descendants of the characters involved. Only about two hundred copies reached private hands; hence its rarity.

1260. Kuykendall, William Littlebury

Frontier days. A true narrative of striking events on the western frontier, by Judge W. L. Kuykendall. [N.p.], J.M. and H.L. Kuykendall, publishers, 1917. Cloth. Scarce.

xi, 251 p. front. (port.). 19 cm.

Appendix: p. 250–251.

Half title.

This book contains some information on the Black Hills outlaws. In a long footnote the author gives another false account of the McCanles-Hickok "fight," has Wild Bill a marshal in Deadwood, and has him killed with buckshot.

It is surprising to find so many inaccuracies in the writing of a man who was the judge at the first trial of Jack McCall, Hickok's killer. Perhaps he may be excused for his faulty account of the McCanles troubles, but for the presiding judge at McCall's trial to declare that Hickok was killed with buckshot is inexcusable. However, two pages later he does state that Hickok was killed with a pistol, "being within six inches of the back of his head."

1261. Kyner, James H.

End of the tracks, [by] James H. Kyner, as told to Hawthorne Daniel. Caldwell, Idaho, the Caxton printers, ltd., 1937. Cloth. OP.

6 p.l., 11–277 p. front. (port.), plates, ports. 23.3 cm.
Half title; pub. device.

Has some material on outlawry.

L

1262. Lackey, B. Roberts

Stories of the Texas rangers, by B. Roberts Lackey. San Antonio, Texas, the Naylor co. [1955]. Cloth.

ix, 105 p. 21.6 cm.
Index: p. 103–105.
Half title.

Has chapters on the Mason County War, the Fort Davis bandits, stage robbery, cattle rustlers, and the killing of Sam Bass. Most of the information on Bass is wrong. The author gives the amount of money secured in the Union Pacific robbery as $20,000 instead of $60,000. He says that Bass went to Round Rock to rob a merchant who was said to have a large amount of money in his safe. He says that Underwood was with the gang at Round Rock, though he had long since left the Bass gang. Oddly enough, except for changes in a few chapter headings, this book is almost word for word the same as *Rangers and Sovereignty*, written by Captain Dan W. Roberts forty-one years earlier. The few changes are in personal pronouns, from first to third person. After I called this discovery to the attention of the publishers, they tipped in the following statement: "Through error, the publishers of *Stories of the Texas Rangers* failed to insert, in this book, a statement to the effect that *Stories of the Texas Rangers* is, to a large extent, a reprinting of *Rangers and Sovereignty*. The author(!) of *Stories of the Texas Rangers* holds the copyright on *Rangers and Sovereignty*."

1263. La Croix, Arda

Billy the Kid. A romantic story founded upon the play of the same name, by Arda La Croix. . . . New York, J.S. Ogilvie publishing co., 1907. Pict. wrappers. Scarce.

3–128 p. front., plates. 17.9 cm.

This little volume has now become scarce and a collector's item. It is based upon the play by Walter Woods and Joseph Santley. The novel version follows the play closely, and, of course, both are fiction.

1264. [La Croix, L. F.]

Graphic tale of most daring and successful train robbery in the history of the northwest, [by L. F. La Croix]. Capture of the desperadoes and their incarceration in the Helena jail, together with the only truthful narrative ever published giving details of escape on the day set for trial. . . . Illustrated. . . . Helena, Mont., State publishing co., publishers, 1909. Wrappers. Rare.

2 p.l., 7–52 p. front. (port.), plates, ports. 23.4 cm.

1265. Ladd, Robert E.

Eight ropes to eternity, [by Robert E. Ladd]. Tombstone, Ariz., published by Tombstone Epitaph [1965]. Pict. wrappers.

3 p.l., 34 p. illus., plates, facsm. 21 cm.
Double column.

Tells about the hangings of Tex Howard, Dan Dowd, Dan Kelly, Red Sample, and William Delaney and the lynching of John Heath.

1266. La Farge, Oliver

Santa Fe. The autobiography of a southwestern town, by Oliver La Farge, with the assistance of Arthur N. Morgan. Foreword by Paul Horgan. Norman, University of Oklahoma press [1959]. Cloth.

xviii p., 1 l., 3–436 p. plates, facsms. 23.5 cm.
Index: p. 421–436.
Half title; "First edition" on copyright p.

This book is composed of excerpts from the early newspaper *The New Mexican*. It has information on the arrest, escape, and death of Billy the Kid, on Elfego Baca, on Wayne Brazil, and on the killing of Pat Garrett. Dave Rudabaugh, Tom Pickett, Bob Olinger, J. W. Bell, and others are also mentioned. The compiler, in a personal comment, makes the common mistake of asserting that the Lincoln County War "was a bitter feud between cattlemen and sheepmen."

1267. La Follette, Robert Hoath

Eight notches, "Lawlessness and disorder, unlimited," and other stories . . ., by Robert Hoath La Follette. Albuquerque, N.M., printed by Valiant printing co., 1950. Pict. wrappers. OP.

3–45 p. illus., plates, ports. 23 cm.

Section I of this unique book deals with Elfego Baca, and Section II consists of forty-five pages printed upside down and entitled "In an Upside-down World."

1268. La Font, Don

Rugged life in the Rockies, by Don La Font. With illustrations by the author and family. Casper, Wyo., Prairie publishing co., 1951. Cloth. OP.

3 p.l., 9–207 p. front. (port.), illus., plates. 23.6 cm.
Vignette; copyright notice on preface page.

This privately printed book gives an account of the killing of Bob Ford by Ed O. Kelly, (whom this author also calls Ed O'Kelly). He makes the statement that Kelly was a friend of Jesse James and had sworn to kill Ford if he ever ran across him. Soapy Smith and Bat Masterson are also mentioned.

1269. Laine, Tanner

Campfire stories, by Tanner Laine. Illustrated by Donald E. Johnson. [Lubbock, Texas, Ranch House publications, 1965.] Stiff pict. col. wrappers.

viii p., 1 l., 3–148 p. illus., map. 21.5 cm.
Illus. t.p.; pub. device and "First edition" on copyright p.

Has a chapter on bank robbery and one on Pink Higgins, the Texas gunman, and mentions the big fight at Tascosa.

1270. Lake, Stuart N.

Wyatt Earp, frontier marshal, by Stuart N. Lake. With illustrations. Boston and New York, Houghton Mifflin co., 1931. Cloth.

xiv p., 1 l., [3]–392 p. front. (port.), plates, ports., facsm. 22.2 cm.
Index: p. [377]–392.
Half title; pub. device; first edition: 1931 under imprint.

Often a typographical error will identify a first printing, for the error is usually corrected in the second printing, but the error "senventy-five" (page 25) appears in all editions as late as 1957, although the earlier error "ellby" for "belly" on page 54 was corrected. The book purports to be a biography of Wyatt Earp, recorded at the instigation of his third wife. Many writers and other men who knew Earp personally held him to be utterly unlike the character portrayed by Lake. This book omits all the shady incidents of his life and does everything possible to glorify him.

The author tells about many events that happened to other people as though they happened to himself, though he waited until all the real participants were dead to do so. To point out all the falsehoods in this book would require many pages (see my *Burs Under the Saddle*, Item 7).

1271. ———

He carried a six-shooter. The biography of Wyatt Earp, by Stuart Lake, with an introduction by Philip Lindsay. London, New York, Peter Nevill, ltd. MCMLII. Cloth.

xi p., 3 l., [3]–392 p. front. (port.), plates, ports. 20.5 cm.
Half title; vignette.

This is the English edition of Item 1270.

1272. Lamar, Robert Howard

Dakota territory, 1861–1889. A study of frontier politics, by Robert Howard Lamar. New Haven, Yale University press, 1956. Cloth. OP.

x p., 2 l., 304 p. ports., map. 23.8 cm.
Bibliographical note: p. 285–291; index: p. 293–304.

Has some mention of Calamity Jane and Wild Bill Hickok. The author seems to have labored under the impression that Hickok's real name was William. He is listed in the index as William Hickok, and the author calls him "Bill" in the text.

1273. ———

The far southwest, 1846–1912. A territorial history, [by] Robert Howard Lamar. New Haven and London, Yale University press, 1966. Cloth.

xii p., 12 l., 23–560 p. plates, ports., fold. maps at end. 24 cm.
Bibliographical essay: p. 505–541; index: p. 543–560.

Has some information about the Lincoln County War. I think that the author is wrong in saying that Charlie Bowdre, Doc Scurlock, and the Coe boys "rode about terrorizing the region." The author also says that Billy the Kid was left-handed. He is mistaken in saying that "soldiers from Fort Stanton surrounded the McSween home and after seven hours of battle forced him and his men into the open by successfully firing the house." He says that Bowdre was "killed by outlaws with whom he was feuding." Bowdre was killed by Pat Garrett at Stinking Springs.

Of Billy the Kid's death by Garrett, he writes: "Cornering him in a dark room at old Fort Sumner, now the house of Pete Maxwell, ..." It was Maxwell's home when the Kid was killed there.

1274. Lamb, Arthur H.

Tragedies of the Osage Hills, as told by Arthur H. Lamb. . . . Pawhuska, Okla., published by the Osage printery [1935]. Pict. wrappers. Scarce.

2 p.l., [5]–203 p. illus., plates. 22.5 cm.
Device.

In dealing with many violent crimes, the author discusses some of the well-known outlaws, such as the Daltons.

1275. Lambert, Oscar Doane

Stephen Benton Elkins, by Oscar Doane Lambert. Pittsburgh, Pa., University of Pittsburgh press, 1955. Cloth. OP.

7 p.l., 336 p. front. (port.), plates, 2 ports. (incl. front.). 22.2 cm.
Bibliography: p. 329–336; index: p. [337]–[348].
Half title.

Has some new material on Cole Younger. The author calls Cole's father Harry. His full name was Henry Washington Younger. He misspells Quantrill's name as Quantrell throughout.

1276. Landrum, Graham

Grayson county. An illustrated history of Grayson county, Texas, by Graham Landrum. . . . Fort Worth, Texas, published by University Supply & Equipment co. [1960]. Padded cloth. Scarce.

2 p.l., 180 p. illus., plates, ports., maps, facsm., plan. 27.5 cm.
Index to pioneers: p. 117–177; bibliography: p. 178–180.
Illus. end papers (dif.); double column.

Contains quite a bit of material on the Lee-Peacock feud of Northeast Texas.

1277. Lane, Allen Stanley

Emperor Norton, the mad monarch of America, by Allen Stanley Lane. Caldwell, Idaho, the Caxton printers, ltd., 1939. Pict. cloth. OP.

9 p.l., [19]–286 p. front., illus., plates, ports., facsms. 23.5 cm.
Acknowledgments: p. [279]–281; bibliography: p. [283]–286.
Illus. half title; illus. end papers (col.); pub. device.

Has some information on lawlessness in San Francisco and the hanging of John Jenkins.

1278. Lang, William W.

A paper on the resources and capabilities of Texas, read by Colonel William W. Lang, before the Farmers' club of the American institute, Cooper union, New

York, March 8th, 1881. . . . To which is appended a paper on the social and economic condition of the state. [New York, Wm. H. Thomas, mercantile printer, 1881.] Wrappers. Rare.

[3]–31 p. large fold. map, tables. 23.2 cm.
Reprinted with additions same year; another enlarged edition with 62 pages and no date.

Part of this paper deals with lawlessness in Texas. Some issues do not include the map.

1279. Langford, Gerald

Alias O. Henry. A biography of William Sidney Porter, by Gerald Langford. New York, the Macmillan co., 1957. Cloth. OP.

xix, 294 p. plates, ports., facsm. 21.5 cm.
Appendix: p. 251–258; notes and references: p. 259–286; index: p. 287–294.
Half title.

Has much material on Al Jennings, with whom Porter was associated in prison and afterward.

1280. Langford, Nathaniel Pitt

Vigilante days and ways. The pioneers of the Rockies; the makers and making of Montana, Idaho, Oregon, Washington, and Wyoming, by Nathaniel Pitt Langford. With portraits and illustrations. Boston, J. G. Cupples co., publishers, 1890. Pict. cloth. Pub. in two volumes. Scarce.

Vol. I, xxvi, 426 p. front. (with tissue), ports. 19.5 cm.
Vol. II, xiii p., 1 l., 485 [6] p. front. (with tissue), ports. 19.5 cm.
Index p. [455]–485.
6 p. adv. at end; vignette on each t.p.
Republished in 1893 and 1895 and in Chicago in 1912. Later issued in one volume.

One of the standard works on the Montana vigilantes and the Plummer gang of road agents.

1281. Lardner, W. B., and M. J. Brock

History of Placer and Nevada counties, California, with biographical sketches of the leading men and women of the counties who have been identified with their growth and development from the early days to the present. History by W. B. Lardner and M. J. Brock. Illustrated. Los Angeles, Historic Record co., 1924. Three-quarter leather. Scarce.

11 p.l., [33]–1255 p. plates, ports. 27.3 cm.

Chapter XIII deals with outlawry in Placer County and gives a long account of

Richard H. Barter, alias Rattlesnake Dick, and Tom Bell. Chapter VI of the history of Nevada County has accounts of Murieta and Tom Bell.

1282. Larson, T. A.

History of Wyoming, by T. A. Larson. Line drawings by Jack Brodie. Lincoln, University of Nebraska press, 1965. Pict. cloth.

xi p., 1 l., 619 p. illus. headpieces, plates, ports., maps., graphs, tables. 23.7 cm.

Appendices: p. 580–582; sources: p. 583–599; acknowledgments: p. 600; index: p. 601–619.

Half title; illus. double t.p.; map on end papers.

Has information on the Johnson County War, Jim Averill, Cattle Kate, Calamity Jane, Nate Champion, Nick Ray, and other characters of Wyoming's wilder days.

1283. Last Raid of the Daltons

A lecture. Tackett's production of the last raid of the Dalton gang at Coffeyville, Kansas, October 5, 1892. [N.p., n.d.] Folder. Rare.

4 p. 19.3 cm.

Double column.

Describes an exhibit of pictures of the Dalton boys.

1284. Lathrop, Amy

Tales of western Kansas. Collected and compiled by Amy Lathrop. [Kansas City, Mo., La Rue printing co., 1948.] Cloth. Scarce.

4 p.l., [13]–152 p. illus., plates, facsms., maps. 23.4 cm.

Half title; illus. t.p.

Has material on Wild Bill Hickok, Billy the Kid, and Pat Garrett. The author claims that Wild Bill was married to "Indian Anne" of Ellsworth, Kansas, and that she had several children by him. The author also makes the statement that Billy the Kid was killed in 1880. She has him born as William Bonney and says that he went to Santa Fe when he was five. She also follows the legend that at twelve he killed a man who had insulted his mother. John Chisum's name is misspelled, and she calls Wayne Brazil's name Wayne Brazee.

1285. [Lathrop, George]

Dark and terrible deeds of George Lathrop, who, after passing through the various degrees of crime, was finally convicted and hung in New Orleans June 5, 1848, for the robbery and murder of his father, March 8, 1847. . . . New Orleans, [E. E. Barclay], published by Rev. W. Stuart, 1848. Wrappers. Rare.

3 p.l., 7–31 [1] p. plates. 22.5 cm.

2 plates before t.p.; 1 plate at end.

1286. Lathrop, Gilbert A.

Little engines and big men, by Gilbert A. Lathrop. Illustrated with photographs. Caldwell, Idaho, the Caxton printers, ltd., 1954. Pict. cloth. OP.

6 p.l., [13]–326 p. front., plates, ports. 21.7 cm.
Half title; pub. device.

Chapter V, entitled "Western Outlaws," and Chapter XXI, entitled "Gunmen of Cimarron," deal with outlaws and lawlessness.

1287. Laughlin, Ruth (Barker)

Caballeros, by Ruth (Barker) Laughlin. Illustrations by Norma van Sweringen. New York, Toronto, D. Appleton and co., inc., 1931. Cloth. Scarce.

4 p.l., 379 [1] p. front., illus. 22 cm.
Index: p. 373–[380].
Half title; vignette; first edition: figure (1) at end of index.

Republished in 1937. Published again in 1945 by the Caxton Printers, ltd., Caldwell, Idaho, with the addition of a glossary.

4 p.l., 418 p. front., illus. 22 cm.
Half title; map on end papers; pub. device.

The author credits Billy the Kid with killing twenty-one men *before* he was twenty-one and says that the Lincoln County War lasted for ten bloody years and that General Lew Wallace was sent "to stop the highwaymen" and arrived just after the war ended.

1288. Laune, Seigniora Russell

Sand in your eye, by Seigniora Russell Laune. Illustrated by Paul Laune. Philadelphia and New York, J.B. Lippincott co. [1956]. Cloth. OP.

4 p.l., 9–256 p. illus. 20.9 cm.
Half title.

Tells of the killing of Ed Jennings by Temple Houston at Woodward, Oklahoma, the event that caused the Jenning boys to turn to outlawry.

1289. Laut, Agnes C.

Pilgrims of the Santa Fe, by Agnes C. Laut . . ., with forty-four illustrations from photographs. New York, Frederick A. Stokes co., MCMXXXI. Cloth. OP.

x p., 1 l., 3–363 p. front. (with tissue), plates. 21 cm.
Index: p. 361–363.
Half title; pict. end papers (col.); untrimmed.

Has a chapter on the Benders.

1290. Lavender, David

The American Heritage history of the great west. By the editors of American Heritage. . . . Editor in charge: Alvin M. Josephy, Jr., Author: David Lavender. Pictorial comment: Ralph K. Andrist. New York, published by American Heritage publishing co., inc., 1965. Buckram.

7 p.l., 15–416 p. illus., plates (part col.), ports., facsms., maps (part col., part double p.). 28.6 cm.

Acknowledgments: p. 410; index (quadruple column): p. 411–416.

Double t.p. (col. illus.); illus. end papers; double column.

Also published in a de luxe edition with slip case.

In the later chapters there is some outlaw material, as well as some mention of such cow-town gunmen as Wild Bill Hickok, Wyatt Earp, Bat Masterson, and Bill Tilghman. There is also some mention of the James boys, the Youngers, the Daltons, Calamity Jane, and Belle Starr. On page 359 is a picture (which appeared on the cover of an early issue of *Great Guns* and later on the cover of an issue of *True West*) alleged to be of the Jameses and Youngers, but the claim is ridiculous and was long ago disproved, and it is high time it ceased to be so identified. There are also two pages on the Johnson County War.

1291. ———

The big divide, [by] David Lavender. Garden City, N.Y., Doubleday & co., inc., 1948. Cloth. OP.

x p., 1 l., 321 p. plates, ports. 22 cm.

Acknowledgments: p. [295]–297; bibliography: p. [301]–307; index: p. [311]–321.

Half title; map on end papers; device; untrimmed; "First edition" on copyright p.

The author touches upon many of the western outlaws, among them Billy the Kid, and upon the Johnson County and Lincoln County wars.

1292. ———

Land of giants. The drive to the Pacific northwest, 1750–1950, by David Lavender. Garden City, N.Y., Doubleday & co., inc., 1958. Cloth. OP.

x p., 1 l., 468 p. 4 double p. maps (col.). 24 cm.

Bibliographical notes p. [447]–457; index: p. [459]–468.

Half title; device.

Has a section on the Montana vigilantes and the Plummer gang.

1293. ———

The Rockies, by David Lavender. New York, Evanston and London, Harper & Row, publishers [1968]. A regions of America book. Cloth.

6 p.l., 404 p. 4 maps (all fold.). 24.5 cm.
Bibliography: p. 371–388; index: p. 389–404.
Half title; double illus. t.p.; "First edition" on copyright p.; untrimmed; pict. end papers.

Has some material on Henry Plummer and his gang and on the vigilantes of Montana.

1294. Lavigne, Frank C.

Crimes, criminals and detectives. By Frank C. Lavigne, chief stock detective, Helena, Montana. . . . Helena, Mont., State publishing co. [1921]. Stiff wrappers. Scarce.

5 p.l., [11]–252 [1] p. plate, port. 19.5 cm.

Contains material on Soapy Smith, the Wild Bunch, train robbers in Montana, and Henry Starr.

1295. [Law and Order Exhibit]

Souvenir pamphlet from the law and order exhibit. [N.p., n.d.] Wrappers. (Cover title.) Scarce.

12 p. 15.2 cm.

Evidently a catalogue written for an unidentified exhibit on outlaws and gunmen. The author touches upon the Youngers, the James brothers, the Ford boys, Ed O. Kelly, William Tilghman, Sam Bass, Wild Bill Hickok, Henry Starr, Cherokee Bill Goldsby, Bill Doolin, Bill Dalton, Ed Nix, Heck Thomas, Rube Burrow, and Belle Starr. He is mistaken in saying that Jim Reed was killed by one of his own gang for the reward, and he errs in the date of Hickok's murder, which occurred in 1877, not 1876.

1296. Lawson, W. B.

Dalton boys and the M. K. and T. train robbery, by W.B. Lawson. New York, Street & Smith, publishers, 1901. Pict. wrappers. Rare.

[128] p. (no pagination). 18.3 cm.
Last 6 p. adv.

1297. ———

The Dalton boys in California; or, a bold holdup at Ceres, by W.B. Lawson. New York, Street & Smith, publishers [1893]. Pict. wrappers. Rare.

1 l. (adv.), [5]–132 p. 19 cm.
Half title; pub. device; 9 p. adv. at end.

A typical wild western, but a rare collector's item. Because of its brittle paper, it has all but disappeared.

1298. ———

Jesse James at Long Branch; or, playing for a million, by W.B. Lawson. New York, Street & Smith, 1898. Col. pict. wrappers. Rare.

[136] p. (no pagination). 18 x 12 cm.
12 p. adv. at end.
No. 14 of Street & Smith, Publishers' Log Cabin Library.

1299. ———

The Indian outlaw; or, Hank Starr, the log cabin bandit, by W.B. Lawson. Orrville, Ohio, Frank T. Fries, printer, publisher, [n.d.]. Pamphlet. (Cover title.) Scarce.

7 p. 24 cm.

Printed on pink paper and unstapled. A tabloid account of the life and bank robberies of Henry Starr.

1300. Lawton, Harry

Willie Boy, a desert manhunt, [by] Harry Lawton. [Balboa Island, Calif.], the Paisano press, [1960.] Pict. cloth.

xii p., 1 l., 224 [2] p. illus., plates, ports. 22.4 cm.
Bibliography: p. 221–224.
Half title; map on end papers; double t.p.; vignette.

The story of Willie Boy, a Paiute Indian turned killer, his chase across the Mojave Desert, and his death.

1301. Layne, J. Gregg

Annals of Los Angeles, from the arrival of the first white man to the Civil War, 1769–1861, by J. Gregg Layne. Special publication number nine. San Francisco, Calif., California Historical society, 1935. Pict. cloth. Illus. label pasted on. OP.

97 p. front., plates (all col. incl. front.). 26.5 cm.
Notes: p. 89–97.
Vignette.

Contains some material on Joaquín Murieta and Jack Powers.

1302. Leach, A. J.

A history of Antelope county, Nebraska, from its first settlement in 1868 to the close of the year 1883, by A. J. Leach. . . . [Chicago, Lakeside press], 1909. Cloth. Scarce.

7 p.l., 9–262 p. 20.7 cm.

Gilt top; untrimmed.

Has several chapters devoted to Doc Middleton and his gang of horse thieves.

1303. Leakey, John

The west that was, from Texas to Montana, by John Leakey, as told to Nellie Snyder Yost. Dallas, Southern Methodist University press [1958]. Cloth.

xii p., 1 l., 3–271 p. plates, ports., facsm. 23.7 cm.
Index: p. 263–271.
Half title; vignette.

Has some new material on King Fisher and a mention of Ben Thompson. I think that the author is mistaken in saying that Ben Thompson had received a message warning him not to come to Jack Harris' Theatre in San Antonio. Fisher told Thompson that if he had the nerve to go, Fisher would go too. The author says that "both were killed as they stepped inside the door, presumably by shots fired from the balcony by someone lying in wait there." But we know that they had been inside and gone to the balcony before the shooting started. The author is also mistaken in saying that Thompson was a U.S. marshal.

1304. Leckenby, Charles H.

The tread of the pioneers. . . . Some highlights in the dramatic and colorful history of northwestern Colorado, compiled by Charles H. Leckenby. Steamboat Springs, Colo., from the Pilot press [1945]. Cloth. Scarce.

6–206 [1] p. plates, ports. 23.6 cm.
Table of contents labeled "index" at end; vignette; copyright notice on verso of flyleaf before t.p.

Privately printed and issued in a small edition, this book contains a chapter on the capture of Harry Tracy and one on Tom Horn.

1305. Leckie, William H.

The buffalo soldiers. A narrative of the Negro cavalry in the west. [By] William H. Leckie. Norman, University of Oklahoma press [1967]. Cloth.

xiv p., 1 l., 3–290 p. illus., plates, ports., maps. 23.5 cm.
Bibliography: p. 262–276; index: p. 277–290.
Half title; t.p. in blue and black; "First edition" on copyright p.

Has an account of the Lincoln County War and Billy the Kid. Also tells of the fight at Blazer's Mill between Brewer's posse and Buckshot Roberts.

1306. Lee, Charles (ed.)

North, east, south, west; a regional anthology of American writing. General editor: Charles Lee. New England, Sarah Cleghorn; Middle Atlantic, Edroin

Seaver; Middle West, A. C. Spectorsky; the West, Joseph Henry Jackson; the South, Struthers Burt. [New York], Howell, Soslin [1945]. Cloth. OP.

> xv p., 1 l., 558 p. 23 cm.
> Bibliography: p. [534]–555; index: p. 556–558.
> Half title.

Another anthology reprinting Edwin Corle's "The Ghost of Billy the Kid" from his *Mojave.*

1307. Lee, John Doyle

History of the Mountain Meadow massacre; or, the butchery in cold blood of 134 men, women and children, by Mormons and Indians, September, 1857. Also a full and complete account of the trial, confession and execution of John D. Lee, the leader of the murderers. . . . [San Francisco], Spalding & Barto, book and job printers, 1877. Wrappers. (Cover title.) Rare.

> 32 p. illus. 23.3 cm.

1308. ———

The Lee trial! An expose of the Mountain Meadow massacre, being a condensed report of the prisoner's statement, testimony of witnesses, charge of the judge, arguments of counsel, and opinions of the press upon the trial, by the Salt Lake Daily Tribune reporter. Salt Lake City, Utah, Tribune printing co., publishers, 1875. Wrappers. Rare.

> 2 p.l., [5]–64 p. 20 cm.

1309. ———

Life, confession and execution of Bishop John D. Lee, the Mormon fiend! His seventeen wives—startling details since his death—implication of Brigham Young—the massacre at Mountain Meadows, also the escape of his daughter. . . . Philadelphia, Pa., issued from the Old Franklin publishing house, 1877. Pict. wrappers. Rare.

> [3]–78 [2] p. illus. 23.2 cm.

1310. ———

The life and confession of John D. Lee, the Mormon. With a full account of the Mountain Meadow massacre and execution of Lee. Helpless women and children butchered in cold blood by merciless Mormon assassins. Philadelphia, Barclay & co., publishers [1877]. Pict. wrappers. Rare.

> 19–46 [1] p. illus., plates. 23.4 cm.
> Republished in an enlarged edition of 64 pages in 1882.

1311. ———

Mormonism unveiled; or, the life and confessions of the late Mormon Bishop John D. Lee (written by himself); embracing a history of Mormonism from its inception down to the present time, with an exposition of the secret history, signs, symbols and crimes of the Mormon church. . . . Illustrated. St. Louis, Mo., Bryan, Brand & co., 1877. Leather. Rare.

xiv, [15]–390 [1] p. front. (port.), plates, ports. 21.6 cm.

Reprinted with appendix added same year. Reprinted in St. Louis in 1881, 1882, and 1889.

Tells about Lee's criminal life, his trial and execution.

1312. ———

The Mormon menace, being the confession of John D. Lee, Danite. An official assassin of the Mormon church under the late Brigham Young. Introduction by Alfred Henry Lewis. With numerous illustrations. New York, Home Protection publishing co. [1905]. Cloth. Scarce.

xxii, [23]–368 p. front., illus. 19.2 cm.

Tells about the murders committed by Lee and, in the appendix, of his execution on March 23, 1877.

1313. Lee, Susan E.

These also served. Brief histories of pioneers. . . . Short stories and pictures relative to Catron, Grant, Sierra, Socorro and Valencia counties of New Mexico, by Susan E. Lee. Drawings by Dorothy S. Covington. Los Lunas, N.M., published by Susan E. Lee, 1960. Pict. cloth.

xiv p., 1 l., 208 p. front. (port.), illus., plates, ports., map. 23 cm.

Half title; illus. t.p.

Has a chapter on the Apache Kid which contains some new material.

1314. Leedy, Carl H.

Golden days in the Black Hills, by "the old timer" Carl H. Leedy. [N.p., n.d.] Stiff pict. wrappers.

2 p.l., 116 p. plates, ports. 21.6 cm.

Has some material on Calamity Jane. The author is mistaken in saying that Belle Starr was Jane's sister and that she married William Hickok, Wild Bill's cousin.

1315. LeFors, Joe

Wyoming peace officer, by Joe LeFors. An autobiography. Laramie, Wyo., Laramie printing co. [1953]. Cloth. Scarce.

xiii p., 2 l., 200 p. front., plates, ports. 24.2 cm.
Appendix: p. 187–192; index: p. 195–200.
Tailpieces.

Published by the author's wife after his death, this book reveals some heretofore unwritten history about the Johnson County War and about Tom Horn and other outlaws of the Northwest. The author was the officer who trapped Horn into a confession. There is also some information on Flat Nose George Curry and the Wild Bunch.

1316. Leftwich, Bill

Tracks along the Pecos, by Bill Leftwich. [Pecos, Texas, Pecos press, 1957.] Pict. wrappers. (Cover title.) OP.

4 p.l., 1 p., 70 p. illus., plates, ports., maps, plans, facsms. 25 cm.

This has material on Jim Miller and John Wesley Hardin. The author gives a detailed description of Miller's killing of Bud Frazier and his later hanging in Ada, Oklahoma.

1317. Lemley, Vernon

The old west, 1849–1929. A short sketch of the old west, and of many characters and historic places, when the prairie schooners crossed the plains, and the change made by the advance of civilization, by Vernon Lemley. Osborne, Kans., [n.d.]. Pict. wrappers. (Cover title.)

8 p. 20.2 cm.

Has some mention of Bat Masterson, Belle Starr, Cherokee Bill, Bob Ford, Wild Bill Hickok, and others.

1318. Lemon, John J. (pseud. of Joseph Have Hanson)

The Northfield tragedy; or, the robber's raid. A thrilling narrative. A history of the remarkable attempt to rob the bank at Northfield, Minnesota. The cold-blooded murder of the brave cashier and an inoffensive citizen. The slaying of two of the brigands. The wonderful robber hunt and capture graphically described. Biographies of the victims, the capture & the notorious Younger and James gang of desperadoes. Illustrated. . . . St. Paul, Minn., published by John Jay Lemon, 1876. Pict. wrappers. Exceedingly rare.

[3]–95 p. plates, ports., map. 21 cm.
Names of contributors for aid of Heywood's family: p. 83–95.

The only copy of this book I was able to locate is in the University of Kansas City Library, where it lay uncatalogued when I examined it. I was allowed to enter the stacks and discovered it on a shelf behind other books, its presence unknown to the librarian. Heywood, the bank's head bookkeeper, was killed in the holdup.

1319. Leonard, Elizabeth Jane, and Julia Cody Goodman

Buffalo Bill: king of the old west. Biography of William F. Cody . . . pony express rider—buffalo hunter—plains scout and guide—master showman, by Elizabeth Jane Leonard and Julia Cody Goodman; edited by James William Hoffman. New York, Library publishers [1955]. Cloth and boards. OP.

9 p.l., 19–320 p. front. (port.), illus., plates, ports. map (double p.), facsm. 20.8 cm.

Notes and appendix: p. 289–302; Cody genealogy: p. 303–308; Frederici genealogy: p. 309–310; bibliography: p. 311–314; index: p. 315–320.

Half title; map on end papers; pub. device.

Has considerable material on Wild Bill Hickok. Unlike most writers who deal with Hickok, these authors do not dwell upon the McCanles "gang," but they do say that he "single-handedly wiped out the McCanles gang, an outlaw band pretending to be attached to the Confederate Army. This courageous exploit made Wild Bill the hero of the hour."

1320. Leopard, John C., Buel Leopard, R. M. McCammon, and Mary McCammon Hillman

History of Davies and Gentry counties, Missouri. Davies county by John C. Leopard and Buel Leopard. Gentry county by R. M. McCammon and Mary McCammon Hillman. Illustrated. Topeka-Indianapolis, Historical publishing co., 1922. Three-quarter leather. Rare.

14 p.l., [65]–1039 p. front. (ports.), plates, ports. 27 cm.

Contains an account of the bank robbery at Gallatin, the Rock Island train robbery in 1881, and the trial of Frank James.

1321. [Lesson, Michael A.]

History of Montana, 1739–1885. A history of its discovery and settlement, social and commercial progress, mines and miners, agriculture and stock-growing, churches, schools and societies, Indians and Indian war, vigilantes, courts of justice. . . . Illustrated. Chicago, Warner, Beer & co., 1885. Three-quarter leather. Scarce.

7 p.l., 15–1367 p. plates, ports., large fold. map (col.) in front. 27.7 cm.

Has much material on the Plummer gang and the Montana vigilantes.

1322. Lesure, Thomas B.

Adventures in Arizona. An informal guide to the sights, legends and history of the Grand Canyon state, by Thomas B. Lesure. San Antonio, Texas, the Naylor co. . . . [1956]. Cloth.

xvi p., 1 l., 3–169 p. plates (col.). 21.7 cm.

Half title; map on end papers.

Has a chapter on Tombstone and the O K Corral fight. The author calls the Earps a "shady clan" and says that the O K battle "lasted only thirty seconds, saw a total of thirty bullets fired and three of the Clanton-McLowery [*sic*] group dead in the dust. And though the Earps were victorious, their marksmanship created a wave of public resentment that later caused them to high-tail it for the sanctuary of Colorado."

1323. Leuba, Edmond

La Californie et les états du Pacifique. Souvenirs et impressions, par Edmond Leuba. Paris, Librairie Sandoz et Thuillier. . . ., 1882. Wrappers. Rare.

2 p.l., [5]–318 p. 19.2 cm.

Chapter XXXII deals with Vásquez and the author's meeting with him as an early-day French visitor to the American West. The author gave information not previously published. At the time he wrote of his experiences in California and of his travels in the southwestern deserts in 1874, he was interested in the borax deposits which had been discovered there. While traveling abroad, Allen L. Chickering came upon a copy of Leuba's book in Paris and translated it into English. In 1893 several chapters from this translation were published by the California Historical Society, under the titles "Bandits, Borax and Bears" and "A Frenchman in the Panamints."

1324. Lewis, Alfred Henry

The sunset trail, by Alfred Henry Lewis. . . . Illustrated. New York, A. S. Barnes & co., 1905. Pict. cloth. Scarce.

x p., 3 l., 393 [6] p. front., illus., plates. 19 cm.

Half title; device; 6 p. adv. at end.

Republished by A.L. Burt in 1906.

Mostly stories of Dodge City and its gunmen, written in fictional form. O. S. Clark, in his *Clay Allison of the Washita*, quotes part of one chapter from this book (see Item 429).

1325. Lewis, Flannery

Suns go down, by Flannery Lewis. New York, the Macmillan co., 1937. Cloth. OP.

4 p.l., 3–226 p. 21 cm.

Half title; untrimmed; "First printing" on copyright p.

Deals with Virginia City, the vigilantes, Jack Davis, Farmer Peel, Sam Brown, and others.

1326. Lewis, John Woodruff (Don Jernado, pseud.)

The true life of Billy the Kid, [by Don Jernado]. New York, Frank Tousey, publisher, August 29, 1881. Pict. wrappers. (Cover title.) Rare.

16 [1] p. 28.7 cm.
Double column.
[Wide Awake Library, Vol. I, No. 451.]
Reprinted in facsimile in 1945 with an introduction by J. C. Dykes.

One of the dime novels that appeared on the stands immediately after the Kid's death. It is utterly false in all details, and very few names are correct. The author says that the Kid was killed on August 14, with a rifle. (It seems that the authors of nearly all the early wild and imaginary tales of western outlaws had little regard for truth; yet they invariably labeled their accounts "true" and used the word "authentic" freely.) The author writes that Mrs. McSween played the piano while her home burned. Such tales may be the source of Walter Noble Burns's account. They were repeated by other writers until they became legendary.

1327. Lewis, Lloyd

It takes all kinds, [by] Lloyd Lewis. New York, Harcourt, Brace and co. [1947]. Cloth. OP.

ix p., 1 l., [3]–276 p. 20.7 cm.
Sources: p. [275]–276.
Half title; "First edition" on copyright p.

A collection of the author's newspaper and magazine articles, written over a period of years. The book contains a chapter on Billy the Kid, and although the author tells the story through a character whom he calls Tom Blevins and who he admits has a reputation for telling tall tales, he does nothing through footnotes or otherwise to correct the preposterous statements made by Blevins. The author himself misnames William Bonney as William Bonner.

According to this tale the Kid went to an eastern college; was a fine musician; was in love with Anne Maxwell, whom he met in Ottaway, Illinois; and by actual count killed forty-five men. The whole chapter is filled with such outlandish tales. The author has Pat Garrett collecting a $12,000 reward from the state and one of $32,000 from the cattle association for killing the Kid. Some reward!

1328. ———, and Henry Justin Smith

Oscar Wilde discovers America [1882], by Lloyd Lewis and Henry Justin Smith. New York, Harcourt, Brace and co. [1936]. Cloth. Scarce.

xiv p., 1 l., 3–462 p. front. (port.), illus., plates, ports. facsms. 24.2 cm.
Notes and bibliography: p. 447–453; index: p. 455–462.

Half title; "First edition" on copyright p.

Chapter 11 is devoted to Jesse James and is accompanied by some unusual pictures. Who would expect to find a chapter on western outlaws in a book of this title? And I am still wondering why the authors included it; it has no connection with the rest of the book. They say that Jesse's greatest sin was the "invention and practice of train robbery," but I fear that he did not invent this great western industry, for the Reno brothers had robbed trains long before Jesse robbed his first one. They repeat the fable about Jesse holding up the landlord to recover the money he had given to the widow to pay off her mortgage. They also have the date of Billy the Kid's killing as July 15. It occurred on the fourteenth.

1329. Lewis, Oscar

High Sierra country, [by] Oscar Lewis. New York, Duell, Sloan and Pearce; Boston, Toronto, Brown and co. [1955]. Cloth. OP.

ix p., 1 l., [3]–291 p. 21.9 cm.
Index: p. [281]–291.
Half title; map on end papers; pub. device.

Chapter VII, entitled "A Gallery of Bad Men," deals with Black Bart, Joaquín Murieta, Chris Evans, George Sontag, and John Sontag, as well as stagecoach and train robberies.

1330. Lewis, Tracy Hammond

Along the Rio Grande, by Tracy Hammond Lewis. Illustrations by Oscar Frederick Howard. New York, Lewis publishing co., 1916. Pict. cloth. Scarce.

5 p.l., 215 p. front., illus. 19.2 cm.

Has a chapter on banditry.

1331. Lewis, Willie Newbury

Between sun and sod, by Willie Newbury Lewis, with illustrations by H. B. Bugbee. Clarendon, Texas, Clarendon press [1938]. Pict. cloth. Scarce.

xv p., 1 l., 244 p. illus., plates. 23.4 cm.
Appendix: p. 229–244.
Half title; vignette.

Chapter XII, entitled "The Law of the West," contains some material on gunmen. The author tells a tale about Wild Bill Hickok (which she spells Hickock) which I very much doubt. It seems that Al Gentry (lately sheriff at Clarendon) was on his way to Texas when Hickok made him dance by shooting at his feet. Later Gentry caught Hickok off his guard and told him that if he did not dance he would kill him, and Wild Bill "danced to the tune of another's playing."

The first printing of this book was recalled because of typographical errors. Newbury was spelled "Newberry" on the title page, and other errors were corrected before it was again released. The first state is thus very scarce.

1332. Lieberson, Goddard (ed.)

The Columbia records legacy collection. The badmen. Songs, stories and pictures of the western outlaws from Black Hills to border, 1865–1900. Produced by Goddard Lieberson. [N.p., n.d.] Stiff boards.

5 p.l., [11]–69 p. illus., plates, ports., map, facsm. 32.3 x 31.2 cm.
Double, triple, and quadruple column.

Issued with records of outlaw songs, and voice recordings of Mrs. Zoe Tilghman, Mrs. Sophie Poe, George Bold, and Homer Croy in a slip case. Has chapters on Quantrill, the James boys, the Youngers, Sam Bass, Billy the Kid, Gregorio Cortez, Ben Thompson, and Belle Starr, and has information on the Daltons, Bill Doolin, Henry Brown, and others.

1333. Liggett, William (Bill), Sr.,

My seventy-five years along the Mexican border, [by] William (Bill) Liggett. New York, Exposition press [1964]. Cloth.

5 p.l., [11]–139 p. 21 cm.
Half title; pub. device; "First edition" on copyright p.

In a chapter entitled "Arizona Lawmen" the author deals with such officers as Burt Mossman, Commodore Perry Owens, Harry Wheeler, John Slaughter, and the Earps. Among the outlaws he writes about are Burt Alvord, Augustin Chacon, the Baca gang, the Apache Kid, and Pearl Hart.

1334. Lillie, Gordon William

Life story of Pawnee Bill, [by Gordon William Lillie. . . . N.p., n.d.) Pamphlet. Scarce.

22 p. 21.3 cm.
Double column.

Contains some material on Jesse James.

1335. Lindquist, Allan Sigvard

Jesse Sweeten, Texas lawman, by Allan Sigvard Lindquist. San Antonio, Texas, the Naylor co. . . ., 1961. Pict. cloth.

xiv, 221 p. front. (port.). 21.7 cm.
Half title; illus. end papers (dif.).

Has much about lawlessness in Texas and some new information about Belle Starr.

1336. Lindsay, Charles

Big Horn basin, by Charles Lindsay. [Lincoln, published by the university, 1932.] Stiff wrappers. Scarce.

6 p.l., 11–274 p. illus., maps (part fold.). 23 cm.
Bibliography: p. 261–274.
Thesis (Ph.D.), University of Nebraska, 1930.
Also issued as University of Nebraska studies, Vol. XXVIII–XXIX.

Has some information about the Johnson County War.

1337. Lindsay, F. W.

The outlaws, by F. W. Lindsay. . . . With pen and ink sketches by Florence Lindsay. [Quesnal, B. C., Canada, 1963.] Pict. col. wrappers.

3 p.l., 7–64 p. illus., plates, ports., map (double p.). 23.5 cm.
Illus. t.p.; double column; "First printing" on copyright p.

The author claims that Quantrill was killed in British Columbia, where he was living under the name Sharp. The author also deals with several outlaws of that section, including Henry Wagner, the Wild McLeans, and Bill Miner.

1338. Linford, Velma

Wyoming, frontier state, by Velma Linford. Drawings by Ramona Bowman. Denver, Colo., the Old West publishing co., 1947. Pict. cloth. OP.

xii p., 1 l., [3]–428 p. front., plates, ports., maps. 23.2 cm.
Bibliography at end of each chapter; appendix: p. 407–414; full bibliography: p. 415–418; pronouncing index: p. 419–428.

Written as a school history, this book contains material on such outlaws as Bill Carlisle and on the Johnson County War.

1339. Lingle, Robert T., and Dee Linford

The Pecos river commission of New Mexico and Texas. A report of a decade of progress 1950–1960. Compiled under the direction of the Pecos river commission, Carlsbad, New Mexico, by Robert T. Lingle and Dee Linford. [Santa Fe, N.M., the Rydal press, 1961.] Stiff wrappers.

xvi p., 1 l., 3–284 p. front. (port.), plates, ports., maps. 22.8 cm.
Appendices: p. 239–274; index: p. 275–284.
Half title; maps on end papers.

Has some information on Pat Garrett, not as a gunman but as a builder of irrigation ditches, as well as material on John Chisum.

1340. Linn, James Weber

James Keeley, newspaperman, by James Weber Linn. . . . Illustrated. Indianapolis, New York, the Bobbs-Merrill co., publishers [1937]. Cloth. Scarce.

6 p.l., 13–286 p. front. (port.), illus., plates, ports., facsms. 24 cm.
Index: p. 281–286.
Half title; untrimmed; "First edition" on copyright p.

In his younger days Keeley was sent by the *Chicago Tribune* to Wyoming to report on the progress of the Johnson County War. The author of this biography states that the trouble "turned out to involve no more than the killing of two inconspicuous ranchmen, Nate Champion and Ray Kelly [*sic*] over a line fence quarrel . . . in a country worthless for ranching." History tells us that Champion's partner was Nick Ray, and the country was good enough for ranching to fight over.

1341. Linthicum, Richard

A book of Rocky Mountain tales (souvenir edition), by Richard Linthicum. [Denver Colo., W. F. Robinson & co., printers, 1892.] Pict. cloth. Scarce.

3 p.l., [9]–158 p. front. (port.), illus. 20.2 cm.

The book was published in an edition of 283 copies. A list of the subscribers and their home towns is given at the end of the book. There is a chapter on Texas Joe, a New Mexico outlaw, and some mention of Billy the Kid.

1342. Linzee, E. H.

Development of Oklahoma territory, by E. H. Linzee, 1940. [Oklahoma City, 1941.] Cloth. Scarce.

[49] p. (no pagination). front., plates, ports. 28.8 cm.

Has material on the Bert Casey gang, Little Breeches, the Daltons, Chris Madsen, Bill Doolin, and Bitter Creek Newcomb.

1343. [List of Fugitives]

for 1887. Compiled from reports of sheriffs received at the adjutant-general's office. Austin, Texas, State printing office, 1887. Wrappers. (Cover title.) Scarce.

101 p. 22.7 cm.
Index: p. [83]–101.
Double column; alphabetized by counties.

1344. ———

for 1889. Part V. Compiled from records of sheriffs received at the adjutant-general's office. Austin, Texas, State printing office, 1889. Wrappers. (Cover title.) Scarce.

19 p. 23.5 cm.
Index: p. 17–19.
Double column.

1345. ——

for 1890. Part VI. Compiled from reports of sheriffs received at the adjutant-general's office. Austin, Texas, State printing office, 1890. Wrappers. (Cover title). Scarce.

22 p. 22.7 cm.
Index: p. [19]–22.
Double column.

1346. ——

For 1900. Compiled from revised reports of sheriffs from fugitive list of 1896, and from subsequent reports of sheriffs received at the adjutant-general's office. Austin, Texas, von Boeckman, Moore & Schutze, state contractors, 1900. Wrappers. (Cover title.) Scarce.

203 p. 22.7 cm.
Index: p. [163]–203.
Double column.

Items 1343 to 1346 were compiled from lists given to the Texas Rangers and were issued annually. They contain the names of many outlaws and other lawbreakers.

1347. Lloyd, John

The invaders. A story of the "Hole-in-the-Wall" country, by John Lloyd. New York, R. F. Fenno & co. [1910]. Pict. cloth. Rare.

9–452 p. front., 3 plates (incl. front.). 19.7 cm.
T.p. in red and black

A fictional account of the Johnson County War, included here because it uses many real names. It is said to have been suppressed; hence its rarity. It has a chapter on Tom Horn and deals with real people, among them Sheriff Angus, Jack Flagg, John Tisdale, Nate Champion, Nick Ray, Jim Averill and others. The man the author calls Captain Stanley is really Frank Canton.

1348. Lloyd-Owen, Frances

Gold Nugget Charlie. A narrative compiled from the notes of Charles E. Masson, by Frances Lloyd-Owen. London, Toronto, Bombay, Sydney, George G. Harrap & co., ltd. [1939]. Cloth. Scarce.

4 p.l., [1] p., 10–259 [1] p. front. (port.), plates, ports. 22.3 cm.
Half title; map on end papers; pub. device.

Has some material on Calamity Jane.

1349. Lockley, Fred

Oregon folks, by Fred Lockley. . . . New York, the Knickerbocker press, 1927. Cloth. Scarce.

vii p., 1 l., 3–220 p. 19.5 cm.

Has a chapter on early-day holdups of stagecoaches in Oregon.

1350. Lockwood, Francis Cummins

Arizona characters, by Frank C. Lockwood. . . . Los Angeles, the Times-Mirror press, 1928. Pict. cloth. Scarce.

xiv p., 1 l., 230 p. front., illus., plates, ports. 20.2 cm.
Half title.

1351. ———

Pioneer days in Arizona, from the Spanish occupation to statehood, by Frank C. Lockwood. . . . New York, the Macmillan co., 1932. Cloth. Scarce.

xiv p., 5 l., 9–387 p. front. (port.), illus., plates, ports., maps. 24 cm.
Index: p. 379–387.
Half title; untrimmed.

Contains considerable material on Arizona outlaws. The author misnames John Heath as Frank Heith. He seems to have a poor opinion of the Earps, and of the O K Corral fight he says that though the Earps were officers of the law they "deliberately brought on the quarrel for the purpose of getting rid of the Clantons and McLowerys [*sic*]." He says that Wyatt Earp "was both a cold-blooded killer and a very suave and crafty dissimulator" and that Wyatt had told the author in detail "how he had killed Curly Bill and John Ringo, but Breakenridge had told conclusively that Earp did not kill either of these men." There is also some information on the Graham-Tewksbury feud.

1352. Lockwood, Francis Cummins, and Capt. Donald W. Page

Tucson—the old pueblo, by Dean Frank C. Lockwood and Captain Donald W. Page. . . . Phoenix, Ariz., the Manufacturing stationers, inc. [n.d.]. Cloth. Scarce.

2 p.l., 5–94 p. front. (map), plates, plan. 23.5 cm.

Has much material on lawlessness.

1353. Logan, Herschel C.

Buckskin and satin. The life of Texas Jack (J. B. Omohundro) buckskin clad scout, Indian fighter, plainsman, cowboy, hunter, guide and actor and his wife Mlle. Morlacchi, premiere danseuse in satin slippers, by Herschel C. Logan, with a foreword by Paul I. Wellman. Harrisburg, Penn., published by the Stackpole co. [1954]. Pict. cloth. OP.

xiv, 218 p. front. (port.), plates, ports., facsms., maps. 22.6 cm.

Chronology: p. 205–207; bibliography: p. 208–211; acknowledgments: p. 212–213; index: p. 214–218.

Illus. half title; illus. end papers; "First edition" on copyright p.

Contains some material about Wild Bill Hickok, primarily about his show life.

1354. Logue, Roscoe

Tumbleweeds and barb wire fences, by Roscoe Logue. Amarillo, Texas, printed by Russell stationery co., 1936. Stiff pict. wrappers. Scarce.

5 p.l., 11–110 p. illus., plates, ports. 23.6 cm.

Vignette; copyright notice on t.p.

The author includes chapters on Sam Bass, Calamity Jane, Belle Starr, and Black Jack Ketchum—all of which are full of errors. In his chapter on Sam Bass, for example, he errs in saying that Bass's first Texas train robbery was the one at Eagle Ford—that was his third robbery. His chapter on Calamity Jane is sympathetic but historically worthless. He has her capturing Jack McCall in a "two-gun play," disarming him, and locking him up. His chapter on Belle Starr is just as unreliable. He also makes some mention of Cattle Kate and the Benders.

1355. ———

Under Texas and border skies, by Roscoe Logue. Amarillo, Texas, printed by Russell stationery co., 1935. Stiff pict. wrappers. Scarce.

4 p.l., 5–111 p. illus., plates, facsm. 23.6 cm.

Vignette; copyright notice on t.p.

In his chapter on Billy the Kid the author is very sympathetic to the Kid. He repeats the legend of the Kid's card game with Bell while a prisoner at Lincoln, as well as the one about the Kid's going to visit his sweetheart at Maxwell's home the night he was killed.

1356. Long, E. Hudson

O. Henry, the man and his work, by E. Hudson Long. Philadelphia, University of Pennsylvania press, 1949. Cloth. OP.

xi [1] p., 1 l., 158 p. front. (port.). 22.2 cm.

Notes: p. 138–148; selected bibliography: p. 149–152; index: p. 153–158.

Half title.

Has some information about Al Jennings when he was in prison with O. Henry.

1357. [Long, Green H.]

The arch fiend; or, the life, confession and execution of Green H. Long. The arch fiend among desperadoes. Who was a member of that celebrated gang, known as the "Banditti of the West," and traveled through the middle, western and southern states, with Hiram Birchead, a notorious English burglar, robbing, counterfeiting, forging, horse-stealing, negro stealing, house burning, gambling, passing counterfeit money, and murdering; carrying devastation, misery, and death, wherever he went, for the space of eleven years, and was finally brought to the gallows, July 27th, 1851, for the treble murder of Col. Darcy, and his two lovely daughters, Beatrice and Juliet. Little Rock, Ark. [New York], published by A. R. Orton, 1851. Pict. wrappers. Exceedingly rare.

2 p.l., [7]–31 [1] p. front., illus. 20.3 cm.

Republished in 1852 with same collation, but with a Little Rock imprint, and reprinted again in 1853.

One of the really rare books dealing with early outlaws. Long committed sixteen murders.

1358. Long, Haniel

Piñon country, by Haniel Long. Edited by Erskine Caldwell. New York, Duell, Sloan & Pearce [1941]. Dec. cloth. Scarce.

xi p., 1 l., 3–327 p. 22.2 cm.

Index: p. 319–327.

Half title; map on end papers; "First edition" on copyright p.

The author includes a chapter on Billy the Kid but tells nothing of his career, merely treating him as a character of interest to tourists.

1359. Long, Katherine W., and Samuel A. Siciliano

Yuma from hell-hole to haven, by Katherine W. Long and Samuel A. Siciliano. Yuma, Ariz., Yuma County Chamber of Commerce, 1950. Stiff pict. wrappers. OP.

2 p.l., 5–63 [1] p. front., illus., plates (3 double p.). 19.6 cm.

Double column.

1360. Longstreth, T. Morris

The silent force. Scenes from the life of the mounted police of Canada, by T. Morris Longstreth. . . . New York, London, the Century co. [1927]. Dec. cloth. Scarce.

xiv p., 1 l., 3–383 p. front., illus., plates, ports., 2 fold. maps. 22.8 cm.

Bibliography: p. 377; index: p. 379–383.

Half title; pub. device.

Has much on lawlessness and a mention of Soapy Smith.

1361. Look, Al

Unforgettable characters of western Colorado, [by] Al Look. Boulder, Colo., Pruett press, inc. [1966]. Cloth.

vii, 231 p. illus., plates, ports., facsms. 22.3 cm.

Contains a long chapter on Doc Shores, an early Colorado sheriff, in which there is mention of many outlaws, such as Butch Cassidy and his Wild Bunch; Alferd Packer, the Colorado cannibal; and Matt Warner. He says that Shores took George and Charlie Marlow, two of the famed Marlow brothers, back to Texas to appear as witnesses—but deputized them first so that they went as officers of the law. There is also some new material on Tom Horn during the time he worked with Shores. Several versions of Kid Curry's death are given.

1362. [López, Rafael]

Utah's greatest manhunt. The true story of the hunt for López, by an eye witness. [Salt Lake, press of the F. W. Gardiner co., n.d.] Pict. wrappers. Scarce.

8 p.l., [19]–142 [1] p. illus. 16.8 cm.
Illus. t.p.; stapled.

The story of a unique manhunt which ended in the underground workings of a mine, though neither López nor his bones were ever found.

1363. Lord, John

Frontier dust, by John Lord. Edited with an introduction by Natalie Shipman. Hartford, Conn., Edwin Valentine Mitchell, 1926. Cloth. (Title label pasted on.) Scarce.

x p., 1 l., 198 [1] p. 22.2 cm.
Half title.
Colophon: "This book has been designed by Robert S. Josephy and a thousand copies have been printed . . . at the shop of Douglas C. McMurtie, N.Y., in December, MCMXXVI."

Although the author says that this book is an autobiography, he makes some statements that we cannot swallow. He claims that Billy the Kid started his career as an outlaw by killing a cook who had thrown hot grease upon him. He also claims that a young Mexican foreman tipped off Garrett that the Kid was in town. Then follows one fantastic tale after another, with the Kid establishing headquarters in the Texas Panhandle and having eighty or ninety men in his gang. The author has him holding up banks, trains, and stagecoaches, crimes the Kid never committed. The author claims that when the U.S. government sent a company of cavalry after the

Kid for robbing the mails, he and his gang whipped the cavalry in an open fight. Lord says that Garrett was a deputy. He was the sheriff.

In telling of the Kid's escape from the Lincoln County jail, the author has him merely tapping the jailer on the head, locking him and his wife in an empty cell, and then riding off. The author claims that he was sleeping in Maxwell's bed the night Garrett arrived, disguised as a Mexican. Garrett got into bed with Lord, and when the Kid arrived, he slid off the side of the bed and shot him. The author states that the Kid was twenty-four years old when he died and had killed twenty-four men. (Writers give varying ages for Billy, but they seldom fail to have him killing a man for every one of those years.)

The author also claims that the James boys, going under the name Thompson, were in the cattle business for a year in an entirely unoccupied section of southwestern New Mexico. The book is filled with such absurd statements.

1364. [Los Angeles County]

An illustrated history of Los Angeles county, California, containing a history of Los Angeles county from the earliest period of its occupancy to the present time. . . . Chicago, the Lewis publishing co., 1889. Dec. cloth. Scarce.

6 p.l., 1 p., 2–835 p. front. (port.), plates, ports. (part with tissues). 30 cm. Double column.

Contains a chapter about Tiburcio Vásquez.

1365. Love, Nat

The life and adventures of Nat Love, better known in the cattle country as "Deadwood Dick," by himself. A true history of slavery days, life on the great cattle ranges and on the plains of the "wild and woolly" west, based on facts, and personal experiences of the author. Los Angeles, Calif. [Wayside press], 1907. Pict. cloth. Scarce.

3 p.l., [7]–162 p. illus., plates, ports. 23.3 cm.

Although the author, a Negro, is supposed to have been writing of his own experiences, he had either a bad memory or a good imagination. He makes the statement that John Chisum (misspelled Chisholm) hired Billy the Kid to steal cattle for him. When Chisum failed to settle satisfactorily with the Kid, the outlaw ran him out of the country. According to one of the author's many preposterous statements, "He [the Kid] would ride up to a bunch of cowboys and enquire if they worked for Chisholm. If they replied in the affirmative, he would shoot them dead on the spot." The author states that the Kid once pointed out a log cabin as the place where he was born. He has Garrett placing the prisoners he captured at Stinking Springs in a boxcar at Las Vegas when the mob was trying to get Rudabaugh. He repeats the story about Judge Bristol's sentence and the Kid's mocking reply.

1366. Love, Robertus

The rise and fall of Jesse James, by Robertus Love. . . . New York, London, G.P. Putnam's sons . . ., 1926. Cloth. Scarce.

ix p., 1 l., 3–446 p. front. (port. with tissue). 22.2 cm.

Probably the most reliable book written about Jesse James to that date. Like most biographers, the author is sympathetic with his subject. He places much of the blame for the James boys' outlawry upon Pinkerton agents and their persecutions. He also repeats the fable about Jesse helping the impoverished widow hounded by the tyrannical landlord. The book contains a chapter on the Union Pacific robbery at Big Springs as an argument against the common belief that Frank and Jesse were connected with this robbery. His account of this event is fairly accurate except that he gives Joel Collins the first name Jim. He states that Jesse "invented train robbing" and that "the first railway train holdup that ever happened has been charged to the James-Younger group." The Renos were the first to rob a train. He also states that Ed Kelly, the killer of Bob Ford, was killed in a sidewalk fight with a town marshal in Texas. He was killed by a city policeman in Oklahoma City.

1367. Lovell, Emily Kalled

A personalized history of Otero county, New Mexico, by Emily Kalled Lovell. Alamogordo, N.M., published by the Star publishing co., inc., 1963. Wrappers.

2 p.l., 4–39 p. plates, ports. 21 cm.
Double column.

Gives some early history of Otero County and its towns. There is also an account of the battle at Blazer's Mill between Buckshot Roberts and Dick Brewer's posse in which Billy the Kid took part.

1368. Lowther, Charles C.

Dodge City, Kansas, by Charles C. Lowther. . . . Illustrated. Philadelphia, Dorrance and co., publishers [1940]. Cloth. OP.

4 p.l., 9–213 p. front., illus., plates. 19.3 cm.
Pub. device.

Tells about the gunmen of Dodge City and includes a chapter about Mysterious Dave Mather.

1369. Lucia, Ellis

Klondike Kate. The life and legend of Kitty Rockwell, the queen of the Yukon, by Ellis Lucia. New York, Hastings House, publishers [1962]. Cloth.

xi p., 7 l., 15–305 p. plates, ports. 21 cm.
Bibliography: p. 293–296; index: p. 297–305.
Half title.

Has some information about Soapy Smith, with slight mention of such characters as Doc Holliday, Belle Starr, Calamity Jane, Big Nose Kate, Cattle Kate, and Wild Bill Hickok.

1370. ———

The saga of Ben Holladay, giant of the old west, by Ellis Lucia. New York, Hastings House [1959]. Pict. boards.

x p., 1 l., 3–374 p. illus., plates, ports., facsm. 21 cm.
Bibliography: p. 361–366; index: p. 367–374.
Half title; illus. double t.p.; map on end papers.

Has a chapter on Joseph Slade, and a chapter entitled "Let 'Em Dangle," which tells about the Plummer gang and the vigilantes who hanged them.

1371. ———

Tough men, tough country, [by] Ellis Lucia. Englewood Cliffs, N.J., Prentice-Hall, inc. [1963]. Two-tone cloth.

xiv p., 2 l., 3–336 p. plates, ports. 23.5 cm.
Bibliography: p. 334–336.
Half title.

Has excellent chapters on the vigilantes of Montana, dealing with Joseph Slade, Henry Plummer, Harry Tracy, and others.

1372. Ludlow, Fitzhugh

The heart of the continent; a record of travel across the plains and in Oregon, with an examination of the Mormon principle, by Fitzhugh Ludlow. With illustrations. New York, published by Hurd and Houghton, 1870. Cloth. Rare.

vi, 568 p. front. (with tissue), plates. 21.8 cm.

Tells about the author's personal meeting with Slade and of Slade's promise to write a story of his life, though he was hanged by the vigilantes before he could do so.

1373. Ludlum, Stuart D. (ed.)

Great shooting stories, edited by Stuart D. Ludlum. Illustrated by Ted Placek. Garden City, N.Y., Doubleday & co., inc., 1947.

xiii p., 2 l., 3–303 p. illus. 22 cm.

Glossary: p. 301–303.

Half title; illus. end papers; vignette; untrimmed; "First edition" on copyright p.

Contains chapters on Wyatt Earp and the O K Corral fight by Stuart Lake and one on John Wesley Hardin by Eugene Cunningham.

1374. Lydston, G. Frank

Panama and the Sierras; a doctor's wander days, by G. Frank Lydston, M.D. Illustrated from the author's original photographs. Chicago, the Riverton press, 1900. Dec. cloth. Scarce.

6 p.l., 13–283 p. front., plates. 21 cm.

Illus. t.p.; untrimmed; privately printed.

Contains some material on Joaquín Murieta and Three-Fingered Jack García. The author says that his father was a member of a posse that chased Murieta. He claims that Murieta wore a suit of mail, which gave the impression that he bore a charmed life until he was shot in the head. The author also says that his father made a special trip to San Francisco to identify Joaquín's head and said that he "never saw Joaquín looking so well." The author spells Murieta as Muriata.

1375. Lyman, Albert R.

Indians and outlaws. Settling of the San Juan frontier, by Albert R. Lyman. Salt Lake City, Utah, Bookcraft, inc. [1962]. Pict. cloth.

5 p.l., [11]–198 p. plates, ports. 23.5 cm.

A story of early Mormon settlement in the San Juan Valley. There are several chapters on the early-day outlaws and horse thieves of the region.

1376. Lyman, George Dunlap

John Marsh, pioneer. The life story of a trail-blazer on six frontiers, by George D. Lyman. Illustrated. New York, Charles Scribner's sons, 1930. Cloth. Scarce.

xii p., 2 l., 3–394 p. front., plates, ports., facsm. 22 cm.

Acknowledgments: p. 339–342; bibliography: p. 343–384; index: p. 387–394.

Half title; map on end papers (dif.); device; untrimmed; first edition: letter "A" on copyright p.

Also published in a limited edition with four facsimiles added, bound in cloth and leather, gilt top, and slip case.

Colophon: "This edition is limited to one hundred and fifty copies of which one hundred and thirty are for sale and twenty are for presentation. No. ——." (Signed).

A chapter entitled "Robbers" has some material on Murieta.

1377. ———

The saga of the Comstock lode. Boom days in Virginia City, by George D. Lyman. . . . Illustrated. New York, London, Charles Scribner's sons, 1934. Cloth. Scarce.

xii p., 1 l., 3–407 p. front., plates, ports. 23 cm.
Acknowledgments: p. 353–355; notes (in part bibliographical): p. 359–399; index: p. 401–407.
Half title; untrimmed; first edition: letter "A" on copyright p.

Has several chapters on the bad men of Washoe, among them "Fighting Sam" Brown and Langford Peel.

1378. Lynch, Lawrence L. (pseud.)

A mountain mystery; or, the outlaw of the Rockies, by Lawrence L. Lynch. Chicago, Laird & Lee, publishers [1894]. Pict. wrappers. Rare.

3 p.l., [11]–600 [8] p. front., illus. 18.6 cm.
Last 8 p. adv.; 3 p. adv. in front.

1379. Lyon, Peter

The wild, wild west, containing the irreducible, rock-bottom, and unadorned facts about such desperadoes, sheriffs, gun slingers, cowtown marshals and assorted riffraff as Wild Bill Hickok, Bat Masterson, Wyatt Earp, Billy the Kid and Jesse James together with various moral lessons and scandalous tales about Calamity Jane and Belle Starr, [by] Peter Lyon. . . . [N.p., n.d., ca. 1960.] Wrappers. (Cover title.)

[15] p. (no pagination). illus., plates, ports. 28 cm.
Double column.

A separate reprint of an article which appeared in the *American Heritage* of August, 1960 (Vol. XI, Number 5). The author attempts to correct the many false legends about these characters and compares them with their fictional counterparts in motion pictures and on television.

1380. Lyons, B. J.

Thrills and spills of a cowboy rancher, [by] B. J. Lyons. . . . New York, Washington, Hollywood, Vantage press [1959]. Cloth. OP.

4 p.l., 9–172 p. front. 21 cm.
Half title; "First edition" on copyright p.

Has a chapter about Harry Tracy. The author spells the name of his accomplice as Morel instead of Merrill.

M

1381. **McAfee, Joseph Ernest**

College pioneering. Problems and phases of life at Park college during its early years; a second volume succeeding "A mid-west adventure in education." By Joseph Ernest McAfee. Kansas City, Missouri, Alumni Parkana committee, 1938. Cloth. Scarce.

7 p.l., 15–264 p. front. (port.). 19.2 cm.
Appendix: p. 259–264.
Half title.

This has some material about Frank and Jesse James.

1382. **[McAuliffe, Eugene]**

History of the Union Pacific coal mines, 1868 to 1940. . . . Omaha, Nebr., the Colonial press [1940]. Morocco. Rare.

4 p.l., 265, x–xliii p. plates, ports., large fold. statement at end. 23.5 cm.
Appendices: p. x–xliii.
Illus. end papers (dif.).

Has some material on Calamity Jane, the hanging of Dutch Charlie, and Big Nose George Parrott. It repeats the legend that Wild Bill Hickok was Calamity Jane's lover.

1383. **McCallum, Henry D., and Frances T. McCallum**

The wire that fenced the west, by Henry D. and Frances T. McCallum. Norman, University of Oklahoma press [1965]. Cloth.

xv p., 1 l., 3–285 p. illus., plates, facsms. 23.5 cm.
Bibliography: p. 268–277; index: p. 278–285.
Half title; "First edition" on copyright p.

Why the authors bring Billy the Kid into the picture is beyond me. He had nothing to do with barbed-wire fencing. Of the Lincoln County War they say that "it was the issue of free range versus land enclosure which caused this fighting" and further that "basically it was the fight of farm settlers and small ranchers struggling against the expanding mesh of wire fencing put up by John Chisum and his fellow cattlemen which developed into the Lincoln County War." Nothing could be further from the truth.

The authors also bring the Johnson County War into the book, and that war had nothing to do with wire fencing. It was a war between large owners and the rustlers and small owners.

1384. McCarty, John L.

Adobe walls bride. The story of Billy and Olive King Dixon, by John L. McCarty. San Antonio, Texas, the Naylor co. [1955]. Cloth.

xi, 281 p. illus., plates, ports. 21.7 cm.

Notes: p. 261–264; bibliography: p. 265–273; index: p. 275–281.

Half title; illus. end papers; illus. t.p.

Has some material on Black Jack Ketchum and his train robberies.

1385. ———

The enchanted west, [by John McCarty. Dallas, Texas, the Doctor Pepper co., 1944]. Stiff pict. wrappers (col.). Scarce.

[38] p. (no pagination). illus. (all col.). 22.7 cm.

Has some material on Billy the Kid, including many of the tales invented by Upson. The author also mentions many western outlaws and gunmen, such as Pat Garrett, Bat Masterson, the Earps, John Slaughter, Bill Tilghman, Clay Allison, Burt Alvord, Black Bart, Sam Bass, Curly Bill Brocius, the Daltons, Jack Helm, John Wesley Hardin, Wild Bill Hickok, Doc Holliday, Bill Longley, the Jameses, Al Jennings, Johnny Ringo, Luke Short, Joseph Slade, Henry Starr, Ben Thompson, and Cole Younger.

1386. ———

Maverick town, the story of old Tascosa, by John L. McCarty, with chapter decorations by Harold D. Bugbee. Norman, University of Oklahoma press, 1946. Pict. cloth.

xiii p., 1 l., 3–277 p. illus., plates, ports. 21 cm.

Bibliography: p. 261–266; index: p. 267–277.

Half title; map on end papers; illus. double t.p.; illus. chapter headings; "First edition" on copyright p.

New and enlarged edition, 1968.

The first complete history of this wild cow town, it tells about its gunmen and gun battles and some of the other outlaws of the Southwest. The chapters on Sostenes l'Archeveque and Billy the Kid are fairly reliable. The author, however, continues the old legends that the Kid was born William H. Bonney and that he killed a man who insulted his mother.

1387. ———

Some experiences of Boss Neff in the Texas and Oklahoma panhandle. [Amarillo, Texas, the Globe-News publishing co., 1941.] Stiff pict. wrappers. (Cover title.) Rare.

[30] p. (no pagination). illus. chap. headings. 27 cm.

Triple column.

"200 copies printed, only 100 of which are offered for sale."

Has a chapter on the famous gunfight at Tascosa. Republished in 1968 by Harry E. Chrisman with marginal corrections by the author.

1388. McCarty, Lea Franklin

The gunfighters, [by] Lea F. McCarty. Berkeley, Calif. [a Mike Roberts color production, 1959]. Stiff pict. wrappers (col.). Hinged.

2 p.l., 44 p. illus., 21 plates (col.), 1 port. 28 cm.

Appendix: p. 43–44.

Vignette; headpieces.

Reproductions of the author's oil paintings of western gunmen, together with a short sketch about each subject on the preceding page. A good-sized pamphlet could be written about the errors the author makes in his text. He has the James boys and the Youngers first cousins and says that the bomb the Pinkertons threw into the Samuel home "literally blew him [Dr. Samuel] sky high." The doctor was unhurt. The author repeats the fable about the McCanles-Hickok "fight" but has only six in the gang. He says that McCall was hanged in Custer City. He was hanged in Yankton.

He has Ben Thompson born in 1883. Thompson was born in 1843, forty years earlier. Many other dates are wrong. The author repeats all the legends about Clay Allison, the Earps, and Billy the Kid. I fail to see why Calamity Jane is included in a list of "gunslingers."

1389. McCauley, James Emmitt

A stove-up cowboy's story, by James Emmitt McCauley. Introduction by John A. Lomax. Drawings by Tom Lea. [Dallas, Texas], published by the Texas Folklore society, Austin, Texas, and the University press in Dallas, 1943. Pict. cloth. Scarce.

xxii p., 1 l., 73 p. front., illus. 22.2 cm.

Illus. end papers.

[Ranch Life series.]

Colophon: "700 copies of this book have been printed and the type melted."

Republished in 1965.

Contains some interesting episodes in the author's life, as well as information about some of the outlaws of Texas and Arizona.

1390. McClintock, James H.

Arizona, prehistoric—aboriginal—pioneer—modern. The nation's youngest commonwealth within a land of ancient culture, by James H. McClintock. Chicago, the S.J. Clarke publishing co., 1916. Three-quarter leather. Pub. in 3 volumes. Scarce.

Vol. I, x, 312 p. front. (port. with tissue), plates, ports., maps. 27 cm.
Vol. II, vii, 313–633 p. plates, ports. 27 cm.
Illus., p. 619–622; index: p. 623–633.
Vol. III, biographical.
Vols. I and II paged continuously; state seal on t.p.

Has reliable chapters on the Arizona outlaws.

1391. McClintock, John S.

Pioneer days in the Black Hills. Accurate history and facts related by one of the early day pioneers. Author John S. McClintock. Deadwood, S.D., edited by Edward L. Senn. Deadwood, S.D., published by John S. McClintock [1939]. Fabrikoid. Scarce.

x p., 2 l., 336 p. front. (port.), plates, ports. 23.5 cm.
Biographical sketches: p. 280–336.
Half title.

Contains much material on the road agents and outlaws of the Black Hills and on Wild Bill Hickok and Calamity Jane. The author knew Calamity Jane very well and tells much of the truth about her. The only mistake I find in his chapter on her is that he says she died August 1, 1903, "lacking one day of being exactly thirty-seven years after the death of Wild Bill Hickok." Wild Bill was killed in 1876, twenty-seven years earlier. The author confirms the fact that Jane's book is full of lies.

1392. McClure, Alexander Kelly

Three thousand miles through the Rocky mountains, by A.K. McClure. Philadelphia, J.B. Lippincott & co., 1869. Cloth. Scarce.

8 p.l., 17–456 p. front. (with tissue), plates. 19.5 cm.
Appendix: p. 453–456.

Contains some information on the Montana vigilantes.

1393. McConnell, H. H.

Five years a cavalryman; or, sketches of regular army life on the Texas frontier, twenty-odd years ago. By H. H. McConnell, late Sixth U.S. Cavalry. Jacksboro, Texas, J.N. Rogers & co., printers, 1889. Cloth. Scarce.

viii p., 1 l., [11]–319 p. 19.6 cm.
Printed on pink paper.

Has some information on the Texas Rangers and on cattle thieves. The author says that Joe Horner (who later left Texas and assumed the name Frank Canton) and "his followers were the typical 'bad men,' the 'shooters from shootersville' of that day."

1394. McConnell, W. J.

Early history of Idaho, by W. J. McConnell . . . who was present and cognizant of the events narrated. Published by authority of the Idaho State Legislature. Caldwell, Idaho, the Caxton printers, ltd., MCMXIII. Cloth. Scarce.

6 p.l., [15]–420 p. 2 ports. (incl. front. with tissue). 23.5 cm.
Appendix: p. [387]–420.

Has much on the Plummer gang of road agents, vigilantes, and robberies.

1395. McConnell, William John

Frontier law. A story of vigilante days, by William J. McConnell, in collaboration with Howard R. Driggs. . . . Illustrated with drawings by Herbert M. Stoops. Yonkers-on-Hudson, N.Y., Chicago, World book co., 1924. Pict. cloth. Scarce.

xii, 233 [8] p. front., illus. 20.2 cm.
"Pioneer Life Series."
Half title; pub. device; headpieces; tailpieces.
8 p. adv. at end.

1396. McCool, Grace

So said the coroner. How they died in old Cochise, by Grace McCool. [Tombstone, Ariz.], Tombstone Epitaph [1968]. Stiff pict. wrappers.

3 p.l., 93 p. 21.3 cm.

This little book tells of the many deaths and murders in Cochise County, Arizona, and has chapters on the Bisbee massacre, the hanging of John Heath, the Earps, and gun battles of the era, especially the one at the O K Corral. The author claims the McLaury brothers spelled their name MacClaughrey. This is the first time I have seen that statement.

1397. McCready, Albert L.

Railroads in the days of steam. . . . Narrative by Albert L. McCready, in collaboration with Lawrence W. Sagle. New York, published by American Heritage publishing co., inc. [1960]. Pict. cloth.

2 p.l., 1 p., 10–153 p. illus., plates (many col., some double p.), ports., maps. 26 cm.

Bibliography: p. 151–152; index: p. 152–153.

Illus. half title; col. illus. double t.p.; pub. device; illus. col. end papers.

Has material on Wyatt Earp, Bat Masterson, the James boys, and the Youngers. The author says that after several more train robberies, "some staged with the help of Cole Younger and his brothers, Jesse James made his first mistake." He says that Jesse decided to branch out and begin robbing banks. Jesse had already robbed quite a few banks, but the author leaves the impression that the bank in Northfield was the first bank he attempted to rob. He also says that Frank and Jesse were "living quite openly in a house in St. Joseph, Missouri, under the name of Howard." Frank not only did not live there but was not even in St. Joseph.

1398. McDade, Thomas M.

The annals of murder. A bibliography of books and pamphlets on American murders from colonial times to 1900. Compiled by Thomas M. McDade. Norman, University of Oklahoma press [1961]. Cloth.

xi p., 1 l., 3–360 p. plates (facsms.). 24 cm.

Index: p. 334–360.

Half title; illus. t.p.; "First edition" on copyright p.

Lists 1,126 books on murders committed throughout the United States. Some of the books deal with western outlaws.

1399. McDearmon, Ray

Without the shedding of blood. The story of Dr. U.D. Uzell, and of pioneer life at old Kimball, [by] Ray McDearmon. San Antonio, Texas, the Naylor co. [1953]. Cloth.

xii, 81 p. 21.6 cm.

Half title.

Chapter 3 deals with bad men and vigilantes.

1400. [McDonald, A.B.]

Murder of the Meeks family; or, crimes of the Taylor brothers. The full and authentic story of the midnight massacre by Bill and George Taylor, of the Meeks family, father, mother and three little children. Flight, pursuit and captures of the murderers, their sensational trials, attempts to bribe juries and guards and their escape from prison. . . . Kansas City, Mo., published by Ryan Walker [1896]. Wrappers. Rare.

[3]–58 p. illus., map. 19 cm.

1401. McDougal, Henry Clay

Recollections, 1844–1909, by Henry Clay McDougal. Kansas City, Mo., Franklin Hudson publishing co., 1910. Cloth. Scarce.

4 p.l., 13–466 p. front. (port. with signature in facsm.). 23.6 cm.
Index: p. 461–466.

In Chapter I there are several pages of new information about the James boys.

1402. McGeeney, P. S.

Down at Stein's Pass. A romance of New Mexico, by P. S. McGeeney. Boston, Angel Guardian press, 1909. Pict. cloth. Scarce.

3 p.l., 114 p. front. (port.). 18.8 cm.

Although fiction, this book is included because it is a collector's item among works on Billy the Kid. The account of the killing of the Kid by Garrett is based upon fact, but the rest is romance.

1403. McGiffin, Lee

Ten tall Texans, by Lee McGiffin. Illustrated by John Alan Maxwell. New York, Lothrop, Lee and Shepard co., inc., 1956. Cloth. Scarce.

2 p.l., 220 p. illus. (9 double p.). 21.5 cm.
Bibliography: p. 220.

This little book, which seems to be slanted toward juvenile readers, contains chapters on ten famous Texas Rangers from Noah Smithwick to Lone Wolf Gonzaullas, a personal friend of mine for many years. The author repeats the fable about John Wesley Hardin shooting a man in the next room because he snored. She is also mistaken in saying that King Fisher was killed by a police officer, and much of her information on Sam Bass is incorrect. She says that Bass held up seven stagecoaches in Nebraska. The holdups took place in South Dakota. She is also mistaken when she writes that Bass "fanned out over Texas, robbing and raiding. Holding up trains became so routine he had a special crew to take over a train while he went down the aisles and fleeced the passengers." Passengers were not robbed in any of Bass's Texas train robberies. There are many more such errors throughout the book.

1404. McGillycuddy, Julia B.

McGillycuddy, agent; a biography of Dr. Valentine T. McGillycuddy, by Julia B. McGillycuddy. Sanford University, Calif. Stanford University press; London, Humphrey Milford, Oxford University press [1941]. Pict. cloth. Scarce.

xi p., 1 l., 3–291 p. front. (port.), ports. 23.5 cm.
Half title; vignette.

In a chapter on Calamity Jane, Dr. McGillycuddy is quoted as saying that he learned about her ancestry from Colonel Dodge and that she was born in Laramie in 1860, the daughter of a soldier named Dalton. He repeated this story so often in letters and conversation that it was generally accepted as true. When one reads Harry Young's book *Hard Knocks,* he is tempted to believe that Mrs. McGillycuddy's book, published twenty-six years later, was taken largely from Young's book, since much of it is word for word as Young wrote his account. Much of the author's material is incorrect, especially her account of the killing of Hickok and the capture of his murderer, McCall.

1405. McGinnis, Edith B.

The promised land, by Edith B. McGinnis. A narrative featuring the life history and adventures of Frank J. Brown, pioneer, buffalo hunter, Indian fighter, and founder of the Quaker settlement of Friendswood. . . . [Boerne, Texas, published by Topperwein publishing co., 1947.] Cloth. OP.

3 p.l., 7–160 p. illus., ports., map. 23.6 cm.
"First edition" on verso of dedication p.

Contains some previously unpublished information on Bat Masterson.

1406. McGinty, Billy

The old west, as written in the words of Billy McGinty [as told to Glenn L. Eyler]. [N.p., 1937.] Stiff wrappers. (Cover title.) Scarce.

108 [2] p. front., illus. 22 cm.
Half title.

Reprinted by the Redlands press, Stillwater, Oklahoma, in 1958.

96 p. 20.8 cm.

Has information on Tulsa Jack Blake and other Oklahoma outlaws. The author tells about the meeting with Ray Daughtery (Arkansas Tom), whose last name he spells Darty. He misspells many other names, among them Mobeda for Mobeetie.

1407. McGivern, Edward

Ed McGivern's book on fast and fancy revolver shooting and police training. . . . Springfield, Mass., the King-Richardson co., 1938. Cloth. Scarce.

8 p.l., 19–484 p. front. (port.), illus., plates, ports. 23.8 cm.
Index: p. 479–484.
Republished many times.

Contains quite a bit of material on many of the outlaws of the West.

1408. McGowan, Edward

Narrative of Edward McGowan, including a full account of the author's adventures and perils while persecuted by the San Francisco vigilance committee of 1856. . . . San Francisco, published by the author, 1857. Pict. wrappers. Excessively rare.

viii, [9]–240 p. plates. 17.6 cm.

Republished in 1917, line for line, page for page from the original edition complete with reproductions, in facsimile of the original illustrations, cover-page title and title page. San Francisco, printed by Thomas C. Russell at his private press. Boards and cloth. Scarce.

viii, 9–240 p. plates (col.). 20.6 cm.

Colophon: "Limited edition of two hundred copies, printed with hand-set type, and type distributed. This is copy ——."

Contains some material on Jack Powers, with whom the author hid out when the vigilance committee was after him.

1409. McGrath, Tom

The vice criminals of the 80's and 90's. Vicente Silva and his forty thieves, by Tom McGrath. [N.p.], 1960. Pict. wrappers.

3 p.l., 1 p., 8–46 p. illus., plates, ports. 22.5 cm.

Appendix: p. 44–46.

1410. McGroarty, John Steven

The pioneer. A fascinating chapter from the pages of California's history, by John Steven McGroarty. . . . [Los Angeles, printed by Press publishing co.], 1925. Pict. wrapper. Scarce.

[18] p. (no pagination). front. (port.). 15.3 x 8.5 cm.

Herman W. Hellman, the subject of this little pamphlet, and at one time a Wells, Fargo shotgun messenger, tells about some of his experiences with Tiburcio Vásquez, the California bandit.

1411. Macguire, H.N.

The Black Hills of Dakota. A miniature history of their settlement, resources, production and prospects, with accurate tables of local distances and a general business directory of the principal towns. Edited and compiled by H. N. Macguire, and published by Jacob S. Gantz. Chicago, 1879. Wrappers. Rare.

[2]–19 p. 16.7 cm.

Tells about the murder of Hickok by McCall. The copy I examined is in the Coe Collection at Yale University.

1412. ——

The coming empire. A complete and reliable treatise on the Black Hills, Yellowstone and Big Horn regions, by H. N. Macguire. . . . Sioux City, Iowa, Watkins & Snead, publisher and stereotypers, 1878. Cloth. Rare.

2 p.l., [6]–177 [12] p. illus., plates, large fold. map in front. 17 cm.
Last 12 p. adv.

Tells about Hickok's death, Calamity Jane, and the early-day lawlessness of the region.

1413. ———

Historical sketch and essays on the resources of Montana, including a business directory of the metropolis. . . . Helena, Mont., Herald book and job printing office, 1868. Wrappers. Rare.

2 p.l., (adv.), [3]–168 p. 22.5 cm.
Adv. on verso of most pages of text.

Has some material about the Montana vigilantes.

1414. ———

The pioneer directory of the metropolis of Montana. [Helena, Mont., Allen & co., 1869.] Exceedingly rare.

[3]–168 p. 20.8 cm.
Adv. on verso of text pages.

Written in three parts. Part 3, by Henry Horr, tells about the Montana vigilantes.

1415. McIntire, James

Early days in Texas. A trip to hell and heaven, by Jim McIntire. Kansas City, Mo., McIntire publishing co. [1902]. Cloth. Rare.

4 p.l., 9–229 p. front., plates, ports. 20.2 cm.
Preface signed: "James McIntire."

The author, himself a fugitive, earlier served as a peace officer in several towns of the West. He tells a great deal about such gunmen as Billy the Kid and Jim Courtright. He was city marshal of Las Vegas, New Mexico, when the mob tried to take Dave Rudabaugh from the train while Dave and the Kid were prisoners of Pat Garrett. He refers to the Kid as the "notorious Mexican outlaw." He tells about running Wyatt Earp and Mysterious Dave Mathers out of Mobeetie for trying to play the old gold-brick game there, and about his later close association with Jim Courtright.

1416. McKee, Irving

"Ben-Hur" Wallace. The life of General Lew Wallace, [by] Irving McKee. Berkeley and Los Angeles, University of California press, 1947.

6 p.l., 301 p. illus., plates, ports. 21.6 cm.
Bibliographical appendix: p. 270–282; index: p. 285–301.
Half Title.

Unlike Wallace's own autobiography, this book devotes some space to the Lincoln County War and tells about Wallace's contacts with Billy the Kid and many of the Kid's exploits during that turbulent time.

1417. McKelvie, Martha

The fenceless range, by Martha McKelvie. Illustrations by John W. Hampton. Philadelphia, Dorrance & co. [1960]. Cloth.

4 p.l., 9–68 [1] p. illus. headpieces, cattle brands on tailpieces. 23.5 cm.

Contains a short and inaccurate chapter on Calamity Jane.

1418. McKennon, C. H.

Iron men. A saga of the deputy United States marshals who rode the Indian territory, [by] C. H. McKennon. Garden City, N.Y., Doubleday & co., inc., 1967. Cloth.

ix p., 1 l., 224 p. plates, ports. 21.5 cm.
Bibliography: p. [209]–217; index: p. [220]–224.
Half title; "First edition" on copyright p.

A book about the Indian Territory and Oklahoma outlaws and the officers who chased them. The author gives a good account of Ned Christie and his death, but is mistaken in saying that Al Jennings had a courtroom altercation with Temple Houston and that Houston killed Ed Jennings there. The killing took place in a saloon after the courtroom fuss. He is also mistaken in saying that Heck Thomas chased Sam Bass all over Texas. There is much information on Cherokee Bill, the Buck gang, the Cook gang, and other outlaws.

1419. McKeown, Martha Ferguson

The trail led north. Mont Hawthorne's story, by Martha Ferguson McKeown. New York, the Macmillan co., 1948. Cloth. OP.

5 p.l., 222 p. 2 maps. 21.5 cm.
Half title.

One of a series of books written about Mont Hawthorne's experiences in the West and in Alaska. This one contains some material on Soapy Smith during his stay in the Klondike.

1420. McKittrick, Myrtle M.

Vallejo, son of California, by Myrtle M. McKittrick. Portland, Oreg., Binfords & Mort, publishers [1944]. Cloth. OP.

6 p.l., 377 p. front. (port.), illus., plates. 23.5 cm.
Bibliography: p. [359]–365; index: p. [367]–377.

Pub. device; "First edition" on copyright p.

Has some information on Joaquín Murieta.

1421. MacLane, John F.

A sagebrush lawyer, [by] John F. MacLane. "Nos morituri te salutamus." [New York, Pandick press, inc., 1953.] Cloth. OP.

viii p., 1 l., 177 p. front. (port.), plates. 23.6 cm.
Half title.

The experiences of a lawyer in the early days of Idaho. Contains some material on Diamondfield Jack Davis.

1422. McLaughlin, Daniel

Chronicles of a Northern Pacific veteran, [by] Daniel McLaughlin, roadmaster, Northern Pacific railway. [Privately printed, Empire printing co., 1930.] Stiff wrappers. Rare.

1 p.l., [3]–56 p. 1 port. 22.3 cm.

A large part of this rare book is about the author's experiences with the Northern Pacific Railway as bridge builder and later as roadmaster. The latter part of the book deals with the noted Montana outlaw Isaac Gravelle and his attempts to get money by dynamiting the Northern Pacific tracks.

1423. McLeod, Alexander

Pigtails and gold dust, by Alexander McLeod. Illustrated. Caldwell, Idaho, the Caxton printers, ltd., 1947. Cloth. OP.

8 p.l., [17]–326 p. front., plates, facsms. 23.5 cm.
Bibliography: p. [323]–326.
Half title; caption title: "A Panorama of Chinese Life in Early California."

Contains a story about Joaquín Murieta and Three-Fingered Jack García and his or the latter's cruelty to the Chinese. The author is among the many who repeat the legend about the reward poster under which Murieta scribbled his defiance.

1424. MacMinn, George R.

The theatre of the golden era in California, by George R. MacMinn. Illustrated. Caldwell, Idaho, the Caxton printers, ltd., 1941. Dec. cloth. OP.

10 p.l., [21]–529 p. front. (col.), illus., plates, ports., facsms. 23.5 cm.
Bibliography: p. [509]–515; index: p. [517]–529.
Half title; pub. device.

Gives some information about the books and plays written about Murieta.

1425. McMurray, Floyd I.

Westbound, [by] Floyd I. McMurray. . . . New York, Chicago, Boston, Atlanta, San Francisco, Dallas, Charles Scribner's sons [1943]. Pict. cloth. OP.

2 p.l., 394 p. plates, ports., map. 20.7 cm.
Bibliography after each chapter; index: p. 389–394.
Half title; double illus. t.p.; map on end papers.

Has material on Wild Bill Hickok and Calamity Jane.

1426. McNeal, Thomas Allen

When Kansas was young, by T.A. McNeal. New York, the Macmillan co., 1922. Cloth. Scarce.

ix p., 1 l., 287 p. 19.5 cm.
Half title.

Contains excellent material on pioneer life in Kansas, including some on outlaws and gunmen, such as Henry Brown and Ben Wheeler, and the robbery of the bank at Medicine Lodge.

1427. McNeill, Cora

"Mizzoura," by Cora McNeill. . . . Minneapolis, Minn., Mizzoura publishing co., 1898. Cloth. Rare.

4 p.l., 391 p. plates, ports. 20.4 cm.
Appendix: p. [365]–390; list of errata: p. 391.

A story of the life of the Younger brothers, said to be the only book written about them which had their personal approval. The author uses fictitious names and writes in a fictional style, though the work is said to be factual and the author provides affidavits in an appendix as proof of its accuracy.

1428. McNutt, G. W.

My twenty-three years' experience as a detective, 1923, by G.W. McNutt. . . . [N.p., 1923.] Cloth. Scarce.

7 p.l., [17]–174 p. front. (port.). 19.6 cm.

1429. McPherren, Ida (Mrs. Geneva Gibson)

Empire builders, by Ida McPherren. A history of the founding of Sheridan. Dedicated to the memory of John D. Loucks, the founder of the town. [Sheridan, Wyo., printed by Star publishing co., 1942.] Stiff pict. wrappers. Scarce.

3 p.l., [6]–72 p. 20.7 cm.

Includes information on such characters as Calamity Jane, Big Nose George Parrott, and Al Jennings and his gang.

1430. ———

Imprints on pioneer trails, by Ida McPherren. Boston, Christopher publishing house [1950]. Cloth. Scarce.

xi p., 2 l., 17–380 [1] p. front., plates. 20.3 cm.
Half title; pub. device.

In this book of personal reminiscences the author includes some material on Henry Plummer and Calamity Jane, none of it very reliable. She states that Calamity Jane died August 2, 1906. She died August 1, 1903.

1431. ———

Trail's end, by Ida McPherren. [Casper, Wyo., printed by Prairie publishing co., 1938.] Pict. cloth. Scarce.

4 p.l., [9]–322 p. front. 20.3 cm.
Half title.

Contains a fictionized account of the Johnson County War.

1432. McReynolds, Robert

Thirty years on the frontier, by Robert McReynolds. . . . Colorado Springs, Colo., El Paso publishing co., 1906. Pict. cloth. Scarce.

4 p.l., 256 p. front., plates, ports. 19.5 cm.

Contains a chapter on outlawry in Oklahoma. Most of the author's information about Bill Doolin is incorrect. He tells about Doolin's escape from the Guthrie jail and the battle at Ingalls (which he calls Ingrim). The author leaves the impression that he went to Ingalls to spy on the outlaws for the marshals who came later and fought the noted battle with the outlaws, but the information on the battle is incorrect, as is his account of Doolin's death.

1433. McRill, Albert

And Satan came also. An inside story of a city's social and political history. By Albert McRill, former city manager of Oklahoma City. [Oklahoma City, 1955.] Col. pict. cloth. OP.

6 p.l., 264 p. front. (port.), plates, ports. 22.5 cm.
Index: p. [260]–264.
Half title; plate on front end paper only.

This work, originally published in the *North Star* under the title "Inside Oklahoma City," is here published for the first time as a book and has been revised and enlarged. It contains much material on the lawlessness of early Oklahoma City and has an account of the killing of Ed O. Kelly, the man who killed Bob Ford in Creede, Colorado, twenty-two years earlier. It also has some information on Bill

Tilghman and Al Jennings. The author says that Kelly's true name was never known but that he was adopted by a Dr. O'Kelly. However, Kelly signed his name as Ed O. Kelly, and in Oklahoma City he was known as Red Kelly.

1434. Madison, Virginia

The Big Bend country of Texas, [by] Virginia Madison. [Albuquerque, N.M.], University of New Mexico press [1955]. Boards. OP.

xv, 263 p. illus., plates, ports. 23.6 cm.
Bibliography: p. 249–256; index: p. 257–263.
Half title; map on t.p.

A chapter entitled "The Bandits Move In" tells about the gang organized by Jesse Evans, John Selman, Black Jack Ketchum, and others.

1435. ———, and Hallie Stillwell

How come it's called that? Place names in the Big Bend country, by Virginia Madison and Hallie Stillwell. [Albuquerque, N.M.], University of New Mexico press [1958]. Boards.

7 p.l., 3–129 p. plates, 1 port. 23.5 cm.
Index: p. 121–129.
Half title; map on end papers.

Has a mention of Black Jack Ketchum.

1436. Mandat-Grancey, Baron Edmond de

Dans les montagnes rocheuses, par le Baron E. de Mandat-Grancey, dessins de Crafty et carte spéciale; Courouné par l'Académie française, prix Montyon. Paris, E. Plon, Nourrit et cie., 1884. Wrappers. Rare.

2 p.l., 314 p. front., plates, fold. map. 18.5 cm.
Reprinted in 1889 and 1894.
Republished in English, translated by William Conn, London, 1887; also published in New York the same year and again in London in 1888 (see Item 477).

The author, a French nobleman, visited the United States and toured the Black Hills. In writing of his experiences, he doubtless based his account of Wild Bill on tall tales fed him by the natives. He claims that Wild Bill made his living "destroying Sioux—so much for the scalp of a man, so much for a woman's and so much for a child's." In dull seasons, the author says, Hickok hung around Deadwood. The author has Jack McCall a bartender in Deadwood and, in his version, when Hickok tried to buy a drink with a handful of bloody scalps, he was refused. He got rough, and McCall shot him *three times.* The whole account is ridiculous.

1437. ———

La brèche aux buffles, par le Baron E. de Mandat-Grancey. Dessins de R.J. de Boisvray. Paris, E. Plon, Nourrit et cie., imprimeurs-éditeurs . . ., 1889. Wrappers. Rare.

xvi, 292 p. front. (double p.), illus. (double p.). 18.5 cm.

Half title; pub. device; tissues; table of contents at end.

Reprinted in 1893 with same collation.

This book has become very scarce. It continues the French nobleman's experiences in America (see Item 1436). He tells something about Calamity Jane and attempts to tell the story of Billy the Kid's escape from the Lincoln jail, when the Kid killed Bell and Olinger. Much of his information seems to have come from Siringo's writings, but in translating those works he seems to have become confused—he has a William Bonny as one of the guards who killed the Kid. As far as I know, this book has never been translated into English.

1438. Mangam, William Daniel

The Clarks. An American phenomenon, by William D. Mangam. With an introduction by Edward Alsworth Ross. . . . New York, Silver Bow press, 1941. Cloth. Scarce.

ix p., 3 l., [7]–257 p. front. (port.), ports., facsm. (fold.). 21 cm.

Critical comment: p. 245–257.

Half title.

Has some information concerning the outlaws of Montana in the vigilante days. It is said that the Clark family bought up and destroyed all the copies of this book that they could find; hence its scarcity.

1439. ———

The Clarks of Montana, by William Daniel Mangam. . . . [New York, the Silver Bow press], 1939. Stiff wrappers. Scarce.

iv, 221 [12] p. front. (port.), plates, ports., facsm. (fold.). 21.2 cm.

Last 12 pages comments on the book by various authorities.

Chapter I tells of Clark's early life in the West at Bannack and Virginia City and deals with such outlaws as Henry Plummer, Ned Ray, Cy Skinner, Buck Stinson, and others of the Plummer gang whom the author knew personally before the vigilantes hanged them.

1440. Mangan, Frank J.

Bordertown, by Frank J. Mangan. Drawings by Fred Carter. El Paso, Texas, Carl Hertzog, 1964. Stiff pict. wrappers.

v, 120 [1] p. illus. 21.6 cm.
Half title.

A rather well-written little history of El Paso, Texas. In a chapter entitled "The Pistoleros" the author tells of the killing of Dallas Stoudenmire and mentions many of the gunmen who lived in or visited El Paso, such as Pat Garrett, Bass Outlaw, John Selman, Jeff Milton, George Scarborough, and Jim Gillett.

1441. Mann, Etta Donnan

Four years in the governor's mansion in Virginia, 1910–1914, Richmond, Virginia, by Etta Donnan Mann. Richmond, Va., the Diet press, publishers, 1937. Cloth. Scarce.

4 p.l., 324 p. front., plates, ports. 23.5 cm.
Appendix (double column): p. 217–324.

Has quite a bit of material on the Allen outlaws.

1442. Manning, William H.

The gold-dragon; or, the California blood-hound. A story of Po-8, the lone highwayman. New York, Beadle and Adams, 1884. Pict. wrappers. (Cover title.) Rare.

31 p. 21.3 cm.
Double column.

One of the Beadle dime novels based on the activities of Black Bart.

1443. Mapes, Ruth B.

Old Fort Smith, cultural center on the southwestern frontier, by Ruth B. Mapes. [Little Rock, Ark., 1965.] Cloth.

viii, 160 p. plates, diagr. 22.2 cm.
Index: p. 151–160.

Contains material on Judge Parker's court and the outlaws he tried. Also has some information on Belle and Pearl Starr.

1444. [Marlow, Charles, and George Marlow]

Life of the Marlows, as related by themselves. Illustrated. Ouray, Colo., Plaindealer print, Kelly & Hulaniski, publishers [1892]. Pict. wrappers. Exceedingly rare.

[5]–181 p. front., illus., plates. 19 cm.
Copyright notice on first flyleaf.

Republished with revisions and edited by William Rathmell, Ouray, Colo., Herald print. W. S. Olexa, publisher [n.d.]. Stiff wrappers. Scarce.

2 p.l., [7]–100 p. 20.4 cm.

The first edition of this work is exceedingly rare, and the second is quite scarce. The chapters following Chapter XVIII are misnumbered XIV, XV, and XVI. The mistake is repeated in the revised edition, in which new material has been added and changes made in the latter part of the book. In these books the Marlows tell their side of the trouble they had with the law. Of the five brothers only the two authors of the book survived.

1445. Marsh, Charles W.

Recollections, 1837–1910, by Charles W. Marsh. Chicago, Farm Implement News co., 1910. Cloth. Scarce.

xv, 299 p. front. (port.), plates. 20.7 cm.

Tells the story of Joseph Slade, his killing of Jules Reni, and his death by hanging at the hands of the vigilantes. There is also a mention of Wild Bill Hickok.

1446. Marshall, James

Elbridge A. Stuart, founder of Carnation company, [by] James Marshall. Los Angeles, Carnation co. [1949]. Limp leather. Scarce.

viii p., 2 l., 3–238 p. front., plates, ports. 26 cm.

Appendix: p. 221–238.

Half title; untrimmed; gilt top.

Colophon: "The volume is number —— of 275 copies issued in memory of Elbridge Amos Stuart founder of Carnation Company on its Fiftieth Anniversary."

Also published in a trade edition.

The author tells about some of his subject's experiences in the wild West around El Paso, Texas, and in New Mexico. He is wrong in saying that Billy the Kid killed twenty-six men and that he was jailed in Las Vegas, "where he killed his two jailers."

1447. ——

Santa Fe, the railroad that built an empire, by James Marshall. New York, Random House [1945]. Cloth. OP.

xvi p., 1 l., 3–465 p. plates, ports., maps, facsms., tables. 22 cm.

Appendices: p. 349–449; index: p. 451–465.

Half title; map on end papers; illus. double t.p.; "First edition" on copyright p.

Another good railroad book containing material on train robberies, such as those by the James boys.

1448. Marshall, Jim

Swinging doors, by Jim Marshall. Illustrated by Gerald Grace. Seattle, Frank McCaffrey, publishers [1949]. Pict. cloth. Scarce.

5 p.l., 11–267 p. front., illus., plates (part col.). 21.2 cm.
Bibliography: p. 266–267.
Illus. chapter headings; untrimmed.

Gives an account of the killing of Hickok by McCall. The author mistakenly says that Hickok had killed three "outlaws" at the Rock Creek "fight." He also gives a wrong account of the killing of Ben Thompson and King Fisher. There is mention of the Earps, Doc Holliday, the McLaurys, and John Ringo. In commenting upon Calamity Jane's claim that she captured McCall with a meat cleaver, the author says that she was "one of the damndest liars who ever infested the plains."

1449. Marshall, Otto Miller

The Wham paymaster robbery, by Otto Miller Marshall. Sponsored and distributed by the Pima Chamber of Commerce [Pima, Arizona], 1967. Pict. col. stiff wrappers.

iii [1] p., 79 [10] p. illus., plates, ports., map, facsms. 23 cm.

A full account of this famous and unsolved robbery though somewhat fictionized. There is also an account of the killing of Glenn Reynolds by the Apache Kid, though the Kid's name is not mentioned. The author writes of Dan Dowd, Red Sample, Bill Delaney, Tex Howard, Dan Kelly, and the robbery at Bisbee.

1450. Marshall, Theodora Britton, and Gladys Crail Evans

They found it in Natchez, by Theodora Britton Marshall and Gladys Crail Evans. New Orleans, Pelican publishing co. [1939]. Cloth. OP.

7 p.l., [11]–236 p. front. (col.), illus., plates, maps, facsms. 23.5 cm.
Index: p. [232]–236.

Has a chapter on such outlaws as John Murrell, the Harpes, and Mason.

1451. [Martin, Charles Lee]

A sketch of Sam Bass, the bandit. A graphic narrative of his various train robberies, his death, and accounts of the deaths of his gang and their history. With illustrations. Dallas, Texas, the Herald steam printing house [Worley and co], 1880. Pict. wrappers. Exceedingly rare.

[3]–153 p. illus., plates. 20.5 cm.
1 p. adv. in front; 2 p. adv. at end.

Reprinted in 1956 by the University of Oklahoma press as No. 6 of the Western Frontier Library series, with an introduction by Ramon F. Adams.

xxiii p., 1 l., 3–166 p. 3 full p. plates. 19.5 cm.
Half title.

This exceedingly rare little book is not to be confused with the Sam Bass volume published in Dallas in 1878. The copy in the Library of Congress is the only original copy of this book known to me. The author says that Sam Bass and Joel Collins drove a herd of cattle to Kansas, where they sold them and then used the money to go to Deadwood, *Idaho Territory*. Aside from the newspaper quotations and the narrative as told by Jim Murphy, much of the rest of the book parallels Hogg's book, published in Denton, Texas (see Item 1001). However, in writing of the lives of some of Bass's confederates, such as Underwood, Barnes, and Arkansas Johnson, this author gives much fuller accounts and gives information not found in the other books about Bass.

The reprint by the University of Oklahoma Press was made from my photostat of the Library of Congress copy. There is a misprint in the introduction: in the third paragraph the date 1876 should be 1878.

1452. Martin, Douglas D.

An Arizona chronology. The territorial years, 1846–1912, [by] Douglas D. Martin. Tucson, University of Arizona press, 1963. Pict. wrappers.

3 p.l., 1 p., [72] p. (no pagination). 22.8 cm.
Bibliography and index: last 12 pages.

1453. ———

The Earps of Tombstone, by Douglas D. Martin. The truth about the O K Corral gun fight and other events in which Wyatt Earp and his brothers participated. This is the story compiled from the files of the Tombstone Epitaph for the years 1880–81–82, as told by this newspaper's early editors. Tombstone, Ariz., published by the Tombstone Epitaph [1959]. Stiff wrappers.

3 p.l., 5–65 p. plan. 22.7 cm.
Partly double column; "First edition" on copyright p.

A collection of exerpts from the *Tombstone Epitaph*. There is a full account of the O K Corral fight and the trial of the Earps. The *Epitaph* was owned by John P. Clum, who was a friend of the Earps, and the account is therefore favorable to them.

1454. ———

Silver, sex and six guns. Tombstone saga of the life of Buckskin Frank Leslie, by Douglas D. Martin. . . . Tombstone, Ariz., published by the Tombstone Epitaph [1962]. Pict. wrappers.

3 p.l., 7–62 p. plates. 22.6 cm.
"First edition" on copyright p.

A history of the life of Buckskin Frank Leslie, telling of his loves and killings as well as his prison life.

1455. ———

Tombstone's Epitaph, [by] Douglas D. Martin. [Albuquerque, N.M., University of New Mexico press, 1951.] Pict. cloth.

xii, 272 p. illus. 23.5 cm.
Half title; illus. end papers (dif.); vignette.

The author has done every student of western history a great favor in gathering together these rare items from the files of the noted Tombstone paper. Naturally, there is much information on the Arizona outlaws and gunmen, some never before published in book form. Since Clum, the publisher of the paper, was a friend of the Earps (see Item 1453), the *Epitaph* excerpts are favorable to them. The book also gives accounts of the O K Corral fight and many other killings in Tombstone and the surrounding region.

1456. Martin, George Washington

The first two years in Kansas; or, where, when and how the Missouri bushwhackers, the Missouri train and bank robber, and those who stole themselves rich in the name of liberty, were sired and reared. An address by George W. Martin. . . . Topeka, State printing office, 1907. Pamphlet. (Cover title.) Scarce.

[3]-30 p. 22.8 cm.

Revelations, based upon original sources, of vital historical facts not found elsewhere. The author's quotations are from exceedingly rare files of pioneer newspapers.

1457. Martin, Jack

Border boss, Captain John R. Hughes, Texas ranger, by Jack Martin. Drawings by Frank Anthony Stanush. San Antonio, Texas, the Naylor co., publishers, 1942. Pict. cloth.

xvi, 236 p. front. (port.). 21 cm.
Bibliography: p. [225]-227; index: p. [231]-236.
Half title; illus. chapter headings; vignette.

The author tells about the killing of John Wesley Hardin by John Selman, the killing of Bass Outlaw, and the lynching of Jim Miller. Ranger Hughes, like several other writers, believes that Pat Garrett was slain by the notorious killer Jim Miller.

1458. Martin, V. Covert

Stockton album through the years, by V. Covert Martin. R. Coke Wood

. . ., Leon Bush . . ., collaborators in writing the manuscript. Stockton, Calif. [Simard printing company], 1959. Cloth. OP.

6 p.l., 13–237 p. illus., plates, ports., facsms., maps. 28.5 cm.
Bibliography: p. 229; index: p. 231–237.
Half title; "First edition" on copyright p.

Has material on Black Bart, Joaquín Murieta, and Three-Fingered Jack García.

1459. Masterson, Vincent Victor

The Katy railroad and the last frontier, by V. V. Masterson. Norman, University of Oklahoma press [1952]. Cloth.

xvi p., 1 l., 3–312 p. illus., plates, ports., facsms., maps, tables. 23.5 cm.
Bibliography: p. 291–297; index: p. 298–312.
Half title; "First edition" on copyright p.

Has a chapter dealing with the Daltons and some of their train robberies, as well as with Belle Starr, and another chapter giving a short history of the Benders.

1460. Masterson, William Barclay (Bat)

Famous gunfighters of the western frontier, by W. B. (Bat) Masterson. Luke Short, Bill Tilghman, Ben Thompson, Doc Holliday, Wyatt Earp. Houston, the Frontier press of Texas, 1957. Cloth.

1 p.l., 5–65 [47] p. plates, ports., facsms. 21 cm.
Last 47 p. pictures from the famous Rose collection.

A reprint in book form of a series of articles which appeared in *Human Life Magazine* in 1907. Only one thousand copies of this book were printed.

1461. ———

The tenderfoot's turn. Six chapters by Bat Masterson. Utica, N.Y., Savage Arms co., 1909. Wrappers. Rare.

24 p. illus. 15.3 cm.

A promotional booklet of the Savage Arms Company containing chapters on Wild Bill Hickok, Billy the Kid, Pat Garrett, Joseph Slade, and Henry Plummer.

1462. Matlock, J. Eugene

Gone beyond the law, by J. Eugene Matlock. Illustrations by J. M. M. Kimberlin. Dallas, Texas, Mathis, Van Nort & co. [1940]. Cloth. Scarce.

6 p.l., 456 p. front., illus. 23 cm.
Half title; map on recto of front binding.

A history of the Regulator-Moderator War of East Texas.

1463. Matthews, Sallie Reynolds

Interwoven, a pioneer chronicle, by Sallie Reynolds Matthews. Houston, Texas, the Anson Jones press, 1936. Cloth. Rare.

x p., 2 l., 3–234 p. front. (port.). 19.8 cm.

Addenda: p. 213–234; letter of introduction by Will James.

Half title.

The author was a sister of Glenn Reynolds, the sheriff of Gila County, Arizona, who was killed by the Apache Kid when he made his escape. She gives a good account of this episode as well as of her own family life.

1464. ———

Interwoven. A pioneer chronicle, by Sallie Reynolds Matthews. Drawings by E. M. Schiwetz. El Paso, Texas, Carl Hertzog, 1958. Two-tone cloth with cattle brands. Scarce.

xiv p., 2 l., 226 [2] p. front., illus., plates, map. 24.3 cm.

Addenda: p. 195–209; index: p. 211–226.

Half title; map on front end papers; family tree on rear end papers; untrimmed.

Colophon: "1500 copies of this book have been printed at El Paso, Texas, by Carl Hertzog."

A reprint of the rare original edition with added introduction, illustrations, and index.

1465. Mattison, Ray H.

Roosevelt and the stockmen's association, by Ray H. Mattison. Reprinted from the *North Dakota History*, Vol. 17, No. 2 (April, 1950); Vol. 17, No. 3 (July, 1950). Bismarck, N.D., the State Historical society of North Dakota [1950]. Stiff wrappers.

[3]–59 [3] p. front. (port.), 3 plates at end. 22.8 cm.

Contains much on horse thieves, rustlers, and vigilantes, as well as the bylaws of the Little Missouri Stockmen's Association and the bylaws of the Montana Stock Growers' Association.

1466. Maury, Gen. Dabney Herndon

Recollections of a Virginian in the Mexico, Indian and Civil wars, by General Dabney Herndon Maury. . . . New York, Charles Scribner's sons, 1894. Pict. cloth. Scarce.

xi, 279 p. front. (port. with tissue). 20.8 cm.

Half title.

Has some material on Captain Jack, the Modoc outlaw.

1467. Maxwell, Hu

Evans and Sontag, the famous bandits of California, by Hu Maxwell. First edition. San Francisco, San Francisco printing co., 1893. Pict. wrappers. Very rare.

3–248 p. illus., plates, ports. 19 cm.

On cover: "The California Library No. 1."

Published the same year in New York under the imprint: "Trade supplied by the American News."

An early account of two California train robbers. Another of those brittle pulp-paper publications that deteriorate so quickly and cause the publication to virtually disappear.

1468. Mayfield, Eugene O.

The backbone of Nebraska. Wherein contained many interesting matters pertaining to pioneer and more modern days, by Eugene O. Mayfield. [Omaha, Neb.], 1916. Wrappers. Rare.

2 p.l., [9]–21 p. plates, ports., map. 22.2 cm.

The author states that Hickok was marshal of Dodge City in the year of 1869. Hickok was never an officer in Dodge. In telling of Hickok's murder the author says that McCall backed up the crowd with a gun until they promised to give him a fair trial. He states further that Hickok and Calamity Jane agreed that when they died they would be buried close together. No such arrangement was made while Hickok was alive.

1469. Maynard, Louis

Oklahoma panhandle. A history and stories of no man's land, by Louis Maynard. . . . [N.P., privately printed], 1956. Pict. wrappers. Scarce.

3 p.l., 70 p. plates, 2 maps. 20.2 cm.

Contains some information about the outlaw William Coe and his capture. There is also a section on Black Jack Ketchum, as well as a mention of Coe and Billy the Kid. I think that the author is mistaken when he says that Ketchum murdered fifteen people, including a mother and her child.

1470. Mazzanovich, Anton

Trailing Geronimo, by Anton Mazzanovich. . . . Edited and arranged by E. A. Brininstool. . . . Some hitherto unrecorded events bearing upon the outbreak of the White Mountain Apache and Geronimo's band in Arizona, 1881–1886. The experiences of a private soldier in the ranks; chief of pack-train service, and scout at Fort Grant; also with the New Mexico rangers. Los Angeles, Calif., Gem publishing co., 1926. Pict. cloth.

9 p.l., 19–277 p. front. (col. with tissue), illus., plates, ports., facsms. 19.7 cm.
Half title; illus. end papers.

Revised edition published in 1931, bound in fabrikoid and privately printed.

13 p.l., 112 p. plates, ports., 1 l., 115–322 p. 20 cm.
Illus. end papers.

Both editions mention the Earps, Doc Holliday, and the Clantons.

1471. Mazzulla, Fred, and Jo Mazzulla

Al Packer, a Colorado cannibal. Colorado cannibal consumes and cashes in on companions, [by] Fred and Jo Mazzulla. [Denver, Colo., 1968.] Pict. cloth.

3 p.l., 1 p., 6–47 [3] p. plates, ports., facsms., maps (1 double p.), plan. 21.8 cm.
Full p. half title, col. with port.

These authors are among the first ones to spell Alferd Packer's first name correctly, as Packer himself spelled it.

1472. ———, and ———

Brass checks and red lights. Being a pictorial pot pourri of (historical) prostitutes, parlor houses, professors, procuresses and pimps, [by] Fred and Jo Mazzulla. [Denver, 1966.] Pict. wrappers (col.).

4 p.l., 9–56 p. illus., plates, ports., facsms., 4 full p. illus. by C. M. Russell (col.). 21.6 cm.
Acknowledgments: p. 55; index: p. 56.

Has some mention of Calamity Jane, Big Nose Kate, Cattle Kate, Bob Ford, and Billy the Kid. I think that the authors are mistaken when they say that Madame Goul "married a half brother of Billy the Kid." The Kid had no half brothers, only an older brother, Joe.

1473. ———, and ———

Outlaw album, by Fred and Jo Mazzulla. Denver, Colo., the A. B. Hirschfeld press [1966]. Stiff wrappers.

1 l., 1 p., 4–48 p. plates, ports. 15.7 cm.
Index: p. 48.

A privately printed little book by authors whose hobby is photographing the West. Most of the portraits in this book are full-page reproductions, each one preceded by a page of text about the subject. Included are Bill Carlisle, Doc Holliday, Big Nose Kate, the hanging of Con Wagner, Asa Moore and Big Ed, Big Steve Long, Dave Rudabaugh, Black Jack Ketchum, Calamity Jane, Jim Averill, Cattle Kate, the Wild Bunch, Billy the Kid, Bob Ford, Ed O. Kelly, Poker Alice, Big Nose George Parrott, Tom Horn, and Alferd Packer.

1474. Meecham, A. B.

The tragedy of the lava-beds; a lecture by Hon. A. B. Meecham, with an appendix containing an account of the rescue, the battles, the betrayal, the capture, trial and execution of the Modoc chief, and the exile of the survivors. [Hartford, Conn.], published by the author, 1877. Wrappers. Rare.

[3]-48 p. front. (port.), plates, ports. 18.5 cm.

Has much on Captain Jack, the Modoc outlaw.

1475. ———

Wigwam and war-path; or, the royal chief in chains. By Hon. A. B. Meecham. . . . Boston, John P. Dale and co., 1875. Cloth. Rare.

xxiii, 700 [1] p. front. (port.), plates, ports. 23.9 cm.
Appendix: p. [685]-700.

Has much on Captain Jack, the Modoc outlaw.

1476. Mencken, August (ed.)

By the neck. A book of hangings selected from contemporary accounts and edited with an introduction by August Mencken. . . . Foreword by H. L. Mencken. Illustrated. New York, Hastings House, publishers [1942]. Pict. cloth. OP.

xx p., 2 l., 264 p. front., illus., plates. 21.4 cm.
Half title; untrimmed.

Chapter XVIII is about the vigilantes of Montana and the hangings of Boone Helm, Jack Gallagher, Frank Parish, Haze Lyons, and Clubfoot George Lane.

1477. Menefee, Eugene L., and Fred A. Dodge

History of Tulare and Kings counties California, with biographical sketches of the leading men and women of the counties who have been identified with their growth and development from the early days to the present. History by Eugene L. Menefee and Fred A. Dodge. Illustrated. . . . Los Angeles, Calif., Historic Record co., 1913. Three-quarter leather. Scarce.

xiv, [5]-890 p. plates, ports., maps. 27.8 cm.
Gilt edges.

Chapter XVI, entitled "Great Train Robberies," deals with the Daltons in California and with the Evans-Sontag gang.

1478. Mercer, Asa Shinn

The banditti of the plains; or, the cattlemen's invasion of Wyoming in 1892 [The crowning infamy of the ages], by A. S. Mercer. [Cheyenne, Wyo., 1894.] Cloth. Exceedingly rare.

5 p.l., [1] p. [12]–139 p. illus., map. 21.3 cm.
Appendix [confession of George Dunning]: p. 107–139.

Rewritten and republished under the title Powder river invasion. War on the rustlers in 1892, by John Mercer Boots. [Los Angeles, 1923.] Cloth. Scarce.

7 p.l., [15]–146 p. 19.8 cm.
Appendix: p. 113–146.

Republished under the title The banditti of the plains, by I. G. McPherren, Sheriden, Wyo., 1930. Wrappers. Scarce.

[80] p. (no pagination). 20.5 cm.

Also published in a new edition, with a foreword by James Mitchell Clarke and illustrations by Arvilla Parker. San Francisco, printed for George Fields by the Grabhorn press, MCMXXXV. Cloth and boards. Scarce.

xiv p., 1 l., 3–136 p. illus. 24.8 cm.
Appendix: p. 111–136.
Illus. chapter headings.

This edition, too, has become quite scarce and expensive.

Reprinted again by the University of Oklahoma press in 1954 as No. 2 of the Western Frontier Library series and with an introduction by the late William H. Kittrell.

The first edition of this book is one of the rarities of western Americana. It had a tempestuous history. Immediately after it was printed, the Wyoming cattlemen objected to having their activities thus exposed, and in the course of a libel suit the entire issue was impounded by a local court and ordered destroyed. The author's sympathies were not with rustlers—he was editor and publisher of a stock journal—but he objected to the highhanded manner in which the large owners were importing paid killers to exterminate other citizens of the region.

While the books were in the custody of the court, a number of copies were stolen and smuggled to Denver, which lay outside the court's jurisdiction. It is claimed that the books were unbound when they were stolen and were later bound in Denver. The rarity of the book is due not only to the impounding and destruction of most of the copies but also to the fact that for many years members of the Wyoming Stock Growers' Association, their sympathizers, and their descendants destroyed every copy they came across. The author's print shop was burned, and he was ordered to leave Wyoming.

1479. Meriwether, Lee

Jim Reed, "sartorial immortal." A biography, by Lee Meriwether. Webster Grove, Mo., the International Mark Twain Society, 1948. Cloth. OP.

4 p.l., 273 ⌈4⌉ p. front. (port.), illus., plates, ports. 22 cm.
Index: p. ⌈272⌉–273.

Has some mention of Jesse James, Jr., and of his trial for train robbery, in which Jim Reed was one of the prosecutors.

1480. Methuin, Rev. J.J.

In the limelight; or, history of Anadarko [Caddo county], and vicinity from the earliest days, by Rev. J. J. Methuin. . . . ⌈Oklahoma City, Walker, Wilson Title co., n.d.⌉ Cloth. Scarce.

iii ⌈1⌉, 137 p. front. (port.), plates, ports. 19 cm.
Last 11 p. adv.
Vignette.

Has much on cattle stealing.

1481. Metz, Leon Claire

John Selman, Texas gunfighter, by Leon Claire Metz. New York, Hastings House, publishers ⌈1966⌉. Cloth.

9 p.l., 19–254 p. front. (double p. illus. map), plates, ports., map. 21 cm.
Notes: p. 207–230; acknowledgments: p. 231–234; bibliography: p. 235–243; index: p. 245–254.
Half title.

Though many books mention John Selman, this is the first biography of him, and the author has done a very good job of both research and writing. The only error I find is that he gives Jack McCall the first name John. There is some material on Billy the Kid, Henry Brown, Fort Griffin, John Wesley Hardin, John Larn, Oliver Lee, Jeff Milton, Jim Miller, Bass Outlaw, George Scarborough, and Jesse Evans and a mention of Butch Cassidy, Wyatt Earp, Jesse James, and John Tunstall.

1482. Michelson, Charles

Mankillers at close range, by Charles Michelson. The "bad man," a western frontier type now practically extinct, his unrighteous life and inglorious death, the stories that illustrate his peculiar moral code. Houston, Frontier press of Texas, 1958. Stiff wrappers.

5–32 p. plates, ports. 17.3 cm.

Reprinted from *Munsey's Magazine* of 1901. Why it was reprinted is beyond me, for in the first place it is of no consequence, and in the second place it is full of errors. It contains material about Wild Bill Hickok, Wyatt Earp, Joseph Slade, Jesse James, King Fisher, Bill Longley, and Billy the Kid. Instead of identifying Billy the Kid's first victim as the man who insulted his mother, as most writers do, this author has him the husband of the Kid's inamorata. He has Wild Bill in charge of the station at Rock Creek when he "fought" and killed "eight out of ten men." His account of the O K Corral fight is most ridiculous, and he has Ike Clanton eloping with Wyatt Earp's sister, Jessie. He has Curly Bill Brocius a cousin of the Earps and says that Ike killed Curly Bill. He has King Fisher killed by a Mexican in Eagle Pass, Texas, instead of being killed in San Antonio. Altogether it is the most confusing and ridiculous account I have ever read. There is not a single sentence in the whole article that is completely accurate, and anyone who knows history will join me in wondering why it was chosen to be reprinted.

1483. Middagh, John

Frontier newspaper: the El Paso Times, by John Middagh. Typography by Carl Hertzog. El Paso, Texas, Texas Western press, 1958. Cloth.

xiv p., 1 l., 333 [1] p. plates, ports., facsm. 23.9 cm.
Index: p. 325–333.
Half title; facsm. of newspaper print on end papers.

Gives an account of John Wesley Hardin's life in El Paso after his release from the penitentiary and of his death. It also has material on the deaths of John Selman, George Scarborough, and Dallas Stoudenmire.

1484. Middleton, John W.

History of the regulators and moderators and the Shelby county war of 1841 and 1842, in the republic of Texas, with facts and incidents in the early history of the republic and state, from 1837 to the annexation, together with incidents of frontier life and Indian troubles, and the war on the reserve in Young county in 1857. By Jonh [*sic*] W. Middleton. . . . Fort Worth, Loving publishing co., 1883. Stiff pink wrappers. Exceedingly rare.

2 p.l., [5]–40 p. 23.2 cm.

Reprinted by John A. Norris, of Austin, Texas, (ca. 1926), in exact duplication (except for wrappers), retaining the misspelled Jonh and carrying a statement at the end from Miss Harriet Smither, archivist of the Texas State Library, concerning the exactness of the duplication. Later the book was again reprinted by H.N. Gammel, of Austin, with the spelling of John corrected and changes in the wrapper. This edition has the same pagination, but measures 23 cm. Both reprints are now scarce. Reprinted again in 1953 by the Frontier Times publishing house of Grand Prairie, Texas, retaining the "Jonh" on the title page.

1485. Millar, Mara

Hail to yesterday, by Mara Millar as told to Page Cooper. Illustrated by George Duncan. New York, Toronto, Farrar & Rinehart, inc. [1941]. Cloth. OP.

viii p., 1 l., 3–302 p. illus. 22 cm.

Half title.

Has a chapter on life in early Oklahoma and deals to a small extent with Al Jennings, the Dalton boys, Chris Madsen, Bill Tilghman, and Heck Thomas.

1486. Miller, Benjamin S.

Ranch life in southern Kansas and the Indian territory, as told by a novice. How a fortune was made in cattle, by Benjamin S. Miller. New York, Fless & Ridge printing co., 1896. Wrappers. Rare.

3 p.l., [7]–163 [1] p. front. (port.). 20 cm.

The author was one of the early presidents of the Cherokee Strip Livestock Association in the seventies. The book contains some firsthand information on Billy the Kid and tells about the attempt of the mob at Las Vegas to take the prisoners away from Pat Garrett, an incident the author witnessed. In reporting the Kid's death, the author mistakenly says that Garrett found the Kid in bed at Maxwell's and "didn't wait to take him prisoner, but poured a load of buckshot into him as he raised up in bed, and that settled it, Billy taking some of the medicine he had been accustomed to administer in such liberal doses to others." A sequel, entitled *Five Years a Cattleman* was supposed to follow this book, but was never published.

1487. Miller, Floyd

Bill Tilghman, marshal of the last frontier, [by] Floyd Miller. Garden City, Doubleday & co., inc., 1968. Cloth.

x p., 1 l., 252 p. plates, ports. 21.5 cm.

Bibliography: p. [241]–245; index: p. [246]–252.

Half title; map on end papers; "First edition" on copyright p.

The author claims that Bat Masterson was "elected sheriff and took office on January 1, 1878." He was elected in November, 1877, and though he did not assume office officially until January 14, 1878, he did act as sheriff for the opening of the January term of the District Court on January 3.

The author is mistaken in calling Wyatt Earp "a Texas cowboy who spent more time in saloons than he did in the saddle." Earp was not from Texas, nor was he ever a cowboy. In fact, he had no use for that species. The author has Ben Thompson, "a printer by trade," killing thirty-two men and Doc Holliday killing twenty-six men—neither count correct.

He has Ingalls, the scene of the fight between the Doolin gang and the marshals, in Kansas, but Ingalls was in Oklahoma Territory. He makes it appear that the marshals first went to Mary Pierce's hotel. They did not go to the hotel until the battle was over and then only to capture Arkansas Tom, the only outlaw they captured in Ingalls.

The author is also mistaken when he writes: "Heck Thomas headed a posse which found him [Doolin] outside of Lawson and in the gun battle that followed, Doolin was shot dead." There was no gun battle. On page 206, the author says that Al Jennings was sentenced to five years at the end of his trial. He was sentenced to a life term on February 17, 1899, but through the intervention of friends President McKinley commuted his life sentence to five years on June 23, 1900. He was released November 13, 1902.

1488. [**Miller, George, Jr.**]

The trial of Frank James for murder, with confessions of Dick Liddil and Clarence Hite, and history of the "James gang." Kansas City, Mo., published by George Miller, Jr. [Columbus, Mo., press of E. W. Stephens, 1898.] Cloth. Scarce.

2 p.l., 5–348 [1] p. front., plates, ports. 19 cm.
Also published in wrappers.

The complete record of the trial, with testimony, addresses to the jury, and the pleas of the attorneys.

1489. Miller, Harry, and Page Cooper

Footloose fiddler, by Harry Miller with Page Cooper. New York, London, Whittlesey House, McGraw-Hill book co., inc. [1945]. Pict. cloth. OP.

vi p., 1 l., 326 p. illus. 26.8 cm.
Half title; vignette.

Though the author is writing of his own experiences, in telling of the death of Ben Thompson he has everything wrong. He says that Thompson had been hanging around the Bella Union for about a month raising a disturbance. He has Thompson killed by a gambler named Martinez while in the Bella Union, where the author was playing the fiddle with an orchestra. Thompson was not killed at any Bella Union in San Antonio, and the author has all the other circumstances wrong. He writes: "But even now old-timers in Southern Texas will talk about the night Ben Thompson was killed in the Bella Union." He fails to mention that King Fisher was killed with Thompson and calls Fisher a local bad man.

1490. Miller, Joaquín

An illustrated history of the state of Montana, containing a history of the state of Montana from the earliest period in its discovery to the present time, together with glimpses of its auspicious future. . . . By Joaquín Miller. . . . Chicago, the Lewis publishing co., 1894. Cloth. Pub. in two volumes. Scarce.

Vol. I, xv, 9–292 p. front., ports. (incl. front., all with tissues). 29.2 cm.
Vol. II, 292 (repeated from Vol. I) –822 p. front., plates, ports. (part with tissues). 29.2 cm.

Volume I contains information on the Montana vigilantes and lawlessness.

1491. Miller, Joseph

Arizona: the last frontier, by Joseph Miller, with drawings by Ross Santee. New York, Hastings House, publishers [1956]. Pict. cloth.

x, 350 p. illus., plates (6 double p.). 21 cm.
Index: p. [343]–350.
Half title; map on end papers; illus. double t.p.

Has chapters on Tombstone during its wild days, the O K Corral fight, and other gunman episodes. It gives a full account of the troubles between the Earps and the Clantons. Most of the other accounts of these troubles have been taken from the *Tombstone Epitaph*, a pro-Earp paper, but this book quotes largely from the *Tombstone Nugget* and the Tucson papers which were not so favorable.

1492. ——— (ed.)

Arizona cavalcade. The turbulent times. Edited by Joseph Miller. Illlustrated by Ross Santee. New York, Hastings House [1962]. Cloth.

7 p.l., [3]–306 p. illus. (6 double p.). 21 cm.
Index: p. [297]–306.
Half title; illus. double t.p.

Mentions Tombstone and some of the Arizona outlaws.

1493. ———

The Arizona story, compiled and edited from original newspaper sources, by Joseph Miller, with drawings by Ross Santee. New York, Hastings House, publishers [1952]. Cloth.

xvii p., 1 l., 3–345 p. illus. 20.8 cm.
Half title; map on end papers; illus. double t.p.

A collection of excerpts from the early newspapers of Arizona, dealing with various subjects from Indians, lost mines, and outlaws to legends and tall tales. Some of the stories, including an account of Pearl Hart, cover various stage robberies, hangings, and shooting scrapes of the outlaws of that region. Some of the outlaws mentioned are Burt Alvord, Apache Kid, the Clantons, the McLaurys, Johnny Ringo, John Heath, Augustin Chacon, Dan Kelly, Billy Stiles, and Frank Stillwell. The Earps, Doc Holliday, Johnny Behan, and the O K Corral fight are also mentioned.

1494. Miller, Nina Hull

Shutters west, by Nina Hull Miller. Denver, Sage books [1962]. Cloth.

5 p.l., 11–152 p. front., plates, ports., facsms. 15.9 x 23.3 cm.

Sources: p. 152.
Half title; pub. device.

Has chapters on the vigilantes of Denver and Laramie. The author tells of the hangings of Con Wagner, Ace Moore, Big Red, Steve Young, and others.

1495. Miller, Nyle H.

Kansas frontier police officers before TV, by Nyle H. Miller, secretary, Kansas State Historical society, Topeka, Kansas. Kansas City, Mo., 1958. Wrappers. (Caption title.) Scarce.

16 p. 22.8 cm.

Reprinted from the *Trail Guide*, published quarterly by the Kansas City Posse of the Westerners, Vol. 3, No. 1, March, 1958. It contains information about Wyatt Earp, Bat Masterson, and Wild Bill Hickok, taken from the contemporary newspapers of their day. While Wyatt Earp was a policeman at Wichita he was mentioned in the *Eagle* only twice and in the *Beacon* only five times, and on none of the occasions was any reference made to brilliant police work. One of the items reported his dismissal. All the Abilene papers refer to him as assistant marshal of Dodge. The many newspaper quotations in this pamphlet take some of the glamour from all three—Wyatt Earp, Bat Masterson, and Wild Bill Hickok.

1496. ———

Some widely publicized western police officers, by Nyle H. Miller. Lincoln, Nebr., reprinted from *Nebraska History*, December, 1958. Stiff wrappers. (Cover title.) Scarce.

303–316 p. 3 ports. 22.9 cm.

Has information about Wild Bill Hickok, Wyatt Earp, and Bat Masterson.

1497. ———, Edgar Langsdorf, and Robert W. Richmond

Kansas, a pictorial history, by Nyle H. Miller, Edgar Langsdorf [and] Robert W. Richmond. Topeka, the Kansas Centennial Commission and the State Historical Society, 1961. Pict. cloth.

viii, 319 p. illus., plates, ports., maps (part col., 4 fold.), facsms. 28.5 cm.
Picture credits: p. 301–302; index: p. 303–316.
Half title; map on front end papers (col.); illus. rear end papers (col.); illus. double t.p.

Has much material on the gunmen of the Kansas cow towns, including Wild Bill Hickok, Wyatt Earp, Doc Holliday, the Dalton gang and their end at Coffeyville, Henry Brown and Ben Wheeler and their end at Medicine Lodge, and others.

1498. ———, and Joseph W. Snell

Why the west was wild. A contemporary look at the antics of some highly publicized Kansas cowtown personalities, by Nyle H. Miller and Joseph W. Snell. Topeka, Kans., published by the Kansas State Historical society, 1963. Cloth.

vii p., 2 l., 5–685 p. illus., plates, ports., map, facsm. 23.5 cm.

Appendix: p. 641–647; acknowledgments and credits: p. 649–650; index: p. 651–685.

Half title; map on end papers.

Reprinted with omissions and in wrappers by the University of Nebraska press.

This work first appeared as a series of articles in the Kansas Historical Society's *Quarterly*. It is a most valuable addition to the history of the Kansas cow towns and their law officers. It should correct some of the false history and legendary trash which has been written about this period. It was taken from the newspaper accounts, governors' reports, court records, and city records of that time. Its authors are two conscientious historians who are connected with the Kansas Historical Society and have access to the excellent newspaper files and other records of the society. I believe this to be one of the most important books on this period.

1499. Miller, Ronald Dean

Shady ladies of the west, by Ronald Dean Miller. Los Angeles, Westernlore press, 1964. Cloth.

ix, 11–224 p. plates, ports. 21 cm.

Bibliography: p. 211–219; glossary: p. 220–224.

Half title; illus. end papers.

The author gives a rather thorough review of prostitution in the West, and has information on such familiar names as Belle Starr, Calamity Jane, Cattle Kate, and Pearl Hart. On page 109 the name Scyene is misspelled Sylene. The author is mistaken when he says, "Then on Saint Valentine's Day, 1866, the James and Younger brothers invented bank robbery in Liberty, Missouri." That story has been disproved. He is also mistaken in saying that Belle Starr's brother had ridden with the James gang and that he was a member of Quantrill's band when he was killed. The author makes it appear that Calamity Jane arrived in Deadwood some time before Hickok. They went together, and he is another who has her death August 2nd, instead of August 1st.

1500. Miller, W. Henry

Pioneering north Texas, by W. Henry Miller. San Antonio, Texas, the Naylor co. [1953]. Cloth.

xi p., 4 l., 303 p. plates, cattle brands, map, facsm. 21.6 cm.
Bibliography: p. 295–297; index: p. 299–303.
Half title; map on end papers.

Has some material on Frank James, Al Jennings, and Cole Younger after the author claims they served prison terms. Frank James never served any prison term, however. In his information about Billy the Kid the author quotes Fred Sutton's false statement in *The Trail Drivers of Texas*, which illustrates how false history can be perpetuated when one writer quotes another as an authority without searching out the truth. The author is mistaken in saying that the Jameses and the Youngers were cousins. He says that Cole Younger spent thirty years in a federal prison, which, of course, is incorrect. Younger spent twenty-five years in a state prison.

The author says that "Sam Bass and his gang terrorized all north central Texas by a series of train robberies *involving almost every railroad company in the state*." Bass only robbed four trains in Texas, the Houston and Texas Central twice and the Texas and Pacific twice.

1501. Miller, William Alexander

Early days in the wild west, by William Alexander Miller. . . . [N.p., press of Franc. E. Sheiry], 1943. Stiff wrappers. OP.

3–15 p. front. (port.), plates, ports. 23 cm.

This little book is an address the author delivered before the District of Columbia Society of the Sons of the American Revolution on Washington's Birthday in 1943. The author tells some new stories about Billy the Kid, stories just as unbelievable as many others which have been told. He also speaks about General Lew Wallace's dread of being killed by the Kid.

1502. Mills, Edward Laird

Plains, peaks and pioneers. Eighty years of Methodism in Montana, by Edward Laird Mills. Portland, Oreg., Binfords & Mort, publishers [1947]. Pict. cloth. OP.

4 p.l., 244 p. plates, ports. 22.2 cm.
Index: p. [237]–244.
Leaf of errata tipped in on back flyleaf; pub. device.

Has a mention of the road agents and of Joseph Slade.

1503. Mills, Lester W.

A sagebrush saga, by Lester W. Mills. Springfield, Utah, Art City publishing co., 1956. Stiff pict. wrappers. OP.

x, 112 p. plates, maps, cattle brands, tables. 35 x 22.8 cm.

Footnotes: p. 107–112.
Half title; double column.

Has a chapter on bandits and one on crimes committed in Nevada.

1504. Mills, William (Bill)

Twenty-five years behind prison bars, by Bill Mills. [N.p., n.d.] Wrappers. (Cover title.) Scarce.

5–60 p. front. 20.2 cm.

Reprinted quite a few years later with different wrappers, some changes in the paragraphing, and with a few last-page changes. At the end of the reprint is a letter by the author dated January, 1951, which gives a clue to a much later printing than the first. The reprint has one additional portrait not included in the first printing.

1505. Mills, William W.

Forty years at El Paso, 1858–1898. Recollections of war, politics, adventure, events, narratives, sketches, etc., by W.W. Mills. . . . Chicago, Press of W.B. Conkey co., 1901.] Dec. cloth. Rare.

4 p.l., 11–166 p. front. (port. with signature in facsm.). 20 cm.

Deals with gun battles and the bloody reign of the city marshals of El Paso. The author misspells Marshal Stoudenmire's name as Studemeir and also misspells John Wesley Hardin's name.

1506. ———

Forty years at El Paso, 1858–1898, by W. W. Mills. With drawings by Tom Lea, introduction and notes by Rex W. Strickland. El Paso, Texas, Carl Hertzog, 1962. Pict. cloth.

xxii p., 2 l., 212 p. illus., plates (4 double p.), facsm. 24 cm.
Appendix: p. 175–199; index: p. 201–212.

In this reissue of Item 1505 both Stoudenmire's and John Wesley Hardin's names are still misspelled. This book was also issued in a numbered, signed, and boxed de luxe edition of one hundred copies.

1507. Milner, Joe E., and Earle R. Forrest

California Joe, noted scout and Indian fighter, by Joe E. Milner. . . . and Earle R. Forrest. . . . With an authentic account of Custer's last fight, by Colonel William H. C. Bowen. . . . Caldwell, Idaho, the Caxton printers, ltd., 1935. Pict. cloth. Scarce.

14 p.l., [29]–396 p. front. (port.), plates, ports. 19.5 cm.

Bibliography: p. [312]; appendix: p. [315]–366; index: p. [367]–396.
Half title; pub. device.

Rich in information about Calamity Jane and Wild Bill Hickok. Contains some new material and has a fairly accurate chapter on the murder of Wild Bill, though there are some misstatements. The authors have Wild Bill holding a pair of jacks and a pair of eights when he was killed and say it was ever afterward known as a "dead man's hand." I thought everyone who knows poker hands is aware that a dead man's hand consists of aces and eights, which was the hand Hickok held. The authors are very critical, and rightly so, of Buel's books.

1508. Miner, Frederick Roland

Outdoor southland of California, by Frederick Roland Miner. With illustrations from photographs and paintings by the author. Los Angeles, Times-Mirror press, 1923. Pict. cloth. Scarce.

6 p.l., [9]–229 p. front. (col.), plates. 20.2 cm.
Half title; illus. chapter headings.

Has a chapter on Joaquín Murieta and Tiburcio Vásquez.

1509. [Missouri]

History and directory of Cass county, Missouri, containing a history of the county, its towns, commercial interests etc. Illustrated. Sold by subscription. Harrisonville, Mo., published by the Cass County Leader, 1908. Cloth. Scarce.

2 p.l., 408 p. illus., plates, ports., large fold. map tipped in. 22.4 cm.

Has a chapter on the James and Younger brothers.

1510. ———

History of Clay and Platte counties, Missouri, written and compiled from the most authentic official and private sources, including a history of their townships, towns and villages. . . . St. Louis, National Historical co., 1885. Cloth. Scarce.

xvi, 1121 [2] p. tables. 25 cm.

Contains much material on the James boys and the Youngers. The book gives a good account of the robbery of the Liberty, Missouri, bank, a story about Jesse and about his death.

1511. ———

The history of Davies county, Missouri. An encyclopedia of useful information, and a compendium of actual facts. . . . Illustrated. Kansas City, Mo., Birdsall & Dean, 1882. Leather. Scarce.

5 p.l., [9]–868 p. plates, ports., large fold. map (col.) in front, tables. 26 cm.

Devotes a section to Jesse James, the robbery of the Gallatin bank and the killing of J. W. Sheets. Also gives an account of the robbery of the Davies county treasurer's safe by John Reno.

1512. ———

History of Greene county, Missouri, written and compiled from the most authentic official and private sources, including a history of its townships, towns and villages. . . . Illustrated. St. Louis, Western Historical co., 1883. Dec. cloth. Scarce.

viii, 919 p. front. (port. with tissue), plates, ports. (part with tissues). 26 cm.

Has a long account of the killing of Dave Tutt by Wild Bill Hickok and the latter's testimony on the killing of James Coleman.

1513. ———

History of Howard and Cooper counties, Missouri, written and compiled from the authentic official and private sources, including a history of its townships, towns and villages. . . . Illustrated. St. Louis, National Historical co., 1883. Cloth. Scarce.

ix, 1167 p. plates. 25.5 cm.

Gives the same information on the killing of Jesse James as that appearing in the same publisher's *History of Marion County.*

1514. ———

The history of Jackson county, Missouri, containing a history of the county, its cities, towns, etc. . . . Illustrated. Kansas City, Mo., Union Historical co., Birdsall, Williams & co., 1881. Leather. Scarce.

xi, [9]–1006 p. front. (with tissue), plates, ports., large fold. map. 25.3 cm.

Contains a chapter on the Youngers.

1515. ———

History of Randolph and Macon counties, Missouri, written and compiled from the most authentic official and private sources, including a history of their townships, towns and villages. . . . Illustrated. St. Louis, National Historical co., 1884. Cloth. Scarce.

xiii, 1223 p. 26.3 cm.

Gives an account of the killing of Jesse James by Bob Ford.

1516. [**Missouri, Kansas and Texas Railway**]

The opening of the great southwest, 1870–1945. A brief history of the origin and development of the Missouri, Kansas and Texas railway. [N.p., 1945.] Stiff wrappers. (Cover title.) Scarce.

3–29 [2] p. illus., plates, maps (1 double p.). 17.7 cm.

Has information on the Spencer gang, train robbers, and the Daltons and their raid on Coffeyville.

1517. Mitchell, John D.

Lost mines of the great southwest, including stories of hidden treasures, by John D. Mitchell. [Phoenix, Ariz., press of the Journal co., inc., 1933.] Cloth. Scarce.

4 p.l., 11–174 p. illus., plates. 20 cm.

This privately printed little book has a chapter containing the author's personal recollections of the James boys and his boyhood search for some of their loot.

1518. Mitchell, Lige

Daring exploits of Jesse James and his band of border train and bank robbers. Containing also some desperate adventures of the Dalton brothers, by Lige Mitchell. Baltimore, Md., I. & M. Ottenheimer, publishers [1912]. Pict. col. wrappers. Scarce.

3 p.l., 7–189 [3] p. illus. 19 cm.

Another example of the cheap early-day novels published by this house.

1519. Mitchell, William Ansel

Linn county, Kansas. A history, by William Ansel Mitchell, written to give and preserve the more intimate knowledge of incidents of world-wide importance and marking an epochal period in the history of the human race. Kansas City, Kans., . . . Campbell-Gates . . ., 1928. Cloth. Scarce.

3 p.l., [5]–404 p. plates, port., map, plan. 23.2 cm.

Contains some material on Jesse James.

1520. Mix, Olive Stokes, and Eric Heath

The fabulous Tom Mix, by Olive Stokes Mix with Eric Heath. Englewood Cliffs, N.J., Prentice-Hall, inc. [1957]. Pict. cloth. OP.

5 p.l., 177 p. plates, ports. 21.9 cm.

Has some material on rustlers and outlaws.

1521. Mix, Tom

The west of yesterday, by Tom Mix, and Tony's story about himself. Compiled and edited by J. B. M. Clark from interviews with the author. Los Angeles, the Times-Mirror press, 1923. Pict. cloth. Scarce.

5 p.l., [11]–162 p. front. (port.), 1 plate. 19.5 cm.

Half title.

Has some information about outlaws during the time Mix served as a sheriff before he went into motion pictures.

1522. Moak, Sim

The last of the mill creeks and early life in northern California, by Sim Moak. Chico, Calif., 1923. Stiff pict. wrappers. Scarce.

[3]–47 [1] p. front. (port.). 24 cm.

Has information about road agents and Black Bart.

1523. Moffett, Cleveland

True detective stories from the archives of the Pinkertons, by Cleveland Moffett. New York, Doubleday & McClure co., 1897. Cloth. Scarce.

4 p.l., 3–250 p. front., 2 ports. (incl. front.). 17 cm.

Reprinted with same collation by G. W. Dillingham co., New York, and later reprinted in Akron, Ohio, by the Superior printing co., without date.

These books have a chapter about the Renos.

1524. Mokler, Alfred James

History of Natrona county, Wyoming, 1888–1922. True portrayal of the yesterdays of a new county and a typical frontier town in the middle west. Fortunes and misfortunes, tragedies and comedies, struggles and triumphs of the pioneers. Map and illustrations. By Alfred James Mokler. . . . Chicago, R. R. Donnelley & sons co., 1923. Cloth. Rare.

xiv p., 1 l., 477 p. front. (with tissue), plates, ports., map, facsm. 23.5 cm.

Index: p. 475–477.

Half title.

Privately printed in a small edition and very scarce, this book has some excellent material on train robberies, the Johnson County War, outlaws, and the hanging of Cattle Kate and of Jim Averill. The author writes that Calamity Jane was a neglected little girl in Miner's Delight when a philanthropic lady took her back East to educate her but that Jane sought bad associates. He also repeats the old legend about her being named Calamity by Captain Egan. He seems to repeat Jane's own autobiography closely and thus repeats many of her wild and untrue tales.

He is in error, too, in saying that Jack McCall (which he spells McCaul) was driving the stage and that Calamity saved him and his six passengers when they were attacked by Indians. In telling about McCall's murder of Wild Bill Hickok, the author writes that "in a very short time McCaul's body was swinging at the end of a rope which had been fastened to the limb of a tree and Calamity Jane was the one who captured McCaul and was the leader of the mob that hanged him." McCall was not lynched but was later legally hanged.

1525. Monaghan, Jay

The great rascal. The life and adventures of Ned Buntline, by Jay Monaghan. With illustrations. Boston, Little, Brown and co., 1952. Cloth. OP.

xi p., 1 l., 3–353 p. front. (port.), plates, ports., facsm. 21.3 cm.

Notes: p. 291–311; bibliography: p. 312–333; acknowledgments: p. 334–336; index: p. 339–353.

Half title.

Has some information about Wild Bill Hickok during his career as a showman.

1526. ———

The legend of Tom Horn, last of the bad men, by Jay Monaghan. Indianapolis, New York, the Bobbs-Merrill co., publishers [1946]. Cloth. OP.

9 p.l., 19–293 p. front. (port.), illus., plates, ports. 22 cm.

Acknowledgments: p. 271–274; list of sources: p. 275–284; index: p. 287–293.

Half title; untrimmed; "First edition" on copyright p.

The author gives some new information about Tom Horn, especially about his ancestry and his boyhood.

1527. ——— (ed.)

The book of the American west, Jay Monaghan, editor-in-chief. Clarence P. Horung, art director; authors, Ramon F. Adams, B. A. Botkin, Natt N. Dodge, Robert Easton, Wayne Gard, Oscar Lewis, Dale Morgan, Don Russell, Oscar Osburn Winther. New York, Julian Messner, inc. [1963]. Pict. cloth.

5 p.l., 11–608 p. illus. (many in col.), plates (many in col.), music, facsms. 28.6 cm.

Suggestions for additional reading: p. 593–595; index: p. 596–607.

Half title; illus. double t.p.; short sketches of editor and authors: p. 608; "First edition" on copyright p.

Also published in a de luxe edition, numbered, bound in leather with an accompanying portfolio of six prints by Frederic Remington, and in slip case.

This unusual book has chapters which cover every phase of western history—mountain men; transportation, mining, and minerals; Indians; the law and the outlaw; the cowboy and his horse; guns; wildlife; folklore; and the art of the west, each written by an expert in his subject. It is included in this work because of the chapter by Wayne Gard on outlaws, in which he deals with many of the well-known outlaws, frontier feuds, and range wars.

1528. Monroe, Arthur Worley

San Juan silver, by Arthur W. Monroe. . . . Historical tale of the silvery San Juan and western Colorado. [Grand Junction, Colo., printed by Grand Junction Sentinel], 1940. Pict. cloth. OP.

ix, 3–250 [1] p. 23.5 cm.

Has much about the lawless days in Colorado. The author speaks of the Jinglebob Ranch of New Mexico and erroneously says that that was where Billy the Kid and Sam Bass got their start. Sam Bass was never in New Mexico. In his chapter on Creede there are some stories about Soapy Smith and Bat Masterson. There is also some new material about Alferd Packer, Black Jack Ketchum, and others.

1529. Montague, Joseph

Wild Bill, a western story, by Joseph Montague. . . . New York, Chelsea House, publishers [1926]. Cloth. Scarce.

3 p.l., [11]–247 [1] p. 19.3 cm.

This is one of the wildest and most unreliable books on Wild Bill ever published. Even if the author intended it for fiction, I fail to see why he did not get his historical facts right. He follows Buel in the account of the trouble with McCanles, and as a whole the book is the product of a rich imagination and dependence upon unreliable secondary sources.

1530. [Montana]

The dynamiters; or, the story of Isaac Gravelle. One of the greatest cases of circumstantial evidence known. Illustrated. Helena, Mont., published by State publishing co. [n.d.]. Wrappers. Very rare.

1 p.l., [3]–113 p. front. (port.), ports. 19 cm.

Gives a full history of Isaac Gravelle, the Montana outlaw.

1531. ———

History of Montana, 1739–1885. A history of its discovery and settlement, social and commercial progress, mines and miners, agriculture and stock growing. . . . Indians and Indian wars, vigilantes, courts of justice. . . . Illustrated. Chicago, Warner, Beers & co., 1885. Three-quarter leather. Scarce.

7 p.l., 15–1397 p. plates, ports., map. 27.8 cm.
Large fold. map in front.

Has a long history of the vigilantes and their hangings.

1532. ———

Montana. An illustrated history of the Yellowstone valley, embracing the counties of Park, Sweet Grass, Carbon, Yellowstone, Rosebud, Custer and Dawson. State of Montana. Spokane, Wash., Western Historical publishing co. [n.d.]. Full leather. Scarce.

xxi, 669 p. front. (port. with tissue), plates, ports. (part with tissues). 29.7 cm.
Double column; gilt edges.

A story of the vigilantes and their troubles with the Plummer gang.

1533. ———

Second annual report of the secretary of the Helena board of trade for the year 1879. Territory of Montana. [Helena, Mont.], Woolford, Macquaid & La Croix, Daily and Weekly Independent, 1880. Wrappers. Rare.

2 p.l., [5]–40 p. fold. map in front. 22 cm.

In a dialogue of questions and answers between a pilgrim and a pioneer, some information is given on the vigilantes of Virginia City, as well as information on Boone Helm, Jack Gallaher, Buck Stinson, Clubfoot George Lane, Henry Plummer, and others.

1534. ———

State of Montana, department of public instruction. Pioneer day manual. . . . Pioneer day, May 31st, 1907. Helena, Mont. [1907]. Pict. wrappers. Scarce.

2 p.l., 5–42 p. 23 cm.
Vignette.

Has a chapter on the Montana vigilantes, Henry Plummer, and the rest of his gang.

1535. Moody, Ralph

Stagecoach west, by Ralph Moody. New York, Thomas Y. Crowell co. [1967]. Cloth.

x, 341 p. front., illus., plates, ports., maps, facsms. 23.3 cm.
Bibliography: p. 323–333; index: p. 335–341.
Half title; map on end papers.

Contains a chapter on Black Bart (Charles Bolton) and his stage robberies. There is some information on Joseph Slade and his killing of Jules Reni, (whom the author mistakenly calls Beni, which could be a typographical error). There is a mention of Wyatt Earp as a shotgun messenger, but it is disappointing that the author omitted so many of the stagecoach robberies in Arizona, the Black Hills, and California.

1536. Moore, Frank L.

Souls and saddlebags, the diaries and correspondence of Frank L. Moore, western missionary, 1888–1896. Edited by Austin L. Moore. Denver, Big Mountain press [1963]. Cloth.

7 p.l., 17–207 p. 22.2 cm.
Index: p. 204–207.
Half title; map on end papers; pub. device.

Includes some information on the hanging of Jim Averill and Cattle Kate.

1537. Moore, Gerald E.

Outlaw's end, by Gerald E. Moore. [N.p., n.d.] Stiff pict. wrappers. Scarce.

3 p.l., 101 p. 19 cm.

Has information about some outlaws of Oklahoma, including Al Spencer and Bud Wells.

1538. Moore, John M. (Tex)

The west, [by] Tex Moore, official cowboy artist of Texas, and old time cow-puncher. [Wichita Falls, Texas, Wichita printing co. 1935.] Pict. cloth. (Cover title.) Scarce.

5 p.l., 147 [1] p. front., plates, facsm. 24 cm.
Half title; no title page.

A little book of personal reminiscences. The author misspells John Chisum's last name as Chisholm. The book is largely an account of the Lincoln County War and Billy the Kid. The author states that Mrs. McSween played "The Star-Spangled Banner" while her home burned and that the bullets were flying thick. No one knows just how this legend started, but it seems to be a favorite with most writers. He continues with the timeworn legends about Billy killing the blacksmith who insulted his mother when he was twelve and his having killed twenty-one men by the time he was twenty-one years old. There are quite a few other errors scattered throughout.

1539. Moore, Langdon W.

Langdon W. Moore. His own story of his eventful life. Boston, published by Langdon W. Moore, 1893. Cloth. Scarce.

xi p., 1 l., 15–659 p. front. (port.), plates, ports., facsm. 22.8 cm.

Experiences of an early-day detective.

1540. Mootz, Herman Edwin

The blazing frontier, by Herman Edwin Mootz. . . . Dallas, Texas, Tardy publishing co., 1936. Cloth. Scarce.

8 p.l., 381 p. plates, ports. 19.5 cm.

A novelized account of some of the Oklahoma outlaw bands, such as the Miller, Doolin, and Jennings gangs.

1541. ———

"Pawnee Bill." A romance of Oklahoma, by Herman Edwin Mootz. . . . Illustrated. Los Angeles, Calif., Excelsior publishing co., publishers [1928]. Pict. cloth. Scarce.

6 p.l., 17–285 [3] p. front. (port.), illus., plates. 20.3 cm.
Half title; last 3 p. newspaper comments.

1542. Morgan, Dale L.

The Humboldt, highroad of the west, by Dale L. Morgan. Illustrated by Arnold Blanch. New York, Toronto, Farrar & Rinehart, inc. [1943]. Cloth. OP.

x p., 1 l., 3–374 p. illus. (1 double p.), plate, map. 20.8 cm.
Bibliography: p. 355–365; index: p. 367–374.
Half title; illus. end papers; illus. chapter headings; first edition: "F R" in device on copyright p.

Contains some information about Butch Cassidy and his Wild Bunch.

1543. Morgan, Edward E. P.

God's loaded dice; Alaska, 1897–1930, by Edward E. P. Morgan in collaboration with Henry F. Woods. . . . Caldwell, Idaho, the Caxton printers, ltd., 1948. Cloth.

5 p.l., [11]–298 p. plates. 23.6 cm.
Half title; head pieces; vignette; pub. device.

Has a chapter on Soapy Smith, his death, and the breaking up of his gang.

1544. Morgan, Jonnie R.

The history of Wichita Falls, by Jonnie R. Morgan. . . . [Wichita Falls, Tex.], 1931. Pict. fabrikoid. Scarce.

5 p.l., [11]–221 p. plates, ports. 23.5 cm.
Bibliography: p. 221.

Contains a section on the robbery of the City National Bank by Kid Lewis and Foster Crawford. The author is mistaken, however, in saying that the robbers were members of the Al Jennings gang.

1545. Morgan, Leon

Shooting sheriffs of the wild west, by Leon Morgan. Racine, Wisconsin, Whitman publishing co. [1936]. Pict. col. boards. Scarce.

2 p.l., 9–422 [6] p. illus. 11.5 cm.

This unusual-size little book deals with Wyatt Earp, Buckey O'Neill, Billy Breakenridge, Pat Garrett, and others but adds nothing new to the many earlier books about these characters. In fact, it continues many false legends.

1546. Morgan, Murray

Skid road. An informal portrait of Seattle, by Murray Morgan. New York, the Viking press, 1951. Cloth. OP.

5 p.l., 3–280 p. 21.8 cm.
Index: p. 275–280.
Republished same year and in 1952. Revised in 1960.

Has some mention of Soapy Smith.

1547. Morgan, Wallace M.

History of Kern county, California, with biographical sketches of the leading men and women of the county who have been identified with its growth and development from the early days to the present. History by Wallace M. Morgan. Illustrated. . . . Los Angeles, Calif., Historic Record co., 1914. Three-quarter leather. Scarce.

xvi p., 1 l., [17]–1556 p. plates, ports. 28 cm.

Contains some material on the career of Tiburcio Vásquez.

1548. Morrel, Ed

The twenty-fifth man. The strange story of Ed Morrel, the hero of Jack London's *Star Rover*, by Ed Morrel, lone survivor of the famous band of California feud outlaws. . . . Montclair, N.J., New Era publishing co. [1924]. Cloth. Scarce.

9 p.l., 390 p. front., illus. 21 cm.
Half title; last 14 p. a bulletin on penology.

A scarce book about the terrible experiences of the last survivor of the Evans-Sontag band of train robbers. The author helped Sontag escape jail and became a hunted man with him.

1549. Morris, Henry Curtis

Desert gold and total prospecting, by Henry Curtis Morris. Illustrated with photographs mostly by the author. Washington, D.C., published by the author, 1955. Cloth. Scarce.

4 p.l., 60 p. plates, ports., map (double p.), facsm. 26 cm.
Half title; illus. t.p.

This privately printed little book has a section on Diamondfield Jack Davis.

1550. Morris, Leopold

Pictorial history of Victoria and Victoria county "where the history of Texas began," by Leopold Morris. [San Antonio, Texas, printed by Clements printing co., 1953.] Cloth. Scarce.

3 p.l., [86] p. (no pagination). plates, ports., maps, facsms., cattle brands. 31.2 cm.

Has some information on the Taylor-Sutton feud and John Wesley Hardin.

1551. Morris, Lerona Rosamond (ed.)

Oklahoma, yesterday-today-tomorrow, edited by Lerona Rosemond Morris. Guthrie, Oklahoma, published by Co-Operative publishing co., December, 1930. Fabrikoid. Scarce.

viii, 9 l., 15–922 [10] p. illus., ports., map. 26 cm.
Index: p. [923–932].
Illus. end papers.

Contains a long chapter on the various outlaws of Oklahoma.

1552. Morris, Lucile

Bald knobbers, by Lucile Morris. Caldwell, Idaho, the Caxton printers, ltd., 1939. Pict. cloth. OP.

8 p.l., [15]–253 p. front. (port.), illus., plates, ports. 23.7 cm.
Bibliography: p. [247]–250; index: p. [251]–253.
Half title; illus. end papers; pub. device.

Concerns outlaws and lawlessness in the Missouri Ozarks.

1553. Morrison, Mrs. Anne L., and John H. Haydon

History of San Luis Obispo county and environs, California, with biographical sketches of the leading men and women of the county and environs who have been identified with the growth and development of the section from the early days to the present. History by Mrs. Anne L. Morrison and John H. Haydon. Illustrated. . . . Los Angeles, Calif., Historic Record co., 1917. Three-quarter leather. Scarce.

7 p.l., [17]–1038 p. plates, ports. 27.7 cm.

Contains a chapter on such outlaws as Murieta, Jack Powers, and Joaquín Valenzuela.

1554. Morrison, William Brown

Military posts and camps in Oklahoma, by William Brown Morrison. . . . Oklahoma City, Harlow publishing corp., 1936. Pict. cloth. Very scarce.

vii [3] p., 180 p. front. (col.), port., drawings (all col.). 23.8 cm.
Bibliography: p. 175–176; index: p. 177–180.
Untrimmed.

On page 21 the author mentions Belle Starr but is mistaken in saying that she was sentenced in Judge Parker's court in 1833. That is evidently a typographical error. He also says that Belle "began her downward career as a spy for Quantrill during the Civil War, and at its close came to the Indian Territory. . . ." She went to Texas with her parents after leaving Carthage, Missouri, before the war was over, and was never a spy for Quantrill. The author also says that she "probably met her death at the hands of her son."

1555. Morse, Frank P.

Cavalcade of rails, by Frank P. Morse. Illustrated. New York, E. P. Dutton & co., inc., 1940. Pict. cloth. OP.

10 p.l., 21–370 p. plates. 24.3 cm.
Index: p. 353–370.
Half title; "First edition" on copyright p.

Chapter XV deals with the James and Younger gang and some of the gang's train robberies. The book also includes a mention of the Renos and the story of Jesse's assassination by Bob Ford.

1556. Moss, William Paul

Rough and tumble. The autobiography of a west Texas judge, by William Paul Moss. New York, Vantage press, inc. [1954]. Cloth. OP.

1 p.l., 177 [19] p. plates, ports., map. 22.2 cm.
Last 19 p. plates and ports.
Pub. device.

Has some mention of Billy the Kid.

1557. Mott, Mrs. D. W. (ed.)

Legends and lore of long ago (Ventura county, California). Contributed by club women of Ventura county. Directed by Mrs. D. W. Mott. Los Angeles, Calif., Wetsel publishing co., inc., 1929. Cloth. Scarce.

6 p.l., 13–223 p. front. (port.), plates, ports. 21.4 cm.
Decorated outer margins; untrimmed.

Has a chapter on Vásquez. The same tale is told about Vásquez that has so often been told about Jesse James and other outlaws—that of giving a widow the money to pay off her mortgage and then robbing the mortgagee. That legend has been told ever since Robin Hood's day.

1558. Muir, Emma M.

Old Shakespeare, by Emma M. Muir. A series of articles from the pages of the *New Mexico Magazine*, by Emma Muir of Lordsburg, who lived in Shakespeare during the last days of the boom of this fabulous mining camp in southwestern New Mexico. . . . [N.p., n.d.] Wrappers. (Cover title.)

16 p. plates, ports., map. 27.8 cm.

Has an account of the hanging of Russian Bill and Sandy King and some information about Curly Bill Brocius.

1559. Mullane, William H. (ed.)

This is Silver City, 1882, 1883, 1884. Volume I. [Silver City, N.M., Silver City Enterprise], 1963. Stiff pict. wrappers.

4 p.l., 74 [16] p. illus., plates, ports., facsms. 27.5 cm.
Double column.

This is a book of excerpts from the *Silver City Enterprise* printed as they appeared in this early frontier newspaper. There is a great deal of material about Joel Fowler and his lynching and various train robberies and murders, and quite a bit of new material on Kit Joy and his trial for murder and train robbery.

1560. ———

This is Silver City, 1885, 1886, 1887. Volume II. [Silver City, N.M., Silver City Enterprise], 1964. Stiff pict. wrappers.

4 p.l., 40 [1] p. plates, ports. 27.5 cm.
Double column.

More excerpts from the *Silver City Enterprise* (see Item 1559). This work continues with the many crimes and murders and outlaws of those years, including the killing of Ike Clanton, and even has news of the killing of Sam Starr, of Indian Territory. It appears that most of the news in the early western newspapers was about robberies, murders, and other crimes.

1561. ———

This is Silver City, 1888, 1889, 1890. Volume III. [Silver City, N.M., Silver City Enterprise], 1965. Stiff pict. wrappers.

3 p.l., 51 p. plates, ports. 27.5 cm.
Double column.

Continues to give news of outlawry and train robberies and tells about the Wham payroll robbery (see Items 1559 and 1560).

1562. ———

This is Silver City, 1891. Volume IV. [Silver City, N.M., Silver City Enterprise], 1967. Stiff pict. wrappers.

3 p.l., 126 p. plates. 27.5 cm.
Double column.

More excerpts from the *Silver City Enterprise* (see Items 1559 to 1561). Contains accounts of many crimes and tells about Bronco Bill Walters.

1563. Mullen, Arthur F.

Western democrat, by Arthur F. Mullen. New York, Wilfred Funk, inc., 1940. Cloth. OP.

xii p., 1 l., 3–360 [1] p. plates, ports. 23.5 cm.
Half title; double t.p.; "First edition" on copyright p.

Gives some excellent information on Doc Middleton and Kid Wade, telling of Middleton's capture, divorce, and marriage to his first wife's sister and the lynching of Kid Wade. The author claims that men of high standing in the community took Wade away from the sheriff and hanged him because they feared he would involve them in his crimes.

1564. Mullin, Robert N.

A chronology of the Lincoln county war, by Robert N. Mullin. Scene: mostly Lincoln county, New Mexico. Time: mainly 1877–1881. [Santa Fe, N.M.], the press of the Territorian [1966]. Wrappers.

3 p.l., 3–39 p. map (double p.). 23 cm.
Press of the Territorian Western Americana series, No. 8.

Gives in chronological order the dates of events and the birth and death dates of many of the participants in the Lincoln County War. Only 100 copies were printed.

1565. Mumey, Nolie

Calamity Jane, 1852–1903. A history of her life and adventures in the west, by Nolie Mumey. Denver, Colo., the Range press, 1950. Boards and leather. Pict. label pasted on. Rare.

xix, 21–146 p. front. (port.), illus. fold. map in front, facsm. of two pamphlets in pocket at end. 26 cm.
Supplement: p. 141–142; index: p. 143–146.
Colophon: "This is number —— of an edition limited to two hundred signed and numbered copies."

The author seems to have made an honest effort to bring to light every facet of

Jane's character, and the book is well annotated. Because of the small edition, it was practically sold out before publication and immediately became a rare item. The author, a well-known Denver surgeon whose hobby is writing historical nonfiction, has his books privately printed in small editions. Consequently all his books command a premium immediately after release.

The author says that Calamity Jane "was supposed to have captured Jack McCall after he shot Wild Bill Hickok and held him captive with a cleaver in a meat market until he was taken into custody." According to his footnote reference, the author obtained his information from Cunningham's *Triggernometry*. This piece of fiction has been repeated until it has become widely accepted as fact. The author also erroneously states that Jack McCall was rearrested in Custer City, and in a footnote he says that Jane married a cab driver in San Antonio, Texas. All other accounts I have seen say that the marriage took place in El Paso, Texas. He also says that Calamity died on August 2, 1903, quoting from Brininstool's *Fighting Red Cloud's Warriors*. She died August 1.

1566. ———

Creede. History of a Colorado silver mining town. With illustrations and a pictorial map, by Nolie Mumey. Denver, Colo., Artcraft press, 1949. Pict. cloth. Scarce.

> xv p., 2 l., [5]–185 p. plates, ports., 2 maps (1 double p.), large fold. map at end. 24.9 cm.
>
> Index: p. [179]–185.
>
> Half title; untrimmed.
>
> Colophon: "Edition limited to five hundred numbered and signed copies."

A good history of this wild mining town in its early days. It contains an accurate account of the killing of Bob Ford. It also has accounts of Soapy Smith and some information on Bat Masterson's stay in Creede.

1567. ———

Hoofs to wings. The pony express, dramatic story of a mail service from east to west which existed one hundred years ago, by Nolie Mumey. Boulder, Colo., Johnson publishing co., 1960. Boards. Scarce.

> 8 p.l., 3–116 p. front. (col. tipped in), illus., plates, facsm. of seals (1 tipped in), fold. col. map at end. 26 cm.
>
> Index: p. 109–116.
>
> Half title; untrimmed; pict. label back of front binding: "Centenary of the Pony Express, 1860–1960;" t.p. in red and black.
>
> Colophon: "This is No. —— of an edition limited to two hundred numbered and signed copies (Signed)."

Accompanying the book is a leather-bound Bible. Stamped in gold on the back of the front binding: "Presented by Russell, Majors & Waddell, 1860."

Has a chapter on Joseph Slade and Wild Bill Hickok.

1568. ———

Poker Alice, Alice Ivers, Duffield, Tubbs, Huckert (1851–1930). History of a woman gambler in the west, by Nolie Mumey. . . . Denver, Colo., Artcraft press, 1951. Pict. art boards. Rare.

6 p.l., 47 p. front. (port. tipped in), plates, ports., large fold. map at end. 27.4 cm.

Colophon: "This is No. —— of a limited edition of 500 numbered and signed copies" (3d prelim. leaf).

To my knowledge, the only book written about this unique and noted western character. The first few copies released had the copyright notice on the verso of the title page, and in the folding map the state of New Mexico was erroneously labeled Nevada. These errors were quickly corrected, but the few copies which escaped correction are now considered as the first state and are very rare.

1569. Munsell, M.E.

Flying sparks, as told by a Pullman conductor, by M. E. Munsell. Kansas City, Tierman-Dart printing co., 1914. Pict. wrappers. Rare.

xvii, 19–159 p. illus., plates, ports. (part with tissues), facsms. 19 cm.

A conductor's experience with some of the Oklahoma outlaws, such as Cherokee Bill, Belle Starr, Jim Reed, and others. The chapter on Belle Starr is strikingly similar to Harman's chapter on Belle in his *Hell on the Border*, much of it word for word except for different paragraphing, and containing the same mistakes. One wonders why the author did not stick to Pullman conducting. He calls Belle a murderess, though she never killed anyone, and he has Fort Smith the headquarters of the "Starr gang." There are many other errors.

1570. Murbarger, Nell

Sovereigns of the sage. True stories of people and places in the great sage-brush kingdom of the western United States, by Nell Murbarger, "Roving reporter of the desert." Palm Desert, Calif., published by Desert Magazine press [1958]. Cloth. OP.

xiv, 342 p. plates, ports., 8 maps. 23.7 cm.

Index: p. [331]–342.

Half title; "First edition" on copyright p.

Has some slight mention of Frank and Jesse James, Butch Cassidy, Soapy Smith, and Bob Ford. A former waitress whom the author interviewed said that Soapy

Smith and Bob Ford always ate at her table in Creede and on Sunday would leave a five-dollar gold piece under a coffee saucer for her.

"They were fine fellows," said the waitress, "both of 'em. I never could understand how Bob could have killed Jesse James as he did."

1571. Murdock, John R.

Arizona characters in silhouette, by John R. Murdock. [N.p.], Fray Marcia de Niza edition, 1939. Stiff pict. wrappers. Scarce.

2 p.l., 7–151 p. illus. (silhouettes). 22.8 cm.
"First published serially in 1933."

Contains material on the Apache Kid and a chapter on Buckey O'Neill and some of the train robbers of Arizona.

1572. [Murieta, Joaquín]

El caballero Chileno bandido en California. Única y verdadera historia de Joaquín Murrieta [*sic*] por le Profesor Acigar. Barcelona, Spain, Biblioteca Hercules [n.d.]. Col. pict. wrappers. Rare.

6 p.l., [13]–206 p. plates. 18.8 cm.
Text in Spanish.

1573. ———

Joaquín Murrieta [*sic*], el bandido Chileno en California. San Antonio, Texas, "Editorial Martinez," 1926. Col. pict. wrappers. Rare.

4 p.l., [9]–264 p. plates. 19 cm.
Index: p. 263–264.
Half title; text in Spanish.

1574. ———

Joaquín Murieta, the brigand chief of California. A complete history of his life from the age of sixteen to the time of his capture and death in 1853. San Francisco, the Grabhorn press, 1932. Pict. boards and cloth. Rare.

vii [1] p., 1 l., 116 [4] p. front. (col.), illus. (col.), fold. lithograph at end. 25.6 cm.
No. 1 Americana reprints.
Bibliography: last four pages.
Double column.
Preface signed in ink by editor, Douglas S. Watson; introduction and bibliography by Francis P. Farquhar.
Published in an edition of 400 copies.

A modern edition of the *Police Gazette* version (see Item 1575). It has become quite rare and valuable.

1575. ———

The life of Joaquín Murieta, the brigand chief of California; being a complete history of his life, from the age of sixteen to the time of his capture and death at the hands of Capt. Harry Love, in the year of 1853. San Francisco, published at the office of the "California Police Gazette," 1859. Pict. wrappers. Exceedingly rare.

[3]–71 [1] p. illus., plates, port. 24.7 cm.
Double column; 1 p. adv. in front; 2 p. adv. at end.

This book was originally published as a serial in the *California Police Gazette* in ten issues (Vol. I, Nos. 34 to 43, September 3 to November 5, 1859). It is an anonymous rewriting of John Rollin Ridge's biography of Murieta. A name is changed here and there, but the book keeps the general story by Ridge, even to much of the dialogue. The writer changed the name of Rosita to Carmela and invented a second mistress named Clarina. Most of the Murieta books which followed, especially the foreign and Latin American ones, relied on this version.

A comparison of this book with Ridge's substantiates Ridge's charge of plagiarism. But this book is much better written than Ridge's. The anonymous writer made some of the conversation more reasonable, and the entire work was re-edited advantageously. Its reissue by the Grabhorn Press in 1932 has made this version more familiar than Ridge's to the modern reader.

The 1859 edition was illustrated by woodcuts from the drawings of Charles Nahl, a well-known artist of the day. It has also become rare; only three or four copies are known to exist. It was republished in 1862 with three of the plates used in the 1859 edition.

1576. ———

Vida y aventuras de Joaquín Murrieta [*sic*]. San Antonio, Texas, imprenta y Librería de Pablo Cruz [1885]. Pict. wrappers. Exceedingly rare.

59 p. 25.5 cm.
Triple column.
Text in Spanish.

Crudely printed on brittle paper, which explains its extreme rarity.

1577. ———

Vida y aventuras del más célebre bandido sonorense Joaquín Murrietta [*sic*]. Sus grandes proezas en California. Mexico, Tip. y encuadernación de I. Paz, 1908. Wrappers. Rare.

[3]–281 [1] p. 8 plates. 17 cm.
Text in Spanish.

1578. ———

Vida y aventuras del más célebre bandido sonorense "Joaquín Murrietta" [*sic*], y sus grandes proezas en el estado de California. Los Ahleles [*sic*], Calif., Editores: O. Pazy cía, imprenta "El libro diario," 1919. Wrappers. Rare.

[3]–128 p. 22 cm.
2 p. adv. in front; 6 p. adv. at end (incl. back wrapper).
Text in Spanish.

1579. ———

Vida y aventuras del más célebre bandido sonorense Joaquín Murrietta [*sic*] y sus grandes proezas en el estado de California. Los Angeles, Calif., C. G. Vincent & co., editores, 1923. Stiff pict. wrappers. Rare.

[3]–110 p. 22.2 cm.
Text in Spanish.

1580. Murphy, Celeste G.

The people of the pueblo; or, the story of Sonoma, by Celeste G. Murphy. Sonoma, Calif., W. T. and C. G. Murphy, MCMXXXV. Cloth. Scarce.

xvi p., 2 l., 3–269 p. front., plates, ports., facsms. 22.7 cm.
Half title.

Contains a chapter on Three-Fingered Jack García.

1581. Murphy, J.W.

Outlaws of the Fox river country. Story of the Whiteford and Spencer tragedies, the assassination of Judge Richardson, the execution of John Baird and the mobbing of J. W. Young . . ., by J. W. Murphy. Hannibal, Mo., Hannibal printing co., 1882. Pict. wrappers. Rare.

2 p.l., [3]–138 p. front., illus., ports. 20.8 cm.

Another history of the outlaws of the Navoo country depicted so well by Edward Bonney. The author, an Alexandria, Missouri, editor, was personally acquainted with many of the desperate characters in this chronicle.

1582. Murphy, Thomas F.

The hearts of the west, by Thomas F. Murphy. Boston, the Christopher publishing house [1928]. Cloth. Scarce.

3 p.l., [9]–194 p. 20.6 cm.
Pub. device.

The author's information on Black Bart is all wrong. He calls this character "a notorious and bloody road agent" and has him at the head of a band of five men. Black Bart was a lone wolf, and he never killed anyone. The author also has California Joe killing Black Bart by shooting him in the stomach in a saloon brawl and says that the state of California gave California Joe a draft for ten thousand dollars as a reward. Black Bart was not killed by California Joe but died a natural death much later.

1583. [**Murrell, John A.**]

Life and adventures of John A. Murrel [*sic*], the great western land pirate, with twenty-one spirited illustrative engravings. Philadelphia, T. B. Peterson and brothers, 1845. Pict. wrappers. Rare.

2 p.l., [5]–126 p. illus., port. 23.4 cm.

Republished, New York, H. Long and brother, 1847.

2 p.l., [5]–126 p. illus. 22.7 cm.
Double column.

1584. ———

Pictorial life and adventures of John A. Murrell, the great western land pirate. By the editors of the New York National Police Gazette. . . . With twenty-one large spirited engravings. . . . Philadelphia, T. B. Peterson and brothers . . . [n.d.]. Wrappers. Rare.

2 p.l., [5]–126 p. illus. 24.3 cm.

Both rare books of the complete histories of the Murrell gang.

1585. Musick, John R.

Stories of Missouri, by John R. Musick. New York, Cincinnati, Chicago, American book co. [1897]. Dec. cloth. Scarce.

3 p.l., 9–288 p. illus. 19 cm.

In the last chapter the author tells about the death of Jesse James and the surrender of Frank James.

1586. Myers, John Myers

Doc Holliday, by John Myers Myers. Boston, Toronto, Little, Brown and co. [1955]. Cloth. OP.

5 p.l., 3–287 p. front. (port.). 21 cm.
Acknowledgments: p. 264–265; bibliography: p. 266–269; index: p. 271–287.
Half title; pub. device; "First edition" on copyright p.

The first, though not the best, book devoted exclusively to this cold-blooded killer.

It is filled with errors. See my *Burs Under the Saddle* (Item 7) for a detailed discussion of them.

1587. ———

The last chance. Tombstone's early years, by John Myers Myers. New York, E. P. Dutton & co., inc., publisher, 1950. Cloth. OP.

4 p.l., 13–260 p. front., plates, ports., maps, plan. 22.2 cm.

Bibliography: p. 244–246; index: p. 247–260.

Half title; map on front end papers; vignette; untrimmed; "First edition" on copyright p.

Republished in 1951 by Grossett and Dunlap under the title *The Tombstone Story.*

On the map facing Chapter I some of the buildings are out of place. Attention is called to these errors because some of the action he writes about could not have happened as it did had the buildings been situated as they appear on the map. The author relies heavily upon the Lake version, and the book contains even more errors than Item 1586. He has Warren Earp killed in Lordsburg, New Mexico, by a rustler. Warren was killed in Willcox, Arizona, by a stage driver named Boyett. The author also says that Doc Holliday "died of tuberculosis in a Colorado sanitorium during or about 1895." He died November 8, 1887. The author corrected this error in his biography of Holliday.

1588. [Myers, Mrs. Peter]

The coming of the white man, [by Mrs. Peter Myers, n.p.]. Milwaukee Land co. [1940]. Pict. wrappers. Scarce.

2 p.l., [5]–38 p. illus., plates. 22.9 cm.

Illus. t.p.

The story of early Montana with some material on the road agents of Henry Plummer's gang and on the vigilantes.

1589. Mylar, Isaac L.

Early days at the mission San Juan Bautista, by Isaac L. Mylar. A narrative of incidents connected with the days when California was young. Watsonville, Calif., published by Evening Pajaronian [1929]. Cloth. Scarce.

6 p.l., [13]–195 p. plates. 23 cm.

Colophon (tipped in): "This book originally appeared in the Evening Pajaronian as a serial. Limited to 300 copies and privately printed."

The author's information about some of the early California bandits such as Chávez and Vásquez is fairly reliable. He gives an account of Vásquez' raid on Paicines, San Benito County.

N

1590. Nadeau, Reni A.

City-makers. The men who transformed Los Angeles from village to metropolis during the first great boom, 1868–'76, by Reni A. Nadeau. Garden City, N.Y., Doubleday & co., inc., 1948. Cloth. Scarce.

xiii p., 1 l., 270 p. 21 cm.
Bibliography: p. [254]–261; index: p. [263]–270.
Half title; map on end papers; untrimmed.

Contains a chapter, entitled "The Reign of Violence," about stage robbers and one, entitled "The Bandidos," about the activities of Vásquez.

1591. Nahm, Milton C.

Las Vegas and Uncle Joe. The New Mexico I remember, by Milton C. Nahm. Norman, University of Oklahoma press [1964]. Cloth.

ix p., 1 l., 3–294 p. 23.5 cm.
Half title; illus. t.p.; "First edition" on copyright p.

The author tells about Pat Garrett bringing Billy the Kid and Dave Rudabaugh to Las Vegas after their capture at Stinking Springs, and he leaves the impression that he believes the skeleton hanging in Dr. Desmarais' office was that of Billy the Kid. The author is mistaken when he writes that "old man Chisum got started on the cattle business by winning a ranch on four sixes." That is the tale told about Burk Burnett and his 6666 brand.

1592. Neal, Dorothy Jensen

Captive mountain waters. A story of pipelines and people, by Dorothy Jensen Neal. Illustrations by Bob Staggs. El Paso, Texas, Western press, 1961. Cloth. Also published in wrappers.

vii p., 2 l., 103 p. illus., plates (mostly col.). 23.9 cm.
Chronology: p. [89]–94; acknowledgments: p. [95]–96; index: p. [97]–103.
Illus. t.p.; limited to 300 copies.

Has some material on Oliver Lee and his battle with Pat Garrett and his men at Wildey Well and some mention of Billy the Kid.

1593. [Nebraska]

Collection of Nebraska pioneer reminiscences. Issued by the Nebraska Society of the Daughters of the American Revolution. By various writers. [Cedar Rapids, Iowa, the Torch press], 1916. Pict. cloth. Scarce.

7 p.l., 11–361 p. front. (port.), plates, ports. 24.6 cm.
Index: p. [343]–361.
Half title; untrimmed.

Has some material on the killing of Jules Reni by Joseph Slade and the killing of McCanles by Hickok.

1594. ———

Pioneer stories of Custer county, Nebraska. Contributed by more than one hundred present and former residents of Custer county. Broken Bow, Nebraska, published by E. R. Purcell, publisher. Custer County Chief, 1936. Stiff wrappers. Scarce.

4 p.l., 193 p. 23.6 cm.
Index to names: p. 186–193.
Double column.

Has much material on I. P. Olive, Luther Mitchell, Ami Ketchum, and Doc Middleton.

1595. ———

Pioneer stories of Furnas county, Nebraska. Compiled from the files of the Beaver City Times-Tribune. University Place, Nebr., Chafin printing co., 1914. Cloth. Scarce.

2 p.l., [7]–212 p. plates, ports. 22.4 cm.

Each chapter, written by a different person, tells of the author's experiences in the early days of the county's settlement. The book gives some false history about the capture of Joel Collins and Old Dad (whoever he was) after the Union Pacific train robbery. The author of this chapter says that Collins was captured at Hays City without the firing of a shot and that he still had sixty thousand dollars in gold in the original sealed packages. We know that Collins and Heffridge were killed at Buffalo Station and that the money had already been divided six ways among the others.

1596. Ned, Nebraska (pseud.)

Buffalo Bill and his daring adventures in the romantic wild west. Complete biography of the world's greatest scout, buffalo hunter, Indian fighter and scout as narrated for the first time by his old comrade and lifelong friend Nebraska Ned. Baltimore, Md., I. & M. Ottenheimer, publishers [1913]. Pict. wrappers. Scarce.

3 p.l., 9–192 p. illus. 19.3 cm.

I can understand why a writer who produced such trash would write under a pseudonym. In this author's account of the Hickok-McCanles "fight" he has ten

McCandles (which he spells McCandlas) men against Buffalo Bill instead of Wild Bill Hickok. Perhaps he was attempting to start a legend of his own. He spells Hickok's name as Hitchcock. Yet even this writer had some effect upon Wilbert Eisele (see Item 668), for some of the conversation in the latter book is in identical words.

1597. Neider, Charles (ed.)

The great west, edited with an introduction and notes by Charles Neider. New York, Coward-McCann, inc. [1958]. Pict. cloth. OP.

5 p.l., [11]–357 p. illus. 16 cm.
Half title; map on end papers (col.); double column.

Has sections on Wild Bill Hickok (a repetition of the Nichols article in *Harper's Magazine*); an excerpt from Pat Garrett's book on Billy the Kid; and an excerpt about Joseph Slade from Mark Twain's *Roughing It.*

1598. Nelson, Bruce

Land of the Dacotahs, by Bruce Nelson. Minneapolis, University of Minnesota press . . . [1946]. Cloth. OP.

6 p.l., 3–354 p. plates, ports., double p. map. 23.5 cm.
Acknowledgments and bibliography: p. 339–343; index: p. 344–354.
Half title; vignette.

The author devotes a chapter to Calamity Jane, debunking her own autobiography and exposing her true character. He writes: "Calamity's claim to being Wild Bill's sweetheart was an infamous slander—a fact which Calamity herself admitted in her declining years—for whatever else may be said of Wild Bill, he was at least fastidious."

But on the whole the author seems to have a poor opinion of Wild Bill, saying that he was not averse to shooting a man in the back. He says that Jack McCall was bribed to kill Wild Bill and was freed at his first trial by a jury packed with men who had paid him to do the job.

1599. Nesbit, Charles Francis

An American family, the Nesbits of St. Clair, by Charles Francis Nesbit. Washington, D.C., 1932. Cloth. Scarce.

4 p.l., [9]–228 p. 21.8 cm.

Has some material on the Youngers and the James boys.

1600. [Nevada]

History of Nevada, with illustrations and biographical sketches of its prominent men and pioneers. Oakland, Calif., Thompson & West, 1881. Cloth. Rare.

xiv p., 2 l., [17]–680 p. plates, ports. (part with tissues), tables. 30.8 cm.

Tells about Sam Langford and Farmer Peel, Nevada's famous gunmen.

1601. ———

Pioneer Nevada. Reno, Nev., lithographed in the United States of America, copyright by Harolds Club, 1951. Stiff pict. wrappers.

1 p.l., 204 [2] p. illus. 35 cm.
Map on end papers; vignette; double column.

Each page of this book is a reprint of one of the advertisements published once a week in the newspapers of Nevada during the years 1946 to 1951, each one representing some phase of history or folklore of the state. Many of the chapters deal with outlaws and gunmen, such as Nickonor Rodregues; Farmer Peel; Fighting Sam Brown; Susie Raper, the lady rustler; Jack Harris; and Milton Sharp. Other chapters deal with Robber's Roost, stage robbers, and the vigilantes.

1602. ———

Pioneer Nevada. Volume Two. Reno, Nev., published by Harolds Club . . ., 1956. Stiff pict. wrappers. OP.

160 p. illus. 35 cm.
Index: p. 160.
Vignette; double column.

1603. Neville, A. W.

The history of Lamar county (Texas), by A. W. Neville. . . . Paris, Texas, published by the North Texas publishing co. [1937]. Fabrikoid. Scarce.

3 p.l., 5–246 p. 1 port. 23.5 cm.
Map on end papers.

Has some material on John Chisum's early life and a mention of Belle Starr.

1604. ———

The Red river valley, then and now, by A. W. Neville. Stories of people and events in the Red river valley during the first hundred years of its settlement. Illustrated by Jose Cisneros. Paris, Texas [designed and produced by Carl Hertzog, El Paso, Texas], 1948. Cloth. Scarce.

xiii p., 1 l., 3–278 p. plate on leaf before each chapter. 24 cm.
Half title; map on end papers; t.p. in red and black; vignette.
Colophon: "Two thousand copies of this book produced at El Paso, Texas. Typography and design by Carl Hertzog; illustrated by Jose Cisneros; silhouettes by Jack Ellis. . . ."

Contains some new material on Jim Reed, Belle Starr, Frank James, and other outlaws. The author tells about the killing of Reed by Morris and repeats the old legend about Belle Starr refusing to identify the body of her husband. He states that Belle married Sam Starr because his family refused to give her part of the money from the Grayson robbery. He also repeats a false tale about how Belle was killed, as told to him by Frank Dalton. The author is mistaken in claiming that she was called Belle Starr even before she married Sam and while she was living with Reed. He also gives a short account of Henry Starr.

1605. Newmark, Harris

Sixty years in southern California, 1853–1913, containing the reminiscences of Harris Newmark. Edited by Maurice H. Newmark [and] Marco R. Newmark. . . . With 150 illustrations. New York, the Knickerbocker press, 1916. Leather and boards. Scarce.

xxviii p., 1 l., 688 p. front. (port. with tissue), plates, ports., facsm. 23.2 cm.
Index: p. 653–688.
T.p. in red and black.
Colophon: "Memorial edition limited to fifty copies. This is No. ——."

Republished in 1926 by the same publishers in a revised edition and augmented to 732 pages with 172 illustrations. Published again in 1930 by Houghton Mifflin company, Boston, in an edition of 744 pages with 182 illustrations.

All these books contain much material on Tiburcio Vásquez and Juan Flores, and Chapter XXXI, entitled "The End of Vásquez," gives a fairly accurate account of his capture.

1606. Newmark, Marco R.

Jottings in southern California history, by Marco R. Newmark. Los Angeles, the Ward Ritchie press [1955]. Pict. boards. OP.

xiv p., 1 l., 3–162 [12] p. plates, ports. 23.3 cm.
Index: p. 157–162.
Half title; illus. t.p.; errata slip tipped in; last 12 p. plates and ports.

Has some mention of Joaquín Murieta and Three-Fingered Jack García.

1607. [New Mexico]

History of New Mexico, its resources and people. Illustrated. Los Angeles, Chicago, New York, Pacific States publishing co., 1907. Cloth. Pub. in two volumes. Scarce.

Vol. I, xxvii, 522 p. plates, ports. (part with tissues). 25 cm.
Vol. II, [523]–1047 p. plates, ports. (part with tissues). 25 cm.

In a chapter entitled "Local Wars and Crimes" the author tells about the Lincoln

County War, Billy the Kid, and others. Many proper names are misspelled. There is material on Vicente Silva, Clay Allison, and other gunmen of the period.

1608. ———

Violent New Mexico. Authentic news stories from New Mexico's wild frontier days. Santa Fe, N.M., published by Ewen Enterprises, [n.d., ca. 1962]. Pict. wrappers. (Cover title.)

[24] p. (no pagination). illus., plates, facsm. 21.5 x 28 cm.

Excerpts from newspapers of the seventies and eighties, telling of the robberies committed by the Ketchums and their battle with Sheriff Farr, stagecoach robberies, the lynching of the Bacas for the murder of Editor Conklin, and information about the marriage of Billy the Kid's mother to Mr. Antrim.

1609. Newsom, J. A.

The life and practice of the wild and modern Indian, by J. A. Newsom. [Oklahoma City, Rev. J. A. Newsom, press of Harlow publishing co., 1923.] Pict. cloth. Scarce. Also published in pict. wrappers.

6 p.l., [7]–219 p. front., illus., ports. 23.6 cm.
Vignette.

Contains material on Oklahoma outlaws and peace officers. The author speaks of the Dalton and Doolin gangs as being in existence at the same time, but Doolin was a member of the Dalton gang until the latter was wiped out at Coffeyville. He then organized his own gang. The author does not seem to know who killed Belle Starr and says that it might have been her son. This volume apparently provided some of the source material for Sutton's *Hands Up* (Item 2171) and Nix's *Oklahombres* (Item 1611).

1610. Nicholl, Edith M. (Mrs. Edith M. Boyer)

Observations of a ranch woman in New Mexico, by Edith M. Nicholl. London, Macmillan and co., ltd.; New York, the Macmillan co., 1898. Dec. cloth.

4 p.l., 271 p. front. (with tissue), plates. 19.4 cm.
Half title; illus. t.p.

Republished, Cincinnati, the Editor publishing co., 1901. Cloth.

3 p.l., 260 p. 19 cm.

Although written by a well-educated woman, the book shows a very careless handling of historical facts with which the author should have been acquainted. According to her, Billy the Kid was a dishwasher when he started his outlaw career after being "ill-used by a big burly man-cook." She says that Tunstall (whom she calls

Morton) was killed from behind on the trail at night and that his body was left for the buzzards. She calls McSween by the name Mackintosh and further states that Billy the Kid's prison guards (Bell and Olinger) went to dinner and left the Kid alone in the jail. While they were gone, he "filed his fetters." She says that there were fifteen people in Mackintosh's (McSween's) home while it burned and that all except Billy the Kid were brutally murdered. She also relates that the Kid went to bed in another room in Maxwell's house the night of his murder, but, "finding himself attacked with the pangs of hunger, arose from his couch and, taking a knife, was proceeding to the storeroom to cut himself some meat. Hearing voices in the room of his host, he opened the door and demanded to know who was there." Then Garrett shot him while the "Kid was standing in the door *with a lamp in his hand*" (italics added).

1611. Nix, Evett Dumas

Oklahombres, particularly the wilder ones, by Evett Dumas Nix, former United States marshal in old Oklahoma territory and the Cherokee strip, as told to Gordon Hines. [St. Louis, 1929.] Pict. cloth. OP.

> xix, 280 p. front., plates, ports., facsms. 23.5 cm.
> Chronology of Oklahoma: p. 279–280.
> Half title; illus. end papers; illus. margins and chapter headings; vignette.

Written entirely about the outlaws of Oklahoma and the peace officers who chased them. It has chapters on the Daltons, the Doolin gang, the Jennings gang, Henry Starr, and others, but there are many mistakes. Most of the incidents the author writes about were secondhand; nearly all the contacts with the outlaws were made by his deputies while he stayed in his office. Too, he dictated this book a number of years after the events took place, by which time his memory was evidently not very good.

1612. Nix, John W.

A tale of two schools and Springtown, Parker county. Being a brief history of the Eearly [*sic*] days in Parker county, with emphasis on the Springtown community, together with a "Tale of Two Schools" and brief biographical sketches of pioneer settlers and their families, by John W. Nix. Ft. Worth, Texas, Thomason & Morrow, printers, 1945. Cloth. Very scarce.

> 5 p.l., 11–347, i–v p. plates, ports. 23.5 cm.
> Index: i–v at end.

Contains some information on the Allen Hill family and their lynching for alleged lawlessness and for conducting a way station for the horse thieves of the region.

1613. Nogales, General Rafael de

Memoirs of a soldier of fortune, [by] General Rafael de Nogales. New York, Harrison Smith, inc., 1932. Cloth. Scarce.

xvi p., 1 l., 380 p. 22.2 cm.
Half title; device; untrimmed.

Has much on lawlessness in many sections of the West.

1614. Nolan, Frederick W.

The life & death of John Henry Tunstall. The letters, diaries & adventures of an itinerant Englishman supplemented with other documents & annotations, compiled and edited by Frederick W. Nolan. [Albuquerque, N.M.], University of New Mexico press [1965]. Cloth.

xvi p., 1 l., 3–480 p. front. (port.), illus., plates, ports., facsms., maps. 24.2 cm.
Appendix: p. 441–446; chronology: p. 447–464; bibliography: p. 465–468; index: p. 469–480.
Half title; notes after each chapter; "First edition" on copyright p.

An excellent book, long overdue. Through diaries, letters, and his own comments we learn of Tunstall's early travels; his experiences as a merchant, his ambition to become a sheep raiser, his attempt at cattle ranching, and his cold-blooded murder, which caused the Lincoln County War to blaze into a shooting war. There is much new material on these troubles, as well as information about Jesse Evans, Billy the Kid, the Coes, and the rest of the Kid's gang. Near the end of the book is much correspondence between John Tunstall's father and the various authorities both in England and in America on the father's long and fruitless attempt to recover the money and property his son had lost through his murder. The book is well done and should assume an important place in the history of Lincoln County, New Mexico. The only fact I question is the author's statement that the Kid was one of the first to escape from the burning McSween home. Most other accounts have him the last to escape.

1615. Nolen, Oren Warder

Galloping down the Texas trail, by Oren Warder Nolen. Anecdotes and sketches of the Texas cowboys, rangers, sheriffs, wild cattle, wild horses and gun and game. Written by a native Texan from the experiences of fifty years in the lone star state. [Odem, Texas, privately printed, 1947.] Cloth. Scarce.

3 p.l., 7–181 p. 23.3 cm.

A little-known book containing some stories of Texas bad men. The author tells one incident about Billy the Kid I have not seen elsewhere.

1616. Nombela, Julio

La fiebre de riquezas; siete años en California. Descubrimiento del oro y exploración de sus inmensos e interesantes relaciones filones. Historia dramática en vista de datos auténticos e interesantes relaciones de los más célebras viajeros, por Julio Nombela, Tomo I. Madrid, Administración, Calle de San Bernardo, Núm. 11, 1871. Wrappers. Pub. in two volumes. Rare.

Vol. I, 547 p. front., plates. 20 cm.
Vol. II, 580 p. plates. 20 cm.
The title page of Volume II is exactly like that of Volume I except for: "Tomo II, Administración, Calle de Serrano, Núm. 14, Barrio de Salamanca, Madrid, 1872."

This book first appeared in Madrid, Spain, as a serial in 1871–72. The author writes of early California in a narrative style, but most of his book consists of flights of fancy. In the second part of the first volume he weaves Murieta into the story and deals with him at length, following the details of the *California Police Gazette* version of Murieta's life very closely—so closely, in fact, that certain parts are merely translations from the English text into Spanish (see Item 1575). He calls upon his imagination in relating Murieta's early life and ancestry.

1617. Nordyke, Lewis

John Wesley Hardin, Texas gunman, by Lewis Nordyke. New York, William Morrow & co., 1957. Boards. OP.

6 p.l., [3]–278 p. map. 21.6 cm.
Acknowledgments: p. [271]–272; index: p. [273]–278.
Half title.

Perhaps the most complete biography of this noted Texas outlaw to date.

1618. ———

The truth about Texas, [by] Lewis Nordyke. New York, Thomas Y. Crowell co. [1957]. Cloth. OP.

x p., 1 l., 276 p. 20.9 cm.
Index: p. 267–276.
Half title; map on end papers.

Tells about the killings of John Wesley Hardin and of John Selman.

1619. Norris, Gordon W.

Golden empire, by Gordon W. Norris. Boston, Bruce Humphries, inc., publishers [1949]. Cloth. OP.

7 p.l., 15–96 p. 21 cm.
Half title; pub. device.

Although this book is poetry, which has generally been avoided in this work, the prose introduction contains some material about Vásquez and Murieta, whom the author claims his father knew personally.

1620. North, Escott

The saga of the cowboy. All about the cattleman, and the part he played in the great drama of the west, by Escott North. . . . London, . . . Jarrolds, publishers, ltd. [1942]. Cloth. Scarce.

xii, 13–192 p. front. (port.), plates, ports., cattle brands. 21.8 cm.
Index: p. 189–192.
Half title.

Written by an Englishman who came to America and worked as a cowboy, this gives much material on western outlaws and the cattle wars. He evidently relies upon Frank Harris and Emerson Hough for his information on Wild Bill Hickok and therefore has many details wrong. His material on Billy the Kid is also inaccurate, and he repeats the fable about Wyatt Earp arresting Ben Thompson in Ellsworth, Kansas. All of his information on outlaws is filled with errors.

1621. [Northern Pacific Railway]

The great northwest. A guide-book and itinerary for the use of tourists and travelers over the lines of the Northern Pacific railroad, the Oregon railway and navigation company and the Oregon and California railroad. . . . With maps and many illustrations. St. Paul, Minn., Northern News co., 1888. Cloth. Rare.

5 p.l., 13–390 p. front., illus., plates. 17.5 cm.

Though the title page calls for maps, there are none listed in the table of illustrations and none in the book. The book has a chapter on the Montana vigilantes.

1622. [Northfield Bank Raid]

A story of the heroism of pioneer citizens of Northfield, Minnesota, who frustrated an attempt by the James-Younger gang to rob the First National Bank of Northfield on September 7, 1876. Northfield, Minn., published by the Northfield News, inc., 1933. Wrappers. Scarce.

2 p.l., 7–32 p. front. (port.), plates, ports., facsm. 20.3 cm.
Later reprinted many times.

1623. ———

The Northfield Bank raid, fiftieth anniversary finds interest undimmed in the oft-told tale of repulse of the James-Younger gang. Reprinted from the Northfield News of August 27, September 3, 10, and 17, 1926. . . . Wrappers.

4 p.l., [5]–22 p. front., plates, ports. 21 cm.
Double column.

Part of this pamphlet is taken from Huntington's *Robber and Hero* (Item 1087), and the latter part was written by old-timers and eyewitnesses to the robbery attempt.

1624. Norvell, Saunders

Forty years of hardware, by Saunders Norvell. Illustrations by Serena Summerfield. . . . New York, published by Hardware Age . . . [1924]. Cloth. Scarce.

2 p.l., 443 p. illus., ports. 19 cm.

The author, who was a traveling salesman for a hardware firm in St. Louis for many years, spins some interesting yarns about his many experiences. In a chapter on Colorado he tells about his acquaintance with Soapy Smith.

1625. Noyes, Alva Josiah

In the land of the Chinook; or, the story of Blaine county, by A. J. Noyes (Ajax). Helena, Mont., State publishing co. [1917]. Cloth. Scarce.

4 p.l., [7]–152 p. plates, ports., facsms. 24 cm.
Index: p. 148–152.
Device.

Contains some material on Kid Curry and his killing of Pike Landusky. The first page, marked "index," is really the table of contents, the true index appearing on the following pages.

1626. ———

The story of Ajax; life in the Big Hole basin, by Alva J. Noyes. Helena, Mont., State publishing co., 1914. Cloth. Scarce.

4 p.l., 158 p. front., plates, ports. 24 cm.
Index: p. [153]–158.
Errata: fourth preliminary leaf.

Said to be the first autobiography published in Montana. It contains some outlaw material.

1627. Nunis, Doyce B., Jr. (ed.)

The golden frontier. The recollections of Herman Francis Reinhart, 1851–1869. Edited by Doyce B. Nunis, Jr. Foreword by Nora B. Cunningham. Austin, University of Texas press [1962]. Cloth.

xxii p., 3 l., 353 p. front. (port.), plates, maps (3 double p.) 23.7 cm.
Appendix: p. [308]–310; bibliography: p. [311]–317; index: p. [319]–353.
Half title; pub. device.

In a chapter entitled "Badmen, Gunmen and Vigilantes" the author tells about Henry Plummer and his gang of road agents.

1628. Nunnelley, Lela S.

Boothill grave yard. A descriptive list of more than 250 graves in Boothill, [by] Lela S. Nunnelley. [Tombstone, Ariz., press of the Tombstone Epitaph], 1952. Pamphlet. Pict. wrappers. (Cover title.)

1 p.l., [12] p. (no pagination). 21.2 x 9.6 cm.

Gives the names on the headpieces and markers on the graves in Boothill, row by row. Many names of gunmen and outlaws are included, among them Billy Clanton, Tom and Frank McLaury, Charley Storm, Dan Dowd, Red Sample, Tex Howard, Bill Delaney, and John Heath.

1629. Nye, Nelson C.

Pistols for hire. A tale of the Lincoln county war and the west's most desperate outlaw William (Billy the Kid) Bonney, by Nelson C. Nye. New York, the Macmillan co., 1941. Cloth. OP.

6 p.l., 196 [1] p. 21 cm.
Half title.

The author admits that this book is fiction but claims that he endeavored to "reveal [the characters] as history actually has portrayed them." He tells his story through a character named Flick Farsom, supposedly a participant in the Lincoln County War. He sticks to well-known facts fairly well, yet he does repeat some erroneous details, such as having Billy the Kid killing Brady from behind an adobe wall and also killing Jimmy Carlisle. His character Farsom takes sides with the Murphy faction, and he makes McSween a crook and a thief and Chisum a cow thief.

O

1630. O'Brien, Robert

California called them. A saga of golden days and roaring camps, by Robert O'Brien. Illustrated by Antonio Sotomayor. New York, London, Toronto, McGraw-Hill book co., inc. [1951]. Cloth. OP.

xv p., 1 l., 3–251 p. illus. 23.5 cm.
Index: p. 245–251.
Half title; map on end papers; headpieces; tailpieces; vignette.

Tells some new stories about Murieta and gives some material on other gold-rush bad men.

1631. O'Byrne, John

"Pike's Peak or bust," and historical sketches of the wild west. By John O'Byrne. Colorado Springs, Colo. . . ., 1922. Cloth. Scarce.

2 p.l., [5]–141 p. front. (port.), plates. 19.6 cm.

A second edition was printed in 1923 with 194 pages and more illustrations.

Another book with false information about Billy the Kid. The author tells about a time he visited Rincon and looked for the jail in which the Kid had been incarcerated but could not find it. No wonder; he was in the wrong town. Like many old-timers, he had heard some tale about the Kid being jailed in Lincoln and years later got it confused with Rincon, probably because of the similarity of the names. Much of the latter part of his book is made up of excerpts from other books.

1632. O'Connor, Richard

Bat Masterson, [by] Richard O'Connor. Garden City, N.Y., Doubleday & co., inc., 1957. Cloth.

7 p.l., 15–263 p. 21.7 cm.

Acknowledgments and bibliography: p. 260–263.

Half title.

One of the most glaring mistakes the author makes occurs on page 46, where he says that "Cynthia Parker had been the wife of a Texas judge. One day they were out riding in a buggy when a band of Comanches swooped down, killed Judge Parker, and carried off his wife." Cynthia Ann Parker was nine years old in 1836, when she was captured by the Indians. The errors in facts and dates are enumerated in my *Burs Under the Saddle* (Item 7).

1633. ———

High jinks on the Klondike, by Richard O'Connor. Indianapolis, New York, the Bobbs-Merrill co., inc., publishers [1954]. Cloth. OP.

4 p.l., 11–284 p. 22.2 cm.

Bibliography: p. 275–277; index: p. 281–284.

Half title; illus. map on end papers; vignette; untrimmed; "First edition" on copyright p.

Has a long chapter on Soapy Smith. There is also some information on Wyatt Earp and the killing of Bob Ford. The author spells Ed O. Kelly's name as Ed O'Kelly.

1634. ———

Pat Garrett. A biography of the famous marshal and the killer of Billy the Kid, [by] Richard O'Connor. Garden City, N.Y., Doubleday & co., inc., 1960. Cloth.

3 p.l., 7–286 p. 21.5 cm.
Bibliography: p. 283–286.
Half title; "First edition" on copyright p.

The author makes his first mistake in his title. Garrett was the sheriff of Lincoln County, not a marshal—and there is a difference. There are many other mistakes, enumerated in my *Burs Under the Saddle* (Item 7).

1635. ———

Wild Bill Hickok, [by] Richard O'Connor. Garden City, N. Y., Doubleday & co., inc., 1959. Pict. cloth.

8 p.l., 17–282 p. 21.6 cm.
Bibliography: p. 279–282.
Half title; "First edition" on copyright p.

Though the author debunks some of the legends about Wild Bill and Calamity Jane, he makes many mistakes, too numerous to enumerate all of them here.

1636. O'Dell, Scott

Country of the sun. Southern California, an informal history and guide, by Scott O'Dell. New York, Thomas Y. Crowell co. [1957]. Cloth. OP.

viii p., 1 l., 310 p. 21 cm.
Glossary: p. 297–298; pronunciation guide: p. 299–300; index: p. 301–310.

Contains some material on Juan Flores and Joaquín Murieta.

1637. Oden, Bill

Early days on the Texas–New Mexico plains, by Bill Oden. Edited by J. Evetts Haley. Canyon, Texas, Palo Duro press, 1965. Pict. cloth.

xi, 69 p. front. (port.), illus., plates (3 double p.) 24 cm.
Half title; illus. map on end papers.
Colophon: "750 copies of this book have been printed at El Paso, Texas."

Reminiscences of an old-time cowboy containing some material on Clay Allison.

1638. Odens, Peter

Outlaws, heroes and jokers of the old southwest, [by Peter Odens, Yuma, Ariz., published by Southwest printers, 1964.] Stiff pict. wrappers.

2 p.l., [72] p. (no pagination). plates, ports. 22.8 cm.

Short tales about various regions of the West, some including outlaws.

1639. O'Flaherty, Daniel

General Jo Shelby, undefeated rebel, by Daniel O'Flaherty. Chapel Hill, University of North Carolina press [1954]. Cloth.

xiv p., 1 l., 437 p. front. (port.), map. 23.5 cm.
Notes: p. 403–422; index: p. 423–437.
Half title.

Has a long chapter on the trial of Frank James.

1640. [O'Hanlon, Rev. John]

Life and scenery in Missouri. Reminiscences of a missionary priest. Dublin, James Duffy & co., ltd., 1890. Cloth. Rare.

xii p., 292 [4] p. 15.3 cm.

Has several pages about the early Mississippi River pirates.

1641. [Oklahoma]

Kay county, Oklahoma. Ponca City, Okla., published by Kay County Gas co. [1919]. Cloth. Scarce.

3 p.l., 7–75 [1] p. illus., plates (9 fold., 8 double p.), ports. (1 double p.), maps (2 double p.), graphs (1 double p.). 22.2 cm.
Copyright notice verso flyleaf.

Contains material on the Daltons, Henry Starr, and Ben Cravens.

1642. ———

Oklahoma, past and present. Brief sketches of men and events in Oklahoma history—from Coronado to the present. Oklahoma City, Frontier publishing co. [n.d., ca. 1907]. Stiff wrappers. Scarce.

4–86 p. front. (port.), illus., plates, ports., map. 24.2 cm.

Has some information about Bill Tilghman, Heck Thomas, Cherokee Bill, and Al Jennings. The author repeats the old legend about Belle Starr refusing to identify Jim Reed as her husband so that his murderer would not get the reward.

1643. ———

Oklahoma, the beautiful land, by the '89ers. Oklahoma City, Okla., published by the Times-Journal publishing co. [1943]. Pict. cloth. Scarce.

3 p.l., 351 p. plates, map. 23.5 cm.

Contains some information on the Daltons, Bill Doolin, Bitter Creek Newcomb, Heck Thomas, Al Jennings, and others.

1644. ———

The saga of no man's land, as seen in 1888 and 1889. Early historical facts of Beaver City, Oklahoma, Cimarron territory, the Oklahoma panhandle. [Beaver, Okla., the Herald-Democrat, n.d.] Stiff wrappers. Scarce.

1 p.l., 5–36 p. front. 19.4 cm.

Has a section on the killing of Billy Olive.

1645. [Oklahoma Authors' Club]

The romance of Oklahoma. Oklahoma Authors' club, [by various members]. Oklahoma City, 1920. Pict. cloth. Scarce.

3 p.l., 86 p. plates, ports. 23 cm.

In Chapter V, "The Triumph of the Law," by Mrs. Zoe Tilghman, there is material on some of the Oklahoma outlaws.

1646. Older, Mrs. Fremont

Love stories of old California, with a foreword by Gertrude Atherton. Illustrated. New York, Coward-McCann, inc. [1940]. Cloth. Scarce.

xvi p., 1 l., 3–306 p. front., plates, ports. 22 cm.
Half title; at head of title: "Mrs. Fremont Older."

Among other love stories, the author tells about Murieta's loves and the illicit loves of Vásquez. In the Murieta chapter she out-Ridges Ridge, using his version of Murieta's life but making it much more romantic.

1647. [Old Settlers]

The old settlers' history of Bate county, Missouri, from its first settlement to the first day of January, 1900. Amsterdam, Mo., published by Tathwell & Maxey [1907]. Cloth. Scarce.

6 p.l., 14–212 p. front. (port.), illus., plates, fold. map. 22.8 cm.

Has some information about the Youngers.

1648. Olson, Edmund T.

Utah, a romance in pioneer years, with historical accounts of turbulent scenes incident to the adjustments of social and political differences between the Latter Day Saints and the government of the United States . . ., by Edmund T. Olson. . . . Profusely illustrated with rare, antique and modern pictures. Salt Lake City, Utah, published by the author, 1931. Dec. cloth. Scarce.

xix [1] p., 345 [1] p. front., illus., plates (4 col. incl. front.), ports., map, facsm. 23.2 cm.
Half title.

Tells about the Hole-in-the-Wall gang, Ben Tasker's gang, stage holdups, the Mountain Meadow Massacre, and John Lee.

1649. Olsson, Jan Olof

Welcome to Tombstone, by Jan Olof Olsson. Translated from the Swedish by Maurice Michael. London, Elek Books [1956]. Cloth. Scarce.

4 p.l., 7–164 p. plates. 22.2 cm.
Half title.

Gives a picture of modern-day Tombstone and tells something about the Earps, Doc Holliday, and the Clantons.

1650. O'Neal, James Bradas

They die but once, the story of a Tejano, by James B. O'Neal. New York, Knight publications, inc., 1935. Cloth. Scarce.

viii p., 2 l., 228 p. 23.5 cm.
Half title.

The subject of this biography, Jeff Ake, upholds the legend that Bill Longley was never hanged. He also says that he was asked by Ben Thompson to go to the Harris Theatre some time after he (Thompson) had killed Jack Harris. When Ake refused to go with him, Thompson went up the street and met King Fisher. Fisher at first also refused to go but finally went, more or less on a dare. History tells us that Fisher and Thompson were in Austin together and later went to San Antonio to visit the theater. And, of course, they were killed there. Ake makes another exaggerated statement when he says that the James and Younger boys must have killed at least fifteen Pinkerton men.

Like many other old-timers, he claims he knew personally nearly all the bad men, such as John Wesley Hardin, Jesse James, Cole Younger, Bill Doolin, and Sam Bass. He says the law got after Bill Doolin and that he went to New Mexico and was killed there (!) and that Bass came to Denison, Texas, and went to work for the sheriff. He means Denton, of course. That is an example of how many old-timers confused place names. There are also many mistakes in the sections about Billy the Kid, Pat Garrett, and others.

1651. [Oregon]

Reminiscences of Oregon pioneers, compiled by the Pioneer Ladies club, Pendleton, Oregon. Pendleton, Oreg., East Oregonian publishing co., 1937. Pict. cloth. OP.

4 p.l., 257 [1] p. 23.2 cm.
Vignette.

Has some material on cattle thieves.

1652. O'Reilly, Harrington

Fifty years on the trail. A true story of western life, by Harrington O'Reilly, with over one hundred illustrations by Paul Frenzeny. London, Chatto & Windus, Piccadilly, 1889. Pict. cloth. Scarce.

xvi, 381 p. front., illus. 19.9 cm.

Device; 32 numbered p. adv. at end.

Reprinted in 1890 and again in 1891 with same imprint and collation; an American edition was made from the same sheets of the London edition in New York in 1889. Also there was a French translation published in Paris the same year with 348 pages. Republished in 1963 by the University of Oklahoma press as one of the Western Frontier Library series, with an introduction by John E. Worchester.

The subject of this book, John Y. Nelson, who says he took part in the hanging of Fly-Specked Billy, tells about Doc Middleton's start in outlawry. There is also some information about Joseph Slade, whom he calls Dan. He names Jules Reni as Jules Berg. Julesburg was the town named after Reni. He is inclined to exaggerate his statements as claiming that forty or fifty men were killed at the battle on Beecher's Island. Only six were killed and eighteen wounded. Nelson had a reputation for "stretching the blanket," and this book, with its errors and exaggerations, bears out that report. He claims that General McKenzie sent for him when he needed advice, and though he lived among the Indians, he apparently did not know a Sioux from a Cheyenne.

1653. Orman, Richard A. van

A room for the night. Hotels of the old west, by Richard A. van Orman. Bloomington and London, Indiana University press [1966]. Cloth.

xiii p., 1 l., 3–162 p. illus., plates. 21.5 cm.

Notes: p. 141–155; index: p. 156–162.

Half title.

Has some mention of Wyatt Earp, Doc Holliday, Wild Bill Hickok, Billy and Ben Thompson, and the Benders.

1654. Orr, Thomas (ed.)

Life of the notorious desperado Cullen Baker, from his childhood to his death, with a full account of all the murders he committed. Thos. Orr, ed. Little Rock, Ark., Price and Barton, printers, 1870. Wrappers. Exceedingly rare.

49 p. 17 cm.

The editor of this little book was a rival of Cullen Baker in a love affair and finally killed the outlaw. His account is therefore rather biased.

1655. Orr, Thomas, Jr.

Life history of Thomas Orr, Jr. Pioneer stories of California and Utah, [by Thomas Orr, jr., Placerville, Calif.], 1930. Stiff wrappers. (Cover title.) Scarce.

5 p.l., 51 [1] p. front. (port.), plates, ports., facsms. 24 cm.

Contains some information on the death of Henry Canfield, an early California outlaw.

1656. Orton, A. R. (pub.)

"The Derienni"; or, land pirates of the Isthmus. Being a true and graphic history of robberies, assassinations, and other horrid deeds perpetrated by those cold-blooded miscreants, who have infested for years the great highways to California, the El Dorado of the Pacific. . . . Five of whom were shot at Panama by the committee of public safety, July 27th, 1852. Together with the lives of three of the principal desperadoes as narrated by themselves. . . . New Orleans, Charleston, Baltimore, and Philadelphia, published by A. R. Orton, 1853. Pict. wrappers. Exceedingly rare.

2 p.l., [17]–44 p. front., plates. 22 cm.

A lurid tale about a gang of cutthroats who operated in Panama, preying upon the California gold seekers who returned to the States by that route.

1657. Osborn, Campbell

Let freedom ring, [by Campbell Osborn]. Tokyo, [Japan], the Inter-Nation co. [1954]. Cloth. OP.

ii p., 2 l., 211 p. map. 17.5 cm.
Half title.

Has a chapter on such Oklahoma outlaws as Bill Doolin, the Daltons, Henry Starr, Al Jennings, Bitter Creek Newcomb, Tulsa Jack, and Dynamite Dick, as well as the marshals. It tells about the fight at Ingalls and the killing of Charlie Bryant and Ed Short. The most surprising thing about this item is that such a book would be published in Japan, especially in English.

1658. Osgood, Ernest Staple

The day of the cattleman, by Ernest Staple Osgood. Minneapolis, University of Minnesota press, 1929. Scarce.

x p., 2 l., 283 p. front., plates, maps (part double p.), facsms., diagrs. 24.6 cm.
Bibliography: p. 259–268; index: p. 269–283.
Half title; illus. end papers; vignette; untrimmed.
Thesis (Ph.D.), University of Wisconsin, 1927. (Without thesis note.)
Reprinted in 1954 and again in 1956, this time in a paper-backed edition, by University of Chicago press.

Contains a tabloid account of the Johnson County War.

1659. Otero, Miguel Antonio

My life on the frontier, by Miguel Antonio Otero. In two volumes.

Vol. I, My life on the frontier, 1864–1882. Incidents and characters of the period when Kansas, Colorado and New Mexico were passing through the last of their wild and romantic years, by Miguel Antonio Otero, former governor of New Mexico. Illustrated by Will Shuster. New York, the Press of the Pioneers, inc., 1935. Cloth. OP.

5 p.l., 293 p. illus., plates. 23.5 cm.

Index: p. 289–293 (triple column).

Half title.

Limited, signed, and numbered edition. In the trade edition the illustrations are omitted.

Vol. II, My life on the frontier, 1882–1897. Death knell of a territory and the birth of a state . . ., by Miguel Antonio Otero, former governor of New Mexico. Albuquerque, N.M., University of New Mexico press, 1939. Cloth. OP.

xi p., 1 l., 306 p. illus. 23.5 cm.

Index: p. 301–306 (triple column).

Half title.

A de luxe edition limited to 400 copies. The trade edition omits the illustrations.

In Volume I the author tells the story of Wild Bill Hickok's murder, repeats many of the legends about Clay Allison, and tells about the attempt of the mob at Las Vegas to take Dave Rudabaugh away from Pat Garrett. He also tells about Jesse James's visit to Las Vegas and his murder by Bob Ford.

In Volume II the author tells about the lynching of Joel Fowler and has a long chapter on Vicente Silva and his gang.

1660. ———

My nine years as governor of the territory of New Mexico, 1897–1906, by Miguel Antonio Otero. Foreword by Marion Dargon, editor. Albuquerque, N.M., University of New Mexico press, 1940. Cloth. OP.

viii p., 1 l., 404 p. front. (port.), ports. 23.6 cm.

Appendix: p. 343–394; index: p. 397–404.

Half title; device.

Colophon: "Four hundred de luxe copies printed of which this is No. ——."

Also published in a trade edition, from which the illustrations are omitted.

In a chapter entitled "The Folsom Train Robberies," the author devotes some space to Black Jack Ketchum and his gang, a few members of which were from Butch Cassidy's Wild Bunch. He also has some information on the Lee-Garrett feud.

1661. ———

The real Billy the Kid; with new light on the Lincoln county war, by

Miguel Antonio Otero. . . . Illustrated from photographs. New York, Rufus Rockwell Wilson, inc., 1936. Cloth. Scarce.

xvii p., 1 l., 200 p. front., illus., plates, ports. 23.4 cm.

Index: p. 197–200.

Half title.

Although this is a relatively recent book, it has become quite difficult to find. The author, like so many other New Mexicans, is very much in sympathy with Billy the Kid. He considers Pat Garrett a cold-blooded killer and cites many opinions to prove that he was a cattle thief and a coward who shot without giving his victim a chance. Although he is critical of Garrett's book, he repeats most of the legends in it created by Ash Upson and makes quite a few mistakes himself.

1662. Outerbridge, Henry

Captain Jack. His story as told to Henry Outerbridge. The life-story to date of a born swashbuckler, two-gun fighter, and world-roving maker of history, including confidential information on the recent disturbances in Mexico, Nicaragua, China and other places where Uncle Sam has irons in the fire. New York and London, the Century co. [1928]. Cloth. Scarce.

xi p., 1 l., 3–377 p. 19.2 cm.

Half title; pub. device.

1663. Ovitt, Mabel

Golden treasure, by Mabel Ovitt. Dillon, Mont., 1952. Pict. cloth. OP.

8 p.l., [17]–252 p. front. (port.), plates, ports., facsms. 23.5 cm.

Appendix: p. [237]–252.

Half title; plan on end papers.

Colophon: "The first printing of Golden Treasure is limited to 1000 copies of which this is No. ——."

A privately printed and well-written book giving much new material on the vigilantes and road agents of Montana.

1664. Owens, Meroe J.

A brief history of Sherman county, Nebraska, by Meroe J. Owens. [Norfolk], printed by the Norfolk News, 1952. Pict. wrappers. Scarce.

5 p.l., 258 p. maps. 22.8 cm.

Has material about the Olives and their murder of Luther Mitchell and Ami Ketchum.

P

1665. Pace, Dick

Golden gulch. The story of Montana's fabulous Alder gulch, by Dick Pace, with sketches by Sindy Cosens. Being a true, quite partial and somewhat humorous history of Alder gulch, Montana, the state's richest placer mining district and the cradle of Montana history. . . . [Butte, 1962.] Stiff pict. wrappers.

vi, 106 p. illus., plates, ports., facsms. 21.3 cm.
Notes and sources: p. 102–103.
Plates on recto and verso of both wrappers.

Has chapters on road agents, including Henry Plummer, Buck Stinson, Haze Lyons, Cy Skinner, Boone Helm, Jack Gallaher, Clubfoot George Lane, and Red Yeager. There is also a chapter with material on Joseph Slade and a mention of Calamity Jane.

1666. Paddock, Capt. B. B. (ed.)

History of Texas. Fort Worth and the Texas northwest edition. Edited by Capt. B. B. Paddock. Chicago, and New York, the Lewis publishing co., 1922. Cloth. Scarce. Pub. in 4 volumes.

Vol. I, xxxv [1]. 439 p. front. (port.), plates, ports. 27.5 cm.
Vol. II, 441–886 p. front., plates. 27.5 cm.
Vol. III, 3–364 p. front. (port.), ports. 27.5 cm.
Vol. IV, 365–752 p. front. (port.), ports. 27.5 cm.

Volume II contains information about Luke Short, Jim Courtright, and Ben Thompson.

1667. Paden, Irene D., and Margaret E. Schlichtmann

The big oak flat road. An account of freighting from Stockton to Yosemite valley, [by] Irene D. Paden and Margaret E. Schlichtmann. San Francisco, Calif., MCMLV. Pict. cloth. OP.

vi, 356 p. front., plates, maps (2 fold.). 24.3 cm.
Notes: p. 301–314; appendix: p. 315–323; bibliography: p. 325–343; index: p. 345–356.
Vignette; untrimmed.
Printed in an edition of 1,000 copies.

Contains material about both Black Bart and Joaquín Murieta.

1668. Page, Henry Markham

Pasadena; its early years, by Henry Markham Page. Los Angeles, privately printed by Lorrin L. Morrison, printing and publishing, 1964. Cloth. Also pub. in stiff wrappers.

xvii p., 2 l., 226 p. front. (ports.), plates, ports., maps (1 double p.). 25.3 cm.
Appendices: p. 217–219; bibliography: p. 221; index: p. 223–226.
Half title; table of contents 1st leaf and recto of back cover.

Contains some slight information on Vásquez, the California outlaw.

1669. Paine, Albert Bigelow

Captain Bill McDonald, Texas ranger. A story of frontier reform, by Albert Bigelow Paine . . ., with introductory letter by Theodore Roosevelt. . . . Special subscription edition. New York, made by J. J. Little & Ives co., 1909. Cloth. OP.

7 p.l., [13]–448 p. front. (port. with tissue), 7 plates (4 col.), facsm. 21.8 cm.
Appendix: p. [399]–448.

A biography of one of the better-known Texas Rangers, this volume deals with many Texas and Oklahoma outlaws. Published by subscription, it was issued in three different bindings simultaneously, each to fit the subscriber's pocketbook. The most expensive was bound in full morocco, the next in red cloth with a portrait of McDonald pasted on, and the third and cheapest, the one most commonly seen, in blue cloth.

1670. Paine, Bayard H.

Pioneers, Indians and buffaloes, by Bayard H. Paine. With foreword by Addison E. Sheldon. Curtis, Nebr., the Curtis Enterprise, 1935. Cloth. OP.

4 p.l., 9–192 p. front. (port.), illus., plates, ports. 21.5 cm.
Index: p. 185–192.

Contains some material on the Olives and their burning of Luther Mitchell and Ami Ketchum.

1671. Paine, Lauran

Texas Ben Thompson, by Lauran Paine. Los Angeles, Westernlore press, 1966. Cloth.

9 p.l., [11]–215 p. front. (port.). 21 cm.
Index: p. [213]–215.
Half title.

I think the author is wrong when he says that "many a drover bought cattle for a dollar a head in Texas and later at the rails' end up in Kansas, sold them for a hundred and fifty dollars a head. No cattle at that time were that high. In a footnote the author claims that after he left Abilene Wild Bill Hickok became embroiled in a fight with Tom Custer and was asked by the town marshal to resign. His affair with Custer happened before he went to Abilene. He is also mistaken in saying that after he accidentally shot Sheriff Whitney Bill Thompson made the statement that he would have shot him "if it had been Jesus Christ." I am glad to say, however, that he does not have Ben Thompson being arrested by Wyatt Earp, as Stuart Lake claims.

1672. ———

Tom Horn: man of the west, [by] Lauran Paine. London, John Long [1962]. Cloth.

4 p.l., 9–190 p. front. (port.). 20.3 cm.
Half title; vignette.
Republished in America in 1963 by Barre publishing co., Barre, Mass.

Though of interest, this book is filled with errors. The author has Sam Bass in Leadville, Colorado. Bass was never in that town, or even in Colorado. He misspells Bat Masterson's middle name as Barkley instead of Barclay. The reason he gives for the outbreak of the Lincoln County War is incorrect, as is his information about the hanging of Cattle Kate and Jim Averill. He says that John Clay was present at the lynching. It is well known who those present were. There are many other errors.

1673. Palmer, Edwin O.

History of Hollywood, by Edwin O. Palmer. Narrative. Volume I, Hollywood, Calif., Arthur H. Cawston, publisher, 1937. Leather. Pub. in two volumes.

Vol. I, 3 p.l., 9–191 p. front., plates, ports., maps. 27.7 cm.
Index: p. 271–292.
Vol. II, biographical.

Has several pages devoted to Tiburcio Vásquez. Volume I was later published as a separate publication.

1674. Pannell, Walter

Civil war on the range, by Walter Pannell. Los Angeles, Calif., published by Welcome News [1943]. Pict. wrappers. Scarce.

(Cover title: "Civil war on the range. An historic account of the battle for the prairies, the Lincoln county war and subsequent events.")

2 p.l., 5–48 p. 15 cm.
[Published with "The empire of the big bend," p. 37–45.]
3 p. adv. at end.

This little pamphlet is filled with errors, so many in fact, that it would take several pages to list them. The author says that Billy the Kid was strictly a hired gunman, "doing murder for wages," and that those wages were paid by John Chisum. His account of the Kid's murder is incorrect. He says that the Kid was in a room next to Maxwell's preparing to go to bed when he decided that he was hungry and went to Maxwell's room to get the key to the smokehouse. He states the Kid pulled the trigger of his gun after Garrett shot him. When he was killed, the Kid carried no gun. On page 26, line 20 is repeated.

1675. Paredes, America

"With a pistol in his hand." A border ballad and its hero, by America Paredes. Austin, University of Texas press [1958]. Pict. cloth.

9 p.l., 7–262 [1] p. front., illus. 23.5 cm.
Bibliography: p. 251–258; index: p. 259–262.
Half title; head and tailpieces; vignette.

The story of Gregorio Cortez, a border bandit.

1676. Park, Robert

History of Oklahoma state penitentiary at McAlester, Okla., by Robert Park. McAlester, Okla., McAlester printing & binding co., publishers, 1914. Pict. wrappers. Scarce.

3 p.l., 144 [4] p. front. (port.), plates, ports. 18.5 cm.

Tells about some of the lesser-known outlaws of Oklahoma.

1677. Parke, Adelia

Memoirs of an old timer, by Adelia Parke. Weiser, Idaho, Signal-American printers [1955]. Stiff pict. wrappers. Scarce.

5 p.l., [3]–65 p. plates. 22.9 cm.
Double column.

Has much on badmen and lawlessness, including John D. Lee, the Mormon fiend.

1678. Parker, B. G.

Recollections of the Mountain Meadow massacre. Being an account of that awful atrocity and revealing some facts never before made public. By B. G. Parker. . . . Plano, Calif., Fred W. Reed, American printer, 1901. Wrappers. Rare.

2 p.l., [4]–31 p. front. (port.). 13.8 cm.

1679. Parker, J. M.

An aged wanderer. A life sketch of J. M. Parker, a cowboy on the western plains in the early days. San Angelo, Texas, headquarters, Elkhorn wagon yard [n.d.]. Pict. wrappers. (Cover title.) Rare.

32 p. front. (port. on verso of cover). 21.3 cm.

Also published under the title "The poor orphan boy, a life sketch of a western cowboy." [N.p., n.d.] Wrappers. (Cover title.) Rare.

2 p.l., [5]–39 [1] p. front. (port.). 16.6 cm.

Both little items are exceedingly rare. The author was an old Texas cowboy who became crippled with paralysis and sold these little books for a livelihood as he wandered over the country. He is another old-timer who claims to have been a close friend of Billy the Kid; yet he is certainly confused in his facts. He says that the first man the Kid killed was his own stepfather, whom he killed for abusing his mother, and that the next man the Kid killed was a blacksmith who hit his horse with a hammer while shoeing him.

He further claims that he was with the Kid when he escaped after the latter killing. Later, he says, he and the Kid were joined by five friends and the officers went after them. The officers set fire to the house, and while it burned, the Kid played the piano (the author adds that he danced to the music). He also claims that he was with the Kid when things got so hot for him "we had to scamper away for the far West and remain in the Rocky Mountains until the spring of 1872." According to his date, this incident would have occurred when the Kid was thirteen years old. He further states that the father of the Kid's sweetheart arranged for Pat Garrett (whom the author calls the "drunken sheriff") to kill the Kid and that Garrett watched his chance and killed the young outlaw while he slept.

1680. Parker, James

The old army memories, 1872–1918, by James Parker . . ., with an introduction by Major General Robert Lee Bullard. Illustrated. Philadelphia, Dorrance & co. [1929]. Cloth. OP.

6 p.l., 13–454 p. front. (port.), plates, ports. 21 cm.

Half title; pub. device.

In Chapter III, entitled "Horsethieves and Outlaws," the author deals with the outlaws Babe Mahardy and Jim and John Anderson.

1681. Parker, Lew

Odd people I have met . . ., [by] Lew Parker. [N.p., n.d.] Wrappers. (Cover title.) Scarce.

3–120 [1] p. front. (port. with tissue), port. 20.8 cm.

Contains some new stories about Wild Bill Hickok and Calamity Jane.

1682. Parker, Watson

Gold in the Black Hills, by Watson Parker. Norman, University of Oklahoma press [1966]. Cloth.

xi p., 1 l., 3–259 p. front., plates, maps. 23.5 cm.
Appendices: p. 204–208; glossary: p. 209–211; bibliography: p. 212–241; index: p. 243–259.
Half title; "First edition" on copyright p.

In a chapter entitled "Badmen of the Hills" the author has material on Sam Bass, Joel Collins, Jim Berry, and Reddie McKemie, as well as on the murder of Wild Bill Hickok by Jack McCall. Many of the lesser-known outlaws of the Black Hills are also mentioned.

1683. Parkhill, Forbes

The law goes west, [by] Forbes Parkhill. Denver, Sage books [1956]. Cloth.

5 p.l., 11–176 p. plates, ports. 22.2 cm.
Index: p. 165–176.
Half title; map on end papers.

Has material on the Espinosas, Joseph Slade, and the Reynolds brothers, Jim and John.

1684. ———

The wildest of the west, [by] Forbes Parkhill. New York, Henry Holt and co. [1951]. Cloth. OP.

x p., 1 l., 3–310 p. plates, ports. 21 cm.
Notes: p. 287; bibliography: p. 289–293; index: p. 295–310.
Half title; "First edition" on copyright p.

Enlarged and reprinted by Sage books, Denver, 1957.

xxxix p., 8 l., (plates and ports), 3–310 p. 21 cm.
Notes: p. 287; bibliography: p. 289–293; index: p. 295–310.
Half title.

Has much material about many of the outlaws of the West, as well as about some of the shady characters of Denver. I am surprised, however, that the author, as familiar as he should be with western history, gives Quantrill's name as Charles W. Quantrell and his alias as Charles Hart. Quantrill's given names were William Clarke. I am disappointed, too, that he has Phil Coe killed in the Bull's Head Saloon and says that Wild Bill Hickok departed from Abilene after the shooting. Coe was killed on the street, and Hickok did not leave Abilene until the following December. He has some of his other killings wrong also and repeats the old legend about Belle Starr holding up a gambling house in Dodge after Blue Duck had lost two thousand dollars he had borrowed from her.

1685. Parks, Charles Caldwell (Carl Gray, pseud.)

A plaything of the gods, by Carl Gray. Boston, Sherman, French & co., 1912. Pict. cloth. Scarce.

3 p.l., 260 p. 20.8 cm.
Device.

A badly done novel about Joaquín Murieta. Based upon the *Police Gazette* version of his life, it gives a new twist by having him drowned when his boat capsized.

1686. Parrish, Joe

Coffins, cactus and cowboys. The exciting story of El Paso, 1536 to present, by Joe Parrish. Book design and illustrations by Russell Parks. [El Paso, Texas, Superior publishing co., 1964.] Stiff wrappers.

4 p.l., 9–93 p. illus., plates, 2 maps (1 double p.), plan. 21.5 cm.
Bibliography: p. 88.

Tells the story of Dallas Stoudenmire and his short reign as marshal of El Paso, as well as other gunmen of that city. He includes John Wesley Hardin, John Selman, Bass Outlaw, George Scarborough, Jeff Milton, Wyatt Earp, and even Billy the Kid because, the author says, the Kid made one brief excursion into El Paso. In this account he follows that old disproved fable about the Kid rescuing his friend Segura. The author is also mistaken when he says that Hardin's first killing was of a Negro, "to avenge a fancied slight." The Negro jumped Hardin after they had had a wrestling match. He is also wrong about Hardin's killing by Selman. Selman did not use a rifle, nor did he shoot Hardin "again and again."

1687. Parrish, Randall

The great plains. The romance of western American exploration, warfare and settlement, 1527–1870, by Randall Parrish. . . . Chicago, A. C. McClurg & co., 1907. Pict. cloth. Scarce.

xiv p., 1 l., 17–399 p. front., plates. 21.5 cm.
Index: p. 385–399.
Half title; pub. device; untrimmed.

Contains a chapter on outlaws. Although the author has long been considered an able historian, he repeats the Nichols fable about the Hickok-McCanles "fight," stating that Wild Bill (whom he calls William Hickok) was attacked by ten men and that he received eleven buckshot and thirteen knife wounds "but had wiped out the M'Kandlas [*sic*] gang." His slight information on Billy the Kid is also wrong.

1688. Parson, Mabel

A courier of New Mexico, [by] Mabel Parson. [N.p., n.d.] Cloth.

3 p.l., [1] p., 2–88 p. 5 double p. maps (col.). 22 cm.
Bibliography: p. 83–88.

Contains some material on Billy the Kid. The author is mistaken in saying that the Kid was the "fighting foreman of a big ranch." She also continues the legend about his killing twenty-one men.

1689. Parsons, George Whitwell

The private journal of George Whitwell Parsons. Prepared by Arizona statewide archival and records project, division of professional and service projects, Works Projects Administration. Phoenix, Ariz., Arizona statewide archival and records project, November, 1939. Stiff wrappers. Photolithographed. Rare.

vi, 335 p. 27.7 cm.

Gives some interesting early history of Tombstone. The author, very partial to the Earps, tells about the killing of Morgan Earp and Frank Stillwell, as well as many of the other troubles the Earps had, including the O K Corral battle.

1690. Parsons, John E.

The peacemaker and its rivals. An account of the single action Colt, by John E. Parsons. New York, William Morrow and co., 1950. Cloth. OP.

viii p., 1 l., 3–184 p. front., illus., plates, facsms., tables. 24 cm.
Notes: p. 159–172; bibliography: p. 173–177; index: p. 178–184.
Half title; facsm. on end papers.

Has references to gunmen and their favorite weapon.

1691. Patch, Joseph Dorst

Reminiscences of Fort Huachuca, Arizona, by Joseph Dorst Patch, Major-General, United States Army, re'd. [N.p., n.d.] Pict. wrappers.

4 p.l., 21 p. [2 l.]. plates, 3 maps (1 double p.). 21.6 cm.

Contains some material on the Earps. The author is mistaken in saying that "Wyatt Earp was sheriff of Tombstone, and his brothers and Doc Holliday were his deputies." He has a poor opinion of Wyatt Earp, saying that both he and Doc Holliday "were professional gamblers and generally shot their victims when they didn't have a chance." He also says that when Earp left Tombstone "the town was more lawless than it was when he first arrived."

1692. Patterson, C. L.

Sensational Texas manhunt, by C. L. Patterson. [San Antonio, Texas, Sid Murray & son, printers, 1939.] Wrappers. Scarce.

2 p.l., 3–30 p. 19 cm.

A story of the tracking down and capture of the killer Gregorio Cortez.

1693. Paxton, W. M.

Annals of Platte county, Missouri, from its exploration down to June 1, 1897, with genealogies of its noted families and sketches of its pioneers and distinguished people. . . . By W. M. Paxton. Kansas City, Mo., Hudson-Kimberly publishing co., 1897. Cloth. Scarce.

1 p.l., 1182 p. front. (port. with tissue). 24.5 cm.
Index: p. 1103–1182.

Contains some material on the James boys and their activities.

1694. Payne, Doris Palmer

Captain Jack, Modoc renegade, by Doris Palmer Payne. Portland, Oreg., Binford & Mort, publishers . . . [1938]. Cloth. OP.

6 p.l., [3]–259 p. ports. 20.3 cm.
Bibliography: p. [257]–259.
Half title; map on end papers.

A history of a bad Modoc Indian who operated in Oregon and northern California.

1695. Payton, William

The last man over the trail, by Col. Wm. Payton. [N.p., 1939.] Stiff pict. wrappers. Scarce.

60 p. illus., plates, map (double p.). 22.8 cm.

Has some information about the Espinosas, the Colorado outlaws.

1696. Peak, Howard W.

A ranger of commerce; or, 52 years on the road, by Howard W. Peak. San Antonio, Naylor printing co. [1929]. Pict. cloth. Scarce.

5 p.l., 262 p. front. (port.). 22 cm.

Contains some material on Sam Bass. The author is mistaken about both dates and incidents.

1697. Pearson, Edmund

Murder at Smutty Nose, and other murders, by Edmund Pearson. London, William Heinemann, ltd., 1927. Cloth. Scarce.

x p., 1 l., 330 p. illus., plates, ports., facsms., map. 21.2 cm.
Appendix: p. 321–330.
Half title.

Chapter X, entitled "Hell Benders," is about the Benders of Kansas and is taken largely from James's *The Benders of Kansas*, Duke's *Celebrated Criminal Cases of America*, and Triplett's *History, Romance and Philosophy of Great American Crimes and Criminals.*

1698. Pearson, Jim Berry

The Maxwell land grant, by Jim Berry Pearson. Norman, University of Oklahoma press [1961]. Cloth.

xiv p., 1 l., 3–305 p. plates, ports., maps. 23.5 cm.
Bibliographical notes: p. 281–294; index: p. 295–305.
Half title; "First edition" on copyright p.

Has some information on Clay Allison, David Crockett, and other gunmen.

1699. Peattie, Roderick (ed.)

The Black Hills, edited by Roderick Peattie. The contributors: Leland O. Case, Badger Clark, Paul Friggens, R. V. Hunkins, Clarence S. Paine, Elmo Scott Watson. New York, the Vanguard press, inc. [1952]. Pict. cloth. OP.

9 p.l., 17–320 p. plates, ports., map. 24 cm.
Index: p. 311–320.
Half title; illus. double t.p.

Contains a long and fairly accurate chapter by Clarence Paine on Wild Bill Hickok and Calamity Jane. The author writes that Wild Bill was appointed marshal "in the rip-roarin' cow town of Abilene, Texas, in April, 1871." I feel certain that the author meant Abilene, Kansas.

1700. ———

The inverted mountain; canyons of the west, edited by Roderick Peattie. Contributors: Weldon F. Heald, Edwin D. McKee, Harold S. Colton. New York, the Vanguard press, inc. [1948]. Pict. cloth. OP.

x p., 1 l., 3–390 p. plates, maps. 24 cm.
Index: p. 379–390.
Half title; illus. double t.p.

Has a mention of Butch Cassidy.

1701. Peavey, John R.

From the thorny hills of Duval to the sleepy Rio Grande. Echoes from the

Rio Grande, by John R. Peavey, 1905 to N-O-W. . . . [Brownsville, Texas, Springman-King co., 1963.] Pict. cloth.

7 p.l., 320 p. illus., plates, map, facsm. 23.5 cm.

Deals with some of the latter-day lawlessness on the Texas-Mexico border.

1702. Peavy, Charles D.

Charles A. Siringo, a Texas picaro, by Charles D. Peavy. . . . Austin, Texas, Steck-Vaughn co. [1967]. Stiff wrappers. Southwest Writers series No. 3.

ii p., 1 l., 41 p. 20.4 cm.
Selected bibliography: p. 39–41.

This little book contains a great deal of material about the outlaws with whom Siringo was associated and about whom he wrote, such as Billy the Kid, the Coes, Tom O'Folliard, Henry Brown, John Middleton, and Charlie Bowdre; and such officers as Pat Garrett, John Poe, and Kip McKinney. The author is mistaken, however, in having the Coes brothers. They were cousins.

1703. Peck, Anne Merriman

Southwest roundup, by Anne Merriman Peck. Illustrated by the author. New York, Dodd, Mead & co., 1950. Cloth. OP.

4 p.l., 248 p. illus., map (double p.). 20.8 cm.
Half title; illus. chapter headings; vignette; untrimmed.
Republished in 1954.

A book, evidently written for young people, covering many aspects of the Southwest. The author touches upon the Lincoln County War and Billy the Kid, but spoils her story by saying that the Kid was "trailed to a friend's house in Fort Sumner where he was cornered by Pat Garrett and shot after a stiff fight."

1704. Peck, Joseph H.

What next, Doctor Peck? [by] Joseph H. Peck, M.D. Englewood Cliffs, N.J., Prentice-Hall, inc. [1959]. Boards and cloth. OP.

xi p., 1 l., 3–209 p. plates, ports. 21 cm.
Half title.

Has a chapter on train robbery and another on robber barons.

1705. Peeples, Samuel Anthony

The dream ends in fury, by Samuel Anthony Peeples. A novel based on the life of Joan [*sic*] Murrieta [*sic*]. New York, Harper & brothers, publishers [1949]. Cloth. OP.

6 p.l., 240 p. 20.8 cm.

Half title; pub. device; untrimmed; "First edition" on copyright p.

Since this is a novel, one does not expect to find many historical facts in it, yet in an introductory note the author attempts to inject a historical element: "Joaquín Murrieta [*sic*] was, beyond doubt, the greatest outlaw in America's history. During the brief four-year murderous career of this man, he personally killed, or caused to be killed, more than 300 men. Estimates of the stolen wealth he accumulated range into millions of dollars." These are pretty broad statements, when one takes into consideration the fact that Murieta was a fictitious character created by a novelist who wrote his book because he needed money.

1706. Peirson, Erma

Kern's desert, by Erma Peirson. Eighteenth annual publication of the Kern county historical society and the county of Kern through its museum, Bakersfield, Calif., 1956. Cloth. Scarce.

viii, 68 p. illus., plates. 23.6 cm.
Map on end papers; vignette.

Has a chapter on Vásquez.

1707. Pelzer, Louis

The shifting cow towns of Kansas, by Louis Pelzer. Reprinted from the transations of the Illinois State Historical society, 1926. Wrappers.

[3]–13 p. 23 cm.

Contains some information on the gunmen of the various wild cow towns of Kansas.

1708. Pence, Mary Lou, and Lola M. Homsher

The ghost towns of Wyoming, by Mary Lou Pence and Lola M. Homsher. New York, Hastings House, publishers [1956]. Boards. OP.

xii p., 1 l., 242 p. illus., plates (1 double p.), ports., facsms., map (double p.). 26 cm.
Acknowledgments: p. 236; index: p. 237–242.
Half title; map on end papers; illus. double t.p.

Has material on the Wild Bunch and their train robberies and on such characters as Jim Averill, Big Nose George Parrott, Calamity Jane, Cattle Kate, Butch Cassidy, Kid Curry, Alferd Packer, Wyatt Earp, Wild Bill Hickok, and others.

1709. Penfield, Thomas

Dig here! by Thomas Penfield. San Antonio, Texas, the Naylor co. . . . [1962]. Pict. cloth.

ix p., 1 l., 240 p. illus. 21.7 cm.

Reading sources: p. 207–235; index: p. 239–240.

Map on end papers; illus. t.p.; pub. device.

Has some material on Black Jack and Sam Ketchum, Burt Alvord, Curly Bill Brocius, John D. Lee, Bob Downing, Billy Stiles, Augustin Chacon, Zwing Hunt, Billy Grounds, Sam Bass, Sandy King, and Sostenes l'Archeveque and on train and stagecoach robberies.

1710. ———

Western sheriffs and marshals. Illustrated by Robert Glauble. New York, Grossett & Dunlap, publishers [1955]. Pict. cloth. OP.

xiv p., 1 l., 3–145 p. front., illus. 28.5 cm.

Bibliography: p. 141–142; index: p. 143–145.

Half title; vignette; headpieces; double column.

Has chapters on Tom Smith, Wild Bill Hickok, Bill Tilghman, Bat Masterson, Jim Courtright, Ben Thompson, Wyatt Earp, Commodore Owens, Frank Canton, Pat Garrett, and other noted marshals and sheriffs. There are glaring errors in every chapter, and many of the dates are wrong. Among other errors the author has Hickok sheriff of Dodge City, with Bat Masterson his deputy; Ben Thompson a marshal of San Antonio, Texas; John Wesley Hardin being killed while playing cards; Billy the Kid being killed with a shotgun. There are many other errors just as inexcusable. It would take several pages to enumerate them all.

1711. Penrose, Charles Bingham

The Johnson county war. The papers of Charles Bingham Penrose in the library of the University of Wyoming, with introduction and notes by Lois van Valkenburgh. Thesis submitted to the department of history and the committee on graduate study at the University of Wyoming, in partial fulfillment of the requirements for the degree of Master of Arts. Laramie, Wyo., 1939. Cloth. Rare.

xxvi p., 1 l., 108–lxxvii.

Photolithographed on one side of paper.

Has much on Tom Horn and, of course, on the Johnson County War. The copy I examined is in the Coe Collection at Yale University.

1712. ———

The rustler business, by Charles B. Penrose. Douglas, Wyo., published by the Douglas Budget, [N.d., ca. 1959.] Pict. wrappers. Rare.

2 p.l., 5–56 p. 21.6 cm.

Much the same as Item 1711, except that it does not have the original introduction or the bibliography. The author was the surgeon who accompanied the invading cattlemen and thus writes with authority.

1713. Penrose, Elder Charles W.

The Mountain Meadow massacre. Who were guilty of the crime. The subject fully discussed and important documents introduced in an address delivered in the Twelfth Ward assembly hall, Salt Lake City, October 26, 1884, by Elder Charles W. Penrose. Reported by John Irvine. Salt Lake City, Utah, printed at Juvenile Instruction office, 1884. Wrappers. Rare.

2 p.l. [5]–80 p. 17.3 cm.

1714. Penrose, Matt R.

Pots o' gold, by Matt R. Penrose. Reno, Nev., A. Carlisle and co. of Nevada, printers and binders [1935]. Cloth. Scarce.

xix, 21–233 p. front. (port.), plates, ports. 20 cm.

The author, at one time superintendent of the Nevada state police and later warden of the state penitentiary, tells about some Nevada bad men, including stage and train robbers. There is some information on Henry Plummer and Farmer Peel, and he gives a good account of the death of Sam Brown, as well as of some of the activities of Jack Davis.

1715. Percy, Adrian

Twice outlawed; a personal history of Ed and Lon Maxwell, alias the Williams brothers. A record of highway robbery, horse stealing, romance and murder, to which is added a detailed and graphic account of the arrest and lynching of Edward Maxwell at Durand, Wisconsin, November 19, 1881, by Adrian Percy. Chicago, W. B. Conkey co., 1884. Pict. cloth. Very scarce.

2 p.l., [7]–194 p. 18.2 cm.
6 p. adv. at end.

1716. Perry, George Sessions

Texas, a world in itself, by George Sessions Perry. Illustrated by Arthur Fuller. New York, London, Whittlesey House, McGraw-Hill book co., inc. [1942]. Cloth. Scarce.

xi p., 1 l., 3–293 p. illus. 23.4 cm.
Index: p. 287–293.
Half title; illus. map on end papers; illus. chapters headings.
Republished by Grossett and Dunlap in 1952.

Included is a short sketch of Sam Bass and his death at Round Rock.

1717. Peterson, P. D.

Through the Black Hills and Bad Lands of South Dakota, by P. D. Peterson. Pierre, S.D., Fred Orlander co. [1929]. Cloth. OP.

4 p.l., 9–189 p. front., illus., plates, ports., maps. 21.8 cm.

Contains a short history of Wild Bill Hickok (which the author spells Hicock) and some information on Calamity Jane. The author writes that Wild Bill "had been hired by Abilene, Kansas, at $1,000 a month to clean up the town and later by Fort Hayes [*sic*] for the same purpose." Hickok was in Hays City (not Fort Hays) in 1869 and at Abilene in 1871.

The writer also claims that Hickok was suggested for chief of police by the good citizens of Deadwood but that the rougher crowd "notified him he would be shot if he did not leave town." Then, the author says, "A notorious outlaw [?] stole quietly through the *side door* of a saloon where Bill was playing cards, drew his gun, and shot Bill through the back of the head, killing him instantly."

1718. Peyton, Green (pseud. of Green Peyton Wertenbaker)

San Antonio, city in the sun, by Green Peyton. New York, London, Whittlesey House, McGraw-Hill book co., inc. [1946]. Cloth. OP.

ix, 292 p. plates, ports., maps (1 fold.). 20.8 cm.
Index: p. 277–292.
Half title.

In Chapter 5 the author mentions some of the outlaws and gunmen who visited San Antonio in the early days and gives a tabloid, but unreliable, account of the killing of Ben Thompson and King Fisher.

1719. Phares, Ross

Bible in pocket, gun in hand. The story of frontier religion, [by] Ross Phares. Garden City, N.Y., Doubleday & co., inc., 1964. Cloth.

4 p.l., 182 p. 21.4 cm.
Notes: p. [167]–182.
Half title; illus. t.p.

Has some mention of Jesse James, John Wesley Hardin, Cole Younger, Al Jennings, and other outlaws. The author spells Tascosa as Tasco and is mistaken when he says that Clay Allison was killed when, in a drunken stupor, he rolled off a loaded wagon and was crushed to death under its wheels. The wheel of Allison's wagon struck a grass clod, and he lost his balance and fell, his head striking a wheel causing a fractured skull.

1720. ———

Reverend Devil, a biography of John A. Murrell, by Ross Phares. New Orleans, Pelican publishing co. [1941]. Pict. cloth. Scarce.

5 p.l., 263 p. illus., plates. 22 cm.
Bibliography: p. [257]–259; index: p. [261]–263.
Half title; map on end papers; headpieces; vignette.

One of the best books written about this early-day outlaw, based upon scholarly research. Murrell was a preacher, and while comparing the religion of various outlaws, the author brings in Jesse James, Cole Younger, and John Wesley Hardin. The spelling of Hardin's middle name as Westley is probably a typographical error.

1721. ———

Texas tradition, [by] Ross Phares, with line drawings by Nick Eggenhofer. New York, Henry Holt and co. [1954]. Pict. two-tone cloth.

xi p., 1 l., 239 p. illus. 21.6 cm.
Half title; "First edition" on copyright p.

A very disappointing book. In a chapter on bad men the author repeats some wild stories about their shooting ability.

1722. [**Philips, John F.**]

Oration of Judge Jno. F. Philips at the funeral of Frank James, February 20th, 1915. [N.p., n.d.] Stiff wrappers. (Cover title.) Scarce.

9 p. 22.8 cm.

This oration was the fulfillment of a promise Judge Philips made to Frank James when they met in Kansas City about a year before Frank died.

1723. [**———, and William H. Wallace**]

Speeches of Judge John F. Philips and Wm. H. Wallace . . . in the trial of Frank James at Gallatin, Missouri, for murder committed while engaged in train robbery. [N.p., n.d.] Wrappers. (Cover title.) Scarce.

151–282 p. 2 ports. 17.3 cm.

1724. Phillips, Michael James

History of Santa Barbara county, California, from its earliest settlement to the present time, by Michael James Phillips. Illustrated. Chicago, Los Angeles, the S. J. Clarke publishing co., 1927. Cloth. Pub. in two volumes. Scarce.

Vol. I, xiv, 15–464 p. front. (port.), plates, ports. 27 cm.

Historical index: p. 453–461; biographical index: p. 463–464.
Vol. II, biographical.

Chapter IX, entitled "Bad Men," deals with Jack Powers and Vásquez.

1725. Pierce, Frank Cushman

A brief history of the lower Rio Grande valley, by Frank C. Pierce. Menasha, Wis., George Banta publishing co., 1917. Cloth. OP.

3 p.l., [7]–200 p. plates, ports., 3 fold. maps. 16.7 cm.

Has a chapter on the Texas Rangers and outlawry along the Mexican border.

1726. Pierce, N. H., and Nugent E. Brown

The free state of Menard. A history of the county. Compiled by N. H. Pierce and Nugent E. Brown. Menard, Texas, Menard News press, 1946. Pict. cloth. Scarce.

3 p.l., 9–213 p. illus., plates, ports. 23.5 cm.
Index: p. 206–213.

Has some information on the lawlessness of this Texas county.

1727. Pinkerton, A. F.

Jim Cummins [*sic*]: or, the great Adams Express robbery. With a portrait of the notorious Jim Cummins [*sic*], and illustrations of scenes connected with this great robbery, by A. F. Pinkerton. Vol. I, March, 1887. The Pinkerton Detective series. . . . Chicago, Laird & Lee, publishers, 1887. Pict. cloth. Scarce.

[17]–162 p. front. (port.), illus. 19.2 cm.

The subject of this book is not the Jim Cummins of the Jesse James gang but a man named Fred Wittrock who used the name Cummins as an alias, though he himself spelled it Cummings.

1728. ———

Jim Cummins [*sic*], oder: der Grosse Adams Express-Raub, Chicago, Laird & Lee, 1887. Col. pict. wrappers. Scarce.

2 p.l., 192 p. illus. 18 cm.

An account of Jim Cummings in German (see Item 1727).

1729. Pinkerton, Allan

Bank-robbers and the detectives, by Allan Pinkerton. . . . New York, G. W. Carleton & co. . . ., 1883. Cloth. Scarce.

1 p.l., v–x, 11–339 p. front., plates. 19 cm.

1730. ———

Criminal reminiscences and detective sketches, by Allan Pinkerton. . . . New York, G. W. Dillingham co., publishers [1878]. Dec. cloth. Scarce.

viii, [9]–324 [6] p. front., plates. 19 cm.
6 p. adv. at end.
Republished in 1879 by G. W. Carleton & Co.

Contains a chapter on Canada Bill, a well-known outlaw.

1731. Pinkerton, William A.

Train robberies, train robbers and the "hold up" men. Address by William A. Pinkerton, annual convention International Association Chiefs of Police, Jamestown, Va., 1907. [N.p.] Wrappers. Rare.

3 p.l., 8–84 p. plates, ports. 17 cm.
Reprinted in Fort Davis, Texas, in 1968.

Most of the author's facts are wrong, and he misspells many names.

1732. Pitts, Dr. James Robert Soda

The life and career of James Copeland, the great southern land pirate who was executed at Augustus, Miss., October 30, 1857, together with the exploits of the Wages clan. By J. R. S. Pitts. New Orleans, La., E. C. Wharton, printer, 1858. Wrappers. Exceedingly rare.

2 p.l., [5]–78 p. 24.4 cm.

I examined a copy of this rare book in the library of the late Thomas W. Streeter, of Morristown, New Jersey.

1733. ———

Life and confession of the noted outlaw James Copeland, executed at Augustus, Perry county, Mississippi. Leader of the notorious Copeland and Wages clan which terrorized the entire southern states, as related by himself in prison after he was condemned to death, giving a list of all members of the clan. Mystic alphabet of the clan for their secret correspondence, with an appendix of profound research, by Dr. J. R. S. Pitts. [Hattiesburg, Miss., 1858.] Pict. wrappers. Rare.

14 p.l., [31]–237 p. front. (port.), illus. 19.7 cm.
Appendix: p. [143]–237.

Strictly speaking, Copeland was not a western outlaw, but he was on the edge of the early West and quite a terror in his day.

1734. ———

Life and bloody career of the executed criminal James Copeland, the greatest southern land pirate . . ., by Dr. J. R. S. Pitts. Jackson, Miss., Pilot publishing co., printers, 1874. Pict. wrappers. Rare.

220 p. 4 plates. 21 cm.

Reprinted again with altered title at Hattiesburg, Miss., in 1909 with 237 pages.

1735. Pleasants, Mrs. J. E.

History of Orange county, California, by Mrs. J. E. Pleasants. . . . Los Angeles, J. R. Finnell & sons publishing co.; Phoenix, Ariz., Record publishing co., 1931. Leather. Pub. in 3 vols. Scarce.

Vol. I, 3 p.l., 7–567 p. front., plates, ports., map. 26 cm.

Index: p. 553–567.

Vols. II and III, biographical.

Chapter IV deals with the killing of Sheriff Barton and the hanging of Juan Flores.

1736. Pleasants, William James

Twice across the plains, 1849, 1856. . . . San Francisco, press of W. M. Brunt co., 1906. Wrappers. Rare.

160 p. front., plates, ports. 17.4 cm.

Has some material on Joaquín Murieta.

1737. Plenn, J. H.

Saddle in the sky. The lone star state, by J. H. Plenn. Illustrated by Agnes Lilienberg Muench. Indianapolis, New York, the Bobbs-Merrill co. [1940]. Cloth. Scarce.

6 p.l., 11–287 p. illus., plates. 22.2 cm.

Half title; map on end papers; "First edition" on copyright p.

Contains some scattered information on the James and Younger boys and devotes several pages to Belle Starr, repeating the old legend about Belle refusing to identify the body of her husband, Jim Reed, to keep his murderer from getting the reward. The author also writes: "There are conflicting stories about her death. The most likely version seems to be that *she was shot at the head of a band robbing a bank*" (italics added). He also tells a wild tale about Belle putting on her "St. Louis clothes," and going to see a banker. He says that she turned on her charm and "did more than captivate him. She actually captured him, abducting him and collecting a nice fat ransom." This incident is pure invention.

1738. ———

Texas hellion. The true story of Ben Thompson, by J. H. Plenn. [New York], published by the American Library [1955]. Stiff pict. wrappers (col.).

2 p.l., 5–160 p. 18 cm.

Contains material about Ben and Bill Thompson, Wyatt Earp, King Fisher, Bat Masterson, and Phil Coe, none of it reliable.

1739. ———, and C. J. LaRoche

The fastest gun in Texas, by J. H. Plenn and C. J. LaRoche. [New York], a Signet book, published by the American Library [1956]. Stiff pict. col. wrappers.

4 p.l., 9–128 p. 18 cm.

A pocket edition of the story of John Wesley Hardin.

1740. Pocock, Roger S.

Following the frontier, by Roger Pocock. New York, McClure, Phillips & co., MCMIII. Pict. cloth. Scarce.

4 p.l., 3–338 p. 20 cm.
Half title; device; untrimmed.
Last 8 p. adv.

In chapters on outlaws, the author touches lightly upon many hunted men of the West from Arizona to Robber's Roost in Wyoming.

1741. Poe, John William

The death of Billy the Kid, by John W. Poe, deputy sheriff under Pat Garrett present at the killing. With an introduction by Maurice Garland Fulton and with illustrations. Boston and New York, Houghton Mifflin co., 1933. Cloth. Scarce.

xi p., 3 l., 3–59 [1] p. front., illus., plates, ports., facsm., plan. 18.8 cm.
Pub. device; first edition: 1933 under imprint.

Though this is an account of the author's personal experience at the death of Billy the Kid, he makes several incorrect statements, such as saying that the Kid, in his escape from the Lincoln jail, "had broken into a room containing firearms, adjacent to where he was guarded, secured a six-shooter, by means of which he immediately proceeded to add two more to his already long list of victims." The Kid did not get into the room containing firearms until after he had killed Bell, and he killed Olinger with his own shotgun.

The author also says that Pete Maxwell "stood in such terror of [the Kid] that he did not dare to inform against him." Actually, Maxwell and the Kid were friends. He also says that the Kid was twenty-three at the time of his death and "had killed a greater number of men than any of the desperadoes and 'killers' I have known or heard of during the forty-five years I have been in the Southwest." He surely must have heard of Wild Bill Hickok or John Wesley Hardin.

1742. ———

The true story of the death of "Billy the Kid" (notorious New Mexico outlaw) as detailed by John W. Poe, a member of Sheriff Pat Garrett's posse, to E. A. Brininstool, 1922. Los Angeles, privately printed by E. A. Brininstool, 1922. Wrappers. Scarce.

3 p.l., [9]–30 p. 19 cm.

Half title; copyright notice tipped in.

This account first appeared in *Wide World* magazine, London, in 1919. This issue was set in type and printed in a limited edition on the printer's own hand press. Of the 350 copies printed, 55 were signed by the printer.

1743. ———

The true story of the killing of "Billy the Kid" (notorious New Mexico outlaw) as detailed by John W. Poe, a member of Sheriff Pat Garrett's posse, to E. A. Brininstool in 1919. Los Angeles, privately printed by E. A. Brininstool, [n.d., ca. 1923]. Wrappers. Scarce.

3 p.l., [7]–15 p. 2 ports. (incl. front.). 22.3 cm.

Colophon (above copyright notice): "Of this booklet, 250 copies were printed for private distribution, each copy numbered. This is No. ——."

Reprinted in 1958 by Frontier press of Texas, Houston.

Three illustrations and a letter from Poe to Brininstool which did not appear in the first printing were added to the second edition. Later the price seems to be the only difference between these editions.

1744. Poe, Sophie (Alberding) (Mrs. John W. Poe)

Buckboard days, by Sophie A. Poe; edited by Eugene Cunningham. Illustrated with many photographs from the famous Rose collection of San Antonio and from private collections. Caldwell, Idaho, the Caxton printers, ltd., 1936. Cloth. Scarce.

8 p.l., [17]–292 p. front., plates, ports., facsm. 23.5 cm.

Notes: p. [269]–287; index: p. [289]–292.

Half title; at head of title: "The thrilling experiences on our southwestern frontier of John William Poe, as Buffalo hunter, U.S. marshal, sheriff, rancher, banker"; map on end papers; illus. t.p.; pub. device.

Mrs. Poe relates many incidents of her husband's life, including the story of their meeting. Her account of the killing of Billy the Kid is very much the same as her husband's, since she obtained her information from him.

1745. Poldervaart, Arie W.

Black-robed justice, by Arie W. Poldervaart. A history of the administration of justice in New Mexico from the American occupation in 1846 until statehood in 1912. [N.p.], Historical Society of New Mexico, 1948. Cloth. Scarce.

xi, 222 p. front. (group port.). 23.5 cm.

Bibliography: p. 213–217; index: p. 219–222.

Half title.

At head of title: "Publications in History, Historical Society of New Mexico, Vol. XIII, September, 1948."

The author, law librarian of the Supreme Court of New Mexico for ten years, writes of the various cases on record up to statehood. He tells about the trial and execution of Black Jack Ketchum, Elza Lay, and train robberies and other lawless activities.

1746. Polk, Stella Gipson

Mason and Mason county: a history, [by] Stella Gipson Polk. Foreword by Fred Gipson. Austin, the Pemberton press, 1966. Cloth.

5 p.l., 119 p. plates. 23.5 cm.

Index: p. [113]–119.

Half title.

Contains a chapter on the Mason County War, the Texas Rangers, and Scott Cooley.

1747. Porter, Henry M.

Pencilings of an early western pioneer, [by] Henry M. Porter. Denver, Colo., the World press, inc., 1929. Cloth. Scarce.

vi p., 1 l., 198 p. 22.3 cm.

Device.

The author tells about some of Clay Allison's shooting scrapes. He is inaccurate and even misspells Allison's name as "Alison."

1748. Porter, Millie Jones (Mrs. J. M.)

Memory cups of Panhandle pioneers, by Millie Jones Porter. A belated attempt at Panhandle history with special emphasis on Wheeler county and her relations to the other counties in the long ago as told by the few remaining old times [*sic*] and the records. Clarendon, Texas, Clarendon press, 1945. Cloth. Scarce.

xv, 648 p. illus., plates, ports., maps. 21.3 cm.

Index: p. [617]–648.

Has some minor material on Jim Courtright and Jim McIntire.

1749. Potter, Jack M.

Cattle trails of the old west, by Col. Jack M. Potter. . . . Clayton, N.M., published by the Leader publishing co., 1935. Stiff pict. wrappers. Scarce.

3–40 p. illus., plates, large fold. map at end. 22.5 cm.
Tailpieces; copyright notice and dedication on t.p.

Republished in 1939 with editing and additions. Edited and compiled by Laura R. Krehbiel, Clayton, N.M., published by Laura R. Krehbiel [1939]. Stiff pict. wrappers. Scarce.

4 p.l., 9–87 p. illus., large fold. map at end. 20.4 cm.
Tailpieces; vignette.

Although the first edition contains no outlaw material, the second has a chapter on Black Jack Ketchum and some information on Mysterious Dave Mathers.

1750. ———

Lead steer and other tales, by Jack Potter. Foreword by J. Frank Dobie. . . . Clayton, N.M., printed . . . by the Leader press, 1939. Stiff pict. wrappers. Scarce.

9 p.l., [13]–116 [1] p. illus., plates, ports. 23 cm.
Copyright notice and dedication on t.p.

This scarce little book contains a chapter on Black Jack Ketchum.

1751. Potter, Theodore Edgar

The autobiography of Theodore Edgar Potter. [Concord, N.H., the Rumford press, 1913.] Cloth. Scarce.

ix p., 1 l., 228 p. front. (port.), ports. 21.5 cm.
Published with half title only.

The manuscript of this book was found after the author's death and published for his children at his written request. The last chapter deals with the capture of the Younger brothers.

1752. Powell, Addison M.

Trailing and camping in Alaska, by Addison M. Powell. New York, A. Wessels, 1909. Pict. cloth. Scarce.

8 p.l., 379 p. front. (with tissue), plates, ports., diagrs. 21 cm.

In Chapter VIII there is some material on the death of Soapy Smith.

1753. Powers, Alfred

Redwood country. The lava region and the redwoods, by Alfred Powers. Edited by Erskine Caldwell. New York, Duell, Sloan & Pearce [1949]. Cloth. OP.

xviii p., 2 l., 292 p. 21.8 cm.
Index: p. 287–292.
Half title; map on end papers; "First edition" on copyright p.

Has quite a bit of material on Captain Jack, the Modoc outlaw.

1754. Powers, Laura Bride

Old Monterey, California's adobe capital, by Laura Bride Powers. Foreword by Dr. Herbert E. Bolton. San Francisco, printed for the San Carlos press, Serra year, 1934. Pict. cloth. Scarce.

xxii p., 1 l., [3]–299 [1] p. front., plates, ports. 21.2 cm.
Bibliography: p. 289–290; index: p. 293–299.
Half title; map on end papers; vignette.

Contains some information on Vásquez and material on Murieta.

1755. Prather, H. Bryant

Come listen to my tale, [by] H. Bryant Prather. Tahlequah, Okla., the Pan press [1964]. Cloth.

viii, 73 p. plates. 22.3 cm.
Half title.

A pleasing little story about the author's life. When he tells about Sam Bass he makes many mistakes, such as having Ranger June Peak securing the services of an informer. The author is referring to Jim Murphy, but Peak had nothing to do with Murphy's treachery. The author has Bass wandering all over the country before reaching Denton. He writes as though Bass's first Texas train robbery was at Cement City "just west of Dallas." That was his third robbery, and it occurred at Eagle Ford. After the battle at Salt Creek, when Arkansas Johnson was killed, the author says that "Murphy was later located in a boarding house on Ross Avenue, Dallas, Texas." That is untrue, as is the author's statement that Murphy told officers "just how and when the bank at Round Rock was to be robbed."

1756. ———

Texas pioneer days, by H. Bryant Prather. Dallas, Texas, the Egan co. [1965]. Cloth.

vi, 75 p. illus., plates, ports. 22.3 cm.
Illus. t.p.

Has a chapter on cattle rustlers and one on the Phillip outlaws of Texas.

1757. Preece, Harold

The Dalton gang. End of an outlaw era, by Harold Preece. New York, Hastings House, publishers [1963]. Cloth.

5 p.l., 11–320 p. plates, ports. (in 1 section). 21 cm.
Notes: p. 289–305; bibliography: p. 306–310; index: p. 311–320.
Half title; dedication on copyright p.

Perhaps the best serious book on the Daltons to date, containing much new material. The author's account of the Northfield raid is unreliable, however. He speaks of the Doolin gang robbing a train at Spearville, Kansas, but it was a bank they robbed. Also in one of his notes he has Chris Evans, of the Evans-Sontag gang, "the younger brother of Jesse Evans," which is incorrect. Though the book is well written, it contains a lot of conversation that no one recorded. Though it makes for more interesting reading, it is out of place in a historical work.

1758. ———

Living pioneers. The epic of the west by those who lived it, [by] Harold Preece. Cleveland, New York, the World publishing co. [1952]. Pict. cloth. OP.

9 p.l., 19–317 p. 21.8 cm.
Half title; vignette; "First edition" on copyright p.

A collection of tales told by pioneers. Several chapters contain information about outlaws, especially those of Indian Territory. In one chapter, written by Joe Pearce, there is a statement that a "trigger-happy" outlaw by the name of Lon Bass had been killed and that he was a brother of Sam Bass. Sam had no brother named Lon. Sam's three brothers were George, Denton, and John. In another chapter there is some information about Sam Bass. The author writes: "Jim Murphy the traitor finally poured poison down his own sorry belly. It was the only decent thing he ever did." Murphy did not commit suicide as legend has it, but accidentally got some eye medicine down his throat, with disastrous results.

1759. ———

Lone star man. Ira Aten, last of the old Texas rangers, by Harold Preece. New York, Hastings House, publishers [1960]. Cloth.

9 p.l., 19–256 p. plates, ports., map. 21.5 cm.
Bibliography: p. 249; index: p. 251–256.
Half title.

Although the author admits that Ira Aten, the subject of this biography, did not join the Texas Rangers until March, 1883, he says that Aten wondered whether he would be sent to capture Frank Jackson, the "uncaught henchman of Sam Bass," or Hendry [*sic*] Brown, "now municipal constable after having been a swaggering gun slinger for Billy the Kid." But he says that Brown was in Tascosa, Texas. The author apparently does not know that Brown served as deputy sheriff under Cape

Willingham at Tascosa in 1880 and had been appointed deputy marshal of Caldwell, Kansas, on July 3, 1882, nearly a year before Aten joined the Rangers.

The author is also mistaken in saying that Johnny Ringo was bushwhacked by Buckskin Frank Leslie in Tombstone. It has been conceded by most authorities that Ringo committed suicide in the desert when his horse escaped from him after he had dismounted to sleep off a drunk. The author says that Black Jack Ketchum was mad at the world because a girl had jilted him, but there is no record that Ketchum's behavior was the result of an unhappy love affair.

1760. Prendergast, Thomas F.

Forgotten pioneers. Irish leaders in early California, by Thomas F. Prendergast. San Francisco, the Trade pressroom, 1942. Cloth.

iv p., 4 l., 178 [1] p. ports. 23.5 cm.
Bibliography: p. 265–268; index: p. 269–278.
Half title.
Colophon: "Of this edition fifteen hundred copies have been printed. . . ."

Has some material on the capture of Murieta and Three-Fingered Jack García.

1761. Prentis, Noble L.

Southwestern letters, by Noble L. Prentis. Topeka, Kans., Kansas publishing house, 1882. Wrappers. Rare.

3 p.l., [5]–133 p. 19 cm.

Tells about some of the tough cow towns in Kansas, among them Newton and Wichita.

1762. Preston, Paul

Wild Bill, the Indian slayer. A tale of forest and prairie life, by Paul Preston. . . . New York, Robert M. DeWitt, publisher [N.d.]. Pict. wrappers. Rare.

2 p.l., [11]–100 p. front. 16 cm.

Another typical dime novel about Wild Bill Hickok.

1763. Prettyman, W. S.

Indian territory. A frontier photographic record, by W. S. Prettyman. Selected and edited by Robert E. Cunningham. Norman, University of Oklahoma press [1957]. Cloth.

xi p., 1 l., 3–174 p. front. (port.), plates, ports. 24.8 cm.
Index: p. 171–174.
Half title; "First edition" on copyright p.

Deals with some of the Indian Territory outlaws.

1764. Price, Con

Memories of old Montana, by Con Price (Masachele Opa Barusha). Hollywood, Calif., the Highland press [1945]. Cloth. Scarce.

4 p.l., 9–154 p. front. 22.8 cm.

"First edition" on copyright p.

Also published in a de luxe edition of 125 copies, numbered and signed by the author and bound in pig skin.

The author has a chapter on Kid Curry in which he tells about the killing of Pike Landusky. There is also a short chapter on the Johnson County War.

1765. Price, G. G.

Death comes to Billy the Kid, by G. G. Price. [Greenburg, Kans., Signal publishing co., 1940.] Pict. wrappers. Scarce.

1 l., 16 [1] p. 22.5 cm.

Port. of author on t.p.

A most ridiculous tale, according to which Billy the Kid was a noble and generous soul persecuted by the cattlemen of New Mexico. The author pictures Pat Garrett (although not mentioning his name) as "tall and angular with a hawklike face and a beak of a nose. His shaggy brows shading deepset eyes, bony hands hanging almost to his knees." On my personal copy, written in ink by the author, he states that he was ten years old when he saw Billy the Kid's "swollen and fly-blown body stretched out on the plaza" awaiting burial. The Kid's corpse had better care than that, and he was not stretched out on any plaza.

1766. Price, Sir Rose Lambart

A summer in the Rockies, by Major Sir Rose Lambart Price. . . . With map and illustrations. London, Sampson Low, Marston & co., ltd., 1898. Cloth. Scarce.

x, 279 p. front. (with tissue), plates, fold. map (col.), tables. 19.8 cm.

Half title; device; untrimmed.

An Englishman's story of his travels in the American West, including an account of the Johnson County War.

1767. Price, S. Goodale

Black Hills, the land of legend, by S. Goodale Price. Illustrations by Charlotte Guishall. Drawings made from actual photographs of the period indicated. Los Angeles, De Vorrs & co., publishers [1935]. Pict. cloth. Scarce.

8 p.l., [21]–139 [1] p. illus., plates, ports., map. 19.6 cm.

Illus. t.p.

Like most books about the Black Hills, this one has some information about Wild Bill Hickok, Poker Alice, and Calamity Jane, none of it very reliable. The author writes that Wild Bill was paid a thousand dollars a month at Abilene, Kansas. That is untrue, as is the author's claim that Hickok's bravery drove the outlaws from the streets of Abilene. He also has the slaying of Wild Bill wrong; he says that Hickok was killed in the Melodian Saloon "after an argument over a gold dust wager."

1768. ———

Ghosts of Golconda. A guide book to historical characters and locations in the Black Hills of western South Dakota, by S. Goodale Price. Deadwood, S.D., Western publishers, inc. [n.d.]. Pict. cloth. OP.

xvi p., 1 l., 2–208 p. illus., plates, ports., map, facsm. 20.6 cm.

Illus. t.p.; 13 p., snapshots and memos at end.

Contains a chapter on Wild Bill Hickok, Calamity Jane, and Poker Alice. The author says that Wild Bill was a marshal of Dodge City, Kansas, and that McCall was captured at Cheyenne after his murder of Wild Bill. Both statements are incorrect. He also mistakenly gives Burlington, Iowa, as Calamity Jane's birthplace.

1769. ———

Saga of the hills, by S. Goodale Price. Illustrations from a rare collection of historical photographs portraying frontier life and events. Hollywood, Calif., Cosmo press, publishers [1940]. Cloth. Scarce.

7 p.l., [3]–245 [1] p. front., illus., plates, ports., facsms. 20.4 cm.

Bibliography: p. 245.

Illus. t.p.; "First edition" on copyright p.

This book contains so many errors that it would take many pages to list them all. The author gives a wild version of the trouble at Rock Creek Station, though he declares that his version is "as nearly correct an account as has yet been published." Though he asserts that the exact truth about the fight will never be known, the truth is known today, and there is no longer any excuse for clinging to the romantic fable Nichols wrote for *Harper's Magazine.*

1770. Pride, W. F.

The history of Fort Riley, by W. F. Pride, captain of cavalry, U.S.A. [N.p.], 1926. Cloth. Scarce.

5 p.l., 15–339 p. front., plates, ports., maps (2 fold.), plan. 23.5 cm.

Gives some examples of Wild Bill Hickok's shooting prowess.

1771. Prince, L. Bradford

A concise history of New Mexico, by L. Bradford Prince. . . . Cedar Rapids, Iowa, the Torch press, 1912. Cloth. Scarce.

5 p.l., [13]–272 p. front., plates, facsms., plan. 22.2 cm.
Half title; pub. device.

Contains some material on the Lincoln County War and Billy the Kid. As a New Mexican of high position, the author should have known better than to spell McSween's name as McSwain.

1772. ———

The student's history of New Mexico, by L. Bradford Prince. . . . Denver, Colo., the Publishers press, 1913. Cloth. Scarce.

4 p.l., [11]–174 p. front., plates, ports., facsm. 20 cm.

Has some material on the Lincoln County War. The author misspells McSween's name as McSwain.

1773. [Prisoner No. 6435]

Sensational prison escape from the Oregon state penitentiary, by Prisoner No. 6435. [N.p., n.d.] Wrappers. Scarce.

3 p.l., [9]–44 p. 20 cm.

Tells about the escape of Harry Tracy and Dave Merrill.

1774. Pruiett, Moman

Moman Pruiett, criminal lawyer. The life story of a man who defended 343 persons charged with murder. The record shows 303 acquittals and the only client to hear the death sentence pronounced was saved by presidential clemency. [Oklahoma City, Okla., Harlow publishing co., 1944.] Cloth. Rare.

xx p. 1 l., 580 p. front., plates, ports. 23.7 cm.

This prominent lawyer had many legal associations with the outlaws of the Southwest. He was hired to defend Joe Allen and Jesse West for the murder of A. A. Bobbitt, but an Ada, Oklahoma, mob hanged them and Jim Miller, destroying Pruiett's case. Of Al Jennings he says: "Al wasn't no gun-fighter. He wasn't no lawyer, and so far as that goes, he wasn't no outlaw." The first edition is very rare, and the second and third printings are very scarce.

1775. Puckett, James L., and Ellen Puckett

History of Oklahoma and Indian territory and homeseekers guide, by J. L. Puckett and Ellen Puckett. Vinita, Okla., Chieftan publishing co., 1906. Cloth. Scarce.

1 p.l., [7]–149 [1] p. front., plates, ports. 22.2 cm.

Gives some information about some of the Oklahoma outlaws, such as the Dick Glass gang.

1776. Pullen, Mrs. Harriet S.

Soapy Smith, bandit of Skagway. How he lived, how he died, by Mrs. Harriet S. Pullen. [Juneau, Alaska, Stroller's Weekly Print, n.d.] Wrappers. Rare.

2 p.l., 18 [1] p. 22.3 cm.
Last unnumbered page has 2 plates of the Pullen house.

Gives a history of Soapy Smith and his gang in Skagway, with some mention of his activities in Denver and Creede as well. The author once owned a museum in Skagway featuring mementos of Soapy Smith.

Q

1777. Quick, Herbert

One man's life. An autobiography, by Herbert Quick. With illustrations. Indianapolis, the Bobbs-Merrill co., publishers [1925]. Cloth. OP.

6 p.l., 408 p. front. (port.), plates, port., facsms. 22.6 cm.
Half title; device; untrimmed.

Chapter VII, entitled "Bandits and Burns," deals with the crimes of the Rainsbargers, outlaws of Iowa.

1778. Quiett, Glenn Chesney

Pay dirt, a panorama of American gold-rushes, by Glenn Chesney Quiett. Illustrated. New York, London, D. Appleton-Century co., inc., 1936. Pict. cloth. Scarce.

xxv p., 1 l., 3–506 p. front., illus., plates, ports., maps. 23 cm.
Bibliography: p. 483–489; index: p. 491–506.
Half title; pub. device; untrimmed; first edition: figure (1) at end of index.

This thick book contains much material on outlaws, but unfortunately most of it is wrong, and the author misspells many proper names. He has Hickok born in the wrong place and in the wrong year. He repeats the legend about the "fight" at Rock Creek Station, though he admits that he read the article in the *Nebraska Historical Magazine* correcting the legend. Evidently he did not believe it. Old legends die hard. He also has Hickok in Abilene in the wrong year and is careless with other dates, saying that Calamity Jane died on August 2 instead of August 1 and that Wyatt Earp was born in 1849 instead of 1848. He has Earp sheriff of Tombstone, which is incorrect, and claims that Wyatt cleaned up Tombstone's disorders, which is also untrue.

1779. Quigg, Lemuel Ely

"Gentleman" George Ives, a Montana desperado, by L. E. Q. Houston, Frontier press of Texas, 1958. Wrappers.

5–32 p. 17 cm.

A separate reprint of one of the letters from *New Empires in the Northwest* (see Item 1780).

1780. ———

New empires in the northwest . . . [by Lemuel E. Quigg]. New York, the Tribune association [1889]. Wrappers. (Cover title.) Rare.

84 p. tables. 26 cm.
Double column.
Cover title: "Library of Tribune Extras, Vol. I, No. 8, August, 1889."

A collection of thirty-seven letters, describing travels through the Dakotas, Montana, and Washington, signed: "L. E. Q." The letters include observations about the cowboys of Wyoming and the reign of outlaws in Montana.

1781. Quinn, John Philip

Fools of fortune; or, gambling and gamblers . . ., by John Philip Quinn. . . . Chicago, [W. B. Conkey], 1890. Pict. cloth. Scarce.

15 p.l., 33–640 p. front. (port.), illus., ports. 23.7 cm.

Has some mention of the James and Younger boys, with whom the author was associated in his earlier years.

1782. Quinn, Vernon

War-paint and powder-horn, by Vernon Quinn . . . with frontispiece in color by H. C. Murphy and three illustrations by Louis G. Schroeder. New York, Frederick A. Stokes co. MCMXXIX. Cloth. OP.

xiv p., 1 l., 298 p. front. (col., with tissue), 4 plates (incl. front.), map. 19.2 cm.
Half title; illus. map on end papers; pub. device; tailpieces.

Contains chapters on outlaws and stagecoach holdups.

R

1783. Raht, Carlisle Graham

The romance of Davis mountains and the Big Bend country. A history by

Carlisle Graham Raht. Drawings by Waldo Williams. El Paso, Texas, the Rathbook co. [1919]. Pict. cloth. Scarce.

3 p.l., 381 p. front. (port.), plates, ports., map (double p.). 20 cm.

Republished in 1963 at Odessa, Texas, in a privately printed edition, with index.

A good history of the Big Bend country. The first edition is now scarce. It has some information on lawlessness and the Texas Rangers of that region. In one place the author mentions Jesse Evans as being the ringleader of Billy the Kid's gang, which is incorrect.

1784. Raine, William MacLeod

Famous sheriffs & western outlaws, by William MacLeod Raine. Garden City, N.Y., Doubleday, Doran & co., inc., 1929. Cloth. OP.

4 p.l., 294 p. 21.3 cm.

Half title; pub. device; t.p. in red and black.

One of the author's earlier nonfiction books, and one in which he covers the subject fairly thoroughly. Like most books about outlaws, it contains some mistakes. He repeats some of the legendary tales about Billy the Kid that were created by Ash Upson, and he says that the Kid and Jesse James were killed in 1881. Jesse was killed in 1882. He has Buckshot Roberts neutral in the Lincoln County War, but Roberts was very active and was with the crowd that killed Tunstall. He also writes that Ben Thompson and King Fisher were killed at the Palace Theatre, but in all other accounts it is called Jack Harris' Variety Theatre. There are other mistakes.

1785. ———

Forty-five caliber law; the way of life of the frontier peace officer, by William MacLeod Raine. [Evanston, Ill., Row, Peterson and co., 1941.] Pict. cloth. OP.

2 p.l., [5]–64 p. illus., ports. 23.5 cm.

Half title: "Way of Life Series"; illus. chapter headings; illus. double t.p.; short biography of author on verso t.p.

One of a series of short books by different authors. This one deals mostly with law-enforcement officers, from marshals and sheriffs to the Texas Rangers and the Northwest Mounted Police. The author is mistaken when he says that Billy the Kid "wantonly killed an Indian agency clerk named Bernstein for no reason except that the young man had seen him stealing horses." This is one killing the Kid should not be saddled with, and he was not on a horse-stealing expedition.

1786. ———

Guns of the frontier. The story of how law came to the west, by William MacLeod Raine. Illustrated. Boston, Houghton Mifflin co., 1940. Cloth. Scarce.

x p., 2 l., 282 p. front., plates, ports., facsm. 21 cm.
Bibliography: p. [271]–274; index: p. [277]–282.
Half title; first edition: 1940 under imprint.

In this book Mr. Raine debunks the fable about the Wild Bill Hickok–McCanles "fight." The author has a very poor opinion of Hickok. He is mistaken in saying that Jack Davis, of the Collins-Bass gang, killed Johnny Slaughter while holding up a stagecoach in the Black Hills. Reddy McKemie was the killer, and the rest of the gang chased him off for that unwise act. The author is also mistaken in saying that Underwood took part in the Union Pacific robbery. Underwood did not join Bass until the latter returned to Texas. His account of the Ketchum gang is filled with errors and misspelled proper names. In his chapter on Ben Thompson he says that Hickok and Phil Coe fought a duel over the favors of one of the queens of the red-light district and that Coe was killed. That story is not true.

1787. ———, and Will C. Barnes

Cattle, by William MacLeod Raine and Will C. Barnes. Garden City, N.Y., Doubleday, Doran & co., inc., MCMXXX. Pict. cloth. Scarce.

xii p., 1 l., 340 p. front., illus., plates, facsms. 21.2 cm.
Appendix: p. 309–324; index: p. 327–340.
Half title; illus. end papers; vignette; "First edition" on copyright p.
Republished under the title *Cattle, Cowboys and Rangers* by Grossett and Dunlap in 1930.

Although primarily about the cattle industry, this book gives much information on western outlaws and feuds. The authors' story of the Lincoln County War is much the same as the one in *Famous Sheriffs and Western Outlaws* (see Item 1784).

1788. ———, et al.

Riders west. A Dell first edition. An original book, with stories and articles by Luke Short, Tom W. Blackburn, J. Frank Dobie, L. L. Foreman, William MacLeod Raine. [New York, published by Dell publishing house, inc., 1956.] Stiff pict. col. wrappers.

2 p.l., [5]–191 p. 16.3 cm.
Cover title: "The Old West in Fact and Fiction as It Really Was."
Double column.

Contains two factual articles and three fiction stories. Raine's article on Wyatt Earp deserves a place in this bibliography because he debunks many of the statements made in Stuart Lake's book.

1789. Rainey, George

The Cherokee Strip, its history, by George Rainey. Illustrated. [Enid, Okla., 1925.] Wrappers. Scarce.

[30] p. (no pagination). illus. 17 cm.

Contains information on the Daltons, the Doolin gang, and other Oklahoma outlaws.

1790. ———

The Cherokee Strip, by George Rainey. Guthrie, Okla., Co-Operative publishing co., 1933. Pict. cloth. Scarce.

x, 504 p. plates, ports. 22 cm.
Index: p. 503–504.
Vignette.

This book is entirely different from Item 1789. It contains information on the Daltons, Dick Yeager, Ben Cravens, and other Oklahoma outlaws, as well as an account of the killing of Ed Short and Charlie Bryant.

1791. ———

No man's land. The historic story of a landed orphan, by George Rainey. [Guthrie, Okla., Co-Operative publishing co.], 1937. Pict. cloth. Scarce.

5 p.l., 245 p. front. (port.), plates, ports., maps, diagrs. 21.8 cm.
Acknowledgments: p. 241–242; index: p. 243–245.
Half title; copyright notice on t.p.

Has some material on the James-Younger gang, the Coe outlaws, and others.

1792. Rak, Mary Kidder

Border patrol, [by] Mary Kidder Rak. Illustrated. Boston, Houghton Mifflin co., 1938. Cloth. Scarce.

ix p., 1 l., 242 [1] p. front., plates. 21.5 cm.
Half title; map on end papers; device; first edition: 1938 under imprint.

"The scope of this book has . . . been limited to the border of Arizona, New Mexico and western Texas"—Foreword.

1793. Ralph, Julian

Our great west. A study of the present conditions and future possibilities of the new commonwealths and capitals of the United States, by Julian Ralph. . . . New York, Harper & brothers, publishers, 1893. Dec. cloth. Scarce.

xi [1], 477 [1] p. front., illus., plates, maps. 23 cm.
Pub. device; 4 p. adv. at end.

Has a chapter on Montana containing some information on the vigilantes and outlaws of that state.

1794. Rambo, Ralph

Trailing the California bandit Tiburcio Vásquez, 1835–1875, by Ralph Rambo. Illustrations and hand-lettered text by the author. [San Jose, Calif., Rosicrucian press, 1968.] Stiff pict. wrappers.

2 p.l., 5–40 p. illus., plates, ports., facsms., map. 23 cm.
Pict. t.p.; signed by the author.

Gives a short but fairly accurate account of the life and execution of the noted California outlaw.

1795. Ramsdell, Charles

San Antonio, a historical and pictorial guide, by Charles Ramsdell. Photographs by Fred Schmidt . . ., and others. Austin, University of Texas press [1959]. Cloth.

xii p., 1 l., 3–308 p. front. plates, ports., 3 maps (double p.). 22 cm.
Note on sources: p. 298–301; index: p. 303–308.
Pub. device.

Has some mention of the killing of Ben Thompson and King Fisher.

1796. Randolph, Vance

Who blowed up the church house? And other Ozark folk tales, collected by Vance Randolph. Illustrations by Glen Rounds with notes by Herbert Halpert. New York, Columbia University press, 1952. Pict. cloth. OP.

xviii p., 2 l., 3–231 p. illus. 22.2 cm.
Notes: p. 183–226; bibliography: p. 227–231.
Half title; illus. double t.p.

Repeats the story about Belle Starr refusing to identify the body of her husband, Jim Reed, to keep the murderer from collecting the reward. This piece of fiction has been retold so often that it has been widely accepted as fact.

1797. Rankin, L.

No. 6847; or, the horrors of prison life. Including many graphic details in the life of John Wesley Hardin, the noted Texas desperado. Three years in the pen. [N.p., printed by No. 6847 himself, ca. 1897.] Wrappers. Exceedingly rare.

xi p., 1 l., 3–67 p. 19.5 cm.
Signed: "L. Rankin"; tailpieces.

Though in the title the author claims to give "graphic details in the life of John Wesley Hardin," he barely mentions him. The book is mostly about the author's life in the Huntsville, Texas, prison.

1798. Rankin, M. Wilson

Reminiscences of frontier days, including an authentic account of the Thornburg and Meeker massacre, by M. Wilson Rankin. . . . Denver, Colo., Photo-lithographed by Smith-Brooks [1938]. Fabrikoid. Scarce.

5 p.l., 140 p. front., illus., plates, maps. 28 cm.

This privately printed book has very crude illustrations. It contains an account of the hanging of Big Nose George Parrott. The author is mistaken in his statement that Joel Collins and Sam Bass fled to Indian Territory after their robbery of the Union Pacific at Big Springs and that they were later arrested and sentenced to a prison term.

1799. Ransom, Rev. A.

A terrible history of fraud and crime; the twin brothers of Texas. Lives, trial, confession and execution at Savannah, Georgia, for the cruel, but mistaken murder of their beautiful sister, Emily Eganus. With full confession of many other awful murders, incendiaries, highway robberies, and garroting, while connected with the lawless band of land pirates of Texas and Kansas. Philadelphia, published by M. A. Milliette [1858]. Pict. wrappers. Exceedingly rare.

[13]–41 [1] p. front., 6 plates, (incl. front. and 1 on back wrapper). 23 cm.
Also published in German the same year under the title *Die Zwilling-Bruders von Texas.*

This rare book is written in the exaggerated style of the period and is full of imaginary conversation. The subjects are supposedly members of the John A. Murrell gang. Other than the title there are no references to the brothers from Texas. The book is signed "Rev. A. Ransom" and is one of several such stories of crime written by ministers of that period. Perhaps such stories served as an escape for them. In my opinion the book is only a piece of bloody fiction, though its rarity has made it a collector's item.

1800. Rascoe, Burton

Belle Starr, "the bandit queen." The true story of the romantic and exciting career of the daring and glamorous lady famed in legend and story throughout the west. . . . The true facts about the dastardly deeds and the come-uppence of such Dick Turpins, Robin Hoods and Rini Rinaldos as the Youngers, the Jameses, the Daltons, the Starrs, the Doolins and the Jenningses. The real story with court records and contemporary newspaper accounts and testimony of the old nesters, here and there in the southwest . . ., by Burton Rascoe. . . . New York, published by Random House . . ., 1941. Cloth. OP.

viii p., 1 l., 3–340 p. front., plates, ports. 23 cm.

Chronology and necrology: p. 277–291; glossary: p. 295–298; bibliographical review: p. 301–336; index: p. 337–340.

This history of Belle Starr is perhaps the most complete work done on the female bandit to date, but when the author brings Billy the Kid into the picture he is rather careless with his facts. He says that the Kid "appeared out of nowhere in Lincoln County, New Mexico, in the fall of 1887, when he was eighteen years old." Unless the date is a typographical error, the author has the Kid "appearing" six years after his death. Later he says that the Kid "was shot to death by Marshal Pat Garrett at Pete Maxwell's house near Fort Sumner, Texas." Garrett was a sheriff, not a marshal, and, of course, Fort Sumner is in New Mexico.

Like so many others, he has the Youngers and the Jameses first cousins and says that Jesse James "invented" train robbery and that the robbery of the Rock Island on July 21, 1873, was the first train robbery in the world. That is incorrect. The Renos held up trains during the 1860's. There are many other errors.

1801. Rascoe, Jesse Ed

Some western treasures, by Jesse E. Rascoe. Cisco, Texas, Frontier book co., 1964. Pict. wrappers.

1 p.l., [3]–80 p. maps. 21.7 cm.

This little book has some new and valuable material on such outlaws as John Kinney, Russian Bill, Clay Allison, Billy the Kid, Bronco Billy Walters, and Frank McNab.

1802. Rath, Ida Ellen

Early Ford county, by Ida Ellen Rath. North Newton, Kans., Mennonite press [1964]. Pict. cloth.

xx, 267 p. plates, ports., maps. 23.5 cm.
Index: p. [265]–267.
Half title.

Contains much on the early history of Dodge City and the killing of Dora Hand, some information on the Dalton gang, and much on the early sheriffs and marshals, such as the Mastersons, Wyatt Earp, Ham Bell, and Bill Tilghman.

1803. ———

The Rath trail. Non-fiction biography of Charles Rath, Indian trader, merchant, buffalo hunter, hide buyer, railroad grader, and organizer of early day towns and trading posts. A friend of Kit Carson and the Bents. A maker of trails. Compiled and written by Ida Ellen Rath, Dodge City, Kansas. Wichita, Kans., McCormick-Armstrong co., inc. [1961]. Pict. cloth.

vii, 204 p. plates, ports., map. 23.7 cm.
Index: p. [197]–204.
"First printing" on copyright p.

Has some material on Dodge City and on Bat Masterson and other lawmen and outlaws.

1804. Ray, Bright

Legends of the Red river valley, by Bright Ray. Illustrations by Frank Anthony Stanush. San Antonio, Texas, the Naylor co., 1941. Cloth.

viii, 258 p. front. 21 cm.

Contains a chapter on the Lee-Peacock feud and some previously unpublished information on Jesse James.

1805. Ray, Clarence E.

The Alabama wolf. Rube Burrow and his desperate gang of highwaymen, by Clarence E. Ray. Illustrated. Chicago, Regan publishing corp. [n.d.]. Pict. wrappers. OP.

2 p.l., 7–188 p. front., illus. 17.8 cm.

1806. ———

The border outlaws, Frank & Jesse James. Chicago, Regan publishing corp. [n.d.]. Col. pict. wrappers. OP.

2 p.l., 7–185 p. front. 17.8 cm.
"Publication Number 3."

1807. ———

Buffalo Bill, the scout. His boyhood days, life on the prairies, trapper, soldier, hunter and showman, by Clarence E. Ray. Chicago, Regan publishing corp. [n.d.]. Col. pict. wrappers. OP.

2 p.l., 189 p. illus. 17.8 cm.
"Publication Number 8."

1808. ———

The Dalton brothers and their Oklahoma cave. A tale of adventure in the Indian territory, together with the desperate and startling criminal career of the gang, by Clarence E. Ray. Illustrated. Chicago, J. Regan & co., publishers [n.d.]. Pict. wrappers. OP.

2 p.l., 7–189 p. front., illus. 18 cm.
3 p. adv. at end.

1809. ———

Famous American scouts . . ., by Clarence E. Ray. Illustrated. Chicago, Regan publishing corp. [n.d.]. Pict. wrappers. OP.

1 p.l., 5–189 p. front., illus. 17.8 cm.

Like all the other books by this author, turned out in mass quantities, this one is most unreliable. On pages 139 to 189 he tells the story of Wild Bill Hickok, locating Rock Creek Station "50 miles west of Topeka," and gives the account of the McCanles "gang" collecting horses for the Confederate army. The rest of his account is the same as that given by Buel and Hough—all wrong.

1810. ———

Harry Tracy, bandit, highwayman and outlaw of the twentieth century, by Clarence E. Ray. Chicago, Regan publishing corp. [n.d.]. Col. pict. wrappers. OP.

2 p.l., 7–188 p. illus. 17.8 cm.
"Publication Number 13."

1811. ———

The James boys; a complete and accurate account of these famous bandit brothers, Frank and Jesse James. An authentic account of their noted band of bank plunderers, train robbers and murderers, by Clarence E. Ray. Illustrated. Chicago, Regan publishing corp. [n.d.]. Pict. wrappers. OP.

2 p.l., 7–192 p. front., illus. 18 cm.

Typical of the cheap books of the period—sensational, but historically worthless.

1812. ———

The James boys and Bob Ford. The downfall of Jesse, by Clarence E. Ray. Illustrated. Chicago, Regan publishing corp. [n.d.]. Pict. wrappers. OP.

2 p.l., 7–187 p. front., illus. 17.8 cm.

1813. ———

Jesse James and his gang of train robbers, by Clarence E. Ray. Illustrated. Chicago, Regan publishing corp. [n.d.]. Pict. wrappers. OP.

2 p.l., 7–187 p. front., illus. 17.8 cm.

1814. ———

Jesse James' daring raid, by Clarence E. Ray. Chicago, Regan publishing corp. [n.d.]. Col. pict. wrappers. OP.

2 p.l., 7–192 p. illus. 17.8 cm.
"Publication Number 2."

1815. ———

The life of Bob and Cole Younger with Quantrell [*sic*]. Daring and startling episodes in the lives of these notorious bandits, by Clarence E. Ray. Chicago, Regan publishing corp., [n.d.]. Pict. wrappers. OP.

2 p.l., 7–189 p. front., illus. 17.8 cm.

1816. ———

The Oklahoma bandits. The Daltons and their desperate gang, by Clarence E. Ray. Illustrated. Chicago, J. Regan & co., publishers [n.d.]. Pict. wrappers. OP.

2 p.l., 7–188 p. front., illus. 18.2 cm.
2 p. adv. at end.

1817. ———

Rube Burrow, king of outlaws and train robbers. A faithful history of his exploits and adventures, by Clarence E. Ray. Illustrated. Chicago, J. Regan & co., publishers [n.d.]. Pict. wrappers. OP.

2 p.l., 7–191 p. front., illus. 18 cm.

1818. ———

Tracy, the bandit; or, the romantic life and crimes of a twentieth century desperado, by Clarence E. Ray. Illustrated. Chicago, Regan publishing corp. [n.d.]. Pict. wrappers. OP.

2 p.l., 7–185 p. front., illus. 18 cm.

1819. ———

The Younger brothers. An authentic and thrilling history of the most noted bandits of ancient or modern times, compiled from reliable sources only, and containing the latest facts in regard to these celebrated outlaws, by Clarence E. Ray. Illustrated. Chicago, J. Regan & co., publishers [n.d.]. Pict. wrappers. OP.

2 p.l., 7–187 p. front., illus. 18 cm.
5 p. adv. at end.

All these sensational books, written by Ray for sale on trains, contain little material of historical value.

1820. Ray, G. B.

Murder at the corners, by G. B. Ray. San Antonio, Texas, the Naylor co. . . . [1957]. Pict. cloth.

xiii p., 4 l., 111 p. plates, ports. 21 cm.
Bibliography: p. 105–106; index: p. 107–111.
Half title.

A history of the Lee-Peacock feud in northeast Texas, with some information on Cullen Baker and Ben Biggerstaff.

1821. Ray, Sam Hill

Border tales. Stories of Texas–New Mexico. The fabulous southwest, by Sam Hill Ray, S.J. [El Paso, Texas, printed by Commercial printing co., 1964.] Stiff pict. wrappers.

5 p.l., [134] p. (no pagination). illus., plates, map. 17.7 cm.

This little book, written by a Catholic priest, describes the country around El Paso and some of the historic sites in New Mexico. There are two chapters on Billy the Kid which follow the Griggs account, a book full of errors. He has the Kid's father killed in Topeka, Kansas, by the Apaches and has a daughter, Jeannie, in the family. It seems that she fell in love with a miner and that when the Kid tried to make the miner marry her, he confessed that he was already married and had six children. The Kid obtained a gun and killed him, making the miner the Kid's first victim. All of this is incorrect. The author is also mistaken in having the Kid's grave marker read: "William H. Bonney, alias Billy the Kid. Died July, 1880." The Kid was killed in 1881.

1822. Ray, Worth S.

Down in the Cross Timbers, by Worth S. Ray (illustrated by the author). Austin, Texas, published by Worth S. Ray [1947]. Cloth. Scarce.

4 p.l., 160 p. illus. 23.5 cm.
"First edition, 500 copies only."

Photolithographed. Crude illustrations. Contains some information about Sam Bass taken from other books.

1823. Rayburn, Otto Ernest

The Eureka springs story, by Otto Ernest Rayburn. Diamond jubilee edition, 1954. Drawings by Gloria Morgan Bailey. Eureka Springs, Ark., the Times-Echo press, 1954. Stiff pict. wrappers. Scarce.

1 p.l., 3–80 p. illus., plates. 21 cm.

Has some information about the James boys I have not seen elsewhere, a chapter on the capture of Bill Doolin by Bill Tilghman, and one on a bank robbery by a remnant of the Henry Starr gang.

1824. ———

Ozark country, by Otto Ernest Rayburn. New York, Duell, Sloan & Pearce [1941]. Cloth. OP.

ix p., 2 l., 3–352 p. 22.2 cm.

Index: p. 347–352.

Half title; map on end papers; "First edition" on copyright p.

Edited by Erskine Caldwell: American Folkway series.

Has some material on the James boys, Belle Starr, and Henry Starr.

1825. Rayfield, Alma Cochran

The west that's gone, [by] Alma Cochran Rayfield. A reflection book. New York, Carlton press, 1962. Cloth.

7 p.l., 128 p. plates. 20.8 cm.

Glossary: p. 123–128.

Has a section on the Medicine Lodge bank robbery by Henry Brown. In a chapter entitled "Law and Order" the author tells about Black Jack Ketchum and his hanging.

1826. Raymar, Robert George

Montana, the land and the people, by Robert George Raymar. Montana biography by special staff of writers. Issued in three volumes. Illustrated. Chicago and New York, the Lewis publishing co., 1930. Leather. Scarce.

Vol. I, xlvi, 3–634 p. front. (port.), plates, ports. 25.7 cm.

Index (in front): p. xv–xlvi.

Vols. II and III, biographical.

In Chapter IX, "How Law Came to Montana," the author has written a great deal about road agents and the vigilantes.

1827. Raymond, Mrs. Dora (Neill)

Captain Lee Hall of Texas, by Dora Neill Raymond; with illustrations by Louis Lundean and Frederic Remington. Norman, University of Oklahoma press, MCMXL. Pict. cloth. OP.

xiii p., 1 l., 3–350 p. illus., plates, ports., fold. map, facsm. 22.4 cm.

Index: p. 345–350.

Half title; illus. chapter headings; illus. t.p.; "First edition" on copyright p.

A well-written biography which shows scholarly research. There are reliable chapters on Sam Bass and the Taylor-Sutton feud and a good account of the killing of Ben Thompson.

1828. Raynor, Ted

Old timers talk in southwestern New Mexico, by Ted Raynor. El Paso, Texas, Texas western press; Mesilla, N.M., Mesilla book center, 1960. Stiff pict. wrappers. Also bound in cloth.

xiii p., 1 l., 86 p. front., illus., plates. 21.6 cm.

Colophon: "2000 copies of this book have been printed of which the first 200 have been bound in cloth."

Has a chapter on Jesse James and some mention of Russian Bill and Sandy King.

1829. Rea, Ralph E.

Boone county and its people, by Ralph E. Rea. Van Buren [Ark.] Press-Argus [1955]. Cloth. OP.

vii p., 2 l., [13]–224 p. 20.5 cm.

Appendix: p. [208]–219; index: p. [220]–224.

Half title.

Arkansas Historical series, Vol. No. 4. Edition limited to 1000 copies.

Has much on Sam Hildebrand, Frank and Jesse James, Cole and Jim Younger, and Henry Starr. The author erroneously says that the Youngers were followers of Hildebrand. Henry Starr was killed at Harrison, Arkansas, by W. J. Myers while robbing the bank. Shirley says that Myers was the bank's cashier (Item 2008), but this author says that he was the bank's president. There is also an account of the hanging of Cherokee Bill.

1830. Redmond, Dennis M.

"Four sixes to beat," by Dennis M. Redmond. [N.p., n.d., El Paso, Texas, ca. 1965.] Stiff wrappers.

10 p. 21.6 cm.

The story of the murder of John Wesley Hardin by John Selman.

1831. Reed, Nathaniel

The life of Texas Jack [by himself]. . . . [Tulsa, Okla., Tulsa printing co., n.d., ca. 1936.] Pict. wrappers. Rare.

3–55 p. front., illus., ports. 22.9 cm.

Port. of author on t.p. and cover.

A little book the author sold for an income in his old age. It has five pages of affidavits on his identity at the end. The author gives much of the same information that he related to Homer Croy, who put it in his book *He Hanged Them High* (see Item 522).

1832. Reese, John Walter, and Lillian Estelle Reese

Flaming feuds of Colorado county, by John Walter Reese and Lillian Estelle Reese. Salado, Texas, the Anson-Jones press, MCMLXII. Pict. cloth.

xxvi p., 1 l., [29]–169 [2] p. front. (group port.), plates, ports. 24.9 cm.

Half title; illus. t.p.; "Limited edition" on t.p.; untrimmed.

A good account of the Reese-Townsend feud and other lawlessness in Colorado County, Texas.

1833. Reid, Col. J. M.

Sketches and anecdotes of the old settlers, and new comers, the Mormon bandits and Danite band, by Col. J. M. Reid. . . . Keokuk, Iowa, R. R. Ogden, publishers, 1876. Wrappers. Rare.

3 p.l., [7]–177 [16] p. illus. 22.7 cm.
Last 7 p. adv. on recto and verso of back wrapper.

Has much on murderers and desperadoes.

1834. Rennert, Vincent Paul

The cowboy, by Vincent Paul Rennert. New York, Crowell-Collier press; London, Collier-Macmillan, ltd. [1966]. Cloth.

vii p., 1 l., 117 p. 21.3 cm.
Bibliography: p. 107–110; index: p. 113–117.

Has material on Jim Averill, Billy the Kid, Sheriff Brady, Nate Champion, Nick Ray, and the Johnson County War. The author mistakenly says that the sheriff's posse arrested Tunstall at his ranch. He makes the statement that fourteen men were in the party at Blazer's Mill. There were eleven in the party. He also says that the battle at Lincoln lasted three days. It lasted five days.

1835. ———

Western outlaws, [by] Vincent Paul Rennert. New York, Crowell-Collier press; London, Collier-Macmillan, ltd. [1968]. Pict. cloth.

7 p.l., 6–152 p. illus., plates, ports., facsms. 21.5 cm.
Bibliography: p. 147–148; index: p. 149–152.
Half title; double t.p.; pub. device; "First printing" on copyright p.

Contains chapters on John Wesley Hardin, the James-Younger gang, Sam Bass, Billy the Kid, Black Bart, Butch Cassidy's Wild Bunch, Rube Burrow, the Daltons, and Bill Carlisle. In his chapter on Sam Bass he has Jim Berry killed, but he says that "Collins and Heffridge were killed later." Collins and Heffridge were the first ones killed after the robbery. He is also mistaken in saying that Bass, in his first Texas train robbery at Allen, secured $3,000. Only $1,280 was taken in this robbery. He is also mistaken in having the express messenger at the Hutchins robbery "shooting it out rather than surrender" and being wounded before he gave up. There was no resistance.

In his chapter on Billy the Kid he has Mesilla in Texas instead of New Mexico and has Jack Long in the sheriff's party when Brady and Hindman were killed.

This is the first account I have seen where Long was included. He is also mistaken in saying that after the Kid mounted a horse to escape "he went over to Olinger and fired the second barrel into him." He did that immediately after his first shot. After the Kid's escape, he says, "for several months Garrett seemed uninterested in the Kid's case or reluctant to go after him." Garrett was very much interested in the Kid's case, but there were plans to be made and information to obtain.

Among other unreliable statements in his chapter on Butch Cassidy and his Wild Bunch, he says that "Ben Kilpatrick and an outlaw named Howard Benson tried to rob the Southern Pacific Express near Sanderson, Texas." The outlaw with Kilpatrick on that attempt was a former cellmate named Ole Buck.

1836. Reno, John

Life and career of John Reno from childhood to the present time, extending over a period of thirty-five years; with illustrations, and including a detailed account of the great safe robbery in Missouri. Written by himself. Indianapolis, Indianapolis Journal co., printers, 1879. Wrappers. Exceedingly rare.

2 p.l., [5]–108 p. illus. 18.2 cm.

Republished in 1940 by Robert W. Shields with notes and offset illustrations and with some editorial changes. Since only 200 copies were printed of this edition, it has also become scarce.

This well-known outlaw tells the story of his life from childhood to his release from prison. It is claimed by some that the entire book was written by L. M. Boland, city editor of the *Seymour Daily Lever* at Reno's dictation. The rareness of the book is largely due to the fact that his relatives, especially his sister, bought every copy they could find, paying all sorts of prices for copies and systematically destroying them. The Reverend Robert W. Shields, who perhaps has done more research on Reno than any other man, told me that Dr. Lucien V. Rule, who had also written an unpublished manuscript on the Renos, owned one of these rare books but that a fire, thought to be the result of arson, gutted his office, destroying the book and all his records. Mr. Shields could scarcely believe that I have a copy in my own library.

1837. Rensch, Hero Eugene, and Ethel Grace Rensch

Historic spots in California. The southern counties, by Hero Eugene Rensch and Ethel Grace Rensch. With an introduction by Robert Glass Cleland. . . . Stanford University, Calif., Stanford University press; London, Humphrey Milford, Oxford University press, 1932. Cloth. Scarce.

xxvii, 267 p. front. (map). 20.7 cm.

Sources: p. 245; index: p. 247–267 (triple column).

Half title; device.

Contains some important material about Murieta and Vásquez, mostly about their hideouts.

1838. ———

Historic spots in California. Valley and Sierra counties, by Hero Eugene Rensch, Ethel Grace Rensch, and Mildred Brooks Hoover. With an introduction by Robert Glass Cleland. . . . Stanford University, Calif., Stanford University press; London, Humphrey Milford, Oxford University press [1933]. Cloth. Scarce.

xxiii, 597 p. front. (map). 20.7 cm.
Index: p. 569–597 (triple column).
Half title; device.

Has material on Murieta and Vásquez. The authors point out and describe the outlaws' hideouts, which were scattered over the state.

1839. Résumé of Facts

connected with the murder of J. H. Tunstall and the plunder of his property in Lincoln county, New Mexico, in 1878. [N.p., n.d., ca. 1882.] Folder. Exceedingly rare.

3 p. 26 cm.

Although this rare little folder has nothing to do with outlaws, I feel that it should be included in this work because the murder of Tunstall was one of the causes of the many killings in the Lincoln County War. Tunstall's family in London failed to recover a cent of the fortune he had invested in New Mexico.

1840. Reynolds, John N.

The twin hells. A thrilling narrative of life in the Kansas and Missouri penitentiaries, by John N. Reynolds, Atchinson, Kansas. Chicago, the Bee publishing co. [1890]. Pict. cloth. Scarce.

5 p.l., 13–331 [1] p. front. (port. with signature in facsm.), illus., plates. 19.2 cm.
Also published by Thompson & Thomas in Chicago.

The author tells about many of his fellow prisoners of the Kansas and Missouri penitentiaries, among them Bill Bryan, a former member of the James gang. Printed on cheap paper.

1841. [Rhoades, William]

Recollections of Dakota territory, [by William Rhoades, Fort Pierre, S.D.], 1931. Wrappers. Scarce.

3-52 p. 23 cm.
Vignette.

Has some mention of the killing of Wild Bill Hickok.

1842. Rhodes, May Davidson

The hired man on horseback. My story of Eugene Manlove Rhodes, by May Davidson Rhodes. Illustrated. Boston, Houghton Mifflin co., 1938. Cloth. Scarce.

xliii [1] p., 1 l., 263 [1] p. front. (port.). 21.4 cm.

Half title; pub. device; first edition: 1938 below imprint.

Contains some information on Billy the Kid, Pat Garrett, and other New Mexico gunmen.

1843. Rich, Everett (ed.)

The heritage of Kansas. Selected commentaries on past times. Edited by Everett Rich. Lawrence, Kans., University of Kansas press [1961]. Cloth.

v [1] p., 359 p. 23.8 cm.

In a chapter entitled "The Outlaw Fringe" there is a section on Kate Bender, by J. P. Harris, and another on the Dalton gang, by Thomas Beer.

1844. Richards, Rev. A. (ed.)

Zilla Fitz James, the female bandit of the south-west; or, the horrible, mysterious and awful disclosure in the life of the Creole murderess, Zilla Fitz James, paramour and accomplice of Green H. Long, the treble murderer, for the space of six years. An autobiographical narrative, edited by Rev. A. Richards. Little Rock, Ark., published by A. R. Orton, 1852. Pict. wrappers. Exceedingly rare.

2 p.l., [7]–31 [1] p. front. (port.), plates. 21.9 cm.

Reprinted with same imprint and collation in 1855. Another edition printed in New York without date.

An unusual story of crime, the specialty of this publisher.

1845. Richardson, Gladwell

Two Guns, Arizona, by Gladwell Richardson. [Santa Fe, N.M., press of the Territorian, 1968.] Pict. wrappers.

1 p.l., 28 p. plates, ports. 23 cm.

Bibliography: p. 25–28.

Illus. t.p.; No. 15 of a series of western Americana.

Contains some material on train roberries and Bucky O'Neill and a mention of Billy the Kid.

1846. Richardson, Rupert Norval

Adventuring with a purpose. Life story of Arthur Lee Wasson, by Rupert Norval Richardson. San Antonio, Texas, the Naylor co. . . . [1951]. Cloth.

xiii p., 4 l., 114 p. plates, ports., double p. map. 21.6 cm.

Tells about Black Jack Ketchum and Sam Bass but adds nothing new. The author is mistaken in saying that Bass had a gang of sixty men and had spies on every train and that Frank Jackson lived out his natural life in New Mexico. Nor did Jim Murphy commit suicide.

1847. ———, and Carl Coke Rister

The greater southwest. The economic, social and cultural development of Kansas, Oklahoma, Texas, Utah, Colorado, Nevada, New Mexico, Arizona and California from the Spanish conquest to the twentieth century, by Rupert Norval Richardson and Carl Coke Rister. . . . Glendale, Calif., the Arthur H. Clark co., 1934. Cloth. OP.

6 p.l., [13]–506 p. 6 maps (all double p. except 1). 24.8 cm.
Index: p. [489]–506.
Half title; references for additional reading after each chapter; pub. device; untrimmed; gilt top.

Contains a chapter on outlaws and vigilantes.

1848. Rickard, T. A.

Through the Yukon and Alaska. By T. A. Rickard. . . . San Francisco, Mining and Scientific press, 1909. Pict. cloth. Scarce.

xiii [1] p., 392 p. front., plates, maps. 23.8 cm.
Index: p. [387]–392.

In a chapter on Skagway the author tells about the reign of Soapy Smith and about his end.

1849. Rickards, Colin

Buckskin Frank Leslie, gunman of Tombstone, by Colin Rickards. Drawings by Russell Waterhouse. El Paso, Texas Western press, 1964. Pict. cloth.

3 p.l., 45 p. front., illus., plates, ports., plan. 24 cm.
References: p. 41–44; acknowledgments: p. 45.
Half title.
Colophon: "450 copies of this book have been printed in El Paso."

Tells the story of Leslie's life, his murders, his marriages, his imprisonment, and his disappearance in his old age.

1850. ———

Mysterious Dave Mathers, by Colin Rickards. Frontispiece by Jose Cisneros. [Santa Fe, N.M., press of the Territorian, 1968.] Cloth.

3 p.l., 42 p. front., plates, ports. 23.6 cm.

References: p. 34–41; acknowledgments: p. 42.

Half title (after t.p.); colophon: "This first edition is limited to 1,500 copies of which this is number ——."

The first complete book written about this noted character, and the first of twelve books to be written for a "Gunfighter and Gunfight" series.

1851. Ricketts, William Pendleton

50 years in the saddle, by W. P. Ricketts. Sheridan, Wyo., Star publishing co., publishers, 1942. Cloth. Scarce.

6 p.l., 198 p. front. (port.), plates, map. 23.2 cm.

Half title; device; "First edition" on copyright p.

A privately printed little book of reminiscences, now very scarce, containing some material on the Hole-in-the-Wall country.

1852. Riddle, Jeff C.

The Indian history of the Modoc war, and the cause that led to it, by Jeff C. Riddle. [N.p., 1914.] Pict. cloth. Scarce.

7 p.l., 15–295 p. front. (port.), plates, ports., maps. 22.8 cm.

Has quite a bit about Captain Jack, the Modoc outlaw.

1853. Ridge, John Rollin (Yellow Bird)

The life and adventures of Joaquín Murieta, the celebrated California bandit, by Yellow Bird. San Francisco, W. B. Cook and co., 1854. Yellow wrappers. Exceedingly rare.

91 p. 2 ports. (incl. front. "Joaquín Murieta, the California Bandit," and "Captain Harry Love" facing p. 49). 21.3 cm.

The first book published about Murieta. Nearly all those that followed were pirated from it. The character Murieta was invented by Ridge, who created a legend out of whole cloth. He even recorded the bandit's conversation and inner thoughts. References to Murieta in standard histories of California are founded upon Ridge's fiction.

The author expected to make money from the book, but his publishers pocketed all of the money from the copies sold and departed, thus failing to circulate the book properly; hence the rarity of the original edition. Before Ridge could finance another edition, the book was copied, reprinted, and translated into several languages with only slight changes.

According to the copyright statement the book was copyrighted under the names of "Charles Lindley and John R. Bridge [*sic*], and the plates were done by Anthony and Baker." It contained a long publisher's preface and a short one by the editor, in which he assured the reader that the book "will be found true."

On page 14 Ridge inserted a poem about Mount Shasta and stated in a footnote that it was written in 1852. The poem was omitted in later editions but holds an honored place in his book of collected poems.

The original edition had no chapter divisions; they were provided in the revised editions. Sabin found but one copy of this rare book (listed by him as No. 51,446), in the New York State Library at Albany, which later burned. The only copy of this edition now said to exist was owned by the late Thomas W. Streeter, of Morristown, New Jersey. From that copy the book was reprinted by the University of Oklahoma Press in 1955, as Number 4 of the Western Frontier Library. The poem on Mount Shasta was included in the reprint, though it has never appeared in any other edition save the original. The long, excellent introduction to this reprint is by the late Joseph Henry Jackson, the man who perhaps has made a more thorough study of the Murieta legend than any other man.

1854. ———

Life and adventure of Joaquín Murieta, the brigand chief of California. Killed by Captain Harry Love, in the year 1853. The third edition of this work, comprising a complete history of the desperado and his gang of outlaws, and giving a detailed account of his most prominent acts of murder and violence, and his subsequent capture and death, together with the shooting and dispersal of his band, by the late John R. Ridge. San Francisco, published by Frederick MacCrellish & co., "Alta California" office, 1871. Wrappers. Rare.

81 p. 22.8 cm.

This revision, made shortly before the author's death, was in reality only the second edition of his book. His new publishers were cautious, however, and considered the *Police Gazette* edition of 1859 so patently based on Ridge's first book that it should be considered the second edition of the work. Therefore they labeled this work the third edition.

In his preface to this edition, Ridge expressed bitterness toward the persons he accused of plagiarism. He wrote in part: "A spurious edition has been foisted upon unsuspecting publishers and by them circulated, to the infringement of the author's copyright and the damage of his literary credit—the spurious work, with its crude interpolations, fictitious additions, and imperfectly designed distortions of the author's phraseology, being by many persons confounded with the original performance."

During the seventeen-year interval between the first edition and the third, the legend of Murieta had grown, and that growth is reflected in this edition. Ridge dropped his Cherokee name "Yellow Bird" and used John R. Ridge. He divided the edition into chapters, with summaries at the head of each chapter. He changed some wording, added a couple of episodes, and enlarged upon others. All of the material in Chapter VI and part of Chapter VII were added. He also used some material from the *Police Gazette* edition which did not appear in his original.

Ridge also made some minor changes in wording and spelling, such as "were" for "have been," "to secure" for "to get hold of," and "Hornitas" instead of "Oanetas." He also made some attempt to document his statements by referring to contemporary newspapers, added some minor adventures of the outlaw, and enlarged upon the dialogue and the references to Murieta's early life and persecution.

1855. ———

Life and adventures of Joaquín Murieta, the celebrated California bandit. Third edition. Revised and enlarged by the author, the late John R. Ridge. San Francisco, Fred'k MacCrellish & co., 1874. Pict. wrappers. Scarce.

2 p.l., [5]–81 p.
[Published with]

Career of Tiburcio Vásquez, the bandit of Soledad, Salinas and Tres Pinos. With some accounts of his capture by Sheriff Rowland of Los Angeles. Compiled from newspaper accounts. San Francisco, F. MacCrellish & co., 1874. Pict. wrappers. Scarce.

[85] p. (no pagination). 22.8 cm.
Cover title: "The Lives of Joaquín Murieta and Tiburcio Vásquez, the California Highwaymen, San Francisco, 1874."
Double column.

1856. Ridings, Sam P.

The Chisholm trail. A history of the world's greatest cattle trail, together with a description of the persons, a narrative of the events, and reminiscences associated with the same, by Sam P. Ridings. Illustrated. Guthrie, Okla., Co-Operative publishing co., publishers [1936]. Pict. cloth. Scarce.

6 p.l., 591 p. front. (port.), plates, ports., fold. map at end. 23.2 cm.
Index: p. 587–591.
Half title.

Although purporting to be a history of the Chisholm Trail, this book also contains much on outlaws, the killing of Ed Short and Charlie Bryant, the Talbot raid, the Lincoln County War, and a chapter on Henry Brown. He continues to follow the many legends about Billy the Kid and misspells many proper names.

1857. Riegel, Robert E.

America moves west, by Robert E. Riegel. . . . New York, Henry Holt and co. [1930]. Cloth. Republished many times.

x p., 1 l., 3–595 p. maps. 22 cm.
Supplementary readings: p. 567–585; index: p. 587–595.
Half title; pub. device.

The author has some scattered material on many of the western outlaws, such as the James and Younger brothers, Sam Bass, and Billy the Kid. He says, "Men like Wild Bill Hickok, Henry Plummer and Sam Bass were all more closely related to the cattle business than to any other phase of life." None of these men had anything to do with cattle, except that on one occasion Sam Bass helped drive a herd north to Kansas. The author says that Hickok had been "born in Vermont, he had been educated for the ministry, and then went West for his health." He repeats the wild tale about Hickok fighting ten men at Rock Creek Station. He also has some unreliable information about Calamity Jane and the Northfield bank robbery and continues that old fable about Billy the Kid killing twenty-one men. There are some typographical errors as well. The book appears to have been written as a history textbook, a fact which makes the errors that much more unjustifiable.

1858. Rifkin, Shepard

King Fisher's road, by Shepard Rifkin. . . . Greenwich, Conn., Fawcet publications, inc. [1963]. Stiff pict. wrappers.

3 p.l., 7–160 p. 18 cm.

Like most of the newsstand books, this one is full of conversation which no one could have recorded and contains more fiction than truth.

1859. Ringgold, Jennie Parks

Frontier days in the southwest. Pioneer days in old Arizona, by Jennie Parks Ringgold. San Antonio, Texas, the Naylor co. [1952].

ix, 197 p. plates, ports., facsms. 21.5 cm.
Index: p. 189–197.
Half title; map on end papers (dif.).

An interesting book of reminiscences about the Southwest when it was wild. The author repeats the legend that Billy the Kid killed the blacksmith alleged to have insulted his mother and has a mention of many of the Arizona outlaws, giving the Apache Kid quite a bit of space. She speaks highly of Johnny Ringo and says that "he loomed far above the opposing gang of outlaws—the Earps, Doc Holliday and the Curly Bill faction in Tombstone's early days."

1860. Ripley, Thomas

They died with their boots on, by Thomas Ripley. Garden City, N.Y., Doubleday, Doran & co., inc., MCMXXXV. Cloth. Scarce.

5 p.l., ix–xx p., 1 l., 285 [1] p. front. (port.), plates, ports. 21.3 cm.

Bibliography included in "Foreword and Acknowledgments."

Half title; illus. end papers; 8 ports. before t.p.; 1 p. adv. at end; pub. device; untrimmed; "First edition" on copyright p.

Primarily concerns John Wesley Hardin and his fellow desperadoes of Texas. The author brings in many gunmen of the early days, tells about the killing of Ben Thompson and King Fisher and the hanging of Bill Longley, and gives some information about Wild Bill Hickok. He refers to Frank Tarbeaux' autobiography and Frank Harris' *My Reminiscences as a Cowboy* as trustworthy books about Hickok, but both are most unreliable.

1861. Rister, Carl Coke

Fort Griffin on the Texas frontier, by Carl Coke Rister. Norman, University of Oklahoma press [1956]. Cloth.

xv p., 1 l., 3–216 p. plates, ports., plan. 21 cm.

Index: p. 209–216.

Half title; "First edition" on copyright p.

In Chapter VIII, entitled "Cowboys, Outlaws and Vigilantes," there is material on the outlaws and the gunmen of West Texas. For some reason the author does not mention John Selman, one of Fort Griffin's most notorious citizens. Since the author died before the book was completed, it is possible that he did not finish the chapter.

General Twigg's initials are incorrectly given as W. A. on page 30 but are corrected to D. E. on page 35. Writing of 1873, he refers to Sherman as "Lieutenant General." Sherman was made a full general in 1869.

1862. ———

No man's land, by Carl Coke Rister. Norman, University of Oklahoma press, 1948. Cloth. OP.

xi p., 1 l., 3–210 p. plates, ports., map. 21 cm.

Bibliography: p. 193–199; index: p. 201–210.

Half title; "First edition" on copyright p.

This book deals with the general lawlessness of the early-day Oklahoma Panhandle and the activities of its vigilantes.

1863. ———

Outlaws and vigilantes of the southern plains, 1865–1885, by Carl Coke

Rister. Reprinted from the *Mississippi Valley Historical Review*, Vol. XIX, No. 4 (March, 1933). Stiff wrappers. OP.

537–554 p. 25.5 cm.

A reprint containing material on Billy the Kid, Tom O'Folliard, Charlie Bowdre, Wild Bill Hickok, and others.

1864. ———

Southern plainsmen, [by] Carl Coke Rister. Norman, University of Oklahoma press, 1938. Cloth. OP.

xviii p., 1 l., 3–289 [1] p. plates, fold. map, facsms. 23.5 cm.
Bibliography: p. 263–279; index: p. 283–289.
Half title; vignette; "First edition" on copyright p.

In a chapter entitled "Frontier Justice" the author gives a general picture of lawlessness in the early-day Southwest.

1865. ———

Southwestern frontier, 1865–1881. A history of the coming of the settlers, Indian depredations and massacres, ranching activities, operations of white desperadoes and thieves, government protection, building of railways, and the disappearance of the frontier, by Carl Coke Rister. . . . Cleveland, Ohio, the Arthur H. Clark co., 1928. Cloth. Scarce.

10 p.l., [25]–336 p. front. (double p. col. map), plates, 2 fold. maps. 24.5 cm.
Bibliography: p. [311]–320; index: p. [323]–336.
Half title; pub. device; untrimmed.

A general picture of lawlessness in the early-day Southwest.

1866. Rittenhouse, Jack D.

Cabezon. A New Mexico ghost town, by Jack D. Rittenhouse. Santa Fe, Stagecoach press, 1963. Cloth.

ix p., 1 l., 13–95 [1] p. plates, ports., maps (1 double p.), cattle brands. 18 cm.
Notes on sources: p. 87–95.
Half title; "First edition" on copyright p.

Chapter 4, entitled "Outlaw Days," has material on the outlaws of Cabezon in its heyday.

1867. ———

The man who owned too much. Together with an 1895 newspaper account of the life of Lucien Maxwell, [by Jack D. Rittenhouse]. Houston, Texas, the Stagecoach press, 1958. Boards, in slip case.

viii p., 2 l., 52 p. front., plates, ports., facsms. 17.5 cm.
Half title; label pasted on.
Colophon: "Printed at the Stagecoach Press in an edition limited to 450 copies. . . ."

Has some mention of Billy the Kid. The author says that, according to legend, Billy the Kid and the slave woman Deluvina were sweethearts, but that is untrue. Deluvina loved the Kid, but not as a sweetheart.

1868. ———

Outlaw days at Cabezon, [by] Jack D. Rittenhouse. Santa Fe, Stagecoach press, 1964. Stiff wrappers. Scarce.

vi p., 1 l., 9–28 p. 17 cm.
Notes on sources: p. 27–28.
Half title; pub. device.
Edition limited to 150 signed and numbered copies.

This little book gives information on many little-known outlaws of New Mexico, most of them of Spanish descent.

1869. Roberts, Bruce

Springs from parched ground, by Bruce Roberts. . . . Drawings on jacket by Emile Topperwein. Uvalde, Texas, printed by the Hornby press. Binding by Highland press, Boerne, Texas [1950]. Cloth. OP.

3 p.l., 177 p. front. (port.), plates, ports., map. 20.6 cm.
Index: p. [167]–177.

This little book was written by a minister and is mostly about his experiences at different churches, but it does have a long chapter on King Fisher. He makes a statement concerning Fisher's trip to San Antonio with Ben Thompson, that I have never seen before: "A number of writers have represented these men as friends, but Mrs. Fisher and others in position to know were positive that the two men had never been up to this time."

1870. Roberts, Daniel Webster

Rangers and sovereignty, by Dan W. Roberts, captain Company "D" of the Texas rangers. San Antonio, Texas, Wood printing & engraving co., 1914. Cloth. Scarce.

5 p.l., 15–190 p. front. (port.). 19.8 cm.
Vignette.

A number of Texas Rangers have written their reminiscences. While this one is not the most important of these accounts, it does contain chapters on the Mason

County War, the Horrell-Higgins feud, and the killing of Sam Bass. Unfortunately, most of the author's information about Bass is incorrect. He says that the Union Pacific robbery yielded twenty thousand dollars in gold. The loot was three times that amount. He says that Bass "and his men" struck south into the Texas Panhandle and "continued down into Denton County." He would have gone a long way out of his way if he had gone through the Panhandle. At the end of the same paragraph he says that "Bass and his party traveled by compass and came nearly straight to Denton County, Texas."

He also says that the "Bass robbers planned to go to Round Rock, Texas, as they had learned that one of the merchants at Round Rock had a big lot of gold in his safe." The Bass gang went to Round Rock to rob a bank. He has Underwood with Bass in Round Rock, but Underwood had quit the gang some time before this. He also has Jim Murphy with the others in the store during the shooting and says that Murphy "ran out with them a little distance, and dodged into a lane and came back into Round Rock." That is also incorrect. Murphy made an excuse to stay in Old Town when Bass, Jackson, and Barnes went into New Town. The author also says that Joel Collins fled to Montana and was pursued by a deputy from Fort Worth, Texas, and killed. Collins and Heffridge were killed in Nebraska soon after the Union Pacific robbery. The author further states that the Bass gang "worked in different states and many a holdup and train robbery committed by them was charged to someone else." It is interesting to compare this book with *Stories of the Texas Rangers* by B. Roberts Lackey (see Item 1262).

1871. Roberts, Lou Conway (Mrs. Dan W.)

A woman's reminiscences of six years in camp with the Texas rangers, by Mrs. D. W. Roberts, "assistant commander," Company D, Texas frontier battalion. Austin, Texas, press of von Boeckmann-Jones co. [N.d., ca. 1928]. Wrappers. Scarce.

3 p.l., 5–64 p. front., plates, ports. 23 cm.

The author tells about some of her husband's encounters with outlaws and feudists.

1872. Roberts, Gov. O. M.

Message of Gov. O. M. Roberts on appropriations and expenditures under control of the governor, to the seventeenth legislature of the state of Texas, convened at city of Austin, in regular session, January 11, 1881. Galveston, Texas, printed at the News book and job office, 1881. Pamphlet. (Cover title.) Rare.

[3]–23 p. 23 cm.

This rare little pamphlet deals mostly with appropriations and expenditures of rewards for the apprehension of outlaws within the state.

1873. Robertson, Frank C., and Beth Kay Harris

Soapy Smith, king of the frontier con men, by Frank C. Robertson and Beth Kay Harris. New York, Hastings House, publishers [1961]. Cloth.

xii, 244 p. plates, ports. 21 cm.
Bibliography: p. 236–237; index: p. 238–244.
Half title; double t.p.

An interesting and well-written book. There are a couple of questionable statements. One is that Calamity Jane and Wild Bill Hickok were once in Creede, Colorado, and the other is that Dave Rudabaugh also went there. The period about which the authors write was the early 1890's, and Rudabaugh was killed in Old Mexico on February 18, 1886.

1874. Robertson, Ruth T.

Famous bandits; brief accounts of the lives of Jesse James, Cole Younger, Billy the Kid and others. . . . Washington, D.C., the Washington bureau [1928]. Stitched folder. Rare.

[4] p. (no pagination). 24 cm.

A condensed account of the outlaws' activities, together with the dates and places of their births and deaths.

1875. Robinson, Doane (Jonah LeRoy Robinson)

Doane Robinson's encyclopedia of South Dakota. First edition. Pierre, S.D., published by the author, 1925. Leather. Scarce.

3 p.l., 7–1003 p. 23 cm.
Addenda: p. 944–987; fourth state census: p. 989–1003.

Contains an abbreviated account of Wild Bill Hickok.

1876. Robinson, W. W.

Panorama, a picture history of southern California. Issued on the 60th anniversary of the Title Insurance and Trust company. Compiled and written by W. W. Robinson. Los Angeles, Title Insurance and Trust co., 1953. Pict. wrappers. Scarce.

[160] p. (no pagination). front. (port.), plates, ports., facsms., maps. 25.3 cm.

Contains some material on Tiburcio Vásquez.

1877. Robinson, William Henry

The story of Arizona, by Will H. Robinson. . . . Illustrated. Phoenix, Ariz., the Berryhill co., publishers [1919]. Cloth. Scarce.

6 p.l., 13–458 p. front., plates, map. 20 cm.
Bibliography: p. 457–458.

In a chapter on saloons and bad men the author tells about the Earp-Clanton and Graham-Tewksbury feuds. He refers to the Earps as the "criminally inclined officers" and says that they were officers "in spite of the fact that both of them [Wyatt and Virgil] were professional gamblers and were suspected of either planning or participating in at least two stage holdups." After the O K Corral fight, the author says, "the Earps at once gave themselves up to friendly authorities who promptly dismissed them." It was not quite as sudden as that.

1878. Rockfeller, John Alexander

Log of an Arizona trail blazer, by John A. Rockfeller. Tucson, Ariz., printed by Acme printing co. [1933]. Pict. cloth. Scarce.

xv, 201 p. front., plates, ports. 21.6 cm.

An account of pioneer Arizona containing some material on the outlaws of that state.

1879. Rockwell, Wilson

New frontier. Saga of the north fork, by Wilson Rockwell. Illustrations by Josephine McKittrick. Denver, Colo., the World press, inc., 1938. Pict. cloth. OP.

xvi p., 1 l., 3–215 p. illus., plates, ports. 20.5 cm.
Appendix: p. 197–207; bibliography: p. 211–215.
Half title; illus. map on end papers.

Contains some minor information on Billy the Kid. The author states that Garrett had thirteen men in the posse that pursued the Kid after his escape from the Lincoln jail. Only John Poe and Kip McKinney accompanied Garrett.

1880. ———

Sunset slope. True epics of western Colorado, by Wilson Rockwell. Jacket and cover design by Velda L. Anglin. Denver, Colo., Big Mountain press [1955]. Pict. cloth. OP.

5 p.l., [11]–290 p. front., plates, ports. 20.4 cm.
Half title; map on end papers; notes after each chapter.

Contains information on George Howard, Bill McCarty, Jim Shirley, Alferd Packer, Harry Tracy, Tom Horn, and others.

1881. ——— (ed.)

Memoirs of a lawman. Edited by Wilson Rockwell. Denver, Colo., Sage books, 1962. Cloth.

12 p.l., [25]–378 p. front. (port.), plates, ports. 23.5 cm.
Half title; pub. device; footnotes after each chapter.

The memoirs of C. W. (Doc) Shores, the sheriff of Gunnison County, Colorado, with much on the early-day lawlessness of the county.

1882. Roe, Edward Thomas

The James boys. A complete and accurate recital of the dare devil criminal career of the famous bandit brothers, Frank and Jesse James, and their noted band of bank plunderers, train robbers and murderers. Specially compiled for the publishers. Chicago, New York, M. A. Donohue & co. [n.d.]. Pict. wrappers. Scarce.

x, 11–248 [6] p. 18.2 cm.
Last 6 p. adv.

One more of the unreliable books about the Jameses.

1883. Roe, G. M. (ed.)

Our police. A history of the Cincinnati police force, from the earliest period until the present day. Edited by G. M. Roe. Illustrated with portraits and etchings. Cincinnati, Ohio [n.d.]. Cloth. Rare.

xii p., 1 l., 19–418 p., plus 68 p. front. (with tissue), plates, ports., plan. 23.6 cm.
Addenda: p. [395]–399; roster of the police force: p. [401]–413; index: p. [414]–418.

In the back of this book is a sixty-eight-page history of the James boys, which seems irrelevant because the Cincinnati police had nothing to do with them. Like so many other early-day histories of outlaws, this one is most unreliable. The author depicts Jesse James as merciless killer from boyhood and claims that he killed two men before he was fifteen. These early killings, the author says, made Jesse's mother's heart "swell with pride and joy." He paints Mrs. Samuel in very dark colors, accusing her of training her sons to be outlaws. He spells Bill Chadwell's last name Caldwell and gets most of his other facts wrong.

1884. Roenigk, Adolph

Pioneer history of Kansas. [Lincoln, Kans.], published by Adolph Roenigk [1933]. Pict. cloth. Scarce.

6 p.l., 365 [7] p. plates, ports. 24 cm.
Index: 5 unnumbered pages at end.
Vignette.
"This material for the first part was collected and written by John C. Baird."

Theophilus Little, who contributed Chapter V of this book of old-timers' reminiscences, tells of the killing of Coe and Williams by Wild Bill Hickok. The author has a very low opinion of Coe and holds Hickok in high esteem. He writes that "for some reason Wild Bill had incurred [Coe's] violent hatred and Coe planned to kill him or rather have him killed, being too cowardly to do it himself. One afternoon Coe got about 200 of the cowboys crazy drunk, his plan being to have them commit some overt act. The marshal would arrest some of them—being so drunk they were to resist, start the shooting and kill the marshal. Some of his friends involved told the marshal of the plot.

". . . the howling mob gathered around but Wild Bill had singled out Phil Coe, who had his gun out, but this marshal had his two deadly guns leveled on Coe and pulled a trigger of each gun and just at that instant a policeman rushed around the corner of the building right between the guns and Coe and he received both bullets and fell dead. The marshal instantly pulled two triggers again and the two lead balls entered Coe's stomach."

Then, the author continues, Wild Bill turned his guns on the crowd, and they scattered like quail, and "in less than five minutes every man of them was on the west side of Mud Creek. Coe did not die that night, and this son of a Presbyterian elder, Wild Bill, got a preacher out of bed and had him go to the dying gambler, Phil Coe, and pray with and for him."

As much as Hickok hated Coe, the detail about having him prayed for is too tall for me. The whole story is false.

1885. Roff, Joe T.

A brief history of early days in north Texas and the Indian territory, by Joe T. Roff. [Allen, Okla., Pontotoc County Democrat], MCMXXX. Stiff wrappers. Scarce.

2 p.l., 5–40 p. 17.5 cm.
Device.

Tells about members of the Lee gang and other lesser-known outlaws.

1886. Rogers, Cameron

Gallant ladies, by Cameron Rogers; with illustrations by Charles O. Naef. New York, Harcourt, Brace and co. [1928]. Cloth. Scarce.

8 p.l., 17–363 p. front., illus., plates. 22.5 cm.
Half title; headpieces; pub. device; untrimmed.

Contains chapters on Belle Starr and Calamity Jane. The author repeats the widely circulated legend about Belle's refusal to identify her husband, Jim Reed, after he was killed to prevent his assassin from collecting the reward. (Reed was identified by a number of other witnesses.)

1887. ——— (ed.)

A county judge in Arcady. Selected private papers of Charles Fernald, pioneer California jurist, with an introduction and notes by Cameron Rogers. Glendale, Calif., the Arthur H. Clark co., 1954. Cloth. OP.

23 p.l., [51]–268 p. front. (port.), plates, ports., facsm. 24.6 cm.
Index: p. [261]–268.
Half title; pub. device; untrimmed.

Fernald, who was sheriff, district attorney, and then county judge from 1851 to 1861, tells some stories about Juan Flores, Joaquín Murieta, and Jack Powers.

1888. Rogers, Fred B.

Soldiers of the Overland. Being some account of the services of General Patrick Edward Conner, & his volunteers in the old west, by Fred B. Rogers, Major, Infantry U.S. Army. San Francisco, the Grabhorn press, 1938. Boards and cloth. OP.

8 p.l., 290 p. front. (port.), plates, ports., facsm., maps (2 large fold.). 26.5 cm.
Appendices: p. 257–273; bibliography: p. 274–277; maps: p. 278; index: p. 279–290.
Colophon: "One thousand copies printed at the Grabhorn Press of San Francisco"; untrimmed.

Contains some material on Joaquín Murieta and Three-Fingered Jack García.

1889. Rogers, John William

The lusty Texans of Dallas, [by] John William Rogers. New York, E. P. Dutton and co., inc., 1951. Cloth.

5 p.l., 11–384 p. front. (port.). 22.3 cm.
Acknowledgments: p. 366–367; index: p. 368–384.
Half title; map on end papers (dif.); vignette; "First edition" on copyright p.
Republished twice since the original edition, the last time in 1964, to keep the stories of Dallas' inhabitants up to date.

Most of his characters are not all that lusty, but he does give some information on Sam Bass, Frank and Jesse James, and Belle Starr, largely confined to their activities in Dallas.

1890. Rojas, Arnold R.

California vaquero, by A. R. Rojas. Fresno, Calif., Academy Library Guild, 1953. Cloth. Scarce.

3 p.l., 11–125 [13] p. front. (port.), plates, ports. 22 cm.
Half title; illus. end papers (dif.); last 6 l., plates and ports.

Contains a bit of information on Vásquez, as well as some mention of Murieta, whom the author admits is more or less an object of folklore.

1891. Rollins, Philip Ashton

The cowboy. His characteristics, his equipment and his part in the development of the west, by Philip Ashton Rollins. New York, Charles Scribner's sons, 1922. Cloth. OP.

xiv p., 1 l., 353 p. 21.2 cm.

Half title; first edition: letter "A" on copyright p.

A second edition with illustrations was published in August, 1922.

1892. ———

The cowboy. An unconventional history of civilization on the old-time cattle range, by Philip Ashton Rollins. Revised and enlarged edition. New York, Charles Scribner's sons, 1936. Cloth. OP.

xx p., 1 l., 402 p. front., plates, double p. map, facsms. 22.3 cm.

Appendix (notes on various statements in the text): p. 387–393; index: 397–402.

Half title; illus. end papers.

A completely revised edition of Item 1891 with another chapter and illustrations added. All three editions contain chapters on cattle rustling and the Johnson County War.

1893. Rollinson, John K.

Hoofprints of a cowboy and U. S. ranger; pony trails in Wyoming, by John K. Rollinson; edited and arranged by E. A. Brininstool; illustrated with photographs. Caldwell, Idaho, the Caxton printers, ltd., 1941. Cloth. Scarce.

7 p.l., [15]–410 [1] p. front., plates, ports., map. 23.6 cm.

Cover title and half title: "Pony Trails in Wyoming;" headpieces; pub. device.

Contains some material on lawlessness and a mention of Tom Horn. It was later reprinted with a glossary added.

1894. ———

History of the migration of Oregon-raised herds to mid-western markets. Wyoming cattle trails, by John K. Rollinson . . ., edited and arranged by E. A. Brininstool; illustrated with photographs and maps. Caldwell, Idaho, the Caxton printers, ltd., 1948. Cloth. Scarce.

9 p.l., [19]–366 p. front. (col.), plates, ports., maps, facsms. 24.2 cm.

Appendices: p. [301]–348; bibliography: p. [349]–351; index: p. [353]–366.

Half title; "Wyoming Cattle Trails;" headpieces; pub. device; untrimmed.

Also published in a de luxe edition.

Colophon: "The limited edition of Wyoming Cattle Trails is 1000 numbered copies, signed by the author, of which this is No. ——. First edition."

This book has a lengthy chapter on the Johnson County War and the hanging of Cattle Kate and Jim Averill and also contains material on Tom Horn and the Wild Bunch.

On page 287 the author writes: "The actual leader of this rampaging outfit was Harry [Harvey] Logan. He had two brothers, Lonnie and John. All three of these Missouri boys settled in Wyoming at a bad spot called Landusky, known as a rendezvous for rustlers, not far from Thermopole." Landusky is in Montana, quite a distance from Thermopole, which is in Wyoming. The author also tells something about Tom Horn's activities. The author, my personal friend, died before the book was released and just after he had signed the unbound signatures of the limited edition.

1895. Rolt-Wheeler, Francis William

The book of cowboys, by Francis Rolt-Wheeler, with 33 illustrations from photographs, sketches and early prints. Boston, Lothrop, Lee & Shepard co. [1921]. Pict. cloth. Scarce.

7 p.l., 13–394 p. front., plates. 20.5 cm.
Half title; pub. device.

In a chapter entitled "Barbed Wire" there is considerable material on the Lincoln County War and Billy the Kid, most of it quoted from Siringo's *Cowboy Detective.* The author makes the introductory statement that "one of the worst of all cattle stealing outfits was Billy the Kid's gang, famous as having held the whole of Lincoln County Texas [!] in a state of guerilla warfare for years." He later gives the correct location of Lincoln County as New Mexico. He gives Jesse Chisholm the first name John but says that Chisholm is "not to be confused with John Chisum who also sold cattle at this time and established the New Mexico trail."

He follows all the old legends about the Kid, having him killing a Negro soldier at the age of fifteen, then a blacksmith in Silver City, and skipping to Old Mexico, and all the rest. The next ten pages are a direct quotation from Siringo's *Cowboy Detective.*

1896. Romer, F.

Makers of history. A story of the development of the history of our country at the muzzle of a Colt. Made into a book by F. Romer. Hartford, Conn., Colt's patent firearms manufacturing co., 1926. Pict. wrappers. Scarce.

[3]–63 [1] p. front., plates. 17 cm.
Errata leaf tipped in.

Deals with many outlaws. The author repeats the legend of the Hickok-McCanles "fight."

1897. Root, Frank A., and William Elsey Connelley

The overland stage to California. Personal reminiscences and authentic history of the great overland stage line and pony express from the Missouri river to the Pacific ocean, by Frank A. Root . . . and William Elsey Connelley. . . . Topeka, Kans., published by the authors, 1901. Dec. pict. cloth. Rare.

xvii, 630 p. front. (with tissue), plates, ports., maps (1 fold. at end). 23.5 cm.
Index: p. 615–627; roll of honor: p. 629–630.
Half title.
Republished in 1950 by the Long Book co., of Columbia, Ohio.

The original is very rare and is considered the standard history of the early stage lines. It has some information on stagecoach robberies, Wild Bill Hickok, and Joseph Slade.

1898. Rorick, Eleanor

The notorious Benders, [by Eleanor Rorick. Cherryvale, Kans., n.d.] Wrappers. (Cover title.) Scarce.

[19] p. (no pagination). 21.6 cm.

This little pamphlet was written for the Bender Museum to celebrate the Cherryvale Centennial. The author gives some new material on these bloody fiends and has quotations from several men who claimed to have been with the posse that captured and did away with them.

1899. Rosa, Joseph G.

Alias Jack McCall. A pardon or death? An account of the trial, petition for a presidential pardon, and execution of John McCall for the murder of Wild Bill Hickok, by Joseph G. Rosa. Kansas City, Mo., Kansas City Posse of the Westerners, 1967. Pict. cloth. Also pub. in wrappers.

3 p.l., 3–32 p. front. (port.), plates, ports., facsms. 23.6 cm.
Notes: p. 30–32.
Half title.
Colophon: "Book Number —— limited to two hundred and fifty copies." Signed by the author.

A revised version of a talk the author gave before the Kansas City Posse of Westerners on October 11, 1966. It gives the first complete description of the legal trial of Jack McCall, at Yankton, Dakota Territory.

1900. ——

The gunfighter, man or myth? [by] Joseph G. Rosa. Norman, University of Oklahoma press [1969]. Cloth.

xv p., 1 l., 3–229 p. plates, ports. 23.5 cm.
Bibliography: p. 212–220; index: p. 221–229.
Half title; double t.p. in red and black; "First edition" on copyright p.

This well-written book deals with the western six-gun and the men who used them, both for and against the law. The author calls Jules Reni by the name Bene. Most authorities claim that Reni is correct. On page 161 he writes that Ben Kilpatrick and Howard Benson "held up a train at San Angelo and were killed by a Wells, Fargo messenger." This happened on the Southern Pacific near Sanderson, Texas (far from San Angelo), and Kilpatrick's companion was a former cell mate, Ole Beck. He spells Henry Brown's first name Hendry, as so many others do, and writes that Brown was "believed to have been a former associate of Billy the Kid." He was, indeed, without question, a former associate of the Kid.

On the whole the book is both interesting and well done and should be a valuable addition to the literature of the gunman.

1901. ———

They called him Wild Bill. The life and adventures of James Butler Hickok, by Joseph G. Rosa. Norman, University of Oklahoma press [1964]. Cloth.

xvii p., 1 l., 3–278 p. front., plates, ports., facsm. 24.2 cm.
Chronology: p. 256–260; bibliography: p. 261–267; index: p. 268–278.
Half title; "First edition" on copyright p.

This is the best biography of Hickok published to date and shows much scholarly research. The author corrects many of the old fables and legends concerning Hickok, and according to my own research, I can find but two errors. The author has Harry Young the bartender at the No. 10 Saloon where Hickok was killed, and he says that Jack McCall entered the saloon by an open rear door. Most of the reliable residents of Deadwood of that day claimed that Anson Tipple was the bartender at No. 10 and that McCall entered by the front door.

1902. Rose, Dan

Prehistoric and historic Gila county, Arizona, by Dan Rose. . . . Phoenix, Ariz., Republic and Gazette printery [n.d.]. Wrappers. Rare.

1 p.l., [3]–37 p. 23 cm.

Contains material on the Tonto Basin War, the Apache Kid, and other Arizona outlaws.

1903. [Rose, Victor M.]

The Texas vendetta; or, the Sutton-Taylor feud, [by Victor M. Rose]. New York, printed by J. J. Little & co. . . . 1880. Wrappers. Exceedingly rare.

[3]–69 p. 17.8 cm.

Republished by Frontier press of Texas, Houston, in 1956.

[3]–69 [17] p. plates, ports. 21 cm.
Last 16 p. plates and ports. from the Rose collection.

Only three copies of the original edition are known to me, one in the Library of Congress, one in the Texas State Library, and the third in private hands. The book gives some information on the Sutton-Taylor feud not found elsewhere.

1904. Rosen, Rev. Peter

Pa-ha-sa-pah; or, the Black Hills of South Dakota. A complete history of the gold and wonder-land of the Dakotas from the original inhabitants, the whites who came in contact with them; opening up of the country to civilization, and its social and political development, by Rev. Peter Rosen, for seven years a missionary in the Black Hills. St. Louis, Mo., Nixon-Jones printing co., 1895. Cloth. Scarce.

xiii, 645 p. front. (port.), illus., plates, ports. 23.5 cm.

Includes an account of the death of Wild Bill Hickok.

1905. Rosenburg, Jay (ed.)

This was in fact the west. [N.p., n.d.] Stiff pict. wrappers.

1 p.l., 2–67 p. illus., plates, ports. 13.8 x 21.6 cm.
Bibliography: p. 62–67.

Mentions most of the outlaws of the West, as well as many of its "shady ladies."

1906. Ross, Edith Connelley

The bloody Benders, by Edith Connelley Ross. Reprinted from collections of the Kansas State Historical Society, 1926–1928, Vol. XVII. Pamphlet. (Caption title.) OP.

15 p. 22.8 cm.

A fairly accurate account of the Benders, containing some material not found elsewhere.

1907. Ross, Nancy Wilson

Westward the women, [by] Nancy Wilson Ross. New York, Albert A. Knopf, 1944. Pict. boards. OP.

5 p.l., 3–199 [1] p. 21.8 cm.
Half title; "First edition" on copyright p.

Has some different material on Calamity Jane.

1908. Rothert, Otto A.

The outlaws of Cave-in-Rock. Historical account of the famous highwaymen and river pirates who operated in pioneer days upon the Ohio and Mississippi rivers and over the old Natchez Trace, by Otto A. Rothert. . . . Cleveland, the Arthur H. Clark co., 1924. Cloth. Scarce.

7 p.l., [17]–364 p. front. (col.), map, facsm. (all with tissues). 24.5 cm.
Bibliography: p. [335]–345; index: p. [349]–364.
Half title; pub. device; untrimmed.

A history of the notorious Harpes.

1909. Rouse, M. C.

A history of Cowboy Flat—Campbell Pleasant valley . . ., by M. C. Rouse, Coyle, Oklahoma. [Privately printed], [n.p., ca. 1960]. Stiff pict. wrappers.

[19] p. (no pagination). 1 plate. 21.7 cm.
Map on t.p.

A picture of early life in Oklahoma, with material on such outlaws as Bill Doolin, Little Dick West, Zip Wyatt Yeager, Bill Powers, Dick Broadwell, Bitter Creek Newcomb, and others, with a mention of the Coffeyville raid.

1910. Rowan, Richard Wilmer

A family of outlaws, by Richard Wilmer Rowan. . . . [Fort Wayne, Ind.], prepared by the staff of the Public Library of Fort Wayne and Allen county, 1955. Pict. wrappers. OP.

3 p.l., 12 p. front. (port.), plates. 21.2 cm.

A reprint of Chapter 14 of *The Pinkertons* (see Item 1911).

1911. ———

The Pinkertons, a detective dynasty, by Richard Wilmer Rowan. Boston, Little, Brown and co., 1931. Cloth. Scarce.

6 p.l., 3–350 p. front. (port.), illus., plates, ports. 22.6 cm.
Index: p. 339–350.
Half title; pub. device; t.p. in red and black.

Most of this book deals with the Civil War and eastern outlaws in the Pinkerton's early work, but it also contains a chapter on the Reno brothers, the first train robbers.

1912. Rush, N. Orwin

Mercer's banditti of the plains. The story of the first book giving an account of the cattlemen's invasion of Wyoming in 1892, by N. Orwin Rush. Tallahassee, Fla., Florida State University library, 1961. Pict. wrappers. OP.

viii, 67 p. front., illus. 21.2 cm.

Bibliography: p. 64–67.

A history of this ruthlessly suppressed book on the Johnson County War.

1913. Russell, Carl Parcher

One hundred years in Yosemite. The romantic story of early human affairs in the central Sierra Nevada, by Carl Parcher Russell. With a foreword by Horace M. Albright. Stanford, Stanford University press; London, Humphrey Milford, Oxford University press, 1931. Cloth. Scarce.

xvi p., 1 l., 3–242 [2] p. front., plates, ports. 22.9 cm.

Chronology and sources: p. 203–216; bibliography: p. 217–230; index: p. 233–242.

Half title; map on end papers.

Contains some information on Black Bart and his holdups.

1914. ———

One hundred years in Yosemite. The story of a great park and its friends, by Carl Parcher Russell. With a foreword by Newton B. Drury. Berkeley and Los Angeles, University of California press, 1947. Cloth. OP.

xviii p., 1 l., 226 p. front., plates, ports. 22.2 cm.

Chronology and sources: p. 179–193; bibliography: p. 197–213; index: p. 217–226.

Half title.

A revision of the first edition (see Item 1913), with many additions and changes and different foreword, subtitle, and illustrations.

1915. Russell, Don

The lives and legends of Buffalo Bill, by Don Russell. Norman, University of Oklahoma press [1960]. Cloth.

x p., 1 l., 3–514 p. plates, ports., 4 maps. 24 cm.

Bibliography: p. 482–493; dime novel list: p. 494–503; index: p. 504–514.

Half title; "First edition" on copyright p.

The most complete as well as the most trustworthy book yet written about Buffalo Bill Cody. The author gives some information about Wild Bill Hickok and gives the correct version of the so-called "fight" at Rock Creek Station. There is also some slight material on Calamity Jane.

1916. Russell, Jesse Lewis

Behind these Ozark hills. History—reminiscences—traditions featuring the author's family, by Jesse Lewis Russell, veteran newspaper man of the Ozark region. Biographical sketches of outstanding descendants of pioneers. New York, the Hobson book press, 1947. Cloth. Scarce.

6 p.l., 205 p. front. (port.). 21.6 cm.
Biographical appendix: p. [175]–205.
Half title; pub. device; double column.

Contains some interesting sidelights on the James brothers, the Youngers, Henry Starr, and others. The author tells of the James boys' hideout near Harrison, Arkansas, but is mistaken in saying that Jim Cummins lived in the brakes of White River, north of Eureka Springs, spending the remainder of his days there. Cummins spent his last days at the Old Soldiers' Home at Higginsville, Missouri, where he died. I corresponded with him at the home. The author tells about Henry Starr meeting his doom in an attempt to hold up a Harrison bank in 1921. He also criticizes Joe Vaughn's *Only True History of Frank James.*

1917. Russell, L. B.

Grandpa's autobiography, by L. B. Russell. . . . Comanche, Texas, printed by the Comanche publishing co. [N.d., ca. 1927]. Stiff wrappers. Scarce.

3–30 p. front. (port.). 23.3 cm.
Privately printed in an edition limited to 300 copies.

Has some mention of John Wesley Hardin and the Taylor-Sutton feud.

1918. Ruth, Kent

Great day in the west. Forts, posts, and rendezvous beyond the Mississippi, by Kent Ruth. Norman, University of Oklahoma press [1963]. Cloth.

xv [1] p., 2–308 p. illus., plates, maps, facsms. 26.7 cm.
Index: p. 296–308.
Half title; illus. t.p.; "First edition" on copyright p.

In his section on Fort Hays the author says that Wild Bill Hickok was "the deputy U.S. Marshal in 1868" at Hays City. Hickok was never a deputy U.S. marshal, but was city marshal of Hays City in 1869. He makes some slight mention of the Earp-Clanton feud, Henry Plummer and the rest of his gang, Billy the Kid, and the Lincoln County War.

1919. ———

Oklahoma, a guide to the Sooner state. Compiled by Kent Ruth and the staff of the University of Oklahoma press with articles by leading authorities and photographic sections arranged by J. Eldon Peek. Norman, University of Oklahoma press [1957]. Cloth.

xxxv p., 1 l., 3–532 p. plates, maps (5 double p., 1 fold.). 21 cm.
Chronology: p. 495–503; selected reading list: p. 504–511; picture sources: p. 512–513; index: p. 515–532.
Half title.

Has material on some of the Oklahoma outlaws.

1920. Rutledge, Col. Dick

A few stirring events in the life of Col. Dick Rutledge, only living Indian scout of the early frontier days of the west, and which occurred during the time he was associated with Kit Carson, Phil Sheridan, Buffalo Bill and others. Some of these tales have never before been revealed, all told in brief form. . . . [N.p., n.d.] Wrappers. Scarce.

18 [1] p. front. (port.). 17.5 cm.

Cover title: "Brief Sketches in the Life of Col. Dick Rutledge, the Last Living Indian Scout."

Contains some material on the James boys, Billy the Kid, and Calamity Jane.

1921. Ryan, Ed

Me and the Black Hills, by the old prospector Man Mountain Ed Ryan. . . . Custer, S.D., published by Ed Ryan, 1951. Pict. wrappers. Scarce.

89 [1] p. illus. 21.3 cm.

Has some material on Wild Bill Hickok, Poker Alice, and Calamity Jane. The author gives his own version of how Calamity received her nickname, claiming that she earned it during a poker game with him. At least it is a different version from the rest, no matter how untrue.

1922. Ryan, J. C.

A skeptic dude in Arizona, by J. C. Ryan. Illustrated by Sid Stone. San Antonio, Texas, the Naylor co. [1952]. Cloth.

xi, 176 p. front. (port.), illus. 21.6 cm.

Appendix: p. 175–176.

Half title; vignette.

Revives the argument pro and con about Wyatt Earp's character and tells the story of the O K Corral fight.

1923. Rye, Edgar

The quirt and the spur; vanishing shadows of the Texas frontier, by Edgar Rye. Chicago, W. B. Conkey co., publishers [1909]. Pict. cloth. Rare.

4 p.l., 9–363 p. front. (port.), plates. 19.8 cm.

Republished in Austin, Texas, in 1967 with an introduction by James M. Day.

A history of Fort Griffin, Texas, in its wild days, containing material on the early life of John Selman and John Larn. The author misspells Selman's name as Sillman.

1924. Rynning, Thomas Harbo

Gun notches. The life story of a cowboy-soldier, by Captain Thomas H.

Rynning, as told to Al Cohn and Joe Chisholm; with a foreword by Rupert Hughes. New York, Frederick A. Stokes co., MCMXXXI. Cloth. Scarce.

> xvii p., 1 l., 332 p. 21 cm.
> Half title; illus. end papers; pub. device.
> Also published in wrappers.

This book deals with many of the Arizona outlaws Rynning pursued while serving as an Arizona Ranger.

S

1925. Sabin, Edwin LeGrand

Wild men of the wild west, by Edwin L. Sabin. . . . New York, Thomas Y. Crowell co., publishers [1929]. Cloth. Scarce.

> xiv, 363 p. front., plates, ports. 21.3 cm.
> Half title; untrimmed.

The author covers practically all the gunmen of the West, from the land pirates of the Mississippi to the outlaws of California. In his sketch of Wild Bill Hickok he tries to correct the legend of the McCanles "fight," but he repeats some of the legends about Hickok's shooting at Hays City and Abilene. He says that Belle Starr was shot by Edgar Watson when she refused his company and that Tunstall was alone when he was murdered. He credits Billy the Kid with many killings committed by others. He repeats the fable about Calamity Jane receiving her nickname from Captain Egan and is also wrong in giving her death date as August 2 instead of August 1.

1926. Safford, Anson P. K.

Message of the governor of Arizona, delivered January 14, 1871, before the Sixth Legislative Assembly. Tucson, Citizen office print, 1871. Wrappers. Rare.

> 13 p. 19.5 cm.

Among other subjects, the governor's message treats of outlawry in Arizona Territory.

1927. ———

Second biennial message of Governor A. P. K. Safford to the Legislative Assembly of Arizona territory at the session commencing January 6, 1873. Tucson, Arizona Citizen print, 1873. Wrappers. Rare.

> [3]–12 p. 21 cm.

Double column.

Has a mention of outlaws.

1928. ———

Fourth biennial message of Governor A. P. K. Safford to the Legislative Assembly of Arizona at the session commencing January 1, 1877. Tucson, Arizona Citizen print, 1877. Wrappers. Rare.

[3]–14 p. 21.3 cm.
Double column.

1929. ———

The territory of Arizona; a brief history and summary of the territory's acquisition, organization, and mineral, agricultural and grazing resources. . . . By authority of the legislature. Tucson, printed by the Citizen office, 1874. Wrappers. (Cover title.) Rare.

[3]–38 p. tables. 22.3 cm.

Has some information about the outlaws of the territory.

1930. Sage, Lee

The last rustler, the autobiography of Lee Sage, with illustrations by Paul S. Clowes. Boston, Little, Brown and co., 1930. Pict. cloth. Scarce.

x p., 1 l., [3]–303 p. illus. 21.6 cm.
Half title; headpieces; tailpieces; vignette.

The autobiography of a man born among the outlaws of Robbers' Roost. His mother took her children from these lawless surroundings back to her old home, but the call of the wild was too great to resist, and the author returned and learned all the tricks of the rustler.

1931. Sahula-Dyckes, Ignatz

Alias Linson; or, the ghost of Billy the Kid, by Ignatz Sahula-Dyckes. New York, Pageant press, inc., 1963. Cloth.

4 p.l., 198 p. front. (from original painting by author). 15.8 cm.
Half title; "First edition" on copyright p.

One of the most ridiculous books on Billy the Kid that I have read.

1932. Salisbury, Albert, and Jane Salisbury

Here rolled the covered wagons, by Albert and Jane Salisbury. Seattle, Superior publishing co. [1948]. Cloth.

7 p.l., 17–256 p. front., illus., plates. 27.7 cm.

Acknowledgments: p. 249; selected bibliography: p. 250–251; index: p. 252–256.

Half title; map on end papers; illus. t.p.; headpieces; vignette.

Colophon: "Two thousand fifty copies of this limited edition have been printed of which two thousand are for sale. This is copy number ——."

Also published in a trade edition.

This excellent book has chapters entitled "Henry Plummer, Sheriff and Bandit Leader," "Virginia City, the Lawless," "The Hanging of George Ives at Nevada City," and "Vigilantes of Virginia City."

1933. Samuels, Charles

The magnificent rube. The life and gaudy times of Tex Rickard, by Charles Samuels. New York, Toronto, London, McGraw-Hill co., inc. [1957]. Cloth. OP.

5 p.l., 301 [1] p. plates, ports. 21 cm.

Bibliography: p. 297–301.

Half title.

The Rickards were neighbors of the James boys, and there is some information about their early life and the time Mrs. Samuel's arm was blown off by a bomb. There is also some information concerning the hanging of the "Slaughter Kid" and Foster Crawford for robbing a bank at Wichita Falls, Texas.

1934. Sanders, Gwendoline, and Paul Sanders

The Sumner county story, [by] Gwendoline and Paul Sanders. [North Newton, Kans., the Mennonite press, 1966.] Pict. cloth.

3 p.l., [7]–190 [1] p. illus., plates, large fold. map at end. 23.5 cm.

Tells about Luke Short's killing of Jim Courtright and of his death at Geuda Springs, Kansas. The authors are mistaken in saying that Short met Bat Masterson for the first time at the Oriental Bar in Tombstone. The two men had been friends in Dodge City earlier. In writing of the Daltons, the authors misspell several names, such as Grant for Grat, Emit for Emmett, and Bradwell for Broadwell. They tell about the killing of Mike Meagher by Jim Talbot and about the bank robbery at Medicine Lodge by Henry Brown and Ben Wheeler, and there is also some mention of the James boys and the Benders.

1935. Sanders, Helen Fitzgerald

A history of Montana, by Helen Fitzgerald Sanders. Illustrated. Chicago and New York, the Lewis publishing co., 1913. Leather. Pub. in three volumes. Scarce.

Vol. I, xxxv, 19–847 p. front. (with tissue), plates, ports., facsm., tables. 27.5 cm.

Double column.
Vols. II and III, biographical.

This scarce history has chapters on the vigilantes of Montana, the road agents, and other outlaws.

1936. ——— (ed.)

X. Beidler, vigilante. Edited by Helen Fitzgerald Sanders in collaboration with William H. Bertsche, Jr., with a foreword by A. B. Guthrie, Jr. Norman, University of Oklahoma press [1957]. Boards.

vii p., 1 l., 3–165 p. plates, ports. 19.7 cm.
Appendices: p. 153–164.
Half title.

This book, Number 8 of the Western Frontier Library, has a great deal about the Montana vigilantes, of whom Beidler was one of the main figures for law and order. Most of this series are reprints, but this one is from an original manuscript.

1937. Sandoz, Mari

The buffalo hunters. The story of the hide men, by Mari Sandoz. New York, Hastings House, publishers [1954]. Cloth.

xii p., 1 l., 3–372 p. plates, map. 21 cm.
Bibliography: p. 369–372.
Half title; map on end papers.

Contains some unreliable information about Wild Bill Hickok. Of the Coe killing the author writes: "On a drunken spree Coe and a friend put on a big brawling and loud-mouth scene until the marshal interfered. . . . Bill's gun brought both Coe and his friend down, as well as a man who came running out of the shadows of an alley." The only men killed were Coe and Williams, the latter Hickok's own deputy.

The author also tells a wild story about "Coe's brother Jim showing up at Cheyenne, saying he had come a thousand miles, from the west coast, to avenge his brother." She admits that the story sounds like Ned Buntline but says, "Wild Bill got caught with only a small double-barreled souvenir pistol Cody gave him in New York, with only one cartridge in it. But Bill saw Coe and a partner in the bar mirror drawing on him. He whirled, killed Jim with the one bullet, threw the gun in the face of the other man, pushed him over backward against the bar, and broke his neck." This story is simply another of those wild tales so commonly told about the early gunmen. In the first place, Wild Bill would never have been caught wearing only a little "souvenir gun," and with only one cartridge in it.

Later she says that Wild Bill "was the man who, it is said, got the nickname of

Wild Bill from the wild account he gave of the McCanles killing at his murder trial of six years ago, the man who had probably killed at least a dozen others besides the Virginian, Dave McCanles [McCanles was from North Carolina], and those with him at the Rock Creek Station of the Overland Stage in Nebraska back in 'Sixty-one.' " In writing of Jack McCall she says that "there are some who said" that McCall was Hickok's brother and that he did resemble him "in a caricatural sort of way." That is ridiculous.

1938. ———

The cattlemen, from the Rio Grande across the far Marias, by Mari Sandoz. New York, Hastings House, publishers [1958]. Cloth.

xiv p., 1 l., 3–527 p. plates, ports. 21 cm.

Notes: p. 499–501; bibliography: p. 503–509; index: p. 511–527.

Half title; map on end papers.

American Procession series; also published in a limited de luxe edition at a ridiculous price.

The author says that Ben Thompson "went to visit his wife, who had apparently been hurt in a runaway in Kansas City," The truth is that when the wife came to visit Kansas, Ben went to Kansas City to meet her, and while he was taking her for a buggy ride the wheel of the buggy hit a hole in the road and overturned, breaking Ben's leg, his wife's arm, and the son's foot. Ben's and the son's injuries healed, but the wife's arm had to be amputated. There are many other mistakes, which I have listed in another work (see Item 7).

1939. ———

Love song of the plains, [by] Mari Sandoz. A Regions of America book. Illustrations and map by Bryan Forsyth. New York, Harper & brothers [1961]. Cloth.

xi, 303 [1] p. illus., fold. map (same as end papers). 21.7 cm.

Bibliography: p. 277–287; acknowledgments: p. [289]; index: p. 291–303.

Half title; map on end papers; vignette; pub. device; illus. chap. headings; untrimmed; "First edition" on copyright p.

In Chapter IX, entitled "A Few Bad Men and Good," the author has some information on Wild Bill Hickok, Doc Middleton, Print Olive and others.

1940. Sands, Frank

A pastoral prince. The history and reminiscences of J. W. Cooper, by Frank Sands. Santa Barbara, Calif., 1893. Pict. cloth. Rare.

xiv p., 1 l., 190 p. front. (port.), ports. 20 cm.

In his chapter on Murieta the author writes: "Today the stories of Murieta look like myths, so enveloped are they with the glamour of enterprise, daring and bravery. Indeed, very many men even doubt the existence of the man, considering him as having been purely a character of fiction, born from the deeds of such men as Jack Powers. Others, admitting that the man actually existed, consider his deeds to have been magnified beyond reason, and affirm that he was only a lieutenant of Powers. But the evidence given by men now living who knew Murieta, both before and during his career of bloodshed and robbery, must count far more than the doubts of people who knew nothing of the matter at all, save from hearsay." It has since been proved that Murieta was the creation of John Rollin Ridge.

1941. Santee, Ross

Apache land, written and illustrated by Ross Santee. New York, Charles Scribner's sons; London, Charles Scribner's sons, ltd., 1947. Pict. cloth. OP.

vii p., 1 l., 216 p. illus. 23.6 cm.

Illus. double t.p.; first edition: letter "A" on copyright p.

In a chapter on the Apache Kid the author gives some new material. Since he was thoroughly familiar with the life and history of Arizona, I consider his account reliable.

1942. ———

Lost pony tracks, by Ross Santee. New York, Charles Scribner's sons, 1953. Pict. cloth. OP.

4 p.l., 303 p. illus. 21.7 cm.

Half title; first edition: letter "A" on copyright p.

Has some information about Kid Curry and his killing of Pike Landusky, some material on Curly Bill Brocious, and some correct information about Billy the Kid's early life. The author is another who says that Wyatt Earp did not kill Curly Bill, saying that Bill Sparks, a close friend of Curly's, denied the claim.

1943. Santerre, George H.

Dallas' first hundred years, 1856–1956 . . ., by George H. Santerre. [Dallas, published by the Book craft, inc., 1856.] Stiff pict. wrappers. OP.

[64] p. (no pagination). plates, ports., plan. 23.4 cm.

4 p. adv. in front; 4 p. adv. at end.

Has the usual material on the activities of Sam Bass and Belle Starr in Dallas.

1944. Saunders, Arthur C.

The history of Bannock county, Idaho, by Arthur C. Saunders. Pocatello, Idaho, the Tribune co., ltd., 1915. Cloth. Scarce.

4 p.l., 11–143 p. 19.4 cm.
Half title; vignette.

In a chapter on stagecoaches the author tells about holdups, road agents, and lynchings.

1945. Saunders, Charles Francis

The southern Sierras of California, by Charles Francis Saunders. . . . Illustrated from photographs by the author. Boston and New York, Houghton Mifflin co., 1923. Pict. cloth. Scarce.

xii p., 1 l., [3]–367 p. front. (with tissue), plates. 21 cm.
Index: p. [365]–367.
Half title; pub. device; untrimmed; first edition: 1923 under imprint.

Contains some material on Murieta and Vásquez.

1946. Savage, James Woodruff, John T. Bell, et al.

History of the city of Omaha, Nebraska, by James W. Savage, and John T. Bell, and South Omaha by Consul W. Butterfield. New York and Chicago, Munsell & co., 1894. Three-quarter leather. Scarce.

xvi, 699 p. front. (port. with tissue), plates, ports. 27.8 cm.
Index: p. 673–699.
State seal on t.p.; gilt edges.

1947. Savage, Pat

One last frontier. A story of Indians, early settlers and old ranches of northern Arizona, by Pat Savage. New York, Exposition press [1964]. Cloth.

5 p.l., [11]–236 p. plates, ports. 21 cm.
Half title; pub. device.

In Chapter XIV, entitled "Range War," the author tells about the Pleasant Valley War between the Grahams and Tewksburys and about the killing of Andy Cooper by Commodore Owens.

1948. Savage, Richard Henry

The little lady of Lagunitas; a Franco-Californian romance, by Richard Henry Savage. . . . New York, the trade supplied by the American News co. [press of J. J. Little & co.], 1892. Cloth. Rare.

3 p.l., [7]–483 p. 20.2 cm.
1 l. adv. at end.

A collector's item, but of no historical value. Although purporting to be the life of Murieta, the book is written in fictional style.

1949. Sawyer, Eugene Taylor

The life and career of Tiburcio Vásquez, the California bandit and murderer; containing a full and correct account of his many offenses against the law, from boyhood up, his confessions, capture, trial, and execution. To which is appended Judge Collins' address to the jury in behalf of the prisoner, by Eugene T. Sawyer. [San Jose, Calif., B. H. Cottle, printer . . ., 1875.] Pict. wrappers. Very rare.

48 p. ports. 21.5 cm.
Port. of Vásquez on cover.

Within a few months of the publication of the above edition, another was published in San Francisco by Bacon and co., book and job printers.

[3]–48 p. ports. 22 cm.

The first edition is one of the rarest of the few books about Vásquez. The author writes with personal knowledge, much of the narrative supposedly coming from Vásquez' lips; in addition, the author traveled through Monterey and San Benito counties, interviewing relatives and old acquaintances of Vásquez, from whom he gathered much information.

1950. ———

The life and career of Tiburcio Vásquez, the California stage robber, by Eugene T. Sawyer. Foreword by Joseph A. Sullivan. Oakland, Calif., Biobooks, 1944. Cloth and boards. Scarce.

viii p., 3 l., 3–91 [1] p. front. 24.7 cm.
Specimen of Vásquez' handwriting; vignette.
"Edition limited to 500 copies;" printed by Grabhorn press, San Francisco.

A modern reprint of the 1875 edition (see Item 1949), now quite scarce.

1951. Scanland, John Milton

The life of Pat F. Garrett and the taming of the border outlaws. A history of the "gun men" and outlaws, and a life story of the greatest sheriff of the southwest, by John Milton Scanland. Published by Carleton F. Hodge, El Paso, Texas. El Paso, Texas, press of the Southwestern printing co. [1908]. Pict. wrappers. Exceedingly rare.

42 p. 4 plates at end. 23.9 cm.
Port. of Garrett with signature in facsimile on front cover; port. of Billy the Kid on verso back cover.

An exceedingly rare and much-sought-after little book. The author begins his narrative by telling about the killing of Pat Garrett by Wayne Brazil, but he barely touches upon the killing of Billy the Kid. He makes an error in stating that the

Kid went to Pete Maxwell's the evening he was killed to meet his "lady love." There are some typographical errors, such as "rade" for "rode" on page 24, and the author misspells some proper names, such as "O'Fallon" for "O'Folliard." Line 15, page 12, is misplaced; it belongs at line 14, page 24. The author makes the statement that the Kid was twenty-two years old when he was killed and had "killed twenty-seven men—perhaps more."

The book adheres to the usual inaccuracies and legends, and the author says that the Lincoln County War was fought between John Chisum and the small ranchers. John J. Lipsey, a book dealer of Colorado Springs, Colorado, published a facsimile of this book in 1952 from a photostat copy from my personal library.

1952. Schaefer, Jack

Heroes without glory. Some good men of the old west, [by] Jack Schaefer. Boston, Houghton Mifflin co., 1965. Cloth.

xix p., 1 l., 323 p. 22 cm.
Half title; "First edition" on copyright p.

Contains chapters on Thomas Smith and Elfego Baca with a mention of John Wesley Hardin, Wild Bill Hickok, and others. The book would be more useful if the author had included an index.

1953. Schatz, August Herman

Opening a cow country. A history of the pioneer's struggle in conquering the prairie south of the Black Hills, by A. H. Schatz. Ann Arbor, Mich., Edwards brothers, inc., 1939. Stiff wrappers. Scarce.

x, 107 p., 1 l., 109–141 p. front., illus., plates, ports., maps, plan. 21 cm.
Appendix: p. 109–141.
Lithoprinted.

This privately printed and scarce little book devotes a chapter to cattle rustling in the Dakotas.

1954. Schell, Herbert Samuel

South Dakota, its beginning and growth, by Herbert Samuel Schell. New York, American book co. [1942]. Cloth. OP.

x p., 1 l., 359 p. front. (double p. map), plates, ports., maps, charts. 20.5 cm.
Appendix: p. 335–344; index: p. 345–359.
Questions and bibliography at end of each chapter.

1955. Schilling, John H.

Scenic trips to the geologic post No. 5. Silver City, Santa Rita, Hurley, New

Mexico, by John H. Schilling. Socorro, N.M., New Mexico Institute of Mining and Technology, 1959. Pict. wrappers. Scarce.

5 p.l., 4–43 p. front. (col.), illus., plates (1 fold.), maps. 24 cm.

Has some information about Billy the Kid and the death of his mother.

1956. Schlesinger, Arthur Meier

The rise of the city, 1878–1898, by Arthur Meier Schlesinger. . . . New York, the Macmillan co., 1933. Cloth. OP.

xvi p., 1 l., 494 p. illus., plates, map (col.), facsms. 22 cm.
Index: p. 475–494.
Half title; illus. end papers.
[Vol. X in the "History of American Life" series.]

Contains material on such outlaws as Billy the Kid, Frank and Jesse James, Joel Fowler, Jesse Evans, and the Daltons.

1957. Schmedding, Joseph

Cowboy and Indian trader, by Joseph Schmedding. Caldwell, Idaho, the Caxton printers, ltd., 1951. Pict. cloth. OP.

8 p.l., [17]–364 p. front., plates, facsm. 23.5 cm.
Half title; map on end papers; headpieces; pub. device; vignette.

Contains some history of Tombstone, Arizona, and the activities of its gunmen. The author tells about the Earps, the Clantons, and their feud, including the O K Corral fight. He states that the bond filed by Virgil Earp when he was appointed chief of police and given by Wyatt was never accepted by the city but that one given by other men was accepted.

1958. Schmidt, Heine

Ashes of my campfire. Historical anecdotes of old Dodge City as told and retold, by Heine Schmidt. . . . Vol. I [only vol. published]. Dodge City, Kans., Journal, inc., publishers [1952]. Stiff pict. wrappers. OP.

3 p.l., 9–72 p. plates, ports. 19.5 cm.
Double column.

Little stories about people, including gunmen, and events in Dodge City.

1959. Schmitt, Jo Ann

Fighting editors. The story of editors who faced six-shooters with pen and won, [by] Jo Ann Schmitt. San Antonio, Texas, the Naylor co. [1958]. Cloth.

xv, 227 p. illus., facsm. at head of each chap. 22.2 cm.

Bibliography: p. 225–227.
Half title; double illus. t.p. in red and black

Has some material on the Earps and the Clantons, including the O K Corral fight.

1960. Schmitt, Martin F. (ed.)

General George Crook, his autobiography. Edited and annotated by Martin F. Schmitt. Norman, University of Oklahoma press [1960]. Cloth.

xx p., 1 l., 3–326 p. plates, ports., maps. 22 cm.
Appendices: p. 302–309; bibliography: p. 310–317; index: p. 318–326.
Half title; map on end papers.

A reprint of the 1946 edition with some new material. Has some information about I. P. Olive and the lynching of Luther Mitchell and Ami Ketchum.

1961. ———, and Dee Brown

The settler's west, by Martin F. Schmitt and Dee Brown. New York, Charles Scribner's sons, 1955. Pict. cloth. OP.

xxvii p., 1 l., 258 p. plates, ports., maps, facsms. 30.5 cm.
Bibliography: p. 253–258.
Half title; vignette; first edition: letter "A" on copyright p.

Mostly a picture book, but there is some material on such western outlaws as the Apache Kid and information on Rose of Cimarron, Cattle Annie, Little Breeches, Calamity Jane, and others.

1962. Schrantz, Ward L.

Jasper county, Missouri, in the Civil War. Compiled by Ward L. Schrantz. Carthage, Mo., the Carthage press, 1923. Cloth. Scarce.

xxi, [23]–269 p. front. (map), plates. 19.7 cm.
Appendix: p. [243]–250; index: p. [251]–269.
Copyright notice on t.p.

Has some information on Jesse and Frank James, Cole Younger, and Belle Starr.

1963. Schultz, Vernon B.

Southwestern town. The story of Willcox, Arizona, [by] Vernon B. Schultz. Tucson, University of Arizona press, 1964. Pict. cloth.

4 p.l., 140 [3] p. front. (port.), map, plan. 23.5 cm.
Notes: p. 119–133; bibliography: p. 134–139; personal interviews: p. 140; index: p. [141]–143.
Half title; pub. device.

Has much on Burt Alvord, both as an officer and as an outlaw. The author tells a great deal about Bill Downing, his crimes, and his death. He also tells about the killing of Warren Earp by Boyett, whom he calls Johnny Boyd. There is also some information about Billy Stiles.

1964. Scobee, Barry

Fort Davis, Texas, 1583–1960, by Barry Scobee. [El Paso, Texas, published by Barry Scobee, 1960.] Cloth. OP.

xiv, 220 p. front., plates, ports. 23.5 cm.

Sources and comments: p. [203]–213; index: p. [215]–220.

In a chapter entitled "The Turbulent Eighteen-Eighties" the author has material on Jesse Evans, Billy the Kid, Jim Gillett, and John Selman.

1965. ———

Old Fort Davis, by Barry Scobee. San Antonio, Texas, the Naylor co. [1947]. Cloth. OP.

ix p., 1 l., 101 p. plates, ports., map. 20.8 cm.

Has material on Jesse Evans, Billy the Kid, Jim Gillett, and John Selman.

1966. ———

The steer branded murder, by Barry Scobee. The true and authentic account of a frontier tragedy. Documented by eye witnesses, it presents the story of cattlemen, cowboys, and the cattle country of far western Texas. . . . [Houston, Texas, Frontier press of Texas, 1952.] Stiff pict. wrappers. OP.

2 p.l., 5–56 [2] p. front., port. 17 cm.

Index tipped in; vignette.

This book is crudely printed, but its author seems to have made an honest effort to dig up the facts concerning this well-known Texas incident, which has become legendary. There is some information about such Texas gunmen as Jim Miller, Mannen Clements, John Wesley Hardin, and John Selman.

1967. Scott, Col. A. W.

Life experiences of a detective, by Col. A. W. Scott, ex-detective, 1878. [Newton, Mass., 1878.] Pict. wrappers. Rare.

2 p.l., 1 p., [6]–51 p. 20.2 cm.

Contains a sketch of Tiburcio Vásquez.

1968. Scott, George Ryley

Such outlaws as Jesse James, by George Ryley Scott. London, Gerald S. Swann, ltd. [1943]. Cloth. Scarce.

2 p.l., [7]–192 p. front., plates. 19 cm.

Has chapters on the James boys, Henry Plummer, Billy the Kid, John Ringo, Ben Thompson, Wild Bill Hickok, the Renos, Sam Bass, Bill Doolin, Rube Burrow, and John Wesley Hardin. The author repeats the old story about the Rock Creek Station "fight" and the false legends about Billy the Kid and gives Hardin the first name Jack.

1969. Scott, George W.

The Black Hills story, written and published by George W. Scott. [Fort Collins, Colo., 1953.] Stiff wrappers. (Caption title.)

97 p. 18.3 cm.

Contains a section on Wild Bill Hickok and Calamity Jane, and one on horse thieves and robbers.

1970. Scott, Hugh Lenox

Some memories of a soldier, by Hugh Lenox Scott, Major-General U. S. Army, retired. Illustrated. New York, London, the Century co. [1928]. Cloth. Scarce.

xvii p., 1 l., 3–673 p. front. (port.), plates, ports., facsm. 22.8 cm.
Appendix: p. 629–635; index: p. 637–673.
Half title; pub. device.

Has some minor information on such outlaws as the Apache Kid, the Daltons, and the James and Younger brothers and tells about the Northfield robbery.

1971. Scott, Kenneth D.

Belle Starr in velvet, by Kenneth D. Scott, as told by Jeannette S. Scott. Tahlequah, Okla., Pan press [1963]. Cloth.

4 p.l., 255 p. plates, ports., facsms. 22.3 cm.
Half title.
Also published in pict. wrappers.

Jeannette Scott claims that she is the granddaughter of Belle Starr, but she does not seem to know her family tree. She says that Belle and her brother Ed were twins. Ed was eight years older than Belle. The author says that the Clay County Savings Association, of Liberty, Missouri, was robbed the day after the robbery of the banks in Northfield, Minnesota. The Clay County bank robbery took place February 13, 1866, and the Northfield robbery occurred on September 7, 1876, more than ten years later.

The author claims that Belle went to Virginia City, Nevada, to look it over for Jesse James and Scout Younger, a statement that I have never seen before. He also tells a different version of the tale about Blue Duck losing his money at Fort Dodge (Dodge City). He says that the money Blue Duck lost was his own, not Belle's, as others have it. Both tales are wrong. The author claims that Belle named her place Younger's Bend after Scout Younger, whom he says she married. That is another ridiculous statement; Scout Younger does not mention it in his own book. Perhaps the author has Scout confused with Cole Younger (though he never married Belle either). He also has Scout Younger at the Northfield robbery and escaping with the James boys. Younger did not take part in that robbery.

The author has Henry Starr living with Sam and Belle Starr and joining Jesse James to rob banks. Jesse did very little robbing after the Northfield raid, which took place in 1876; and since Henry Starr was born December 2, 1873, he would have been a little young for such strenuous work. Starr was only nine years old when Jesse was murdered. The author has Sam Starr killed in a country schoolyard. Sam was killed in the yard of "Aunt Lucy" Surratt during a country dance. The author has Pearl, Belle's daughter, joining Buffalo Bill's wild West show as a trick rider working under the name Rose of Cimarron. That name was attached to Rose Dunn, of Bill Doolin's day, and I have never seen any record that Pearl was with Buffalo Bill. The author does not mention that she was first a prostitute and later a madam. He is also mistaken in having Belle's son, Ed, joining Henry Starr's gang.

The author has Jesse James in love with Belle and proposing to her, but Jesse loved his wife and family. He says that Jim July's name was Jim Starr, and is apparently unacquainted with the fact that Belle made Jim change his name to Starr after Sam's death. The author is also mistaken in having Henry Starr's favorite occupation holding up trains. He was a bank robber and never attempted to rob a train.

1972. Secrest, William B.

Joaquín, by William B. Secrest. Fresno, Calif., Saga-West publishing co. . . . [1967]. Stiff pict. wrappers.

2 p.l., 5–40 p. plates, ports., map, facsms. 23 cm.

A story of Murieta and his depredations in the gold mines of California.

1973. Seeley, Charles Livingstone

Pioneer days in the Arkansas valley in southern Colorado and history of Bent's fort, by Charles Livingstone Seeley. . . . Denver, Colo., Charles Livingstone Seeley [1932]. Stiff wrappers. Scarce.

3–20 p. front. (port.), illus. 20 cm.

Illus. t.p.

Has a chapter on Jesse James, telling about his murder by Bob Ford.

1974. Segale, Sister Blandina

At the end of the Santa Fé trail, [by] Sister Blandina Segale. [Columbia, Ohio, published by the Columbia press, 1932.] Pict. cloth. Scarce.

5 p.l., [3]–347 p. illus., plates, ports. 20.3 cm.
Copyright notice on verso of "author's note" (2d p).

Republished by Bruce publishing co., Milwaukee, 1948 and 1949.

xi p., 1 l., 298 p. front. (port.), plates, ports. 20.3 cm.
Footnotes: p. 285–290; bibliography: p. 291–294; index: p. 295–298.
Half title.

This book first appeared serially in the *Santa Maria Magazine*, October, 1926, to January, 1931. It contains material on Billy the Kid. The author is confused about information and dates. She was told that the Kid was "attacking every mail coach and private conveyence." She was not afraid of him, she says, because she had met him earlier in Trinidad and had done him a favor for which he had promised never to bother her. She claims to have visited the Kid in jail May 16, 1882, nearly a year after his death, and she records his death as September 8, 1882. She says it was only then that she learned that his true name was William H. Bonney. His death, she says, "ends the career of one who began his downward course at the age of twelve years by taking revenge for the insult that had been offered to his mother." The reprint omits some material that appears in the first printing.

1975. Sell, Henry Blackman, and Victor Weybright

Buffalo Bill and the wild west, by Henry Blackman Sell and Victor-Weybright. New York, Oxford University press, 1955. Pict. boards and cloth. OP.

x p., 1 l., 3–278 p. front. (col.), illus., plates, ports., facsms., plan. 26 cm.
Bibliography: p. 265–269; picture credits: p. 271–273; index: p. 274–278.
Half title; illus. map on end papers; pict. t.p.; double column.

Tells much about the association between Wild Bill Hickok and Buffalo Bill Cody. The authors barely mention the McCanles affair, but do correctly state that only three men were killed. This volume repeats some of the other "lives" of Buffalo Bill word for word—sometimes whole paragraphs. There are many errors, too: the Studebaker plant was not in Fort Wayne but in South Bend; Spotted Tail was not the leader of the Custer massacre; the Sioux were at war from 1876 to 1891; Mlle Morlacchi was not an obscure Italian actress but a very famous dancer. There are other errors.

1976. Senn, Edward L.

"Deadwood Dick" and "Calamity Jane." A thorough sifting of facts from fiction, written and published by Edward L. Senn. Deadwood, S.D., [1939]. Pamphlet. (Cover title.) Scarce.

3–15 p. 18.3 cm.

The author makes an effort to debunk some of the unreliable statements of earlier writers. Some of his dates are wrong.

1977. ———

"Wild Bill" Hickok, "prince of pistoleers." A tale of facts and not fiction and romance, written and published by Edward L. Senn. Deadwood, S.D. [1939]. Pamphlet. (Cover title.) Scarce.

16 p. 18.3 cm.

An abbreviated sketch of Wild Bill, in which the author does much to debunk the fables written about this noted gunman, especially those about the McCanles "fight." The author, a newspaper man, made an honest effort to straighten out some garbled history.

1978. Settle, William A., Jr.

Jesse James was his name; or, fact and fiction concerning the careers of the notorious James brothers of Missouri, by William A. Settle, Jr., Columbia, Mo., University of Missouri press [1966]. Pict. cloth.

6 p.l., 263 p. plates, ports., maps (1 double p.), facsms. 24.2 cm.
Notes: p. 203–231; bibliography: p. 233–251; index: p. 253–263.
Half title; illus. double t.p.

A well-written and well-annotated history of the James boys, one of the few reliable accounts.

1979. Sexton, Maj. Grover F.

The Arizona sheriff, by Maj. Grover F. Sexton, the deputy from Yavapai. Illustrated by Benton H. Clark. [N.p.], published by the Studebaker corp. of America, 1925. Pict. wrappers. (Cover title.) Scarce.

2 p.l., 5–46 p. illus., plates, ports., map. 23 cm.

A historically unimportant little pamphlet.

1980. Shackleford, William Yancey

Belle Starr, the bandit queen. The career of the most colorful outlaw the Indian territory ever knew, by William Yancey Shackleford. Girard, Kans., Haldemann-Julius publications [1943]. Wrappers. OP.

[3]–24 p. 21.5 cm.

The author makes an effort to clear up some points about Belle Starr's life. He compares his information with that of other writers.

1981. ———

Buffalo Bill Cody, scout and showman, [by] William Yancey Shackleford. Girard, Kans., Haldemann-Julius publications [1944]. Wrappers. OP.

1 p.l., [3]–24 p. 21.5 cm.

Tells something about Wild Bill Hickok's life as a showman.

1982. ———

Gun-fighters of the old west, [by] William Yancey Shackleford. Girard, Kans., Haldemann-Julius publications [1943]. Wrappers. OP.

1 l., [3]–24 p. 21.5 cm.

This booklet contains short sketches of some of the best-known outlaws of the West. The author attempts to cover outlaws from the Ohio River pirates of 1800 to the Daltons. He repeats all the false legends about Wild Bill Hickok, his "fight" with ten men at Rock Creek Station, and all the rest. He admits that his account of the Lincoln County War was taken from Emerson Hough's writings, which he says give the first authentic (!) account of this affair. He exposes his ignorance of the West by saying that "John Chisum of Lincoln County fame is the same man who gave his name to the famous cattle trail that the radio cowboys are still caterwauling about." His account is full of errors, and his information about the Jameses, the Youngers, and the Daltons is just as unreliable.

1983. [Shackleton, B. Close]

Handbook of frontier days of southeast Kansas, [by B. Close Shackleton, n.p.], privately printed, 1961. Stiff pict. wrappers.

viii p., 1 l., 141 p. 3 plates. 22.8 cm.

Has some mention of the James and Younger boys and the Benders.

1984. Shaner, Dolph

The story of Joplin, by Dolph Shaner. New York, Stratford House, inc. [1948]. Cloth. Scarce.

xi, 144 p. 14 full p. plates. 21.6 cm.

Contains some material on the James and Younger brothers and tells about their visit to Joplin.

1985. Sharp, Paul F.

Whoop-up country. The Canadian-American west, 1865–1885, by Paul F. Sharp. Minneapolis, University of Minnesota press [1955]. Pict. cloth. OP.

xiii p., 1 l., 3–347 p. plates, ports., maps. 22.5 cm.
Footnotes: p. 319–336; index: p. 337–347.
Half title; vignette.

Contains some information about Henry Plummer and the Montana vigilantes.

1986. Shaw, Luella

True history of some of the pioneers of Colorado, [by] Luella Shaw. Hotchkiss, Colo., published by W. S. Coburn, John Patterson and A. K. Shaw, 1909. Stiff wrappers. Scarce.

vi, [9]–268 [1] p. front. (port.), plates, ports. 19.8 cm.

Has an account of Jim Reynolds and his gang, noted outlaws of Colorado.

1987. Shay, John C.

Twenty years in the backwoods of California, by John C. Shay. Being the actual experiences and observations of a native son of California, covering a period of twenty years in one locality, while engaged in prospecting, gold mining, homesteading, stock raising and the roadside smithy. Boston, the Roxburgh publishing co. [1923]. Cloth. Rare.

4 p.l., [9]–142 p. 20 cm.
Half title.

Chapter VI is devoted to stage robberies.

1988. Shea and Patten

The "Soapy" Smith tragedy, compiled and copyrighted by Shea and Patten. Skagway, Alaska, [Daily Alaskan print], 1907. Pict. wrappers. Three-hole tie. Rare.

[23] p. (no pagination). 13 plates (incl. t.p.). 24 x 15.3 cm.
Text on verso of plates.

This exceedingly rare little book is said to have been written by H. B. LeFevre, of Skagway. It is a condensed history of the reign of terror and outlawry in White Pass and the Skagway country in 1898, the formation of the vigilance committee, Soapy Smith's counter organization of thugs and cutthroats known as the "Law and Order Committee of 303," and the killing of Soapy and the breaking up of his gang.

1989. Sheldon, Addison Erwin

Nebraska old and new. History, stories, folklore, by Addison Erwin Sheldon. . . . Lincoln, Nebr., University publishing co. [1937]. Pict. cloth. OP.

x, 470 p. front. (map), illus., plates, ports., facsms., plan. 20.8 cm.
Index: p. 465–470.
Half title; vignette.

In a chapter entitled "War On the Rustlers" the author tells about the hanging of Kid Wade and the capture of Doc Middleton.

1990. Sheldon, Lionel A.

Message of Gov. Lionel A. Sheldon to the legislature of New Mexico at its session commencing January 2nd, 1882. Santa Fe, N.M., Charles W. Greene, public printer, 1882. Wrappers. (Cover title.) Rare.

20 p. 22 cm.

Discusses crime and appeals for law enforcement.

1991. Shell, Leslie Doyle, and Hazel M. Shell

Forgotten men of Cripple Creek, by Leslie Doyle Shell and Hazel M. Shell. Denver, Colo., Big Mountain press, 1959. Cloth.

6 p.l., 13–160 p. plates, ports., facsm. 22.3 cm.
Acknowledgments: p. 157–160.
Half title; pub. device; map on end papers.

Has a chapter entitled "Outlaws of Florissant."

1992. Sheller, Roscoe

Bandit to lawman, by Roscoe Sheller. Yakima, Wash., Franklin press, inc., 1966. Cloth.

x, 176 p. plates, ports. 22 cm.
Map on end papers.

A fictionalized account of the life of Matt Warner. The author adheres closely to the historical facts, however, and uses real names.

1993. ———

Ben Snipes, northwest cattle king, by Roscoe Sheller. Portland, Oreg., Binsford & Mort, publishers [1957]. Pict. cloth. OP.

4 p.l., 205 p. plates, ports. 22.3 cm.
Appendix: p. 203–205.
"First edition" on copyright p.

Gives an account of the robbing of the Benjamin S. Snipes Bank in Roslyn, Washington, by Matt Warner and the McCarty brothers.

1994. Sheridan, Sol N.

History of Ventura county, California, by Sol N. Sheridan. Chicago, the S. J. Clarke publishing co., 1926. Cloth. Pub. in two volumes. Scarce.

Vol. I, xviii p., 1 l., 21–472 p. plates. 27.2 cm.

Index: p. 461–472.
Vol. II, biographical.

In Chapter XXIII, entitled "The Days of the Bandit," the author deals at length with the life of Vásquez.

1995. Sherlock, Herbert Arment

Black powder snapshots, by Herbert Arment Sherlock. [Huntington, W.Va., Standard publications, inc., 1946.] Pict. boards. In slip case. Scarce.

6 p.l., [7]–[53] p. (no pagination). illus., plates, maps. 35.7 cm.

Has a chapter on the murder of Wild Bill Hickok.

1996. Sherwell, Samuel

Old recollections of an old boy, by Samuel Sherwell, M.D. . . . New York, the Knickerbocker press, 1923. Cloth. Scarce.

ix [1] p., 3–271 p. front. (port. with tissue). 20.8 cm.

Tells about the capture and death of Espinosa, and the hanging of Joseph Slade.

1997. Shields, Robert William

Illustrations for Mule's Crossing, a history of the Reno era; the story of the Reno brothers, the world's first train robbers, America's pioneer wild west gang, and the only criminals ever lynched from the custody of the United States. . . . Franklin, Ind., R. W. Shields, 1944. Stiff wrappers. Exceedingly rare.

1 p.l. 46 plates (incl. ports., facsms.). 27.5 x 21.5 cm.
"Twelve copies . . . printed. . . ."

There is no text in this book, which contains only the plates used in the back of the book *The Reno Gang of Seymour*. These twelve issues were made up as souvenirs for Shields's friends. "Mule's Crossing" was the early name of Seymour, Indiana, from which the Renos operated.

1998. ———

Seymour, Indiana, and the famous story of the Reno gang who terrorized America with the first train robberies in world history . . ., by Robert W. Shields. . . . Indianapolis, Ind., H. Lieber and co., 1939. Stiff wrappers. Scarce.

3 p.l., 44 [1] p. illus., fold. map. 26.8 cm.
Mimeograph dry-stencil process on one side of paper.

One of the few books written about the Renos. It is reliable.

1999. Shinkle, James D.

Fifty years of Roswell history—1867–1917, by James D. Shinkle. . . . Roswell, N.M., Hall-Poorbaugh press, inc. [1964]. Cloth.

x, 294 p. plates, ports. 23.5 cm.

Appendices: p. 277–283; notes: p. 284–294.

Contains material on the Horrells and their war in Lincoln County.

2000. ———

Reminiscences of Roswell pioneers, by James D. Shinkle. . . . Roswell, N.M., Hall-Poorbaugh press, inc. [1966]. Cloth.

ix, 270 p. plates, ports., map. 23.6 cm.

An anthology of recollections written by various old-timers of Roswell. A chapter by Ernest Matthews, the son of Jacob B. (Billy) Matthews, tells about his father's activities as a deputy sheriff when Billy the Kid and his gang killed Sheriff Brady and Deputy Sheriff George Hindman. The writer says that his father shot the Kid in the leg as he was trying to get the sheriff's gun. In another chapter there is much material on the Lincoln County War, John Chisum, Alexander McSween, and others. In a chapter by Mary Hudson Brothers the writer makes the mistake of giving J. W. Bell the first name George. There is some information on the Horrell War of Lincoln County, an account of Bill Cook's capture in New Mexico, material about the killing of Huston Chapman, and some information about Black Jack Christian. In a later chapter there is a statement that the Lincoln County War was fought between John Chisum "and all the other cattle owners combined," a claim that is known to be incorrect.

2001. Shinn, Charles Howard

Graphic description of Pacific coast outlaws. Thrilling exploits of their arch-enemy, Sheriff Harry N. Morse. Some of his desperate hand-to-hand encounters with bandits, by Charles Howard Shinn. . . . [San Francisco, R. R. Patterson, 1887.] Wrappers. (Caption title.) Rare.

[3]–32 p. front. (port.). 17 cm.

Caption title.

A very rare little book dealing with Vásquez, Murieta, and other California outlaws of Spanish descent.

2002. ———

Graphic description of Pacific coast outlaws. Thrilling exploits of their arch-enemy, Sheriff Harry N. Morse (for many years the terror of brigands of California—a man of intrepid courage, wonderful skill, and splendid leadership). Some of his desperate hand-to-hand encounters with bandits, by Charles Shinn from the Bancroft library, University of California, Berkeley. Introduction and notes by J. E. Reynolds, Los Angeles, Westernlore press, 1958. Pict. cloth. OP.

ix p., 11 p., 37–107 p. plates, ports., facsms. 20.8 cm.
Index: p. 103–107.
Half title; illus. end papers.

A reprint of the original edition with added notes and introduction. Though Reynolds says that the original edition was published "sometime between 1890 and 1895," the copy I once owned, which was listed in the first edition of *Six-Guns and Saddle Leather*, carried the date 1887.

2003. ———

Mining camps. A study in American frontier government, by Charles Howard Shinn. New York, Charles Scribner's sons, 1885. Cloth. Scarce.

xi, 316 p. 21.2 cm.
Authorities consulted: p. 299–307; index: p. 309–316.
Half title; 4 l. adv. at end.
Reprinted by Alfred A. Knopf, New York, in 1948.

Although the author mentions Murieta only briefly, he deals at length with the lawlessness of the early California mines.

2004. Shinn, Capt. Jonathan

The memories of Capt. Jonathan Shinn. Greeley, Colo., Weld County Democrat, 1890. Wrappers. Rare.

[3]–88 p. 18.3 cm.

Has much on lawlessness, horse thieves, and vigilantes.

2005. Shipman, Mrs. O. L.

Letters, past and present . . ., by Mrs. O. L. Shipman. [N.p., n.d.] Stiff wrappers. Scarce.

5 p.l., 9–137 p. ports. 22.8 cm.
Index: p. 131–137.

A series of letters to the author's nephews and nieces containing some material on Billy the Kid, Bill Cook, Tom O'Folliard, and Pat Garrett. The author tells about the killing of O'Folliard by Garrett, and says: "On account of his method in killing young O'Folliard and Billy the Kid, Pat Garrett became very unpopular in New Mexico."

2006. ———

Taming the Big Bend. A history of the extreme western portion of Texas from Fort Clark to El Paso, by Mrs. O. L. Shipman. [Marfa, Texas, 1926.] Cloth. Scarce.

viii p., 1 l., [3]–215 p. front. (with tissue), ports., fold. map at end. 23.7 cm.
Index: p. [209]–215.

In a chapter entitled "Law West of the Pecos" the author deals with the Texas Rangers and lawlessness. In another chapter there is mention of the Lincoln County War, Billy the Kid, John Wesley Hardin, John Selman, and other gunmen of the Southwest.

2007. Shippey, Lee

It's an old California custom, [by] Lee Shippey. New York, the Vanguard press, inc. [1948]. Pict. cloth. OP.

6 p.l., 3–392 p. illus. 21.2 cm.
Half title; illus. t.p.; headpieces; untrimmed.

A chapter entitled "To Engage in Banditry" contains information on some of the California outlaws, such as Murieta, Tiburcio Vásquez, Black Bart, Jack Powers, and Rattlesnake Dick. He uses the spelling Murrietta and also spells Vásquez' first name as Tibursio.

2008. Shirley, Glenn

Buckskin and spurs. A gallery of frontier rogues and heroes, by Glenn Shirley. New York, Hastings House, publishers [1958]. Cloth.

xi p., 1 l., 191 p. plates, ports., facsms. 21 cm.
Bibliography: p. 185–191.
Half title.

This book has chapters on Ben Cravens and Henry Starr, with information on other outlaws such as Burt Alvord, Bill Downing, Billy Stiles, and Augustin Chacon.

2009. ———

Heck Thomas, frontier marshal. The story of a real gunfighter, by Glenn Shirley. Philadelphia and New York, Chilton co. [1962]. Cloth.

xii, 231 p. plates, ports., maps. 21 cm.
Half title.

A biography of a famous deputy U.S. marshal containing much information on many of the Oklahoma outlaws.

2010. ———

Henry Starr. Last of the real badmen, by Glenn Shirley. New York, David McKay co., inc. [1965]. Cloth.

xi p., 1 l., 208 p. plates, ports. 21 cm.

Notes: p. 193–199; index: p. 201–208.
Half title.

Perhaps the most complete history of this outlaw to date.

2011. ———

Law west of Fort Smith. A history of frontier justice in the Indian territory, 1834–1896, by Glenn Shirley. Illustrated with photographs. New York, Henry Holt and co. [1957]. Cloth.

xi [1] p., 1 l., 3–333 p. plates, ports., map, facsms. 21.3 cm.
Appendices: p. 209–301; notes: p. 305–321; bibliography: p. 325–333.
Half title; "First edition" on copyright p.

A book about Judge Parker's court, dealing with many Oklahoma outlaws. The book would have been much more valuable if it had been provided with an index.

2012. ———

Outlaw queen. The fantastic true story of Belle Starr—the most notorious gun-girl in the west, [by] Glenn Shirley. Derby, Conn., Monarch books, inc. [1960]. Stiff col. pict. wrappers.

2 p.l., 5–141 [3] p. 18 cm.

A typical newsstand paper-back book. Though in his title the author writes that it is a true story, like so many others he follows some of the legends that have grown up about his character. He is mistaken in having the Jameses and the Youngers first cousins. He claims that they "invented bank robbery," saying that they robbed the Clay County Savings Association at Liberty, Missouri. Historians deny that they were the first bank robbers. He repeats the fable about Belle refusing to identify the body of her husband, Jim Reed, after he was killed by Morris, and is also mistaken in claiming that Blue Duck was a white man. He also repeats the legend about Belle holding up a gambling house in Fort Dodge (!) after Blue Duck had lost some of her money there. Fort Dodge was a military post, and there were no gambling joints on the post. The author is also mistaken in having John Middleton, Belle's lover, the same Middleton who had been with Billy the Kid's gang. They were two different persons. To further fictionize his story, the author depicts some bold love scenes between Belle and her amorous companions.

2013. ———

Pawnee Bill. A biography of Major Gordon W. Lillie, by Glenn Shirley. Albuquerque, N.M., University of New Mexico press, 1958. Cloth.

6 p.l., 13–256 p. illus., plates, ports., facsms. 23.7 cm.
Bibliography: p. 234–247; index: p. 248–256.
Half title; illus. t.p.; "First edition" on copyright p.

Has some material on Henry Brown, Wild Bill Hickok, and some of the Oklahoma marshals. The author states of Buffalo Bill: "In the fall of 1871, he guided the Grand Duke Alexis of Russia . . . ." It was in January, 1872, that Buffalo Bill acted as the duke's guide. There are other minor errors too, but as a whole it is a good book.

2014. ———

Six-gun and silver star, by Glenn Shirley. Albuquerque, N.M., University of New Mexico press, 1955. Pict. cloth.

vii p., 1 l., 235 p. front. (map). 23.4 cm.
Bibliography: p. 217–228; index: p. 229–235.
Half title.

About the Oklahoma outlaws and the marshals who extinguished them.

2015. ———

Toughest of them all . . ., by Glenn Shirley. [Albuquerque, N.M., University of New Mexico press, 1953.] Cloth. OP.

ix, 145 p. 21 cm.
Bibliography: p. [137]–141; index: p. [143]–145.
Half title.

This book adds nothing new to outlaw literature. The author is mistaken in saying that Billy the Kid "had gotten rid of his handcuffs and leg irons" while Olinger was running across the street from the hotel to the courthouse after hearing the shot that killed Bell. It was not that swift and easy. In fact, the Kid did not completely free himself from his leg irons until he reached a friend's house much later. On page 14 the author repeats the erroneous date of Pat Garrett's death given in Coe's *Frontier Fighter*. Of the battle at the McSween home he says: "The Kid ran the gauntlet of blazing guns, drawing the fire, enabling Brown and the others to escape into the night." The Kid was one of the last to leave the burning house, and I have never seen any evidence that Brown was in the McSween home at that time. On page 103, "Border" is spelled "Boarder." There are chapters on Kate Bender, Henry Brown, the Marlows, Cherokee Bill, the Daltons, and others.

2016. ——— **(ed.)**

Buckskin Joe; being the unique and vivid memoirs of Edward Jonathan Hoyt, hunter-trapper, scout, soldier, showman, frontiersman, and friend of the Indians, 1884–1918. Taken from his original manuscript notes and edited by Glenn Shirley. Lincoln, Nebr., University of Nebraska press [1966]. Cloth.

xii p., 1 l., 194 p. plates, ports., facsm. 23.7 cm.

Index: p. 187–194.

Half title.

Has some mention of the Dalton boys, their bank robberies, and their fiasco at Coffeyville and tells about the robbery of a bank by the James boys in the author's home town.

2017. Shockley, Martin

Southwest writers anthology, by Martin Shockley. . . . Austin, Texas, Steck-Vaughn co. [1967]. Stiff wrappers.

xvii p., 1 l., 328 p. 21 cm.

Index: p. 325–328.

Half title.

A collection of writings by Southwest writers, including a chapter on Sam Bass from Walter Prescott Webb's *The Texas Rangers.*

2018. Shoemaker, Floyd C. (ed.)

Missouri, day by day, [by] Floyd C. Shoemaker. [Jefferson City, Mo., Mid-State printing co.], 1942. Cloth. Pub. in two volumes.

Vol. I, v, 446 p. 23.2 cm.

Index: p. 429–446.

Vol. II, 499 p. 23.2 cm.

Biographical abbreviations: p. 473–475; index: p. 477–499.

Republished in 1943.

Volume I has material on the Jameses and Youngers, Bob Ford, Clell Miller, Belle Starr, and others. Volume II has a sketch of Bob Dalton, some material on Charley Bryant, Emmett Dalton, Hildebrand, and the bank robbers at Gallatin. Both volumes have accounts of Jesse James's murder.

2019. Shumard, George (pub.)

The ballad and history of Billy the Kid. Facts and legends. [Clovis, N.M., Tab publications, 1966.] Pict. wrappers. (Cover title.)

31 p. illus., plates, ports., maps. 27 cm.

I am glad the unknown author of this book used the word "legends" in his title, because he repeats many of those created by Ash Upson, especially about the Kid's early years. He gives Buckshot Roberts the first name Buck, and he claims that Sheriff Brady and Deputy Hindman were putting up "wanted" posters when they were killed. They were going to the courthouse to post a notice of the postponement of court. He also says that the Kid was wounded in the shoulder at this time. He repeats the legend that the Kid was playing cards with Bell at the time he killed the latter. His whole account seems to follow Garrett's book closely. He has the Kid killed on July 18 instead of the fourteenth. He corrects the date later. He says that Garrett was killed by an unknown assassin, but most historians claim that he was killed by Jim Miller. The author also continues the legend about the Kid having killed twenty-one men by the time he was twenty-one years old.

2020. Siddons, Leonora

The female warrior. An interesting narrative of the sufferings, and singular & surprising adventures of Miss Leonora Siddons. . . . Full and interesting particulars, written by herself. New York, printed for and published by E. E. Barclay, 1843. Wrappers. Exceedingly rare.

[5]–21 p. front. 22.2 cm.

Reprinted in New York, 1844, and in 1847 with same collation.

Miss Siddons could in no sense be classed as an outlaw or gunman, but I believe that her little book should be included in this work because she was a unique character and her book is a rare collector's item. She joined the Texas army under General Sam Houston, and during the Battle of San Jacinto she was shot and left for dead. Recovering the next morning, she was captured by the Mexicans. After an attempted escape, she was recaptured and taken to Vera Cruz. From there she was made to walk barefooted over the burning sands to Mexico City, where she was imprisoned. She escaped and returned to her friends in 1843.

2021. Simmons, Frank E.

History of Coryell county, by Frank E. Simmons. [N.p.], published by Coryell County News, 1935. Stiff wrappers. OP.

4 p.l., 102 p. 20 cm.

A chapter entitled "Era of Lawlessness" gives some information about the outlaws of this Texas county.

2022. Simmons, Lee

Assignment Huntsville. Memoirs of a Texas prison official, [by] Lee Simmons. Austin, University of Texas press [1957]. Cloth. Scarce.

xvi p., 1 l., 3–233 p. front., plates, ports. 23.5 cm.

Index: p. 227–233.

Half title; pub. device.

Has material on Milt Good, Matt Kimes, Tom Ross, and many more modern outlaws. The author, my personal friend, died soon after this book was published.

2023. Simpson, C. H.

Life in the far west; or, a detective's thrilling adventures among the Indians and outlaws of Montana, by C. H. Simpson. Chicago, Rhodes & McClure publishing co., 1893. Cloth. Scarce.

4 p.l., 9–264 [4] p. illus., plates. 20 cm.
Republished in 1896.

2024. Simpson, S. R.

Llano estacado; or, the plains of west Texas, by S. R. Simpson. San Antonio, Texas, the Naylor co. . . . [1957]. Cloth.

6 p.l., 41 p. plates, ports. 21.7 cm.
Index: p. 39–41.
Half title.

Mentions Sam Bass, Calamity Jane, Wild Bill Hickok, the James and Younger boys, the Ketchums, and Ben Kilpatrick.

2025. Sims, Judge Orland L.

Gun-toters I have known, with an introduction by Joe B. Frantz. Austin, the Encino press, 1967. Two-tone cloth. OP.

ix p., 1 l., 3–57 p. plates, ports. 25.5 cm.
Half title; illus. t.p.; colophon: "The Encino Press has produced *con mucho* 750 copies of this book according to the design by William D. Wittliff. This is copy number ——."

Has material on Wild Bill Hickok, Captain Bill McDonald, Wyatt Earp, and Clay Allison. The author tells about Ben Kilpatrick, Black Jack Ketchum and the Wild Bunch, Will Carver, Harvey Logan, Harry Longabaugh, and Butch Cassidy.

2026. Siringo, Charles A.

A cowboy detective. A true story of twenty-two years with a world-famous detective agency; giving the inside facts of the bloody Coeur d'Alene labor riots, and the many ups and downs of the author throughout the United States, Alaska, British Columbia and Old Mexico. Also exciting scenes among the moonshiners of Kentucky and Virginia, by Chas. A. Siringo. . . . Chicago, W. B. Conkey co., 1912. Pict. cloth. Scarce.

6 p.l., 11–519 p. front. (port.), plates (2 double p.), ports. 19.7 cm.
Published the same year in wrappers by J. S. Ogilvie.
Republished in Santa Fe in 1914 with wrappers and without publisher's imprint.

The author uses the name Dickenson for Pinkerton. When he autographed this book for me a few years before his death, he took his pen, and at the chapter heading of Chapter I, scratched out Dickenson and wrote Pinkerton. He also wrote Tom Horn beneath the picture of this character, which was labeled Tim Corn. His original title was *Pinkerton's Cowboy Detective*, but the agency held up publication of the book through superior court action until he changed the title to *Cowboy Detective*, changed the name Pinkerton, and substituted other fictitious names.

This book has had an interesting history. When Siringo signed a contract with the Pinkerton Agency, he agreed to never disclose any information secured by him other than to the agency itself. When he left the agency and wrote a book about his experiences, it was widely advertised before publication with large and bright posters at various railway-station stands. A member of the agency saw one of these posters and tried to purchase the book but was told it had not yet been published. He made his report to the agency and they succeeded in securing the galley sheets. Both Siringo and his publisher, W. B. Conkey, were served with injunctions. Siringo had settled in Santa Fe, New Mexico, by this time and was served there.

The injunctions halted publication of the book, but the author subsequently agreed to eliminate some of his experiences and to change many names of the Pinkerton personnel and their clients. When the book appeared, the Pinkertons again found names and references to confidential information which they would not allow to be published and obtained another injunction for the book's suppression. It was issued in 1914 without the publisher's imprint.

2027. ———

Further adventures of a cowboy detective. A true story of twenty-two years with a world-famous detective agency. Giving the inside facts of the bloody Coeur d'Alene labor riots, and the many ups and downs of the author throughout the United States, Alaska, British Columbia and Old Mexico . . ., by Charles A. Siringo. New York, J. S. Ogilvie publishing co. [1912]. Col. pict. wrappers. Rare.

3 p.l., [247]–519 p. 17.4 cm.
3 p. adv. at end.

When Ogilvie published *A Cowboy Detective* (see Item 2026), the publisher retained the title and issued the work in two volumes, this being the second. The two books were paper-bound, being numbered 127 and 128 in the Railroad Series. Both these paper-bound books are exceedingly scarce today though at one time every newsboy carried a plentiful supply.

2028. ———

History of "Billy the Kid." The true life of the most daring young outlaw of the age. He was the leading spirit in the bloody Lincoln county, New Mexico, War . . ., by Chas. A. Siringo. . . . [Santa Fe, N.M., the author, 1920.] Stiff pict. wrappers. Rare.

2 p.l., [5]–142 [1] p. 18 cm.
1 p. adv. at end.

Republished in facsimile, with an introduction by Charles D. Peavy, by Steck-Vaughn, Austin, Texas, 1967.

This rare little book further strengthened some of the legends about the Kid which by the time were so well established. The author repeats the many legends about the Kid's early life that were created by Ash Upson and follows the Garrett book very closely, even to the misspelled proper names. The book is full of errors, as have been pointed out in my *Burs Under the Saddle* (Item 7).

2029. ———

The lone star cowboy, being fifty years' experience in the saddle as cowboy, detective and New Mexico ranger, on every cow trail in the woolly old west. Also the doings of some "bad" cowboys, such as "Billy the Kid," Wes Harding [*sic*], and "Kid Curry," by Chas. A. Siringo. . . . Santa Fe, N.M., 1919. Pict. cloth. Scarce.

4 p.l., 291 [1] p. front., plates, ports., facsm. 20.5 cm.

Contains many of the stories related in the author's earlier books. The author states in his preface: "This volume is to take the place of *A Texas Cowboy*" (see Item 2032).

2030. ———

Riata and spurs. The story of a lifetime spent in the saddle as cowboy and detective, by Charles A. Siringo, with an introduction by Gifford Pinchot, and with illustrations. Boston and New York, Houghton Mifflin co., 1927. Pict. cloth. Very scarce.

xiv p., 1 l., 276 p. front., plates, ports., facsm. 21.2 cm.

Vignette; first edition: 1927 under imprint.

"Certain parts of the book are reprinted, in revised form, from the author's privately printed narrative called the *Lone Star Cowboy* and *Cowboy Detective*." —p. *x*.

The first half of this book was taken from the author's *A Cowboy Detective* (see Item 2026), with real names in place of fictional ones. Siringo was a persistent soul and seemed determined to use the enjoined material in all his books; but when the publisher's attention was called to this objectionable material, the books were recalled and a corrected and revised edition was released. Pages 120 to 268 were suppressed in the new edition, and all references to the author's experiences with the Pinkerton Agency were cut out and material on bad men substituted. Only a few copies of the original printing survived; hence its scarcity. Siringo helped perpetuate some of the false legends about Billy the Kid. He says that the Kid killed Carlyle, and he has the sheriff's posse taking him and his gang to Fort Sumner after their capture at Stinking Springs. He says that Ash Upson told him the history of the Kid's birth and early years, just as Upson wrote about them in Garrett's book. Like so many others, he has the Kid dancing a jig on the upstairs porch after killing Bell and Olinger, but I think that even the Kid would have found it difficult to dance a jig wearing leg irons.

In speaking of the killing of Sam Bass at Round Rock, Texas, he says that Sam was killed by "Detective George Harold . . . although a Mr. Ware got the credit for it." He says that Dad Jackson and Underwood escaped, but he is mistaken in referring to Jackson as Dad, and Underwood had left the gang before the Round Rock incident.

2031. ———

Riata and spurs. The story of a lifetime spent in the saddle as cowboy and ranger, by Charles A. Siringo, with an introduction by Gifford Pinchot, and with illustrations. Revised edition. Boston and New York, Houghton Mifflin co. [1927]. Pict. cloth. OP.

xiv p., 1 l., 261 p. front., plates, ports., facsm. 21.2 cm.

Half title; vignette.

"Letters from Gifford Pinchot and Emerson Hough to the author" (1 l. inserted between p. 260 and 261).

In this revised edition, issued after the recalling of the first printing, the entire last half of the book is changed, but without explanation. The author substituted material on bad men that he had intended for another book. The word "ranger" was substituted for "detective" in the second printing.

In this volume the author deals with many gunmen. He tells some of the legends about King Fisher. He is mistaken in saying that Ben Thompson "was a vicious cowboy bad man." Thompson had nothing to do with cattle at any time. He repeats the Billy the Kid material he used in the original edition and again makes many mistakes about Bass and his gang, as well as about Wild Bill Hickok.

2032. ———

A Texas cowboy; or, fifteen years on the hurricane deck of a Spanish pony. Taken from real life, by Chas. A. Siringo, an old stove-up "cowpuncher," who has spent nearly twenty years on the great western cattle ranges. Chicago, Ill., M. Umbdenstock & co., publishers, 1885. Pict. cloth. Exceedingly rare.

2 p.l., [ix]–xii, [13]–316 p. double p. front. (col.), illus., ports. 20 cm.

Added t.p. illus. in color; dec. end papers.

Republished in 1886 under the imprint of Siringo and Dobson, with the same title page and with an addendum (pages 317 to 347), an index to the addendum, and a dedication. The second frontispiece of the first edition was used as the only frontispiece of the second printing. This frontispiece was later used as the cover for the paper-backed newsstand editions.

This book was reprinted many times between 1914 and 1926 by various publishers, such as the Eagle Publishing Company; Rand, McNally and Company; and finally in a cheap pulp edition by J. S. Ogilvie. It was one of the first books written about the cowboy and perhaps received wider circulation than any other of its time. Yet it is now hard to find a copy, and it is nearly impossible to find a copy of the first edition.

Again republished in 1950:

A Texas cowboy; or, fifteen years on the hurricane deck of a Spanish pony—taken from real life, by Charles A. Siringo. With bibliographical study and introduction by J. Frank Dobie and drawings by Tom Lea. Typography by Carl Hertzog. New York, William Sloane Associates [1950]. Cloth. OP.

xl p., 3 l., 7–198 p. illus., facsm. 22 cm.
Half title; illus. double t.p.; headpieces; first edition: pub. device with "WSA" on copyright p.

2033. ———

Two evil isms, Pinkertonism and anarchism, by a cowboy detective who knows, as he spent twenty-two years in the inner circle of Pinkerton's National Detective Agency, by Charles A. Siringo. . . . Chicago, Ill., Charles Siringo, publisher, 1915. Stiff pict. wrappers. Exceedingly rare.

2 p.l., 109 [1] p. front., illus. 19.7 cm.
Device; table of contents verso of t.p.
Republished in facsimile by Steck-Vaughn, Austin, Texas, 1967.

The first edition was out of print by the time it came off the press. From the time Siringo severed connections with the Pinkertons and started writing, he seemed determined to reveal what he knew of them, and they were just as determined to suppress his efforts. This book apparently originated in the mind of a Matthew Pinkerton, no relation to the detective Pinkertons. Somehow he got possession of the original plates of *A Cowboy Detective* (see Item 2026), cut out a great part of it, added some material, and had it published under the above title. He had it printed by one company, bound by a second, and distributed by a third. Thus it was hard to trace, but the Pinkerton Agency soon obtained an injunction and had the court seize all copies on hand and destroy them. A small lot had been shipped west and escaped, thus making the book exceedingly rare. I had the good fortune to own one of these copies.

2034. Skelton, Charles L.

Riding west on the pony express, [by] Charles L. Skelton. Illustrated by Paul Quinn. New York, the Macmillan co., 1937. Cloth. OP.

5 p.l., 196 p. front., illus. 21 cm.

Author's note: "Riding West has some factual matter never before published, including a correct description of J. A. Slade, the most colorful individual connected with the pony express."

2035. Skinner, Emory Fiske

Reminiscences, by Emory Fiske Skinner. Chicago, Vestal printing co., 1908. Cloth. Scarce.

xi, 358 p. front. (port.). 21.8 cm.

Has some information about the road agents around Virginia City, Montana, in the 1860's.

2036. Sloan, Richard E.

Memories of an Arizona judge, by Richard E. Sloan. . . . Stanford University, Calif., Stanford University press; London, Humphrey Milford, Oxford University press, 1932. Cloth. Scarce.

xii, 250 p. 20 cm.

Index: p. 247–250.

Half title.

Contains accounts of stage robberies, the Earp-Clanton feud, and the Graham-Tewksbury (spelled Tukesbury) feud.

2037. ———

History of Arizona. Hon. Richard E. Sloan, supervising editor, Ward R. Adams, author, assisted by an advisory council. Issued in four volumes, profusely illustrated. Arizona biography by special staff of writers. Phoenix, Record publishing co., publishers, 1930. Full leather. Scarce.

Vol. I, 8 p.l., 21–525 p. front. (port.), plates, ports., maps, plan. 27.5 cm.

Vol. II, 2 p.l., 7–530 p. front., plates, map, plan. 27.5 cm.

Device; gilt tops.

Vols. III and IV, biographical.

Volumes I and II have good history on the cattle wars and of the many outlaws of Arizona.

2038. Sloter, Jim

Eloy, [by Jim Sloter, Eloy, Ariz., n.d.]. Pict. cloth. (Cover title.) Scarce.

[3]–64 p. front. (port.), plates, ports. 23.5 cm.

The story of Eloy, Arizona, and the many killings there.

2039. Small, Floyd B.

Autobiography of a pioneer, by Floyd B. Small; being an account of the personal experiences of the author from 1867 to 1916. . . . Seattle, Wash., F. B. Small, 1916. Stiff pict. wrappers. Scarce.

2 p.l., 7–106 p. illus. 23.4 cm.

"Do not read paragraphs marked in red until you come to those marked in blue. This was a transposition made by the printer and will be corrected in the next edition. . . ."—The author.

The author claims to have been a close neighbor of Wild Bill Hickok's sister; yet he spells the name Hecock. He errs in saying that Wild Bill was killed in August, 1877, and makes a bigger mistake when he says that Jack McCall was hanged in Virginia City, Montana. He is wrong, too, in saying that Wild Bill spent the last ten years of his life in the employ of the United States government as a scout. He also gives an account of his meeting with the James boys.

2040. Small, Joe Austell (ed.)

The best of true west, edited by Joe Austell Small. New York, Julian Messner, inc. [1964]. Pict. cloth.

7 p.l., 15–317 p. illus. headpieces. 24 cm.

Half title; "First edition" on copyright p.

A collection of stories taken from the first five years of *True West Magazine.* It contains several chapters on gunmen, including one on the death of Old Man Clanton; one on the Johnson County War and the killing of Nate Champion and Nick Ray; one on the hideouts of the Oklahoma outlaws; one on the capture of Augustin Chacon, written by Cap Mossman; and one on Clay Allison, written by Norman B. Wiltsey. The chapter on Allison is full of errors, for example, the author's description of the manner in which Allison became a cripple, the false legend about his meeting Wyatt Earp in Dodge, and the often-repeated tale about his pulling the dentist's teeth. His account of Clay's killing of Chunk Colbert and Clay's own death are entirely wrong.

2041. Small, Kathleen Edwards, and J. Larry Smith

History of Tulare county, California, by Kathleen Edwards Small, and Kings county, California, by J. Larry Smith. Illustrated. Chicago, the S. J. Clarke publishing co., 1926. Cloth. Pub. in two volumes. Scarce.

Vol. I, 6 p.l., 15–637 p. front. (port.), plates, map. 27.4 cm.

Index: p. 627–637.

Vol. II, biographical.

Contains a long chapter on train robbery and the activities of Grat and Bill Dalton in California and of the Evans-Sontag gang. The King County section has some material on Murieta and Vásquez.

2042. Smith, Alson Jesse

Brother Van, a biography of the Rev. William Wesley Van Orsdel, by Alson Jesse Smith. New York, Nashville, Abingdon-Cokesbury press [MCMXLVIII]. Cloth. Scarce.

6 p.l., 13–240 p. front. (port.), illus., plates, ports. 20.3 cm.
Index: p. 237–240.
Decorative half title; map on end papers; illus. t.p.

A biography with some scattered material on Henry Plummer and his gang, Joseph Slade, and the vigilantes.

2043. Smith, Benjamin

A fugitive from hell, by Benjamin Smith (Frank Davis). Fifteen years an outlaw. [Joplin, Mo., 1935.] Cloth. Scarce.

4 p.l., 9–122 [1] p. front. (port.), plate at end. 19.6 cm.

Another of those little books, often hard to come by, of reminiscences written by former outlaws and convicts.

2044. Smith, C. Alphonso

O. Henry biography, by C. Alphonso Smith. . . . Illustrated. Garden City, New York, Doubleday, Page & co., 1916. Cloth. Scarce.

v p., 3 l., 3–258 p. front. (port.), plates, ports., facsm. 24 cm.
Index: p. 253–258.
Half title; pub. device; untrimmed.

Contains some information about Al Jennings, who was associated with O. Henry during his prison days.

2045. Smith, Charles A.

A comprehensive history of Minnehaha county, South Dakota. Its background, her pioneers, their record of achievement and development, by Charles A. Smith. Mitchell, S.D., Educator supply co., 1949. Fabrikoid. OP.

xviii [3] p., 504 p. front., plates, ports. 25.6 cm.

Contains an account of the James boys when they were making their escape after the bank robbery at Northfield.

2046. Smith, D. B.

Two years in the slave-pen of Iowa, by the author, D. B. Smith. Kansas City, Mo., H. N. Farey & co., printers and binders, 1885. Cloth. Rare.

ix, [5]–205 p. 17.7 cm.

Has some information on the robbery of the state treasury at Lincoln, Nebraska, and on Polk Wells and other outlaws.

2047. Smith, Edward H.

You can escape, by Edward H. Smith. . . . With a preface by Edward Hale Bierstadt. New York, the Macmillan co., 1929. Cloth. OP.

xiv p., 1 l., 264 p. 19.8 cm.
Bibliography: p. 263–264.
Half title; untrimmed.

Has a chapter devoted to Harvey Logan and the Wild Bunch. The author tells about Logan's killing of Pike Landusky and about his many escapes from prison. He tells nothing about the incidents leading up to the killing of Pike, however, and the details of the killing itself are wrong. In writing of the Wild Bunch, he is also wrong in stating that "this chief of banditti was Black Jack Ketcham [*sic*]." He says that Harvey Logan "succeeded to leadership because Black Jack was hanged."

2048. Smith, Helena Huntington

The war on Powder river, [by] Helena Huntington Smith. New York, London, Toronto, McGraw-Hill book co. [1966]. Cloth.

xiii p., 320 [1] p. front. (map), plates, ports. 23.5 cm.
Notes: p. 287–306; bibliography: p. 307–311; index: p. 313–320.
Half title; "First edition" on copyright p.
Reprinted by University of Nebraska press, Lincoln, in wrappers in 1967.

Undoubtedly the best and most nearly complete history of the Johnson County War thus far. The work shows a great deal of scholarly research.

2049. Smith, Stephe R.

A journalist's account of the outlaw Rande. His remarkable career and pending trial . . ., (by Stephe R. Smith). [Burlington, Iowa, Hawkeye printing co., 1878.] Pict. wrappers. Rare.

42 p. 22.5 cm.

2050. Smith, T. Marshall

Legends of the war of independence and of the earlier settlements in the west, by T. Marshall Smith. Louisville, Ky., J. F. Brenan, publisher, 1855. Dec. cloth. Rare.

xvi, [17]–397 p. 22 cm.

Contains several chapters on the Harpes.

2051. Smith, Tevis Clyde, Jr.

From the memories of men, by T. C. Smith, Jr. . . . Brownwood, Texas, published by T. C. Smith, Jr. [1954]. Wrappers. OP.

3 p.l., [7]–66 p. 22.7 cm.
1 p. adv. in front; business cards scattered throughout.

Has some information on the James boys, John Wesley Hardin, and some lesser-known outlaws.

2052. ———

Frontier's generation. The pioneer history of Brown county, with side-lights on the surrounding territory, by Tevis Clyde Smith, Jr. Brownwood, Texas, published by the author [1931]. Stiff wrappers. OP.

4 p.l., [5]–63 p. front., plates, ports. 22.2 cm.
Advertisements scattered throughout.

One section tells about John Wesley Hardin, some of his killings, and his capture, trial, and death.

2053. Smith, Waddell F. (ed.)

The story of the pony express. Edited by Waddell F. Smith. San Francisco, Hesperian House [1960]. Pict. cloth.

xii p., 13–195 p. illus., plates (4 col.), ports., facsms. 24 cm.
Bibliography: p. 185; index: p. 187–195.
Half title; illus. double t.p.; map on end papers.

The editor has Doc Brink (whom he calls Dock) an express rider and says that he made a good record but that his chief fame was gained in a fight at Rock Creek Station, in which he and another " 'cleaned out' the McCandless [*sic*] gang of outlaws." Then he tells us that Doc's associate was Wild Bill. Heretofore Wild Bill has received all the credit for this deed. In a footnote he adds that "as marshal of Abilene, Kansas, and other wild frontier towns [Hickok] became a terror to bad men and compelled them to respect the law and order when under his jurisdiction." There is also some mention of Joseph Slade.

2054. Smith, Wallace

Garden of the sun, by Wallace Smith. A history of San Joaquin valley, 1772–1939. Los Angeles, Calif., Lymanhouse [1939]. Cloth. Scarce.

v, 558 [i]–iii p. plates, maps, plan. 23.4 cm.
Appendix: p. 541–558; index: p. [i]–iii (at end).
Half title.

Has much material on Joaquín Murieta, Tiburcio Vásquez, the Dalton brothers, and Evans and Sontag, the train robbers. The author makes the mistake of stating that the first published account of Murieta appeared in the *California Police Gazette* of September 3, 1859. This did perhaps become the best-known account because of the scarcity of the first issue of Ridge's book, published in 1854.

2055. ———

Prodigal sons. The adventures of Christopher Evans and John Sontag, by Wallace Smith. Boston, the Christopher publishing house [1951]. Cloth. Scarce.

7 p.l., 15–434 p. front. (port.), plates, ports. 22.3 cm.
Appendix: p. 416–434.
Half title; pub. device.

The most extensive book on Evans and Sontag to date, and also the most authentic. The author tells more of Evans' childhood and family life than is revealed in any other book I have examined. He has done a scholarly work, and his book can be considered reliable. The word "fact" is repeated consecutively on lines 17 and 18 of page 37, a typographical error which may be an identifying characteristic of the first printing.

2056. Smith, Wallace

Oregon sketches, by Wallace Smith. New York, and London, G. P. Putnam's sons, 1925. Cloth. Scarce.

xii p., 1 l., 3–247 p. front. (with tissue), illus. 22 cm.
Illus. end papers.

This has a chapter on Captain Jack, the Modoc outlaw. This author is not the same Wallace Smith as the author of Items 2054 and 2055.

2057. Smith, William Fielding

Diamond six, by William Fielding Smith. Edited by Garland Roark. Garden City, N.Y., Doubleday & co., 1958. Pict. cloth. OP.

4 p.l., 9–383 p. 21.7 cm.
Half title; map on end papers; cattle brands on t.p.; "First edition" on copyright p.

Has some material on John Wesley Hardin.

2058. Smythe, William E.

The conquest of arid America. . . . Illustrated. By William E. Smythe. . . . New York, the Macmillan co.; London, Macmillan & co., ltd., 1905. Cloth. Scarce.

xxv [1] p., 2 l., 3–360 p. front. (port. with tissue), plates, ports., map. 21 cm.
Appendices: p. 333–349; index: p. 351–360.
Half title; untrimmed.

Contains some information about the Johnson County War.

2059. Snell, Joseph W.

Painted ladies of the cowtown frontier, by Joseph W. Snell. Kansas City, Kansas City Posse of Westerners, 1965. Cloth.

3 p.l., 3–24 p. front., illus. 23.5 cm.

Colophon: "Book Number —— (Signed). Limited to two hundred and fifty autographed copies."

Footnotes: p. 23–24.

Half title; illus. t.p.

Tells about the killing of Ed Masterson, and has a mention of such gunmen as Bat Masterson, Wild Bill Hickok, Ben and Bill Thompson, and Rowdy Joe Lowe. It is strange that the author does not mention Wyatt Earp, though Earp's common-law wife was one of the painted ladies. I think the author is wrong in listing Rose of Cimarron as one of the cowtown prostitutes. This little book originally appeared in wrappers as Vol. X, No. 4, of *The Trail Guide*, the Kansas City Westerners' quarterly publication.

2060. [Soito, Patricia]

A hundred years of Pleasanton. "The most desperate town of the West. . . ." Sketches by Raymond Safreno. Photos by Bene Jesse and others. San Francisco, printed by Philips & Van Orden co. Cuts by Poor Richard photo engraving co. . . ., 1949. Stiff pict. wrappers. OP.

1 p.l., 3–30 [2] p. illus., plates, ports., map. 27.8 cm.

Double column.

Published as a souvenir of the Pleasanton Centennial, this little book gives some information on the death of Narcisco Borjorques, repeats many of the fables about Murieta and has some information about Vásquez.

2061. Sollis, Roberta Beed

Calamity Jane. A study in historical criticism, by Roberta Beed Sollis. . . . [Helena, Mont.], published by the Western press, Historical Society of Montana. Correlated and edited by Vivian A. Paladin. Indexed by John Hakola . . ., 1958. Cloth.

xiv, 147 p. plates, ports., facsms. 23.6 cm.

Bibliography: p. 131–137; picture notes: p. 139–141; index: p. 143–147.

Vignette.

Colophon: "This is No. —— of 2,000 numbered copies."

This book corrects a lot of false history that has been written about Calamity Jane and has some information about Wild Bill Hickok and his murderer, Jack McCall.

2062. Sonney, Louis S.

The American outlaw. Issued by officer L. S. Sonney, of Sonney's Historical Museum. . . . [N.p., n.d., ca. 1931.] Pict. wrappers (Cover title.) Scarce.

28 [1] p. 23 cm.

Has some information about Alferd Packer, Harry Tracy, Dave Merrill, Black Bart, Jesse James, Roy Gardner, and others.

2063. ———

Life history of Roy Gardner, the smiling bandit. A strangely interesting and true story, by Louis S. Sonney. [N.p., n.d.] Pict. wrappers. Scarce.

32 p. 19.5 cm.

2064. Sonnichsen, Charles Leland

Alias Billy the Kid. ". . . I wanted to die a free man. . . ." By C. L. Sonnichsen [and] William V. Morrison. Albuquerque, N.M., University of New Mexico press, 1955. Cloth. OP.

xi p., 1 l., 136 p. plates, ports. 23.5 cm.
Appendices: 91–131; index: p. 133–136.
Half title.

An attempt to prove that Billy the Kid lived until 1955 under the alias Brushy Bill Roberts. "Roberts" tells a very plausible story, but anyone who had read the many accounts of the Kid's life could have done as well—or better, for a better impersonator might not have made the statement that there was a "gunfight" at Maxwell's the night the Kid was killed. "Roberts" seems to forget that there were other witnesses to the events of that night in the persons of John Poe, Kip McKinney, Pat Garrett, Pete Maxwell, and others.

2065. ———

Billy King's Tombstone. The private life of an Arizona boom town, by C. L. Sonnichsen. Illustrated. Caldwell, Idaho, the Caxton printers, ltd., 1942. Pict. cloth. Scarce.

7 p.l., [15]–233 p. front., plates, ports. 23.5 cm.
Half title; plan on end papers; pub. device.

A different picture of Tombstone from that given in other books on the subject. A story of a bartender who knew every character in this wild town, it throws some new light upon such characters as Buckskin Frank Leslie, Burt Alvord, and Sheriff John Slaughter.

2066. ———

Cowboys and cattle kings. Life on the range today, by C. L. Sonnichsen. Norman, University of Oklahoma press [1950]. Cloth. OP.

xviii p., 2 l., 5–316 p. plates, ports. 23.5 cm.
Bibliography ("Not from Books"): p. 296–304; index: p. 305–316.
Half title; illus. t.p.

Has some information about Cattle Kate Watson and Belle Starr.

2067. ———

I'll die before I'll run. The story of the great feuds of Texas, by C. L. Sonnichsen. New York, Harper & brothers, publishers [1951]. Cloth. OP.

xviii p., 1 l., 3–294 p. plates, ports. 21.8 cm.
Sources and notes: p. 267–294.
Half title; illus. map on end papers; pub. device; "First edition" on copyright p.

A book that shows serious research. It does not cover all the Texas feuds, but feuds are difficult to write about since descendants of the participants may still be living. In his "Sources and Notes" (page 285) the author states that "the only appearance in print of the Marlow feud is in a story by William McLeod [*sic*] Raine." The Marlows themselves wrote a book about this feud in 1892 (see Item 1444). The author has since told me that he corrected this error. The book would be more useful if it were provided with an index.

2068. ———

Outlaw. Bill Mitchell alias Baldy Russell. His life and times, [by] C. L. Sonnichsen. Denver, Colo., Sage books [1965]. Cloth.

6 p.l., 11–197 p. plates, ports. 22.2 cm.
Acknowledgments: p. 172–175; notes: p. 176–188; bibliography: p. 189–193; index: p. 194–197.
Half title; map on end papers.

The life story of this little-known man who became an outlaw because of a family feud with a neighbor whom his father had befriended and caused the father to be unjustly hanged.

2069. ———

Ten Texas feuds, by C. L. Sonnichsen. Albuquerque, N. M., University of New Mexico press, 1957. Pict. cloth.

5 p.l., 3–248 p. 23.7 cm.
Notes and bibliography: p. 217–243; index: p. 244–248.
Half title.

Has a good chapter on Jim Miller. Like many other historians of the Southwest, the author holds to the theory that Jim Miller fired the shot that killed Pat Garrett. There is also information on Scott Cooley, John Wesley Hardin, and John Selman.

2070. ———

Tularosa. Last of the frontier west, [by] C. L. Sonnichsen. New York, the Devin-Adair co., 1960. Pict. cloth.

6 p.l., 3–336 p. plates, ports. 21 cm.
Sources: p. 293–299; notes: p. 300–324; index: p. 327–336.
Half title; map on front fly leaf.

This excellent book gives some new history on the life and feuds of the Tularosa country of New Mexico, with material on Billy the Kid, Pat Garrett, the murder of Albert J. Fountain, the feud between Garrett and Oliver Lee, and other information.

2071. Sorenson, Alfred R.

Early history of Omaha; or, walks and talks among the old settlers. A series of short sketches in the shape of a connected narrative of the events and incidents of early times in Omaha . . ., by Alfred Sorenson. Illustrated with numerous engravings, many of them being from original sketches drawn especially for this work by Charles S. Huntington. Omaha, Nebr., printed at the office of the Daily Bee, 1876. Cloth. Scarce.

6 p.l., [9]–248 p. illus., plates, ports. 22.5 cm.
Chapter decorations; pages 229 through 248 advertisements.
Republished in 1889 with additions in an edition of 342 pages.

Has a chapter on horse thieves and vigilantes.

2072. ———

"Hands up!" or, the history of a crime. The great Union Pacific express robbery, by Al Sorenson. Illustrated. Omaha, Nebr., published by Barkalow brothers, 1877. Wrappers. Exceedingly rare.

5 p.l., [11]–139 p. plates. 16.5 cm.
Half title; 6 p. adv. at end.
Later reprinted by C. B. Dillingham, New York. Also rare.

The first book published about the robbery of the Union Pacific at Big Spring, Nebraska, by Joel Collins, Sam Bass, and company. It was published soon after the robbery took place and gives a detailed account of the robbery.

2073. ———

The story of Omaha from the pioneer days to the present time, by Alfred

Sorenson. . . . Illustrated. The third edition revised, rearranged and enlarged. Omaha, Nebr., printed by the National printing co., 1923. Cloth. Scarce.

5 p.l., 661 [5] p. front. (port.), plates, ports., facsm. 22.5 cm.
Last 5 p. adv.

Chapter XXXIII is a condensation of the author's "Hands Up!" published in 1877 (see Item 2072).

2074. Sowell, Andrew Jackson

History of Fort Bend county, containing biographical sketches of many noted characters . . ., by A. J. Sowell. Houston, Texas, W. H. Coyle and co., printers, 1904. Cloth. Rare.

xii, 373 p. front. (port.). 22.5 cm.

This book was printed in an edition of fewer than one hundred copies. It contains material on the Jaybird-Woodpecker feud of Texas.

2075. Sparks, William

The Apache Kid, a bear fight and other true stories of the old west, by William Sparks. Los Angeles, Skelton publishing co., 1926. Stiff pict. wrappers. Scarce.

3 p.l., [9]–215 p. 4 plates. 20 cm.

A collection of articles, among them stories of the Apache Kid and the Diablo Canyon train robbery.

2076. Spaulding, William A.

History and reminiscences, Los Angeles city and county, California. Compiled by William A. Spaulding. Los Angeles, Calif., published by J. R. Finnell & sons publishing co. [n.d.]. Leather. Pub. in three volumes. Scarce.

Vol. I, 5 p.l., 13–558 p. front. (port. with tissue), plates, ports. 27.4 cm.
Index: p. 523–558.
Vols. II and III, biographical.

Contains a chapter on Vásquez and some material on Murieta.

2077. Speer, Marion A.

Western trails, [by Marion A. Speer, Huntington Beach, Calif., printed by the Huntington Beach News, printers, publishers, 1931.] Cloth. Scarce.

4 p.l., [11]–377 [1] p. front. (port.), plates. 23.7 cm.
Half title only.

Has some material on Tom Horn and some information on Tascosa, Texas, and its Boot Hill.

2078. Spencer, Mrs. George E.

Calamity Jane. A story of the Black Hills, by Mrs. George E. Spencer. New York, Cassell and co., ltd. [1887]. Wrappers. Rare.

2 p.l., [5]–172 p. 17.8 cm.
12 p. adv. at end.

A book of fiction, and a collector's item among Calamity Jane materials. It is said to be the first book of fiction published by a South Dakotan.

2079. Spindler, Will Henry

Rim of the sandhills. A true picture of the old Holt county horse thief–vigilante days, by Will Henry Spindler. . . . Mitchell, S.D., published by the Educator supply co. [1941]. Cloth. Scarce.

7 p.l., [15]–346 p. front., plates, ports. 19.8 cm.

A story of Kid Wade, a horse thief and outlaw hanged by the vigilantes of Nebraska.

2080. ———

Yesterday's trails, [by] Will H. Spindler. [Gordon, Nebr., Gordon Journal publishing co., 1961.] Stiff pict. wrappers. (Cover title.)

2 p.l., 5–80 p. front. (port.), plates, ports. 23.5 cm.

Has chapters about Kid Wade and Doc Middleton.

2081. Spivak, John L.

The devil's brigade. The story of the Hatfield-McCoy feud, [by] John L. Spivak. [New York], Brewer and Warren, inc. [n.d.]. Cloth. OP.

5 p.l., 7–325 [1] p. 22.5 cm.
Half title.

2082. Splawn, Andrew Jackson

Ka-Mi-Akin, the last hero of the Yakimas, by A. J. Splawn. [Portland, Oreg., Press of Kilham stationery & printing co., 1917.] Cloth. Scarce.

6 p.l., 436 [6] p. front., plates, ports. 23.5 cm.
Last 6 p. biography and eulogy.
Reprinted in 1944 in an edition of 500 pages.

Has much information on lawlessness in the Northwest and some previously unrecorded material on Boone Helm.

2083. Sprague, Marshall

Money mountain. The story of Cripple Creek gold, by Marshall Sprague. With illustrations. Boston, Little, Brown and co. [1953]. Cloth. OP.

xx p., 1 l., [3]–342 p. front., plates, ports. 22 cm.

Appendices: p. [297]–302; notes: p. [303]–319; bibliography: p. [321]–327; acknowledgments: p. [328]–330; index: p. [333]–342.

Half title; map on end papers; pub. device; "First edition" on copyright p.

Contains some new material on Soapy Smith and tells much about the lawlessness of this mining town.

2084. Spring, Agnes Wright

The Cheyenne and Black Hills stage and express routes, by Agnes Wright Spring. . . . Glendale, Calif., the Arthur H. Clark co., 1949. Cloth.

7 p.l., [17]–418 p. plates, ports., facsm. (all in one section near end), fold. map at end. 24.5 cm.

Appendices: p. [341]–365; bibliography: p. [367]–371; index: p. [405]–418.

Half title: American Trail Series VI; pub. device; untrimmed.

Republished with omissions as a Bison Book by the University of Nebraska press in 1958 with wrappers.

One of the best books written about the Black Hills and the outlaws of that region, revealing much scholarly research by an able historian. The chapters on the road agents and other outlaws deal with Dunc Blackburn, Reddy McKemie, Joel Collins, Sam Bass, Bill Heffridge, and many others. The author is mistaken in saying that Wild Bill Hickok killed several soldiers in Abilene. On page 159 she writes: "It was related of him that he had on one occasion broken all records, made by one man against great odds, in his fight with what is known as the McCanless [*sic*] gang. In it he killed or seriously crippled ten well-armed men and lived to tell the tale."

She then gives a footnote referring to George Hansen's article in the *Nebraska Historical Magazine*, which corrects this false history. Mrs. Spring must know the truth about this legend, for she is an able historian and researcher. But I think she made a mistake in leaving the statement dangling without correcting it. Many have read her account who have not read the magazine article and therefore did not know the true details of the "fight."

2085. ———

Colorado Charley, Wild Bill's pard, by Agnes Wright Spring. Boulder, Colo., Pruett press, inc., 1968. Cloth.

xvi, 144 p. plates, ports., facsms. 22.3 cm.

Bibliography: p. [129]–136; index: p. [137]–144.

Half title.

The first and only book devoted to Colorado Charley. It tells about his friendship with Wild Bill Hickok and Bill's assassination. There is also some information about Calamity Jane and Joel Fowler.

2086. ———

William Chapin Deming, of Wyoming, pioneer publisher, and state and federal official. A biography, by Agnes Wright Spring. . . . Glendale, Calif., privately printed in a limited edition, by the Arthur H. Clark co., 1944. Cloth. Scarce.

9 p.l., [21]–531 p. front. (port. with tissue), plates, ports., facsms. 24.5 cm.
Appendices: p. [495]–511; index: p. [513]–531.
Half title; pub. device; untrimmed.

Contains some material on Tom Horn.

2087. Stambaugh, J. Lee, and Lillian J. Stambaugh

A history of Collin county, Texas, by J. Lee Stambaugh and Lillian J. Stambaugh. Austin, the Texas State Historical association, 1958. Pict. cloth. OP.

x p., 1 l., 3–303 p. front. (2 ports.). 24 cm.
Bibliography: p. 279–282; index: p. 283–303.
Half title; map on end papers; pub. device.
Vol. III of Texas County and Local History series, H. Bailey Carroll, general editor.

Tells about Sam Bass's first Texas train robbery at Allen, and devotes several pages to the Lee-Peacock feud. The authors are mistaken in stating that "Jesse James married in 1874 and immediately moved to Sherman [Texas], where he spent most of the rest of his life."

2088. Stanley, Clark

The life and adventures of the American cow-boy; life in the far west, by Clark Stanley, better known as the Rattlesnake King. [N.p.], published by Clark Stanley, 1897. Pict. wrappers. Scarce.

3 p.l., [7]–39 p. illus., ports. 23.5 cm.
"History of Snakes" and "Antidotes for Snake Bite": p. 32–39; index. 2d prelim. p.; 10 p. adv. at end.

Another edition, same title. [N.p., n.d.]

[78] p. (no pagination). illus., plates. 22.2 cm.

2089. ———

True life in the far west, by the American cowboy, Clark Stanley. Worcester, Mass., published by Clark Stanley by Messenger printing co. [N.d., ca. 1898.] Pict. wrappers. Scarce.

2 p.l., [5]–78 [2] p. front., illus. 22.2 cm.
Vignette.

There are some differences in the illustrations in this first and subsequent printings. Another edition, with additions, was bound with:

Something interesting to read, [by] Clark Stanley, the Texas cowboy.

8 p.

23 p. adv. at end.

Has a mention of Calamity Jane and Luke Short.

2090. Stanley, Edwin J.

Life of Rev. L. B. Stateler; or, sixty-five years on the frontier. Containing incidents, anecdotes, and sketches of Methodist history in the west and northwest, by Rev. E. J. Stanley. . . . Introduction by Bishop E. R. Hendrix. Illustrations by E. S. Paxson. Nashville, Tenn.; Dallas, Texas, publishing house of the M. E. Church South . . ., 1907. Pict. cloth. Scarce.

xvii, 365 [1] p. front., plates, ports. 19.6 cm.
Reprinted with same imprint in 1916.

Contains a chapter on outlaws and the vigilantes of Montana. The author tells about the hanging of Henry Plummer and many of his gang and how the vigilantes brought law into that raw land.

2091. Stanley, F. (pseud. of Father Stanley Crocchiola)

The Alma (New Mexico) story, by F. Stanley. [N.p., n.d.] Stiff wrappers. (Cover title.)

18 p. 21.5 cm.

Has material on the Ketchums, Butch Cassidy, William McGinnis (Elza Lay), Harvey Logan, and others of the Wild Bunch.

2092. ———

The Antonchico (New Mexico) story, by F. Stanley. [N.p., n.d.] Stiff wrappers. (Cover title.)

18 p. 21.5 cm.

Has some mention of Billy the Kid and Pat Garrett.

2093. ———

Clay Allison, by F. Stanley. [Denver, Colo., World press, inc., 1956.] Cloth. Scarce.

xi, 236 p. 22.3 cm.

Bibliography: p. 229–236.
Half title.

The most complete biography of this noted gunman to date, printed in a small edition, which was exhausted immediately after publication and hence was scarce from the beginning.

2094. ———

The Clayton (New Mexico) story, by F. Stanley. [N.p., n.d., ca. 1960.] Stiff wrappers. (Cover title.)

42 p. 21.5 cm.

Has material on Black Jack Ketchum and other Clayton outlaws.

2095. ———

Dave Rudabaugh, border ruffian, by F. Stanley. [Denver, Colo., World press, inc., 1961.] Cloth.

viii, 200 p. plates, facsm., plan. 21.5 cm.
Bibliography: p. 197–200.
Half title.

This is the only biography to date of this outlaw companion of Billy the Kid. The author is mistaken when he says that Doc Holliday, because of "the depression of 1873, as well as poor health, was induced to try Fort Worth as a place of business." Holliday set up his dental parlor in Dallas, not in Fort Worth. The author is further mistaken in saying that "since Holliday did not wear sidearms until he came to Fort Worth it is quite possible that friend Rudabaugh taught him how to use his six-shooter." Holliday met Rudabaugh, not in Fort Worth, but later in Fort Griffin, and he was a killer before their meeting.

In quoting from Stuart Lake's book on Wyatt Earp, Father Stanley inserts, in parenthesis, that Rudabaugh never killed a jailer in his life. He did kill one at Las Vegas, and that was the reason the mob wanted him after his capture at Stinking Springs.

The author is also mistaken in saying that when Tom O'Folliard was killed at Fort Sumner it was a dark and foggy night and that Tom fell from his horse when he was shot. It was a snowy night and therefore could not have been foggy; besides, snow lightens the night to quite a degree. Also, O'Folliard did not fall from his horse but rode back a short way toward his retreating companions and then returned toward the place where he had been shot and begged his killers not to shoot again. He was helped from his horse by Garrett's men.

Writing of the death of Curly Bill Brocius, the author says that the Cattlemen's Association offered a thousand dollars for Curly Bill dead or alive and that Earp used this reward "to buy fresh mounts and provisions for his men." There is no record that any such reward was paid, and no proof that Curly Bill was killed at that time.

2096. ———

Desperadoes of New Mexico, by F. Stanley. [Denver, Colo., printed by the World press, inc., 1953.] Cloth. OP.

xv, 320 p. plates, ports. 22.3 cm.

Bibliography: p. 317–320.

Half title.

Colophon: "Limited edition of New Mexico Desperadoes. This book number —— of an edition limited to eight hundred volumes."

A book which covers practically all the well-known outlaws of New Mexico. The author tells some things that do not appear in other books on the subject. He also, however, repeats many of the legends about Billy the Kid. Like many writers, he has Mrs. McSween playing her piano while her home burned, an act she emphatically denied. The book has many typographical errors.

In his chapter on Dick Brewer the author has the killing of Tunstall all wrong, and he leaves the impression that Morton was the only one present at the killing. He is wrong again when he writes that Widenmann made demands on Tunstall and that when Tunstall did not fulfill them Widenmann turned against him.

He quotes as fact material from the *Santa Fe New Mexican* that is completely incorrect. He quotes the paper as saying that Brady and Hindman were killed when they were fired upon from McSween's home and that for this killing McSween, Robert Wildman [*sic*] and W. P. Shields were arrested and taken to Fort Stanton, "where they were held prisoners." In this account the paper also says that George Coe was shot through the head. None of these details were true. This chapter of the book is largely quoted from this paper, which is historically unreliable.

The author is mistaken in saying that Black Jack Ketchum always used ten men in his train holdups and that he robbed the passengers. He is also wrong in saying that Billy the Kid had heard so much about William Coe, the outlaw, that he wanted to be like him. Again he is wrong in saying that Bob Ford was killed "as an actor on how he killed Jesse James." Ford did travel for a time with a cheap melodramatic show called *The James Boys in Missouri*, but he was a saloon man in Creede, Colorado, when he was killed. There are many other errors.

2097. ———

The Duke City. The story of Albuquerque, New Mexico, 1706–1956, [by F. Stanley]. [Pampa, Texas, Pampa print shop, 1963.] Cloth.

xiii, 267 p. 22 cm.

Bibliography: p. 235–249; index: p. 251–267.
Half title.

A chapter entitled "The Law—Both Sides" deals with some of the outlaws and gunmen of Albuquerque, including Elfego Baca and Clay Allison.

2098. ———

The Elizabethtown (New Mexico) story, by F. Stanley. [N.p., 1961.] Stiff wrappers. (Cover title.)

1 p.l., 3–19 p. 21.8 cm.

Has some mention of Clay Allison, Wall Henderson, and other gunmen of the period.

2099. ———

The Folsom (New Mexico) story, by F. Stanley. Pantex, Texas, F. Stanley, February, 1962. Stiff wrappers. (Cover title.)

3–20 p. 21.5 cm.

Has some material on William Coe, the outlaw, and on Black Jack Ketchum and his train robberies and capture.

2100. ———

Fort Bascom, Comanche-Kiowa barrier, by F. Stanley. . . . [Pampa, Texas, Pampa print shop, 1961.] Cloth. OP.

v, 224 p. 22.2 cm.
Bibliography: p. 215–224.

Has material on Clay Allison, Chunk Colbert, Davy Crockett, Jim Courtright, Wyatt Earp, Bat Masterson, Gyp, Joe, Jim, and Mannen Clements, Billy the Kid, and others.

2101. ———

Fort Stanton, by F. Stanley. . . . [Pampa, Texas, Pampa print shop, 1964.] Cloth.

iv, 265 p. 22.3 cm.
Bibliography: p. 245–254; index: p. 255–263.
Half title.
"Limited to 500 copies."

Gives a history of Fort Stanton from Civil War days to the present. There is much on the Lincoln County War and Billy the Kid. Much of the book is composed of quotations from other sources, and the author persists in writing in long paragraphs, some of which are three or four pages long. The book is an improvement over most of his other books in that the author has provided an index.

2102. ———

Fort Union (New Mexico), by F. Stanley. [N.p., 1953.] Cloth.

xiii p., 1 l., 305 p. plates, ports. 22.3 cm.
Bibliography: p. 301–305.
Half title.

Contains a chapter on some of the lawlessness in New Mexico and tells some new stories about Clay Allison, as well as giving some information on Bill Coe and David Crockett, the outlaws.

2103. ———

The grant that Maxwell bought, by F. Stanley. [Denver, Colo., printed by the World press, 1952.] Cloth. Very rare.

4 p.l., 256 p. 15 p. plates and ports. at end; fold. map in pocket at end. 28.7 cm.
Bibliography: p. 254–256.
Colophon: "Limited edition of Grant That Maxwell Bought. This book number —— of an edition limited to two hundred and fifty volumes." (Signed.)

This limited edition was immediately sold out and is now very rare. In a long chapter on Clay Allison the author tries to correct some of the legends about that notorious gunman.

2104. ———

Jim Courtright, two gun marshal of Fort Worth, by F. Stanley, in collaboration with Lulu Courtright Hart, daughter of Jim Courtright who contributed the pictures and new material. Henry Meyerhoff, who traveled for much of the material. Mrs. Henry Meyerhoff . . ., who contributed much and traveled extensively for documents. [Denver, Colo., World press, inc., 1957.] Cloth. OP.

xii, 234 p. plates, ports. (all in one section). 22.2 cm.
Bibliography: p. 229–234.
Half title.
Colophon: "This edition limited to 500 copies of which this is ——."
Reprinted the following year.

The author devotes quite a few pages to Sam Bass, telling about his Texas train robberies and other activities. I fail to understand why so much space in a book about Courtright should be devoted to Bass, because Courtright's only connection with the outlaw was to join a posse trying to "hole him up." The author continues: "The outlaw proved too shrewd. Courtright gave up the chase."

I think he is mistaken when he writes: "When McIntyre [*sic*] wrote his book [*Early Days In Texas*], taking credit for ordering Courtright about in Mobeetie and having himself a hero of many of the escapades involving Courtright and himself, Courtright was already in his grave fifteen years and unable to set McIntyre right or contradict any of his statements."

2105. ———

The Kingston (New Mexico) story, by F. Stanley. Pantex, Texas, F. Stanley, August, 1961. Stiff wrappers. (Cover title.)

3–20 p. 21.5 cm.

Has some information on various gangs of New Mexico, including the Toppy Johnson gang and the Kinney gang. He mentions Jim Courtright and his part with the posse going into Spring Valley after the outlaws. The author intimates that Kinney was sent to prison in Leavenworth, but he was sent to the Kansas State Penitentiary. The author has A. J. Fountain boarding a special train at Mesilla on March 25. Fountain left Las Cruces on March 21. He also says that Fountain was tried in Spring Valley. No such trial occurred. He has Fountain arresting Irwin and Colville and says that Irwin was a butcher. Colville was the butcher. The author also misspells some names, such as Kinny for Kinney, Asque for Askew, Tomas for Thomas, and Rynerston for Rynerson.

2106. ———

The La Belle (New Mexico) story, by F. Stanley. Limited to 500 copies. Pantex, Texas . . ., 1962. Stiff wrappers. (Cover title.)

3–19 p. 21.5 cm.

Has some material on the Ketchums and McGinnis.

2107. ———

The Lake Valley (New Mexico) story, by F. Stanley. . . . Pep, Texas, 1964. Stiff wrappers. (Cover title.)

3–20 p. 21.5 cm.

Contains some information on Jim McIntire and Jim Courtright.

2108. ———

The Lamy (New Mexico) story, by F. Stanley. (Limited to 400 copies.) Pep, Texas, June, 1966. Stiff wrappers. (Cover title.)

20 p. 21.5 cm.

Early Lamy was noted for its lawlessness. There is material on robberies, horse stealing, Ike Stockton, Joel Fowler, the Ketchums, and others.

2109. ———

The Las Vegas story (New Mexico), by F. Stanley. . . . [Denver, Colo., World press, inc., 1951.] Cloth. Rare.

xi p., 1 l., 340 p. plates, ports. 22.3 cm.
Bibliography: p. 335–340.
Half title.

Has a chapter on Vicente Silva and another on outlaws and lawlessness. His account of the capture of Billy the Kid and Rudabaugh at Stinking Springs is quoted from the *Las Vegas Optic*. He spells Rudabaugh as Radabaugh. There is some material on Doc Holliday and many others of Las Vegas' lawless days.

2110. ———

The Lincoln (New Mexico) story, by F. Stanley. Pep, Texas, 1964. Stiff wrappers. (Cover title.)

1 p.l., 3–26 p. 21.5 cm.

A story of Lincoln County and its troubles. The author tells about the Horrells and the murder of Tunstall. He is mistaken in saying that Billy the Kid attended Tunstall's funeral. The Kid was being held by the Murphy crowd at that time.

2111. ———

The Mogollon (New Mexico) story, by F. Stanley. . . . Pep, Texas, 1968. Stiff wrappers. (Cover title.)

1 p.l., 3–23 p. 21.5 cm.

This little pamphlet, limited to four hundred copies, contains some material on the Butch Cassidy gang, Billy the Kid, and his stepfather, William Antrim.

2112. ———

No more tears for Black Jack Ketchum, by F. Stanley. [Denver, Colo., World press, inc., 1958.] Stiff wrappers.

x, 148 p. 21.7 cm.
Bibliography: p. 147–148.
Half title.
Colophon: "Only 500 copies printed of which this is No. ——."

The author quotes from the *Santa Fe New Mexican* about a Frank O'Phallard who was the "last of the Sam Bass gang of train robbers who cleaned out the customs house at El Paso many years ago." The author admits that Sam Bass's biographers fail to mention this incident but says that it may have been "overlooked in the light of the Bass exploits in East Texas." Bass was never in El Paso, and he did not operate in East Texas. Nor was there ever an O'Phallard in his gang. Many of the Wild Bunch are mentioned in this book, since they were more or less connected with the Ketchum gang.

2113. ———

Notes on Joel Fowler, by F. Stanley. Limited to 500 copies. Pep, Texas . . ., 1963. Stiff wrappers. (Cover title.)

1 p.l., 3–19 p. 21.5 cm.

Gives some highlights on Fowler's life, his murder of James Cale, and his own lynching.

2114. ———

One half mile from Heaven; or, the Cimarron story. Compiled by F. Stanley for the Raton Historical society. . . . [Denver, Colo., World press publishing co., 1949.] Stiff pict. wrappers. Rare.

6 p.l., 3–155 p. plates, ports., plan. 21.5 cm.
Bibliography: p. 145–147; notes: p. 148–155.
Half title.

Contains much material on Clay Allison and other gunmen of Cimarron.

2115. ———

The Otero (New Mexico) story, by F. Stanley. Limited to 500 copies. Pantex, Texas, April, 1962. Stiff wrappers. (Cover title.)

3–20 p. 21.5 cm.

Has some mention of Clay Allison and Mace Bowman.

2116. ———

The private war of Ike Stockton, by F. Stanley. [Denver, Colo., World press, inc., 1959.] Cloth.

x, 169 p. 22.2 cm.
Half title.
Colophon: "Limited edition of which this is copy No. ——." (Signed.)

This book is largely made up of excerpts from other books and newspapers. It includes the life of the Stocktons, bad men of the first order, the story of the Colfax County War, and an account of the San Juan County War and touches on the Lincoln County War. He repeats the statement that Billy the Kid was a pallbearer at Tunstall's funeral. The author also deals with other history irrelevant to his subject.

2117. ———

Raton chronicle. Compiled by F. Stanley for the Raton Historical society.... [Denver, Colo., World press publishing co., 1948.] Pict. stiff wrappers. Rare.

7 p.l., 3–146 p. plates, ports. 21.5 cm.
Notes: p. 133–143; bibliography: p. 144–146.
Half title.

Has some material on early-day lawlessness in Raton, New Mexico, and some information on Bob Ford's stay in Raton.

2118. ———

The San Marcial (New Mexico) story, [by F. Stanley]. [n.p., 1960.] Stiff wrappers. (Cover title.)

18 p. 21.5 cm.

Has some material on Dave Rudabaugh.

2119. ———

The Seven Rivers (New Mexico) story, by F. Stanley. Limited to 500 copies. Pep, Texas, 1963. Stiff wrappers. (Cover title.)

2–20 p. 21.5 cm.

Has some information on the Beckwiths, Billy the Kid, Bob Olinger, Tom Pickett, Billy Wilson, Dave Rudabaugh, and others.

2120. ———

The Shakespeare (New Mexico) story, by F. Stanley. Pantex, Texas, F. Stanley, October, 1961. Stiff wrappers. (Cover title.)

3–20 p. 21.5 cm.

The author says that Russian Bill was arrested by Deputy Sheriff Jack Rutland in Deming, but contemporary newspaper accounts reported that he was arrested by Tom Tucker. The author says that Russian Bill's real name was Feador Telfin, but it was Woldemar Tetenborn. He also says that Sandy King bought a silk handkerchief from the Smyth Mercantile store and that when the clerk asked him to pay for it King shot off the tip of the clerk's index finger. The shot attracted a crowd of men who, the author says, overpowered King and put him in jail. Again, according to contemporary newspaper reports, King was captured in Lordsburg after the clerk shot him in the neck. The author also says that Russian Bill and Sandy King were hanged from a beam in the barroom of the Grant House. They were hanged in the dining room because there were no trees nearby and the crossbar of the corral had been taken down.

The author does not mention some of the other important events in Shakespeare, such as the capture of the famous outlaw John Kinney by the Shakespeare Guards.

2121. ———

Socorro: the oasis, by F. Stanley. [Denver, Colo., World press, inc., 1950.] Cloth. Rare.

8 p.l., 221 p. plates, ports. 22.3 cm.
Bibliography: p. 215–221.
Half title.

Has some history of early-day Socorro, with a chapter on Joel Fowler and his lynching, as well as information on the vigilantes and on Elfego Baca.

2122. ———

The Springer (New Mexico) story, by F. Stanley. Pantex, Texas, F. Stanley, January, 1962. Stiff wrappers. (Cover title.)

2–24 p. 21.5 cm.

Has some mention of Black Jack Ketchum and his gang.

2123. ———

The White Oaks (New Mexico) story, by F. Stanley. [N.p., 1961.] Stiff wrappers. (Cover title.)

23 p. 21.5 cm.

Has some information about Billy the Kid, Pat Garrett, Dave Rudabaugh, Joel Fowler, and others.

2124. Stanley, Henry M.

My early travels and adventures in America and Asia, by Henry M. Stanley. With two maps and two photogravure portraits. London, Sampson Low, Marston and co., ltd. . ., 1895. Cloth. Pub. in two volumes. Scarce.

Vol. I, xxi, 301 p. front. (port. with tissue), fold. map (col.). 19.6 cm.
Index: p. [293]–301.
Vol. II, ix, 424 p. front. (port. with tissue), fold. map (col.). 19.6 cm.

In an interview the author asked Wild Bill Hickok how many white men he had killed, and the answer was "considerably over a hundred." Hickok said that he was twenty-eight when he killed his first man. The killing took place in Leavenworth when five men entered his room to rob him while he lay asleep. Hickok said: "I kept perfectly still until just as the knife touched my breast; I sprang aside and buried mine in his heart, and then used my revolver on the others right and left. One was killed and another wounded and then, gentlemen, I dashed through the room and rushed to the fort, where I procured a lot of soldiers, and returning to the hotel, captured the whole gang of them, fifteen in all. We searched the cellar, and found eleven bodies buried in it—the remains of those who had been murdered by those villains." This is a sample of the tall tales Wild Bill loved to feed to easterners, especially writers.

2125. Stansbery, Lon R.

The passing of the 3D ranch, by Lon R. Stansbery. [Tulsa, Okla., printed for the author by George W. Henry printing co., n.d., ca. 1930.] Pict. cloth. (Cover title.) Rare.

92 p. illus., plates, ports. 19.4 cm.

Reprinted in New York in 1967.

This rare little book gives some heretofore unpublished facts about the Daltons, Bill Doolin, the Jennings gang, the Cook gang, Cherokee Bill, and other Oklahoma outlaws. The author is mistaken in saying that Grat Dalton was caught robbing a bank in California. It was a train that he was supposed to have robbed. The author gives Dick Broadwell's first name as Nick, and he is mistaken in saying that Bill Dalton was killed near Guthrie. He was killed near Ardmore.

2126. Stanton, G. Smith

"When the wildwood was in flower." A narrative, covering fifteen years' experiences of a New Yorker on the western plains, [by] G. Smith Stanton. . . . New York, J. S. Olgivie publishing co. [1910]. Cloth. Scarce.

5 p.l., 11–123 [2] p. plates, ports. 19.8 cm.

2 p. adv. at end.

Has some information about Canada Bill, a noted outlaw of the Northwest.

2127. [Starr, Belle]

Bella Starr, the bandit queen; or, the female Jesse James. A full and authentic history of the dashing female highwayman, with copious extracts from her journal. Handsomely and profusely illustrated. . . . New York, Richard K. Fox, publisher, 1889. Stiff col. pict. wrappers. Exceedingly rare.

2 p.l., [5]–64 [8] p. front., illus. 21 cm.

8 p. adv. at end.

Various issues of this same edition had different numbers of pages of advertisements.

Published in facsimile in a de luxe edition by the Steck Company, Austin, Texas, 1960, with an introduction by R. H. Porter and with new plates and ports., some col., and in a slip case. A few copies were published in wrappers similar to the original, without an introduction. The de luxe copies were presented to friends and customers as Christmas presents (the publisher reprints some rare book every year for this purpose).

The first edition of this book is a rare collector's item, but is historically worthless. I am sorry to say that it has been the source of most accounts of Belle Starr by earlier historians, and its contents have been repeated so often and so widely that even some modern historians use materials from it, unaware of its inaccuracies or its source. It is highly imaginative fiction, presented as fact by an anonymous writer on the *Police Gazette* staff. Names, dates, and other details are wrong, even to the spelling of Belle's first name. The excerpts alleged to have been taken from her letters are pure fiction, and she kept no journal. Most writers of the yellow-journalism school of the period used such vehicles to give their writing an air of authenticity.

The author states that Belle started her career to avenge the killing of her younger brother in about 1867. The Civil War was over by that time, and the records show that her brother was killed in 1863 and that he was eight years older than Belle. This book, like many others after it, makes Belle a beautiful young woman. Perhaps she was when she was in her teens, but all the pictures of her that I have seen show her to be common and unattractive.

In an article in *Real West Magazine* (Vol. 2, No. 6, February, 1959) a writer made the claim that this book was written by a free-lance writer named Alton B. Myers. According to the *Real West* article, Myers did not even know who Belle Starr was until someone told him she was a "two-bit whore," and he suddenly got the idea to write a book about her. To judge from the unreliability of the rest of the article, there is little truth to this claim.

2128. Starr, Henry

Thrilling events; life of Henry Starr, famous Cherokee Indian outlaw narrates his many adventures from boyhood to date. Written in the Colorado penitentiary by himself. . . . [N.p., (Tulsa, Okla.)], 1914. Col. pict. wrappers. (Cover title.) Exceedingly rare.

50 [1] p. 19.8 cm.
Port. of author on cover.

A well-written and most interesting little book about this outlaw's life and his many lawless acts. There are many typographical errors, stretches of misplaced text, and a repetition of two sentences on page 23. The author ends his narrative with a bitter tirade against society and has many comments to make on graft in the courts, especially Judge Parker's court. The only copy known to me is in the library of the Oklahoma Historical Society, Oklahoma City.

2129. Steckmesser, Kent Ladd

The western hero in history and legend, by Kent Ladd Steckmesser. Norman, University of Oklahoma press [1965]. Cloth.

xiii [1] p., 1 l., 3–281 p. plates, ports., facsms. 23.5 cm.
Bibliography: p. 256–271; index: p. 272–281.
Half title.

Contains several chapters on Billy the Kid and on Wild Bill Hickok. The author, I am happy to say, is another historian who is trying to correct some false history.

2130. Steele, Rev. John

In camp and cabin. Mining life and adventures in California during 1850 and later, by Rev. John Steele. . . . Lodi, Wisc., published by J. Steele, 1901. Wrappers. Rare.

81 p. 23.5 cm.
Double column; untrimmed.

Contains a story about Joaquín Murieta.

2131. Steele, S. B.

Forty years in Canada. Reminiscences of the great north-west with some account of his service in South Africa, by Colonel S. B. Steele, C.B.M.V.O., late of the N.W.M. Police and the S. Africa Constabulary. Edited by Mollie Glenn Niblett, with an introduction by J. G. Coleman. . . . New York, Dodd, Mead & co., 1915. Cloth. Scarce.

xvii p., 1 l., 428 p. front. (port. with tissue), plates, ports. 22 cm.
Index: p. 413–428.
Half title.

Has quite a bit of material on Soapy Smith. The author tells a different, but equally preposterous, tale about Wild Bill Hickok and his battle with *ten* men. His version of the big "fight" is that Hickok's partner asked him to drop by his home and see how his wife and children were getting along. The family "lived five miles out of town on a lonely plain." Hickok started out with six cartridges in his revolver, but shot a prairie chicken on the way. After he arrived and had chatted with his partner's wife for a few moments, he noticed a rifle hanging over the mantelpiece. The wife told him that "Blank's (no names were called) gang passed there awhile ago, and they were coming back soon, and if they see your horse at the door they will come in and murder you." Soon they came, guns in hand, and Wild Bill "killed the first five with his pistol and a sixth with the rifle, brained two with the barrel, and in a desperate struggle dispatched the last two with his bowie knife, ten men dead and he not disabled."

I fail to see why this fairy tale should have been included in a book about Canada.

2132. [Steele, William]

Report of the adjutant general of the state of Texas for the year 1874. Houston, A. C. Gray, state printer, 1874. Wrappers. Rare.

[3]–13 p. tables (2 fold.). 21.3 cm.

Tells about the wounding of John Wesley Hardin by Captain Waller, though Hardin made good his escape on that occasion.

2133. Steen, Ralph W. (ed.)

The Texas news. A miscellany of Texas history in newspaper style. Ralph W. Steen, editor. Austin, Texas, the Steck co., publishers [1955]. Pict. cloth. Scarce.

iii, 187 p. plates, ports. 20 cm.

Index: p. 179–186; acknowledgments: p. 187.

Triple column; illus. t.p.

Also published in a special Christmas edition (boxed), col. front., with a supplement by Curtis Bishop and illustrated by Elizabeth Rice.

A collection of newspaper excerpts giving information on many of the Texas outlaws, such as Cullen Baker, Sam Bass, Billy the Kid, John Wesley Hardin, Frank Jackson, and Ben Thompson. It gives an account of Jim Murphy killing himself out of fear of Jackson, and this account may be the origin of that fable that Murphy committed suicide.

2134. Stegner, Wallace

Mormon country, by Wallace Stegner. Edited by Erskine Caldwell. New York, Duell, Sloan and Pearce [1942]. Cloth. OP.

x p., 1 l., 3–362 p. 22.2 cm.

Index: p. 351–362.

Half title; map on end papers; "First printing" on copyright p.

Contains a chapter on Butch Cassidy and his Wild Bunch.

2135. Stellman, Louis J.

Mother lode. The story of California's gold rush, by Louis J. Stellman. Cover design and decorations by Paul Rockwood. San Francisco, Calif., Harr Wagner publishing co., [1934]. Cloth. OP.

xv, 304 p. front. (port.), plates, ports. 19.3 cm.

Index: p. 299–304.

Illus. end papers.

The author's account of Murieta follows the Ridge version, though he states that at one time Murieta's band was composed of almost as many women as men. There is also some information on Black Bart and his capture.

2136. Stephens, Lorenzo Dow

Life sketches of a jayhawker of '49, by Lorenzo Dow Stephens. Actual experiences of a pioneer told by himself in his own way. [N.p.], San Jose, [privately printed, 1916.] Stiff wrappers. Scarce.

2 p.l., [7]–68 p. ports. 23.6 cm.

There are said to have been only three hundred copies of this book printed. The author gives some fresh material on Murieta.

2137. Stephens, Robert W.

Tribute to a ranger. Captain Alfred Y. Allee, company D, Texas rangers, [by] Robert W. Stephens. [N.p., 1968.] Stiff wrappers.

3 p.l., [1]–4 p. port. 21 cm.
Colophon: "Number —— of 200 copies privately printed May, 1968."

2138. Stephenson, Terry E.

Caminos viejos. Tales found in the history of California of especial interest to those who love the valleys, the hills and the canyons of Orange county, its traditions and its landmarks, by Terry E. Stephenson. Published on the press of the Santa Ana High School and Junior College by its director Thomas E. Williams. Illustrated with photographs, with maps and with woodcuts, the latter by Miss Jean Goodwin and Arthur Ames. Santa Ana, Orange county, Calif., 1930. Dec. fabrikoid. Very scarce.

9 p.l., 111 p. front., illus., plates, maps (2 double p., 1 large fold. at end). 25.5 cm.
Half title; illus. end papers; untrimmed.
Colophon: "This book is one of the de luxe edition of two hundred and fifty copies of which this is No. ——." (Signed by author and printer.)

Reprinted in another de luxe edition of 500 signed and numbered copies the same year. This edition was marked "Revised Edition" on the verso of the second flyleaf. Both editions are now very scarce. The press discontinued operation in 1942.

Has a long chapter on outlawry in Orange County and tells of the killing of Sheriff Barton and the hanging of Juan Flores.

2139. Sterling, Hank

Famous western outlaw-sheriff battles, by Hank Sterling. New York, Rainbow books [1954]. Col. pict. wrappers.

2 p.l., 5–126 [1] p. illus. 19.2 cm.

Has chapters on the James boys, the Daltons, Bill Doolin, the Earp-Clanton feud, Sam Bass, Wild Bill Hickok, Billy the Kid, and the Ed Short–Charlie Bryant killing. There are mistakes in every chapter, too many to enumerate here.

2140. [Sterling, Thomas]

Autobiography of Tom Sterling. Seven years of thrilling adventures of a western peace officer. . . . Santa Monica, Calif., Weaver publishing co., 1941. Pict. cloth. Scarce.

2 p.l., 3–118 p. front. (port.), plates, ports. 24.5 cm.
7 blank p. at end.

Privately printed in a small edition, this book is now scarce. It has some material on the gunmen of Dodge City, Kansas.

2141. Sterling, William Warren

Trails and trials of a Texas ranger, by William Warren Sterling. Drawings by Bob Schoenke. [N.p., 1959.] Half leather. Privately printed. Scarce.

xvi p., 1 l., 3–524 p. illus., plates, ports., facsms., map, music. 24.2 cm.
Half title; illus. t.p.; illus. end papers.
Reprinted in 1969 by University of Oklahoma press, Norman.

Has chapters on the Bandit War and material on Sam Bass, Frank Jackson, Gregorio Cortez, and other Texas badmen. The chapter on Bass is largely correct, but there are several errors in other sections.

2142. Stewart, A. J. D. (ed.)

The history of the bench and bar in Missouri. With reminiscences of the prominent lawyers of the past, and a record of the law's leaders of the present. A. J. D. Stewart, editor. Illustrated. St. Louis, Mo., the Legal publishing co., 1898. Leather. Scarce.

3 p.l., 7–664, i–viii p. plates, ports. (with tissues). 28.8 cm.
Index: p. i–viii.

Has much material on the James brothers and the trial of Frank James.

2143. Stewart, Marcus A.

Rosita; a California tale, by Marcus A. Stewart. San Jose, Calif., Mercury steam print, 1882. Cloth. Rare.

3 p.l., [5]–72 p. 20 cm.

In this epic poem the author tries to create another legend about Murieta by having him escape death and return to Mexico to live a happy life. He makes Rosita the wife of one of Murieta's lieutenants rather than the wife of Murieta himself.

2144. Stoll, William T.

Silver strike. The true story of silver mining in the Coeur d'Alenes, as told by William T. Stoll to W. H. Whicker. With illustrations. Boston, Little, Brown and co., 1932. Cloth. Scarce.

vii p., 2 l., [3]–273 p. front., plates, ports. 21 cm.
Half title; pub. device.

Contains much on the outlawry of the Coeur d'Alenes and on Charlie Siringo's adventures as a detective.

2145. Stone, Arthur L.

Following old trails, by Arthur L. Stone . . ., with illustrations. Missoula, Mont., Morton John Elrod, 1913. Cloth. Scarce.

7 p.l., 17–304 p. front., plates, ports. 23.5 cm.
Half title; device.

Has a chapter on the Montana vigilantes telling about some of the hangings they carried out in their efforts to bring law and order to the frontier.

2146. Stone, Will Hale

Twenty-four years a cowboy and ranchman in southern Texas and old Mexico. Desperate fights with the Indians and Mexicans, by Will Hale. Illustrated. Hedrick, O. T., published by W. H. Stone [1905]. Stiff wrappers. Exceedingly rare.

5–268 p. illus. 19 cm.
Reprinted in 1959 by University of Oklahoma press, Norman as No. 12 of the Western Frontier Library, with an introduction by A. M. Gibson.

This book, rare in the first edition, was written as an autobiography, but in my opinion it is nothing more than an attempt at sensational dime-novel writing. Other than because of its rarity as a collector's item, I wonder why such a historically worthless book was reprinted. The author claims to have lived for twenty-four years in a Spanish-speaking section of the country; yet he had to have a girl friend teach him the language. He seems to be entirely unacquainted with his geography. He claims to have lived within a hundred miles of the Pecos River, yet only a few hours' ride from Matamoros. He claims to have taught General Taylor how to fight Indians and claimed that there were Negro soldiers in the army long before the army enlisted Negroes.

Though he claims to be a cattleman, he makes some statements a cattleman would ridicule. Apparently he did his calf branding in the middle of the screw-worm season. He seems to have been proud of his stealings and killings.

He devotes several chapters to Billy the Kid, all of them filled with errors. He says that the Kid was seventeen when his parents moved to Silver City. He tells a preposterous tale about the battle at Lincoln and says that the burning house was surrounded by soldiers and some Seven River Indians and that the Kid played the piano all the while the battle was going on, to "entertain the crowd outside." He further states that no one escaped except Tom O'Folliard (which he spells O'Phollard) and the Kid. The author puts himself into much of the action, claiming to have been in the battle at Lincoln, with Garrett when O'Folliard was killed, and with the posse at Stinking Springs; but his name has never been mentioned in any other account. He spells many names wrong, such as Caralyle for Carlyle, Sirrango for Siringo, and Tunsal for Tunstall.

The copy of the first edition that I examined, in the Library of Congress, was almost too brittle to handle.

2147. Stong, Phil

Gold in them hills. Being an irreverent history of the great 1849 gold rush, [by] Phil Stong. Garden City, N.Y., Doubleday & co., inc., 1957. Cloth. OP.

5 p.l., [11]–209 p. 21.7 cm.
Bibliography: p. [205]–209.
Half title; map on end papers; vignette; "First edition" on copyright p.

Has some material on Murieta, Tom Bell, Joseph Slade, and others. The author speaks disparagingly of the early Texas Rangers, saying that "they were about the worst gang of murderous cutthroats in the world." This is the first such accusation I have ever read about that body of lawmen.

2148. Stout, F. E.

Rube Burrows [*sic*]; or, life, exploits and death of the bold train robber, by F. E. Stout. Aberdeen, Miss., 1890. Pict. wrappers. Very rare.

2 p.l., [5]–78 p. ports. 15.5 cm.
Port on t.p. and front wrappers.

Said to be the rarest of all the books about this outlaw, it tells about his life from childhood to the day of his death. The author is wrong in saying that Rube Burrow was on the train at the time of Jackson's capture and that he made his escape disguised as a woman.

2149. Stout, Tom (ed).

Montana, its story and biography. A history of aboriginal and territorial Montana and three decades of statehood. Under the editorial supervision of Tom Stout. Chicago and New York, the American Historical society, 1921. Full leather. Pub. in three volumes. Scarce.

Vol. I, xlix, 894 p. front., plates, ports. 27 cm.
Vols. II and III, paged continuously, biographical, double column.

Volume I contains a long chapter on the outlaws and vigilantes of Montana, based largely on Dimsdale's and Langford's books on the subject.

2150. Stover, Elizabeth Matchett (ed.)

Son-of-a-gun stew; a sampling of the southwest, edited by Elizabeth Matchett Stover; foreword by John William Rogers; illustrated by Harold D. Bugbee. Dallas, University press in Dallas, Southern Methodist University, 1945. Cloth. Scarce.

x p., 1 l., 216 p. illus. 21.5 cm.
Half title; illus. double t.p.
Also published in wrappers; later republished by Grossett and Dunlap.

An anthology of articles published in the *Southwest Review*, 1915 to 1945, published to commemorate the first Southwest Book Fair held in Dallas in 1945. One article, entitled "Horse Thieves," by J. Evetts Haley, tells about outlaws and other persons who became outlaws. The author is mistaken when he says that Jesse Evans was killed by Billy the Kid at the outbreak of the Lincoln County War.

2151. Strauss, Levi (pub.)

Levi's round-up of western sheriffs. [San Francisco, Levi Strauss & co., n.d.] Pict. folder. OP.

[11] p. (no pagination). illus. 14.8 cm.

Has material on Tom Smith, John Owens, Wild Bill Hickok, Bill Tilghman, Dallas Stoudenmire, King Fisher, and others.

2152. Strahorn, Carrie Adell

Fifteen thousand miles by stage. A woman's unique experience during thirty years of path finding and pioneering from the Missouri to the Pacific and from Alaska to Mexico, by Carrie Adell Strahorn. With 350 illustrations from drawings by Charles M. Russell and others, and from photographs. New York, London, G. P. Putnam's sons, 1911. Cloth. Pict. label pasted on. Scarce.

xxv p., 1 l., 673 p. front. (port. with tissue), illus., plates (4 col. with tissues), ports. 23.4 cm.
T.p. in red and black.
Reprinted with same collation in 1915.

Gives accounts of the Montana vigilantes and the Plummer gang.

2153. Street, Julian Leonard

Abroad at home; American ramblings, observations, and adventures of Julian Street. With pictorial sidelights, by Wallace Morgan. New York, the Century co., 1914. Cloth. Scarce.

xiv p., 1 l., 3–517 p. front., plates. 22.8 cm.

Half title; device; untrimmed.

Reprinted in 1916 and 1918.

Chapter XXVI, entitled "The Tame Lion," is about Frank James.

2154. Streeter, Floyd Benjamin

Ben Thompson, man with a gun, by Floyd B. Streeter. With an introduction by William F. Kelleher. New York, Frederick Fell, inc., publishers [1957]. Boards.

18 p.l., 21–217 p. plates, ports., facsms. 21.3 cm.

Citations and comments: p. 205–210; bibliography: p. 211–217.

Port. on t.p.; untrimmed.

This reliable book, whose author died before its publication, shows good research. It has material on Wild Bill Hickok, Phil Coe, Wyatt Earp, Ben Thompson, King Fisher, and others. The author ridicules the statement made by Stuart Lake in his Wyatt Earp biography that Earp arrested Ben Thompson after the killing of Sheriff Whitney in Ellsworth. Lake's account first appeared in his "Tales of the Kansas Cowtowns," published in the *Saturday Evening Post*, November 8, 1930.

"When this account appeared in print," writes Mr. Streeter, "the writer began a long and exhaustive search for all the evidence on the subject. The investigation included interviews with five eyewitnesses; municipal, county, and state records; files of contemporaneous Kansas newspapers and out-of-state dailies; and printed reminiscences of the period. A study of the evidence convinced the author that Wyatt Earp did not arrest Ben Thompson and that the account in the local paper, which closes with the following statement, is correct: "Thus the city is left without a police force, with no one but Deputy Sheriff Hogue to make arrests. He received the arms of Ben Thompson on the agreement of Happy Jack to give up his arms" (*Ellsworth Reporter*, August 21, 1873).

2155. ———

The Kaw; the heart of a nation, by Floyd Benjamin Streeter; illustrated by Isabel Bate and Harold Black. New York, Toronto, Farrar & Rinehart, inc. [1941]. Cloth. Scarce.

ix [1] p., 1 l. 3–371 p. illus., map. 21 cm.

Rivers of America series.

Acknowledgments: p. 351–352; bibliography: p. 353–359; index: p. 361–371.

Half title; illus. end papers; illus. t.p.; first edition: letters "FR" in device on copyright p.

Contains material on the gunmen of the cow towns of Kansas, such as Wild Bill

Hickok and Ben Thompson. On page 348, line 32, the words "the Congressional school" should read "the Congregational school." The author gives a full account of the troubles with the Thompsons in Ellsworth when Sheriff Whitney was killed, but he makes no mention of Wyatt Earp disarming Ben Thompson, as Earp claimed.

2156. ———

Prairie trails & cow towns, [by] Floyd Benjamin Streeter; with illustrations from old prints. Boston, Chapman & Grimes [1936]. Cloth. Very scarce.

5 p.l., 11–326 p. front., plates, ports. 20.8 cm.

Notes (biographical): p. 219–225; index: p. 227–232; bibliography: p. 233–236.

Vignette; untrimmed.

Republished by Devin-Adair, New York, in 1963.

This able historian gives a good picture of the various cow towns of Kansas and the activities of the gunmen who lived in them.

2157. ———

Tragedies of a Kansas cow town, by F. B. Streeter. Reprint from the *Aerend*, Vol. V, Nos. 2 and 3 (Spring and Summer, 1934). Published quarterly by the faculty of the Fort Hays Kansas State College [n.d., ca. 1934]. Wrappers. (Cover title.) Scarce.

81–162 p. 23 cm.

A thoroughly reliable, well-annotated history of Ellsworth in its early days. It tells about the killing of Sheriff Whitney by Bill Thompson and does not mention Stuart Lake's claim that Wyatt Earp arrested Ben Thompson.

2158. Strevell, Charles Nettleton

As I recall them, [by] Charles Nettleton Strevell. [N.p., n.d., ca. 1943.] Leather. Scarce.

5 p.l., 11–304 [4] p. plates, ports. 22.4 cm.

Index: p. [306]–[308].

This privately printed book has some mention of Calamity Jane and the hanging of Big Nose George Parrott, as well as the hanging of Cold Turkey Bill and his gang, and Beaver Creek Jake and his bunch of rustlers.

2159. Strong, Capt. Henry W.

My frontier days & Indian fights on the plains of Texas, by Captain Henry W. Strong. [N.p. (Dallas, Texas), n.d., ca. 1926.] Pict. wrappers. (Cover title.) Scarce.

122 p. 1 port. 22 cm.

Has some material on the Benders and on some early-day lawlessness in Texas. The author gives quite an account of the outlaw career of one Joe Horner, who later turned up in Wyoming as Frank Canton.

2160. Stuart, Granville

Forty years on the frontier as seen in the journals and reminiscences of Granville Stuart, gold-miner, trader, merchant, rancher and politician; edited by Paul C. Phillips. Cleveland, the Arthur H. Clark co., 1925. Cloth. Pub. in two volumes. Scarce.

Vol. I, 10 p.l., [23]–272 p. front. (port. with tissue), plates. 24.4 cm.

Vol. II, 5 p.l., [13]–265 p. front., plates. 24.4 cm.

Index: p. [243]–265

Half title: Northwest Historical series II (both volumes); pub. device; untrimmed; gilt top.

Written by a well-educated and influential pioneer of early Montana, this work contains valuable history. The author did much to organize a group of latter-day vigilantes to break up a band of horse and cow thieves who became so bold in their operations that drastic measures had to be taken. He gives a good account of the killing of Rattlesnake Jake Fallon and Long-Haired Owens.

2161. Stuart, Hix C.

The notorious Ashley gang. A saga of the king and queen of the Everglades, by Hix C. Stuart. Stuart, Fla., St. Lucie printing co., inc. [1928]. Cloth. Scarce.

3 p.l., 7–80 p. front., plates, ports. 19.5 cm.

Though the Ashley gang were not western outlaws, they operated in much the same manner.

2162. Sullivan, Dulcie

The L S Brand. The story of a Texas panhandle ranch, by Dulcie Sullivan. Introduction by Loula Grace Erdman. Austin & London, University of Texas press [1968]. Cloth.

11 p.l., [23]–178 p. illus., plates, ports. (all in 1 section), cattle brands. 22.5 cm.

Index: p. [169]–178.

Half title; pub. device; No. 6 of the M. K. Brown Range series.

A most interesting little book which tells of life on the famous L S Texas ranch. There is some material on Billy the Kid, the cowboy strike, and the big fight at Tascosa when Ed King, Fred Chilton, and Jesse Sheets were killed by Lem Woodruff and his friends.

2163. Sullivan, Edward Dean

The fabulous Wilson Mizner, by Edward Dean Sullivan. . . . New York, N.Y., the Henkle co., publishers [1935]. Pict. cloth. Scarce.

xi p., 1 l., 15–324 p. front. (port.), plates, ports. 23.6 cm.
Half title; "First published July, 1935" on copyright p.

This tells of Mizner's acquaintance with Soapy Smith during his stay at Skagway and of his killing.

2164. Sullivan, Frank S.

A history of Meade county, Kansas, by Frank S. Sullivan. Topeka, Kans., Crane & co., printers, binders, publishers, 1916. Cloth. Scarce.

6 p.l., 13–184 p. plates, ports., tables. 23.2 cm.

Has a chapter on lawlessness.

2165. Sullivan, W. John L.

Twelve years in the saddle for law and order on the frontiers of Texas, by Sergeant W. J. L. Sullivan, Texas ranger, co. B, frontier battalion. Austin, Texas, von Boeckmann-Jones co., printers, 1909. Cloth. Port. pasted on. Exceedingly rare.

4 p.l., [3]–284 p. front., plates, ports. 21 cm.
Errata on verso of third prelim. leaf.
Republished in 1966 by the Buffalo-Head press, New York.

Tells about the life of this Texas Ranger and contains chapters about the hanging of Bill Longley, the Cook gang, and some Texas feuds and bank robberies.

2166. [Sunday, William E.]

Gah dah gwa stee, [by W. E. Sunday, Pryor, Okla., printed by Byron Smith, 1953.] Cloth. Scarce.

4 p.l., 172 p. plates, ports., cattle brands. 24 cm.

Gives an account of an arrest of the Daltons before the Coffeyville raid.

2167. [Supreme Court of the United States]

Henry Starr, plaintiff in error *vs.* the United States. Brief of plaintiff in error. In error to the Circuit Court of the United States for the western district of Arkansas. [N.p., 1892.] Wrappers. (Cover title.) Rare.

53 p. 21.7 cm.

Documents the trial of Henry Starr for the killing of Floyd Wilson in Indian Territory in 1892.

2168. Sutherland, William Alexander

Out where the west be-grins, by William Alexander Sutherland. [Las Cruces, N.M., Southwest publishing co., 1942.] Stiff wrappers. Scarce.

2 p.l., 5–94 [1] p. 23.4 cm.
Port. on cover.

Gives a short sketch of the killing of Bob Olinger by Billy the Kid.

2169. Sutley, Zachary Taylor

The last frontier, by Zach T. Sutley. New York, the Macmillan co., MCMXXX. Cloth. Scarce.

vi p., 2 l., 350 p. fold. map. 22.5 cm.
Half title; untrimmed.

Contains material on the hanging of Lame Johnny and on Jesse James, Wild Bill Hickok, and Calamity Jane. The author has Calamity Jane "born of Mormon parents in Salt Lake City, but [ran] away with a freighter when she was a girl of fifteen." The author says that he "heard a shot in the Bell-Union Theater" and ran to the door of the dance hall to find that Wild Bill had been shot by McCall. He states that Wild Bill had been a stock tender at one of the Overland Stage stations and that he "began his career by defending his station against a bandit gang which tried to steal his stock and hold up the stage." Wild Bill, he writes, "was not the popular hero he has been pictured by later writers but was a bully whom men feared but did not respect." He claims that he was a witness at the trial of McCall at Yankton and that he was also in Northfield when the James-Younger gang held up the bank there. These old-timers seemed to have been everywhere.

2170. Sutton, Ernest V.

A life worth living, by Ernest V. Sutton. Introduction by Lee Shippey. End paper painting "When the West Was Young" and chapter headings by Clarence Ellsworth. Pasadena, Calif., Trail's End publishing co., inc. [1948]. Cloth. Scarce.

xiv p., 1 l., 350 p. front. (port.), ports. 22.6 cm.
Index: p. 347–350.
Illus. end papers (col.); illus. chapter headings; double t.p.; pub. device; untrimmed; "First edition" on copyright p.
Edition limited to 2,000 signed copies.

Contains some material on the Benders and Chris Evans.

2171. Sutton, Fred Ellsworth

Hands up! Stories of the six-gun fighters of the old wild west, as told by

Fred E. Sutton and written down by A. B. MacDonald. Illustrated. Indianapolis, the Bobbs-Merrill co., publishers [1927]. Pict. cloth. Scarce.

7 p.l., 13–303 p. front., plates, ports. 21.5 cm.
Half title; untrimmed.

The author makes many questionable statements. According to his narrative he appears to have been personally acquainted with all the outlaws of the West, but in view of his age at his death in 1927, such acquaintances would have been impossible. He claims that he saved the life of Billy the Kid in Dodge City, but he would have been only three years old at the time, and I can find no record that the Kid was in Dodge City. The author claims to have been present at many exciting events in the lives of outlaws; for example, he claims to have seen the body of Jesse James immediately after he was killed by Bob Ford. He also, he says, happened to be in Dodge when Wagner and Walker killed Ed Masterson and says he held Masterson's head on his knee while the gunman was dying.

Despite the author's claim that Bat Masterson was wounded in Tascosa, Texas, in a row with a gang of Texas cowpunchers, Masterson was wounded by Sergeant King in Mobeetie, Texas. The author's accounts of Billy the Kid, Wild Bill Hickok, and all the rest have many errors, too numerous to list here. On the whole, it is a most unreliable book. The author and I corresponded frequently while we were both writing feature stories for the *Dallas Morning News.*

2172. Swallow, Alan (ed.)

The wild bunch, edited by Alan Swallow. Denver, Sage books [1966]. Cloth.

6 p.l., 13–136 p. front. (port.), maps. 22.3 cm.
Half title.

Has much on bank and train robberies, dealing with many outlaws, such as Butch Cassidy, Harvey Logan, Ben Kilpatrick, the Ketchums, Harry Longabaugh, Elza Lay, Tom O'Day, and Bill Carver. On page 78 there is this error: "Several years later, about 1908, Siringo published his first book, *Riata and Spurs.* It was reported that this publication was suppressed. Siringo then published his revised edition in 1912." *Riata and Spurs* was Siringo's last book, not his first and it was published in 1927 and the revised edition later in the same year.

2173. Swan, Oliver G. (ed.)

Frontier days, edited by Oliver G. Swan. Philadelphia, Macrae-Smith co., publishers [1928]. Pict. cloth. Scarce.

6 p.l., 13–512 p. front. (col.), 12 col. plates (incl. front.). 24.8 cm.
Illus. end papers (col.); illus. t.p.
Also published in a de luxe edition and in slip case.

An anthology containing material on bad men, road agents, Black Bart, Henry Plummer, Billy the Kid, and others. There are many mistakes in the book, especially in the articles by Arthur Chapman, "The Men Who Tamed the Cow-Towns," and the one on Billy the Kid. See my *Burs Under the Saddle* (Item 7) for an enumeration of the errors.

2174. Sweet, Alex E., and J. Amory Knox

On a Mexican mustang through Texas, from the Gulf to the Rio Grande. By Alex E. Sweet and J. Amory Knox. . . . Illustrated. Hartford, Conn., S. S. Scranton & co. . . ., 1883. Pict. cloth. Scarce.

7 p.l., 15–672 p. front., illus., plates, facsms. 22.8 cm.
Headpieces; tailpieces.

A rather facetious account of life in Texas in the early days, with some material on John Wesley Hardin, the Taylor-Sutton feud, and other lawlessness.

2175. Sweetman, Luke D.

Back trailing on open range, by Luke D. Sweetman. Illustrated by L. D. Cram. Caldwell, Idaho, the Caxton printers, ltd., 1951. Pict. cloth. OP.

6 p.l., 13–248 p. front. (col.), illus., map. 23.5 cm.
Half title; illus. end papers; headpieces; vignette; pub. device.

A book about ranching in Montana containing some material on Calamity Jane.

T

2176. Taber, Louise E.

California gold rush days. Stories from the radio series broadcast, by Louise E. Taber. Vol. I, No. 2. [N.p., n.d. (San Francisco), 1936.] Pict. wrappers. Scarce.

3 p.l., 7–55 [1] p. front. (port.), illus., plates, map, (double p.). 23.4 cm.

One of a series of little books published in the form of magazines. This issue contains a chapter on Black Bart.

2177. Tabor, Silver Dollar

Star of blood, by Silver Dollar Tabor. . . . [Denver, Colo., 1909.] Stiff wrappers. Rare.

[3]–74 p. illus., port. 22.3 cm.
Device.

An amateurish story about Allen Dowmen, the outlaw.

2178. Talbot, F. L. (ed.)

St. Louis police department. Illustrated. St. Louis, press of Woodward & Tiernan printing co. [N.d.]. Stiff wrappers. (Cover title.) Scarce.

[260] p. (no pagination). illus., plates, ports., 1 large fold. scene. 23.4 x 31.2 cm.

Adv. and business cards scattered throughout.

Tells about the capture of Ben Kilpatrick and Laura Bullion, members of the Butch Cassidy gang, in St. Louis.

2179. ———

Souvenir. St. Louis police department. [St. Louis, press of Woodward & Tiernan printing co.], 1902. Thin cloth. Rare.

2 p.l., [256] p. (no pagination). plates (many full p.), ports. 23.5 x 31 cm.

Adv. and business cards scattered throughout.

Historical section double column.

Tells about the robbery of the Frisco train at Glendale, Missouri, and the final capture of Marion Hudgepeth, the leader of the gang. It also tells about the capture of Ben Kilpatrick and Laura Bullion, members of the Butch Cassidy gang.

2180. Tallent, Annie D.

The Black Hills; or, the last hunting ground of the Dakotahs. A complete history of the Black Hills of Dakota from their first invasion in 1874 to the present time, comprising a comprehensive account of how they lost them; of numerous adventures of the early settlers; their heroic struggles for supremacy against the hostile Dakotah tribes, and their final victory; the opening of the country to white settlement, and its subsequent development, by Annie D. Tallent. St. Louis, Mo., Nixon-Jones printing co., 1899. Cloth. Scarce.

xxii, 713 p. front. (port. with tissue), plates, ports. 23.6 cm.

Tailpieces.

The author has Billy the Kid a horse thief and a member of the Exelbee (*sic*) gang in the Black Hills. Although she has the Kid named McCarthy, this was not the Billy the Kid of New Mexico, for the latter was certainly never in the Black Hills. The book also contains some information on Wild Bill Hickok, Jack McCall, Dunc Blackburn, and other outlaws.

2181. Targ, William (ed.)

The great American west. A treasury of stories, legends, narratives, songs & ballads of western America, edited with an introduction by William Targ. Cleveland and New York, World publishing co. [1946]. Pict. cloth. OP.

xii p., 1 l., 3–595 p. 21.8 cm.

Glossary of western words: p. 587–591; acknowledgments: p. 593–595.

Half title: "Tales and Legends;" vignette.

An anthology of western stories and articles, among them "Stick 'Em Up," from *Guns of the Frontier*, by William MacLeod Raine; and "Dick Yeager," from *The Cherokee Strip*, by Marquis James.

2182. Tate, Charles Spencer

Pickway, a true narrative, by Charles Spencer Tate. Chicago, Ill., the Golden Rule, 1905. Wrappers. Rare.

3 p.l., 9–150 [5] p. front. (2 ports.), illus. 19.4 cm.

5 p. adv. at end.

The author, who was a gambler of the early West, tells some stories of Liver-Eatin' Johnson and the death of Billy the Kid, but this is not the famous Kid of New Mexico.

2183. Taylor, Drew Kirksey

Taylor's thrilling tales of Texas, being the experiences of Drew Kirksey Taylor, ex-Texas ranger and peace officer on the border of Texas. Written by himself and narrating true incidents of frontier life. [San Antonio, Texas, Guaranty bond printing co.], 1926. Cloth. Scarce.

2 p.l., 7–93 p. front. (port. with tissue), illus. 22 cm.

The author tells about some gunmen he knew, such as John Selman, John Larn, Clay Allison, and John Wesley Hardin. He also claims to have known Billy the Kid personally, and he is another who has him killing a man for each year of his life, and says that the Kid was twenty-three when he was killed. There are many more mistakes.

2184. Taylor, Joseph Henry

Kaleidoscopic lives. A companion book to *Frontier and Indian Life*, by Joseph Henry Taylor. Illustrated. Washburn, N.D., printed and published by the author, 1896. Cloth. Scarce.

3 p.l., [5]–206 [4] p. front., illus. (part on col. paper), ports. 20 cm.

Republished in 1902.

Has some material on lawlessness, including horse stealing and the vigilantes of the Dakotas.

2185. Taylor, Nat M.

A brief history of Roger Mills county, by Nat M. Taylor. [N.p., n.d.] Cloth. (Cover title.) Scarce.

2 p.l., 5–64 p. plate. 22 cm.

2186. Taylor, Ralph C.

Colorado, south of the border, [by] Ralph C. Taylor. Denver, Colo., Sage books [1963]. Cloth.

7 p.l., 15–561 p. illus., plates, ports., maps. 21.6 cm.
Index: p. 550–561.
Half title; pub. device.

Has chapters on the noted Colorado outlaws, the Espinosas, the Reynolds gang, Bat Masterson, and the more modern outlaw gang of Jake Fleagle, as well as Sister Blandina Segale's association with Billy the Kid. The author tells about the robbery of the Amity Bank in Colorado. He gives Kid Wilson the first name Kit, and is also mistaken in saying that Henry Starr was Belle Starr's husband. Though he says that Wilson was never caught, he was.

The author repeats all the mistakes Sister Blandina made in her book and says that Billy the Kid committed twenty-six murders and that "it might have been 30 if he had not been talked out of violence against four Trinidad doctors by Sister Blandina." He has the Kid a newsboy and bootblack in New York before he landed in *Denver* and became an outlaw at the age of sixteen. He has the Kid returning to Kansas after his father and mother died, and has him killed at the age of twenty-six. He says that while Bat Masterson was still on crutches from the wound given him by Sergeant King, *Marshal* Wyatt Earp sent him an urgent call to come to Dodge and help him enforce the law there. We know that Earp was not the marshal and had no authority to hire anyone.

2187. Taylor, Thomas Ulvan

Bill Longley and his wild career, by T. U. Taylor. Bandera, Texas, Frontier Times [n.d.]. Wrappers. (Cover title.) Scarce.

31 p. 22 cm.
Reprinted from the *Frontier Times* in 1926.

A fairly accurate account which the author culled from contemporary newspapers, state records, and interviews with personal friends of the outlaw. It contains some typographical errors.

2188. ———

The Chisholm trail and other routes, by T. U. Taylor. San Antonio, Texas, printed for the *Frontier Times* by the Naylor co., 1936. Cloth. Scarce.

xi, 222 p. front. (map), port., maps. 19.7 cm.
Index: p. 189–194; appendix: p. 195–222.
Half title.

Gives a brief description of Billy the Kid and his association with John Chisum.

2189. ———

The Lee-Peacock feud, by T. U. Taylor. . . . Bandera, Texas, published by *Frontier Times* [n.d.]. Wrappers. Scarce.

10 p. 26.4 cm.
Double column.
Reprinted in 18 p. by the *Frontier Times* publishing house, Grand Prairie, Texas.

A separate reprint of an article on this feud which appeared in the *Frontier Times.*

2190. Terrell, Charles Vernon

The Terrells. Eighty-five years, Texas from Indians to atomic bomb . . ., [by] C. V. Terrell. Austin, Texas, printed for the author by Wilkinson printing co., Dallas, Texas, 1948. Fabrikoid. Scarce.

6 p.l., 13–336 p. plates, ports. 23.3 cm.
Vignette.

Reminiscences of an old-timer. The author is mistaken in saying that Sam Bass started his career in bank and train robbing in Denton County; in fact, he never did any robbing in Denton County at all, and he certainly never robbed a bank at any time, though he was planning to rob one when he was killed.

2191. [Texas]

Moscow memories, 1841–1961. Moscow, Texas, published by the Parent-Teacher Association. . . . [N.d., ca. 1961.] Fabrikoid. Scarce.

2 p.l., 5–128 p. plates, ports. 27.5 cm.
Last 31 p. adv.
Illus. end papers.

Contains an account of John Wesley Hardin and the place where he killed his first man.

2192. ———

Report of the adjutant general of the state of Texas for the year ending August 31st, 1876. Galveston, Shaw & Blaylock, state printers, 1876. Wrappers. Rare.

[3]–13 p. 23 cm.

Reports on lawlessness in the state.

2193. ———

Report of special committees on lawlessness and violence in Texas. Published by order of the convention. Austin, printed at the office of the Daily Republican, 1868. Wrappers. Rare.

[3]–14 p. 21.2 cm.

This report, sent to the carpet-bag governor, E. J. Davis, deplores the many killings of Negroes and troubles with the whites. It was in this period that so many of the noted Texas outlaws, such as John Wesley Hardin and Bill Longley, got their start.

2194. ———

Texas frontier troubles. House of Representatives, 44th Congress, 1st Session report No. 343 [1876]. Sewn. (Caption title.) Rare.

xxi, 180 p. 22.8 cm.

Testimony presented to the special committee on Texas frontier troubles and cattle thefts.

2195. Thane, Eric (pseud. of Ralph Chester Henry)

High border country, by Eric Thane. Edited by Erskine Caldwell. New York, Duell, Sloan & Pearce [1942]. Cloth. Scarce.

ix p., 1 l., 3–335 p. 22 cm.
Index: p. 333–335.
Half title; map on end papers; "First edition" on copyright p.

Contains quite a bit of material on the Montana vigilantes, Boone Helm, Henry Plummer, Joseph Slade, and the Wild Bunch of later days.

2196. ———

The majestic land. Peaks, parks & prevaricators of the Rockies & highlands of the northwest, by Eric Thane. Illustrated. Indianapolis, New York, the Bobbs-Merrill co., inc., publishers [1950]. Cloth. OP.

5 p.l., 11–347 p. plates. 22.2 cm.
Index: p. 333–347.
Half title; map on end papers; "First edition" on copyright p.

Contains some material on Montana outlaws.

2197. Thomas, D. K.

Wild life in the Rocky mountains; or, the lost million dollar gold mine, by D. K. Thomas. Illustrated by Alice Moseley and M. Reynolds. . . . [N.p.], C. E. Thomas pub. co., 1917. Cloth. Pict. label pasted on. Scarce.

5 p.l., 13–221 p. front., illus., plates. 19.5 cm.

Contains chapters on road agents, desperadoes, and the Montana vigilantes.

2198. Thomes, William Henry

The whaleman's adventures in the Sandwich islands and California, by Wm.

H. Thomes. . . . Illustrated. Boston, Lee and Shepard, publishers; New York, Lee, Shepard and Dillingham, 1872. Cloth. Scarce.

5 p.l., 9–444 p. front. (with tissue), plates. 19.7 cm.
"Ocean Life Series."

This book was evidently a popular one in its day, for it was republished in 1874, 1876, 1882, 1885, 1889, and 1890 by various publishers. It tells about the author's supposed encounter with Joaquín Murieta.

2199. Thompson, Albert W.

The story of early Clayton, New Mexico, [by] Albert W. Thompson. [Clayton, N.M., printed by the Clayton News, 1933.] Wrappers. (Cover title.) Rare.

95 p. plates, ports. (last 5 pages). 21.5 cm.

The last half of this little book deals with the life, crimes, and hanging of Black Jack Ketchum.

2200. ———

They were open range days; annals of a western frontier, by Albert W. Thompson. Denver, Colo., the World press, inc., 1946. Cloth. Scarce.

viii p., 1 l., 3–193 [1] p. plates, ports., map, plan. 21.5 cm.
Half title; untrimmed; copyright notice on t.p.
Edition limited to 500 copies.

Contains much material on Black Jack Ketchum and the Coe gang and some information on Billy the Kid and the big fight at Tascosa, Texas.

2201. Thompson, George G.

Bat Masterson; the Dodge City years, by George G. Thompson. Topeka, printed by Kansas State printing plant . . ., 1943. Wrappers. Scarce.

3–55 p. 22.8 cm.
Appendix: p. 47–54; bibliography: p. 55.
Fort Hays Kansas State College studies. Language and Literature series, No. 1, F. B. Streeter, editor. General series, No. 6.

This excellent little treatise is reliable and well annotated. The author claims that his account of Bat's killing of Sergeant King, an entirely different version from the account by Stuart Lake, was told to him by Bat's son. He has Wyatt Earp assistant marshal of Dodge serving under Bassett. Most of his information is taken from contemporary newspaper reports and personal interviews with old-timers and Masterson's son.

2202. Thompson, George Washington

Five years of crime in California; or, the life and confession of G. W. Strong, alias G. W. Clark, who was tried, convicted and hung, August 31st, 1866 at Ukiah City, Mendocino county, California, for the murder of Frances Holmes. A truthful record of this most extraordinary man . . . together with evidence . . . legal proceedings . . . rulings of the courts before whom he was tried. . . . Compiled and arranged by deputy sheriff and one of his prison guards, George Washinton [*sic*] Thompson. Ukiah City, Mendocino County, Calif., published by Peter A. Forsee, January 25th, 1867. Wrappers. Rare.

46 p. 23.3 cm.

2203. Thompson, Henry C.

Sam Hildebrand rides again, by Henry C. Thompson. Bonne Terre, Mo., printed and published by Steinbeck publishing co., 1950. Stiff wrappers. OP.

3 p.l., 113 p. front., 4 plates. 22.2 cm.

One of the few books written about this notorious Missouri outlaw.

2204. Thompson, Mrs. Mary, et al.

Clayton, the friendly town of Union county, New Mexico. A limited edition . . ., [by] Mrs. Mary Thompson, William H. Halley—collaborator: Simon Herstein. [Denver, Colo., published by the Monitor publishing co., 1962.] Stiff pict. wrappers.

iv, 168 [1] p. illus., maps. 21.5 cm.

These authors, like some others, say that Black Jack Ketchum whittled a wooden six-shooter while in prison. One wonders how a one-armed man could do it. There is quite a bit on Ketchum's life in this little book, including some information I have not seen elsewhere. There is some mention of such gunmen as Clay Allison, Billy the Kid, Tom O'Folliard, and Charlie Bowdre. The authors are mistaken in saying that the last three "were buried in one grave."

2205. Thorndike, Thaddeus

Lives and exploits of the daring Frank and Jesse James, containing a graphic and realistic description of their many deeds of unparalleled daring in the robbing of banks and railroad trains, by Thaddeus Thorndike. Baltimore, I. & M. Ottenheimer, publishers, 1909. Pict. wrappers. OP.

vi, 7–185 p. front., illus. 19 cm.

3 p. adv. at end.

Another cheap, unreliable book on the James boys, printed on unusually bad paper.

2206. Thorp, Nathan Howard (Jack)

Story of the southwestern cowboy, pardner of the wind, by N. Howard (Jack) Thorp . . . in collaboration with Neill M. Clark. Illustrated. . . . Caldwell, Idaho, the Caxton printers, ltd., 1945. Cloth. OP.

10 p.l., [21]–309 p. front., plates, ports., music. 23.6 cm.
Appendix: p. [285]–301; index: p. [303]–309.
Half title: "Pardner of the Wind;" pub. device.

One of the best later western books. The author gives some frank opinions of Billy the Kid, Sam Bass, and other outlaws. He claims that a man in Socorro named Jack with an assumed surname was actually Joe (Frank) Jackson, a member of the Sam Bass gang who escaped at Round Rock. Most other accounts I have examined claim that Bill Downing was Jackson, and Downing himself said so. The author is also mistaken in saying that Bass bossed the herd of cattle he helped drive north. Joel Collins was trail boss. His chapter on Billy the Kid is more accurate than most. The author did not live to see his book in print.

2207. Thorp, Raymond W.

Spirit gun of the west; the story of Doc W. F. Carver, plainsman, trapper, buffalo hunter, medicine chief of the Santee Sioux, world's champion marksman, and originator of the American wild west show, by Raymond W. Thorp. . . . Glendale, Calif. . . ., the Arthur H. Clark co., 1957. Cloth.

9 p.l., [19]–266 p. front., plates, ports., facsms. 24.7 cm.
Bibliography: p. [247]–253; index: p. [254]–266.
Half title: Western Frontiersman series VII; pub. device; untrimmed.

Has some material on Wild Bill Hickok.

2208. Thrapp, Dan L.

Al Sieber, chief of scouts, by Dan L. Thrapp. Norman, University of Oklahoma press [1964]. Cloth.

xvi p., 1 l., 3–432 p. plates, ports., map. 23.5 cm.
Bibliography: p. 411–420; index: p. 421–432.
Half title; illus. t.p.; "First edition" on copyright p.

Contains two chapters on the Apache Kid and some scattered material on Tom Horn.

2209. Tibbles, Thomas Henry

Buckskin and blanket days. Memoirs of a friend of the Indians. Written in 1905, by Thomas Henry Tibbles. Garden City, N.Y., Doubleday & co., inc., 1957. Cloth. OP.

8 p.l., 17–336 p. 21.6 cm.

Half title; untrimmed.

Contains some material on Jesse James and the bank robbery at Liberty, Missouri.

2210. Tilden, Freeman

Following the frontier with F. Jay Haynes, pioneer photographer of the old west, [by] Freeman Tilden. New York, Alfred A. Knopf, 1964. Cloth.

xi [1] p., 1 l., 3–406 p., i–vii [1]. front., plates, (11 double p.), ports., map (double p.). 26 cm.

Appendix: p. 399–406; index: p. i–v; index of illustrations: p. vi–[viii].

Has some mention of Calamity Jane and Wild Bill Hickok. The author is mistaken when he says that Hickok had been city marshal of Deadwood before he was killed. He held no office while he was in Deadwood.

2211. Tilghman, Zoe Agnes (Stratton)

Marshal of the last frontier. Life and service of William Matthew (Bill) Tilghman for 50 years one of the greatest peace officers of the west, by his wife Zoe A. Tilghman. Glendale, Calif., the Arthur H. Clark co., 1949. Cloth.

9 p.l., [19]–406 p. front. (port.), plates, ports., fold. map at end. 24 cm.

Index: p. [397]–406.

Half title: Western Frontiersmen series III; pub. device; untrimmed.

This book, the only complete biography of this noted peace officer, tells about his experiences with the gunmen of Dodge City and the outlaws of Oklahoma and about his tragic death.

2212. ———

Outlaw days. A true history of early-day Oklahoma characters, revised and enlarged from the records of Wm. Tilghman, by Zoe A. Tilghman (Mrs. Bill Tilghman). [Oklahoma City, Okla.], Harlow publishing co., 1926. Pict. wrappers. Scarce.

iii p., 1 l., 138 p. front., ports. 17.3 cm.

This book has been used extensively as source material by later writers, but it contains the same mistakes as those in the Graves book (see Item 859). The author says that Heck Thomas was an express messenger on a train that was held up by Sam Bass "between Galveston and Denison" and that Thomas saved twenty-two thousand dollars by hiding the money in a stove and giving the robbers a bundle of papers. She also says that Thomas helped break up the Bass gang. Thomas had nothing to do with the finish of the Bass gang. She repeats the old legend about Belle Starr refusing to identify her dead husband to keep his assassin from collecting the reward. Both this volume and Newsom's *The Life and Practice of the Wild and Modern Indian* were issued by the same publisher, and there are many similarities between them.

2213. ———

Spotlight. Bat Masterson and Wyatt Earp as U.S. deputy marshals, by Zoe A. Tilghman. San Antonio, Texas, the Naylor co. [1960]. Stiff pict. wrappers.

3 p.l., 21 p. 19 cm.

Mrs. Tilghman did a great deal of research trying to determine whether or not Masterson and Earp held the office of deputy U.S. marshal. It seems that Masterson received an appointment from Theodore Roosevelt after he left the West and went to New York and that Earp was appointed to the office just before he left Tombstone.

2214. Tillotson, F. H.

How to be a detective. A complete text book of the methods and practices used by the best detectives in dealing with the criminal, together with a criminal vocabulary. Illustrated. By F. H. Tillotson. . . . Kansas City, Mo., Hailman printing co., 1909. Cloth on thin boards. Scarce.

2 p.l., [5]–187 [1] p. illus., plates, ports., facsm. 17 cm.

Most of this book deals with safe blowers, but there is some information about Pat Crowe and the Oklahoma outlaw Ben Cravens.

2215. Timmons, William

Twilight on the range. Recollections of a latterday cowboy, [by] William Timmons. Austin, University of Texas press [1962]. Cloth.

7 p.l., 3–223 p. plates, ports. 23.5 cm.
Index: p. 215–223.
Half title; illus. t.p.; errata slip laid in; pub. device.
Number 2 of the M. K. Range Life series.

Has some mention of Billy the Kid, Pat Garrett, the Daltons, and Temple Houston.

2216. Tinkham, George H.

California men and events. Time 1769–1890, by George H. Tinkham. . . . [Stockton, Calif., Record publishing co., 1915.] Cloth. Scarce.

6 p.l., 15–336 p. illus., plates, ports. 20.3 cm.

Chapter XI, though entitled "Crimes and Criminals," does not deal with any particular outlaws of the West.

2217. ———

History of San Joaquin county, California, with biographical sketches of the leading men and women of the county who have been identified with its growth and development from the early days to the present. History by George H. Tinkham. Illustrated. Los Angeles, Historic Record co., 1923. Three-quarter leather. Scarce.

ix, [33]–1640 p. plates, ports. (part with tissues). 29.3 cm.
Double column.

Chapter XXII, entitled "Courts and Criminals," contains information about Tom Bell and Black Bart.

2218. ———

A history of Stockton from its organization up to the present time, including a sketch of the San Joaquin county, comprising a history of the government, politics, state of society, religion . . . and miscellaneous events within the past thirty years, by George H. Tinkham. San Francisco, W. H. Hinton & co., printers, 1880. Cloth. Scarce.

xvi p., 1 l., 397 p. front. (port. pasted in), illus., plates, ports. 22.5 cm.
Appendix: p. [387]–397.

Has some mention of Murieta.

2219. Tittsworth, W. G.

Outskirt episodes. . . . W. G. Tittsworth, the author. [Avoca, Iowa, 1927.] Cloth. Rare.

3 p.l., [7]–232 [1] p. 20 cm.
Port. of author tipped in on t.p.

This rare book is the personal narrative of the author's life and adventures in the Wyoming country and his experiences among the Rocky Mountain outlaws in the days when the Union Pacific was building westward. The author tells about Tom Horn's killings and his execution.

2220. Tolbert, Frank X.

An informal history of Texas. From Cabeza de Vaca to Temple Houston. Illustrated. [By] Frank X. Tolbert. New York, Harper & brothers, publishers [1961]. Cloth.

viii p., 1 l., 275 [1] p. illus., plates, 3 maps (1 double p.). 21.7 cm.
Notes: p. 245–260; sources: p. 261–263; index: p. 265–275.
Half title; map on end papers; untrimmed.

Has some information on Al Jennings, a mention of Billy the Kid and Bat Masterson, and some information on Temple Houston.

2221. [Tombstone]

Souvenir of Tombstone. [N.p., n.d.] Wrappers. OP.

[13] p. (no pagination). plates, ports., plan. 22.5 cm.
5 p. adv. at end and adv. on rear wrapper.

This little pamphlet gives some information on the Earp-Clanton feud.

2222. Tompkins, Stuart Ramsay

Alaska, promyshlennik and sourdough, by Stuart Ramsay Tompkins. Norman, University of Oklahoma press, 1945. Cloth.

xiv p., 1 l., 3–350 p. plates, ports., maps. 21 cm.
Bibliography: p. 305–338; index: p. 339–350.
Half title; outline map on t.p.

Contains some minor material on Soapy Smith.

2223. Tompkins, Walker A.

Santa Barbara's royal rancho, the fabulous history of Los Dos Pueblos, by Walker A. Tompkins. Berkeley, Calif., Howell-North, 1960. Pict. cloth.

viii p., 1 l., 282 p. plates, ports., facsms. 23.5 cm.
Half title; map on end papers.

Contains several chapters on the activities of Jack Powers and a mention of Murieta.

2224. Toole, K. Ross

Montana, an uncommon land, [by] K. Ross Toole. Norman, University of Oklahoma press [1959]. Cloth.

x p., 1 l., 3–278 p. plates, ports., maps. 23.5 cm.
Bibliography: p. 259–269; index: p. 270–278.
Half title; double t.p.; "First edition" on copyright p.

Has some information on Henry Plummer and the Montana vigilantes.

2225. Toponce, Alexander

Reminiscences of Alexander Toponce, pioneer, 1839–1923, [written by himself]. [Ogden, Utah, Mrs. Kate Toponce, 1923.] Morocco. Very scarce.

7 p.l., 15–248 p. front. (port.), plates, ports. 18 cm.
Device.

This privately printed book has several chapters on the road agents and vigilantes of Montana.

2226. Torchiana, Henry Albert William van Coenen

California gringos, by H. A. van Coenen Torchiana. . . . San Francisco, Calif., Paul Elder and co. [1930]. Cloth. Scarce.

5 p.l., 281 p. front. (port.), plates. 19.6 cm.

Contains some material on Murieta, Black Bart, Chris Evans, the Sontags, and other California outlaws.

2227. ———

Story of the mission Santa Cruz, by H. A. van Coenen Torchiana. . . . San Francisco, Calif., Paul Elder and co., 1933. Cloth. Scarce.

xix p., 2 l., 5–460 p. front., plates, maps, facsms. 24 cm.
Appendix: p. 403–447; index: p. 449–460.

Contains some material on Murieta based upon the *Police Gazette* account.

2228. Towle, Virginia Rowe

Vigilante woman, by Virginia Rowe Towle. South Brunswick, N.Y., A. S. Barnes and co., inc.; London, Thomas Yoseloff, ltd. [1966]. Cloth.

10 p.l., [21]–182 p. plates, ports., facsm. 21.5 cm.
Bibliography: p. [177]–182.
Half title; pub. device.

Has a chapter on Electra Bryan, who married Henry Plummer, and tells about Plummer's early life and some of his crimes. In a chapter on Maria Virginia Slade there is much information on Joseph A. Slade, her husband, and a bad man when drunk. In spite of his meanness she stuck to him until his death at the hands of vigilantes.

2229. Towne, Charles W.

"Her majesty Montana." Highlights in the history of a state fifty years old in 1939. A series of 28 radio broadcasts, by C. W. Towne on the program of the Montana Power co. [N.p., n.d., ca. 1939.] Wrappers. (Cover title.) Scarce.

2–72 p. illus., map. 23 cm.
Illus. chap. headings.

Has a chapter on the Plummer gang and the Montana vigilantes.

2230. ———

"Her majesty Montana." The pioneer period: 1743–1877; the industrial period: 1878–1938. Text by Charles W. Towne. Illustrated by Frank Ward and Bob Hall. [N.p., n.d., ca. 1939.] Wrappers. Scarce.

150 p. illus. 22.5 cm.

Has a chapter on Henry Plummer and the Montana vigilantes.

2231. Townshend, R. B.

The tenderfoot in New Mexico, by R. B. Townshend. London, John Lane. the Bodley Head, ltd. [1923]. Cloth. Scarce.

ix p., 1 l., 257 p. front., plates, ports. 22.5 cm.
Half title; untrimmed.
American edition published by Dodd, Mead co., New York, in 1924.

One of a series of books by this English author, who spent some time in the American West and wrote about his travels. In this book he tells of meeting Billy the Kid in New Mexico.

2232. Tracy, Rev. Henry

A confession of the awful and bloody transactions in the life of Charles Wallace, the fiend-like murderer of Miss Mary Rogers, the beautiful cigar-girl of Broadway, New York, whose fate has for several years past been wrapt in the most profound mystery; together with an authentic statement of the many burglaries and murders of Wallace and the notorious and daring thief, Snelling; and an account of the murder and robbery of Mr. Parks, of Newport, Kentucky, also perpetrated by Wallace; a thrilling narrative of his intercourse with the Brown murderess, Emeline Morere. . . . From his own memoranda, given at the burning stake, to Rev. Henry Tracy. New Orleans, published by E. E. Barclay & co., 1851. Pict. wrappers. Extremely rare.

vi, 7–31 p. illus., plates. 23 cm.

Characteristic of earlier publications on criminals. Note that this one is also edited by a minister.

2233. Train, Arthur

On the trail of the bad men, by Arthur Train. . . . New York, Charles Scribner's sons, 1925. Cloth. Scarce.

xviii p., 3 l., 5–427 p. 21 cm.
Half title; untrimmed.

The first chapter deals with some outlaws of Arizona and with the Earp-Clanton feud. The author makes a mistake in saying that Wyatt Earp was a U.S. marshal at that time. He has a character telling him about the O K Corral fight and has him saying that Virgil Earp used a shotgun and that when the Earps opened fire all the Clantons except Ike were killed.

2234. Travers, James W.

California. Romance of clipper ships and gold rush days, by James W. Travers. Los Angeles, Calif., Wetzel publishing co., inc. [1949]. Cloth. OP.

8 p.l., 17–309 p. plates, ports., facsms. 21 cm.

The author gives some material on Murieta, Black Bart, and other stagecoach robbers.

2235. Trelawney-Ansell, E. C.

I followed gold, by E. C. Trelawney-Ansell. London, Peter Davies [1938]. Cloth. Scarce.

6 p.l., 13–320 p. 20.3 cm.
Half title.
Published in New York by Lee Furnam, inc., in 1939.

The author, who knew Soapy Smith personally, tells about some of his activities and his death.

2236. Trenholm, Virginia Cole

Footprints on the frontier. Saga of the La Ramie region of Wyoming, by Virginia Cole Trenholm. [Douglas, Wyo., printed by Douglas Enterprise co., 1945.] Cloth. Scarce.

10 p.l., [21]–384 p. front., plates, ports. 23.5 cm.
Bibliography: p. [362]–365; index: p. [366]–384.
Half title; vignette.
Colophon: "Edition limited to one thousand copies of which this is No. ——."

The author is mistaken in saying that Calamity Jane was the first white woman to enter the Black Hills; Calamity Jane did not go into the Black Hills until several years after the rush began into the region. The author repeats the legend that Jane got her nickname by rescuing Captain Egan, but says this was Buffalo Bill's story.

The author writes: "She is said to have saved the life of Jack McCaul [*sic*], a stage driver, and his six passengers by driving the coach to safety after McCaul had been wounded by Indians. McCaul, a number of years later, assassinated Wild Bill at Deadwood, . . . and in turn was lynched by a mob supposed to have been led by Calamity Jane." Only the information about the killing of Wild Bill is correct. The book also contains some information about Tom Horn and the Johnson County War.

2237. ——, and Maurine Carley

Wyoming pageant, by Virginia Cole Trenholm and Maurine Carley. Casper, Wyo., Prairie publishing co. [1946]. Pict. cloth. OP.

4 p.l., [9]–272 p. front., illus. (2 col.), ports., map, tables. 20.2 cm.
Bibliography: p. 256–262; index: p. 263–272.
Map on end papers.

Has some information about the Johnson County War and the Wyoming gunmen of that period, such as Tom Horn, Nate Champion, Nick Ray, and Joseph Slade, as well as about Cattle Kate and Calamity Jane.

2238. Triggs, J. H.

History of Cheyenne and northern Wyoming, embracing the gold fields of the Black Hills, Powder River and Big Horn counties . . ., by J. H. Triggs. Omaha, Nebr., printed at the Herald steam book and job printing house, 1876. Wrappers. Exceedingly rare.

3 p.l., 7–144 p. front. (fold. map). 22.5 cm.
Advertisements: p. 132–144 and back wrapper.
Republished in Laramie in 1955.

A very rare early imprint with some material on the vigilantes.

2239. ———

History and directory of Laramie City, Wyoming territory, comprising a brief history of Laramie City from its first settlement to the present time, together with sketches of the characteristics and resources of the surrounding country; including a minute description of a portion of the mining region of the Black Hills. Also a general and business directory of Laramie City, by J. H. Triggs. Laramie City, Daily Sentinel print, 1875. Wrappers. Exceedingly rare.

[3]–91 p. 22.3 cm.
Official directory: p. 62–63; general directory: p. 64–91.
Full p. adv. on verso of first 23 pages.
Republished in Laramie in 1955.

This exceedingly rare imprint gives a frank history of Laramie in its turbulent days and reign of violence.

2240. ———

A reliable and correct guide to the Black Hills, Powder River and Big Horn gold fields. Full description of the country, how to get to it, including a correct map of the gold regions . . ., by J. H. Triggs. Omaha, Nebr., printed at the Herald steam book and job printing house, 1876. Wrappers. Exceedingly rare.

1 p.l., [3]–144 p. front. (fold. map). 22.2 cm.
Adv. on verso front wrapper and last 13 pages.
Another edition published in 1878.

With the exception of the first sixteen pages, this book is identical with the author's *History of Cheyenne and Northern Wyoming* (Item 2238). Only three or four copies are known to exist. It contains a chapter on the vigilantes.

2241. Trimble, William J.

The mining advance into the inland empire. A comparative study of the beginnings of the mining industry in Idaho and Montana, eastern Washington and Oregon, and the southern exterior of British Columbia and the institutions and laws based upon that industry, by William J. Trimble. . . . A thesis submitted for the degree of Doctor of Philosophy, the University of Wisconsin. Madison, Wisc., 1914. Stiff wrappers. Rare.

3 p.l., [7]–254 p. front. (map). 23.2 cm.

Bulletin of the University of Wisconsin, No. 638. History series, Vol. 3, No. 2.

Has a long chapter, entitled "The Evolution of Order and Law In the American Territories," dealing with the vigilantes and outlaws of Montana and Idaho.

2242. Trinka, Zena Irma

Out where the west begins, being the early and romantic history of North Dakota, by Zena Irma Trinka. . . . Illustrated from photographs by D. F. Barry, the noted Indian photographer. Map and 74 illustrations. St. Paul, Minn., the Pioneer co., 1920. Pict. fabrikoid. Scarce.

xvi p., 1 l., 432 p. front. (port. with tissue), plates (1 col.), ports., fold. map. 22 cm.

Index: p. 427–432.

Contains a chapter on the North Dakota vigilantes.

2243. Triplett, Col. Frank

Conquering the wilderness; or, new pictorial history of the life and times of the pioneer heroes and heroines of America . . ., by Colonel Frank Triplett . . . with 200 portraits from life, original and striking engravings from the designs by Nast, Darley and other eminent artists. New York and St. Louis, N. D. Thompson publishing co., 1883. Cloth. Scarce.

xxxix p., 1 l., 43–742 p. front., illus., plates, ports. 23.5 cm.

Republished several times.

This book contains some very uncomplimentary statements about Wild Bill Hickok. Among other things the author says: "This fellow was a red-handed murderer without a single redeeming trait, not even possessing the fearless bravery that usually characterizes the western desperado. It is extremely doubtful if, in his whole career, Wild Bill ever killed an enemy who had an even chance. His killings, despite all that his admiring biographers may say, were brutal murders, in which he relentlessly 'took the drop,' as men of his class express it, and slaughtered his foe, as the butcher does the unsuspecting ox, and with little mercy and remorse."

2244. ———

History, romance and philosophy of great American crimes and criminals; including the great typical crimes that have marked the various periods of American history from the foundation of the republic to the present day . . ., by Col. Frank Triplett . . . with over 150 fine engravings, representing scenes, incidents and personal portraits. St. Louis, N. D. Thompson and co., 1884. Pict. cloth. Scarce.

xxxix p., 1 l., 43–742 p. front., illus., plates, ports. 23.5 cm.

Republished by Park publishing co., Hartford, Conn., 1885.

The author gives sketches of outlaws from Murrell, the Harpes, and Joseph Hare down through the years to the Benders, Ben Thompson, the Jameses, and the Youngers.

2245. ———

The life, times and treacherous death of Jesse James. The only correct and authorized edition. Giving full particulars of each and every dark and desperate deed in the career of this most noted outlaw of any time or nation. The facts and incidents contained in this volume were dictated to Frank Triplett by Mrs. Jesse James, wife of the bandit, and Mrs. Zerelda Samuel, his mother. Consequently every secret act—every hitherto unknown incident—every crime and every motive is herein truthfully disclosed. . . . Chicago, Ill., St. Louis, Mo., Atlanta, Ga., J. H. Chambers & co., 1882. Pict. cloth. Exceedingly rare.

xvi p., 1 l., [17]–416 p. front., illus., plates, ports. 19 cm.

Running title: "Life and Times of Jesse and Frank James."

Republished several months later with a front., port. of Jesse James. Published again in an enlarged edition, including details about Frank James's surrender and with an added plate.

The few copies in existence are usually in poor condition. In a fairly reliable chapter on the Union Pacific robbery by the Collins-Bass gang, the author denies that Jesse James took part, as stated by many other writers. He does, however, make the mistake of giving Joel Collins the first name Jim.

This book has had an interesting history. Of two editions, one is thought to have been issued in the summer of 1882 and the second in early November of the same year and both suppressed shortly afterward. The second edition has an additional chapter on Frank James's surrender, his portrait, and a total of 425 pages. Its publication caused a great deal of trouble to both its publisher and its author. It is purported to have been dictated to the author by Jesse James's wife and his mother, but both women emphatically denied it. In an interview with a reporter for the *St. Louis Post-Dispatch*, published May 1, 1882, James's wife makes the following statement:

". . . my soul revolts at the suggestion of lending my name and sanction to any publication of Jesse James' career, yet I have been represented as dictating such a book, and coming to St. Louis to revise such matter as has already been prepared for the publication. Though I have frequently and publicly declared that I know absolutely nothing concerning any and all crimes charged to the commission of my husband, and that under no circumstances would I lend my name to any publication descriptive of his career, yet I am again required to reassert all that I have previously said, and to also particularize the cause for this repetition. A publisher in St. Louis, named J. H. Chambers, has circulated broadcast an assertion that he was having prepared by a writer named Frank Triplett a book on the lives and careers of Frank and Jesse James, and that all matter it would contain would be furnished by me. This statement is absolutely false, as I am not, never have been, and never will—because I can not—furnish any facts criminating either Frank or Jesse James."

To contradict this statement the *Kansas City Evening Star* published the following comment:

"Her [Mrs. James's] arrangement with Chambers, the St. Louis publisher, has fallen through. It appears she furnished material for the book and was to be allowed to see the proofs and make any changes or alterations she might choose; in fact it was to contain nothing of which she disapproved, she claims that Chambers violated his agreement, and would not allow her to see 92 out of 220 pages of the book. Thereupon she informed him that she would withdraw from all connections with the book and publish a card disavowing and repudiating it."

To quote again from the *St. Louis Post-Dispatch* of May 1, 1882:

"Persons entertaining any doubt as to the sources of our information or [the book's] full and reliable character can have all doubts removed by calling at our office, corner Third and Locust Streets, and inspecting the contract, letters, receipts etc., signed by Mrs. James and Mrs. Samuel." Below this statement the paper printed a facsimile of a receipt for $50 in advance royalty signed by both women.

The author devotes a long chapter to accusing Governor Crittenden in strong language of conspiring with Bob and Charlie Ford to murder Jesse. It appears that several months passed before Governor Crittenden heard of this book. When he did, he saw to the destruction of every copy he could lay his hands upon. To make matters worse, the publisher was sued by Mrs. James, and on top of it all Frank James objected to the book because it accused him of moral misconduct. All this made the history of the book a rugged one. One does not wonder at its rarity.

2246. Truman, Benjamin Cummings

Life, adventures and capture of Tiburcio Vásquez, the great California bandit and murderer, by Maj. Ben C. Truman, editor of *Los Angeles Star*. [Los Angeles], printed at the Los Angeles Star office, 1874. Pict. wrappers. Exceedingly rare.

[3]–44 p. front. (map), diagr. 22.8 cm.
Port. on front wrapper.

The frontispiece on the recto of the first flyleaf after the cover is a map showing the location of Vásquez' capture. There are advertisements on the inside of the front wrapper, inside the back wrapper, and outside the back wrapper. On pages 34 to 44 is an account in Spanish of Vásquez' capture. Among the rarest books about this outlaw.

Reprinted in 1941 by the Clyde Brownes at the Abbey San Encino press, Los Angeles. Cloth and leather. Scarce.

3 p.l., [7]–43 [1] p. front. 24.4 cm.
Half title.
Colophon: "This edition of Tiburcio Vásquez, designed by the Clyde Brownes, father and son, was set by the latter in Linotype Garamond No. 3, and printed on Strathmore Old Laid Book by Frank Masley of the Abbey. The portrait of Vásquez, taken from two dissimilar ones of his day, was drawn by artist Vince Newcomes, the cover fashioned by Earle A. Gray. One hundred copies of this book have been printed, of which this is No. ——."

This reprint is not complete, only the first thirty pages of the original being included.

2247. ———

Occidental sketches, by Major Ben C. Truman. . . . San Francisco, San Francisco News co., publishers, 1881. Cloth. Rare.

4 p.l., [11]–212 [12] p. 17.8 cm.
Vignette; 12 p. adv. at end.

Chapter VII, entitled "Three Extinct Citizens," is about outlaws and stage robbers. Chapter XI deals with the capture and hanging of Vásquez.

2248. [Tuolumne County]

A history of Tuolumne county, California. Compiled from the most authentic records. San Francisco, published by B. F. Alley, 1882. Calf. Scarce.

xi, 509 p. ports. 21.5 cm.
Appendix: p. [3]–48 at end.

Contains a chapter on Murieta.

2249. Turilli, Rudy

I knew Jesse James, by Rudy Turilli. Stanton, Mo. . . ., 1966. Pict. wrappers.

[80] p. (no pagination). plates, ports., facsms. 25.8 cm.
Partly double column.

This author is another who claims that the late J. Frank Dalton was the original Jesse James. He goes to some length to prove his point, including notorized affidavits, but I am sure that Jesse was laid in his grave in 1882.

2250. Turner, John Peter

The north-west mounted police, 1873–1893, by John Peter Turner. . . . Inclusive of the great transition period in the Canadian west, 1873–1893, when the law and order was introduced and established. Ottawa, Edmund Cloutier. . . . King's printer and controller of Stationery, 1950. Stiff wrappers. Pub. in two volumes.

Vol. I, xiii, 686 p. plates, ports., fold. map at end. 24.8 cm.
Half title; pub. device.

Vol. II, 610 p. plates, ports. 24.8 cm.
Index: p. 577–610.
Half title; pub. device; errata at end.

Has much on lawlessness, cattle rustling, and murders.

2251. Turner, Mary Honeyman Ten Eyck (Mrs. Avery Turner)

Avery Turner, pioneer railroad and empire builder of the great southwest, by Mrs. Avery Turner. Amarillo, [Texas]. Southwestern printing co., 1933. Stiff wrappers. Rare.

3–46 p. front. (port. with tissue), plates, ports. 23.3 cm.

This privately printed little book has some slight information about Billy the Kid, John Poe, and Wyatt Earp.

2252. ———

These high plains, by Mary Honeyman Ten Eyck Turner (Mrs. Avery Turner). Amarillo, Texas, [printed by the Russell stationery co.]), 1941. Cloth. Col. pict. label pasted on. Rare.

4 p.l., 11–94 p. front. (port.), plates. 24 cm.
Half title.
"Limited to 150 books." Privately printed.

The author states that Billy the Kid was born July, 1881, the month and year in which he was killed, and that he was "a murderer at 12 years of age and had 21 notches on his gun, one for each victim." She further states that he was killed when Pat Garrett shot him in the back.

2253. Tuttle, Rev. D. S.

Reminiscences of a missionary bishop, by Rev. D. S. Tuttle. . . . New York, Thomas Whittaker [1906]. Dec. cloth. Scarce.

v, 498 p. front. (port. with tissue), ports. 21.2 cm.
Index: p. 491–498.
Untrimmed.

Has much on Virginia City, the vigilantes' dealings with Henry Plummer, George Ives, and the others.

2254. Twitchell, Ralph Emerson

The leading facts of New Mexico history, by Ralph Emerson Twitchell. . . . Cedar Rapids, Iowa, the Torch press, 1911–1917. Cloth. Pub. in four volumes. Scarce.

Vol. I, xxi p., 3 l., 3–506 p. front. (col.), plates, ports., facsms., fold. map. 24.8 cm.
Index: p. [487]–506.
Vol. II, xxi p., 3 l., 3–631 p. front. (port.), plates, ports., facsms., 3 fold. maps. 24.8 cm.
Index: p. [611]–631.
Half title.
Vols. III and IV, biographical.
Published in a subscriber's edition of 1,500 numbered and signed copies.

The author tells about the Lincoln County War and claims that Billy the Kid killed only nine men. He misspells Bowdre as Bowder, McSween as McSwain, and Tunstall as Tunstel.

2255. Tyler, George C.

Whatever goes up. The hazardous fortunes of a natural born gambler, by George C. Tyler in collaboration with J. C. Furnas. With a word of introduction by Booth Tarkington. Illustrated. Indianapolis, the Bobbs-Merrill co., publishers [1934]. Cloth. Scarce.

xvii p., 1 l., 21–317 p. front. (port.), plates, ports., facsm. 22.6 cm.
Index: p. 307–317.
Half title; untrimmed; "First edition" on copyright p.

Has some information on the James boys, Bat Masterson, and Dodge City.

2256. Tyler, George W.

The history of Bell county, by George W. Tyler; edited by Charles W. Ramsdell. San Antonio, Texas, the Naylor co., 1936. Cloth. Scarce.

xxiii p., 1 l., 425 p. front. (port.), plates, ports., 2 fold. maps. 23.4 cm.

Index: p. 405–425.

"At [the author's death] the writing was incomplete and some was in the form of rough notes. It was left to the editor . . . to revise and condense the manuscript, and, in a few instances, to fill out the narrative" (p. ix).

Contains some material on Sam Bass, Bill Longley, and other Texas outlaws.

U

2257. Upshur, George Lyttleton

As I recall them. Memories of crowded years, by George Lyttleton Upshur. Introduction by Rufus Rockwell Wilson. New York, Wilson-Erickson, inc., 1936. Cloth. Scarce.

xi p., 1 l., 271 [1] p. front., plates, ports. 23.5 cm.

Index: p. 261–271.

Half title.

Colophon: "Of this limited edition of As I Recall Them seven hundred and fifty copies have been printed, and all have been signed by the author ——. This is copy No. ——."

The author claims to have been on the stagecoach when Bud Philpot was killed by stage robbers, and he claims that Wyatt Earp and Doc Holliday did the high-jacking. He writes that "the Earps invariably laid murders like these on 'bad cowboys,'" and says that "the former were eventually driven from the state of Arizona." He tells about Curly Bill Brocius and John Ringo and claims that Ringo committed suicide when he found himself in the desert crazed by thirst and without a horse, his animal having run away while he took a drunken nap. "The lead in the cartridges that remained," he writes, "had been chewed to pieces in his effort to create saliva to assuage his thirst. So died John Ringo, the best and most powerful of all the cowboy gang leaders."

2258. Upton, Charles Elmer

Pioneers of El Dorado, by Charles Elmer Upton. . . . Placerville, Calif., Charles Elmer Upton, publisher, 1906. Cloth. Scarce.

3 p.l., [3]–201 [1] p. plates. 20.6 cm.

Appendix: p. [181]–201.

The appendix gives a complete "history" of Joaquín Murieta based upon the Ridge account.

2259. Urquhart, Lena M.

Roll call. The violent and lawless, by Lena M. Urquhart. Denver, Colo., Golden Bell press [1967]. Stiff pict. wrappers.

3 p.l., 7–57 p. illus., plates (1 double p.), ports., map, facsm. 21.5 cm.
Bibliography: p. 56–57.

Has a chapter on Doc Holliday during his stay at Glenwood Springs and another on Kid Curry. Some of the author's story of Curry is unreliable.

2260. [U.S. House of Representatives]

Depredations on the Texas frontier. U.S. House of Representatives, 43rd Congress, 1st Session, Report No. 395. [Washington, 1874.] Scarce.

3 p. 22.8 cm.

A report on cattle stealing on the Mexican border.

2261. ———

43rd Congress, 2nd Session, Ex. Doc. No. 175. Western Judicial District of Arkansas. Letter from the Attorney-General relative to the claim arising from expenditures of the marshal's office of the Western Judicial District of Arkansas. [N.d.]. Sewn. Rare.

156 p. 22.8 cm.

Contains some information on the early law enforcement out of the court at Fort Smith, Arkansas.

2262. ———

44th Congress, 1st Session, Report No. 343. Texas frontier troubles. [N.J.]. Sewn. Rare.

xxi, 180 p. large fold. map. 22.8 cm.

Has a great deal on the lawlessness of the frontier of Texas.

V

2263. Vandor, Paul E.

History of Fresno county, California, with biographical sketches of the leading men and women of the county who have been identified with its growth and development from the early days to the present. History by Paul E. Vandor.

Illustrated. . . . Los Angeles, Calif., Historic Record co., 1919. Three-quarter leather. Pub. in two volumes. Scarce.

Vol. I, 12 p.l., [31]–1286 [1] p. plates, ports. (part with tissues). 27.8 cm.
Vol. II, biographical.

Several chapters are devoted to California outlaws, one to Vásquez, one to the Evans-Sontag gang, and another to various criminals of the county, including Murieta.

2264. Van Doren, Mark (ed.)

An autobiography of America. Edited by Mark Van Doren. New York, Albert & Charlie Boni, MCMXXIX. Cloth. Scarce.

xiv p., 1 l., 3–737 p. 21.4 cm.
Bibliography: p. 731–733; index: p. 735–737.

Has a chapter on Billy the Kid quoted from Siringo's book *Riata and Spurs.*

2265. Verckler, Stewart P.

Cowtown-Abilene. The story of Abilene, Kansas, 1867–1875, [by] Stewart P. Verckler. New York, Carlton press, 1961. Cloth.

5 p.l., 76 p. front. (map), illus., plan. 21.8 cm.
Half title.

This little book has quite a few errors in it, especially in the account of the killing of Phil Coe by Wild Bill Hickok.

2266. Vernon, Joseph S., and Capt. Henry Booth

Along the old trail. A history of the old and a story of the new Santa Fe trail. Cimarron, Kans., Larned, Kans., Tucker-Vernon co., publishers [1910]. Cloth. Scarce.

190 p. front. (col.), plates (2 col. incl. front.), ports. 21.7 cm.
Vignette; published in three parts.

Contains information on Dodge City and on Mysterious Dave Mathers and other gunmen of that cow town.

2267. Vestal, Emmett

"Texas Slim. . . ." My ten years in hell, [by] Emmett Vestal. . . . [Montgomery, Ala., printed by Johnson printing co., n.d.] Stiff wrappers. Scarce.

3 p.l., 7–135 p. front., plates, ports. 19.3 cm.

A little-known western outlaw who later became an evangelist tells the story of his life.

2268. Vestal, Stanley (pseud. of Walter S. Campbell)

The Missouri, by Stanley Vestal. Illustrated by Getlar Smith. Maps by George Annand. New York, Toronto, Farrar & Rinehart, inc. [1945]. Cloth. OP.

x p., 2 l., 5–368 p. illus., maps (1 double p.). 21 cm.

Rivers of America series.

Notes: p. 335–343; acknowledgments: p. 345–347; bibliography: p. 349–354; index: p. 355–368.

Half title; illus. end papers; illus. t.p.; first edition: "FR" in device on copyright p.

Contains some material on Jesse James and the other Missouri outlaws.

2269. ———

Queen of cowtowns, Dodge City. "The wickedest little city in America," 1872–1886, by Stanley Vestal. New York, Harper & brothers [1952]. Cloth. OP.

viii p., 2 l., 285 p. plates, ports. 21.5 cm.

Notes: p. 271–279; bibliography: p. 281–282; acknowledgments: p. 283–285.

Half title; pub. device; untrimmed; "First edition" on copyright p.

Though the author makes several mistakes, this is still one of the best books on Dodge City. Most of its gunmen come in for some attention. Under the bottom illustration opposite page 21 the caption should read "Civilian model" instead of "Pavillion model." The author told me that he had asked the publishers to make this correction. If the book is reprinted, this error will be a mark of identity of the first state.

2270. ———

Short grass country, by Stanley Vestal. Edited by Erskine Caldwell. New York, Duell, Sloan & Pearce [1941]. Cloth. Scarce.

x p., 1 l., 3–304 p. 22 cm.

Index: p. 299–304.

Half title; map on end papers; "First edition" on copyright p.

In two chapters the author deals extensively with lawlessness in the short-grass country. Such officers as Bat Masterson, Bill Tilghman, and Wyatt Earp are mentioned.

2271. ———

Wagons west. Story of the old trail to Santa Fe, by Stanley Vestal. Illustrations by Irwin Shope. New York, published by American Pioneer Trails association, 1946. Stiff col. pict. wrappers. Rare.

2 p.l., 50 p. illus., map (double p.). 17.7 cm.

Contains material on Dodge City, Luke Short, Bat Masterson, Wyatt Earp, and Mysterious Dave Mathers.

2272. **Vickers, C. L. (ed.)**

History of the Arkansas valley, Colorado. Illustrated. Chicago, O. L. Baskin and co., 1881. Morocco. Scarce.

vii p., 1 l., [11]–889 p. front., plates, ports. 25.3 cm.
Double column.

Contains chapters on the vigilantes and outlaws of Colorado.

2273. **Visscher, William Lightfoot**

Buffalo Bill's own story of his life and deeds. This autobiography tells in his own graphic words the wonderful story of his heroic career. . . . His autobiography is brought up to date including a full account of his death and burial, written by his boyhood chum and life-long friend, William Lightfoot Visscher. . . . [N.p., 1917.] Cloth. Port. pasted on. Scarce.

xiii, 15–352 p. front., illus., plates, ports. 21.5 cm.

Like most of the books about Buffalo Bill, this one also contains some material on Wild Bill Hickok; but unlike most of them, it does not mention the McCanles "fight."

2274. **Vivian, A. Pendarves**

Wanderings in a western land. By A. Pendarves Vivian, with illustrations from original sketches by Mr. Albert Bierstadt and the author. London, Sampson Low, Marston, Searle & Rivington, 1880. Pict. cloth. Scarce.

xvi, 426 p. front. (with tissue), illus., plates, large fold. map. 22.5 cm.
Half title; vignette; 32 numbered pages at end listing other books of these publishers.

Of Wild Bill Hickok, the author says: "Once in a gambling saloon in Montana he was set upon by three brother rowdies, and disposed of the whole three with his bowie knife. Eventually he lost his life while playing cards somewhere in the Black Hills of Dakota. A man he had been gambling with had lost heavily to him, and avenged himself for his losses by shooting 'Wild Bill' through the back of the head, as he sat playing with another set. Such was the public indignation against the perpetrator that he was lynched there and then without further ceremony." None of this is true except that Hickok was killed.

2275. **Vivian, Martha Campbell**

Down the avenue of ninety years. Reminiscences of Martha Campbell

Vivian, with twenty illustrations from daguerreotypes and photographs. [N.p.], privately printed, 1924. Cloth. Rare.

6 p.l., 137 [1] p. front. (port. with tissue), plates, ports., facsms. (2 fold.). 19.7 cm.

Half title; untrimmed.

Published in an edition of 300 copies.

The author, a southern girl, condemns the Kansas Redlegs and says: "It was men of this sort who drove the James boys from their home, pillaged it, and committed other atrocities on them and their parents. The James boys could not get to the Southern Army and were persecuted and hunted, their home destroyed and their lives attempted to make an honest living. I think these facts should be borne in mind before we too severely condemn Jesse James and his brothers [*sic*] for their acts of outlawry." The author displays some bias and exaggeration.

2276. Volland, Robert Frederick

The Reno gang of Seymour, by Robert Frederick Volland. . . . [N.p., 1948.] Fabrikoid. Rare.

ii p., 1 l., 332 p., 1 l., plus 34 p. plates, liii p. plates, ports., facsms. 28 cm.

Plates: p. i–xxxiv; appendix: p. i–xxx; bibliography: p. xxxi–xxxv; index: p. xxxvi–liii.

Mimeograph dry-stencil process on one side of paper.

Twenty-five copies of this book were made, after which the stencil was destroyed. The volume was copyrighted by Reverend Robert W. Shields, who told me that it served as the author's thesis for the degree of Master of Arts at the University of Indiana.

The first few copies of the book were bound in black imitation leather with pages sewn through punched margins. Later copies were bound in red imitation leather and fully sewn. These copies are scattered through a few libraries, such as the Library of Congress and the Indiana State University; a number went to various Pinkerton officials; one was presented to the descendants of the Renos; and one went to the Seymour, Indiana, Public Library, where it will be released for circulation after twenty-five years. I was fortunate enough to purchase the last copy that was for sale.

It is the best book yet published on the Renos and is well documented. Because of the method of reproduction, it is a thick book.

2277. Voorhees, Luke

Personal recollections of pioneer life on the mountains and plains of the great west, by Luke Voorhees. [Cheyenne, Wyo., privately printed, 1920.] Cloth. Scarce.

3 p.l., [7]–75 p. front. (port.). 22.5 cm.
Device.
Published in an edition of 125 copies.
Reprinted with additions at Philadelphia in 1927.

Contains some information on stage robbers and Slade's killing of Jules Reni.

W

2278. Walden, Arthur Treadwell

A dog-puncher on the Yukon, by Arthur Treadwell Walden, with an introduction by Walter Collins O'Kane and with illustrations. Boston and New York, Houghton Mifflin co., 1928. Pict. cloth. OP.

xviii p., 1 l., 289 p. front., plates. 22.2 cm.
Half title; map on end papers; vignette; first edition: 1928 under imprint.

Robbery and murder on the trails. The author tells much about Soapy Smith and gives a different account of the guard who killed him.

2279. Waldo, Edna La Moore

Dakota, an informal study of territorial days gleaned from contemporary newspapers, by Edna La Moore Waldo. Bismarck, N.D., Capital publishing co. [1932]. Cloth. OP.

9 p.l., [3]–297 [3] p. 25.3 cm.
Bibliography: p. [299–300].
Half title; vignette; untrimmed.
Reprinted in 1936 with index and 459 pages.

Contains some material on Calamity Jane and tells the story of Wild Bill Hickok's murder and the hanging of Jack McCall.

2280. Walgamott, Charles Shirley

Reminiscences of early days. A series of historical sketches and happenings in the early days of Snake river valley, by C. S. Walgamott. Cloth. Pub. in two volumes. Rare.

Vol. I, [n.p., 1926].
3 p.l., 127 [1] p. front., ports. 23.3 cm.
Double column.

Vol. II, [Twin Falls, Idaho, the Idaho Citizen, 1927].
4 p.l., 9–127 [1] p. front., illus., plates (1 col. and tipped in). 23.3 cm.

Has a chapter on Diamondfield Jack Davis and another on the vigilantes.

2281. ———

A series of historical sketches of early days in Idaho. Six decades back, [by] Charles Shirley Walgamott. Illustrated by R. H. Hall. Caldwell, Idaho, the Caxton printers, ltd., 1936. Cloth. Scarce.

8 p.l., [17]–358 p. front. (col. with tissue), illus., plates. 23.5 cm.
Half title; illus. end papers (dif.); pub. device.

This book is practically the same as the two-volume set (Item 2280). It contains some material on the vigilantes, stage robberies, and other outlaw material.

2282. Walker, Franklin

San Francisco's literary frontier, by Franklin Walker. New York, Alfred A. Knopf, MCMXXXIX. Cloth. OP.

xii p, 1 l., 3–400, i–xxv p. plates, ports., facsms. 24.2 cm.
Bibliography: p. 363–370; notes and references: p. 371–400; index: p. i–xxv.
Half title; pub. device; untrimmed.

Contains material on Joaquín Murieta, whose life the author admits is a legend. Also mentions Three-Fingered Jack García.

2283. Walker, Henry J.

Jesse James, "the outlaw," by Henry J. Walker. [Des Moines, Iowa, Wallace-Homestead co., 1961.] Volume I (all published). Cloth.

8 p.l., 17–283 p. plates, ports. 19.8 cm.
"First edition" on copyright p.

Another of those ridiculous books filled with preposterous statements. The author believed that the old faker J. Frank Dalton was the original Jesse James. There are mistakes on every page, too many to enumerate here. See my *Burs Under the Saddle* (Item 7).

2284. [**Walker, Robert C.**]

Report of the secretary of the Helena board of trade for 1878. Helena, Herald print, 1879. Wrappers. Rare.

32 p. fold. map. 22.2 cm.

Has material on road agents and the vigilantes.

2285. ———

Second annual report of the secretary of the Helena board of trade for the year 1879. Territory of Montana. [Helena], Mont., Woolfolk, Macquaid and Lacrois, daily and weekly *Independent*, 1880. Wrappers. Rare.

40 p. fold. map in front. 22.2 cm.

Has some outlaw and vigilante material.

2286. Walker, Stanley

Home to Texas, by Stanley Walker. New York, Harper & brothers [1956]. Cloth. OP.

v p., 1 l., 307 p. 21.5 cm.
Half title; untrimmed; "First edition" on copyright p.

Has some information on the Horrell-Higgins feud and on outlaws of the Southwest.

2287. Walker, Tacetta B.

Stories of early days in Wyoming; Big Horn basin, by Tacetta B. Walker. Casper, Wyo., Prairie publishing co. [1936]. Cloth. Scarce.

iv p., 1 l., 271 p. plates, ports., maps. 23.5 cm.
Bibliography: p. 268; index: p. [269]–271.
Map on end papers.

This privately printed book contains chapters on the Johnson County War and on the outlaw period, dealing with Butch Cassidy and his gang and the hanging of Tom Horn.

2288. Wallace, Andrew (ed.)

Sources & readings in Arizona history. A checklist of literature concerning Arizona's past. Edited by Andrew Wallace. Decorations by Anne Merriman Peck. Tucson, Arizona Pioneers' Historical society, 1965. Pict. cloth. Also pub. in wrappers.

xiv p., 1 l., 181 p. illus. (headpieces). 23.7 cm.
Author index: p. 171–181.
Half title; illus. double t.p. in red and black.

Section X, entitled "Outlaws and Lawmen," is a checklist on this subject compiled by Ramon F. Adams.

2289. Wallace, Betty

Gunnison country, by Betty Wallace. Denver, Sage books [1960]. Cloth.

7 p.l., 13–208 p. front. (map), plates, ports., facsms., map. 22 cm.
Acknowledgments: p. 205; bibliography: p. 206–207; interviews: p. 207–208.
Half title; map on end papers; pub. device.

Has some information on Alferd Packer, Bob Ford, Ed O. Kelly, Wyatt Earp, and Doc Holliday.

2290. ———

History with the hide off, [by] Betty Wallace. Denver, Colo., Sage books [1965]. Fabrikoid.

5 p.l., 7–276 p. front. (plan), illus., plates, ports., map (double p.), facsms. 22.2 cm.

Index: p. 266–276.

Half title; map on end papers; pub. device.

Has some information on Alferd Packer and Wyatt Earp and a mention of Bat Masterson.

2291. Wallace, Charles (comp.)

The cattle queen of Montana. A story of the personal experiences of Mrs. Nat Collins, familiarly known to western people as "The Cattle Queen of Montana," or "The Cowboy's Mother," in which is included narratives of thrilling adventures . . . and descriptions of the plains, the mines, cattle raising industry and other features of western life, learned during forty years' residence in the far west; compiled by Charles Wallace. Illustrations from special photographs. St. James, Minn., C. W. Foote [Chicago, printed by Donohue and Henneberry, 1894.] Stiff wrappers. Very rare.

xiii, [15]–249 p. front. (port.), illus., plates. 19 cm.

Revised and edited by Alvin E. Dyer and republished by press of Dyer printing co., Spokane, Wash. [1902]. Stiff wrappers. Rare.

5–260 p. front. (port.), illus., plates, ports. 20 cm.

The editor of the original edition states that he wrote this book while attending the University of Washington. Of the one thousand copies that were printed, he sold about twelve and gave a few copies away. The remaining copies he burned, an act he later regretted. Thus it is now almost impossible to find a copy of the original edition. Both editions contain some information on the Montana vigilantes, the hanging of George Ives, Joseph Slade, Plummer, and the others.

2292. Wallace, Lew

Lew Wallace; an autobiography. Illustrated. New York and London, Harper & brothers, publishers, MCMVI. Cloth. Pub. in two volumes.

Vol. I, ix p., 2 l., 501 [1] p. front. (port. with tissue), illus., plates, ports., map. 21.3 cm.

Vol. II, vii [1] p., 2 l., 503–1027 [1] p. front. (port. with tissue), ports., map, facsms., diagrs. 21.3 cm.

Index: p. 1005–[1028].

Pub. device; paged continuously.

Although General Wallace was sent to New Mexico as governor to quell the Lincoln County War, he does not say much about these troubles in his autobiography. He gives some incorrect information about John Chisum, saying that he imported "about seventy men—murderers, thieves and dangerous men of all classes" from Texas to protect his herds.

2293. Wallace, William H.

The closing speech for the state in the trial of Frank James for murder, held at Gallatin, August and September, 1883. Kansas City, 1883. Wrappers. Scarce.

65 p. 19 cm.

Reprinted with additions in an edition of 131 pages in 1890.

2294. ———

Closing speech for the state made by Wm. H. Wallace, Esq., prosecuting attorney for Jackson county, Missouri, in the trial of Frank James for murder, held at Gallatin, Davies county, Mo., in Aug. and Sept. 1883. Kansas City, Mo., press of Ramsey, Miller & Hudson, 1884. Wrappers. Scarce.

[2]–64 p. 21.7 cm.

Port. on cover.

Contains speeches on "Law and the Bandit" and the "Frank James Trial."

2295. ———

Speeches and writings of William H. Wallace; with autobiography. Kansas City, Mo., the Western Baptist publishing co., 1914. Cloth. Scarce.

6 p.l., [13]–308 p. front. (port.), plates, ports. 24 cm.

Lettering on cover: "Introduction by S. M. Brown."

In the latter part of the book is the author's autobiography, in which he tells much about the crimes and trials of the James boys and about his prosecution of Frank James.

2296. Waller, Brown

Last of the great western train robbers, by Brown Waller, South Brunswick, N.Y., A. S. Barnes and co.; London, Thomas Yoseloff, ltd. [1968]. Cloth.

8 p.l., 17–272 p. front. (port.), plates, ports. 21.5 cm.

Bibliography: p. 265–267; index: p. 268–272.

Half title; pub. device.

This book is about Harvey Logan and his train-robbing activities. The author follows Logan's career very closely; however, he misspells proper names such as Longbaugh for Longabaugh, Barry Ketchum for Berry Ketchum, Nath Champion for Nat Champion, Mount Morish for Mount Moriah, and Point Rock for Paint Rock, though the last is likely a typographical error, since he later spells it correctly. He is mistaken in having Black Jack Ketchum born in New Jersey. He was born in San Saba County, Texas.

He is also mistaken in saying that "Seven Rivers, south of Roswell, was the lower extremity of the Chisholm Trail." He says that George Scarborough died on "April 4, four years to a day from the time he had killed John Selman." Scarborough was wounded on April 5 and died on April 6. He is also mistaken in having Ed Welsh as Ben Kilpatrick's companion when the two men were killed attempting to hold up the Southern Pacific near Sanderson, Texas. Kilpatrick's companion was Ole Beck, a cellmate of Kilpatrick's in the Atlanta prison.

2297. Wallis, George A.

Cattle kings of the Staked plains, by George A. Wallis. Dallas, Texas, American Guild press [1957]. Cloth.

5 p.l., 11–180 p. plates, ports. 19.6 cm.

Map on front end papers; cattle brands on rear end papers; "First edition" on copyright p.

Republished by Sage books, Denver, Colo., in 1965.

Has a chapter on John Chisum containing some confused material on Billy the Kid. The errors in the book are too numerous to list all of them here. In describing the burning of the McSween home, he says that McSween and Billy the Kid "remained until the last and kept up a brisk fire while the others crawled away." It is a well-known fact that McSween refused to touch a gun and was killed before the others left.

Of the killing of Sheriff Brady and Deputy Hindman, he writes that "the enraged Tunstall boys, led by Billy the Kid, boldly rode into Lincoln and shot it out with Sheriff Brady and his deputies." It was not a "shoot out" but an ambush. The chapter on Billy the Kid is even more confused. The author says that the Kid "wore his pistol on his left side and fired with deadly aim with his left hand." This description is the result of the well-known picture of the Kid that was developed backwards. The Kid was right-handed. The author tells an entirely new, and equally incorrect, story about the Kid's killing of Bell. He also misspells many proper names.

2298. Walsh, Richard John

The making of Buffalo Bill. A study in heroics, by Richard J. Walsh, in collaboration with Milton S. Salisbury. Illustrated. Indianapolis, the Bobbs-Merrill co., publishers [1928]. Cloth. OP.

vii p., 3 l., 15–391 p. front. (port.), illus., plates, ports., facsms. 22.6 cm.

Bibliography: p. 365–370; index: p. 373–391.

Half title; illus. front end papers; map on rear end papers; device; "First edition" on copyright p.

The author here quotes William E. Connelley in trying to correct the false story of the Hickok-McCanles "fight."

2299. Walter, William W.

The great understander. True life story of the last of the Wells, Fargo shotgun express messengers. Compiled by William W. Walter. Aurora, Ill., published by William W. Walter [1931]. Pict. cloth. Scarce.

5 p.l., 11–315 p. front. (port.). 19.6 cm.

The life of Oliver Roberts de la Fontaine, his experiences in the early West, and his contacts with stage robbers and other lawless persons. He tells of witnessing a holdup by Vásquez and his gang and spells this outlaw's name "Vasquaz," but this could be a typographical error.

2300. Walters, Lorenzo D.

Tombstone's yesterdays, by Lorenzo D. Walters, with illustrations. Tucson, Ariz., Acme printing co., 1928. Cloth. Very scarce.

7 p.l., [11]–293 p. front. (port.), illus., ports. 23.5 cm.

Pub. device.

"Tombstone's Yesterdays has been appearing as a serial in the 'Progressive Arizona and the Great Southwest,' a Ward Shelby publication, during the past two years and has now been revised and enlarged and offered to the public in book form." (On 2d prelim. leaf.)

A book filled with errors. The author includes chapters about Pat Garrett and Billy the Kid, though neither man had anything to do with Tombstone. Most of his information on the Kid is wrong, from his childhood (when, he says, the Kid was a bootblack in New York) to his death. Most of his information about the Earps and the Clantons is unreliable as is his account of virtually every other gunman he mentions. Most of the errors are enumerated in my *Burs Under the Saddle* (Item 7).

2301. Walton, Augustus Q.

A history of detection, conviction, life and designs of John A. Murel [*sic*], the great western land pirate; together with his system of villainy, and plan of exciting a Negro rebellion. Also a catalogue of the names of four hundred and fifty-five of his mystic clan fellows and followers, and a statement of their efforts for the destruction of Virgil A. Stewart, the young man who detected him. To which is added a biographical sketch of V. A. Stewart, by Augustus Q. Walton. Cincinnati, [U. P. James, n.d.]. Pict. wrappers. Rare.

2 p.l., [19]–84, [iii]–xii p. front. (port.), plates. 21.6 cm.

Pages [iii]–xii at end give a sampling of a book entitled *A History of the Feud Between the Hill and Evans Parties. . . .*, J. J. Thompson.

Published in Athens, Tenn., by G. White in 1835, and in Lexington, Ky., the same year in two issues, one of 84 pages and another of 89 pages. Republished in 1836 with 60 pages, and again in 1837 with 86 pages.

2302. Walton, William M.

Life and adventures of Ben Thompson, the famous Texan. Including a detailed and authentic statement of his birth, history and adventures, by one who has known him since a child, by W. M. Walton. Austin, Texas, published by the author [printed by Edwards and Church, newsdealers], 1884. Pict. wrappers. Exceedingly rare.

4 p.l., [5]–229 p. front. (port.), plates. 17 cm.

Reprinted by Frontier Times, Bandera, Texas, 1926. Wrappers.

Reprinted again in 1954, by the Frontier press of Texas, Houston, in cloth.

5–232 p. plates, ports. 21.7 cm.

Last 5 p., plates and ports. This reprint omits the original preface, illustrations, and chapter headings.

Republished in facsimile in 1956 by the Steck co., Austin, Texas, and given as Christmas gifts to the publisher's friends and customers. This reprint is in a de luxe, boxed edition with colored plates and bound in boards.

2 p.l., [5]–229 p. front. (port.), 14 plates (all col.). 21 cm.

A few copies also published with pict. wrappers. Both editions now scarce.

I can remember when a copy of the original paperback could be bought for ten cents from a bushel basket that sat in front of an Austin, Texas, bookstore. Now this book is exceedingly rare and exceedingly high in price when one is fortunate enough to locate a copy. It was written by a man who was Thompson's close friend and his attorney and naturally sympathetic. The book gives an accurate account of the death of Sheriff Whitney in Ellsworth, Kansas, and, unlike Stuart Lake's account, does not mention that Wyatt Earp was there.

2303. Waltrip, Lela, and Rufus Waltrip

Cowboys and cattlemen, by Lela and Rufus Waltrip. Decorations by Larry Toschik. New York, David McKay co., inc., 1967. Pict. cloth.

6 p.l., 179 p. illus. 21 cm.

Notes: p. 166–167; bibliography: p. 168–178; about the authors: p. 179.

Half title; illus. t.p.

In a chapter on John Chisum, the authors deal with the Lincoln County War. They say that there were fourteen men in the McSween home when it was attacked. They are also mistaken in saying that Alexander Grzelachowski was a friend of Billy the Kid. Nor were the Kid and Dolan "the only surviving leaders of the opposing forces in the cattle war." They say that Billy "became a fugitive of the law and was finally hunted down, and slain by Pat Garrett in 1881, after killing a deputy sheriff." He killed two deputies, not one.

In their chapter on Burt Mossman, they tell about some of his experiences as a ranger and his dealings with Burt Alvord, Billy Stiles, and Augustin Chacon.

2304. Walz, Edgar A.

"Retrospection," by Edgar A. Walz. [N.p., October, 1931.] Imt. leather. Exceedingly rare.

2 p.l., 5–31 [1] p. front. (port. tipped in). 18 cm.

This privately printed little book, which gives some sidelights on the Lincoln County War, is exceedingly rare. It was written by a man who was in Lincoln County at the time of the conflict.

2305. Ward, Don (ed.)

Bits of silver. Vignettes of the old west. Edited by Don Ward. New York, Hastings House, publishers [1961]. Cloth and boards.

x p., 1 l., 3–306 p. 21.5 cm.
Half title.

An anthology of some of the books published by Hastings House to celebrate its Silver Anniversary. In the chapter on Silver Camps, the author spells the name of Ed O. Kelly as O'Kelly as so many others do. In Frazier Hunt's chapter on Billy the Kid Olinger's name is spelled Ollinger. There are several chapters on western outlaws, such as Billy the Kid, Rube Boyce, and Soapy Smith, and such gunmen as Doc Holliday, Print Olive, Bob Ford, and the Earps.

2306. Ward, Joseph O.

My grandpa went west, by J. O. Ward. Caldwell, Idaho, the Caxton printers, ltd., 1956. Pict. cloth.

6 p.l., [13]–130 p. front. (col.), illus., plates. 21.6 cm.
Half title; head and tailpieces; map on end papers; pub. device.

Tells about a brush "grandpa" had with the James gang after their robbery of a bank in Russellville, Kentucky.

2307. Ward, Margaret

Cimarron saga, by Margaret Ward. [N.p., n.d., ca. 1940.] Cloth. OP.

88 p. front. (port.), plates, ports., facsms. 22.4 cm.

Has some material on Clay Allison and Elfego Baca.

2308. Ward, William

The Dalton gang, the bandits of the far west. The most desperate train robbers that ever lived. The first true history of the raids and robberies of the gang who terrorized five states . . . as told by a U.S. deputy marshal and set forth by William Ward. Cleveland, published by the Arthur Westbrook co. [n.d.]. Col. pict. wrappers. Scarce.

3 p.l., [7]–179 [12] p. front., illus. 17.3 cm.
12 p. sampling of the author's book on Harry Tracy.

The Ward books listed in these pages are examples of the books on various outlaws by this hack writer. Although he claims that this book is "the first true history" of the Daltons, there is very little truth in the account.

2309. ———

Harry Tracy, the death dealing Oregon outlaw, by William Ward. Profusely illustrated. . . . Cleveland, published by the Arthur Westbrook co. [1908]. Col. pict. wrappers. Scarce.

191 p. illus. 18 cm.

2310. ———

The James boys of old Missouri. Only true account of the outlaw deeds of the bandit king of the far west, and the assassination of Jesse James by Bob Ford, as told by an eye-witness and written down by William Ward. Adventure Series No. 2. Cleveland, published by the Arthur Westbrook co. [1907]. Col. pict. wrappers. Scarce.

[3]–190 [1] p. illus. 18 cm.

Early-day hack writers commonly included the word "true" in their titles. This writer also tried to make it appear that the story had been told to him by an eye-witness, apparently to give the tale authenticity.

2311. ———

Jesse James' dash for fortune; or, the raid on the Kansas City fair, by William Ward. Adventure Series No. 9. Cleveland, the Arthur Westbrook co. [n.d.]. Col. pict. wrappers. Scarce.

3 p.l., [7]–191 p. illus. 18 cm.

2312. ———

The Younger brothers, the border outlaws. The only authentic history of the exploits of these desperadoes of the west. From facts supplied by Cole and Bob and written down by William Ward. Illustrated. Adventure Series No. 6. Cleveland, published by the Arthur Westbrook co. [1908]. Col. pict. wrappers. Scarce.

2 p.l., [5]–162 [28] p. illus. 18 cm.
28 p. adv. at end.

Again, the title claims that this account is the only true and authentic one, but it is as unreliable as the rest.

2313. Warden, Ernest A.

Infamous Kansas killers . . ., by Ernest A. Warden. . . . [Wichita, Kans., McGuin publishing co., 1944.] Pict. wrappers. (Cover title.) OP.

2 p.l., [5]–48 p. ports. 18.8 cm.
[Volume III of "Thrilling Tales of Kansas"].
"An accurate history of all the legal hangings executed by the State of Kansas up to the present time." (Prelim. page.)

2314. ———

Thrilling tales of Kansas, by Ernest Warden. [Wichita, Kans., printed by the Wichita Eagle press [1932]. Wrappers. Scarce.

2 p.l., 5–112 p. 19.6 cm.
Device.

Contains material on the Benders, the Daltons, and bank robbers Henry Brown and Ben Wheeler.

2315. ———

Thrilling tales of Kansas, from 1873 to 1938, [by] Ernie Warden. [Wichita, Kans., "second revised edition," 1938.] Pict. wrappers. Scarce.

2 p.l., 3–100 [1] p. 19.3 cm.

Although this book has much the same title as the 1932 edition (Item 2314), it is practically a new book, containing new material and retaining only a few chapters from the first printing.

2316. Warman, Cy

Frontier stories, by Cy Warman. New York, Charles Scribner's sons, 1898. Dec. cloth. Scarce.

4 p.l., [3]–246 p. 18.2 cm.
Half title.

Contains a chapter on outlaws and tells about the killing of Jesse James by Bob Ford, and about the later killing of Ford himself. The book also tells something about the career of Frank Rand, as well as about Soapy Smith.

2317. ———

The story of the railroad, by Cy Warman. . . . Illustrated. New York and London, D. Appleton and co. [1898]. Pict. cloth. Very scarce.

xix, 280 p. front., plates, fold. map. 19.3 cm.

Tells about the fight at Newton, Kansas, and about life at Dodge City, with information on Dog Kelly and Bat Masterson.

2318. Warner, Frank W. (comp.)

Montana territory. History and business directory, 1879. Illustrated. Distances, fares, and altitudes. Counties, towns, mining camps. Commercial, mineral, and agricultural interests. With a sketch of the vigilantes. Helena, Mont., Fisk brothers, printers and binders [1879]. Boards and cloth. Rare.

3 l. (adv.), 3 p.l., 218 p. illus., plates, fold. map. 21.5 cm.

Prefatory note signed: "F. W. Warner."

Advertising l. interspersed (in part unpaged) and on inside of front and back wrappers.

Contains a twenty-chapter reprint of Dimsdale's *Vigilantes of Montana.*

2319. Warner, Matt

The last of the bandit riders, by Matt Warner, as told to Murray E. King. Illustrated with photographs. Caldwell, Idaho, the Caxton printers, ltd., 1940. Pict. cloth. Very scarce.

10 p.l., [21]–337 p. front., plates, ports. 23.4 cm.

Appendix: p. [329]–337.

Half title; pub. device; vignette.

An excellent book on the outlaw career of Matt Warner and his association with Butch Cassidy and his Wild Bunch.

2320. Warner, Opie L.

A pardoned lifer. Life of George Sontag, former member notorious Evans-Sontag gang of train robbers. Written by Opie L. Warner. [San Bernardino, Calif., the Index print, 1909.] Cloth. Scarce.

7 p.l., 15–211 p. front. (port.). 19.4 cm.

George Sontag tells about his activities as a member of the Evans-Sontag gang, his life in prison, and his reason for turning against Evans. Some of his statements do not agree with other published material about this gang of train robbers. There are several typographical errors, such as "wears" for "years" on page 48, "leace" for "leave" on page 57, "letts" for "letter" on page 60, and "persuads" for "persuade" on page 69.

2321. Waters, Frank

The Colorado, by Frank Waters. Illustrated by Nicolai Fechin, maps by George Annand. New York, Toronto, Rinehart & co., inc. [1946]. Cloth. OP.

xii p., 2 l., 3–400 p. illus. (1 col.), maps (1 double p.). 20.8 cm.
Reference appendix: p. 389–393; glossary: p. 395–396; index: p. 397–400.
Half title; illus. t.p.

Contains some material on Wyatt Earp, mostly very uncomplimentary.

2322. ———

The story of Mrs. Virgil Earp. The Earp brothers of Tombstone, by Frank Waters. New York, Clarkson N. Potter, inc., publisher [1960]. Cloth.

5 p.l., 3–247 p. 21.5 cm.
Acknowledgments: p. 235–237; citations and comments: p. 241–247.
Half title; map and plan on end papers; pub. device; "First edition" on copyright p.

At last we have a book which dares to tell the truth about the Earps, refuting the many highly romantic and imaginary tales told by Burns and Lake. We now see them, not as the ideal officers of the law and the heroes they are commonly thought to be, but as the saloonkeepers, gamblers, whoremongers, and gunmen that they were. The author relates many inside stories as told by a member of the family and gives us information not recorded before. The author makes a few mistakes himself, but they are of little importance.

This book had its beginning with the dictated recollections of Mrs. Virgil Earp, but because of a threatened suit by both Stuart Lake and Wyatt Earp's third wife the manuscript lay in the files of the Arizona Historical Society for twenty-five years. In 1959 the author found new documentary evidence to substantiate the account, and the book was published.

The book would be more useful if it had been provided with an index and if the author's citations were less difficult to follow. Yet it is a giant move in the right direction toward taking Wyatt Earp off his pedestal and placing him where he belongs, among human beings, and revealing him as something less than the invincible hero most readers have held him to be ever since the publication of Stuart Lake's book.

2323. Waters, L. L.

Steel tracks to Santa Fe, by L. L. Waters. Lawrence, Kans., University of Kansas press, 1950. Cloth. OP.

11 p.l., [9]–500 p. plates, ports., maps, graphs, tables. 23.6 cm.
Half title; map on end papers.

Contains some material on Newton, Kansas, and its gun battles.

2324. Waters, William

A gallery of western badmen, by William Waters. [Covington, Ky., Americana publications, 1954.] Stiff pict. wrappers. (Cover title.) OP.

33 p. plates, ports. 21.6 cm.
Double column.

Short sketches of many of the leading outlaws and gunmen. The book, typical of cheap paperbound books, is filled with errors. The author follows all the well-known legends concerning Wild Bill Hickok, Sam Bass, Clay Allison, Billy the Kid, and Wyatt Earp. The errors are listed in detail in *Burs Under the Saddle* (Item 7).

2325. Watrous, Ansel

History of Larimer county, Colorado. Collated and compiled from historical authorities, public reports, official records and other reliable sources . . ., by Ansel Watrous. Illustrated. Fort Collins, Colo., the Courier printing & publishing co., 1911. Leather. Scarce.

4 p.l., 7–513 p. front. (port. with tissue), plates, ports. (part with tissues). 29 cm.
Index: p. 505–513.
Double column; gilt edges.

Contains material on Joseph Slade and other outlaws.

2326. Watson, Frederick

A century of gunmen; a study in lawlessness, by Frederick Watson. London, Ivor Nicholson & Watson, ltd., 1931. Cloth. Scarce.

vii [1] p., 295 [1] p. 22 cm.
Acknowledgments: p. 291; index: p. 292–[296].
Half title; vignette.

Although the author has written an interesting book, most of his quotations have been taken from unreliable sources, such as Sutton's *Hands Up*, Frank Harris' *Reminiscences of a Cowboy*, Emerson Hough's *Story of the Outlaw*, and Lord's *Frontier Dust*. The author seems to have had a talent for picking the least reliable of the many books he could have cited.

Wyatt Earp did not arrest Ben Thompson in Ellsworth; Billy the Kid was not a Texas gunman, nor did he kill twenty-four men; Pat Garrett was not a deputy sheriff, but a sheriff; and Bass did not fall prey to the pistol of one of his own band.

2327. Way, Thomas E.

Frontier Arizona, [by] Thomas E. Way. A milestone book. New York, Carlton press, 1950. Cloth.

xvi, 279 p. 20.8 cm.
Half title.

Although the blurb on this book says that it is "well-documented and informative," I find very little documentation and much erroneous information. When he describes Buckskin Frank Leslie as propped against a tree in the desert, he has Leslie confused with Johnny Ringo. He has Old Man Clanton and his son Finn in the O K Corral battle, and he has the killing of Andy Cooper by Commodore Perry Owens wrong, as well as the hanging of Russian Bill. There are many other doubtful statements.

2328. ———

Sgt. Fred Platten's ten years on the trail of the redskins, by Thomas E. Way. Illustrations by Frances Wells Roberts. . . . Williams, Ariz., Williams News press [1963]. Stiff pict. wrappers.

4 p.l., 44 p., 2 l. illus., plates, port., facsm. 28.2 cm.
Double column; adv. 1 p. in front and verso front wrapper; 3 p. adv. at end and both recto and verso back wrapper.

Has some information on the Pleasant Valley War, the Apache Kid, and Tom Horn and a slight mention of Wild Bill Hickok. The author's account of the killing of Andy Cooper by Owens is incorrect.

2329. Way, W. J. (Jack)

The Tombstone story, by W. J. "Jack" Way. The astonishing tale of "the town too tough to die." [Tucson, Ariz., the Livingston press], 1965. Stiff wrappers.

1 p.l., 3–40 p. front. (port.), plates, ports., facsm., map, plan. 21 cm.

A short history of Tombstone with information on the Earps, Doc Holliday, Bat Masterson, Luke Short, Buckskin Frank Leslie, the Clantons, McLaurys, Frank Stillwell, Sheriff Behan, and Curly Bill Brocius. The author is mistaken in saying that, when Wyatt Earp left Prescott, "accompanying him, or soon to follow were his second wife, Mattie, his brothers Virgil, Morgan, James and Warren. . . ." Virgil and his wife and Wyatt and his wife went to Tombstone from Prescott together. The author also says that Wyatt bought a quarter interest in the Oriental Saloon, but he was given an interest in exchange for protecting the place.

2330. Weadock, Jack

Dust of the desert. Plain tales of the desert and the border, by Jack Weadock. Illustrations by Jack Van Ryder, with an introduction by George H. Doran. New York, London, D. Appleton-Century co., inc., 1936. Pict. cloth. Scarce.

xx p., 1 l., 3–306 p. front., illus. 24.5 cm.
Half title; illus. end papers; pub. device; first edition: figure (1) at end of text.

In his chapter on Billy the Kid, the author gives an inaccurate account of the killing of Jimmy Carlyle.

2331. Webb, W. E.

Buffalo land; an authentic account of the discoveries, adventures, and mishaps of a scientific and sporting party in the wild west; with graphic descriptions of the country . . . replete with information, wit and humor. The appendix comprising a complete guide for sportsmen and emigrants, by W. E. Webb. . . . Profusely illustrated from actual photographs and original drawings by Henry Worrall. Cincinnati and Chicago, E. Hannaford & co. . . ., 1872. Pict. cloth. Rare.

xxiii, 25–503 p. front., plates, ports. 22.6 cm.

Appendix: p. 431–503.

Contains some material on Wild Bill Hickok (which the author spells Hickock). He admits that Wild Bill gained his reputation "through *Harper's Magazine*" and says that "much that has been written about him is fiction." He does not mention the McCanles trouble, and claims that Buffalo Bill told him Wild Bill was his cousin—perhaps another of Cody's many tall tales.

2332. Webb, Walter Prescott

The story of the Texas rangers, by Walter Prescott Webb. Illustrated by Nicholas Eggenhofer. New York, Grossett & Dunlap, publishers [1957]. Pict. cloth. OP.

vi p., 1 l., 152 p. illus. 28.5 cm.

Half title; illus. end papers; illus. t.p.

An entirely different book from Item 2333, written for younger readers. It has a lot of information about the many outlaws and feuds of Texas.

2333. ———

The Texas rangers, a century of frontier defense. Illustrated with drawings by Lonnie Rees and with photographs. Boston and New York, Houghton Mifflin co., 1935. Cloth. Scarce.

xiv p., 2 l., 3–583 [1] p. front., illus., ports., facsms. 24.4 cm.

Half title; part tailpieces; pub. device; first edition: 1935 under imprint.

At head of title: "Walter Prescott Webb."

Also published in a de luxe edition limited to 200 copies. The trade edition has gone through several printings. Republished by the University of Texas press, Austin, 1965.

The most thorough work to date on the Texas Rangers. It naturally deals with many Texas outlaws.

2334. ——— (ed.)

The handbook of Texas. Walter Prescott Webb, editor-in-chief. H. Bailey Carroll, managing editor. . . . In two volumes. . . . Austin, Texas State Historical association, 1952. Pict. cloth.

Vol. I, xv p., 1 l., 977 p. 25 cm.
Half title; double column.

Vol. II, ix p., 1 l., 953 p. 25 cm.
Half title; double column.

Biographical sketches of many of the Texas outlaws and gunmen, such as Cullen Baker, Bill Longley, John Wesley Hardin, Belle Starr, and Ben Thompson.

2335. [Weber, Charles W.]

Jack Long; or, shot in the eye. A true story of Texas border life, [by Charles W. Weber]. New York, W. H. Graham, 1846. Wrappers. Rare.

[3]–30 p. 21 cm.

A story of the Moderator and Regulator War in Texas.

2336. Wellman, Paul I.

The blazing southwest. The pioneer history of the American southwest, by Paul I. Wellman. New York, Toronto, Cape Horn, Sydney, published for the Fireside press by W. Foulshar & co., ltd., London [1961]. Cloth. Scarce.

5 p.l., [11]–240 p. plates, ports., maps. 22 cm.

The author's account of Billy the Kid and the Lincoln County War contains the same errors he has made in his other books. He has the Kid's mother moving to New Mexico after her marriage to Antrim. His account of the fight at Blazer's Mill is all wrong, and he is also incorrect in his account of the Earp-Clanton feud.

2337. ———

A dynasty of western outlaws, [by] Paul I. Wellman. Illustrated by Lorence Bjorklund. Garden City, N.Y., Doubleday & co., inc., 1961. Cloth.

8 p.l., [17]–384 p. illus. chap. headings. 24 cm.
Bibliography, evaluated: p. [355]–368; index: p. [369]–384.
Half title; illus. map on end papers.

This is a well-written book, though I find errors of fact throughout. The author says that the Youngers and the Jameses were first cousins, but they were not related. He says that "the dubious honor of being the first bank held up in American history was bestowed upon Jesse by a local institution, the Clay County Savings and Loan Association, of Liberty. . . ." It has been proved that Jesse James did not take part in this robbery but was at home in bed recovering from an earlier wound.

The author spells Ed O. Kelly's name as Ed O'Kelly. He also says that Henry Starr's father was Hopp Starr, a brother of Sam Starr, one of Belle's husbands. Henry's father was named George, not Hopp, and he was not Sam's brother.

In the first paragraph of Chapter 7 the author makes a statement that I must challenge: "It should be stated that the outlaws of the West, after the first post–Civil War period, were almost without exception cowboys." Many were cowboys, but most were buffalo hunters and renegades from other walks of life.

In his bibliography the author states that Appler's *The Younger Brothers* was printed as a book in 1892. It was originally published in 1875. He also says that Anthony Gish's *American Bandits* was "in most cases surprisingly accurate . . ." and "quite rare." I find Gish's book most unreliable and not even scarce. He defends the book *Hands Up*, Sutton's dictation to A. B. McDonald, and states that McDonald was a reliable reporter, a winner of a Pulitzer prize. That may be true, but McDonald certainly swallowed Fred Sutton's tall tales without investigating their truthfulness.

2338. ———

Glory, God and gold, a narrative history. By Paul I. Wellman. Garden City, N.Y., Doubleday & co., inc., 1954. Cloth. OP.

xii p., 1 l., [3]–402 p. 7 maps. 24 cm.

Midstream of America series.

Some books to read: p. [389]–390; index: p. [391]–401.

Half title; map on end papers.

One of a series of books edited by Lewis Gannett. In the latter part of the book the author tells about Billy the Kid, repeating all the well-worn legends created by Ash Upson. Most of the statements about the Kid are wrong, from the killing of Baker and Morton to the statement that he was going to Maxwell's to see his sweetheart when he was killed. The author is mistaken in saying that the Brewer posse went to Blazer's Mill to hunt Buckskin Roberts. Roberts was looking for them and happened to arrive at the mill after Brewer did. There are also many mistakes in the account of the battle at McSween's home.

The author says that O'Folliard and Bowdre were killed in what he calls a battle at Stinking Springs, but there was no battle. Bowdre was shot early one morning when he went out to feed the horses, and O'Folliard had been slain several days earlier at Fort Sumner. There are many other mistakes, some of them having to do with Wyatt Earp.

2339. ———

Spawn of evil. The invincible empire of soulless men which for a generation held the nation in a spell of terror, [by] Paul I. Wellman. Drawings by Lorence Bjorklund. Garden City, N.Y., Doubleday & co., inc., 1964. Pict. cloth.

ix, 350 p. illus. headpieces. 24 cm.
Bibliography: p. [337]–342; index: p. [343]–350.
Half title; illus. map (col.), on end papers; illus., t.p.; "First edition" on copyright p.

This book pretty well covers the outlaws of our early day western rivers and traces, including the Mason gang, the Cave-in-Rock gang, Sile Doty, the Harpes, John A. Murrell, and others.

2340. ———

The trampling herd, [by] Paul I. Wellman; illustrations by F. Miller. New York, Carrick & Evans, inc. [1939]. Cloth. OP.

6 p.l., 13–433 p. illus. 21.8 cm.
"Some books to read": p. 417–419; index: p. 421–433.
Half title; map on end papers; illus. t.p.
At head of title: "The Story of the Cattle Range of America."
Later reprinted by Doubleday & Co., Garden City, N.Y.
Another impression made by J. S. Lippincott, Philadelphia, in 1939.

Although this is primarily a cattle book, it contains much on outlaws and the range wars of Lincoln and Johnson counties. The author again repeats all the legends concerning Billy the Kid's early life, and most of his account of this young outlaw is wrong.

He has a different version of the start of the trouble between Phil Coe and Wild Bill Hickok. He says that it started over cards when Hickok caught Coe cheating. His account of the O K Corral fight is also inaccurate.

2341. Wells, Evelyn, and Harry C. Peterson

The '49ers, by Evelyn Wells and Harry C. Peterson. Garden City, N.Y., Doubleday & co., inc., 1949. Cloth. OP.

5 p.l., 273 p. 22 cm.
Half title; vignette; untrimmed.

In Chapter 11, entitled "Bad Men," there is a tabloid biography of Joaquín Murieta.

2342. Wells, Polk

Life and adventures of Polk Wells (Charles Knox Polk Wells), the notorious outlaw, whose acts of fearlessness and chivalry kept the frontier trails afire with excitement, and whose robberies and other depredations in the Platte purchase and elsewhere, have been a most frequent discussion to this day, all of which transpired during and just after the Civil War. Written by himself. [N.p. (Halls, Mo.), published by G. A. Warnica, his life long friend and chief financial support, n.d., ca. 1907.] Cloth. Scarce.

2 p.l., [7]–259 p. front. (2 ports.), illus. 22.8 cm.

Although Wells was not as popular a subject among writers as others of his ilk, he was quite an outlaw in his day.

2343. Wendt, Lloyd, and Herman Kogan

Bet a million! The story of John W. Gates, by Lloyd Wendt and Herman Kogan. Indianapolis, New York, the Bobbs-Merrill co., publishers [1948]. Cloth. Scarce.

4 p.l., 9–357 p. front., plates, ports. 22.2 cm.
Bibliography: p. 335–342; index: p. 345–357.
Half title; untrimmed.

Gives some mention of John Wesley Hardin and the killing of Ben Thompson. The authors are mistaken when they say that Rowdy Joe Lowe was killed while holding up a Union Pacific train at Big Spring, Kansas. The hold-up took place at Big Spring, Nebraska.

2344. West, John O.

Billy the Kid, hired gun or hero, [by] John O. West, Texas Western College, reprinted from The Sunny Slopes of Long Ago, Texas Folklore Society publication XXXIII. Dallas, published by Southern Methodist University press, 1966. Wrappers.

70–80 p. 23 cm.

The author rightfully criticizes some of the published works about the Kid.

2345. West, Ray B., Jr. (ed.)

Rocky mountain cities, edited by Ray B. West, Jr., with an introduction by Carey McWilliams. New York, W. W. Norton & co., inc. [1949]. Cloth. OP.

14 p.l., 29–320 p. 21.8 cm.
Notes on contributors: p. 318–320.
Half title; pub. device; "First edition" on copyright p.

Contains a chapter dealing with Cheyenne, Wyoming, and the Johnson County War.

2346. Westerners' Brand Book (Chicago Posse)

The westerners' brand book, 1944. Being a collection of the original papers presented at meetings of the westerners and also of the discussions in which they participated during the first year, March 1944 to March 1945, at Chicago, Illinois [1945]. Pict. cloth. Scarce.

5 p.l., 9–151 p. illus., facsm. 23.5 cm.
Index: p. [157–160].
Half title.

Contains chapters on Calamity Jane and Jesse James.

2347. ———

The westerners' brand book, 1945–'46. Being the papers presented during the second year of the westerners (1945–'46), together with some original papers rescued from manuscripts and ephemera. Chicago, Ill. [1947]. Pict. cloth. Scarce.

5 p.l., 9–166 [4] p. illus. 23.5 cm.
Index: p. [169–170].
Half title; illus. end papers.

Contains papers on Calamity Jane, the James boys, and the Johnson County War. In this volume Clarence Paine offers the theory that Calamity Jane might be a hermaphrodite, but there is no evidence to support this theory.

2348. Westerners' Brand Book (Denver Posse)

1945 brand book, containing twelve original papers relating to western and Rocky mountain history, edited by Herbert O. Brayer. Denver, Colo., the Westerners [printed by Bradford-Robinson printing co.], 1946. Pict. cloth. Scarce.

xiii, 251 p. illus., map. 23.6 cm.
Appendix: p. [219]–237; index: p. [241]–251.
Half title.
Colophon: "Three hundred and fifty copies of which this is No. ——."

Contains a chapter on the hanging of Tom Horn.

2349. ———

1946 brand book. Twelve original papers pertaining to the history of the west, edited by Virgil V. Peterson. Denver, Colo., [the Artcraft press], 1947. Pict. cloth. Scarce.

xii p., 1 l., 242 p. front. (fold. col. panorama), plates, (1 col.), ports., maps, facsms. 23.6 cm.
Index: p. 232–242.
Half title.
Colophon: "Five hundred copies of which this is number ——."

Has chapters on Bill Carlisle, the Wyoming train robber, and on Alferd Packer.

2350. ———

1948 brand book. Twelve original papers pertaining to the history of the west, edited by Dabney Otis Collins. Denver, Colo., the Westerners [printed by the Artcraft press, 1949]. Pict. cloth. Scarce.

xx p., 2 l., 271 p. illus., plates, ports., map. 23.6 cm.
Index: p. 265–271.
Half title; facsm. of newspaper advertisements on end papers.
Colophon: "Limited edition of 500 copies of which this is No. ——."

The author of a chapter entitled "Typing the Western Gunman" attempts to compare types of gunmen in build, color of eyes, hair, and quality of courage. Every notable gunman comes under his examination, but his hardest words are reserved for Billy the Kid. He says, in part, "his photograph shows a young man whom any physician would diagnose as an adenoidal moron, both constitutionally and emotionally inadequate to a high degree."

2351. ———

1950 brand book. Vol. VI, edited by Harold H. Dunham. Denver, Colo., University of Denver press [1951]. Pict. cloth. Scarce.

ix [1] p., 5–312 p. front., plates, ports., map, facsm. 23.6 cm.
Index: p. [307]–312.
Half title; illus. end papers.
Colophon: "Regular edition of seven hundred copies of which this is number ——."

In a chapter on Cattle Kate the author claims that the proper spelling of Jim Averill (as commonly spelled) should be Averell. He presents a well-annotated and reliable account of the life of Cattle Kate after her association with Averill.

2352. ———

1952 brand book. Sixteen original studies in western history. Edited by Elvon L. Howe, with special sketches by H. D. Bugbee. Denver, Colo., the Westerners [1953]. Pict. cloth. Scarce.

xxi p., 2 l., 297 p. plates, ports. 23.6 cm.
Index: p. 279–297.
Half title; copyright notice on verso 2nd p. after t.p.
Colophon: "Regular edition of five hundred copies. This is No. ——."

Contains a chapter in which I criticize some books about Wild Bill Hickok and Billy the Kid, my first published effort to set the record straight.

2353. ———

The Denver westerners' 1953 brand book IX. Maurice Frink, editor, Francis

B. Rizzard, assistant editor, Nick Eggenhofer, illustrator. Denver, Colo., the Westerners, 1954. Pict. cloth. Scarce.

11 p.l., [3]–331 [1] p. illus., plates, facsms. 23.6 cm.
Appendix: p. [309]–315; index: p. [317]–331.
Half title; cattle brands on end papers; illus. double t.p.
Colophon: "Regular edition of five hundred copies."

Has a chapter of material on the Johnson County War, and another on Spanish songs, some of them concerning Billy the Kid.

2354. ———

1954 brand book. Edited by Erl H. Ellis with assistance from Alan Swallow and sketches by Jeannie Pear as Volume Ten of the Denver posse of westerners. [Boulder, Colo., printed by the Johnson publishing co., 1955.] Pict. cloth. Scarce.

xxii p., 1 l., [3]–368 p. plates (1 fold.), ports., map. 23.6 cm.
Index: p. 346–368.
Half title; illus. end papers.
Colophon: "This is No. —— of the regular edition which is limited to 500 copies."

Has a chapter on Buckskin Frank Leslie and another containing some information on Calamity Jane and Wild Bill Hickok.

2355. ———

1955 brand book, being Volume Eleven of the Denver posse of the westerners, edited by Alan Swallow with original sketches by Muriel Sibell Wolle. [Boulder, Colo., Johnson publishing co., 1956.] Pict. cloth. Scarce.

10 p.l., 21–454 [1] p. plates, ports., facsm., 2 fold. maps. 23.6 cm.
Index: p. 449–454.
Half title; map on end papers.
Colophon: "This is No. —— of the regular edition limited to five hundred copies."

Contains a chapter on the Lincoln County War and Billy the Kid.

2356. ———

1956 brand book of the Denver westerners. Edited by Charles S. Ryland, drawings by Frank L. Philips. Denver, Colo., the Westerners, 1957. Pict. cloth. Scarce.

9 p.l., 3–383 p. illus., plates, ports., facsm., maps (2 fold., 1 in pocket at end). 23.6 cm.
Corresponding members of posse: p. 367–373; index: p. 376–383.
Half title.
Colophon: "This is No. —— of 500 copies of the regular edition."

Has a chapter on the death of Jesse James, one on Wild Bill Hickok and the myth of his shooting, and one on cattle rustlers. There is also a chapter on the Reynolds gang of Colorado and one on Murphy of the Lincoln County War. There is a new version of the killing of Bob Ford by Ed O. Kelly (which the author spells Ed O'Kelly). The writer says that Soapy Smith, boss of Jimtown (Creede), "was unable to force Ford into making his game crooked so he tried another way. He talked O'Kelly into the idea that by killing Ford he would become famous." I am afraid the writer has his facts wrong.

2357. ———

1957 brand book of the Denver westerners. Edited by Numa L. James. [Boulder, Colo., the Johnson co., 1948.] Pict. cloth. Scarce.

6 p.l., [3]–436 [1] p. illus., plates, facsms., maps. 23.6 cm.
Index: p. 422–436.
Half title; illus. end papers.
Colophon: "This is No. —— of the regular edition which is limited to five hundred copies."

A chapter entitled "Rougher Than Hell" deals with Ike Stockton and his gang. There is also a chapter on Clay Allison and another on Tom Horn.

2358. ———

A collection of articles relating to the west. 1958 brand book of the Denver westerners. Edited by Nolie Mumey. Boulder, Colo., Johnson publishing co., 1959. Boards and cloth. Scarce.

xi [1] p., 3–361 p. front. (col.), illus., plates, ports. 23.6 cm.
Index: p. [351]–361.
Half title; untrimmed.

Contains some material on Soapy Smith.

2359. ———

The 1962 brand book of the Denver posse of the westerners. Eighteenth annual volume. Edited by John J. Lipsey. Drawings by Archie Musick. Denver, Colo. [composed, printed and bound by Johnson publishing co.], 1963. Pict. cloth. Scarce.

11 p.l., 3–397 [1] p. illus., plates, ports. (1 fold.), maps, (1 fold.). 23.6 cm.
Index: p. 377–397; sketch of the author preceding each article.
Half title; illus. end papers.

Has chapters on the Lincoln County War, the members of the Earp family, and guns and two-gun men.

2360. ———

The 1963 all posse-corral brand book of the Denver posse of the westerners. 19th annual edition. Edited by Robert B. Cormack, with illustrations and sketches by George Catlin, Will James, and Robert B. Cormack. Denver, Colo., 1964. Fabrikoid. Scarce.

> xviii [2] p., [3]–475 [2] p. illus., plates, ports., maps, facsms. 23.6 cm.
> Index: p. [463]–475.
> Half title; illus. end papers; various colored paper throughout; text partly double column.
> Colophon: "This is copy number —— of the regular edition limited to 725 copies."

Has chapters on Cattle Kate Watson and Mountain Charley; some material on Jules Reni; whom the author calls Beni; and some information on Tom Horn, Joseph Slade, and Dodge City Boot Hill.

2361. ———

Brand book of the Denver westerners, edited by Francis B. Rizzard. Illustrated by Guy M. Herstrom. [Boulder, Colo., Johnson publishing co., 1965.] Pict. Fabrikoid. Scarce.

> 10 p.l., [5]–404 [12] p. illus., plates, ports., facsms. 23.6 cm.
> Index: last 10 unnumbered pages.
> Half title: "A Publication of the Denver Posse of Westerners for 1964."
> Colophon: "Regular edition limited to a total of six hundred and fifty copies. Number ——."

Has chapters containing material on such gunmen as Burt Alvord, Frank Baker, Billy the Kid, Black Jack Christian, Doc Middleton, Bronco Bill Walters, Butch Cassidy, Augustin Chacon, Calamity Jane, Kid Curry, Pat Garrett, Jesse James, Lincoln County War, Jeff Milton, George Musgrove, Tom O'Folliard, Alferd Packer, Big Nose George Parrott, Joseph Slade, and Tom Ketchum.

In a chapter entitled "Hero Makers" the author states that Billy the Kid was living in Silver City at the age of eight. The Kid's mother and stepfather did not move to Silver City until after they were married in 1873. Thus, if the Kid was born in 1859, as the author says, he would have been fourteen years old when they married. The author also repeats the legend about the Kid killing a blacksmith who had insulted his mother. He also has the Kid murdering Indian trappers for their pelts and has him the one who shot Frank Baker and Billy Morton "out of the saddle while trying to escape."

In another chapter, entitled "Outlaws," the author gives Code Young the first name Cole and says that he was killed during a train robbery on October 2, 1896.

The robbery took place on October 22 of that year. Both errors could be typographical ones.

2362. ———

Brand book of the Denver westerners, edited by Arthur L. Campa. Illustrated by Raul Rossell. [Boulder, Colo., Johnson publishing co., 1966.] Pict. cloth.

9 p.l., 3–411 p. illus., plates (4 col.), ports., facsms., map. 23.6 cm.

Index: p. 401–411.

Half title: "Annual publication of the Denver Westerners Posse, 1965, Volume XX."

Colophon: "This is No. —— of the regular edition. Limited to seven hundred thirty-five copies."

Contains a chapter on Kit Joy, the train robber; one on Joel Fowler, the noted gunman; and one on the killing of Wild Bill Hickok.

2363. Westerners' Brand Book (Los Angeles Posse)

The westerners' brand book, Los Angeles corral, 1947. [Los Angeles, 1948.] Cloth and leather. Scarce.

8 p.l., 19–176 p. front., illus., plates, ports. 26 cm.

Bibliography: p. 161–168; errata: p. 169; index: p. 170–173.

Half title; illus. end papers.

Colophon: "The Westerners' Brand Book Los Angeles 1947 is limited to 600 copies."

In E. A. Brininstool's chapter on Billy the Kid he repeats all the old legends about the Kid's early life. There is nothing new in the entire article, and he recommends Walter Noble Burns's *Saga of Billy the Kid* as "by far the most truthful account of the Kid's activities before the killing. . . ." If he considers Burns's book history, it is no wonder he accepts the false tales about the Kid. The volume also contains a chapter on Jeff Milton and copies of newspaper clippings about Tombstone, Arizona, and its troubles.

2364. ———

The westerners' brand book. Los Angeles corral, 1949. [Los Angeles, 1950.] Cloth and leather. Scarce.

7 p.l., 17–263 [1] p. front., illus. (84 col.), plates, ports., cattle brands, fold. facsm., large fold. map. 26 cm.

Bibliography: p. 251–254; index: p. 257–262.

Half title; illus. end papers; vignette.

Colophon: "The Westerners' Brand Book, Los Angeles Corral, 1949 is limited to 400 copies."

Among the historical papers is a chapter on Black Bart, one on the killing of Ed Masterson, and one on Colonel Dudley and the part he played in the Lincoln County War.

2365. ———

Westerners' brand book, 1950. Los Angeles corral. [Los Angeles, 1951.] Leather. Scarce.

8 p.l., 17–232 p. illus., plates (3 col.), cattle brands, earmarks, facsms. 26 cm.

Contributors: p. 211–214; bibliography: p. 215–226; index: p. 227–230.

Half title; illus. end papers (col.); illus. t.p.

Colophon: "The Westerners' Brand Book, Los Angeles Corral, 1950 limited to 400 copies."

In one article some mention is made of Billy the Kid and Black Jack Ketchum. In an article on the Bell Ranch of New Mexico, the author speaks of the graves of Henry (Charlie) Bowdry (Bowdre) and Tom O'Fallord (O'Folliard).

2366. ———

Westerners' brand book, Los Angeles corral. Book five. [Los Angeles, 1953.] Cloth. Scarce.

7 p.l., 17–180 p. illus., plates, (1 double p., col.), ports., maps, facsms. 26 cm.

Contributors: p. 165–168; bibliography: p. 169–172; index: p. 173–178.

Half title; illus. t.p.; illus. end papers.

Colophon: "The Westerners' Brand Book of Los Angeles Corral is limited to 400 copies."

Contains a chapter on Henry Brown, one on the Apache Kid, and one on books about outlaws.

2367. ———

Westerners' brand book. Los Angeles corral. Book six. Los Angeles, 1956. Pict. cloth. Scarce.

7 p.l., 17–163 [1] p. illus., plates, ports., map, facsm. 26 cm.

Contributors: p. 147–151; bibliography: p. 153–158; index: p. 159–162.

Half title; illus. t.p.; map on end papers.

Colophon: "The Westerners' Brand Book of Los Angeles Corral is limited to 400 copies."

Has chapters on Billy the Kid's stepfather, William Antrim, and on John Wesley Hardin.

2368. ———

The westerners' brand book, Los Angeles corral. Book number seven. [Los Angeles, 1957.] Pict. cloth. Scarce.

5 p.l., 15–293 p. illus., plates, ports., facsms. 26 cm.

Contributors: p. 287–293.

Half title; illus. end papers.

Colophon: "Book 7 the Westerners' Brand Book of Los Angeles Corral is limited to 475 copies."

Has chapters on the murder of Dora Hand and Dodge City, the start of the Lincoln County War, and the Pinkerton's bombing of the home of Jesse James.

2369. ———

The westerners' brand book. Book eight. Los Angeles corral, [Los Angeles, 1959.] Pict. cloth. Scarce.

7 p.l., 15–229 [2] p. illus., plates, ports., maps. 26 cm.

Contributors: p. 227–229.

Half title; illus., end papers; illus. t.p.

Among the chapters that deal with gunmen are "Dodge City's Boothill," by Earle Forrest; "Guns of Death Valley," by James Severn; "Murder of I. Chapman," by Philip J. Rasch; and "A Dynasty of Western Outlaws," by Paul I. Wellman. In the last article there are many mistakes, some of which are listed in Item 2337. Wellman seems to agree with Burton Rascoe that the book *The Only True History of Frank James*, by "himself," is true, though it is the most spurious document it has been my privilege to examine.

2370. ———

The westerners' brand book. Book ten. [Los Angeles], Los Angeles corral, 1963. Two-tone cloth. OP.

5 p.l., 11–241 [1] p. illus., plates (part col., 1 large fold.), ports., maps, graph, plan. 26 cm.

Index: p. 230–241.

Half title; illus. end papers; illus. t.p.

Colophon: "The Westerners' Brand Book, Book Ten of Los Angeles Corral is limited to 525 copies."

Has a splendid chapter by Don Meadows, entitled "Juan Flores and the Manillas," dealing with this California outlaw. All the Brand Books (with the exception of those issued in Chicago) are published annually. Those listed here are the only ones to date containing material on western outlaws.

2371. Western Writers of America

Legends and tales of the old west. By members of the western writers of America. Edited by S. Omar Barker. Garden City, N.Y., Doubleday & co., inc. [1962]. Cloth.

xiv p., 2 l., 408 p. 21.5 cm.
Half title.

Contains several chapters on such gunmen and outlaws as Joaquín Murieta, Black Bart, Tom Horn, Cole Younger, King Fisher, Luke Short, Bat Masterson, Diamondfield Jack Davis, and others. Since most of these authors are writers of fiction, the stories contain more fiction than history.

2372. Wetmore, Helen Cody

Last of the great scouts. The life story of Col. William F. Cody, (Buffalo Bill) as told by his sister Helen Cody Wetmore. [Duluth, Minn., the Duluth press printing co., publishers, 1899.] Cloth. Scarce.

xiii. 296 p. front., illus., plates. 21 cm.
Half title; device.

Another edition published same year with one less chapter and with different illustrations. The preface, table of contents, and preliminary leaves are in different order, and some of the paragraphing, as well as some tenses, are changed.

Republished, New York, International book and publishing co., 1900.
On cover: "Special Limited Edition."

Republished again by Grossett and Dunlap in 1918. In this reprint pages 321 to 333 are by Zane Grey.

2373. Wharton, Clarence Ray

L'Archeveque, by Clarence R. Wharton. Houston, Texas, the Anson Jones press [1941]. Wrappers. Scarce.

21 p. 22.6 cm.

The story of Sostenes L'Archeveque, an outlaw of the Texas Panhandle.

2374. ———

Wharton's history of Fort Bend county, by Clarence R. Wharton. . . . San Antonio, Texas, the Naylor co., 1939. Cloth. Scarce.

xi, 250 p. front. plates (1 col.), ports., maps (1 fold.), facsms. 23.5 cm.
Appendix: p. 233–235; bibliography: p. 237–238; index: p. 239–250.
Half title; illus. t.p.

Contains an account of the Jaybird-Woodpecker feud and other lawlessness.

2375. Wheeler, Col. Homer Webster

Buffalo days; forty years in the old west. The personal narrative of a cattleman, Indian fighter and army officer, by Colonel Homer W. Wheeler. . . . With an introduction by Major-General James G. Harbord. Indianapolis, the Bobbs-Merrill co. [1925]. Cloth. Scarce.

12 p.l., 369 p. front. (port.), plates, ports. 22 cm.
Index: p. 365–369.
Half title; vignette.
Later republished by A. L. Burt co.

This book was rewritten from the author's *The Frontier Trail* (see Item 2376). It has a chapter on Wild Bill Hickok and one entitled "Western Bad Men." For comment, see Item 2376.

2376. ———

The frontier trail; or, from cowboy to colonel. An authentic narrative of forty-three years in the old west as cattleman, Indian fighter, and army officer, by Colonel Homer W. Wheeler. . . . Los Angeles, published by Times-Mirror press, 1923. Pict. cloth. Scarce.

9 p.l., [15]–334 p. front. (port.), plates, ports., facsms. 23.2 cm.

In his chapter on Wild Bill Hickok, the author does not attempt to tell about the McCanles "fight" in his own words, but quotes from an article written by Buffalo Bill for *Hearst's Magazine*, published in the January, 1917, issue. The amazing thing to me is that in the preceding paragraph he writes that "many untrue stories have been circulated in Eastern magazines regarding Wild Bill." In spite of Wheeler's confidence in him, Buffalo Bill apparently had a knack for inaccuracies, as one can judge from the following excerpt:

"Coming into his swing station at Rock Creek one day in December, 1870 [both month and year are wrong], Bill failed to arouse anyone with shouts for a fresh mount, which was an indication of trouble. It was the stock-tender's business to be on hand with the relief pony the instant the rider came in. The Pony Express did not tolerate delays. Galloping into the yard, Bill dismounted and hurried to the stable, where he found, in the doorway, the stock-tender lying dead. At the same instant a woman's voice rang out from the cabin nearby. Turning about, Bill found himself face to face with a ruffian who was rushing from the house brandishing a six-shooter." Then, the author says, Bill killed the fellow and another one before entering the house, where he was met with a fusillade from four men, and of course he killed all of them.

In the first place, Hickok was not a pony-express rider, but a stable boy at the station. This account is different from some of the others Cody wrote, but just as far from the truth. He did not have Hickok wounded, which is the only truthful feature of the whole account.

2377. [Wheeler, Rev. C. C.]

[Confessions of some California murderers. Sacramento, Calif., Daily Union print, 1853.] Sewn. (Caption title.) Exceedingly rare.

16 p. 24.5 cm.

The trials, confessions, and executions of George Stewart, Benny Ackerman, and others. This rare item was examined in the Coe Collection at Yale University.

2378. Whisenand, Emma Boge

This is Nebraska, by Emma Boge Whisenand. Drawings made from prints by Esther Boquest Boardman. Kansas City, Mo., Burton publishing co., publishers [1942]. Pict. cloth. OP.

3 p.l., 9–150 [7] p. front., illus. 20.5 cm.
Last 7 p. index.
Half title; map on end papers.

Contains some material on Calamity Jane and Wild Bill Hickok. It repeats the fiction that Calamity Jane was among those who captured Jack McCall.

2379. White, Dale (pseud. of Mrs. Howard Place)

Bat Masterson, by Dale White. New York, Julian Messner, inc. [1960]. Cloth.

3 p.l., 7–191 p. 21.7 cm.
Bibliography: p. 185–186; index: p. 187–191.
Half title; pub. device.

The fact that this book was written for young readers makes its inaccuracies all the more irritating. Young minds should be exposed to historical truths, not legends originated by early-day dime novelists. The author repeats the fiction about Wyatt Earp arresting Ben Thompson in Ellsworth. The book is filled with errors.

2380. White, Michael C.

California all the way back to 1828, by Michael C. White. Written by Thomas Savage for the Bancroft Library, 1877. Introduction & notes by Glen Dawson. Illustrations by Clarence Ellsworth. Los Angeles, Glen Dawson, 1956. Cloth. OP.

xvi p., 17–93 p. front. (port.), illus., map (fold.). 19 cm.
Half title; map on end papers (dif.).
"Limited to 300 copies."
No. XXXII of "Early California Travel series."

Contains a chapter on the early California bandits with material on Juan Flores and Joaquín Murieta.

2381. White, Owen Payne

The autobiography of a durable sinner, [by] Owen P. White. New York, G. P. Putnam's sons [1942]. Cloth. OP.

vi p., 1 l., 3–344 p. 22 cm.
Index: p. 339–344.
Half title.
At head of title: "Owen P. White."

Owing to a threatened suit, the first printing of this book was recalled for deletions before release date. Only a few copies reached private hands (including my own); thus copies of the first state are rare. Pages 239 to 244 were deleted, and new material was tipped in. The book contains quite a bit of material on the gunmen of the Southwest. Clay Allison is the author's hero, but his remarks about the Earps and Pat Garrett are very disparaging.

According to all other accounts I have read of John Selman's killing of Bass Outlaw, the author has his facts mixed. He also speaks of Pat Garrett as a frequenter of the Coney Island Saloon in El Paso and writes: "Noteworthy of these bad characters was Pat Garrett, whose only claim to fame was that from a hiding place *behind a bed* he murdered Billy the Kid" (italics added).

In this autobiography White gives us some insight into why so many of his articles in *Collier's* were written without research. He promised the editor to make these articles "true and vivid," but they were anything but true.

"My first eight stories for *Collier's*," he writes, "with my old gun-fighting murderers promoting the sale of the magazine by killing someone in almost every paragraph, were written in record time. I began them in August, finished them in September. . . ." He admits that he was "allowed, even encouraged, to write about anything I wanted to whether I knew anything about it or not."

In an article he wrote for *American Mercury* about Quantrill, entitled "Buckets of Blood," he spelled his subject's name incorrectly. Yet he says that the demand for "the true tales of blood and murder was so great that *Collier's* ordered me off to the West to search for material from which to concoct another batch." This is not the attitude of the true historian. He would have done better to go to a library and read a few reliable histories.

2382. ———

Lead and likker, by Owen P. White. New York, Minton, Balch & co., 1932. Cloth. Scarce.

vii p., 1 l., 3–274 p. 21.2 cm.
Half title; pub. device; untrimmed.

Contains chapters on many of the outlaws, from Henry Plummer, John Wesley

Hardin, Ben Thompson, and Belle Starr to Chris Evans of California. Most of these chapters are unreliable, especially the one on Belle Starr. In this book, as in some of his others, the author says that Henry Brown was hanged by the Medicine Lodge mob. Brown was killed, first by being shot as he tried to escape, then by being hanged with the others.

2383. ———

My Texas 'tis of thee, by Owen P. White. New York, G. P. Putnam's sons, 1936. Cloth. OP.

6 p.l., 274 p. 19.6 cm.

Half title; pub. device; untrimmed.

Contains a not too reliable chapter on Luke Short and his killing of Jim Courtright, as well as the activities of some other gunmen.

2384. ———

Out of the desert. The historical romance of El Paso, by Owen P. White. El Paso, Texas, the McMath co., publishers, 1923. Cloth. Rare.

6 p.l., 442 p., 2 l. (1 errata). plates, ports. 23.8 cm.

Section two, biographical: p. [329]–442.

Half title; vignette; errata leaf.

Reprinted in 1924 with same imprint in 345 pages, omitting the biographical and newspaper section.

Mr. White's first book and perhaps his best. It contains much material on the lawlessness of El Paso. It also has a chapter on Dallas Stoudenmire and much on gunplay in the frontier town of El Paso.

2385. ———

Texas, an informal biography, by Owen P. White. New York, G. P. Putnam's sons [1945]. Cloth. OP.

ix p., 1 l., 3–268 p. front. (port.), illus., plates, ports., facsm. 20.5 cm.

Index: p. 265–268.

Half title; map on end papers.

The last book written by this author before his death, and his poorest. It contains much unreliable material on gunmen. His account of Sam Bass is confused, both in the planning of the Union Pacific robbery and in the amount obtained. He says that the robbers seized $120,000 in "20 dollar gold pieces"—double the amount they actually got. He says that there was "deep sorrow" when word came that Joel Collins and Bill Heffridge (misspelled Hefferide) were killed on their way to San Antonio (he pictures early-day Texans in general as champions of outlaws). He says that each robber's cut was $40,000. He has Underwood taking part in the robbery, which is incorrect, and he further states that Underwood and Berry lived in Texas under assumed names for the rest of their lives—also incorrect. Berry was killed near his home in Missouri shortly after the robbery.

The author says that Davis and Bass showed up in Denton and gave out interviews to the press about their future plans and that Davis, with a bride on his arm, declared that he would go to South America and reform. Davis did not go to Denton, but left Bass in Fort Worth, and not with any bride. The author says that when Bass gathered a gang and held up his first train in Texas "west of Dallas," it "threw the entire state into a frenzy of delight." The first train Bass held up in Texas was at Allen, *north* of Dallas. He makes the citizens of Texas appear ridiculous by saying that they thought so much of Bass that he could have been elected governor of the state and that they were proud of all the robbers of the Union Pacific because it was the biggest one in history and prayed nightly for their safety. Mr. White does not seem to have known what happened in his own state.

He is mistaken in saying that Jim Courtright belonged to the "kill 'em for cash" profession and "was good at it." He says that Courtright "had bumped off, at so much per head, perhaps a dozen unarmed jumpers and unoffending nesters." (One could almost write another book on the mistakes in this one.) He paints Ben Thompson with a black brush and an inaccurate one. He does not have much to say about Black Jack Ketchum, but what he does say is incorrect.

"From a Sunday School class in Knickerbocker (near San Angelo)," he writes, "came a whole covey of outlaws who, headed by Black Jack and Barry [Berry] Ketchum, were finally all hanged in Clayton, New Mexico." Berry, the oldest brother, was not an outlaw, and only Black Jack was hanged in Clayton. He says that Wyatt Earp was in Abilene "endeavoring to short-card the poor unprotected cowboys out of their hard earned cash before the gals could get their hands on it." Earp was in Dodge City, not in Abilene.

2386. ———

Them was the days; from El Paso to prohibition, by Owen P. White, with drawings by Ross Santee. New York, Minton, Balch & co., 1925. Pict. cloth. Scarce.

6 p.l., 3–235 p. front., illus. 21.4 cm.
Half title; pub. device; untrimmed.

Has a chapter, entitled "The Psychology of Gun-Men," about the feud between John Wesley Hardin and John Selman.

2387. ———

Trigger fingers, by Owen P. White. . . . New York, London, G. P. Putnam's sons, 1926. Cloth. Very scarce.

vii p., 1 l., 3–323 p. 19.2 cm.

This book contains several chapters on various gunmen of the Southwest, and, as usual, most of them are unreliable. The author repeats most of the Upson legends about Billy the Kid and claims his first victim was a "black nigger" who tried to cheat him in a card game. He also says that the Kid killed twenty-six men, "not counting Indians," and that he killed Bernstein with no more provocation than that he "didn't like Jews nohow." He not only has Dave Wall, instead of J. W. Bell, as the Kid's guard, but has the circumstances of his killing all wrong. He is another writer who spells O'Folliard's name as O'Phalliard.

His account of the Hickok-McCanles "fight" is unreliable, and he says that Dave McCanles (which he spells McCandless) was the leader of a bunch of horse thieves. He admits that there are many different versions of this "fight." One writer, he says, has Wild Bill "killing ten men and having been stabbed and shot eighteen or twenty times himself," while another writer says Wild Bill only shot five of the enemy, "while a third in my opinion sticks to the truth. I will use the story as told by the last one." But the story he follows is also completely false. He gives Jack McCall the first name John and makes many other mistakes.

In his chapter on Sam Bass he has Henry Underwood taking part in the Big Springs robbery, though Underwood joined Bass after his return to Texas. He has one of the party, after the robbery, going to Ogallala and arousing the suspicion of a clerk by an unusual purchase, but this suspicious purchase was made before the robbery when one of the men bought six bandannas. He says that the total take of the robbery "must have come to a grand total of $114,000." He further says that the young clerk saw the robbers dividing the money and that the sight "frightened him to death." He makes the statement that "everybody in the state of Texas of course knew that Denton was honored by having had one of its local boys take part." That is ridiculous. The citizens of Texas were no fonder of outlaws than were any other law-abiding people.

He says that the first Texas train robbery took place when the Bass gang "held up a west-bound train at a small station a few miles west of Dallas." By direction, that would have been the holdup at Eagle Ford, but the first holdup was at Allen, north of Dallas. He has the second holdup east of Dallas, which would have been the robbery at Mesquite, but that was Bass's fourth and last holdup.

He has Jim Murphy captured when Arkansas Johnson was killed, but Murphy was not one of the gang at that time. He says that a Babe Daniels was a member of the gang, a character I have never read about elsewhere. He ends the chapter by saying that Jackson was hanging around Denton after the Round Rock incident waiting for a chance to kill Murphy, who "in a few weeks committed suicide." Jackson never returned to Denton, and Murphy did not commit suicide. In his chapter on Clay Allison he repeats many of the legends about this gunman, and his information is just as unreliable as that in his other writings.

2388. Whiting, F. B.

Grit, grief and gold. A true narrative of an Alaskan pathfinder, by F. B. Whiting, M.D. Seattle, Wash., Peacock publishing co., MCMXXXIII. Pict. fabrikoid. Scarce.

xvi [1], 247 p. front. (port.), plates, ports. 20.2 cm.
Half title.

Has several chapters on Soapy Smith, giving some different information on his gang provided by the doctor who performed the autopsy on Soapy after his death.

2389. Whittemore, Margaret

One-way ticket to Kansas. The autobiography of Frank M. Stahl, as told to Margaret Whittemore. Illustrated by the author. Lawrence, University of Kansas press, 1959. Cloth. OP.

5 p.l., 146 p. illus., plates, ports., facsm. 21.7 cm.
Index: p. [143]–146.
Half title.

The author says that Wild Bill Hickok came to Kansas to become a stage driver on the Santa Fe Trail, and was later killed in Deadwood "by a drunken gambler."

2390. Wickersham, James

Old Yukon. Tales, trails and trials, by Hon. James Wickersham. . . . Washington, D.C., Washington law book co., 1938. Cloth. Scarce.

xi, 514 p. front. (map), illus., plates, ports., map. 23.6 cm.
Index: p. 489–514.

Chapter II contains some new and interesting material on Soapy Smith.

2391. Wildwood, Warren

Thrilling adventures among the early settlers embracing desperate encounters with Indians, tories and refugees; daring exploits of Texas rangers and others, and incidents of guerilla warfare; fearful deeds of the gamblers and desperadoes, rangers and regulators of the west and southwest . . ., by Warren Wildwood, Esq. . . . Illustrated by 200 engravings. Philadelphia, John E. Potter and co. [1861]. Dec. cloth. Rare.

7 p.l., 15–384 p. front. (with tissue), illus. 19.5 cm.
Half title; illus. t.p.

Contains several chapters on crime and early-day desperadoes, such as John A. Murrell.

2392. Wilhelm, Stephen R.

Cavalcade of hooves and horns, [by] Steve Wilhelm. San Antonio, the Naylor co. [1958]. Pict. cloth.

xv, 218 p. illus. 22.2 cm.
Bibliography: p. 209–210; index: p. 211–218.
Half title; illus. double t.p.; head and tail pieces.
Also published in a de luxe edition.

Has some material on Billy the Kid. The author continues the legend that the Kid had killed twenty-one men by the time he was twenty-one years of age. There is also some material on Print Olive and his death. In speaking of rustlers, the author writes: "One of the worst of these was a woman, Ella Watson, better known as 'Cattle Kate.' Kate had a variety of taking ways, chief among them that of 'acquiring' any cattle that drifted near her place and superimposing her own brand on them." Cattle Kate did no rustling at all. Cowboys gave her stolen cattle (mostly calves) as the price for spending the night in her arms. She and her paramour, Jim Averill, were considered rustlers, however, and they were finally seized and hanged as such.

2393. ———

Texas, yesterday and tomorrow, by Steve Wilhelm. Houston, Texas, Gulf publishing co. [1947]. Cloth. Scarce.

4 p.l., 134 p. 20.7 cm.
Index: p. 132–134.

The author gives some unusual, and unreliable, information on Sam Bass, such as saying that when Bass planned to rob a train "he would hide four horses five miles apart on his getaway route and thus, after he accomplished his robbery, he would have a fresh horse under him and could easily out-distance the pursuing posse. . . ." He also states that Bass got started in outlawry to get money to pay his gambling debts, which is untrue. He claims that "tradition has it that Sam Bass left upwards of one hundred and fifty thousand dollars in gold hidden in various parts of Texas during his train robbing spree, which lasted over a period of years." Since Bass started his train-robbing career with the Union Pacific in the latter part of 1877 and got killed in mid-1878, his career was a short one and did not last "over a period of years." Also, on his way to Round Rock, where he was killed, Bass spent the last twenty-dollar gold piece he had seized in the Union Pacific robbery; and since his Texas train robberies never exceeded more than a few hundred dollars, he certainly did not have much gold buried in scattered caches throughout Texas.

2394. Willcox, R. N.

Reminiscences of California life, being an abridged description of scenes which the author has passed through in California and other lands . . ., by R. N. Willcox. Avery, Ohio, Willcox print, 1897. Cloth. Rare.

3 p.l., 5–290 p. 21.5 cm.

It is said that only seventy-five copies of this book were issued. A portrait is inserted in some copies. There is some material about Tom Bell, the California outlaw.

2395. Willett, Edward

Clip, the contortionist; or, the vigilantes of Montana, by Edward Willett. . . . New York, Beadle & Adams, 1884. Pict. wrappers. Rare.

14 p. 28.5 cm.
Beadle's Half Dime Library, Vol. XIV, No. 340.
Triple column.

2396. Williams, Albert N.

The Black Hills, mid-continent resort, by Albert N. Williams. American Resort series No. 4. [Dallas, Texas], Southern Methodist University press, 1952. Cloth. OP.

xiv, 130 p. illus., plates, ports. 20.5 cm.
Bibliography: p. 126; index: p. 127–130.
Half title; vignette.

Tells about the military and early history of the Black Hills. In writing about Wild Bill Hickok, the author states that Hickok received most of his fame through dime novels. That is incorrect. He gained much of his reputation during his lifetime, primarily through his interview with Nichols for *Harper's Magazine*. In his version of the Rock Creek Station "fight" the author calls Hickok the station manager and says, "No one today knows for certain how many men were killed, for eye-witness accounts have included reports ranging all the way from one to six, all of them presumably slain by Hickok." The author has McCall captured in a stable and says that after his trial McCall "hurried back to Cheyenne to escape the reach of Hickok's friends."

He says that Sam Bass was the inventor of stage robbery in the Black Hills and that he was killed in a barber shop, both statements incorrect. There are many other errors.

2397. Williams, Brad, and Choral Pepper

The mysterious west, [by] Brad Williams and Choral Pepper. Cleveland and New York, the World publishing co. [1967]. Cloth.

6 p.l., 13–192 p. plates, ports., facsm., map. 23.4 cm.

Half title; double t.p.; pub. device; "First edition" on copyright page.

Contains a chapter on Joaquín Murieta, in which the authors misspell Murieta's name. They repeat the legend about Billy the Kid killing twenty-one men by the time he was twenty-one years of age and claim that Murieta killed more than three hundred men. According to the authors, Murieta had a special hatred for Orientals and "more than 200 of his victims were Orientals." There is some mention of Calamity Jane, Belle Starr, and Alferd Packer.

2398. Williams, Charlean Moss

Washington, Hemstead county, Arkansas. Gateway to Texas, 1835, Confederate capital, 1863, by Charlean Moss Williams. "The old town speaks." Houston, Texas, the Anson-Jones press, MCMLI. Cloth. Scarce.

13 p.l., 338 p. front. (port.), plates. 24.2 cm.

Maps on end papers (dif.); untrimmed.

Contains a short chapter on John A. Murrell.

2399. Williams, Emma Inman

Historic Madison. The story of Jackson and Madison counties, Tennessee. From the prehistoric moundbuilders to 1917, by Emma Inman Williams. A contribution to the sesquicentennial celebration of Tennessee statehood in 1946. With illustrations. Jackson, Tenn., published by Madison County Historical Society, 1946. Cloth. Scarce.

xiv p., 17 l., 553 p. illus., plates, ports., facsms., maps, tables. 25.2 cm.

Index: p. 533–553.

Half title; illus. end papers; gilt top.

Has a chapter on John A. Murrell, the land pirate.

2400. Williams, Harry

Texas trails; legends of the great southwest, by Harry Williams . . ., pen and ink sketches by Hans Reuter. San Antonio, Texas, the Naylor co. [1932]. Pict. cloth. OP.

vii p., 2 l., 269 p. 24 cm.

Index: p. 263–269.

Half title; illus. end papers; tailpieces; vignette.

"These stories, some now revised and altered, appeared in the 'Texas Trail' column of the *San Antonio Light* between the years 1927 and 1931" (Foreword.)

A collection of short articles, among which are tales about Joel Fowler, John Wesley Hardin, and Ben Thompson.

2401. Williams, Henry Llewellyn

"Buffalo Bill" (the Hon. William F. Cody). Rifle and revolver shot; pony express rider; teamster; buffalo hunter; guide and scout. A full account of his adventurous life with the origin of his "Wild West" show, by Henry Llewellyn Williams. London, George Routledge and sons . . ., 1887. Cloth. Rare.

vi, [7]–192 p. front. 20 cm.

Half title.

This is said to be the rarest book about Buffalo Bill. It is founded upon the many dime novels of its day and is thus, of course, unreliable. In one place the author, an Englishman, says, "Lest the authenticity of this early exploit be demurred at let us hasten to say it is recorded by Colonel Prentis Ingraham." Ingraham was one of the prolific and wildly imaginative dime novelists of his day and certainly no authority on anything historical. The whole book is a ludicrous attempt to write about the American wild West.

2402. ———

Joaquín (the Claude Duval of California); or, the marauder of the mines. A romance founded on truth. New York, Robert M. DeWitt, publisher [1865]. Pict. wrappers. Rare.

160 p. 23.5 cm.

Republished, New York, Pollard & Moss, 1888. Dec. cloth.

[3]–206 p. 19 cm.

2 p. adv. at end.

Reprinted again with same imprint in 1889.

Another fictitious account based on the *California Police Gazette* version of Murieta's "life."

2403. Williams, Jean

The lynching of Elizabeth Taylor, by Jean Williams. [Santa Fe, N.M.], press of the Territorian [1966]. Stiff wrappers.

1 p.l., 3–40 [1] p. plates. 22.8 cm.

Western Americana series, No. 7, limited to 1,000 copies.

Acknowledgments: p. [41].

Has some material on Jim Averill, Cattle Kate Watson, and Print Olive.

2404. Williams, John G.

The adventures of a seventeen-year-old lad and the fortunes he might have won, by John G. Williams. Boston, printed for the author by the Collins press, 1894. Cloth. Scarce.

x, [11]–308 p. front. (port. with tissue), illus. 23.8 cm.

A privately printed book in which the author gives an account of his encounter with Joaquín Murieta and Three-Fingered Jack García.

2405. [Williams, Joseph S.]

Old times in west Tennessee. Reminiscences—semi-historic—of pioneer life and the early emigrant settlers in the Big Hatchie country, by a descendent of one of the first settlers. Memphis, Tenn., W. G. Cheeney, printer and publisher, 1873. Cloth. Rare.

5 p.l., [7]–295 p. 19.5 cm.

Devotes several pages to the early history of the Murrell gang.

2406. Williams, Llew

The Dalton brothers in their Oklahoma cave. A tale of adventure in the Indian territory, by Llew Williams. . . . Together with the desperate and startling criminal career of the gang. With illustrations from life and the actual scenes of their crimes. Chicago, M. A. Donohue & co. [n.d.]. Pict. cloth. Rare.

1 p.l., 5–234 p. illus. 19.8 cm.

An early-day fantastic tale containing not one word of truth; one of the cheap "thrillers" typical of its time.

2407. Williams, Judge Oscar Waldo

A city of refuge, by O. W. Williams. [N.p., n.d.] Wrappers. Rare.

8 p. 22.9 cm.

Has some descriptions of citizens of Silver City, New Mexico, and some information about Billy the Kid and his first arrest.

2408. ———

[Letter to J. O. Williams. Fort Stockton, 1925.] Pamphlet. Rare.

[14] p. (no pagination). 21.7 cm.

Gives an account of the bank robbery at Liberty, Missouri. The holdup was attributed to the James boys, but the author says that he later talked to a Mrs. Pool, of Marfa, Texas, who claimed that she had cooked supper for the James boys a hundred miles away from Liberty on the same day the bank was robbed.

2409. ———

The old New Mexico, 1879–1880. Reminiscences of Judge O. W. Williams. [N.p., n.d.] Wrappers. Rare.

48 p. 22.9 cm.

An interesting little pamphlet of reminiscences with some references to lawlessness in New Mexico and a mention of Billy the Kid. At the end are the words "To be continued," but if the second volume was ever published, I have not been able to find it.

2410. ———

Pioneer surveyor, frontier lawyer. The personal narrative of O. W. Williams, 1877–1902. Edited with annotations by S. D. Myers. Introduction by C. L. Sonnichsen. El Paso, Texas, Texas Western College press, 1966. Cloth and leather.

xii p., 1 l., 3–350 p. front. (port.), illus., plates, ports., maps (3 illus. and double p.). 24.2 cm.

Notes after each chapter; epilogue: p. 303–317; appendices: p. 325–333; acknowledgments: p. 335–336; index: p. 337–350.

Half title; t.p. in red and black; pub. device.

Also published in a de luxe edition in slip case, signed by the editor, the writer of the introduction, the artist, the researcher, and the designer-producer.

Colophon: "One hundred fifty copies of this Fort Stanton edition have been specially printed, boxed and signed, May 20, 1966. . . . This is copy number ——."

The author, a well-educated man with no ambition to become a professional writer, had many little privately printed pamphlets published from his notes, letters, and diaries. They were written in such a clear and interesting style, revealing so many little-known historical facts, that they were sought by historians and collectors all over the country. The supply was so limited that they got into very few hands. Here is a collection of many of his writings in their proper relation and context.

The author lived in the West during its raw period as surveyor, miner, and lawyer and knew personally many notable and notorious men. During his stay in Shakespeare, New Mexico, he knew Sandy King and Russian Bill when they were hanged. He was a friend of J. W. Bell long before the latter became a deputy and was killed by Billy the Kid. He gives an account of this killing in one chapter. There is also some mention of Curly Bill Brocius, Johnny Ringo, Bob Olinger, and others. Living in that age and with his talents, the author has left us many dependable firsthand accounts of the period.

2411. Williams, R. H.

With the border ruffians. Memories of the far west, 1852–1868, by R. H. Williams, sometime lieutenant in the Kansas rangers, and afterward captain in the Texas rangers. Edited by E. W. Williams. With portrait. London, 1907. Cloth. Scarce.

xviii p., 1 l., 3–478 p. front. (port. with tissue), plates, ports. 22.3 cm.

Index: p. 473–478.

Half title.

Reprinted with same collation in 1908; American edition, New York, E. P. Dutton and co., 1907 with same collation; another edition printed in Toronto in 1919.

Deals with life during the lawless days of Kansas and Texas.

2412. Williams, Walter, and Floyd Calvin Shoemaker

Missouri, mother of the west, by Walter Williams, Ll.D., and Floyd Calvin Shoemaker, A.B., A.M., assisted by an advisory council. Missouri biography by special staff of writers. Issued in five volumes. Vol. II. Illustrated. Chicago, New York, the American Historical Society, inc., 1930. Fabrikoid. Scarce.

2 p.l., 7–629 p. front. (port.), plates, ports. 26.4 cm.

Volume II contains material on the Jameses and the Youngers.

2413. Williamson, Thames

Far north country, by Thames Williamson. Edited by Erskine Caldwell. New York, Duell, Sloan & Pearce [1944]. Cloth. OP.

xi p., 1 l., 3–236 p. 22 cm.

Index: p. 233–236.

Half title; map on end papers.

Gives a brief story about Soapy Smith.

2414. Williard, James F., and Collin B. Goodykoontz (eds.)

The Trans-Mississippi west. Papers read at a conference held at the University of Colorado, June 18–June 21, 1929. Edited by James F. Williard and Collin B. Goodykoontz. Boulder, University of Colorado, 1930. Cloth. Scarce.

xi, 366 p. 20.4 cm.

Index: p. 343–366.

Half title.

In a chapter entitled "The American Picaresque" there is material on Jesse James, Joaquín Murieta, and others.

2415. Willison, George Finlay

Here they dug the gold, by George F. Willison. . . . New York, Brentano's publishers [1931]. Pict. cloth. Scarce.

xiii p., 1 l., [3]–299 p. illus. 22.5 cm.

Half title; map on end papers; pub. device.

Republished in 1935. In 1946 a revised and enlarged edition was published by Reynal & Hitchcock, New York.

Contains much material on the lawlessness in the mining camps of Colorado.

2416. Willson, Roscoe G.

No place for angels. Roscoe G. Willson's stories of old Arizona days. Illustrations by Frank King. Phoenix, Ariz., the Arizona Republic; Tucson, Ariz., Arizona Silhouettes [1958]. Cloth. OP.

6 p.l., 275 p. front., illus. 23.5 cm.
Half title; vignette.

2417. Wilson, Edward

An unwritten history. A record from the exciting days of early Arizona, by Edward Wilson. Cover design by O. D. Brown. [Phoenix, Ariz., the McNeill co., 1915.] Pict. cloth. Rare.

3 p.l., 7–77 p. 17.3 cm.

Reprinted in Santa Fe by the Stagecoach press in 1966 with added footnotes and index as No. 4 of the Stagecoach press Southwestern series, limited to 750 copies.

xi p., 1 l., 15–62 [1] p. 17.8 cm.
Index: p. 61–62.

Among other stories about early Arizona the author gives accounts of the Apache Kid; Grant Wheeler, the train robber; and a man called Black Jack—evidently Black Jack Christian, for the author says he was not Tom Ketchum.

2418. Wilson, Isaac A.

Four years in a home made hell, by Isaac A. Wilson. Siloam Springs, Ark., the Herald printing co., 1894. Wrappers. Exceedingly rare.

62 p. front. (port.). 19.5 cm.

I know of but one copy of this rare little book. A member of the Reno gang, the author writes an account favorable to them, but he gives some accurate information on how the vigilantes worked.

2419. Wilson, Neill Compton

Silver stampede, the career of Death Valley's hell-camp, old Panamint, by Neill C. Wilson. Illustrated. New York, the Macmillan co., 1937. Cloth. Scarce.

xiv p., 1 l., 319 p. illus., plates, ports., facsms. 22.3 cm.
Index: p. 315–319.
Half title; map on end papers; "First printing" on copyright p.

The history of Panamint in the days of its bad men.

2420. ———

Treasure express. Epic days of the Wells Fargo, by Neill C. Wilson. Illustrated. New York, the Macmillan co., 1936. Pict. cloth. OP.

xii p., 1 l., 322 p. illus., plates, ports., facsm. 22.2 cm.
Acknowledgments: p. 309–311; index: p. 313–322.
Half title; illus. end papers; untrimmed.

A well-written book dealing with stagecoaches and the men who robbed them. The author intimates that Doc Holliday was in the group that held up the stage when Bud Philpot was killed.

2421. ———, and Frank J. Taylor

Southern Pacific. The roaring story of a fighting railroad, [by] Neill C. Wilson and Frank J. Taylor. New York, London, Toronto, McGraw-Hill book co., inc. [1952]. Cloth. OP.

viii p. 1 l., 256 p. plates, ports. 23.5 cm.
Appendix: p. [211]–245; bibliography: p. [247]–248; index: p. [249]–256.
Half title; map on end papers.

Contains a chapter on train robbery, the Daltons, the Evans-Sontag gang, Big Jack Davis, and the De Autrements.

2422. Wilson, Rufus Rockwell

A noble company of adventurers, by Rufus Rockwell Wilson. . . . Illustrated from drawings by May Fratz and from photographs. New York, B. W. Dodge and co., 1908. Pict. cloth. Rare.

2 p.l., 219 p. front., plates. 19 cm.
Device.

In a long chapter on the Texas Rangers the author gives accounts of their clashes with outlaws and Texas gunmen.

2423. ———

Out of the west, by Rufus R. Wilson. . . . Illustrations by E. Fletcher. New York, the press of the Pioneers, 1933. Cloth. Scarce.

7 p.l., 452 p. illus. 24.5 cm.

Republished, New York, Wilson-Erickson, inc., 1936.

xvii, 480 p. front., illus. 24 cm.
Bibliography: p. 461–468; index: p. 469–480.
Half title.
Colophon: "Of this edition of Out of the West, three hundred copies have been signed by the author. This is copy No. ——."
Published same year in a revised and enlarged edition.

In a chapter entitled "Turbulent Tombstone" the author makes Wyatt Earp quite a hero and superman. In the battle of the O K Corral he has all the Clanton crowd armed except Ike Clanton and portrays Sheriff Behan as a coward. The author's version of the killing of Stillwell is quite different from other accounts, and most of this chapter is inaccurate; for example, the author has Wyatt Earp arresting Ben Thompson in Ellsworth when Sheriff Whitney was killed.

In another chapter, entitled "Frontier Peace Officers," the author repeats the legends about Wild Bill Hickok and tells about his impossible shooting feats. He writes that after Hickok's murder McCall "was tried, found guilty and hanged." McCall was released after his first trial, later bragged about his feat, was rearrested, tried in a court of law at Yankton, and then hanged.

2424. ———, and Ethel M. Sears

History of Grant county, Kansas, by R. R. Wilson and Ethel M. Sears. [Wichita, Kans., printed by Wichita press, 1950.] Cloth. OP.

3 p.l., 13–278 p. front. (port.), maps. 20.5 cm.

2425. Wilstach, Frank Jenners

Wild Bill Hickok, the prince of pistoleers, by Frank J. Wilstach. Garden City, N.Y., Doubleday, Page & co., 1926. Cloth. OP.

xviii p., 1 l., 304 p. front. (port.), plates, ports. 21.4 cm.

Half title; t.p. in red and black; vignette; untrimmed; "First edition" on copyright p.

Republished in 1939 by Sun Dial press under the title *The Plainsman, Wild Bill Hickok*.

The author apparently made a sincere effort to depict the true character of David McCanles. He tells a more accurate story of the McCanles "fight" with Wild Bill than most writers. He labels the Nichols, Buel, and Hough accounts "pure fable," but he is extremely partial to the subject of his own biography. He repeats much of Buel's fanciful fiction, such as Hickok's duel with Conquering Bear, his fight with four cowboys, and many other incidents. He has a different version of the trouble between Coe and Hickok at Abilene, saying that Hickok had ordered Coe to move his gambling layout from the back room to the front of the building, claiming that players were being drugged and robbed in the back room. He is among the writers who say that Wild Bill's body was reburied at Mt. Moriah on August 3, 1879.

2426. Winch, Frank

Thrilling lives of Buffalo Bill, (Col. Wm. F. Cody), last of the great scouts, and Pawnee Bill, Maj. Gordon W. Lillie (Pawnee Bill), white chief of the Pawnees. . . . [New York, S. L. Parson and co., inc., 1911.] Wrappers. Scarce.

224 p. front., illus., plates, ports., facsm. 19 cm.

2427. Winchell, Lilbourne Alsip

History of Fresno county, and the San Joaquin valley. Narrative and biographical, by Lilbourne Alsip Winchell. Under the editorial supervision of Ben R. Walker. . . . Fresno, Calif., A. H. Cawston, publisher [1933]. Dec. cloth. Scarce.

2 p.l., [5]–323 p. front. (port.), plates, ports., map. 27.4 cm.

Has a chapter on Murieta and Vásquez.

2428. Winget, D. H.

Anecdotes of Buffalo Bill which have never before appeared in print, by his boyhood friend and "pard," D. H. Winget. Clinton, Iowa, June, 1912. Pict. cloth. Scarce.

4 p.l., 13–224 p. front. (port.), illus., plates, ports. 19.8 cm.
Port on t.p.

The author tells about his meeting with Jesse James.

2429. ———

Anecdotes of "Buffalo Bill" that have never appeared in print, by Dan Winget, the last of the old scouts. Chicago, Historical publishing co., 1927. Cloth. Scarce.

5 p.l., 13–230 p. front. (port.), illus., plates, ports., facsm. of letter. 20 cm.
Illus. chap. headings; tailpieces; vignette.

Contains some intimate short stories about Buffalo Bill and the author, among them one about Jesse James. The author again tells the old story about the cruel mortgage holder and the widow but gives it a different setting. Although the author claims to have known all the early notorious gunmen intimately, he misspells many of their names, such as Quantrail for Quantrill, Hitchcock for Hickok, and Simon Slade for Joseph Slade.

2430. Winn, Mary Day

The macadam trail. Ten thousand miles by motor coach, by Mary Day Winn. Illustrated by E. H. Suydam. New York, Alfred A. Knopf, MCMXXXI. Cloth. Scarce.

xiv p., 1 l., 3–319, i–xii p. front. (col.), full p. illus. 23 cm.
Index: p. i–xii.
Half title; illus. end papers; illus. chap. headings; vignette; "First edition" on copyright p.

Chapter V is about Bill Carlisle, the Wyoming train robber. The book also contains material on the Johnson County War, Jesse James, Billy the Kid, and Calamity Jane, but none of the author's information adds anything of value.

2431. Winslow, Kathryn

Big pan-out, [by] Kathryn Winslow. New York, W. W. Norton & co., inc. [1951]. Cloth. OP.

x, 3–247 p. plates. 21.8 cm.

Half title; map on end papers; "First edition" on copyright p.

Republished in London by the Travel Book club in 1953 with 11 photographs and 2 maps, and an added index.

Both editions contain some material on Soapy Smith during the time he was in Skagway.

2432. Winther, Oscar Osburn

The great northwest. A history, by Oscar Osburn Winther. New York, Alfred A. Knopf, 1947. Cloth. Scarce.

xv p., 1 l., 3–383 p., xxv p. plates, ports., maps. 21.7 cm.

Bibliography: p. 346–383; index: p. i–xxv.

Half title; pub. device; untrimmed.

Has material on Henry Plummer, George Ives, Ned Ray, Jack Gallaher, Clubfoot George Lane, and the others of the Plummer gang.

2433. ———

The old Oregon country. A history of frontier trade, transportation, and travel, [by] Oscar Osburn Winther. . . . Stanford, Calif., Stanford University press; London, Oxford University press [1950]. Cloth. Scarce.

xvi p., 1 l., 3–348 p. front., plates, ports., maps. 26 cm.

Bibliography: p. 305–323; index: p. 327–348.

Half title.

A special bound edition was published by Indiana University press as No. 7 in its "Social Science Series."

In a chapter on stagecoach travel the author tells about many of the road agents, such as Stove Pipe Sam, George Ives, Henry Plummer, and Black Bart.

2434. ———

The transportation frontier; Trans-Mississippi west, 1865–1890, [by] Oscar Osburn Winther. . . . New York, Chicago, San Francisco, Toronto, London, Holt, Rinehart and Winston [1964]. Cloth.

xiv, 224 p. plates, maps (2 double p.), facsms. 23.2 cm.

Notes: p. [165]–192; bibliographical notes: p. [193]–210; index: p. [211]–224.

Half title; maps on end papers.

In a chapter entitled "Indians, Outlaws and Wayfarers" the author has some material on such outlaws as Black Bart, the Plummer gang, the Jameses and the Youngers, and the Sam Bass gang.

2435. ———

Via western express & stagecoach, by Oscar Osburn Winther. Stanford University, Calif., Stanford University press [1945]. Pict. cloth. Scarce.

xi, 158 p. plates, ports., facsms. 26 cm.
Bibliographical notes: p. 149–150; index: p. 151–158.
Half title; maps on end papers; illus. double t.p. (col.); illus. chap. headings.

Contains material on Murieta, Vásquez, Tom Bell, and other California bandits.

2436. Wister, Fanny Kemble (ed.)

Owen Wister out west. His journals and letters. Edited by Fanny Kemble Wister. [Chicago], University of Chicago press [1958]. Pict. cloth and boards. OP.

xix [2] p., 2–269 p. illus., plates, ports. 22.8 cm.
A Wister bibliography: p. 262–264; acknowledgments: p. 265–266; index: p. 267–269.
Half title; pub. device.

The author gives some of his recollections of life in the West, the Johnson County War, his trip to Tombstone, Arizona, and the Earps, the Clantons, Doc Holliday, and the McLaurys. Bud Philpot's name is misspelled as Bud Philfit, and the author evidently does not know that Philpot's death could be laid to his changing places with Bob Paul, the messenger. The author misspells some proper names, such as Bekan for Behan, though this one may be a typographical error.

2437. Wolle, Muriel Sibell

The bonanza trail, ghost towns and mining camps of the west, by Muriel Sibell Wolle. Illustrated by the author. Bloomington, Ind., Indiana University press, 1953. Cloth. OP.

xiv p., 2–510 p. front., illus., maps. 26 cm.
Glossary: p. 477–482; selected bibliography: p. 483–489; index: p. 491–510.
Half title; illus. end papers.

The author gives a wealth of material on the vigilantes and the outlaws and gunmen who followed the mining camps of the West.

2438. ———

Montana pay dirt. A guide to the mining camps of the treasure state, [by] Muriel Sibell Wolle. Denver, Sage books [1963]. Cloth.

7 p.l., 11–436 p. illus., plates, maps. 28.2 cm.

Bibliography: p. 411–416; index: p. 417–436 (triple column).
Half title; illus. end papers (col.); double column.

A most interesting book on ghost towns of Montana, which also contains much material on the Plummer gang of Virginia City, a new story about Calamity Jane, and a chapter on Kid Curry and his Wild Bunch, as well as the killing of Pike Landusky.

2439. Wood, M. W. (pub.)

History of Alameda county, California, including its geology, topography, soil and production; together with a full and particular record of the Spanish grants. . . . Separate histories of each of the townships, showing their advancement and progress. . . . Illustrated. Oakland, M. W. Wood, publisher, 1883. Calf. Rare.

vii p., 1 l., [9]–1001 p. front. (port.), ports., tables. 26.8 cm.

In a long chapter entitled "Criminal History of the County" the book takes up the story of crime from 1853 to 1881. The better-known outlaws dealt with are Juan Soto, Vásquez, and Rondado, alias Procopio.

2440. Wood, R. E. (ed).

Life and confessions of James Gilbert Jenkins; the murderer of eighteen men. . . . Photographically reorted [*sic*] and arranged for the press by R. E. Wood. Napa City, Calif., published by C. H. Allen and R. E. Wood. Printed by William P. Harrison & co., 1864. Pict. wrappers. Rare.

3 p.l., [7]–56 p. front., illus. 23 cm.

An exceedingly rare little book on one of the early outlaws of California.

2441. Wood, Raymund F.

California's agua fria. The early history of Mariposa county, by Raymond F. Wood. Fresno, Calif., Academy Library guild, 1954. Cloth. Scarce.

4 p.l., 11–112 p. front., plates, map. 22 cm.
Notes: p. 95–[99]; appendix: p. 101–106; index: p. 107–112.
Half title; map on end papers.

Makes some mention of the Mexican outlaws of California.

2442. Wood, Richard Coke

Calaveras, the land of skulls (the Calaveras country), [by] Richard Coke Wood. . . . [Sonora, Calif., published by the Mother Lode press, 1955.] Cloth. OP.

vii, 158 p. plates, ports. 23.8 cm.
Appendix: p. 148–149; bibliography: p. 150–153; index: p. 154–158.
Half title; device; notes at end of each chap.; "First edition" and copyright notice on verso of half title.

Includes a chapter entitled "Crime and Miner's Justice," which deals with Sam Brown, Black Bart, Joaquín Murieta, and Three-Fingered Jack García.

2443. ———

Murphys, queen of the Sierra. A history of Murphys, Calaveras county, California, by Richard Coke Wood. Angel's Camp, Calif., published by Calaveras Californian [n.d.]. Stiff pict. wrappers. OP.

3 p.l., 88 p. front. (port.), illus., plates, ports., fold. map. 19.6 cm.
Notes: p. 83–87; bibliography: p. 87–88.

Has much material on Joaquín Murieta and Three-Fingered Jack García.

2444. ———

Tales of old Calaveras, by Richard Coke Wood. . . . [N.p., n.d.] Cloth. Scarce.

3 p.l., 5–94 [2] p. front. (map), plates, ports. 23.5 cm.
Notes and references after each chap.; index: p. [95]–[96].
Preface on verso of t.p.

Contains chapters on Murieta and Black Bart.

2445. Woods, Betty

Ghost towns and how to get to them, by Betty Woods. Maps by M. T. Williams. Scene: New Mexico. Time: the present. [Santa Fe, N.M.], press of the Territorian [1964]. Wrappers.

1 p.l., [3]–36 p. maps (1 double p.). 23 cm.
Ghost towns not shown: p. 34–36.
Number 4 of a series of Western Americana.

Several of the ghost towns mentioned were the homes or hideouts of some of the New Mexico outlaws, such as Billy the Kid, Curly Bill Brocius, Johnny Ringo, Black Jack Ketchum, Russian Bill, and Sandy King.

2446. [Woods, H. Clay]

Memorandum, headquarters department of the Columbia. Portland, Oreg., April 17, 1873. Folder. Rare.

4 p. 19.2 cm.

A memorandum by H. Clay Woods, assistant adjutant general, giving an account of the murder of General Edward Camby by the Indian outlaw Captain Jack.

2447. Woods, Henry F., and Edward E. P. Morgan

God's loaded dice. Alaska, 1897–1930, by Edward E. P. Morgan in collaboration with Henry F. Woods. . . . Caldwell, Idaho, the Caxton printers, ltd., 1948. Cloth. OP.

5 p.l., [11]–298 p. plates. 23.7 cm.
Half title; vignette; headpieces; pub. device.

Has some information on Soapy Smith during his Skagway days, and on his death.

2448. Woods, Rev. James

Recollections of pioneer work in California, by Rev. James Woods. . . . San Francisco, Joseph Winterburn & co., book and job printers . . ., 1878. Cloth. Rare.

3 p.l., [5]–260 p. 19.4 cm.

Contains some material on Joaquín Murieta.

2449. Woods, S. D.

Lights and shadows of life on the Pacific coast, by S. D. Woods. New York and London, Funk & Wagnalls co., 1910. Cloth. Scarce.

4 p.l., 474 p. front. (port. with tissue). 20.6 cm.

Has some information about the Evans-Sontag train robbers.

2450. Woodson, William H.

History of Clay county, Missouri, by W. H. Woodson. Illustrated. Topeka, Indianapolis, Historical publishing co., 1920. Three-quarter leather. Scarce.

12 p.l., [65]–777 p. front. (port.), plates, ports. 27.7 cm.
"Biographical history": p. [338]–777.

Contains a full chapter on the James boys, including their robbery of the bank at Gallatin.

2451. Wooldridge, Maj. J. W.

History of the Sacramento valley, California, by Maj. J. W. Wooldridge. . . . Illustrated. Chicago, the Pioneer Historical publishing co., 1931. Cloth. Pub. in three volumes. Scarce.

Vol. I, xxii, 508 p. front., plates, ports. 26.7 cm.
Vols. II and III, biographical.

In a long account about Murieta, the author follows the Ridge version.

2452. Wooten, Mattie Lloyd (ed.)

Women tell the story of the southwest. Compiled and edited by Mattie Lloyd Wooten. . . . San Antonio, Texas, the Naylor co., 1940. Cloth. OP.

xvii, 394 p. front. 23.5 cm.

Glossary: p. 375–376; index: p. 379–394.
Half title; device.

Contains a chapter on Billy the Kid and Pat Garrett, telling about their first meeting.

2453. Workman, Boyle

Boyle Workman's the city that grew, as told to Caroline Walker. Illustrations a series of original pen drawings by Harriet Morton Holmes; with additional drawings by Orpha Klinker Carpenter; drawings from old photographs by Daniel S. MacManus. Los Angeles, the Southland publishing co., 1935. Cloth and leather. OP.

xiv p., 2 l., [5]–430 p. front. (port.), illus., plates, ports. 22.5 cm.
Index: p. 393–430.
Illus. chap. headings; untrimmed.
Also published in a de luxe edition and reprinted three times in 1936.

Has a chapter on Vásquez, his robbery of Allessandro Repetto, and his final capture. There is also a mention of Murieta.

2454. Wright, Carolyn, and Clarence Wright

Tiny Hinsdale of the silvery San Juan, [by] Carolyn and Clarence Wright. [Denver, Colo.], Big Mountain press [1964]. Cloth.

5 p.l., 11–196 p. front. (map), illus., plates, ports. 22.3 cm.
Acknowledgments: p. 193–194; bibliography: p. 195–196.
Half title; pub. device.

In a chapter on crime the authors tell about many killings and lynchings, as well as the hanging of Billy LeRoy at Del Norte, Colorado. There is also a chapter on Alferd Packer, whose first name the authors, like most other writers, call Alfred.

2455. Wright, Muriel Hazel

The story of Oklahoma, by Muriel H. Wright. Editorially assisted by Joseph B. Thoburn. Oklahoma City, Okla., Webb publishing co. [1930]. Cloth. Scarce.

xix, 342 p. front., plates, ports., maps. 19.6 cm.
Bibliography: p. 320–325; vocabulary: p. 327–330; index: p. 331–342.
"Points to be remembered" (a summary) after each chapter.

Contains some information on Oklahoma outlaws and Judge Parker's court.

2456. Wright, Robert Marr

Dodge City, the cowboy capital, and the great southwest in the days of the wild Indian, the buffalo, the cowboy, dance halls, gambling halls, and bad men, by

Robert M. Wright. . . . [Wichita, Kans., Wichita Eagle press, 1913.] Pict. cloth. Rare.

6 p.l., 9–344 p. front. (col.), plates, ports. 20.3 cm.
Copyright notice on recto of front.

It is said that most of this edition was destroyed by the printer; hence its rarity. A later edition without date or colored frontispiece is sometimes confused with the first edition. The first edition may be identified by the colored frontispiece with the copyright date on the recto. The second edition has a black-and-white picture of the author and son, this picture appearing after the title page in the first edition. Because the author knew Wyatt Earp well, I think that his spelling of Earp's name as Wyat Erb must be a typographical error. This book, one of the first written about Dodge City, reveals intimate knowledge of the gunmen of that wild cow town. The author says that Bat Masterson was elected sheriff of Ford County in 1876. Masterson was elected in 1877. He is also incorrect when he says that Charlie Bassett was in the posse with Masterson that went after the Kingsley train robbers.

The author says that burials at Boot Hill were stopped in 1874, but, according to the files of the *Dodge City Globe*, 1878 and 1879, no official action was taken until January, 1879. The records also show that Jack Wagner, George Hoy, Dora Hand, and several others were buried there in 1878. Some copies of this book were released with the word "capitol," rather than "capital," on the spine.

2457. Wright, William (Dan de Quille, pseud.)

History of the big bonanza; an authentic account of the discovery, history, and working of the world-renowned Comstock silver lode of Nevada . . ., by Dan de Quille. Profusely illustrated. Sold by subscription only. Hartford, Conn., American publishing co.; San Francisco, Calif., A. L. Bancroft & co., 1876. Dec. cloth. Scarce.

xvi, 17–569 [1] p. double p. front. (with tissue), illus. 22.8 cm.
Appendix: p. 567–569.

Has some material on Fighting Sam Brown and his death and on other outlaws and vigilantes.

2458. Wyllys, Rufus Kay

Arizona, the history of a frontier state, by Rufus Kay Wyllys. Phoenix, Ariz., Hobson & Herr [1950]. Cloth. OP.

xiii p., 1 l., 408 p. illus., plates, ports., 9 maps, facsm. 22 cm.
Guide to reference: p. 365–384; index: p. 387–408.
Half title ("Frontier" misspelled "Frintier"); t.p. in red and black; vignette; "First edition" on copyright p.

Also published in a de luxe edition limited to 406 copies and signed by the artist, cartographer, designer, and author.

Contains some scattered material on the gunmen of Arizona, the Earps, the Clantons, Curly Bill Brocius, and others.

2459. Wyman, Walker D.

Nothing but prairie and sky. Life on the Dakota range in the early days. Recorded by Walker D. Wyman from the original notes of Bruce Siberts. Norman, University of Oklahoma press [1954]. Two-tone cloth. OP.

xiii p., 1 l., 3–217 p. plates, ports., map (double p.). 22 cm.
Index: p. 209–217.
Half title; double t.p.

Has some mention of Tom Horn and the Johnson County War.

2460. Wynn, Marcia Rittenhouse

Desert bonanza. Story of early Randeburg, Mojave desert mining camp, by Marcia Rittenhouse Wynn. Illustrated. Culver City, Calif., M. W. Samelson, publisher, 1949. Cloth. Scarce.

xv p., 1 l., [3]–263 p. front., plates, map. 22 cm.
Notes: p. [257]–260; glossary: p. [261]–263.
Half title; "First edition" on copyright p.

Has a chapter on the activities of Vásquez in the Mojave.

2461. [Wyoming]

Casper chronicles. [Mountain States Litho.] Published by Casper Zonta club, 1964. (Cover title.) Stiff pict. wrappers.

3 p.l., 7–107 p. plates, ports. 21.6 cm.

Contains a short chapter on Bill Carlisle, the "Lone Bandit" of Wyoming, and another chapter on the war between the cattlemen and the sheepmen.

2462. ———

Star valley and its communities. Material collected and written by University of Wyoming extension class in Education 603, School and Community Relations, in August and September, 1951. Art and map work by Mrs. Beatrice Murray. . . . [N.p., n.d., ca. 1951.] Stiff pict. wrappers. Scarce.

4 p.l., 2–129 p. illus., plates, maps. 27.5 cm.
Crudely mimeographed on one side of gray paper.

Has a section on such outlaws as Matt Warner, Tom McCarthy, and Butch Cassidy.

Y

2463. York, Mary E.

The Bender tragedy. To the memory of my husband, Dr. W. H. York, murdered in Labette co., Kansas, March, 1873 . . ., by Mary E. York. . . . Mankato, [Kans.], Geo. W. Neff, book and job printer, 1875. Wrappers. Rare.

42 p. plan. 22 cm.

The author tells about the Benders' murder of her husband, a murder that was part of the beginning of the end of the Benders

2464. Yost, Nellie Snyder

The call of the range The story of the Nebraska Stock Growers association, by Nellie Snyder Yost. Denver, Colo., Sage books [1966]. Cloth.

7 p.l., 13–437 p. plates, ports., facsms., fold. map at end. 26 cm.
Appendix: p. 409–426; index: p. 427–437.
Half title; map on end papers; pub. device.

The author tells about the Union Pacific train robbery by Joel Collins and his gang. The author is mistaken in saying that John Underwood took part in this robbery. She also says that Sam Bass "was supposed to have confessed to burying his share of the Big Springs robbery loot there as he fled south. Though hordes of people moved mountains of earth in the vicinity, no U.P. gold was ever found, so far as is known." No wonder, for Bass did not bury his gold but took it to Texas, where he spent it lavishly. He spent his last gold piece on his way to Round Rock just before he was killed.

The author also tells about the Olives and the killing of Luther Mitchell and Ami Ketchum, and about the careers of Doc Middleton, the noted horse thief, and Kid Wade, who was lynched because what he knew would be detrimental to some of the "better citizens."

2465. Young, Charles E.

Dangers on the trail in 1865. A narrative of actual events, by Charles E. Young. Geneva, N.Y. [press of W. Y. Humphrey], 1912. Pict. cloth. Scarce.

3 p.l., [7]–248 p. illus., plates, map. 19.5 cm.

Has some mention of outlawry in Denver's early days.

2466. Young, Harry (Sam)

Hard knocks. A life story of the vanishing west, by Harry (Sam) Young.

Portland, Oreg. [Wells & co., printers and publishers, 1915.] Boards and cloth. Very scarce.

4 p.l., [9]–242 p. plates, ports. 19.6 cm.

Although published the same year in Chicago by Laird and Lee with the same number of pages and bound in cloth, but with 7 fewer plates, the Portland edition is said to be the first printing. It is printed on much better paper than the Chicago edition.

The author claims to have known Wild Bill Hickok personally, but he continues the Nichols legend about the McCanles "fight." He says that the stage company sent Hickok to Rock Creek Station from St. Louis to take care of the desperate situation. That statement is incorrect. The author has Hickok killing eight men at one time when he first arrived at Abilene. He also claims that he was the bartender at Saloon 66, where, he says, Wild Bill was killed. All the old-timers and eyewitnesses say that the bartender was Anson Tipple, and we know that the killing took place in Saloon No. 10. He has Calamity Jane born at Fort Laramie, Wyoming, in 1860, the daughter of a soldier named Dalton. Twenty-six years later, Dr. McGillycuddy repeats much of Young's information word for word. He has Calamity Jane passing away August 2, 1906, "on the same day and month, and in the same hour, Wild Bill was assassinated thirty years before." She died August 1, 1903, but sentiment demanded that her death take place the same day and month as Hickok's. There are many, many other errors which I have dealt with in *Burs Under the Saddle* (Item 7).

2467. Young, Herbert V.

Ghosts of Cleopatra hill. Men and legends of old Jerome, by Herbert V. Young. Jerome, Ariz., Jerome Historical society [1964]. Pict. wrappers (col.).

6 p.l., 151 p. illus., plates (part col.), ports., map. 20.3 cm.
Half title.

This book, primarily about prominent early settlers and mining men of Jerome, contains three chapters on various lawmen and touches upon the Pleasant Valley War and other lawlessness.

2468. [Young, S. Glenn]

Life and exploits of S. Glenn Young, world-famous law enforcement officer. Compiled by a friend and admirer from data furnished by the hero, with the exception of the last chapter which was completed by another of the hero's intimate friends. . . . Herrin, Ill., published by Mrs. S. Glenn Young, [n.d., ca. 1924.] Cloth. Scarce.

4 p.l., 9–253 p. front. (port.), plates, ports. 21 cm.

Experiences of a law enforcement officer among the outlaws, especially in Texas and Oklahoma.

2469. Young, Dr. S. O.

True stories of old Houston and Houstonians. Historical and personal sketches, by Dr. S. O. Young, Houston, Texas. Galveston, Texas, Oscar Springer, publisher, 1913. Stiff wrappers. Scarce.

2 p.l., [5]–244 p. 22.2 cm.

Has some information on Billy the Kid, Ben Thompson, Billy Thompson, King Fisher, and other noted gunmen.

2470. Younger, Cole

The story of Cole Younger, by himself. Being an autobiography of the Missouri guerrilla captain and outlaw, his capture and prison life, and the only authentic account of the Northfield raid ever published. Illustrations made expressly for this book. Chicago, press of Henneberry co., 1903. Stiff wrappers. Excessively rare.

5 p.l., [7]–123 [2] p. front. (3 large ports.), illus., plates, ports., plan. 21.8 cm.
Reprinted in 1955 by the Frontier press of Texas, Houston, in an edition of 135 pages and bound in cloth. Pages 124 to 135 are plates and ports. from the Rose collection.

The author says that he wrote this book because when he was released from prison he found that hundreds of books had been published about him and his brothers and that in all these books there was "not to be found six pages of truth."

Many of the books on Younger's life state that Belle Starr's daughter was his illegitimate child, but Younger here claims that though at the time Belle herself made some claims to be his wife, he had never heard of her. It was only after someone explained to him that Belle Starr was the Belle Shirley or Belle Reed he had known in earlier days that he realized who she was. He further states that Frank and Jesse James were not in the Northfield robbery, but that statement is doubtful.

2471. Younger, Scout (Bison Bill)

True facts of the lives of America's most notorious outlaws, as told by Scout Younger (Bison Bill). [N.p., n.d.] Pamphlet. Wrappers. (Cover title.) Scarce.

1 p.l., 2–15 p. 20.4 cm.

Has short sketches of the James boys, the Younger brothers, Bob Ford, Red [Ed] Kelly, Belle Starr, Henry Starr, Cherokee Bill, Sam Bass, Bill Doolin, Dick Broadwell, and others.

The author's account of Wild Bill Hickok is both ridiculous and unbelievable. He says that Hickok killed more than two hundred men in the line of duty and that he was the first chief of police at Fort Dodge. Fort Dodge was a military fort and had no chief of police, and Hickok never served as an officer in Dodge City. The author also claims that Hickok had killed nine men in Dodge before he had been there twenty-four hours.

2472. [Younger Brothers]

Younger brothers of the great west. [Racine, Wisc., Whitman publishing co., n.d.] Wrappers. Scarce.

3–182 [5] p. 16.2 cm.
5 p. adv. at end.

Another of the pulp publications sold by the train butcher boys. The anonymous writer of this tale says that the Younger brothers had a cattle ranch in Texas "which they called home." Neither the Jameses nor the Youngers were ever cattlemen.

Z

2473. Zink, Wilbur A.

The Roscoe gun battle. Younger brothers vs. Pinkerton detectives, by Wilbur A. Zink. . . . [Appleton City, Mo.], Democrat publishing co., inc., 1967. Stiff pict. wrappers.

4 p.l., 29 [1] p. plates, ports., map. 23 cm.
"Limited first edition" and copyright notice on t.p.
Bibliography on p. 1.

A history of the killing of John Younger and Detective Daniels and the wounding of Detective Lull.

2474. Zornow, William Frank

Kansas. A history of the Jayhawk state, by William Frank Zornow, Norman, University of Oklahoma press [1957]. Cloth.

xii p., 1 l., 3–417 p. illus., plates, ports., maps. 24.2 cm.
Bibliography: p. 379–400; index: p. 401–417.
Half title; device; "first edition" on copyright p.

Addenda

2475. Bruce, Leona

Banister was there, [by] Leona Bruce. Fort Worth, Branch-Smith, inc., 1968. Boards.

2 p.l., [1]–196 p. plates, ports., facsm. 23.5 cm.
Bibliography: p. 188; index: p. [189]–196.
Pub. device; "first printing" on copyright p.

In telling about the Union Pacific robbery by Joel Collins and his gang, the author quotes James Gillett's false statement that John Underwood was a member of the gang. She also says that this Underwood was a brother of Henry Underwood, who later joined Sam Bass in his new gang at Denton, Texas. Otherwise, the author's account of Bass is fairly correct.

2476. Carson, John

The Union Pacific. Hell on wheels, by John Carson. [Santa Fe, N.M., press of the Territorian, 1968]. Stiff wrappers.

2 p.l., 5–36 p. plates. 23 cm.
Western Americana series, No. 16.

The author tells about the Union Pacific robbery by Joel Collins and his gang. He is mistaken in having eight men taking part in this robbery. There were only six. He also mentions Doc Middleton and Bear River Tom Smith.

2477. Chrisman, Harry E.

Fifty years on the owl hoot trail. Jim Herron, the first sheriff of No Man's Land, Oklahoma territory, by Harry E. Chrisman, from an original manuscript by Jim Herron. Introduction by Edward Everett Dale. Chicago, Sage books [1969]. Cloth.

xxiii p., 2 l., 3–355 p. plates, ports., facsms. 23.5 cm.

Appendix: p. 301–303; notes: p. 305–333; bibliography and sources: p. 335–341; photo credits: p. 342–343; index: p. 345–355.

Half title; map on end papers; pub. device; "first edition" on copyright p.

An interesting story of a rancher in No Man's Land who had to follow the Owl Hoot Trail for fifty years because of a frame-up of a powerful cattlemen's association.

The author is mistaken in saying that the Dalton boys were related to the James boys through the Youngers. The Daltons were related to the Younger boys but not to the Jameses. The author has Billy the Kid a vicious killer who "had only one desire at the end of his short career, and that was to kill another man." He also says that some of the men the Kid killed "were store clerks and barbers who were unarmed. He bushwhacked and shot others in the back." Billy was far from being that vicious, and he never killed any clerks or barbers.

The author is also mistaken in having Henry and Belle Starr holding up a bank together. Belle never held up any bank, and these two never worked together. Henry was a mere boy when Belle was murdered.

2478. Coan, Charles Florus

A history of New Mexico, by Charles F. Coan . . ., assisted by a board of advisory editors. . . . Chicago and New York, the American Historical society, inc., 1925. Leather. Pub. in three volumes.

Vol. I, xlviii, 586 p. front., illus., plates, ports., maps, tables. 26.7 cm.

Bibliographies at end of some chaps.

Vols. II and III, biographical.

Volume I contains a chapter on the livestock industry, with an account of the Lincoln County War. The author is careless with the spelling of proper names, such as Chisom for Chisum, McSwain for McSween, and Tunsel for Tunstall. His account of Billy the Kid follows the false legends of Ash Upson.

2479. Coburn, Walt

Pioneer cattleman in Montana. The story of the Circle C ranch, by Walt Coburn. Norman, University of Oklahoma press [1968]. Cloth.

xii p., 1 l., 3–338 p. plates (1 col. fold.), ports. 23.5 cm.

Appendices: p. 290–329; index: p. 331–338.

Half title; "first edition" on copyright p.

This excellent book gives a fine picture of one of the famous ranches in Montana and tells about some of that state's outlaws. The author tells about the killing of Pike Landusky and some stories about Butch Cassidy and his Wild Bunch. I am proud to say that this author is a personal friend.

2480. Dillon, Richard

Wells Fargo detective. The biography of James B. Hume, by Richard Dillon. New York, Coward-McCann, inc. [1969]. Cloth.

11 p.l., 23–320 p. illus., plates, ports., facsms. 22 cm.
Sources: p. 301–302; index: p. 303–320.
Half title; double t.p.; pub. device.

Has much on stagecoach and train robberies and a long chapter on Black Bart, as well as a long chapter on the Southern Pacific War, dealing with the Evans-Sontag gang of train robbers.

2481. Flagg, Oscar H. (Jack)

A review of the cattle business in Johnson County, Wyoming, since 1882, and the causes that led to the recent invasion, by Oscar H. "Jack" Flagg. Cheyenne, Wyo., the Vic press [1967]. Stiff wrappers. Scarce.

2 p.l., 5–50 p. 2 plates. 22.8 cm.
Limited to 500 numbered copies.

Articles which originally appeared in the Buffalo Bulletin about the Johnson County War, the hanging of Jim Averill and Cattle Kate and the killing of Nat Champion and Nick Ray. Printed on buff paper.

2482. Gregg, Andy

Drums of yesterday. The forts of New Mexico, by Andy Gregg. [Santa Fe, N.M., press of the Territorian, 1968.] Stiff wrappers. (Cover title.)

3–40 p. front., plates, map (double p.). 23 cm.
Western Americana series, No. 17.

Under a section about Fort Sumner the author tells about the killing of Billy the Kid by Pat Garrett, and in a section about Fort Stanton he tells about the Lincoln County War.

2483. Grover, David H.

Diamondfield Jack. A study in frontier justice, by David H. Grover. Reno, Nev., University of Nevada press, 1968. Cloth.

xi p., 1 l., 3–189 p. illus., plates, ports. 21 cm.
Notes after each chapter; bibliography: p. 179–182; index: p. 183–189.
Half title.

The first and only book to deal with Diamondfield Jack Davis and his crimes.

2484. Lake, Carolyn (ed.)

Under cover for Wells Fargo. The unvarnished recollections of Fred Dodge.

Edited by Carolyn Lake. Foreword by Neil Morgan. Illustrated with photographs. Boston, Houghton Mifflin co., 1969. Cloth with facsimile signature of F. J. Dodge.

xx p., 1 l., 3–280 p. plates, ports. 21.6 cm.
Index: p. 267–280.
Half title; map on end papers; "first printing" on copyright p.

The author has Wyatt Earp the marshal of Dodge City and says that after he had tamed the town he turned in his badge to Mayor Dog Kelly and told him that "he was through with the marshal business." He also has Wyatt a U.S. marshal at Tombstone long before he was appointed to that office.

In parenthesis the editor says that the *Tombstone Nugget* was owned by Johnny Behan and the rustlers, but that statement is incorrect. Of the O K Corral fight the author says that "on arriving in town Ike Clanton had made it known that his gang had come after the Earps." The Clantons were not hunting trouble, and the author is also mistaken in having the Clantons opening fire when they were told by Virgil Earp that they were under arrest.

The author has Charlie Bryant arrested by Ed Short at a friend's house in El Reno, Oklahoma. Bryant was arrested while ill in bed in his room at a hotel. The author also says that Billy Thompson, the brother of Ben Thompson, was a friend "whom I had known in Tombstone days." I have never seen an account reporting that Billy Thompson was ever in Tombstone.

2485. Looney, Ralph

Haunted highways. The ghost towns of New Mexico, by Ralph Looney. New York, Hastings House, publishers [1968]. Cloth.

7 p.l., 13–220 p. front., plates, ports. 25.5 cm.
Sources: p. 213–214; index: p. 215–220.
Half title; map on end papers; double column.

Has a chapter on the Lincoln County War and the career of Billy the Kid. The author gives a fairly accurate account of these incidents, though when writing of the battle of McSween's home he hints that Mrs. McSween played the piano during the fight. However, he prefaces his statement with the phrase "It was reported." After the Kid had killed J. W. Bell, the author says, "someone called Olinger [who had taken some prisoners across the street for a meal], who left his prisoners at the Wortley and ran to the courthouse." No one called Olinger. He heard the pistol shot that killed Bell and thought that Bell had killed the Kid. In writing of the Kid's death, the author is also mistaken in saying that "two bullets from Garrett's Colt cut [the Kid] down in a darkened room at Fort Sumner." It is true that Garrett fired twice, but only the first bullet found its mark.

There is a chapter on Elfego Baca and his famous fight at Frisco—one man against an army of cowboys. There is also some information about Clay Allison, and in a chapter on the town of Shakespeare there is an account of the hanging of Sandy King and Russian Bill.

2486. Metz, Leon Claire

Dallas Stoudenmire: El Paso marshal, by Leon Claire Metz. Austin and New York, the Pemberton press . . ., 1969. Two-tone cloth.

xii, [1]–162 p. plates, ports. 23.6 cm.

Footnotes: p. [129]–145; bibliography: p. [147]–151; acknowledgments: p. [153]–155]; index: p. [157]–162.

Half title. illus. double t.p.

The first complete biography of this famous gunman and officer.

2487. Mullin, Robert N.

The boyhood of Billy the Kid, by Robert N. Mullin. With a gallery of photographs. [El Paso, Texas, Texas Western press, 1967.] Stiff wrappers.

1 p.l., 3–26 [2] p. plates, ports. 23 cm.

Southwestern Studies Vol. V, No. 1, Monograph No. 17.

References: p. 24–26.

An interesting and valuable addition to the literature on Billy the Kid, filled with new material about the Kid's childhood.

2488. Rickards, Colin

Charles Littlepage Ballard, southwesterner, by Colin Rickards. [El Paso, Texas, Texas Western press, 1966.] Stiff wrappers. (Cover title.)

2 p.l., [5]–40 p. plates, ports. 22.7 cm.

Southwestern Studies, Vol. IV, No. 4, Monograph No. 16.

References: p. 31–39; acknowledgments: p. 40.

Contains material on Billy the Kid, the killing of Huston Chapman, and the pursuit of Black Jack Christian, George Musgrave, and the rest of his gang.

2489. Scott, George W.

The Black Hills story, written and published by George W. Scott. Fort Collins, Colo., 1953. Stiff wrappers.

2 l., 1 p., 4–97 p. 18.4 cm.

Contains a section on the killing of Wild Bill Hickok and one on Calamity Jane.

2490. Secrest, William B.

Juanita, by William B. Secrest. Fresno, Calif., Saga-West publishing co. [1967]. Stiff pict. wrappers.

2 p.l., 5–31 p. plates (1 double p.), ports., map, facsm. 23 cm.

The story of the only woman lynched in the California gold-rush days.

2491. [**Wyoming**]

100 years in the wild west. A pictorial history of Rawlins, Wyoming. [Rawlins, Wyo., Times stationers, 1968.] Stiff wrappers.

[98] p. (no pagination). plates, ports., map (double p.), facsms. 26.5 cm.

Has some material on the hanging of Big Nose George Parrott.

Index

All index numbers refer to items, not to pages. Authors are arranged alphabetically in the text and are not repeated in the index. Even though the entry is not mentioned in the item, it is included in the indicated work.

C

D

L

N

P

W

Z

The paper on which this book is printed bears the watermark of the University of Oklahoma Press and has an effective life of at least three hundred years.